ARCHITECTURES FOR COMPUTER VISION

ARCHITECTURES FOR COMPUTER VISION

FROM ALGORITHM TO CHIP WITH VERILOG

Hong Jeong

Pohang University of Science and Technology, South Korea

WILEY

This edition first published 2014

Registered office
John Wiley & Sons Singapore Pte. Ltd., 1 Fusionopolis Walk, #07-01 Solaris South Tower, Singapore 138628.

For details of our global editorial offices, for customer services and for information about how to apply for permission to reuse the copyright material in this book please see our website at www.wiley.com.

Library of Congress Cataloging-in-Publication Data

Jeong, Hong.
Architectures for computer vision : from algorithm to chip with Verilog / Hong Jeong.
pages cm.
Includes bibliographical references and index.
ISBN 978-1-118-65918-2 (cloth)
1. Verilog (Computer hardware description language) 2. Computer vision. I. Title. II. Title: From algorithm to chip with Verilog.
TK7885.7.J46 2014
621.39–dc23

2014016398

Set in 9/11pt Times by Aptara Inc., New Delhi, Indiae Ltd

1 2014

Contents

About the Author

Hong Jeong joined the Department of Electrical Engineering at POSTECH in January 1988, after graduating from the Department of EECS at MIT. He has worked at Bell Labs, Murray Hill, New Jersey and has visited the Department of Electrical Engineering at USC. He has taught integrated courses, such as multimedia algorithms, Verilog HDL design, and recognition engineering, in the Department of Electrical Engineering at POSTECH. He is interested in filling in the gaps between computer vision algorithms and VLSI architectures, using GPU and advanced HDL languages.

Preface

This book aims to fill in the gaps between computer vision and Verilog HDL design. For this purpose, we have to learn about the four disciplines: Verilog HDL, vision principles, vision architectures, and Verilog design. This area, which we call *vision architecture*, paves the way from vision algorithm to chip design, and is defined by the related fields, the implementing devices, and the vision hierarchy.

In terms of related fields, vision architecture is a multidisciplinary research area, particularly related to computer vision, computer architecture, and VLSI design. In computer vision, the typical goal of the research is to design serial algorithms, often implemented in high-level programming languages and rarely in dedicated chips. Unlike the well-established design flow from computer architecture to VLSI design, the flow from vision algorithm to computer architecture, and further to VLSI chips, is not well-defined. We overcome this difficulty by delineating the path between vision algorithm and VLSI design.

Vision architecture is implemented on many different devices, such as DSP, GPU, embedded processors, FPGA, and ASICs. Unlike programming software, where the programming paradigm is more or less homogeneous, designing and implementing hardware is highly heterogeneous in that different devices require completely different expertise and design tools. We focus on Verilog HDL, one of the representative languages for designing FPGA/ASICs.

The design of the vision architecture is highly dependent on the context and platform because the computational structures tend to be very different, depending on the areas of study – image processing, intermediate vision algorithms, and high-level vision algorithms – and on the specific algorithms used – graph cuts, belief propagation, relaxation, inference, learning, one-pass algorithm, etc. This book is dedicated to the intermediate vision, where reconstructing 3D information is the major goal.

This book by no means intends to deal with all the diverse topics in vision algorithms, vision architectures, and devices. Moreover, it is not meant to report the best algorithms and architectures for vision modules by way of extensive surveys. Instead, its aim is to present a homogeneous approach to the design from algorithm to architecture via Verilog HDL, that guides the audience in extracting the computational constructs, such as parallelism, iteration, and neighborhood computation, from a given vision algorithm and interpreting them in Verilog HDL terms. It also aims to provide guidance on how to design architectures in Verilog HDL so that the audience may be familiarized enough with vision algorithm and HDL design to proceed to more advanced research. For this purpose, this book provides a Verilog vision simulator that can be used for designing and simulating vision architectures.

This book is written for senior undergraduates, graduate students, and researchers working in computer vision, computer architecture, and VLSI design. The computer vision audience will learn how to convert the vision algorithms to hardware, with the help of the simulator. The computer architecture audience will learn the computational structures of the vision algorithms and the design codes of the major algorithms. The VLSI design audience will learn about the vision algorithms and architectures and possibly improve the codes for their own needs.

This book is organized with four independent parts: Verilog HDL, vision principle, vision architecture, and Verilog design. Each chapter is written to be complete in and of itself, supported by the problem sets and references. The purpose of the first part is to introduce the vision implementation methodology, the Verilog HDL for image processing, and the Verilog HDL simulator for designing the vision architecture. Chapter 1 deals with the taxonomy of the general and specialized algorithms and architectures that are considered typical in vision technology. The pros and cons of the different implementations are discussed, and the dedicated implementation by Verilog HDL design addressed. Chapter 2 introduces the basics of Verilog HDL and coding examples for communication and control modules. These modules are general building blocks for designing vision architectures. Chapter 3 introduces Verilog circuit modules, such as processor, memory, and pipelined array, which are the building blocks of the vision architectures. The vision architectures are designed using processors, memories, and possibly pipelined arrays, connected by the communication and control modules. Chapter 4 introduces the Verilog vision simulators, specially built for designing vision architectures. The simulator consists of the unsynthesizable module, which functions as an interface for image input and output, and the synthesizable module, which is a platform for building serial and parallel architectures. This platform is tailored to the specific architectures in later chapters.

The second part, comprising Chapters 5–7, introduces the fundamentals of intermediate vision algorithms. Instead of treating diverse fields in vision research, this part focuses on the energy minimization, stereo, motion, and fusion of vision modules. Chapter 5 introduces the energy function, which is a common concept in computer vision algorithms. The energy function is explained in terms of Markov random field (MRF) estimation and the free energy concept. The energy minimization methods and the structure of a typical energy function are also explained. Chapter 6 is dedicated to stereo vision. Instead of surveying the extensive research done, this chapter focuses on the constraints and energy minimization. A typical energy function that is subsequently designed with various architectures is discussed. Chapter 7 deals with motion estimation and fusion of vision modules. Instead of an extensive survey, this chapter focuses on the motion principles and the continuity concept that unify the various constraints in motion estimation. This chapter also deals with the fusion of vision modules, directly with intermediate variables, bypassing the 3D variables, which give strong constraints for determining the intermediate vision variables. This chapter closes with a set of equations linking the 2D variables directly, i.e. blur diameter, surface normal, disparity, and optical flow.

The third part, which comprises Chapters 8–10, introduces the algorithms and architectures of the major algorithms: relaxation, dynamic programming (DP), belief propagation (BP), and graph cuts (GC). The computational structures and possible implementations are also discussed. Chapter 8 introduces the concept underlying the relaxation algorithm and architecture. In addition to the Gauss–Seidel and Jacobi algorithms, this chapter introduces other types of architectures: specifically, extensions to the Gauss–Seidel–Jacobi architecture. In Chapter 9, the concept underlying the DP algorithm and architecture is introduced, and the computational structures of various DP algorithms discussed. Finally, the algorithms and architectures of BP and GC are addressed in Chapter 10, and their computational structures and possible implementations discussed.

The fourth part, which comprises Chapters 11–14, is dedicated to the Verilog design of stereo matching with the major architectures: relaxation, DP, and BP. All the designs are provided with complete Verilog HDL codes that have been verified by function simulation and synthesis. Chapter 11 addresses the Verilog design of the relaxation architecture. Chapter 12 deals with the Verilog design of serial architectures for the DP. The design is aimed at executing stereo matching with the serial vision simulator. Chapter 13 introduces the systolic array in Verilog HDL. This chapter explains in detail how to design the control module and the systolic array, connected by local neighborhood connections. Finally, Chapter 14 deals with BP design for stereo matching. This chapter also explains in detail the design methods with Verilog HDL.

All the designs are accompanied by complete source codes that have all been proven correct via simulation and synthesis tests. A package of the codes in the textbook, and the complementary codes, is provided separately for readers. The codes are carefully provided with the general constructs in standard Verilog HDL, which is free from IPs and vendor-dependent codes. I hope that this book will provide an important opportunity that stirs the reader's ability to develop more advanced vision architectures for various vision modules, to deal with the topics that are not dealt within this book because of space constraints, and to fill in the gaps between computer vision and VLSI design.

Much of the work was accomplished during my one year sabbatical leave from POSTECH from September 2012 to August 2013, inclusive. This work was supported by the "Core Technology Development for Breakthrough of Robot Vision Research" and the "Development of Intelligent Traffic Sign Recognition System to cope with Euro NCAP" funded by the Ministry of Trade, Industry & Energy (MI, Korea). During the writing of this book, Altera Corporation provided necessary equipment and tools through the Altera University Program. I would like to thank Michelle Lee at Altera Korea and Bruce Choi at Uniquest, Inc. for helping me to participate in the program. I am also grateful to Peter Lee at Vadas, Inc. for supporting my laboratory financially through projects and Jung Gu Kim at VisionST, Inc. for providing required data and equipment. Some of the programs and bibliography searches were done with help from my students, In Tae Na, Byung Chan Chun, and Jeong Mok Ha. Other students, Jae Young Chun, Seong Yong Cho, and Ki Young Bae, helped with preparation, editing, and proofreading. I sincerely appreciate publisher James Murphy for choosing my writing subject and editor Clarissa Lim for helping me with various pieces of advice and notes. I also remember my colleagues, Prof. Rosalind Picard at MIT Media Lab and Prof. C.-C. Jay Kuo at USC. I thank Professors, Jae S. Lim, Alan V. Oppenheim, Charles E. Leiserson, and Eric Grimson at MIT, Prof. Bernard C. Levy at UC Davis, Prof. Stephen E. Levinson at University of Illinois, and Prof. Jay Kyoon Lee at Syracuse University. Finally, I sincerely appreciate Prof. Bruce R. Musicus at MIT for his generous support and guidance.

Hong Jeong
hjeong@postech.ac.kr

Part One

Verilog HDL

1

Introduction

This chapter addresses the status of the vision architectures in four major fields: computer architectures, vision algorithms, vision devices, and design methodologies. Computer architecture, which is characterized by serial, parallel, pipelined, and concurrent computation, must be tuned to the underlying computational structures – parallel, iterative, and neighborhood computation – that are used in intermediate computer vision. Vision algorithms, which have evolved from heuristic methods to generic structured algorithms at each level of computer vision from low level to high level, must be investigated in terms of computational structures. The vision devices, ranging from CPUs to very-large-scale integration (VLSI) chips, must be investigated in terms of their flexibility and computational complexity. Finally, the design flow from vision to chip, which is not well-defined, must be defined and delineated using a general methodology.

1.1 Computer Architectures for Vision

Vision architectures are special forms of more general computer architectures. In the early 1970s, a general point of view on computer architecture was to see it as an information flow of data and instructions into a processor (Figure 1.1). Flynn's taxonomy (Flynn 1972) is the most universally accepted method of classifying computer systems. The instruction stream is defined as the sequence of instructions performed by the processing unit. The data stream is defined as the data traffic exchanged between the memory and the processing unit. According to Flynn's classification, the instruction stream and data stream can both be either singular or multiple in nature.

Flynn's taxonomy classified architectures into single instruction single data stream (SISD), Single instruction multiple data stream (SIMD), multiple instruction single data stream (MISD), and multiple instruction multiple data stream (MIMD). In this classification system, an SISD machine is the traditional serial architecture where instructions and data are executed serially. This is often referred to as the Von Neumann architecture. An SIMD machine is a parallel computer, where one instruction is executed many times with different data in a synchronized manner. An extreme example is the *systolic array* (Kung and Leiserson 1980; Kung 1988; Leiserson and Saxe 1991). In an MISD machine, each processing unit operates on the data independently via independent instruction streams. This computational technique is also called *pipelining*. A set of pipelined vectors is referred to as a superscalar. An MIMD machine is a fully parallel machine where multiple processors execute different instructions and data independently.

This concept can be formalized by a set of state machines, such as the Moore machine or the Mealy machine. Suppose a processing element (PE) in a state Q_k receives date D_k and instruction I_k and

Architectures for Computer Vision: From Algorithm to Chip with Verilog, First Edition. Hong Jeong.

Companion Website: www.wiley.com/go/jeong

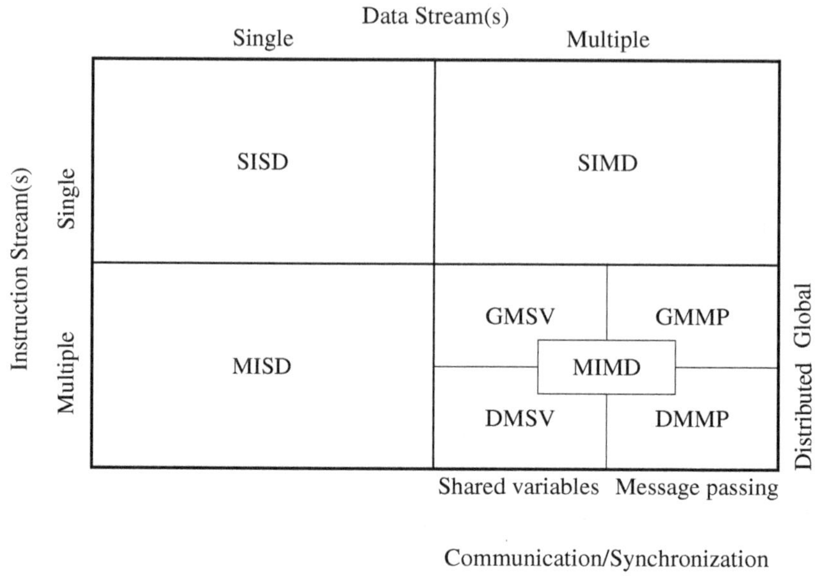

Figure 1.1 Flynn–Johnson taxonomy of computer architectures

generates output O_k, $(k = 0, 1, \ldots)$ according to the state transition $T(\cdot)$ and output generation $H(\cdot)$. Then, the SISD machine is modeled by a Mealy machine:

$$\begin{cases} Q_{k+1} = T(Q_k, D_k, I_k), \\ O_k = H(Q_k, D_k, I_k), \quad k = 0, 1, 2, \ldots. \end{cases} \tag{1.1}$$

Other machines can be modeled by a set of PEs by combining data and instructions in various ways. As such, an SIMD machine is modeled as a set of identical PEs, operating on different data but controlled by the same instruction set:

$$\begin{cases} Q^l_{k+1} = T\left(Q^l_k, D^l_k, I_k\right), \\ O^l_k = H\left(Q^l_k, D^l_k, I_k\right), \quad \forall l \in [0, N-1], \end{cases} \tag{1.2}$$

where N denotes the number of PEs. The MISD machine is modeled as

$$\begin{cases} Q^l_{k+1} = T^l\left(Q^l_k, O^{l-1}_k, I^l_k\right), \\ O^l_k = H^l\left(Q^l_k, O^{l-1}_k, I^l_k\right), \quad \forall l \in [0, N-1], \end{cases} \tag{1.3}$$

where the data input is $O^{l-1}_k = D^l_k$ and the output is O^{N-1}_k. The MIMD machine is a set of different machines:

$$\begin{cases} Q^l_{k+1} = T^l\left(Q^l_k, D^l_k, I^l_k\right), \\ O^l_k = H^l\left(Q^l_k, D^l_k, I^l_k\right), \quad \forall l \in [0, N-1]. \end{cases} \tag{1.4}$$

Nowadays, the MIMD category includes a wide variety of different computer types and as a result, taxonomies have been added to the MIMD class. The Flynn–Johnson taxonomy, which is one of many classification methods, proposed a further classification of such machines based on their memory structure (global or distributed) and the mechanism used for communications/synchronization (shared variables or message passing).

A global memory shared variable (GMSV) machine is a machine with shared memory multiprocessors. A global memory message passing (GMMP) machine is a machine that uses global memory and message passing. This type of machine is rarely used. In distributed memory shared variables (DMSV) machines, memory resources are distributed to the processors and the variables are shared. In distributed memory message passing (DMMP) machines, memory resources are distributed and message passing is used. In this classification system, DMSV and DMMP machines are loosely coupled machines, and GMSV and GMMP machines are tightly coupled machines. In addition to data and instructions, this classification system introduces two more variables: memory M and message m,

$$\begin{cases} Q_{k+1}^{l} = T^{l}\left(Q_{k}^{l}, D_{k}^{l}, I_{k}^{l}, M_{k}^{l}, m_{k}^{l}\right), \\ O_{k}^{l} = H^{l}\left(Q_{k}^{l}, D_{k}^{l}, I_{k}^{l}, M_{k}^{l}, m_{k}^{l}\right), \quad \forall l \in [0, N-1]. \end{cases} \tag{1.5}$$

The differences between the four machine types are based on the various combinations of the memory M, shared by a set of processors, and the messages m, passed between a set of processors.

Modern computer processors, such as central processing units (CPUs), digital signal processors (DSPs), field-programmable gate arrays (FPGAs), embedded processors (EPs), and graphics processing units (GPUs), tend to evolve into huge systems that use more computational resources – more pipelines, multi cores, more shared memory, more distributed memory, and multi-threading.

For computer vision, the computational architectures depend on the levels of vision (early, intermediate, and high-level vision) and the algorithms (relaxation, graph cut, belief propagation, etc). Starting from serial algorithms for general computers, we usually search for more structured algorithms and architectures for better implementation. The passage from low to intermediate vision is characterized by high-levels of resource usage for numerical computations and memory space, and the structures that are used are usually parallel, repetitive, or local neighborhood structures. High-level vision, on the other hand, is characterized by high-level resource usage for symbolic computation, and the structures that are used are usually concurrent, heterogeneous, modular, and hierarchical computational structures. The intermediate level is closer to the regular, SIMD, and MISD architectures and the high level is closer to the general, SISD, and MIMD architectures. From early to intermediate level, the computational structures are characterized by pixel or local neighborhood computations, recursive updating, and scale-dependent (hierarchical or pyramidal) and parallel computations. We will concentrate on designing architectures for such early- to intermediate-level operations that are parallel and iterative and rely on neighborhood computations.

Similar to general computer architecture, vision architecture can be modeled by state machines. Assume an image plane $\mathcal{P} = \{(x, y) | x \in [0, N-1], y \in [0, M-1]\}$ and an image defined over $\mathcal{P}$, $I = \{I(p) | p \in \mathcal{P}\}$. A neighborhood N_p is a set of (topologically) connected pixels around $p \in \mathcal{P}$, and a window A_p is a set of pixels around $p \in \mathcal{P}$. A typical operation is to update the state of a pixel using the neighborhood values along with the image input. The operation is repeated for all pixels until the values converge. The outputs are the pixel states in equilibrium. The state equation for parallel iterative neighborhood computation is defined as follows:

$$\begin{cases} Q^{(k+1)}(A_p) = T(Q^{(k)}(N(A_p)), I(A_p)), & k = 0, 1, \dots, K-1, \\ O(A_p) = Q^{(K-1)}(A_p), & \forall p \in \mathcal{P}, \end{cases} \tag{1.6}$$

where the superscript denotes the iteration and K denotes the maximum number of iterations. The parallelism can be achieved by the set of window A_p. The iteration means the recursive computation of the states. The neighborhood computation is represented by the local neighborhood function $N(A_p)$. This is a basic computational structure in low to intermediate vision that generally uses large amounts of spatial and temporal resources. The run-time is $O(MN\mathcal{A}\mathcal{N}K)$, which is proportional to the image size MN, the window size A, and the number of iterations. The required space is $O(MN)$, which is proportional to the image size MN.

1.2 Algorithms for Computer Vision

With regards to stereo vision, there are survey papers (Brown *et al.* 2003; Kappes *et al.* 2013; Scharstein and Szeliski 2002; Szeliski *et al.* 2008) and a site (Middlebury 2013), where state-of-the-art algorithms are listed and test datasets are stored.

The algorithms can be categorized into local matching and the global matching methods. Local matching algorithms use matching costs from a small neighborhood of target pixels. Most local matching algorithms adopt a three-step procedure for matching – cost computation, aggregation, and disparity computation. The first and the third steps are common both in local and global matching methods. The aggregation step gathers measured matching costs in pre-defined matching support, whose definition varies depending on the kind of algorithm. On the other hand, global matching algorithms use matching costs from every pixels on the image to determine single-pixel correspondence. Global matching methods commonly consist of the optimization step instead of the aggregation step. In the optimization step, the algorithm aims to search acceptable solution that minimizes or maximizes some kind of *energy function*. Energy functions have various constraints about geometries and appearances of two views.

Though some of the local matching algorithms show acceptable performance based on error rate and processing speed, most top-ranked algorithms are global matching methods, such as belief propagation (BP) and graph cuts (GC), which are based on energy functional models. In general, global matching methods require more computations and more memory than local methods.

The vision algorithms consist of a set of basic general algorithms that can be combined in various manners. Some of the general algorithms are listed in Table 1.1.

Conceptually, the exhaustive search is a kind of benchmark for the global solution, ignoring all the other practical requirements such as time and space requirements. The Gauss-Seidel and Jacobi methods and relaxation algorithm are the fundamental algorithms in iterative optimization methods. The dynamic programming algorithm is an efficient algorithm for divide-and-conquer type problems. The simulated annealing (SA) algorithm is an intelligent sampling strategy for statistical optimization,

Table 1.1 Comparison of major vision algorithms

Technology	Performance	Parallelism	Time	Flexibility
Exhaustive Search	Ultimate goal	No	NP-hard	General
Gauss–Seidel	Low	Serial	Fast	General
Jacobi	Low	Parallel	Fast	General
Relaxation	Medium	Parallel	Medium	General
DP	Good	Parallel	Fast	1D problem only
SA	Good	No	Slow	General
BP	Near best	Parallel	Slow	General
GC	Best	Serial	Slow	General

cf. DP: dynamic programming, SA: simulated annealing, BP: belief propagation, and GC: graph cuts.

which is guaranteed to converge to the global minima if some ideal conditions, such as *generation probability*, *acceptance probability*, and *annealing schedules*, are satisfied. The BP is the result of the long evolution of stochastic relaxation that determines marginal distributions iteratively in a Bayesian tree. The GC algorithm has evolved from max-flow min-cut problems to the current swap move and expansion move algorithms (Boykov *et al.* 2001). Owing to the BP and GC algorithms, the performance of vision algorithms has improved dramatically. Some research has even reported that due to the two algorithms there may be no more margins than a few percent to the global optimum. The two algorithms are general problem solvers but require vast resources for computation and space. The GC algorithm requires global communication that may in turn require serial computation. The BP algorithm is based on MRF and neighborhood computation that may require parallel computation.

There are also common optimization techniques in computer vision fields such as expectation maximization (EM), Bayesian filtering, Kalman filtering, particle filtering, and linear programming relaxation (LPR).

1.3 Computing Devices for Vision

The lifespan of hardware systems is very short compared to the life spans of algorithms and software systems. In spite of the poor documentation and the difficulty of surveying the field, we can get a feel for the state of the field from the survey lists for device types, performance, and trends (Lazaros *et al.* 2008; Nieto *et al.* 2012; Tippetts *et al.* 2011, 2013).

In image processing, the most dedicated devices are FPGAs and ASICs (refer to the books on FPGAs and image processing (Ashfaq *et al.* 2012; Bailey 2011; Gorgon 2013, 2014; Samanta *et al.* 2011). They are fast enough for real-time processing, yet small enough for portability and mass production.

The flow from algorithm to architecture to device is characterized by the constraints and requirements. The algorithms and architectures are closer to concepts, and the device is the reality with a smaller degree of freedom. Therefore, any algorithm, targeted for implementation, must be developed from the beginning so as to satisfy the device constraints.

Although there are numerous types of devices, they can be classified into roughly six categories: Generic CPUs, EPs, DSPs, GPUs, FPGAs, and ASICs. All of these six platforms, except dedicated digital circuits, are common tools for hardware realization. The major differences between these platforms are speed, flexibility, and development time. In addition, there may be other relevant factors such as cost, power consumption, and time required for updates.

The major devices and factors are summarized in Table 1.2. With regards to performance and cost, single-purpose, dedicated ASICs are rated best, and the generic processors, which are targeted for general application, are rated lowest. However, with regards to flexibility, which deals with major updates or modifications, the order is reversed: ASICs are rated lowest and the generic processors are the best.

Table 1.2 Comparison of major devices

Technology	Performance/cost	Time until running	Speed	Flexibility
ASIC	Very High	Very long	Very high	No
FPGA	Medium	Long	High	Low
GPU	High	Medium	High	Medium
DSP	High	Medium	Medium	High
EP	Low	Short	Low	High
Generic CPU	Low to medium	Very short	Very low	Very high

cf. EP: Embedded Processor.

In terms of development time, ASICs take the longest amount of time and the generic processors only require programming time.

We want to explore the pure computational structures of the vision algorithms and use them as much as possible in developing dedicated architectures. Because of this, we exclude algorithms that need sophisticated software control. Devices such as GPU, DSP, EP, and generic processor are heavily dependent on software. This book focuses on the FPGA/ASIC because they are genuinely dedicated hardware solutions that do not require software interventions.

1.4 Design Flow for Vision Architectures

The task of researchers is to define vision problems, explore vision algorithms, and build software or hardware systems. For hardware realization, the vision algorithm can be coded into devices such as embedded processors, GPUs and CPUs with hyper-threading, and streaming SIMD extensions (SSE). ASICs, FPGAs, and programmable logic devices (PLD) are more dedicated devices. The chip design process is separate from the vision algorithms. The algorithms cannot be applied directly to chip design. The vision algorithm is inherently serial and the chip is inherently concurrent.

There must be an intermediate stage between the vision algorithm and the chip design. This stage, called vision architecture, must integrate the vision algorithm, which is mostly serial, into the design architectures, which are concurrent. The overall design flow is illustrated in Figure 1.2.

The design flow consists of the three parts: vision, architecture, and chip design. The vision part means the ordinary vision research and the algorithms for programming. In the vision architecture, the vision algorithms are analyzed in terms of computational structure, and redesigned using processing elements, memory, and connections into architecture. Given the architecture and specifications, the chip

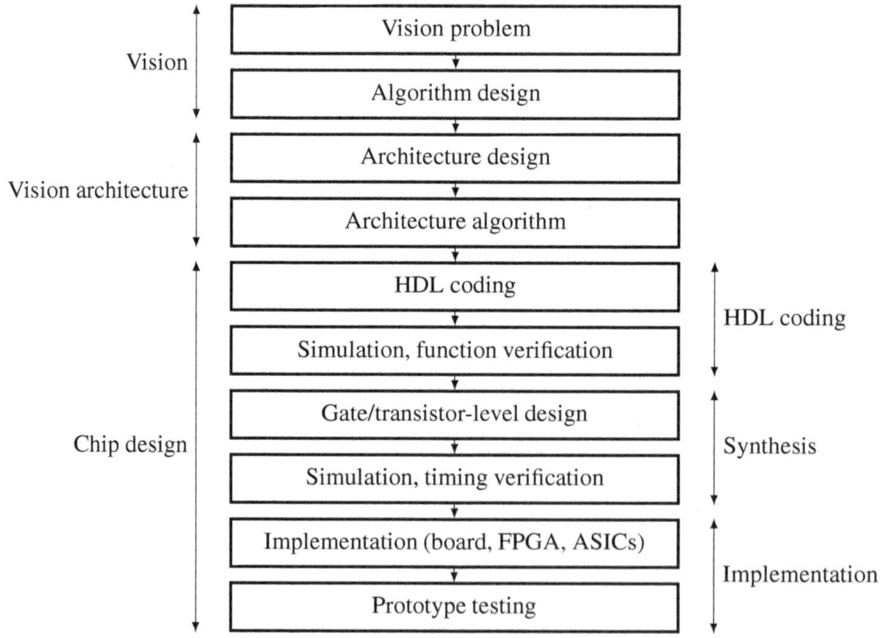

Figure 1.2 Design flow from vision to chip

design progresses sequentially from hardware description language (HDL) coding, to synthesis, and then to implementation. The HDL coding programs the architecture description into the register transfer language (RTL) format. This code is converted into circuits, i.e. net list, in the synthesis stage. Each stage is a loop consisting of design and testing. There are variety of potential realizations for the net list, such as FPGA (i.e. programming) and ASICs (i.e. hard copy) and full custom.

The FPGA design consists of the following stages.

1. Define a new project and enter the design using VHDL or Verilog HDL languages. The design can also be entered using schematic diagrams that can be translated to any HDL.
2. Compile and simulate the design. Find and fix timing violations. Obtain power consumption estimates and perform the synthesis.
3. Download the design to the FPGA using either a parallel port or a USB cable. Designs can also be downloaded via the Internet to a target device.

Once an FPGA design is verified, validated, and used successfully, there is an option to migrate it to a structured ASIC. This option is known as hard copy. Using hard copy, FPGA design can be migrated to a hard-wired design removing all configuration circuitry and programmability so that the target chip can be produced in high volume. Hard-copied chips use 40% less power than FPGAs and the internal delays are reduced.

Vision algorithms can be implemented using computational structures that are either serial or parallel and either iterative or recursive. Therefore, we have to reinterpret the vision algorithms in terms of architectural modalities and describe them in architectural terms. To expand the vision research to architecture, vision engineers have to learn two principles:

- Architecture design: Given an algorithm, analyze the computational structures in terms of data structures – memory, queue, stack, and processing – and express them in a hardware algorithm.
- HDL coding: Code the algorithm in HDL and test.

The first task is to convert vision algorithms into hardware algorithms. Vision algorithms are free from the constraints of a specific realization and as a result can rely on generic programming. The hardware, on the other hand, must be described in terms of memory, data structure, communication, and control. Likewise, the vision algorithm can be coded in a high-level programming language, but the architecture must be designed using the lower-level HDL programming language.

There are integrated programming environments such as Quatus by Altera, Inc. and ISE by Xilinx, Inc. They are the software tools for synthesis and analysis of HDL designs, which enable the developer to synthesize their designs, perform timing analysis, examine RTL diagrams, simulate a design's reaction to different stimuli, and configure the target device. We will use Quartus tools as a reference design tool and Verilog as a design language. Verilog is preferred in this book because it closely resembles C, which is one of the most prominent languages in vision research.

Problems

1.1 [Architecture] Explain the advantages and disadvantages of SISD. How are problems addressed in DSP?

1.2 [Architecture] What are the pros and cons of SIMD and MISD?

1.3 [Architecture] What are the problems with shared and distributed memory systems?

1.4 [Architecture] For GMSV and GMMP, how must Equation (1.5) be defined?

1.5 [Architecture] Express an average operation (one-pass) in terms of Equation (1.6).

1.6 [Architecture] Express a difference operation (one-pass) for $\frac{\partial}{\partial x}I$ and $\frac{\partial}{\partial y}I$ in terms of Equation (1.6).

1.7 [Devices] Explain the processors – CPU, DSP, EP, GPU, FPGA, and ASIC – in terms of their core functions and specifications. In addition, what are the state-of-the-art technologies for each device?

1.8 [Algorithm] Understanding vision algorithms in terms of computational structure is very important. Name some vision algorithms that make use of (1) one-pass/multi-pass, (2) neighborhood operation, (3) iteration, and (4) hierarchical structures.

1.9 [Algorithm] The labeling problem assigns labels $l \in [0, L-1]$ to the pixels in $\mathcal{P} = \{(x, y) | x \in [0, N-1], y \in [0, M-1]\}$. How many cases are there in labeling? If the labels of the neighbors are equal, how many cases are there? Discuss the role of constraints in the labeling problem.

1.10 [Design] Download Altera Quartus or Xilinx ISE and acquaint yourself with the tools. What are the major functions of these tools? How can vision algorithms be designed into circuits?

References

Ashfaq A, Hameed T, and Mehmood R 2012 *FPGA Based Intelligent Sensor for Image Processing: Image Processing with FPGA*. Lambert Academic Publishing.

Bailey DG 2011 *Design for Embedded Image Processing on FPGAs*. Wiley-IEEE Press.

Boykov Y, Veksler O, and Zabih R 2001 Fast approximate energy minimization via graph cuts. *IEEE Trans. Pattern Anal. Mach. Intell.* **23**(11), 1222–1239.

Brown M, Burschka D, and Hager G 2003 Advances in computational stereo. *IEEE Trans. Pattern Anal. Mach. Intell.* **25**(8), 993–1008.

Flynn M 1972 Some computer organizations and their effectiveness. *IEEE Trans. Computer* **C-21**, 948–960.

Gorgon M 2013 *FPGA Imaging: Reconfigurable Architectures for Image Processing and Analysis*. Springer.

Gorgon M 2014 *FPGA Imaging: Reconfigurable Architectures for Image Processing and Analysis*. Springer.

Kappes JH, Andres B, Hamprecht FA, Schnorr C, Nowozin S, Batra D, Kim S, Kausler BX, Lellmann J, Komodakis N, and Rother C 2013 A comparative study of modern inference techniques for discrete energy minimization problems *EMMCVPR 2013*.

Kung H and Leiserson C 1980 Algorithms for VLSI processor arrays In *Introduction to VLSI Systems* (ed. Mead C and Conway L) Addison-Wesley Reading, MA pp. 271–291.

Kung S 1988 *VLSI Array Processors*. Prentice-Hall, Englewood Cliffs, NJ.

Lazaros N, Sirakoulis GC, and Gasteratos A 2008 Review of stereo vision algorithms: from software to hardware. *International Journal of Optomechatronics* **2**(4), 435–462.

Leiserson C and Saxe J 1991 Retiming synchronous circuitry. *Algorithmica* **6**(1), 5–35.

Middlebury U 2013 Middlebury stereo home page http://vision.middlebury.edu/stereo (accessed Sept. 4, 2013).

Nieto A, Vilarino D, and Sanchez V 2012 *Towards the Optimal Hardware Architecture for Computer Vision* InTech chapter 12.

Samanta S, Paik S, and Chakrabarti A 2011 *Design & Implementation of Digital Image Processing using FPGA: FPGA-based digital image processing*. Lambert Academic Publishing.

Scharstein D and Szeliski R 2002 A taxonomy and evaluation of dense two-frame stereo correspondence algorithms. *International Journal of Computer Vision* **47**(1-3), 7–42.

Szeliski RS, Zabih R, Scharstein D, Veksler OA, Kolmogorov V, Agarwala A, Tappen M, and Rother C 2008 A comparative study of energy minimization methods for Markov random fields with smoothness-based priors. *IEEE Trans. Pattern Anal. Mach. Intell.* **30**(6), 1068–1080.

Tippetts BJ, Lee DJ, Archibald JK, and Lillywhite KD 2011 Dense disparity real-time stereo vision algorithm for resource-limited systems. *IEEE Trans. Circuits Syst. Video Techn* **21**(10), 1547–1555.

Tippetts BJ, Lee DJ, Lillywhite K, and Archibald J 2013 Review of stereo vision algorithms and their suitability for resource-limited systems http://link.springer.com/article/10.1007%2Fs11554-012-0313-2 (accessed Sept. 4, 2013).

2

Verilog HDL, Communication, and Control

As C/C++ is a major language for programming vision algorithms, Verilog HDL/VHDL is a major language for designing analog/digital circuits. These two types of languages share common properties: a textual description consisting of expressions, statements, and control structures. One important difference is that HDLs explicitly include the notion of time and connectivity. As in other types of high-level programming languages, there are numerous design languages such as Impulse C, VHDL, Verilog, SystemC, and SystemVerilog, to name a few. In addition, Verilog HDL is one of the most widely used HDLs, along with VHDL, and its syntax is very similar to that of C, allowing vision engineers to be comfortable starting a circuit design.

This HDL was standardized in IEEE Standard 1364-2005 (IEEE 2005), resembles C, and covers a wide range constructs, from gate level to system level. SystemVerilog in IEEE Standard 1800-2012 (IEEE 2012) is a superset of Verilog-2005. In addition to the modules in Verilog-2005, SystemVerilog defines more design elements such as the program, interface, checker, package, primitive, and configuration. In addition, the language interface, VPI, in Verilog-2005 is generalized into DPI. This book is mostly based on Verilog-2005 (IEEE 2005).

This chapter introduces the Verilog syntax, the communication, and control modules. For the Verilog syntax, we will learn the minimal amount of syntax and grammar necessary for designing a vision architecture. (Refer to (Stackexchange 2014; Tala 2014) for introduction and questions.) The behavioral model, which is a high-level description similar to C, is adopted in various pieces of coding throughout this book. For the design method, we will learn the concept of communication, such as synchronous and asynchronous communication, and that of control, such as datapath method and distributed control.

2.1 The Verilog System

The overall structure of a design system consists of two modules: a test bench (TB) (a.k.a. test fixture) and unit under test (UUT) (a.k.a. device under test). The UUT is a target design that is to be implemented on hardware to execute a certain algorithm. The TB is not a part of the design, but a utility for testing the UUT (Figure 2.1). Aided by a simulator, the TB generates pattern vectors as inputs to the simulated UUT, gathers the output, and compares it with the expected values, generating a warning message or counting the errors, allowing any incorrect design to be accurately caught. After simulation and testing, the UUT

Architectures for Computer Vision: From Algorithm to Chip with Verilog, First Edition. Hong Jeong.

Companion Website: www.wiley.com/go/jeong

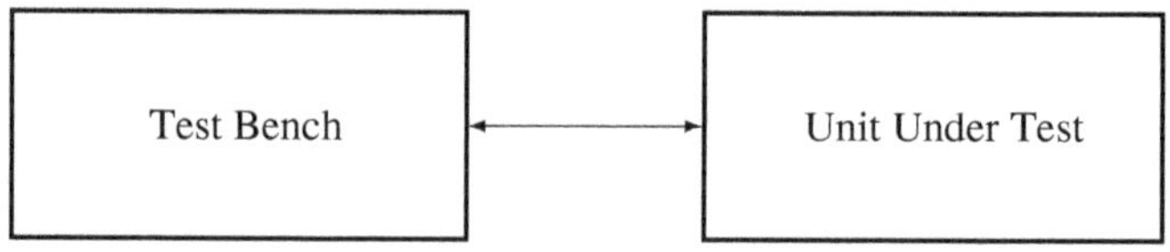

Figure 2.1 The Verilog system: TB-UUT modules

is synthesized for devices such as FPGA, CPLD, and ASIC, aided by synthesis tools and libraries. While the two modules are programmed by the same HDL language, their properties differ greatly. The target module must consist of synthesizable Verilog codes only, but the test bench can consist of both synthesizable and unsynthesizable Verilog codes.

For a vision system, the UUT can be considered as hardware that executes a certain vision algorithm, receives a series of images, and emits the results through input and output ports. For proper testing, the TB must provide a set of representative image examples to detect any possible blind spots in the algorithm or design that were not noted at the programming stage. For example, if we are designing a stereo matching system, the TB must supply a pair of images to the UUT and assess the output from the UUT by comparing the results with the predicted disparities.

Because our concern is a vision system, in the next chapter we will develop a TB-UUT system, called a *vision simulator*, dedicated to vision.

2.2 Hello, World!

To become familiar with Verilog HDL, let us start by comparing it with C language. Simply put, the syntax of Verilog is very similar to that of the C programming language. The major features in common are the case sensitivity, control flow keywords, and operators. The major differences are the logic values, variable definition, data types, assignment, concurrency, procedural blocks with begin/end instead of curly braces, and compilation stages. While a C program must be compiled once, aided by a compiler, an HDL program may undergo two stages, *RTL* in the HDL and *netlist* in the synthesizer.

Because the level of language is high enough, many algorithms in vision can be written in Verilog HDL, if not for synthesis. For example, the 'hello world' examples for Verilog and *C* are listed side by side below.

Hello world in Verilog

```
module main;
   initial
   begin
      $display("Hello, world!\n");
      $finish;
   end
endmodule
```

Hello world in C

```
#include<stdio.h>
main();
   {
        printf("Hello, world!\n");
   }
```

When executed using a Verilog simulator, the program outputs the same string as that of the C program. A program in Verilog always starts with **module** and ends with **endmodule**, after some possible headers. The scope is delimited by **begin** and **end** instead of the curly braces in C. In addition, there are many common features between the two languages. To make this program work, a file containing the above contents, `hello.v`, is provided and executed with a Verilog simulator to obtain the string, `Hello, world!` with a one-line feed. There are numerous simulators available, such as Verilog-XL,

NCVerilog, VCS, Finism, Aldec, ModelSim, Icarus Verilog, and Verilator, to name a few. In addition, there are integrated development environments (IDEs) such as Altera Quartus and Xilinx ISE for editing, simulating, debugging, synthesis, testing, and programming.

When programming in Verilog HDL, there are three hardware description methods: *structural description, behavioral description*, and *mixed description.* A structural description is used to describe how the device is connected internally at the circuit and gate level. A behavioral description is used to describe how the device should operate in an imperative manner (cf. object-oriented and declarative in SystemVerilog). Considering the complexity of vision algorithms, we will follow the behavioral description method most of the time in this book.

As the next step, let us design a simple adder, a four-bit adder, using the behavioral model.

$$c = a + b, \tag{2.1}$$

where a, b, and c are all four-bit integers. The source codes are included in the file, `adder.v`.

Listing 2.1 A 4-bit adder: `adder.v`

```
'timescale 1ns/1ps                          //unit time/precision
module adder(                               //ports
   input [3:0] a, b,                        //input ports
   output [3:0] c                           //output ports
   );

   assign c= a+ b;                          //continuous assignment
endmodule
```

The module `adder` is the target design module, written in RTL syntax, to be simulated and possibly synthesized. It can be considered a procedure having two input arguments `a` and `b` and one output argument `c`, considered a *call by value* protocol (instead of *call by reference*). In the declaration section, three *ports* (similar to *arguments* in C) are declared as **`input`** and **`output`**. However, the argument directions are not formally specified in C. The statement **`assign`** `c=a+b` indicates that `c` is changed as soon as `a` or `b` is changed. This assignment, called a *continuous assignment*, is designed for the behavior of the combinational circuit.

In addition to the main modules, a TB must also be used to examine the adder module. The test bench, `tb.v`, is shown below.

Listing 2.2 A test bench: `tb.v`

```
'timescale 1ns/1ps
module tb;                                  //no ports
   //declaration
   reg [3:0] a, b;                          //reg type for storage
   wire [3:0] c;                            //wire for connection

   //instantiation
   adder UUT (.a(a),.b(b),.c(c));           //run UUT
```

```
    //test vector generation
    initial begin                              //run once for simulation
       //initialize Inputs
       a = 0;                                  //execute sequentially
       b = 0;
       #100;                                   //wait 100 ns
       //add stimulus here
       repeat (1000) begin                     //repeat 1000 times
          a = a + 1;                           //execute sequentially
          b = b + 2;
          #100;                                //wait 100 ns
       end                                     //repeat end
    end                                        //initial end
endmodule
```

Because this module was designed only for testing, no port declaration is needed. It consists of two concurrent constructs: *instantiation* and an *initial block*, which may appear in arbitrary order. Instantiation is used to activate the adder module by calling the module as a statement. This module will be activated whenever the input values are changed. Unlike C, where all variables must be declared and defined before the statements referencing them, the input variables may not be defined lexically before instantiation but must be defined somewhere inside the same module. In the initial block, the values for the input ports are generated according to the designer's scheme. In a more elaborate system, the desired values must be generated according to the target algorithm, be compared to the actual values, and indicate the location of the errors.

In a typical IDE system such as Altera Quatus (with ModelSim) and Xilinx ISE (ISIM or ModelSim), the Verilog simulator shows the values of the variables in a timing diagram (Figure 2.2). The left side of the figure shows the data and variables along with their values, in binary format. The horizontal axis is a time axis with the units specified in the target module. In this diagram, the variable values are shown in both numeric and signal forms. After a successful simulation, the system enters the synthesis stage during which a net-list file is generated, which can be observed in a schematic diagram.

2.3 Modules and Ports

An arbitrarily large system can be built by connecting small modules with input and output ports in a hierarchical manner. As such, a hierarchical hardware description structure is realized that allows the modules to be embedded within other modules. In C, this mechanism is realized through procedure calls with parameter passing, forming nested calls. In Verilog HDL, each module definition stands alone, and the modules are not nested. To connect the modules, higher-level modules create instances of lower-level

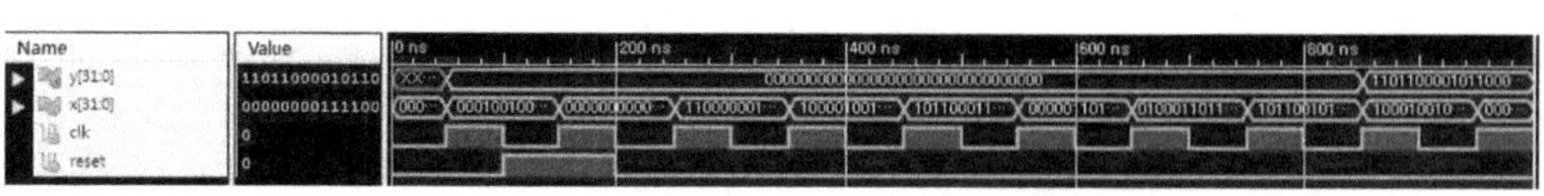

Figure 2.2 The simulator output: timing diagram

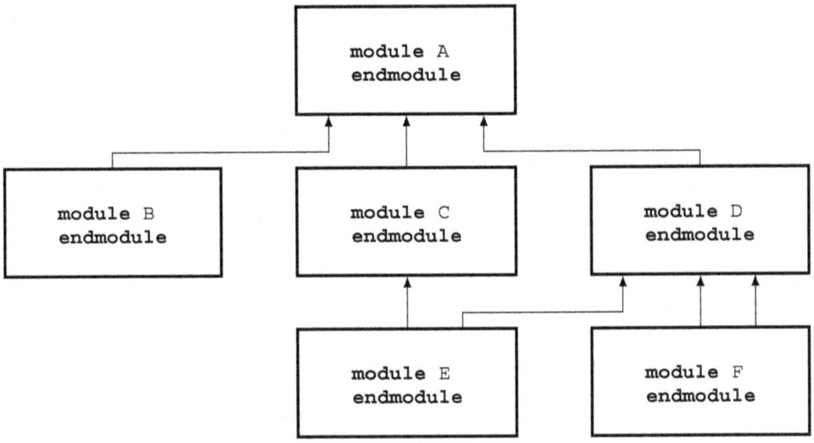

Figure 2.3 A hierarchy of modules

modules and communicate with them through input, output, and bidirectional ports. In this sense, an *instantiation* is similar to a function call in C.

Figure 2.3 illustrates a system consisting of six modules in a hierarchical connection. In this system, the top module `A` calls (i.e. instantiates) `B`, `C`, and `D`; `C` calls `E`; and `D` calls `E` and `F` twice. An instantiation creates a circuit, and thus the code means that `E` and `F` are created twice, respectively.

To avoid a naming conflict, every identifier must have a unique hierarchical path name. The hierarchy of modules and the definition of items such as tasks and named blocks within the modules must have unique names. As with the connected modules, the hierarchy of names forms a tree structure, where each module instance, generated instance, task, function, named begin-end, or fork-join block defines a new hierarchical level or scope in a particular branch of the tree. The name of the module or module instance is sufficient to identify the module and its location in the hierarchy. Therefore, a module can reference a module below it (downward referencing), a module above it (upward referencing), and a variable (variable referencing).

Communication between modules is specified through ports, similar to arguments in C. However, there are significant differences between the two languages in terms of the nature of the arguments used. Unlike C, the direction of the ports must be specified using an **`input`**, **`output`**, or **`inout`**. In addition, the port types must be specified in terms of net-type and reg-type only, regardless of whether scalar or vector data are used. Typically, the input-output pair must be declared as **`reg-wire`**. The variable **`reg`** retains its value until it is changed by executing corresponding statements, and the variable **`wire`** simulates a passive wire whose value is determined by the driver, **`reg`**.

Figure 2.4 illustrates this concept. Module A calls module B with two arguments, `a` and `b`. In this figure, the pair, `a-c`, is declared by **`reg-wire`**, and the pair, `b-d`, is declared by **`wire-reg`**. (In actuality,

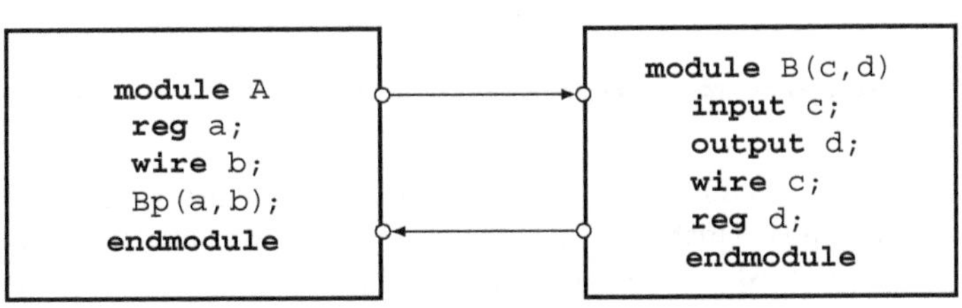

Figure 2.4 Connecting two modules by ports

wire b and **wire** c are omitted.) This concept holds, in general, for a reg-net type pair, which simulates a driver-physical wire.

The net data types represent physical connections between structural entities such as gates. A net will not store a value (except for the **trireg** net), but its value will be determined by the values of its drivers. If no driver is connected to a net, its value has to have a high-impedance (z).

There are two ways to name the ports: *positional* (a.k.a. in-place) and *named association*, without allowing a mixed association. In the example, instantiation `p(.d(b), .c(a))` in a named association is equivalent to instantiation `p(a,b)` in a positional association. The ports are either scalar or vector in reg-type and net-type but not in arrays or variables.

A module is the region enclosed between the keywords **module** and **endmodule** that contains all of the Verilog constructs except *compiler directives* having a certain structure.

Listing 2.3 Module constructs

```
module module_name (port-name, port-name,...,port-name)
   //port declarations
   input declarations                       //port directions
   output declarations
   inout declarations

   //type declarations
   net declarations                         //data and variable declarations
   variable declarations
   parameter declarations                   //parameter declarations

   //functions and tasks
   function declarations                    //function definition
   task declarations                        //task definition

   //execute once for TB
   initial begin                            //one-time execution statements
      instantiations                        //instantiation of other modules
   end

   //procedural statements
   always begin                             //statements for a design
      procedural statements
   end
endmodule
```

Followed by the keyword, **module** is the module identifier and port list. The main body of the module consists of a port declaration, variable declaration, function and task definition, and statements in the initial and procedural blocks, which are defined between **begin** and **end**. Among them, the initial block, which is executed once, is provided for a test bench. The order of all constructs, except the statements inside **begin** and **end**, does not matter.

The port list can be specified by the in-place or name list. The I/O declaration defines the direction of data flow for the ports. The variables are declared into three types: net type, variable type, and parameter. The function and task correspond to a function and procedure in C: a function returns a result, but a procedure does not. In addition, a procedure itself can be a statement, but a function cannot. The initial block is executed once and is therefore used for a design simulation. The module under test herein must put in the initial block. The main statements appearing in the procedure statements are specified by **always**.

2.4 UUT and TB

As previously mentioned, a design usually consists of a main module called the device under test (DUT) (or UUT), and another module called the test bench (TB) (or test fixture). A UUT is designed for synthesis, but a test bench is not. A test bench consists of test vectors (test suite or test harness), a UUT, and an instantiation. A set of test vectors must be generated and applied to an instantiated UUT as a stimulus so that the responses may be observed. Just like any other module description, a test bench is written in Verilog. A language-based test bench is portable and reproducible. The syntax of a TB is as follows.

Listing 2.4 The test bench constructs

```
module testbench_name
   instantiation                          //instantiation of UUT

   initial                                //one time execution
      begin
         procedural-statement             //test vector generation
            ...                           //checking and
         procedural-statement             //report
      end
endmodule
```

The structure consists of an instantiation and initial block. The purpose of an instantiation is to call the UUT, similar to a procedure call in C. However, unlike C, the argument values are defined later in the initial block. The purpose of an initial block is to provide argument values to the UUT and observe the output from the UUT and to provide other jobs such as comparing the output with the expected values, counting errors, and issuing warnings, all under the control of the designer.

A detailed description is shown in Figure 2.5. As shown on the left, the TB sends test signals to the DUT and receives the response in return. The internal structure of the TB is illustrated in detail on the right. A simulation with the TB is realized by an instantiation in the **initial** block. The pattern generator provides a set of test patterns including critical input cases that are supplied to both the DUT and the algorithm, which is to be executed by the UUT. Both responses from the TB and algorithm are collected, observed, and compared by the comparator to see if any mismatches exist. The observation results are reported outside by characters, diagrams, or graphs.

2.5 Data Types and Operations

Thus far, we have learned the concepts of the UUT-TB and module-port. Now, let us describe in detail the syntax needed for constructing such modules. A *value set* is a set of data types designed to represent the data storage and transmission elements in a digital system. The Verilog value set consists of four basic values, `0` and `1`, for ordinary logic, and `x` and `z` for unknown and high-impedance states. For example,

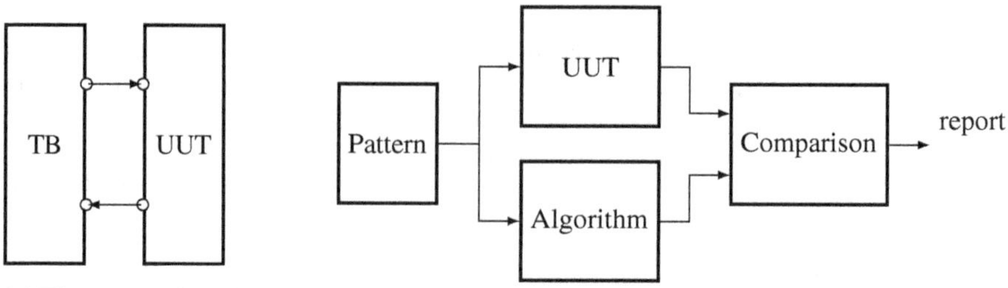

(a) The connection of UUT-TB

(b) The TB structure

Figure 2.5 The UUT and the TB

one bit can have the values, `1'b0`, `1'b1`, `1'bx`, and `1'bz`, where the bases are `'b` (binary),`'o` (octal), `'d` (decimal), which is the default value, and `'h` (hexadecimal).

There are three groups of data types: *net data type*, *variable data type*, and *parameter*. The net data type represents physical connections and thus does not store a value (except **`trireg`**). Its value is determined by the values of its drivers and thus has high impedance if disconnected. The exception is **`trireg`**, which holds the previously driven value even when disconnected from the driver. The driver connection is represented by a continuous assignment statement. The net type consists of *wired logic* (**`wire`**, **`wand`**, and **`wor`**), *tri-state* (**`tri`**, **`triand`**, **`trior`**, **`tri0`**, **`tri1`**, and **`trireg`**), and *power* (**`supply0`** and **`supply1`**).

Among the net types, the **`wire`** and **`tri`** nets are used for nets that are driven by a single gate or continuous assignment. The **`wire`** net is used when a driver drives a net, and the **`tri`** net is used when multiple drivers drive a net. A wired net is used to model wired logic configurations. The **`wor/trior`** nets create a wired-or, such that if the value of any of the drivers is 1, the resulting value of the net is 1. Similarly, the **`wand/triand`** nets represent a wired-and, such that when the value of any driver is 0, the value of the net is 0.

The **`trireg`** net stores a value to model the charge storage nodes. It can be in one of two states: a driven state or a capacitive state, each of which corresponds to either a connected or disconnected state. The **`tri0`** and **`tri1`** nets represent nets with resistive pull-down and resistive pull-up devices on them. The **`supply0`** and **`supply1`** nets are used to model the power supplies in a circuit.

The variable type is an abstraction of a data storage element, as in C. The values are initially default and are determined later through *procedural assignment* statements. The variable data types are **`reg`**, **`integer`**, **`real`**, **`time`**, and **`realtime`**. The **`reg`** type is for a register that stores data temporarily in a procedural assignment. It is used to represent either a combinational circuit or a register that is sensitive to edges or levels of signals. The **`integer`** and **`time`** variable data types are not for hardware elements but for a convenient description of the operations. The **`integer`** and **`real`** types are general-purpose variables used for manipulating quantities that are not regarded as hardware registers. The **`time`** variable is used for storing and manipulating simulation-time values in cases where timing checks are required and for diagnostics and debugging purposes.

The net and variable types can be configured as arrays. An n-dimensional array is represented by a variable identifier and multiple indices: `[MSB_1:LSB_1]...[MSB_n:LSB_n]`, where MSB and LSB are integers.

Listing 2.5 Arrays

```
[MSB_1:LSB_1]...[MSB_n:LSB_n] variable_identifier
                    [MSB_1:LSB_1]...[MSB_m:LSB_m]
```

The index convention is a *row-major* order, that is, the LSB changes most rapidly. A variable identifier is presented between the indices. The indices before and after the variable are called *packed* and *unpacked*, respectively. Packed arrays can have any number of dimensions. They provide a mechanism for subdividing a vector into subfields, which can be conveniently accessed as array elements. A packed array differs from an unpacked array, in that the whole array is treated as a single vector for arithmetic operations. An unpacked array differs from a packed array in that the whole array cannot be accessed, but rather each element has to be treated separately. (Unfortunately, the multidimensional packed array is possible only in SystemVerilog.) The memory is realized with a reg-type array.

Example 2.1 (Arrays) *Examples of arrays are as follows.*

```
reg a[7:0];                                        //8 1-bit scalar register
reg [7:0] b;                                       //1 8-bit vector register
reg c[7:0][0:255];                                 //8 x 256 array of 1-bit
reg [0:7] d [0:255];                 //256 8-bit vector indexed from 0 to 7
//The followings are allowed only in SystemVerilog.
reg [1:3][7:0] e;                                  //24-bit 3-field vector
reg [1:3][7:0] f[0:255]                            //256 24-bit 3-field vectors
reg [1:3][7:0] g[1:2][0:255]                       //512 24-bit 8-field vectors
```

In the example, **reg** could have been replaced with any of the net or variable types.

Parameters do not belong to either a net or variable type but are constants. There are two types of parameters: *module parameters* (**parameter**, **defparam**) and *specify parameters* (**specify**, **specparam**). The parameters cannot be modified at runtime, but can be modified at compilation time to have values that are different from those specified in the declaration assignment, allowing a customization of the module instances. The non-local parameter values can be altered in two ways: the **defparam** statement, which allows assignment to parameters using their hierarchical names, and the module instance parameter value assignment, which allows values to be assigned in line during module instantiation.

The net types are further specified by the drive strength and propagation delay. There are two types of strengths: *charge strength* for **trireg** and *drive strength* for net signals. The types of drive strength are **supply**, **strong**, **pull**, and **weak**. A signal with drive strength propagates from a gate output and a continuous assignment output. The charge strength specification is used with **trireg** with **small**, **medium**, and **large**. The net delay is specified with triple delays (rise, fall, transition), which indicate a rise delay, fall delay, and transition to a high-impedance value. Each of these delays can be further specified through (min:typ:max) keywords.

Example 2.2 (Strengths and delays) *Some typical examples are as follows:*

```
trireg a;                                   //charge strength medium
trireg (small) #(0,0,100) b;                //charge strength and delay
trireg (large) unsigned [0:7] c;            //charge with range
and #(10) and1 (out,input1,input2);         //delay
and #(10,20) and2 (out,input1,input2);      //delay
bufif0 #(1,2,3) buff0 (io1,io2,dir);        //delay
bufif0 #(1:2:3,4:5:6,7:8:9) buff1 (io1, io2, dir);  //delay
```

Now, let us consider the operators defined for the data types. Verilog defines a set of unary, binary, and ternary operators. For bit-wise logic, `~`, `&`, and | represent NOT, AND, and OR, respectively; ^ and `~^`/`^~` represent XOR and XNOR, respectively. The logical operators are !, `&&`, and || for NOT,

AND, and OR, respectively. The reduction operators are unary operators, `&`, `~&`, `|`, `~|`, `^`, and `~^/^~` representing AND, NAND, OR, NOR, XOR, and XNOR, respectively.

The arithmetic and shift operators are `+`, `-`, `~`, `*`, `/`, `%`, and `**` for add, subtract, 2's complement, multiply, divide, modulus, and exponent, respectively. The relational operators are `>`, `<`, `>=`, and `<=`. In addition, the operators, `==` and `=!` are used for comparing two numbers excluding `x` and `z`. The operators, `===` and `==!` are used for numbers with all four states considered.

The shift operators are `>>` and `<<` for logical, and `>>>` and `<<<` for arithmetic shifts. The operators `{,}`, `{{}}`, `?:`, and `,` are concatenation, replication, conditional, and event-or, respectively.

Example 2.3 (Expressions) *Some examples are as follows.*

```
&4'b1001=0                              //reduction
false: 4'b0000!, true: 4'b0010!         //logic value
{2'b10,2'b01} = 4'b1001                 //concatenation
4'b0100 & 4'b01xz = 4'b0100             //bit-wise logic
~2'b10 = 2'b01                          //bit-wise complement
16'b0,8'bz01 = 8'bzzzzzz01              //bit-wise
true: 2'b10 < 4'b010                    //logic statement
2'h06 == 4'b0110                        //logic statement
X ? Y:Z                                 //if X is true then Y, else Z
```

An event-or can be used instead of **`or`** in the following case: the expressions, `@(clock or trig) regb = rega` and `@(clock,trig) regb = rega`, are identical, indicating an assignment occurring when an event occurs on clock or trig. The delay expression is a triplet, `(minimum:typical:maximum)`, as in `(16'd10:16'd50:16'd100)`. The compiler directives are **`'include`**, **`'define`**, and **`parameter`**, where **`'define`** is used as a global, and **`parameter`** as a local to a module.

2.6 Assignments

Unlike in C, where only one type of assignment exists, there are two basic forms of assignments in Verilog: *continuous assignment* to drive the nets and *procedural assignments* to update the variables. Roughly speaking, they are introduced to specify explicitly whether an assignment is for combinational or sequential circuits.

The purpose of a continuous assignment is to represent a signal change in a combinational circuit by assigning values to the nets. The assignment operator is the pair **`assign`** and `=`. As in combinational logic, the left-hand side of this operator is changed whenever the value of the right-hand side changes.

Example 2.4 (Continuous assignments) *The two expressions are effectively the same.*

Continuous declaration	Declaration, assignment
`wire (strong1, pull0) b = a;`	`wire b;` `assign (strong1, pull0) b = a;`

In the example, the two expressions are identical.

A delay, called a *net delay*, can be introduced by either a declaration or an assignment.

Example 2.5 (Delays) *The continuous assignment with delay.*

```
wire #100 a;
assign wire c = (#20) a + b;
```

In the first expression, any change of `a` will take effect after 100 unit times from the cause event. In a continuous assignment, changes in `a` or `b` will take effect with a change of `c` in 20 time units.

Similar to a delay, strength can be used as a declaration or an assignment. This applies only to assignments to scalar nets of the following types: **wire**, **tri**, **trireg**, **wand**, **triand**, **tri0**, **wor**, **trior**, and **tri1**. In other types, the strengths are fixed. For example, the strength value is always 1 for the following net types: **supply1**, **strong1**, **pull1**, **weak1**, and **highz1**. Similarly, the strength value for an assignment is always 0 for the following: **supply0**, **strong0**, **pull0**, **weak0**, and **highz0**.

Example 2.6 (Strengths) *The strengths for a continuous assignment.*

```
assign (strong1, pull0) b = a;          //the same as below
assign (pull0, strong1) b = a;
assign (pull0, pull1) b = a;            //wrong
```

In the example, the first two expressions are identical: the order does not matter. The third expression is wrong: the strengths conflict with each other.

In the behavioral model, all of the statements are contained through the following procedures: initial construct, always construct, task, and function. The activity starts at the control constructs, **initial** and **always**. All of the initial and always constructs are enabled at the beginning of the simulation and run separately and concurrently. However, the initial construct is executed only once, but the always construct is permanently executed. There is no implied order of execution between the initial and always constructs. There is also no limit to the number of initial and always constructs that can be defined in a module.

An initial block is executed once and is externally concurrent. The assignments are either sequential (=) or concurrent (<=). This construct is not for a synthesis but for a simulation. Contrarily, an always block is executed permanently until **$finish** or **$stop** appears and is internally concurrent. The assignments are either sequential (=) or concurrent (<=). This construct is provided for synthesis.

The behavioral model is characterized by procedural assignments that are used to place values in variables. Unlike a continuous assignment, a procedural assignment does not have duration but holds a value until the next procedural assignment occurs for that variable. Procedural assignments appear within procedures such as **always**, **initial**, **task**, and **function**. These assignments can be thought of as triggered assignments that happen when the flow of execution in the simulation reaches an assignment within a procedure. Reaching the assignment can be controlled by event controls, delay controls, if statements, case statements, and looping statements.

There are three types of procedural assignments: = for *blocking*, <= for *nonblocking*, and **assign-deassign** and **force-release** for *procedural continuous* assignments. The first type of procedural assignment is blocking assignments that are executed before the execution of the statements that follow in a sequential block. The second type is nonblocking assignments, which are all concurrent, independent, and order-free within the same parallel block. All of the nonblocking assignments in a parallel block undergo a two-step execution: the first step (evaluation, execution, and scheduling) and an update.

Example 2.7 (Blocking and nonblocking assignments) *Swapping values.*

Blocking statements

```
always @(posedge clock) begin
 c = a; //temporary variable c
 a = b;
 b = c;
end //always
```

Nonblocking statements

```
always @(posedge clock) begin
 b <= a; //RHS for the 1st step
 a <= b; //LHS for the 2nd step
end //always
```

The swapping can be realized by both blocking and nonblocking assignments. With blocking assignments, a temporary variable is needed. With nonblocking assignments, two assignments are concurrent. The variables on the right-hand side are old values, and the ones on the left-hand side are new values obtained after the swapping.

The third type is a procedural continuous assignment with **assign-deassign**, which assigns values only when active and prevents ordinary procedural assignments from affecting the values of the assigned registers when inactive. This allows expressions to be driven continuously onto variables or nets. The **assign** part in a procedural continuous assignment statement overrides all procedural assignments to a variable. The **deassign** part in a procedural statement terminates a procedural continuous assignment to a variable. The value of the variable remains the same until the driver **reg** is assigned a new value through a procedural assignment or procedural continuous assignment. Yet another type is a procedural continuous assignment with **force-release**, which overrides a procedural assignment or procedural continuous assignment such that the variable resumes its original value when released.

Example 2.8 (assign-deassign) *The procedural continuous assignment.*

```
always @(posedge clock)
   Count = Count + 10;          //Count generation
always @(reset or set)
   if (reset)                   //asynchronous reset
      assign Count = 0;         //prevents counting, until reset goes low
   else if (set)                //asynchronous set
      assign Count = 1;         //prevents counting, until set goes low
   else
      deassign Count;           //resume counting on next posedge clock
```

This is a counting example that contains a blocking procedural assignment and procedural continuous assignments. The counting event in the first always block is suppressed by the events in the second always block.

2.7 Structural-Behavioral Design Elements

Two design elements are possible: *structural* and *behavioral*. A structural design aims at a faithful hardware realization and uses fourteen gates such as **and**, **or**, **not**, **nand**, **nor**, **xor**, **xnor**, **buf**, **buf0**, **buf1**, **notif0**, and **notif1** and twelve switches including **cmos**, **nmos**, **rtran**, and **tran** (see IEEE1364-2005 for a full list). In a structural model, an instance statement has the following form.

Listing 2.6 Instantiation

```
component-name instance_identifier (expr, expr, ..., expr);
```

Here, the component name indicates the built-in gate.

Example 2.9 (Structure of module) *An inhibition gate can be built as follows.*

```
module Inhibitor (in, invin, out);      //BUT-NOT
   input in, invin;                     //port declaration
```

```
    output out;
    wire notinvin;                       //variable
    not Q1 (.out(notinvin),.in(invin));  //instantiation
    and Q2 (out,in,notinvin);            //instantiation
endmodule
```

This example is for an inhibitor designed by two built-in gates. The arguments can be specified by either an in-place or a naming method.

As previously stated, all procedures in the behavioral model are defined in the following four statements: initial construct, always construct, task, and function. The initial and always constructs are enabled at the beginning of a simulation. The initial construct is executed only once, but the always construct is permanently executed. There is no implied order of execution between the initial and always constructs, and there is no limit to the number of initial and always constructs that can be defined in a module.

The behavioral (procedural) design is characterized by a procedural assignment for the blocking and nonblocking processing, a **begin-end** block for the scope, and a sensitivity list for the synchronization.

Listing 2.7 Procedural assignments

```
Blocking assignment: variable-name = expression
Non-blocking assignment: variable-name <= expression
```

The statements with a blocking assignment are executed in order, but those with a nonblocking assignment are executed concurrently.

The scope is determined by the **begin-end** pair.

Listing 2.8 Scopes

```
begin: block-name
   variable declaration
   parameter declarations
   procedural statements
end
```

A scope consists of declarations and procedural statements. The always block consists of a sensitivity list.

Listing 2.9 always block

```
always @(signal-name or signal-name) procedural statements
```

Whenever any signal in the list is changed, the procedural statements in the scope are executed sequentially for blocking and concurrently for nonblocking.

The behavioral design is a high-level programming environment consisting of the following control flows: condition (**if**, **case**), loop (**for, repeat, while, forever**), and **fork/join**, which are all analogous to those in C.

Listing 2.10 Conditionals

```
if (condition) procedural-statement                  //if condition
else procedural-statement

case (selection-expression)                          //case statement
   choice,...,choice: procedural-statements
      ...
   choice,...,choice: procedural-statement
endcase

for (loop-index=first, loop-index <= last);          //for loop
   loop-index = loop-index+1;)
   procedural-statement

repeat (index-expression) procedural-statement       //repeat loop

while (logical-expression) procedural-statement      //while loop

forever procedural-statement                         //forever loop

fork                                                 //fork statement
   procedural-statement
join
```

Here, a forever statement indicates an infinite loop. The **fork/join** pair is used for parallel processes. All statements (or blocks) between a **fork/join** pair begin their execution simultaneously upon the execution flow hitting the fork. The execution continues after the join upon completion of the longest-running statement or block between the fork and join.

Example 2.10 (fork/join) *A simple example.*

```
initial fork
   $write("A");                          //print A
   $write("B");                          //print B
   begin #5                              //wait 5 time units
      $display("C");                     //display C
   end
join
```

As a result of the simulation, we may have either sequence 'ABC' or 'BAC' printed out. In actuality, the order of simulations between the first and second writes depends on the simulator implementation.

Procedure assignments have two methods for timing control: *delay control* and *event control*. Delay control is used to specify the time duration between when a statement is first reached and when the statement is actually executed. The event control expression allows a statement execution to be delayed until a simulation event occurs in a concurrently executing procedure. There are two types of simulation events: implicit and explicit. An implicit event indicates a change of value on a net or variable, and an explicit event indicates the occurrence of an explicitly named event triggered from other procedures.

The timing controls are realized through three methods: # for delay control, @ for event control, and **wait** for a combination of an event control and a loop. The event control can be made sensitive to signal edges with **posedge** and **negedge**.

Example 2.11 (Timing control) *The timing control example.*

```
#100 b = a;                              //delay 100 time units
@c b = a;                                //at the change of c
@ (posedge clock) b = a;                 //positive edge of clock
always @(a or b, c) d= a+b+c;            //event logical
always @(*) c = a+b;                     //equivalent to @(a or b)
always @* begin                          //equivalent to @(a,b,c,d)
   c = a; d = b; e = c + d;
end
wait (!enable) b = a;                    //at the change of enable
```

The *intra-assignment delay* and *event controls* are the timing controls specified within an assignment statement. They delay the assignment of a new value to the left-hand side, but the right-hand side expressions are evaluated before the delay.

Example 2.12 (Intra-assignment) *The example is as follows.*

```
always @Swap                      always @Swap
   fork                              fork
      #10 a = b;//at 10,                a = #10 b;//at 0, tmp1=b, tmp2=a
      #10 b = a;//a=b and b=a           b = #10 a;//at 10, a=tmp1, b=tmp2
   join                              join
```

In the code on the left, both a and b are sampled and set at the same simulation time, resulting in a *race condition*. In the code on the right, the assignment is deferred 10 time units from the sampling.

Finally, a block of statements is a means for grouping two or more statements together so that they act syntactically as a single statement. There are two types of blocks: a sequential block with **begin-end** and a parallel block with **fork-join**.

2.8 Tasks and Functions

As in C, tasks and functions are common procedures that can be executed in different locations in a program. In addition, they are building-blocks of large procedures, and thus, the source descriptions can be easily built and debugged.

However, the two procedures have many different characteristics. Unlike those in C, a function must execute in one simulation time unit, but a task can execute in multiple time units, according to time-controlling statements. Another difference is that a function cannot enable a task, but a task can enable other tasks and functions. As for the arguments, a function has at least one input type argument and does not have an **output** or **inout** type argument, but a task can have zero or more arguments of any type. A function returns a single value, but a task does not return a value. A function has no output, but a task can have zero or more arguments of **output** and **inout**.

A function responds to an input value by returning a single value, but a task can return multiple values. Because of this response, a function is used as an operand in an expression, but a task is used as a statement.

A task is enabled from a statement that defines the argument values to be passed to the task and to the variables that receive the results. Control is passed back to the enabling process after the task has completed. If a task has timing controls inside it, then the time of enabling a task can be different from the time at which the control is returned. A task can enable other tasks, which in turn can enable still other tasks with no limit on the number of tasks enabled. Regardless of how many tasks have been enabled, control does not return until all enabled tasks have completed.

There are two forms for tasks: task name-endtask and task name-parenthesis-endtask.

Listing 2.11 Tasks and functions

```
task task_name;
   input declarations
   output declarations
   variable declarations
   parameter declarations
   procedural-statements
endtask
function result-type function-name;
   input declarations
   variable declarations
   parameter declarations
   procedural-statements
endfunction
```

The standard formats of task and function are shown.

Tasks without and with the optional keyword **automatic** are called *static tasks* and *automatic task*, respectively. In a static task, all declared items are statically allocated and shared across all uses of the task executing concurrently. In an automatic task, all declared items are allocated dynamically for each invocation and cannot be accessed by hierarchical references. An automatic task can be invoked through the use of its hierarchical name.

Because a function is limited in a unit simulated time, it cannot contain any time-controlled statements with #, @, or **wait** and thus cannot enable tasks. A function definition contains at least one **input** argument but not **output** or **inout**. A function must include an assignment of the function result value to the internal variable that has the same name as the function name. Finally, a function should not have any nonblocking assignments.

To see the differences between tasks and functions, let us look at the factorial example, which is a typical example of recursion. The recursion can be realized by either a function or a task.

Example 2.13 (Factorial) *The use of tasks and functions in factorial.*

Task

```
module factorial_task;
 //define the task
 task factorial (level,result);
  input [31:0] level;
  output integer result;
  integer i;
  if (level >= 2)
   factorial (level-1,result);
   result = result * level;
  else
   result = 1;
 endtask

 //test the task
 integer result;
 integer n;
 initial begin
 for (n = 0; n <= 7; n = n+1)
  begin
   factorial(n,result);
   $display("%0d factorial=%0d",
             n, result);
  end
 end
endmodule //factorial_task
```

Function

```
module factorial_function;
 //define the function
 function automatic integer factorial;
  input [31:0] level;
  integer i;
  if (level >= 2)
   factorial = factorial (level - 1)
             * level;
  else
   factorial = 1;
 endfunction

 //test the function
 integer result;
 integer n;
 initial begin
  for (n = 0; n <= 7; n = n+1)
  begin
   result = factorial(n);
   $display("%0d factorial=%0d",
             n, result);
  end
 end
endmodule //factorial_function
```

On the left, the task calls itself recursively, and on the right, the function is called iteratively. The factorial is a good example that shows the relationship between recursion and iteration.

2.9 Syntax Summary

The typical structure of a module is shown below, containing as many as possible Verilog constructs.

Listing 2.12 Summary of syntax

```
module arch_vision (Q1,Q2,Q3,Q4);
   //declaration
   input Q1,Q2;                                //ports
   output[7:0] Q3;
   inout Q4;
   reg[&:0] Reg1,Mem1[1:254];                  //variables
   wire Wire1,Wire2,Wire3,Wire4;
   parameter String = "vision architecture";
   //one time execution for Test bench
```

```
    initial                                    //for simulation only
    begin: BlockName
       Statements
    end
    //continuous assignments
    assign Wire1 = Expression;
    assign wire[3:0] Wire2 = Expression;
    //procedural assignments
    always @(sensitivity-list)
       begin
          procedural-statements;
       end
    //module instances, COMP defined in other module
    COMP Q (Wire3,Wire4);                      //external module call
    Task(.A(Q1),.B(Q4),.C(Q3));                //procedure call
    Q3 = Function(Q1);                         //function call
    //procedures definition
    task Task:
       input A;                                //ports
       inout B;
       output C;
       begin                                   //main part
          Statements
       end
    endtask

    //function definition
    function[7:0] Function;
       input A;                                //ports
       begin
          Function = Expression;               //use Function <= RHS
       end
    endfunction
endmodule
```

The module consists of declaration, initial block, procedural blocks, task, and function; the order may be arbitrary, and the execution is concurrent.

In addition, typical Verilog statements are listed below.

Listing 2.13 Summary of statements

```
#delay                                 //delay expressions
wait (Expression)
@(A or B or C)                         //triggering statements
@(posedge Clk)
```

```
Reg = Expression;                       //assignment statements
Reg <= Expression;
assign Reg = Expression;
deassign Reg;
TaskEnable(...);                        //event control
disable TaskOrBlock;
->EventName;                            //event trigger
```

The list contains continuous and procedural assignments, along with even triggers.

2.10 Simulation-Synthesis

Once the vision algorithm is written in the Verilog HDL complying with the Verilog syntax and grammar, the file with extension v must be compiled for simulation and then synthesis. In the simulation stage, the Verilog syntax is analyzed in the compilation stage, some design constructs such as **`generate`** are interpreted in the elaboration stage, and the compiled code written in Verilog grammar is executed in the simulation stage. The synthesis stage generates the standard design in the register-transfer level (RTL) and the target specific net-list, which needs to be downloaded into the devices such as field-programmable gate arrays (FPGAs), complex programmable logic devices (CPLDs), and application-specific integrated circuits (ASICs).

Because the synthesis is far more restricted than the simulation, we have to know the requirements for the constraints and use them in the design stage. There are three types of synthesis: logic gate synthesis, RTL synthesis, and behavioral synthesis. A logic gate synthesis is a synthesis from logic equations to logic gate diagrams; it is the simplest level of synthesis. In an RTL synthesis, all operations involve the transfer of data between registers using only a subset of the Verilog HDL. This is the state of the art of synthesis. A behavioral synthesis aims to convert a high-level description, like C, to desired circuits. Naturally, the HDLs have evolved toward this type of synthesis. For example, SystemVerilog is a superset of Verilog-2005 that has many high-level constructs, seemingly like C++. The behavioral design in Verilog-2005 HDL is a natural choice for vision algorithms, which involve complicated operations. In the future, SystemVerilog might play a significant role in designing vision algorithms, together with OpenCV.

Some of the guidelines in the synthesis stage are stated below. A combinational logic can be synthesized with continuous statements with **`assign`** and blocking statements with **`always`**. Continuous assignment can be used to represent simple circuits and must be used outside of always or initial blocks. Assign is used in top-level statements that are executed concurrently and continuously with all other top-level statements in the module. The left-hand side (LHS) of a continuous assignment statement must be a wire signal, whereas the variables on the right-hand side can be reg or wire signals.

The **`always`** blocks can represent complex combinational circuits; continuous assignment alone is not enough for complex combinational circuit. All circuit inputs must be included in the event control clause of the **`always`** block. No other signals must be included in the event control clause. No statements should be sensitive to rising or falling signal edges.

The sequential logic synthesis is designed by **`always`** blocks, in which statements execute concurrently and infinitely. Always blocks use an event control clause in order to prevent inefficient simulation behavior. The LHS of an assignment in an always block must be the type of reg. Within the same module, values must not be assigned to a single signal in two or more different always blocks. Use of both positive and negative edges of the same clock signal in an event control should be avoided. The common code template for Moore/Mealy-type finite state machines, available in mode Verilog platforms, may be useful.

Verilog consists of synthesizable and unsynthesizable Verilog code. For synthesis, the following must be considered. System functions and tasks are not for synthesis but for simulation and debugging. Verilog directives are not for synthesis. The **`initial`** block is not for synthesis. The values `x` and `z` are difficult to use in synthesis and should typically be avoided, unless there is a very specific reason to use them. Strength and delay statements cannot be synthesized. In conditional constructs (e.g., **if**, **case**), the default should be used, and don't-care values should be assigned to the output in order to simplify logic. Latches are inferred from incomplete if statements.

2.11 Verilog System Tasks and Functions

For simulation purposes, the Verilog HDL defines a set of system functions and tasks, analogously to those in C libraries. They are divided into ten categories: display tasks, file I/O tasks, timescale tasks, simulation control tasks, PLA modeling tasks, stochastic analysis tasks, simulation time functions, conversion functions, probabilistic distribution functions, command line input, and math functions. Knowing the system functions and tasks is essential to building a sophisticated system. Here, the format is the same as the normal tasks and functions.

One of the most useful system functions might be the display tasks, called **$display**, **$write**, **$strobe**, and **$monitor**.

Listing 2.14 Display-write tasks

```
display_task_name (list_of_arguments);
```

The display tasks may have a suffix such as b, o, d or h for binary, octal, decimal, and hex numbers, respectively; *d* is the default format for unspecified arguments. The basic display is write, and an advanced one is display, which adds a newline. In addition, strobe provides the ability to display simulation data at a selected time, and monitor provides the ability to monitor and display the values of any variables or expressions specified as arguments. The list of arguments includes strings, formats, and variables.

Example 2.14 (Display task) *Examples of display tasks.*

```
$write ("value = %b", bval);            //binary data
$write ("value = %0d", dval);           //suppress leading zeroes
$display ("value = %0", dval):          //dval is written in octal
$display ("time = %t", $time);          //simulation time
$strobe ("time = %0d", dval);           //at each simulation time
$monitor ("value = %0d", dval);         //displays at dval change
```

The system tasks and functions for file I/O are divided into the following four groups: open/close, file write, variable write, and read file. The file open and close tasks are $fopen and $fclose, respectively, which are very similar to those in C.

Listing 2.15 File open-close

```
multi_channel_descriptor = $open ("file_name");
file_descriptor = $open ("file_name", type);
$fclose (multi_channel_descriptor);
$fclose (file_descriptor);
```

The multichannel and file descriptors are 32-bit numbers. The argument `type` is a character string such as `r` for read, `w` for write, or `a` for append. A single bit in the multichannel descriptor represents the channel number and open/close. Thus, because multichannel descriptors are combined into one descriptor that contains all the open channel positions, multiple files can be written. A file descriptor is used to open a file according to `type`. The **`$fclose`** system task closes an open file.

The file output task names are **`$fdisplay`**, **`$fwrite`**, **`$fstrobe`**, and **`$fmonitor`**, defined similarly to the standard output, **`$display`**, **`$write`**, **`$strobe`**, and **`$monitor`**.

Listing 2.16 File output

```
file_output_task_name (multi_channel_descriptor,list_of_arguments);
file_output_task_name (file_descriptor, list_of_arguments);
```

]The first argument is either a multichannel descriptor or a file descriptor, which indicates where to direct the file output.

The system tasks, **`$swrite`** and **`$sformat`**, are used to write strings.

Listing 2.17 String output

```
$swrite (output_reg, list_of_arguments);
$sformat (output_reg, format_string, list_of_arguments);
```

The **`$swrite`** is the same as **`$fwrite`** except that the first argument is a **`reg`**. The **`$sformat`** is used for formatted writing. Files that are opened by file descriptors can be read only if they were opened with `r` type values.

Character or string is read by the following commands:

Listing 2.18 Character-string-text input

```
character = $fgetc (file_descriptor);
code = $ungetc (character, file_descriptor);
code = $fgets (reg, file_descriptor);
code = $fscanf (file_descriptor, format, arguments);
code = $sscanf (reg, format, arguments);
code = $fread (dest, file_descriptor, start, count);
$readmemb (file_reg, memory_name, start, finish);
$readmemh (file_reg, memory_name, start, finish);
```

For the file and string input, system functions are provided for character (**`$fgetc`**, **`$ungetc`**), line (**`$fscanf`**, **`$sscanf`**), register (**`$fread`**), and text (**`$readmemb`**, **`$readmemh`**). **`$fgetc`** reads a character, and **`$ungetc`** returns the pointer to the previous position. **`$fgets`** reads a line until **`reg`** string is filled, a newline character is read and transferred to string, or an EOF condition is encountered. **`$fscanf`** and **`$sscanf`** are used for formatted reading from a file descriptor and **`reg`** string, respectively. **`$fread`** is used for reading binary data to fill the destination, which is **reg** or memory. The optional arguments start and count specify the starting point and the number of reading data, respectively. **$readmemb** and **$readmemh** read and load data from a test file to a memory. The text file may contain white spaces, comments, binary, or hexadecimal numbers. The start and finish addresses are optional. In addition, the addresses may be specified in the data file with the @ sign. The **integer** code represents an error condition.

For file access, the following commands are provided:

Listing 2.19 File positioning

```
position = $ftell (file_descriptor);
code = $fseek (file_descriptor, offset, operation);
code = $rewind (file_descriptor);
```

The system function **$ftell** returns the offset between the beginning of the file and the file descriptor. **$fseek** is used to reposition the file to the position. **$rewind** is equivalent to **$fseek**(file_descriptor,0,0). **$flush** writes any buffered output to the opened files. During the file I/O system task and function, incidental errors might occur. **$ferror** is a system function that returns an error code. There are also command line inputs including the following: **$test**, **$value**, and **$plusargs**.

Example 2.15 (File I/O) *The I/O examples are as follows.*

```
integer messages, broadcast,
   r_color, g_color, b_color;
initial begin
   r_color = $fopen("r.dat");
   if (r_color == 0) $finish;
   g_color = $fopen("alu.dat");
   if (g_color == 0) $finish;
   b_color = $fopen("mem.dat");
   if (b_color == 0) $finish;
   messages = r_color|g_color|b_color;
   //broadcast std output
   broadcast = 1 | messages;
end

$fdisplay (broadcast,
   "file opened at %d", $time);
$fdisplay (messages,
   "Error on r_color at %d",
      $time);
```

The simulation control tasks are **$finish** and **$stop** for exit and suspend, respectively. There are a set of system tasks and functions for queue and stack: **$q_initialize**, **$q_add**, **$q_remove**, **$q_full**, **$q_exam**.

Listing 2.20 Queue

```
$q_initialize (q_id, q_type, max_length, status);
$q_add (q_id, job_id, inform_id, status);
$q_remove (q_id, job_id, inform_id, status);
$q_full (q_id, status);
$q_exam (q_id, q_stat_code, q_stat_value, status);
```

$q_initialize creates a queue (q_type=1) or stack (q_type=2) with the given queue id and maximum length. The push and pop operations are simulated with **$q_add** and **$q_remove**, respectively.

The `job_id` is an integer input for identification. The `inform_id` is a user-defined integer. **`$q_full`** checks spaces in the queue, and **`$q_exam`** provides statistical information about queue activity. The status code is an integer that represents the error warning condition.

The simulation time can be observed by the following system functions: **`$time`**, **`$stime`**, and **`$real-time`**. There are system functions that convert numbers between different formats: **`$rtoi`** for real to integer, **`$itor`** for integer to real, **`$realtobits`** for real to binary, and **`$bitstoreal`** for binary to real. There are a set of random number generators: **`$random`**, **`$dist_uniform`**, **`$dist_normal`**, **`$dist_exponential`**, **`$dist_poisson`**, **`$dist_chi_square`**, **`$dist_t`**, and **`$dist_erlang`**.

There are integer and real math functions in Verilog system functions, which are identical to those in C. In addition to the Verilog system tasks/functions, there is a program interface with foreign functions written in C. With this interface, called VPI, the Verilog program can call user-defined functions and tasks and obtain the results. In image processing, the file transfer is the most essential operation between C programs and Verilog programs, which is not feasible in such operations.

2.12 Converting Vision Algorithms into Verilog HDL Codes

Computer-aided hardware design has evolved from the FSM, algorithmic state machine (ASM), HDL, and high-level synthesis (HLS). In the FSM method, the algorithm is represented by the state table and the state diagram. The design is in the logic equations and the minimization. In the FSM method with HDL, the representation is in the RTL (register transfer level) and the state diagram. The goal is to design the control logic from the state diagram and the datapath from the RTL. In ASM, the algorithm is represented by the RTL and the ASM chart. The control logic and the data path are designed by ASM chart and the RTL that are provided. The high-level synthesis works at a higher level of abstraction, starting with an algorithmic description in a high-level language such as SystemC, ANSI C/C++, OpenCL (Acceleware 2013), or HLS (Xilinx 2013). At the start, the designer develops the module functionality and the interconnect protocol manually. After that, the high-level synthesis tool constructs the architecture and transforms the functional codes into fully timed RTL codes. In the end, the RTL codes are used directly in a conventional logic synthesis flow to create a gate-level implementation.

One of the most fundamental abstractions is the control structure. The basic types of control structures are sequential, conditional, and loop. Most vision algorithms consist of mixtures of these control structures. Sequential computation means that statements are executed sequentially during each clock tick. Consider an algorithm consisting of N such statements. There are two ways to interpret the sequential computations in Verilog HDL (refer to the following codes).

Listing 2.21 Sequential

```
always @(posedge clock) begin
   a = b;
   c = d;
   e = f;
   g = h;
   ...
   y = z;
end //always
always @ (posedge clock) begin
   if (reset) state <= 1;
   else begin
      state <= state + 1;
```

```
      case (state) begin
         1: begin
               a <= b;
            end
         2: begin
               c <= d;
            end
            ...
         N: begin
               y <= z;
            end
      endcase
   end
end //always
```

In the first code, the statements are executed sequentially by the blocking assignments. In the second code, the same is true for the sequential execution. However, there is a considerable difference between the two code segments. In the first code, the statements in a block are executed in one clock period, but in the second code, the statements are executed in each clock period. This mechanism is possible by the always-case combination. The sequential order is forced by the state and the statements are divided into blocks. Notice that the state increment and case block are concurrent.

In Verilog HDL, the available loop statements are **for**, **while**, **repeat**, and **forever**. The codes segments, with one exception, are listed side by side in the following. The one exception is **forever**, which represents permanent iteration. The assignments are all blocking, but they can also all be nonblocking, if necessary. For *N* statements, the loops need *NT* clocks for blocking and *T* clocks for nonblocking.

for

```
for (t=0;t<T;t=t+1)
   begin
      a = b;
      c = d;
      ...
      y = z;
   end
```

while

```
t = 0;
while (t<T)
   begin
      t = t + 1;
      a = b;
      ...
      y = z;
   end
```

repeat

```
repeat (T)
   begin
      a = b;
      c = d;
      ...
      y = z;
   end
```

Regardless of the type of loop, all the statements in a block are executed in one clock period. Even for the blocking assignments, all of the statements in a block are executed in one clock time period. Actually, the loop is unfolded into a cascade of combinational modules, with each module executing each statement. (See *unfolding* (Wikipedia 2013b).)

In many cases, the statements must be separated and executed sequentially in a clock period, and repeated iteratively up to a predetermined number of times. Inserting delay statements between each blocking assignment is useless because the delay statements are not synthesized. It is possible to implement the sequential mechanism by combining case and if key words.

Loop 1

```
always @ (posedge clock) begin
   if (reset) begin
      state <= 1; t <= 1;
   end else begin
      state <= state + 1;
      case (state) begin
         1: a <= b;
         2: c <= d;
         ...
         N: begin
            y <= z;
            if (t < T) begin
               state <= 1;
               t <= t + 1;
            end
         end
      endcase
   end
end //always
```

Loop 2

```
always @ (posedge clock) begin
   if (reset) begin
      state <= 1; t <= T;
   end else begin
      state <= state + 1;
      case (state) begin
         1: a <= b;
         2: c <= d;
         ...
         N: begin
            y <= z;
            if (t > 0) begin
               state <= 1;
               t <= t - 1;
            end
         end
      endcase
   end
end //always
```

The code segments on the right also execute the statements iteratively up to the maximum number of iterations. (The statements can be either blocking or nonblocking, but not a mixture. Each statement can be replaced with a block of statements, which are either blocking or nonblocking.) In the Verilog loop statement, one iteration occurs in just one clock period. In this code, on the other hand, one iteration occurs in N clock periods.

There are many ways to code loops. First, the counter can be either auto-incrementing or auto-decrementing. The code segments above use both types of counters. There is another variation of the loop. The position of the if-statement can be either at the beginning or at the end of the statement block.

Autoincrement

```
always @ (posedge clock) begin
   if (reset) begin
      state <= 1; t <= 1;
   end else if (t < T) begin
      state <= state + 1;
      t <= t + 1;
      case (state) begin
         1: a <= b;
         2: c <= d;
         ...
         N: y <= z;
      endcase
   end
end //always
```

Autodecrement

```
always @ (posedge clock) begin
   if (reset) begin
      state <= 1; t <= T;
   end else if (t > 0) begin
      state <= state + 1;
      t <= t - 1;
      case (state) begin
         1: a <= b;
         2: c <= d;
         ...
         N: y <= z;
      endcase
   end
end //always
```

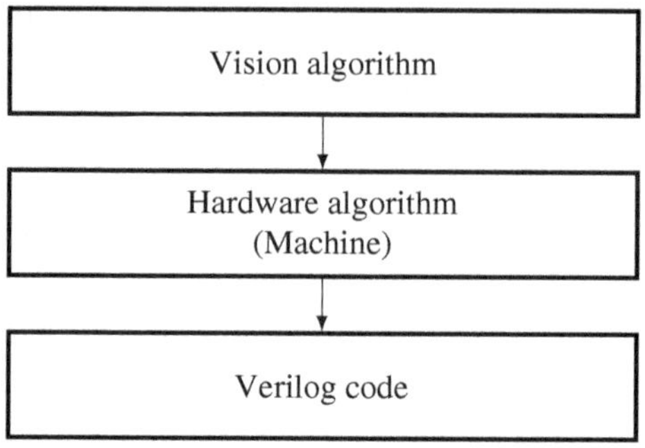

Figure 2.6 The three-step design method for vision architecture

Unlike the previous code segments, the if-statement in this code is placed before the statement block. Like the previous code segments, two types of counters can be implemented. Therefore, there are four ways to configure the loops, depending on the if-statement positions and the counter types. If the assignment types are considered as well, then there are eight types of loops.

2.13 Design Method for Vision Architecture

Verilog HDL includes many design aids that transform the codes in high-level languages or diagrams to the codes in HDL. For example, the 'C to HDL tools' convert C program code into an HDL (or RTL) (Wikipedia 2013a). In the future, high-level languages might evolve to manage both software and hardware with the same unified compiler. Among others, the two packages, Altera OpenCL (Acceleware 2013) and Xilinx HLS (Xilinx 2013), are evolving rapidly. The design can be downloaded to the FPGAs (i.e. programming), converted to the hard copy of the ASIC chips (i.e. hard copy), or the full custom ASIC chips.

As an alternative, this book suggests a systematic method in designing a vision architecture. This method consists of three steps: 1) to prepare a vision algorithm, 2) to prepare a hardware algorithm, and 3) to code in Verilog HDL (see Figure 2.6). The first step is to provide a vision algorithm that consists of clear definitions of input and output, step-by-step procedures, (i.e. in time) for computing output, and all parameters and variables.

The second step is to provide a hardware algorithm that represents a state machine. Consider that $q(t)$ is the state, $\{x(t), y(t)\}$ is an input-output pair, and $T(\cdot)$ and $H(\cdot)$ are the state transition function and the observation function, respectively. Then, a Moore machine is represented by the state equation:

$$\begin{cases} q(t+1) = T(q(t), x(t)), \\ y(t) = H(q(t)). \end{cases} \tag{2.2}$$

This equation represents the general operations in vision algorithms, including sequential operation, parallel operation, iterative operation, neighborhood operation, recursive computation, and various memory structures.

A block diagram is shown in Figure 2.7(a). The state machine expresses how the state evolves and how the output is generated, as a function of time. To be a hardware algorithm, the standard representation, Equation (2.2), is not enough, because the use of resources (i.e. memory, ports, and connection) is not explicitly defined. A state equation must clearly specify which place of the memory must be read in order for the state to be updated, and which place of the memory must be replaced by the updated values.

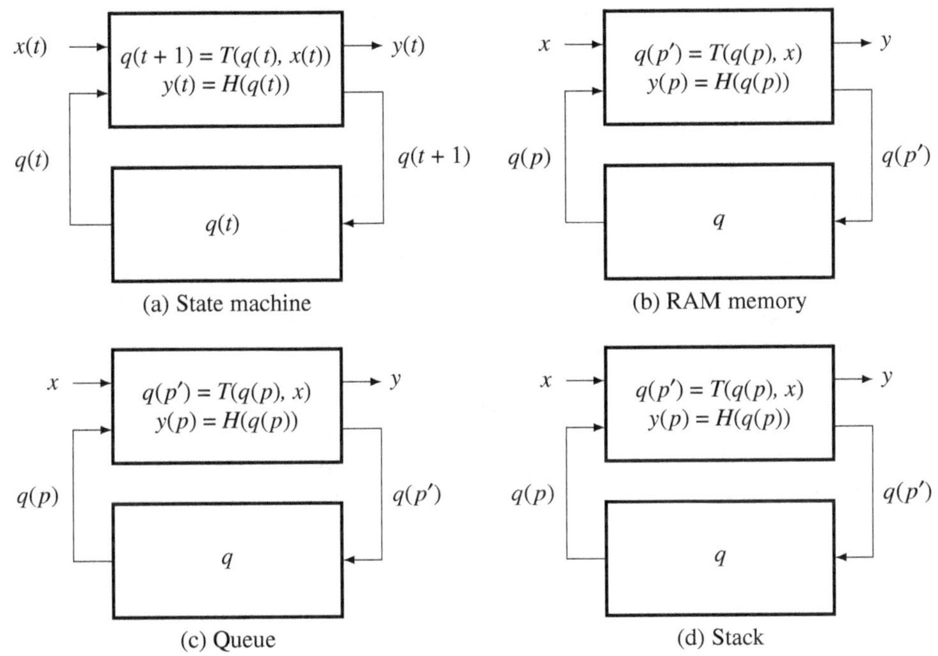

Figure 2.7 State machines for vision

That is, the state equation must be rewritten in terms of the state memory and connectivity. To examine this further, we must specify the types of memories used most often in vision algorithms: RAM (random access memory), queue, and stack (Figures 2.7(b)–(d)). With RAM, an algorithm may access an arbitrary address in a memory for memory read and write. It may be a vector or a plane memory, often like an image plane. With a queue memory, an algorithm may push the data in one end and read data from another position of the queue. With a stack, an algorithm may read or write the memory by pop or push operations. A complicated system may consist of one or more such memories.

Let us denote the reading and writing positions of a memory by p and p', respectively. Then the new state equation is

$$\begin{cases} q(p') \leftarrow T(q(p), x), \\ y \leftarrow H(q(p)). \end{cases} \tag{2.3}$$

Here, the time index is omitted, because this equation is executed in every clock tick in a sequential circuit. Instead, an index, which represents the connectivity between memory and processor, is specified. The positions of a state memory, p for reading and p' for writing, must be defined explicitly. Also, the assignment can be any of the Verilog assignments, continuous assignment (`assign =`), blocking (=) or nonblocking (i.e. <=). (The assignment, $\leftarrow$, collectively represents the three types of assignments.) In a neighborhood system, the access points must be a set of addresses within a neighborhood window. In most vision algorithms, the addresses are not random; they are fixed. Therefore, deriving addresses of the memory is one of the major tasks for specifying a hardware algorithm. To differentiate a hardware algorithm from a software algorithm, we use the term '(state) machine' for hardware algorithm. Once the hardware algorithm is provided, we can express the architecture more easily by the Verilog HDL.

2.14 Communication by Name Reference

For vision processing, large amounts of data must sometimes be transferred between modules very rapidly. The data may be as small as a scalar or a vector or it may be as large as a set of image arrays or maps. The data width and data length are usually constant or known in advance. Verilog HDL allows only a scalar and a vector to be transferred between two ports. Therefore, the data must be a scalar, a byte, or a long vector constructed from a large array. The data must be transferred sequentially. There are basically two methods for building channels between modules: the *reference-based method* and the *port-based method.* In addition, there must one or more control programs that copy the original image and write the copy to the other module.

The reference-based method is useful when a large amount of image data must be transferred between modules, especially during simulations. Instead of using the physical ports, this method uses the name referencing in the hierarchical name referencing in Verilog HDL. Depending on where the control mechanism exists, there are three methods. Assume that a sender contains an image and a receiver wants copies of it, and that the two modules are instantiated as SENDER and RECEIVER in the third module. The first possibility is that the sender is active and the receiver is passive during the copying process.

Listing 2.22 Referencing method: active sender and passive receiver

```
'define DATA_WIDTH 8
'define DATA_SIZE 10
module sender(input clock, reset);
   reg ['DATA_WIDTH-1:0] image [0:'DATA_SIZE-1];     //image to be sent
   integer i;                                        //counter
   //send data
   always @(posedge clock) begin
      if (reset) begin                               //pseudo data
         for (i=0; i<'DATA_SIZE; i=i+1) begin        //by random
            image[i] <= $random % 256;               //number generation
         end
      end
      else begin
         //copy data by name reference
         for (i=0; i<'DATA_SIZE; i= i+1) begin       //send data
            RECEIVER.image[i] <= image[i];           //by referencing
         end
      end
   end //always
endmodule

module receiver(input clock, reset);
   reg ['DATA_WIDTH-1:0] image [0:'DATA_SIZE-1];     //image to be copied
endmodule
```

The image data is stored in the sender module and it is copied into the image in the other module. Without loss of generality, the image is filled by a random number generator for test purposes. In actual applications, the image must be an actual image or set of vectors or a scalar. (The same method is used repeatedly in the following for dealing with test images.) In the main part, an image element of the other module is referenced and copied using the image element in this module. Meanwhile, the receiver module contains an empty image. Because the receiver is passive, it does nothing, and the sender performs the copying process. No other module is necessary, though the sender and the receiver must be able to receive common signals: clock and reset signals.

The second possibility is the opposite of the method above. In this case, the sender is passive and the receiver is active in the transfer control process.

Listing 2.23 Referencing method: passive sender and active receiver

```
`define DATA_WIDTH 8
`define DATA_SIZE 10
module sender(input clock, reset);
   reg [`DATA_WIDTH-1:0] image [0:`DATA_SIZE-1];     //image to be sent
   integer i;                                        //counter
   //send data
   always @(posedge clock) begin
      if (reset) begin                               //pseudo data
         for (i=0; i<`DATA_SIZE; i=i+1) begin        //by random
            image[i] <= $random % 256;               //number generation
         end
      end
   end //always
endmodule

module receiver(input clock, reset);
   reg [`DATA_WIDTH-1:0] image [0:`DATA_SIZE-1];     //empty image
   integer i;                                        //counter
   //copy data
   always @(posedge clock) begin
      //copy data by name reference
      for (i=0; i<`DATA_SIZE; i= i+1) begin          //copy data
         image[i] <= SENDER.image[i];                //by referencing
      end
   end //always
endmodule
```

In this case, the sender does nothing but prepare the image data. The receiver copies the image from the sender into its own image. The receiver references the image in the sender and copies its contents into the image.

The third possibility is the case where there is a third module that controls the copy process from the sender to the receiver. In this case, the sender and the receiver are both passive, and the third module is a controller for the communication process. The sender contains an image that is filled by a random number generator.

Listing 2.24 Referencing method: active third module

```
`define DATA_WIDTH 8
`define DATA_SIZE 10
module sender(input clock, reset);
   reg [`DATA_WIDTH-1:0] image [0:`DATA_SIZE-1];   //image to be sent
   integer i;                                        //counter
   //send data
   always @(posedge clock) begin
      if (reset) begin                               //pseudo data
         for (i=0; i<`DATA_SIZE; i=i+1) begin        //by random
            image[i] <= $random % 256;               //number generation
         end
      end
   end //always
endmodule

module receiver(input clock, reset);
   reg [`DATA_WIDTH-1:0] image [0:`DATA_SIZE-1];   //image to be copied
endmodule

module third_module(input clock, reset);

   //instantiation
   sender SENDER (clock, reset);
   receiver RECEIVER (clock, reset);

   //control by a third module
   integer i;                                        //counter
   always @(posedge clock) begin
      for (i=0; i<`DATA_SIZE-1; i= i+1) begin        //send data
         RECEIVER.image[i] <=  SENDER.image[i];      //copy image
      end
   end //always
endmodule
```

The receiver contains an empty image to be filled. In this case, the third module plays the role of transferring data between the sender and receiver. Any module can access the variables in the other modules by the hierarchical name referencing mechanism in Verilog HDL.

2.15 Synchronous Port Communication

Unlike in the simulation modules, the data in the synthesis modules must be transferred through ports. Because the port is one-dimensional, sending a multidimensional array through the port requires special care. On the sender side, the array must first be flattened into one-dimensional vectors and must be sent iteratively via the data stream. On the receiver side, the flattened vector must be popped out into the original array.

There are two methods that can be used to send a stream of data: synchronous and asynchronous data transfer. In synchronous transfer, the sender and the receiver start simultaneously. The role of the sender is to send the data units synchronously, one at a time, according to the clock. The role of the receiver is to receive the data synchronously, one at a time, from the common clock. There is no checking mechanism between the beginning and the end of the transfer, which is called a *transaction*, except by the common clock. The clock should allow for a slight delay between the times of sending and receiving.

For synchronous communications, there can be a third module that instantiates the sender and receiver and connects them by generating control signals.

Listing 2.25 Synchronous communication: third module control

```
'define DATA_WIDTH 8
'define DATA_SIZE 10
module third_module (input clock, reset);
   integer i;                                   //counter
   wire [7:0] data;                             //connection
   reg  state, req_send, req_receive;           //control variables
   //instantiation
   sender SENDER (clock, reset, req_send, data); //sender
   receiver RECEIVER (clock, reset, req_receive, data); //receiver

   //control
   always @(posedge clock) begin
      if (reset) begin
         i <= 0; state <= 1; req_send <= 0; req_receive <= 0;
      end
      else begin
         case (state)
         0: begin
            state <= 1;i <= i + 1;req_send <= 1; req_receive <= 0;
            end
         1: if (i < 10) begin                   //trigger both modules
            state <= 1;i = i + 1;req_send <= 1;  req_receive <= 1;
            end
            else if (i == 10) begin             //trigger once more
               i <= i + 1; req_send <= 0;  req_receive <= 1;
            end
            else req_receive <= 0;
         default: state <= 0;
         endcase
      end
   end //always
endmodule
```

```
module sender(input clock, reset, req, output reg [7:0] data);
   reg [7:0] image [0:9];                        //image data
   //sending data
   integer i;                                    //counter

   //fill the image
   always @(posedge clock)
      if (reset) begin                           //provide data
         for (i=0; i<10; i=i+1) begin image[i] <= $random % 256;
      end

   always @(posedge clock) case (req)            //monitor req_send
      0: i <= 0;
      1: begin i <= i + 1; data <= image[i]; end
      endcase
endmodule

module receiver(input clock, reset, req, input [7:0] data);
   reg [7:0] image [0:9];                        //empty image
   //sending data
   integer i;                                    //counter
   always @(posedge clock) case (req)            //sense req_receive
         0: i <= 0;
         1: begin i <= i + 1; image[i] <= data; end
      endcase
endmodule
```

The third module must be careful to trigger the sender first during the request for the transaction and keep the receiver triggered at the end of the transaction. That is, the beginning and end of the transaction are delayed by one clock period between the sender and the receiver. Unlike the third module, the control program is the same in both the sender and the receiver.

Another alternative is that the sender controls the data communication.

Listing 2.26 Sender active receiver passive

```
`define DATA_WIDTH 8
`define DATA_SIZE 10
module sender(input clock,reset,output reg req,output reg [7:0]data);
   //image
   reg [7:0] image [0:9];                        //image
   //variables
   integer i;                                    //counter
   reg state;                                    //state
```

```
    //fill the image
    always @(posedge clock) begin
       if (reset) begin                                //fill the image
          for (i=0; i<10; i=i+1) image[i] <= $random % 256;
    end //always

    //sedn data
    always @(posedge clock) begin
       if (reset) begin state <= 0; i <= 0; end
       else begin
          case (state)
          0: begin
             state <= 1; i <= i + 1; data <= image[i]; req <= 1;
             end
          1: if (i < 10) begin
                i <= i + 1; data <= image[i]; req <= 1;
             end
             else if (i == 10) begin i <= i + 1;   req <= 1; end
             else req <= 0;
          endcase
       end
    end //always
endmodule

module receiver (input clock,reset,req,input [7:0] data); //receiver
    //empty image
    reg [7:0] image [0:'DATA_SIZE-1];                 //empty image
    //variables
    reg state;                                        //state
    integer i;                                        //counter
    //main part
    always @(posedge clock) begin
       case (req)                                     //monitor request
          0: i <= 0;                                  //idle
          1: if (i < 10) begin i <= i + 1; image[i] <= data; end
          else i <= 0;
       endcase
    end //always
endmodule
```

The sender controls the receiver by sending a request signal. Meanwhile, the receiver monitors for the request signal and continues to copy data as long as the request signal is asserted.

Note that the request signal is still active for one more clock period even after the counting ends. There is one clock period delay between the sender and the receiver.

2.16 Asynchronous Port Communication

For secure communication, the transaction must include a two-phase or four-phase *handshaking* protocol. In both cases, when the two ports are linked, the data transfer is synchronized by a common clock. In the four-phase handshaking protocol, the quiet (i.e. idle) state is when neither the request nor the acknowledgement are zero. In the first step, the sender provides data and raises the request signal. In the second step, the receiver detects the rise in the request signal, receives the data, and raises the acknowledgement signal. In the third step, the sender detects the rise in the acknowledgement signal, lowers the request signal, and stops the data transfer. In the fourth step, the receiver detects the low request signal and lowers the acknowledgement signal. The four steps are repeated again as needed.

The two-phase handshaking protocol is a simplified version. There are two quiet states. The request and acknowledgement are both either zero or one. In the first step, the sender provides data and changes the request signal. In the second step, the receiver detects the change in the request signal, receives the data, and changes the acknowledgement signal. In the third step, the sender detects the change in the acknowledgement signal and the transaction ends. The loop is repeated forever.

The control mechanism on the sender's side is shown below. It consists of two states – one state for idling and the other state for sending data. The assumption is that the database to be sent is provided already before the transfer. This template shows that the database is a vector and that the transfer unit is a scalar in the vector. However, the database can be easily expanded to an image array. A counter is used to count the number of data units that are transferred.

Listing 2.27 Handshaking

```
`define DATA_WIDTH 8
`define DATA_SIZE 10
module third_module (input clock, reset);          //call the modules
   //variables
   wire [`DATA_WIDTH-1:0] data;                     //connecting the modules
   //instantiation
   sender SENDER (clock,reset,req,ack,data);        //sender
   receiver RECEIVER (clock,reset,req,ack,data); //receiver
endmodule

module sender(input clock,reset,output reg req,input ack,
   output reg [7:0] data);
   //image
   reg [`DATA_WIDTH-1:0] image [0:`DATA_SIZE-1]; //image for transfer
   //variables
   integer i;                                       //counter
   reg state;                                       //state
   //main part for sending
   always @(posedge clock) begin
      if (reset) begin                              //fill the image
         for (i=0; i<10; i=i+1) image[i] <= $random % 256;
         i <= 0; state <= 1; req <= 0;              //initialization
      end else begin
```

```
            case (state)
            0: if (!ack) begin state <= 1; req <= 0; end  //alt states
            1: if (i == 0) begin
                   state <= 0; i <= i+1; data <= image[i]; req <= 1;
               end
               else if (ack) begin
                   if (i < 10) begin
                   state <= 0; i <= i + 1; data <= image[i]; req <= 1;
                   end
                   else begin state <= 0; i <= 0;   req <= 0;
                   end
               end
            default: state <= 0;
            endcase
        end
    end //always
endmodule

module receiver (input clock,reset,input req,output reg ack,
    input [7:0] data);
    //empty image
    reg ['DATA_WIDTH-1:0] image [0:'DATA_SIZE-1]; //to be filled
    //variables
    reg state;                                   //state
    integer i;                                   //counter
    //main part for sending
    always @(posedge clock) begin
        if (reset) begin i <= 0; state <= 1; ack <= 0; end
        else begin
            case (state)
            0: if (!req) begin state <= 1; ack <= 0; end
            1: if (req) begin
               if (i < 10) begin
                   state <= 0; i <= i + 1;  image[i] <= data; ack <= 1;
               end
               else begin state <= 0; i <= 0;   ack <= 0;
               end
            end
            default: state <= 0;
            endcase
        end
    end //always
endmodule
```

The sender provides the data to be sent and sends the request signal to the receiver. At each clock signal, the sender sends new data unit until the number of data units reaches a predefined number. Because the sender and the receiver know the number of data units, the acknowledgement signal is not necessary. On the receiver side, the control mechanism must be designed similar to the state machine. The receiver monitors for the request signal from the sender and begins to capture the data at each rising clock signal. When the number of data units that are captured reaches the predefined number, the receiver sends the acknowledgement signal to the sender.

The control mechanism must monitor the request bit from the sender and respond immediately when the request is asserted. At each clock signal, the data is captured and stored and the counter is incremented. The amount of received data is the same as that of the sent data. Upon completion, an acknowledgement signal is sent to the sender, which is not necessary in this simple case.

In this case, the handshaking protocol marks the beginning and end of the entire data transfer. During the transfer process, the data transfer and packet communication are synchronous. For secure communication, when the clock may be somewhat unreliable due to broadcasting, the handshaking protocols can be inserted between each data unit, resulting in asynchronous communication. There is a large difference between synchronous and asynchronous communications. For image transfer, a faster method is typically used, because the amount of data to be transferred is usually large.

Among the event-sensitive and level-sensitive control statements, the **wait** statement can be used for synchronizing or handshaking between the concurrent processes. (Unfortunately, it is not synthesizable in most systems.) It is sensitive to levels, as opposed to events, and is thus useful for handshake control (Lin 2008). In addition to the control mechanism, two *semaphores* (or *messages*) are needed, 'send' and 'receive' for example. The process waits until the expression of the semaphores is true, and then executes the statement. There are two types of handshake protocols: two-phase and four-phase. Further, each protocol has two alternative methods: sender-initiated and receiver-initiated (Lin 2008). The following is an example of a receiver-initiated code for the four-phase handshake protocol:

Listing 2.28 Port communication: Four phase handshake

```
`define DATA_WIDTH 8
`define DATA_SIZE 100

module tb;                                            //testbench
   reg clock, reset;
   wire ['DATA_WIDTH - 1:0] data;                     //connection
   wire send, receive;                                //semaphores
   integer i;                                         //counter

   //instantiation
   sender SENDER (clock, reset, send, receive, data);     //sender
   receiver RECEIVER (clock, reset, send, receive, data);   //receiver

   //initialization
   initial begin
      clock = 0; reset = 0;          //initialize clock and reset
      for(i=0;i<'DATA_SIZE;i=i+1) SENDER.image[i] = $random % 256;
      #50; reset = 1; #150; reset = 0;              //reset
   end
```

```
   //clock generation
   always #50 clock =  ~clock;
endmodule

module sender (                                  //sender
   input clock, reset,
   input send,                   //receive message from receiver
   output reg receive,              //send message to receiver
   output reg ['DATA_WIDTH-1:0] data
   );

   reg ['DATA_WIDTH-1:0] image [0:'DATA_SIZE - 1];        //data

   integer i;                                    //variable

   always @(posedge clock) begin: SENDER
      if (reset) begin i <= 0; end               //initialize variable
      else if (i < 'DATA_SIZE) begin
            receive = 0;                         //don't receive yet
            wait (send) data = image[i];         //wait for send
            receive = 1;                         //receive my data
            wait (!send) receive = 0;            //wait while receiving
            i = i + 1;                           //next data
         end
   end //always
endmodule

module receiver (
   input clock, reset,
   output reg send,
   input receive,
   input ['DATA_WIDTH-1:0] data
   );

   reg ['DATA_WIDTH-1:0] image [0:9];
   integer i;

   always @ (posedge clock) begin: RECEIVER
      if (reset) begin i = 0; end                //initialize variable
      else begin
         send = 1;                               //send data
         wait (receive) image[i] = data;         //wait for receive
            send = 0;                            //don't send
```

```
        wait (!receive) send = 1;                    //wait
        i = i + 1;                                   //next data
      end //else
    end //always
endmodule
```

Both modules run concurrently, and therefore, the messages are initialized (send = 1, receive = 0). Because it was initiated (send = 1), the sender provides data and sends a message (receive = 1). The receiver receives the data and acknowledges the successful transfer (send = 0). The sender then asks the receiver if it is ready to receive data whenever the sender is ready (receive = 0). This triggers the last wait statement in the receiver to change the state (send = 1). Finally, the two processes are back in their initial states waiting to repeat the above procedure.

The four-phase handshake is based on the semaphore levels, which results in four states, 0/0. 0/1, 1/0, and 1/1, for send/receive semaphore pairs. Conversely, the two-phase handshake can be designed by event-sensitive control. It has two states – 0/0 and 1/1 – for send/receive semaphores:

Listing 2.29 Port communication: two-phase handshake

```
'define DATA_WIDTH 8
'define DATA_SIZE 100

module tb;                                           //testbench
  reg clock, reset;
  wire ['DATA_WIDTH - 1:0] data;                     //connection
  wire send, receive;                                //semaphores
  integer i;                                         //counter

  //instantiation
  sender SENDER (clock, reset, send, receive, data);     //sender
  receiver RECEIVER (clock, reset, send, receive, data);    //receiver

  //initialization
  initial begin
    clock = 0; reset = 0;            //initialize clock and reset
    for(i=0;i<'DATA_SIZE;i=i+1) SENDER.image[i] = $random % 256;
    #50; reset = 1; #150; reset = 0;                 //reset
  end
  //clock generation
  always #50 clock = ~clock;
endmodule

module sender (                                      //sender
  input clock, reset,
  input send,                  //receive message from receiver
```

```
   output reg receive,            //send message to receiver
   output reg ['DATA_WIDTH-1:0] data
   );

   reg ['DATA_WIDTH-1:0] image [0:'DATA_SIZE - 1];        //data

   integer i;                                        //variable

   always @(posedge clock) begin: SENDER
      if (reset) begin receive = 0;i <= 0;end        //initialize variable
      else if (i < 'DATA_SIZE) begin
            receive =  ~receive;                     //don't receive yet
            wait (send) data = image[i];             //wait for send
            i = i + 1;                               //next data
         end
   end //always
endmodule

module receiver (
   input clock, reset,
   output reg send,
   input receive,
   input ['DATA_WIDTH-1:0] data
   );

   reg ['DATA_WIDTH-1:0] image [0:9];
   integer i;

   always @ (posedge clock) begin: RECEIVER
      if (reset) begin send = 0; i = 0; end          //initialize variable
      else begin
            send =  ~send;                           //send data
            wait (receive) image[i] = data;          //wait for receive
      end //else
   end //always
endmodule
```

Many problems exist in both the four-phase and two-phase (a.k.a. XOR) handshakes. In general, the two-phase handshake will have less overhead and better efficiency if a common clock drives the communicating modules. On the other hand, the four-phase handshake is more reliable and efficient when there is no such common clock.

Finally, the handshake and synchronous communication can be mixed, similar to packet communication, if the data size is very large. Between semaphore exchanges, a large amount of data can move between the sender and the receiver in an interval of many clocks.

2.17 Packing and Unpacking

For image processing, the transfer unit is usually a vector or a set of images or maps. The processor must access a pixel, a set of pixels for neighborhood operation, or the entire image for internal storage in an array. Regardless of the type of data, the transfer unit must be a vector, which is a simple byte for a pixel or a set of bytes for neighborhood pixels. Providing the input and output ports is not enough. The transfer mechanism introduced above must be embedded into both the sender and receiver ports.

For synthesis, the data communication must be based on the ports. If the size of the data to be transferred is identical to that of the port, the data can be transferred between the modules through the input and output ports. The port connections can be either scalar or vector, and no additional circuitry is needed if the port size is correct.

If the design resource allows for large ports, larger pieces of data can be transferred by assembling the sending data on the sender's side so that it fits the data bus and reassembling the data received at the receiver's side into data with the original size.

Listing 2.30 Communication: flattening the data

```
`define WIDTH 8
`define SIZE 10
module tb;
   reg clock, reset;

   initial begin
      clock = 0; reset = 0;#100;                  //initialize
      reset = 1; #100; reset = 0;                 //reset
   end

   always #50 clock =   ~clock;                   //clock

   //fill the memory for test
   integer j;
   always @(posedge clock) begin
      if (reset) for (j = 0; j < `SIZE; j=j+1)    //not for synthesis
         SENDER.image[j] <= $random % 256;        //use name reference
   end //always

   //main part for data connection
   wire [`WIDTH * `SIZE - 1:0] data;              //very big wire

   sender SENDER (clock, reset, data);            //sender
   receiver RECEIVER (clock, reset, data);        //receiver
endmodule

module sender(                                    //sender
   input clock, reset,
   output [`WIDTH * `SIZE - 1:0] data
   );
```

```
    reg ['WIDTH - 1:0] image [0:'SIZE -1];          //image to be sent

    //make a single big data
    genvar i;
    generate                                         //use generate
       for (i = 0; i < 'SIZE; i= i + 1) begin: GEN //fill the fields
       assign data['WIDTH*i +:'WIDTH] = image[i];
       end
    endgenerate
endmodule

module receiver(                                     //receiver
    input clock, reset,
    input ['WIDTH * 'SIZE - 1:0] data               //big bus
    );

    reg ['WIDTH - 1:0] image [0:9];                  //image data

    //disassemble the data
    integer i;
    always @*
       for (i = 0; i < 'SIZE; i = i + 1)
          image[i] <= data['WIDTHG*i +:'WIDTH];     //original size
endmodule
```

In this code, the **generate** block in the sender assembles a long data with the original data and the **for** block in the receiver disassembles the data back into the original data. This method involves the use of a very wide bus that fits the data. In actuality, there is a limit on the connection resource in a chip, which therefore limits the use of this method.

2.18 Module Control

A typical vision system may consist of one or more modules, thus requiring a control mechanism to execute the modules in systematic order: sequentially, concurrently, or partially in serial and partially concurrently. There are two basic control methods: centralized control and distributed control. In centralized control, a single control unit controls all the modules, whereas in distributed control, no separate control module exists, and therefore the modules control themselves interactively via some trigger (or strobe) signals.

The centralized control can be realized by decomposing the vision system into *control unit* and *datapath* (Hennessy and Parrerson 2012; Patterson and Hennessy 2012). In this control, the overall system consists of a controlling module and controlled modules, analogous to the control unit and datapath, respectively, in a typical computer. Between the control unit and the datapath, two types of signals are transferred: status and control signals. The control unit examines the status and determines the next order; the datapath operates according to the order and reports the status.

Let us consider how to control three modules, each printing A, B, C, respectively.

Listing 2.31 Control: FSM

```
module tb;                                         //testbench
   reg clock, reset;
   wire [2:0] q;                                   //connection

   //instantiation
   control CONTROL (clock,reset,q,ackA,ackB,ackC); //control module
   moduleA A (clock, reset, q, ackA);              //module A
   moduleB B (clock, reset, q, ackB);              //module B
   moduleC C (clock, reset, q, ackC);              //module C

   //clock and reset
   initial begin
      clock = 0; reset = 0; #50;                   //initialize
      reset = 1; #50; reset = 0;                   //reset signal
      forever #50 clock =  ~clock;                 //clock signal
   end
endmodule

//control unit
module control (                                   //control unit
   input clock, reset,
   output reg [2:0] q,                             //control signal
   input ackA, ackB, ackC                          //status
   );

   //build input status vector
   wire [2:0] qi;
   assign qi[0] = ackA ;
   assign qi[1] = ackB;
   assign qi[2] = ackC;

   //determine next state
   always @ (negedge clock, posedge reset) begin //negedge used
      if (reset) begin q <= 3'b000; end
      else case (q)                                //moore machine
         3'b000: q <= 3'b001;
         3'b001: if (qi == 3'b001) q <= 3'b010;  //next state
         3'b010: if (qi == 3'b010) q <= 3'b100;
         3'b100: if (qi == 3'b100) q <= 3'b000;
         default: q <= 3'b000;
      endcase
```

```
   end //always
endmodule

//datapath modules
module moduleA (input clock,reset,input[2:0]q,output reg ack);//a
   always @ (posedge clock, posedge reset) begin //posedge used
      if (reset) ack <= 0;                       //reset the status
      else if (q[0]) begin                       //monitor the control
         $display("A");                          //arbitrary statements
         ack <= 1;                               //assert the status
      end else ack <= 0;                         //reset the status
   end //always
endmodule

module moduleB (input clock,reset,input[2:0]q,output reg ack);//b
   always @ (posedge clock, posedge reset) begin
      if (reset) ack <= 0;
      else if (q[1]) begin
         $display("B");
         ack <= 1;
      end else ack <= 0;
   end //always
endmodule

module moduleC (input clock,reset,input[2:0] q,output reg ack);//c
   always @ (posedge clock, posedge reset) begin
      if (reset) ack <= 0;
      else if (q[2]) begin
         $display("C");
         ack <= 1;
      end else ack <= 0;
   end //always
endmodule
```

The control unit consists of two parts: a status vector builder and an FSM. The status signals coming from each module are first assembled into an input vector via continuous assignment. The FSM then determines the next state depending on the present state and the input vector. The rule can be generally represented by case statements. (In this example, the rule is simple because the order of execution is sequential.) There is a delay in both the module response, from control output to status report, and the control unit response, from status input to control output. If we use negedge instead of posedge, the cycle time is only one clock instead of two clocks. (See the problems at the end of this chapter.)

The distributed control system needs trigger (strobe) signals to start the first module. Unlike handshaking, there are no feedback signals from the excited module to the exciting module. However, this mechanism can be realized via the event-sensitive and level-sensitive controls (@ and **wait**). The activated module may subsequently trigger other modules. This mechanism is repeated for all the modules, triggering the entire modules in a chain-reaction manner. Each module needs two trigger signals, one for triggering itself and another for triggering others at the end of the current process. The same problem can be coded in this method as follows:

Listing 2.32 Control: distributed

```
module tb;                                        //testbench
   reg clock, reset;
   reg run;                                       //triggering signal
   //instantiation
   moduleA A (clock, reset, run, ackA);           //module A
   moduleB B (clock, reset, ackA, ackB);          //module B
   moduleC C (clock, reset, ackB, ackC);          //module C

   //clock and reset
   initial begin
      clock = 0; reset = 0; run = 0;#50;          //initialize
      reset = 1; #50; reset = 0;                  //reset signal
      run = 1; #100; run = 0;                     //run signal
   end
   always #50 clock =  ~clock;                    //clock signal
endmodule

module moduleA (input clock, reset, input run, output reg ack);//a
   always @ (posedge clock, posedge reset) begin
      if (reset) ack <= 0;                        //reset the status
      else if (run) begin                         //monitor the control
         $display("A");                           //arbitrary statements
         ack <= 1;                                //assert the status
      end else ack <= 0;                          //reset the status
   end //always
endmodule

module moduleB (input clock, reset, input run, output reg ack);//b
   always @ (posedge clock, posedge reset) begin
      if (reset) ack <= 0;                        //reset the status
      else if (run) begin                         //monitor the control
         $display("B");                           //arbitrary statements
         ack <= 1;                                //assert the status
      end else ack <= 0;                          //reset the status
   end //always
endmodule

module moduleC (input clock, reset, input run, output reg ack);//c
   always @ (posedge clock, posedge reset) begin
```

```
      if (reset) ack <= 0;                   //reset the status
      else if (run) begin                    //monitor the control
         $display("C");                      //arbitrary statements
         ack <= 1;                           //assert the status
      end else ack <= 0;                     //reset the status
   end //always
endmodule
```

For this purpose, there must be a trigger signal supplied from the outside, which may be used to trigger the first module. There can be many variations of this method. Depending on the trigger signal, we may use either event-sensitive or level-sensitive control (@ and **wait**). The number of executions can be controlled by introducing the counters. This method is very efficient in its simplicity. However, if there are many modules, the complicated control needed cannot be easily designed. Furthermore, contentions may arise in the input trigger, because one or more modules might possibly try to control the same module. The other problem is the possibility of the occurrence of a loop, which cannot be easily detected in a system with many modules. This method is especially efficient when the number of modules is small and the control flow is sequential.

2.19 Procedural Block Control

Inside the module, controlling of procedural blocks is an important issue in designing vision processors that must do reading, writing, and buffer updates, in addition to the main task of vision processing. The most fundamental approach is to use a large state machine that contains all the operations classified into states. Consider writing ABCABC..., using a three-state machine:

Listing 2.33 Controlling procedural block: state machine

```
module tb;
   reg clock, reset;
   reg [1:0] state;

   initial begin
      clock = 0; reset = 0; #50; reset = 1; #50; reset = 0;
   end
   always #50 clock = ~clock;

   always @(posedge clock) begin
      if (reset) begin
         state <= 0;
      end
      else case (state)
         0: begin
               state <= 1;
               $display("A");
            end
```

```
            1: begin
                 state <= 2;
                 $display("B");
               end
            2: begin
                 state <= 0;
                 $display("C");
               end
            default: state <= 0;
        endcase
    end
endmodule
```

The **$display** function must be replaced with appropriate vision operations. For a more sophisticated task, the state can be further divided into smaller states, in a hierarchical manner. The advantage of this method is the ability to use global variables, such as memory and array, which often contain huge amounts of image data. The disadvantage is that each state, which may be a large machine, cannot be simulated and synthesized separately.

The next approach is to divide the large state machine into separate procedural blocks, which are themselves state machines, even though the sizes are smaller.

Listing 2.34 Controlling procedural blocks: semaphores

```
module tb1;

    reg clock, reset;
    reg [1:0] state_A, state_B, state_C;
    reg do_A, do_B, do_C;

    initial begin
        clock = 0; reset = 0; #50; reset = 1; #50; reset = 0;
    end
    always #50 clock = ~clock;

    always @(posedge clock) begin: BLOCK_A
        if (reset) begin
            state_A <= 0;
            do_B <= 0;
        end
        else case (state_A)
            0: begin
                    if (do_A) begin
                        state_A <= 1;
                        do_C <= 0;
```

```
                end
                else begin
                    state_A <= 0;
                    do_B <= 0;
                end
            end
        1: begin
                state_A <= 0;
                $display("A");
                do_B <= 1;
            end
        default: state_A <= 0;
    endcase
end

always @(posedge clock) begin: BLOCK_B
    if (reset) begin
        state_B <= 0;
        do_C <= 0;
    end
    else case (state_B)
        0: begin
                if (do_B) begin
                    state_B <= 1;
                    do_C <= 0;
                end
                else begin
                    state_B <= 0;
                    do_C <= 0;
                end
            end
        1: begin
                state_B <= 0;
                $display("B");
                do_C <= 1;
            end
        default: state_B <= 0;
    endcase
end

always @(posedge clock) begin: BLOCK_C
    if (reset) begin
        state_C <= 0;
        do_A <= 1;
    end
```

```
        else case (state_C)
           0: begin
                 if (do_C) begin
                    state_C <= 1;
                    do_B <= 0;
                 end
                 else begin
                    state_C <= 0;
                    do_A <= 0;
                 end
              end
           1: begin
                 state_C <= 0;
                 $display("C");
                 do_A <= 1;
              end
           default: state_C <= 0;
        endcase
     end

endmodule
```

Control of this system must be done by exchanging messages that they can use to control each other. In this case, situations in which a variable is driven by more than two procedural blocks have to be avoided.

The other alternative is to use a control unit, which is a small state machine that receives states from the procedural blocks and sends control signals to them in return.

Listing 2.35 Controlling procedural blocks: control unit

```
module tb;
   reg clock, reset;
   reg [1:0] state, state_A, state_B, state_C;
   reg do_A, do_B, do_C, done_A, done_B, done_C;

   initial begin
      clock = 0; reset = 0; #50; reset = 1; #50; reset = 0;
   end
   always #50 clock = ~clock;

   always @(posedge clock) begin
      if (reset) begin
         state <= 0;
         do_A <= 1;
         do_B <= 0;
```

```
      do_C <= 0;
   end
   else case (state)
      0: if (done_A) begin
            do_A <= 0;
            do_B <= 1;
            state <= 1;
         end
      1: if (done_B) begin
            do_B <= 0;
            do_C <= 1;
            state <= 2;
         end
      2: if (done_C) begin
            do_C <= 0;
            do_A <= 1;
            state <= 0;
         end
      default: state <= 0;
   endcase
end

always @(posedge clock) begin: BLOCK_A
   if (reset) begin
      done_A <= 0;
   end
   else if (do_A) begin
      $display("A");
      done_A <= 1;
   end
   else
      done_A <= 0;
end

always @(posedge clock) begin: BLOCK_B
   if (reset) begin
      done_B <= 0;
   end
   else if (do_B) begin
      $display("B");
      done_B <= 1;
   end
   else
      done_B <= 0;
end
```

```
    always @(posedge clock) begin: BLOCK_C
       if (reset) begin
          done_C <= 0;
       end
       else if (do_C) begin
          $display("C");
          done_C <= 1;
       end
       else
          done_C <= 0;
    end
endmodule
```

This code actually generates AABBCCAA..., which can be corrected by counting the number of executions. This scheme is often called the datapath method, which consists of control unit and datapath. In the example, the states are `done_A`, `done_B`, and `done_C`. The control signals are `do_A`, `do_B`, and `do_C`.

Another method is to transfer the control in a daisy-chain manner, without relying on the control unit.

Listing 2.36 Control: internal trigger

```
module tb;                                              //testbench
    reg clock, reset;
    reg run;                                            //first module trigger

    //instantiation
    moduleABC ABC (clock, reset, run);                  //moduleABC

    //clock and reset
    initial begin
       clock = 0; reset = 0; run = 0;                   //clock, reset, run
       #50; reset = 1; #50; reset = 0;                  //reset signal
       run = 1; #100; run = 0;                          //run signal
    end
    always #50 clock =  ~clock;
endmodule

module moduleABC (input clock, reset, input run);
    reg ack, ackB, ackC;
    always @ (posedge clock, posedge reset) begin: A
       if (reset) ackB <= 0;                            //reset the status
       else @ (run) begin                               //monitor the trigger
          $display("A");                                //arbitrary statements
```

```
         ackB <= 1;
      end
   end

   always @ (posedge clock, posedge reset) begin: B
      if (reset) ack <= 0;                      //reset the status
      else @ (ackB) begin                       //monitor the trigger
         $display("B");                         //arbitrary statements
         ackC <= 1;
      end
   end

   always @ (posedge clock, posedge reset) begin: C
      if (reset) ack <= 0;                      //reset the status
      else @ (ackC) begin                       //monitor the trigger
         $display("C");
      end
   end
endmodule
```

The first module is initiated by the trigger signal coming from another module, except that the processes are initiated by the trigger signals from other processes executing in the same module. This computation has many variations: the shape of the trigger signal, the number of executions, the use of event-sensitive or level-sensitive control, or conditional statements.

When the states or the procedural blocks are too large to be designed in the above manner, they must be designed with modules. In these large systems, the control structures must also be expanded to module control. The first alternative is the datapath method, in which a control unit receives states from each module, determines the next state, and then sends control signals to the modules. The second alternative is the use of semaphores, which are exchanged between modules, as a handshake, to control themselves.

The decision as to which entities, i.e. state, procedural block, or module, and which type of control, i.e. data path and handshake, to use depends on the nature and size of the vision problem.

Problems

2.1 [Handshake] Design two always blocks, where one block sends a sequence of random data to the other via a four-phase handshake. The transfer is synchronized to a common clock.

2.2 [Handshake] Design two always blocks, where one block sends a sequence of random data to the other via a two-phase handshake. The transfer is synchronized to a common clock.

2.3 [Handshake] Design two modules, where one module sends a sequence of random data to the other via a four-phase handshake. The transfer is synchronized to a common clock.

2.4 [Handshake] Design two modules, where one module sends a sequence of random data to the other via a two-phase handshake. The transfer is synchronized to a common clock.

2.5 [Packed and unpacked] Design a circuit that converts an unpacked array into a packed array.

2.6 [Packed and unpacked] Design a circuit that converts a packed array to an unpacked array.

2.7 [Control] In Listing 2.31, the negedge trigger is used in the control unit to prevent each state occupying two clock periods. What happens if, instead of negedge, posedge is used for the trigger?

2.8 [Control] Write a code that writes ABAB..., using two always blocks and semaphores `do_A` and `do_B`.

2.9 [Control] The following code contains a summation loop:

```
module loop(input clock, reset, input [7:0] x, output reg [7:0] y);

   reg [7:0] sum, i;

   always @(posedge clock) begin
      if (reset) y = x;
      else begin
         for (i=0; i<10; i=i+1)
            y = 2 * y + i;
      end
   end //always
endmodule
```

What happens in synthesis time in terms of the circuit structure?

2.10 [Control] Convert the previous code, so that the summation may be synchronized to the clock. Use the keyword **`if`** in front of the statement block.

References

Acceleware 2013 OpenCL Altera http://www.acceleware.com/opencl-altera-fpgas (accessed May 3, 2013).

Hennessy JL and Patterson DA 2012 *Computer Architecture – A Quantitative Approach (fifth edn.)*. Morgan Kaufmann.

IEEE 2005 *IEEE Standard for Verilog Hardware Description Language*. IEEE.

IEEE 2012 *IEEE Standard for SystemVerilog*. IEEE.

Lin MB 2008 *Digital System Designs and Practices: Using Verilog HDL and FPGAs*. John Wiley & Sons.

Patterson DA and Hennessy JL 2012 *Computer Organization and Design – The Hardware / Software Interface (Revised 4th Edition)* The Morgan Kaufmann Series in Computer Architecture and Design. Academic Press.

Stackexchange 2014 Verilog tag in stackoverflow http://stackoverflow.com/ (accessed Feb. 25, 2014).

Tala DK 2014 Welcome to Verilog page http://www.asic-world.com/verilog/index.html (accessed Feb. 25, 2014).

Wikipedia 2013a C to HDL http://en.wikipedia.org/wiki/C_to_HDL (accessed May 3, 2013).

Wikipedia 2013b Unfolding (DSP implementation) http://en.wikipedia.org/wiki/Unfolding_(DSP implementation) (accessed May 16, 2013).

Xilinx 2013 High level synthesis http://www.xilinx.com/training/dsp/high-level-synthesis-with-vivado-hls.htm (accessed May 3, 2013).

3

Processor, Memory, and Array

This chapter introduces the general structure of an image processing system and the basic architectures of its major constituents, processors, and memories.

In general, a vision algorithm can be considered as a systematic organization of small algorithms, which, in many cases, can be divided further into even smaller algorithms recursively, until the algorithms cannot be divided further into meaningful units. The final divided algorithms tend to have simple and regular computational structures and thus can be considered fundamental algorithms. We are concerned with the architectures consisting of processors and memories that correspond to the fundamental algorithms. In an ordinary architecture, the constructs are the accumulators, arithmetic circuits, counters, gates, decoders, encoders, multiplexors, flip-flops, RAMs, and ROMs. However, in image processing, the constructs are bigger units, such as the neighborhood processor, forward processor, backward processor, BP processor, DP processor, queues, stacks, and multidimensional arrays.

When considered in the algorithm hierarchy, processors and memories are located at the leaf of the tree and play the role of building blocks of the algorithms. Before we begin to design the full system, it is helpful to provide processors and memories, collectively called processing elements (PEs), that are optimally designed in parameterized libraries. We will learn how to define the processing elements and connect them in an array, allowing us to build a larger system from a set of smaller systems. This chapter discusses some processors, memories, and processor network in HDL code.

3.1 Image Processing System

In order to process images, possibly in real time, the hardware system must be built with at least two devices: a frame buffer connected to a camera and an image processing (IP) chip (Figure 3.1(a)). The frame buffer, or video RAM (VRAM), is a fast memory where the captured images are stored in a full frame and reading is possible when the buffer contents are being renewed. The IP chip, realized in the form of CPLD, FPGA, or ASIC, reads the images from the frame buffer, processes them according to the algorithm, and sends the results to the ports. This is a rough general configuration, and the nature of the processor and memory may vary, depending on the application.

The internal operations are represented with Verilog modules, as shown on the right side of Figure 3.1. The images in the frame buffer must be transferred to the image memory so that the PE can quickly access the image. The memory may be installed externally if the image is too large to be stored inside the chip. The PE may need additional memory, which we call state memory, to store the

Architectures for Computer Vision: From Algorithm to Chip with Verilog, First Edition. Hong Jeong.

Companion Website: www.wiley.com/go/jeong

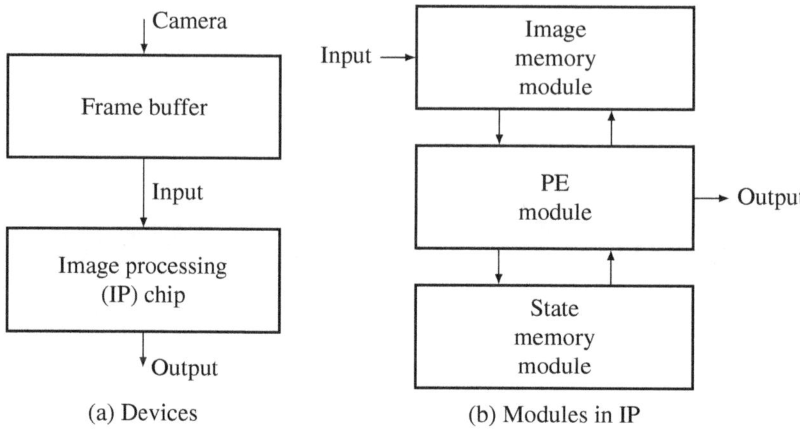

Figure 3.1 The general structure of image processing system

intermediate results and retrieve them rapidly. This memory can also be located outside if the data is too large to be stored inside the chip. The PE is the main processor that computes the main portion of the algorithm, in addition to port control such as sync and I/O signals. In a compact system, all three modules reside in the chip, while in a large system, the three modules may be located in separate chips.

We are concerned with the structure of the modules: PEs and memories. Just as there are many algorithms and architectures, there are also many PEs and memories. In an effort to determine the basic PEs and memories, we have to first investigate the nature of algorithms, as in the following section.

3.2 Taxonomy of Algorithms and Architectures

In order to derive efficient hardware systematically from the given algorithm, we need some design stages and representation schemes. Let us consider the following three stages: vision algorithm, architecture design, and HDL coding. As a starting point, the vision algorithm needs a detailed description of the computation, with statements listed in serial order. The ordinary representation is almost free, but it generally follows an Algol- or Pascal-like syntax. The architecture design attempts to interpret the algorithm in terms of hardware resources, such as PEs and memories, describing their connections and operations. At this stage, we need to specify the structure of the memory and the access points, the connections between the processor and memory, and the control mechanism, in addition to the detailed computation. The Verilog code converts the designed architecture into a behavioral description (and ultimately a circuit description). Similar to the relationship between a high-level language, assembly language, and machine code, the Verilog HDL code is converted to RTL and net-list by compilers and synthesizers. Some algorithms may be simple enough to be designed directly in the HDL coding, skipping a hardware description. However, other algorithms may need a detailed description of the hardware before moving on to HDL coding. (In this case, the hardware design paradigm is shifted to high-level synthesis, such as Altera's Vivado and Xilinx's HLS) missed.

In general, algorithms can be decomposed into smaller algorithms recursively until some well-known algorithms are reached. There are numerous well-known algorithms, such as FFT, relaxation, recursion, iteration, DP, BP, Kalman filtering, particle filtering, Bayesian filtering, graph cuts, and EM. The well-known algorithms can then be decomposed into even smaller algorithms, again recursively until the

Table 3.1 PEs and memories for fundamental algorithms

Memory/Processor	a) Multi-dimensional array	b) Local register	c) Global queue	d) Local stack
1) Neighborhood processor	IN algorithm GC algorithm		SAT algorithm	
2) BP processor	BP algorithm			
3) Viterbi processor				HMM, DP algorithms
4) Forward/ backward processor		HMM algorithm		

cf. IN: iterative neighborhood, BP: belief propagation, GC: Graph cuts and SAT: sum area table.

smallest algorithms are reached. The smallest algorithms are elements of the many well-known algorithms, often having no names, and thus we may call them *fundamental algorithms*. Examples include the neighborhood algorithm, iteration, recursion, sorting, shortest path algorithm, forward processing in the Viterbi algorithm, forward/backward processing in the hidden Markov model (HMM), inside/outside algorithm in parsing, and one-pass processing in the sum area table (SAT) algorithm (Viola and Jones 2001). (Because we cannot enumerate all such algorithms, we will focus only on the algorithms that will be used later.) The fundamental algorithms can be modeled by some architecture, which is organized by well-defined processors and memories, which we may call the *fundamental architecture*. The architectural description is the blueprint for the HDL coding.

In this light, we now present the algorithm hierarchy consisting of the fundamental algorithm:

- Fundamental architecture – HDL coding. Each level of description must follow this order.
- Algorithm, architecture, HDL.

In vision, as limited to the intermediate processing in this book, the fundamental algorithms can be decomposed into the processors and memories, as listed in Table 3.1. In this table, the top row and the left column represent memories and processors, respectively. The processors are the devices that execute the most basic operations. The memories are the devices that store temporary, input, and output data. The table entries are a few examples of fundamental algorithms, which may consist of more than one processor and memory. They may also need some other processors and memories, which are omitted from this table due to lack of regular and well-defined structures. For example, the HMM can be realized with the Viterbi processor for solving the decoding problem, and the forward/backward processor for solving the evaluation and learning problems. The DP can be realized with the Viterbi processor.

The neighborhood processor executes neighborhood operations regardless of the definition of the neighborhood and internal operation. Thus, the neighborhood processor includes a general processor that receives an arbitrary number of inputs, such as a pixel for pixel processing or a window of pixels for concurrent processing. The IN and SAT algorithms use this type of processor. The BP processor is the main processor in the BP algorithm; it receives neighbor values and emits output values to the neighbors. The forward/backward processor provides the values for evaluation and learning in HMM. The Viterbi processor finds the shortest path in the Viterbi algorithm, which is used in DP and HMM. The processors may be decomposed into smaller units, but at some point, the meaning of the processor may be lost because the remaining operations are purely mathematical and logical.

As data structures, memories can be classified as arrays, registers, queues, and stacks. An array is a data structure in which the data can be accessed randomly and be used to store intermediate results of the neighborhood. A register symbolizes small data, such as variables, reg type, and parameters, that are stored inside a processor. A queue is a data structure mostly used in one-pass algorithms, such as SAT, as we shall see later. A stack is another data structure for storing pointers in the Viterbi algorithm. On the device side, memories can be implemented in many different ways. First, they may be provided inside or outside the chip. Next, memories can be realized with various devices, such as SRAM, SDRAM, or EEPROM. A detailed specification of the target device and memory is needed at the time of synthesis.

In the following sections, we will design some essential processors and memories and provide code templates.

3.3 Neighborhood Processor

Processors are the main engine where most operations occur for updating system states. In neighborhood processing, the two major related algorithms are the iterative neighborhood (IN) and SAT algorithms. The IN algorithm receives four or eight neighbor values, updates the pixel values, and sends out the value to its neighbors, repeating this process until convergence. We can replace a pixel with a window to represent concurrent processing. This kind of operation is typical in many image processing systems, such as filtering, morphological processing, and relaxation. The SAT algorithm is an abstraction of the SAT algorithm for pattern recognition (Crow 1984; Tapia 2011; Viola and Jones 2001). It receives the values of three neighbors, updates the pixel value, and stores it until a later computation recalls it.

The neighborhood processor executes one of the basic operations, a local operation, which determines the attribute of a pixel based on neighborhood values. The obtained value is again used by the neighbors in the next iteration. This basic operation can be considered a state machine in which a pixel's state is determined by the neighborhood states.

Let us consider an architecture for a four-neighborhood system. For a given pixel, $(x, y) \in \mathcal{P}$, the typical neighborhood is the set of pixels $\{(x, y), (x+1, y), (x-1, y), (x, y-1), (x, y+1)\}$. However, for the SAT algorithm, the neighbors are the set of pixels $\{(x, y), (x-1, y), (x, y-1), (x-1, y-1)\}$. Without loss of generality, let us use the former definition.

For each pixel, $(x, y) \in \mathcal{P}$, the state equation is

$$\begin{aligned} Q(x,y) &\leftarrow T\{I(x,y), Q(x,y), Q(x+1,y), Q(x-1,y), Q(x,y-1), Q(x,y+1)\}, \\ O(x,y) &\leftarrow H(Q(x,y)), \end{aligned} \tag{3.1}$$

where $I(\cdot)$ is an image, $Q(\cdot)$ is a state, and $O(\cdot)$ is an output. $T(\cdot)$ and $H(\cdot)$ are the state transition and observation transformation, respectively. All the complex operations are abstracted by $T(\cdot)$ and all the state memories are represented by $Q(\cdot)$. The operations are repeated as needed based on the predefined number of iterations. This statement means that a processor receives data from neighbors including itself as well as the image input, updates its state, and produces an output.

Figure 3.2 illustrates this concept. At the top left, there is an image plane with $M \times N$ pixels (i.e. $\mathcal{P} = \{(x, y) | x \in [0, N-1], y \in [0, M-1]\}$). $PE(x, y)$ is defined for each pixel $(x, y) \in \mathcal{P}$ that is connected with its neighbors. The four neighborhood systems are shown in the next figure. A pixel's state is determined by the image and the four neighbor states. As shown at the bottom, a PE is a system that receives inputs and produces an output. The repetition in plane $\mathcal{P}$ and in time can be controlled by nested loops.

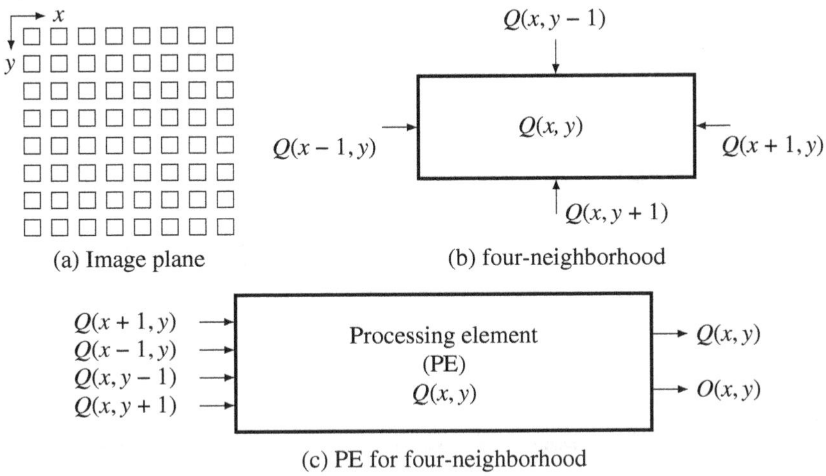

Figure 3.2 Processing elements for neighborhood computation

There are two possible approaches for the system memory. In a distributed system, each processor possesses a memory register for storing Q. A global memory scheme, on the other hand, includes a large memory unit, $Q = \{Q(x, y)|x \in [0, N-1], y \in [0, M-1]\}$, and all the processors access it as needed. Without loss of generality, we follow the second scheme.

This PE can be realized by a Moore machine with two states, which can be represented by a scheme with one bit in *binary coding* and two bits in a *one-hot coding* scheme. The following code is used in the binary coding:

Listing 3.1 The neighborhood processor: `pe_neighbor.v`

```
module pe_neighbor #(parameter DATA_WIDTH=32) (
   input clock, reset,
   input signed [DATA_WIDTH-1:0] image,       //pixel value
   input signed [DATA_WIDTH-1:0] q_east, q_west,
      q_south, q_north                        //neighbor states
   output reg signed [DATA_WIDTH-1:0]q, result//state and result
   );
   //Moore machine
   parameter STATE1 = 1'b0, STATE2 = 1'b1;    //assign states
   //initialize state
   reg [1:0] state = STATE1;
   always @(posedge clock) begin
      if (reset) begin                        //reset
         state <= STATE2;                     //next state
         q <= 0;
      end
```

```
        else case (state)
          STATE1 : begin                          //idle state
            state <= STATE1;
            q <= 0;
          end
          STATE2 : begin                          //main operation
            q <= T(image, q, q_east, q_west,
                   q_south, q_north);             //state transition
            result <= H(q);                       //observation
          end
        endcase
    end //always
endmodule
```

In the above coding, a pixel-centered coordinate system (i.e. east, west, south, north, center) is used for convenience. Two states are used to define the idling and the main operation. State transition and output generation are written in the same block. If specified, $T(\cdot)$ must be replaced with an actual code. As a whole, this processor receives five values (one pixel image and four neighborhood states) and computes the pixel state and output. To form a complete system, the processors must be connected with an external global memory (i.e. RAM) where their states are stored.

3.4 BP Processor

A more complicated type of PE can be found in BP. In this PE, the states are dependent on both input and output directions, and a different state is needed for different outputs. For a node (x, y), let us define the four states $\{Q_e, Q_w, Q_s, Q_n\}$. The corresponding state equation is described in Equation 3.2. The subscripts represent the pixel-centered coordinates – east, west, south, and north. In a simple system, the four transition functions T_e, T_w, T_s, and T_n will be identical. In an actual BP system, more terms exist, such as smoothness terms (i.e. prior) that relate two nodes with costs and normalization terms that prevent overflow and underflow.

$$\begin{aligned}
Q_e(x,y) &\leftarrow T_e\{I(x,y), Q_s(x,y+1), Q_w(x-1,y), Q_n(x,y-1)\},\\
Q_w(x,y) &\leftarrow T_w\{I(x,y), Q_e(x+1,y), Q_s(x,y+1), Q_n(x,y-1)\},\\
Q_s(x,y) &\leftarrow T_s\{I(x,y), Q_e(x+1,y), Q_w(x-1,y), Q_n(x,y-1)\},\\
Q_n(x,y) &\leftarrow T_n\{I(x,y), Q_e(x+1,y), Q_s(x,y+1), Q_w(x-1,y)\},\\
O(x,y) &\leftarrow H\{I(x,y), Q_w(x-1,y), Q_e(x+1,y), Q_s(x,y+1), Q_n(x,y-1)\}.
\end{aligned} \tag{3.2}$$

In BP, the states are called *beliefs* and must be updated until convergence. This operation is accomplished by iterating the image plane many times. After the convergence, all four states are used to generate the outputs, as denoted by the transformation $H(\cdot)$. The operations – initialization, update scheduling, along with the state transition functions – are the major factors for designing such a system.

Figure 3.3 represents a PE. On the left figure, there is a pixel that is connected bidirectionally with its four neighbors. The right side of the figure shows the PE that receives four inputs and gives four outputs. The outputs will only be stable after the states are stabilized.

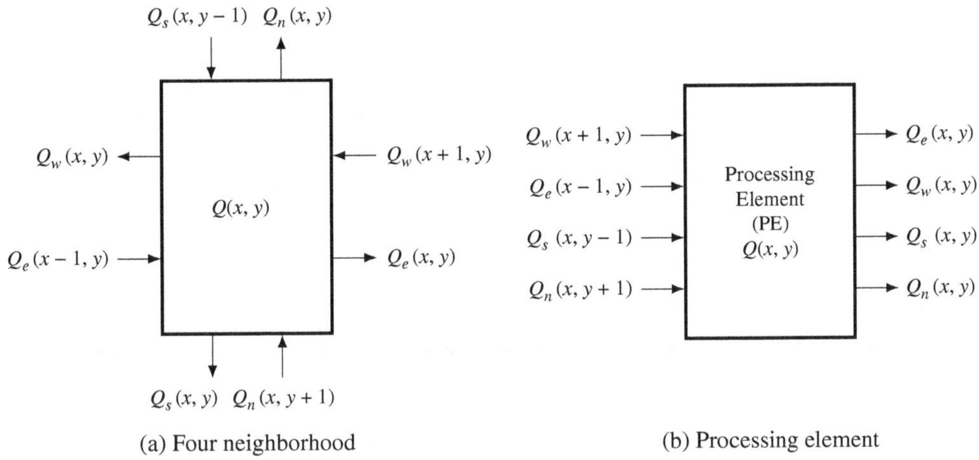

Figure 3.3 A processing element with four states

In HDL code, this processing element can be represented as follows.

Listing 3.2 The BP processor: `pe.v`

```
module pe #(DATA_WIDTH=32) (
   input clock, reset,
   input signed [DATA_WIDTH-1:0] image,        //pixel image
   input signed [DATA_WIDTH-1:0] i_east, i_west,
         i_south, i_north                      //neighbor states
   output reg signed [DATA_WIDTH-1:0] o_east, o_west,
         o_south, o_north,                     //new states
   output reg signed [DATA_WIDTH-1:0] result, //result
   );
   //define states
   parameter STATE1 = 1'b0, STATE2 = 1'b1;     //assign states
   //initialize state
   reg [1:0] state = STATE1;
   always@(posedge clock) begin
      if (reset) begin                         //reset
         state <= STATE2;                      //next state
         result <= 0;
      end
      else case (state)
         STATE1 : begin                        //idle state
            state <= STATE1;
            result <= 0;
         end
```

```
        STATE2  : begin                          //state transition
           o_east <= T_e(image,i_south,i_west,i_north); //east out
           o_west <= T_w(image, i_east,i_south,i_north);//west out
           o_south <= T_s(image, i_east,i_west,i_north);//south out
           o_north <= T_n(image, i_east,i_west,i_south);//north out
           result <= H(i_east,i_west,i_south,i_north);  //result
        end
     endcase
  end //always
endmodule
```

The operation is represented by a two-state Moore machine. The machine may start in the idle state but can jump to the normal state when it is reset. In an actual PE, the internal operation is more complicated, depending on the image input, a prior term, and a normalization factor. The image and the states may be different in data size, but for the sake of simplicity, we have made them the same here.

3.5 DP Processor

In DP and the HMM (Lawrence *et al.* 2007; Rabiner and Juang 1993), the Viterbi algorithm is commonly used for solving the decoding problem. Let us call the processor that is dedicated to the Viterbi algorithm the *Viterbi processor*. The search space consists of $N_q \times N$ nodes, where N_q is the number of states and N is the time parameter. The shortest path in this space is found via two phases: the forward processing phase and the backward processing phase. In the forward processing phase, each node determines a pointer to one of the N_q nodes and pushes it into its stack. If the parent nodes are limited to a small neighborhood around the node, then it is possible to solve this problem with a linear systolic array. Otherwise, serial processing is unavoidable because the number of connections is too large to be implemented in an array. In this case, the processor structure is very simple, like the forward processor that will be explained soon in terms of HMM. For the linear array, let us design a processor so that in later chapters we can reuse it for implementing a full DP system.

Let the position of a PE be (i, j), where $j \in [0, N_q - 1]$ for states and $i \in [0, N - 1]$ for image width. The PEs are connected linearly, forming an array $\{(i, 0), (i, 1), \dots, (i, N_q - 1)\}$ for a variable $i \in [0, N - 1]$. Each PE possesses a private stack, $Q = \{q_0, q_1, \dots, q_{N-1}\}$, with the top being q_0 and the bottom being q_{N-1}. During the forward processing, the PE determines the minimum cost, $\phi(i, j)$, and the parent index, $\eta(i, j)$, which is related to the minimum cost. The costs and pointers are determined using the following equation:

$$\begin{cases} \phi(i, j) = \min_{k \in [0, N_q - 1]} \phi(i - 1, k) + \mu(k, j) + \rho(i, j), \\ \eta(i, j) = \arg\min_{k \in [0, N_q - 1]} \phi(i - 1, k) + \mu(k, j), \quad j \in [0, N_q - 1]. \end{cases} \tag{3.3}$$

Here, $\mu(\cdot)$ represents a function and $\rho(\cdot)$ is a local cost. A pair of neighbor processors is blocked by a register. The N_q processors on the array are all concurrent.

The corresponding circuit is shown in Figure 3.4. The left image is the linear array where the PEs are connected with neighbors via up and down links. The PEs are blocked by registers with neighbor PEs, as indicated on the edges, so that the data moves synchronously. The PE determines the cost and the pointer that is to be pushed into the stack. The function μ and the local parameter ρ are determined locally in each PE. All of the processors can update the costs and the pointers concurrently.

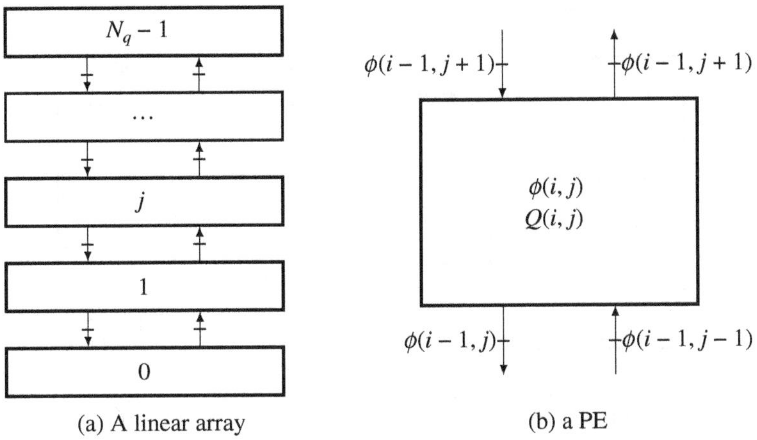

Figure 3.4 A linear array and the PE in forward processing

The HDL code needs an external stack that can be accessed by instantiation.

Listing 3.3 Viterbi forward processor: pe.v

```
module forward_processor #(parameter DATA_WIDTH = 16,
   STACK_DEPTH = 100)(
   input clock, reset,
   input signed [DATA_WIDTH-1:0] rho, phiu, phid, //up down and queue
   output reg [1:0] eta, pushpop              //pointer to queue
   );
   //variables
   parameter mu = 1, muu = 2, mud = 2;
   reg [DATA_WIDTH-1:0] phi;                   //cost
   integer epsilon = 1;                        //threshold
   always @ (posedge clock) begin
      pushpop = 0;                             //no operation
      if (phiu + muu - phid - mud > epsilon) begin //choose smaller
         phi <= phid + mud;                    //new cost
         eta <= 2'b11;                         //new pointer
      end
      else if (phiu + muu - phid - mud > epsilon)begin
         phi <= phiu + muu;
         eta <= 2'b01;
      end
      else begin                               //choose itself
         phi <= phi + mu;                      //new cost
         eta <= 2'b00;                         //new pointer
      end
```

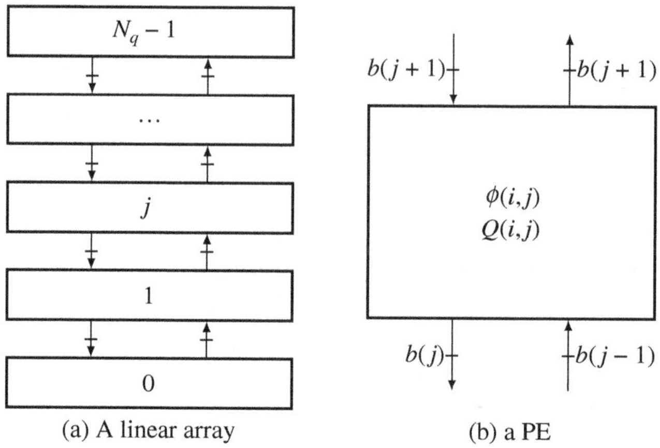

Figure 3.5 A linear array and the PE in the backward processing

```
      pushpop = 2'b01;                          //push
   end //always
endmodule
```

To avoid exact equality, which is highly improbable, a threshold parameter `epsilon` is introduced. This module accesses an external stack via the value `eta` and the action `pushpop`. Each processor has its own stack. Thus, there are N_q processors and stacks. The state update operations and stack operations are concurrent for all processors.

In the backward processing phase, the PE executes completely different tasks (refer to Figure 3.5). Each PE contains a bit flag that indicates whether the node is located on the shortest path or not. To search for the shortest path, each PE must pop from the stack and, if its own flag is set to one, activate the flag in the upward or downward PE, based on the popped pointer. Since `eta` $\in \{-1, 0, 1\}$, indicating the upward, current, and downward positions, it is easy to find the correct parent. For a flag bit $b(j)$ at j-th PE, the new flag bit is determined by the following logic:

$$b(j + \eta(j)) \leftarrow 1, \text{if } b(j) \cdot \eta(j) = 1, \tag{3.4}$$

where $\eta(j)$ is the pointer that has been popped from the stack.

The HDL code is as follows:

Listing 3.4 Viterbi Backward processor: `backward_processor.v`

```
module backward_processor (
   input clock, reset,
   input [1:0] fu, fd,                        //flag input
   output [1:0] qu, qd,                       //flag output
   output [1:0] pushdown,                     //pop
```

```
    input [DATA_WIDTH-1:0] q                     //popped data
    );

    reg flag = 0;                                //current flag

    always @ (posedge clock) begin
       qu = 0; qd = 0;                           //initialize output
       pushpop = 2'b11;                          //issue pop
       if (flag & q == 2'b01) qu <= 1;           //activate upward
       else if (flag & q == 2'b11) qd <= 1;      //activate downward
       else if (flag) flag <=0;                  //keep unchanged
       else flag <= 0;                           //turn off the flag
    end //always
endmodule
```

This module shares the same stack with the forward phase module. In order to access the stack, this module issues the pop command and receives the stack output.

In order to realize the Viterbi algorithm, an array of N_q processors and stacks must be activated. During the forward processing phase, the processors fill the stacks with the pointers. During the backward processing phase, the opposite actions take place. The output is popped pointers from the active processors. The pointers are relative and thus must be accumulated for the absolution position of the shortest path.

3.6 Forward and Backward Processors

In HMM, the search space is defined over the $N_q \times N$ nodes, where N_q is the number of states and N is the time parameter. In this space, the forward probability $\alpha(i, j)$ and the backward probability $\beta(i, j)$ can be computed using the forward and backward algorithms. Given the initial values $\{\alpha(0,j)|j \in [0, N_q - 1]\}$ and the local measures $\{\rho(j,k)|j,k \in [0, N_q - 1]\}$, it is possible to compute the forward and backward probabilities:

$$\begin{cases} \alpha(i,j) = \sum_{k\in[0,N_q-1]} \alpha(i-1,k) + \mu(k,j) + \rho(i,j), \\ \beta(i,j) = \sum_{k\in[0,N_q-1]} \beta(i+1,k) + \mu(j,k) + \rho(i+1,k), \end{cases} \tag{3.5}$$

where $i = 0, 1, \ldots, N-1$ and $j \in [0, N_q - 1]$. Here, $\mu(j, k)$ denotes the cost between the states j and k. The purpose is to obtain the result $\{\alpha(N-1, j)|j \in [0, N_q - 1]\}$. The backward probability can be obtained similarly, but in reverse time order. These algorithms are similar to the Viterbi forward algorithm, except that summation is used instead of minimum. However, unlike the Viterbi algorithm, no pointers or stacks are involved here. The memory locations are local registers.

A forward processor is shown in Figure 3.6. It is similar to the backward processor, except that the direction is reversed. The processor takes N_q inputs and produces one output. The processor cannot be implemented in a linear array, as the Viterbi processor can, because the number of inputs is too high to allow for adequate connections in an array. Instead, the computation must be executed sequentially in a double loop: $j = 0, 1, \ldots, N_q - 1$ for each $i = 0, 1, \ldots, N - 1$.

The processor takes N_q inputs and produces one output. The processor cannot be implemented in a linear array, as the Viterbi processor does, for there are too many inputs to be connected in an array.

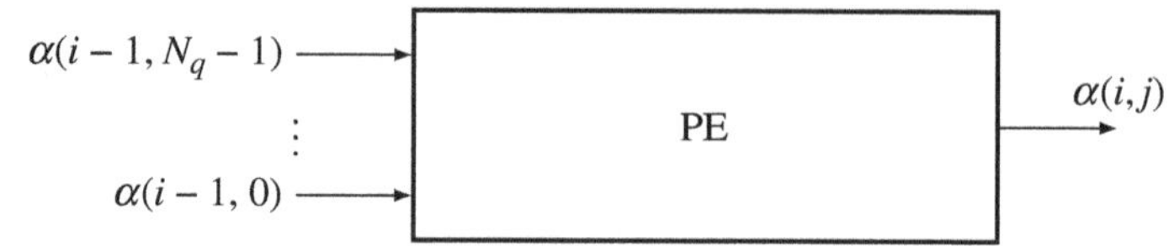

Figure 3.6 A forward processor

Instead, the computation must be executed sequentially in a double loop: $j = 0, 1, \ldots, N_q - 1$ for each $i = 0, 1, \ldots, N - 1$.

For a large N_q, the processor may even perform iterations in order to process N_q inputs: $k = 0, 1, \ldots, N_q - 1$ for the node pair (k, j).

Listing 3.5 Forward processor: `pe.v`

```
module forward_processor #(parameter DATA_WIDTH = 16)(
   input clock, reset,
   input signed [DATA_WIDTH-1:0] rho, alpha, //input
   output reg signed [DATA_WIDTH-1:0] q,     //output
   );
   //variables
   parameter mu = 1;

   always @ (posedge clock) begin
     if (reset) q <= 0;
     else q <= q + alpha + mu + rho;
   end //always
endmodule
```

For simplicity, mu is set to an arbitrary value. In addition to the processor, a RAM is needed to store N_q instances of α. Since this is a simple processor, the full computation requires three nested loops: $\{(i, j, k) | i = 0, 1, \ldots, N - 1, j = 0, 1, \ldots, N_q - 1, k = 0, 1, \ldots, N_q - 1\}$. Thus, the complexity is $O(NN_q^2)$. The backward processor can be coded similarly. The forward and backward algorithms can be generalized to the outside and inside algorithms (Baker 1979; Manning 2001).

3.7 Frame Buffer and Image Memory

Before proceeding further, let us first present common modules for the frame buffer and the image memory. The frame buffer must be external to the chip. For simulation purposes, the following code may be used:

Listing 3.6 Frame buffer: `fbuffer.v`

```
module fbuffer
   #(parameter DATA_WIDTH=8, parameter ADDR_WIDTH=10)(
   input we, clock,
```

```
    input  [(DATA_WIDTH-1):0] data,             //input data
    input  [(ADDR_WIDTH-1):0] read_addr, write_addr, //address
    output reg [(DATA_WIDTH-1):0] q             //output data
    );
    //declare the RAM variable
    reg [DATA_WIDTH-1:0] ram[0: 2 ** ADDR_WIDTH-1];

    always @ (posedge clock) begin
       //write and read
       if (we) ram[write_addr] <= data;         //write data
       q <= ram[read_addr];                     //read data
    end //always
endmodule
```

This is a simple template of a dual-port RAM with a single clock, where the data can be written and read simultaneously. In one port, the video stream is written continuously, and in the other port the data is read out continuously. There are templates and libraries for advanced RAMs in most EDA tools. Initial values may be prepared with a hex editor in a binary file with a `hex` or `mif` extension.

The image memory is the workspace, in which the PE can execute the algorithm and possibly modify the contents. This memory may be designed inside the chip for a small dataset or outside the chip for a large dataset. This memory must be written to and read from concurrently. This memory can be realized by the dual-port memory as in the following template:

Listing 3.7 2D array: `imem.v`

```
module imem #(parameter DATA_WIDTH=8, parameter ADDR_WIDTH=10)(
    input we_a, we_b, clock,
    input  [(DATA_WIDTH-1):0] data_a, data_b,   //input data ports
    input  [(ADDR_WIDTH-1):0] addr_a, addr_b,   //addresses
    output reg [(DATA_WIDTH-1):0] q_a, q_b      //output data ports
    );
    //declare the RAM variable
    reg [DATA_WIDTH-1:0] ram[0: 2 ** ADDR_WIDTH-1];
    //port A
    always @ (posedge clock)
    begin
       if (we_a)
       begin
          ram[addr_a] <= data_a;                //write data
          q_a <= data_a;                        //store the address
       end
       else q_a <= ram[addr_a];                 //output data
    end //always
    //port B
```

```
    always @ (posedge clock)
    begin
       if (we_b)
       begin
          ram[addr_b] <= data_b;                    //write data
          q_b <= data_b;                            //store the address
       end
       else q_b <= ram[addr_b];                     //output the data
    end //always
endmodule
```

Note that the array is written only when `wena` or `wenb` are asserted. Otherwise, the array is always read out. All of the systems that follow will use the same frame buffer module and the same image memory module.

3.8 Multidimensional Array

For the design of state memories, there are many alternative methods that depend on the available resources in a given device. The most general method is to use the standard Verilog array construct, which does not specify any available resources. A more advanced method is to use the parameterized libraries and IPs that are available in EDA tools. If the target devices, such as CPLD or FPGA, are specified, the library modules can be further tuned to the target devices. In an FPGA, there are several types of memories, such as registers, ROM, SRAM, and RAM. The registers, as portions of *logical elements* (LEs), are very limited in number and usage. For large memories, as required in most vision algorithms, one or more external RAMs must be connected via appropriate ports. In this section, we consider a simple design method that uses the standard Verilog construct and does not assume a particular device or commercial tool.

In image processing, the state memory is often a 2D array, $Q = \{q(x,y)|x \in [0, N-1], y \in [0, M-1]\}$, defined over an image plane, $I = \{I(x,y)|x \in [0, N-1], y \in [0, M-1]\}$. Unfortunately, the RAM is organized as a 1D array, $RAM = \{RAM(z)|z \in [0, MN-1]\}$. To move from a 2D coordinate, (x, y), to a 1D coordinate, z, the address must be flattened via concatenation: $z = \{x, y\}$. Therefore, $RAM(\{x,y\}) \leftarrow q(x,y)$ signifies concatenation. To move from 1D to 2D, the address z must be popped to (x,y). That is, $q(x,y) \leftarrow RAM(\{x,y\})$. This concept can be expanded to the case where a set of addresses must be accessed. Figure 3.7 illustrates such a memory.

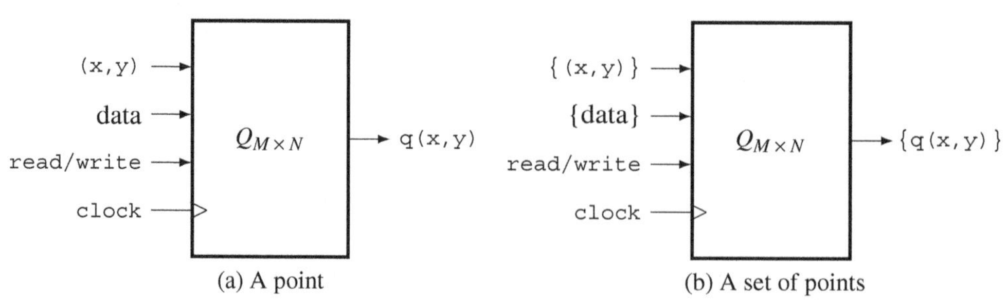

Figure 3.7 A 2D memory, Q: `(x,y)` for address, data for input, `q` for output, `read`, `write`, and `clock` for control and clock signals

The processor accesses the memory as a 2D array, but internally the memory is an ordinary 1D RAM. For accessing neighbors and a window, the address and the outputs must be a set of data, as shown on the right of Figure 3.7.

One of the simplest RAMs is a single-port RAM having a single read/write address bus. In certain vision algorithms, the memory may be used to store the initial image values. This operation can be accomplished by initializing the contents. The following code is a template for a 2D array:

Listing 3.8 Module: `ram2d.v`

```
module ram #(parameter DATA_WIDTH=32, ADDR_WIDTH=10)(
   input we, clock,
   input [DATA_WIDTH-1:0] data,                  //input data
   input [ADDR_WIDTH-1:0] x,y,                   //address
   output [DATA_WIDTH-1:0] q                     //output data
   );
   //declare the variables
   reg [DATA_WIDTH-1:0] ram[0:2 ** (2 * ADDR_WIDTH)-1]; //RAM
   reg [ADDR_WIDTH-1:0] x_reg, y_reg;            //hold address
   //write data
   always @ (posedge clock) begin
      if (we) ram[{x,y}]                         //write
      x_reg <= x; y_reg <= y;                    //store address
   end //always
   //read data
   assign q = ram[{x_reg,y_reg}];                //output
endmodule
```

When synthesized, this array is actually implemented by RAM or registers. There are more advanced RAMs that have multiple ports and need multiple clocks so that reading and writing can be executed concurrently. To initialize the 2D memory, there must be an initialization process that reads the external RAM and writes to the internal 2D array.

For accessing points in a neighborhood or a window, this simple template will not work and thus must be modified to include a list of address ports. The indexed part select used in stacks can be very useful in dealing with long flat addresses.

3.9 Queue

The data structure queue (or FIFO buffer) is the main data structure in the fast relaxation equation (FRE) machine, which will be introduced in Chapter 8. The queue is special in that its size (width and depth) is constant, the data always enters from one end (i.e. the head) and leaves from the other end (i.e. the tail), a set of fixed locations are accessed concurrently, and the queue element is a window, thus forming a parallelepiped.

Let us start with a simple queue. A queue, Q, with width N_w and depth N_q is an array of $N_w \times N_q$ elements:

$$Q = \{\mathbf{q}(1), \mathbf{q}(2), \ldots, \mathbf{q}(N_q)\}, \tag{3.6}$$

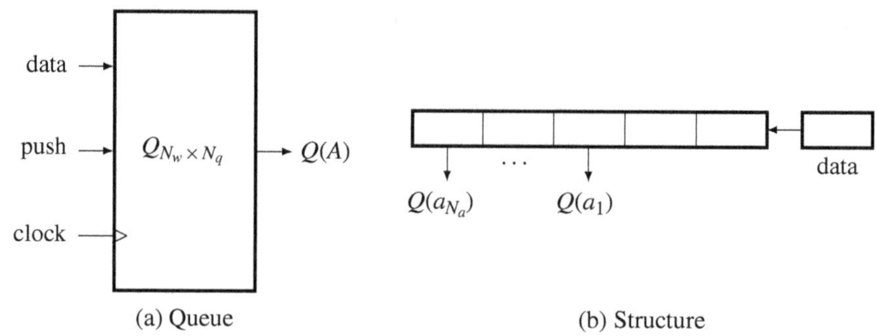

Figure 3.8 A queue Q: q for input, A for fixed addresses, $Q(A)$ for output, shift and clock for control and clock signals

where $\mathbf{q}(1)$ and $\mathbf{q}(N_q)$ are the head and tail, respectively. The access addresses are the set $A = \{a_1, a_2, \ldots, a_{N_a}\}$, where N_a is the number of access points. (In the FRE machine, A is a neighborhood of addresses, as we shall see in later chapters.) The output must always be available for the PE. (No loading command is needed.)

A hardware queue can be considered as a system, as shown in Figure 3.8. Initially, the queue is empty. It is then filled until it is completely full. Thereafter, the queue is always full. In order to access the data in the queue, either the head or the tail address can be used as a pointer. Mathematically, for an input x, the push operation is given by

$$Q \xleftarrow{push} x. \tag{3.7}$$

There are three techniques for implementing a hardware queue: *systolic*, *shift register*, and *circular buffer*. A systolic queue is a systolic array where the registers are cascaded in a linear configuration. A shift register is a register in which all data is shifted into the put operation. A circular buffer is a memory with head and tail pointers sliding along the memory buffer.

Out of these three options, we choose the shift register, which is the simplest. We design the core part of the queue using the shift register. Usually, the input data is a set of data in a window. Since the port does not allow arrays, the data must be flattened first and then it must be popped out internally. The following code illustrates this approach:

Listing 3.9 Queue: `queue.v`

```
module queue #(parameter DATA_WIDTH=8, DATA_NUM = 2, QUEUE_DEPTH=10,
   ADDR0 = 0, ADDR1 = 10)(
   clock, push, data, q0, q1);
   input clock, push;
   input signed [DATA_WIDTH * DATA_NUM - 1:0] data; //input data
   output reg  signed [DATA_WIDTH-1:0] q0, q1;       //output data

   //define variables
```

```
    reg [DATA_WIDTH-1:0] ram [0:QUEUE_DEPTH * DATA_NUM -1]; //ram
    integer i,j;
    //push the data
    always @(posedge clock) begin
       if (push) begin
          for (j = DATA_NUM; j > 0; j = j - 1) begin
             for(i = QUEUE_DEPTH * DATA_NUM - 1; i > 0; i = i - 1)
                ram[i] <= ram[i-1];                 //shift data
             //pop out and push the data (indexed part select)
             ram[0] <= data[(j * DATA_WIDTH - 1) -: DATA_WIDTH];
          end
             q0 <= ram[ADDR0]; q1 <= ram[ADDR1]; //read data
       end
    end //always
endmodule
```

Note the indexed part select in the data pop-out and push. The output data is a set of queue elements in a set of pre-defined positions. If the queue size is large, then it may not be possible to complete the shift operations in one clock cycle. In that case, the clock must be slowed down or counted until a block of data is pushed completely into the queue. If the queue size is large, then the circular shift buffer, which uses memory, could be used alternatively.

3.10 Stack

The stack data structure is used heavily in DP and HMM and thus must be optimized. In both algorithms, the stack is used to store a parent index and possible costs. The parent index is the node from the previous stage, which has been chosen as a parent from a set of possible options. The stack is defined by an $N_w \times N_q$ array $Q = \{\mathbf{q}(1), \ldots, \mathbf{q}(N_q)\}$, where N_w is the data width and N_q is the stack depth. The stack is illustrated in Figure 3.9.

The data is an input to be pushed into the stack and q is an output to be popped from the stack. The stack is parameterized by the data width and the stack depth. The push and pop controls are coded by the state.

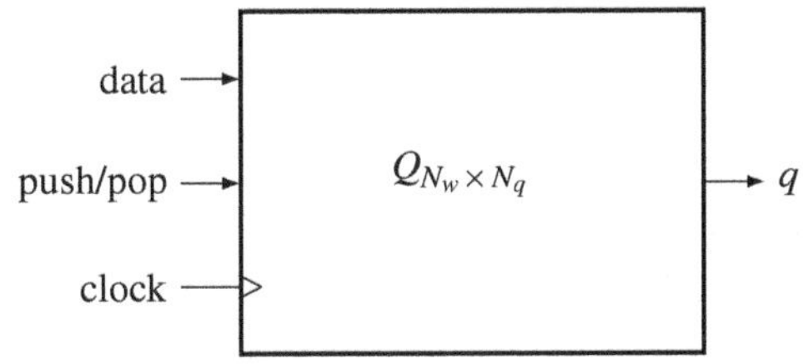

Figure 3.9 A stack Q: data for input, q for output, push, pop, and clock for control and clock signals

Listing 3.10 Stack: `stack.v`

```
module Stack #(parameter DATA_WIDTH = 8, STACK_DEPTH = 100)(
   input clock, reset,                          //clock and reset
   input [1:0] state,                           //state
   input [DATA_WIDTH-1:0] data,                 //input data
   output reg [DATA_WIDTH-1:0] q                //output data
   );
   //declaration memory
   reg [DATA_WIDTH-1:0] ram[0:STACK_DEPTH-1]; //stack
   //integer variables
   integer stack_address, i;
   //assign states
   parameter STATE_IDLE = 0, STATE_PUSH = 1, STATE_POP = 2; //states
   //always block
   always @ (posedge clock) begin
      if (reset) begin                          //reset
         for (i=0; i < STACK_DEPTH; i=i+1) ram[i] <= 0;
         stack_address <= 0;
         end
      else case (state)
         STATE_IDLE : q <= 8'hZZ;               //idle state
         STATE_PUSH : begin                     //push state
            if (stack_address == 0) begin
               ram[0] <= data;
               stack_address <= stack_address + 1;
            end else if (stack_address < STACK_DEPTH - 1) begin
               ram[stack_address] <= data;
               stack_address <= stack_address + 1;
            end else begin
               ram[stack_address] <= data;
               stack_address <= stack_address;
            end
         end
         STATE_POP : begin                      //pop state
            if (stack_address == 0) begin
               q <= ram[stack_address];
               ram[stack_address] <= 0;
               stack_address <= stack_address;
            end else begin
               q <= ram[stack_address];
               ram[stack_address] <= 0;
               stack_address <= stack_address - 1;
            end
         end
```

```
        default : begin                              //fault recovery
           q <= 8'hZZ;
        end
      endcase
    end //always
endmodule
```

The combination of various PEs and memories will result in different types of PE memory models.

3.11 Linear Systolic Array

Now, let us design a simple architecture that can execute a linear filter. Through the projects, we will learn the following concepts: designing processing elements (PEs) with state machine, designing network systems, and designing test benches. In addition, the linear pipelined array, which will be used in this chapter, is an important computational structure for DP and HMM, which is frequently used in solving computer vision problems. In later chapters, such arrays will be derived and designed for computer vision algorithms.

Once a PE is designed, a set of such elements can be connected in various ways to form different topologies. One of the possible connections is the linear arrangement, which is often called *systolic array* (Kung and Leiserson 1980; Petkovic 1992). The systolic arrays are very convenient for VLSI because of properties such as pipelining, nearest-neighbor connection, and identical processors. This structure is also essential for designing the DP or HMM, which will be investigated in later chapters.

As an example, let us consider a linear convolution. A signal $x(t)$ is convolved with weights w, and the output $y(t)$ is obtained. For a *finite impulse response* (FIR) filter, the system equation becomes

$$y(t) = \sum_{k=0}^{K-1} w_k x(t-k). \tag{3.8}$$

Here, K is the number of filter taps. Computationally, this simply means a weighted sum, with shifted input signals and weights.

The serial algorithm is as follows. For the sake of simplicity, we use only three taps for the filter.

Algorithm 3.1 (Serial algorithm) *Compute the following:*

- *input:* $x(t)$.
- *output:* $y(t)$.
- *parameters:* $\{w_0, w_1.w_2\}$.

1. *for* $t = 0, 1, \ldots$
   (a) $y \leftarrow w_0 x(t) + w_1 x(t-1) + w_2 x(t-2) + \cdots + w_{K-1}(t-k)$.
   (b) *output:* y.

This can be realized with a PE. (See the problems at the end of this chapter.) However, here, we consider designing a systolic array. A given function can have many systolic arrays that are different in topology and registers. Obtaining different arrays is possible, because the registers can be redistributed by *retiming* (Leiserson and Saxe 1991), and the topology can be modified by topological transformation (Jeong 1984).

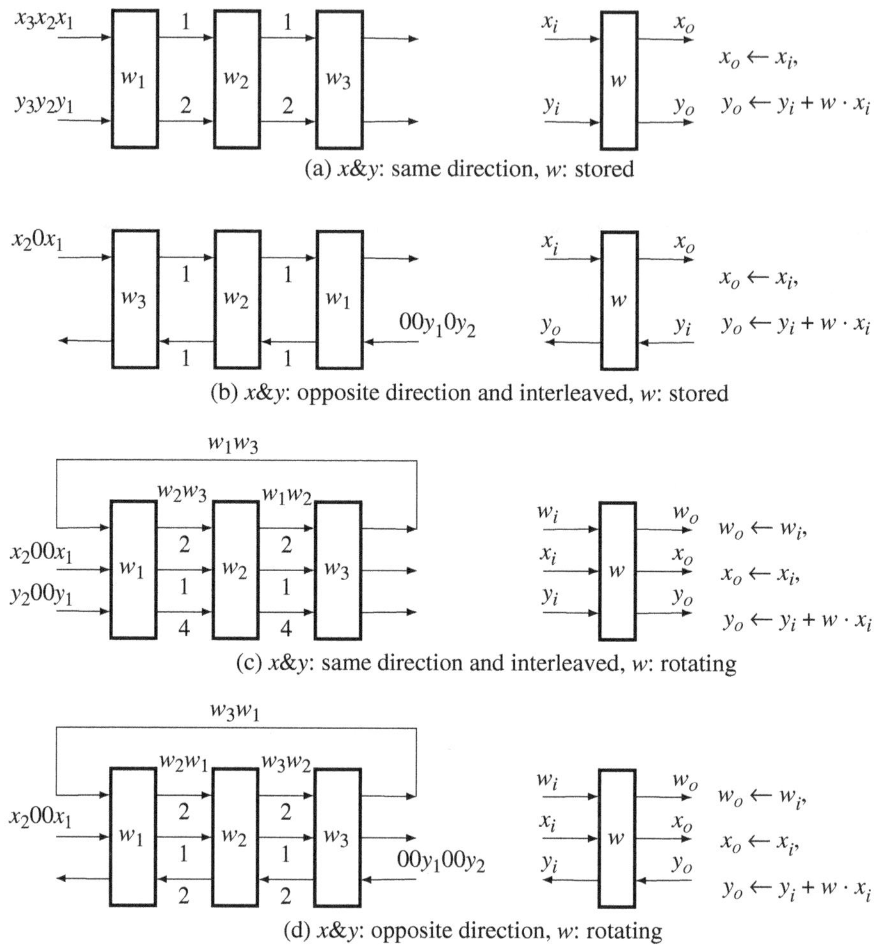

Figure 3.10 Linear systolic arrays for convolution (Numbers represent the number of registers. PEs are on the right.)

Furthermore, interleaved circuits, which are collectively called a *k-slow* circuit, can be obtained by adding more registers (Leiserson and Saxe 1991). If the transformations in timing and topology are combined, numerous circuits may result (Jeong 1984).

Among the many circuits, four are shown in Figure 3.10 (Jeong 1984). Only three taps are used here, but the circuits can be easily expanded for longer taps. The numbers on the edges represent the number of registers that block the PEs. The array is shown on the left, and the PE is shown on the right. For a given array, all the PEs are performing the same operations. The data stream is permanently arranged by the fixed connections and delays. In each clock tick, all the data move in a lock-step manner, like a machine. The four circuits differ in the direction of input, output, and weight and in the number of registers. The zeroes, which are introduced between signals, represent interleaving, and independent signals can be put in those places. In (b), the weights are stored in the PEs, but the directions of input and output are opposite. In this configuration, the number of registers is reduced, but the signals must be interleaved. A set of different signals can be processed in such an interleaved system. In (c), the PE does not store weights, and thus all the signals and weights are supplied externally. The first and second arrays are dual, and thus, the third and the fourth arrays must also be dual.

Let us design only the first array (Figure 3.10(a)). The design consists of three modules: four identical PEs, a network, and a test bench. The network module connects the four PEs in a cascaded configuration by using the output of one module as the input of the other module. The overall system is a Moore machine.

A PE consists of a weight memory, a register for the x output, and two registers for the y output. Using the memories, we express the internal operation of a PE by the hardware algorithm.

Algorithm 3.2 (PE(k)) *For a PE(k), do the following:*

- *input:* $\{xi(k), yi(k)\}$.
- *memory:* $w(k), xo(k), \{y(k), yo(k)\}$.
- *output:* $\{xo(k), yo(k)\}$.

1. *initialization:* $w(k)$.
2. *for each clock*
   (a) $y = yi(k) + w(k)xi(k)$.
   (b) *output:* $xo(k) \Leftarrow x(k), yo(k) \Leftarrow y$.

Here, k means the id of the PE. The Verilog procedural assignments are used – blocking (=) and nonblocking (<=), to clarify the serial and concurrent processing.

For Algorithm 3.2, we can write the module, `pe.v`.

Listing 3.11 Module: `pe.v`

```
'timescale 1ns / 100ps                                //unit time/ precision
'define DATA_WIDTH 32                                 //parameter
//module pe, the signals are signed for 2's complement arithmetic.
module pe(
    input signed ['DATA_WIDTH-1:0] xi,                //signal input
    output reg signed ['DATA_WIDTH-1:0] xo,           //signal output
    input signed ['DATA_WIDTH-1:0] yi,                //output input
    output reg signed ['DATA_WIDTH-1:0] yo,           //output output
    input clock,
    input reset
    );
    //Moore machine
    parameter STATE1 = 2'b00;                         //idle state
    parameter STATE2 = 2'b01;                         //input weights
    parameter STATE3 = 2'b10;                         //store weights
    parameter STATE4 = 2'b11;                         //main operations

    reg [8:1] clock_count;                            //for weight input
    reg [1:0] state = STATE1;                         //initialize state
    reg signed ['DATA_WIDTH-1:0] w;                   //weight
```

```
    reg signed ['DATA_WIDTH-1:0] y;                  //simulate output
                                                       register

    (* FSM_ENCODING='SEQUENTIAL', SAFE_IMPLEMENTATION='YES',
       SAFE_RECOVERY_STATE='<recovery_state_value>' *) //attributes
    always@(posedge clock) begin                     //sequential circuit
       if (reset) begin                              //synchronous reset
          state <= STATE2; xo <= 0; yo <= 0; clock_count <= 0;
       end else
       (* PARALLEL_CASE, FULL_CASE *) case (state)//attributes
       STATE1 : begin                                //idle state
          state <= STATE1; xo <= 0; yo <= 0;
       end
       STATE2 : begin                                //input/ load weights
          if (clock_count < 4) begin
                state <= STATE2;
                clock_count <= clock_count + 1;
                xo <= xi; yo <= 0;
          end else begin
                state <= STATE3;
                w <= xi; xo = xi; yo <= 0;
          end
       end
       STATE3 : begin                                //main operations
          state <= STATE4;
          xo <= xi;
          y <= yi + w * xi;
       end
       STATE4 : begin                                //for delay
          state <= STATE3;
          xo <= xi;
          yo <= y;
       end
       default : begin                               //fault Recovery
          state <= STATE1;
          $display ("%0t State error occurred!", $time );//for debugging
       end
       endcase
    end                                              //always
endmodule
```

In coding the PE, it is convenient to use four states: state 1 for idle state, state 2 for loading filter weights, state 3 for the weighted sum, and state 4 for output. In the idle state, a PE stays unchanged until the system is reset. Once it is reset, the system goes to state 2, where the input, which is the weight, is loaded into the internal memory. It is economical to share the input port for the weight and data input, in time-sharing – weights first and data next. When all the weights are loaded, the system goes to state 3, where a multiplication-accumulation is performed. The state then goes to 4, where the output signals are shifted into the registers. Afterward, states 3 and 4 are visited alternately until the system power is turned off.

The next stage is to define a network module that configures the PEs, connecting their outputs and inputs. The hardware algorithm is shown below.

Algorithm 3.3 (Network) *Connect* $\{PE(k)|k \in [0,2]\}$.

- *input:* x.
- *output:* $yo(2)$.

1. *for each clock tick, do the following:*

$$xo(-1) \Leftarrow x, xi(k) \Leftarrow xo(k-1), yi(k) \Leftarrow yo(k-1), k \in [0,2].$$

In this network, the two outputs of a previous PE become the two inputs of a subsequent PE, except in the case of the first PE, which receives the two inputs from outside. The output of the last PE is the system output. Like PEs, the network is described by the connection points instead of the system clock, which is already implicit in the hardware.

For Algorithm 3.3, we can build a module, *network.v*.

Listing 3.12 Module: `network.v`

```
'timescale 1ns/100ps                               //unit time/ precision
'define DATA_WIDTH 32                              //parameter
//network for connecting PEs
module network(
   input signed ['DATA_WIDTH-1:0] xi,              //input
   output signed ['DATA_WIDTH-1:0] yo,             //output
   input clock,                                    //clock input
   input reset                                     //reset input
   );
   //nets and variables
   wire signed ['DATA_WIDTH-1:0] xo;               //actually dummy
   wire signed['DATA_WIDTH*3:1] t,s;               //connection nets
   //chain of instances
   pe p[1:4] ({t,xi}, {xo,t}, {s,0}, {yo,s},clock,reset);
endmodule
```

There are three methods for connecting modules in a chained topology. The first method is to enumerate all the PEs and their ports directly. The better method is to use the *communication net*, which is used in this example. By this method, we used two intermediate variables – `t` and `s` – to form a chained configuration. There is another method using the Verilog construct **`generate`**.

Finally, the network must be tested with a test bench, `tb.v`.

Listing 3.13 Module: `tb.v`

```
`timescale 1 ns / 100 ps                          //unit time/ precision
`define DATA_WIDTH 32                             //parameter
//a test bench
module tb;                                        //test bench
  //inputs
  reg signed[`DATA_WIDTH-1:0] x;
  reg clock, reset;
  //outputs
  wire signed [`DATA_WIDTH-1:0] y;
  //instantiate UUT
  network UUT (                                   //supply x and receive y
    .xi(x),
    .yo(y),
    .clock(clock),
    .reset(reset)
  );
  //execute once for simutation
  initial begin
    x = 0; clock = 0; reset = 0;                  //initialize inputs
      #100 reset = 1;                             //generate reset
      #100 reset = 0;
  end
  always #50 clock = ~clock;                      //clock generation
  always @(posedge clock) begin                   //generates weights
  if (reset == 1) assign x = 0;                   //assign-deassign
  else x = $random;                               //random numer used here
  deassign x;                                     //assign-deassign
  end
endmodule
```

In the code, the network is instantiated with the name UUT, and the signals are supplied by the codes expressed thereafter. In the signal stream, simulated by the random number generator, the first four input data are used as weights, and the remaining data are used as signals. There is some latency because of the tap size, weight preparation, and other initialization processes.

The three modules `tb.v`, `network.v`, `pe.v` collectively construct the overall system and can be simulated. The simulated signals are shown in Figure 3.11. In the left panel, the input and output reset and clock are listed. The right panel shows the signals' corresponding nets and variables.

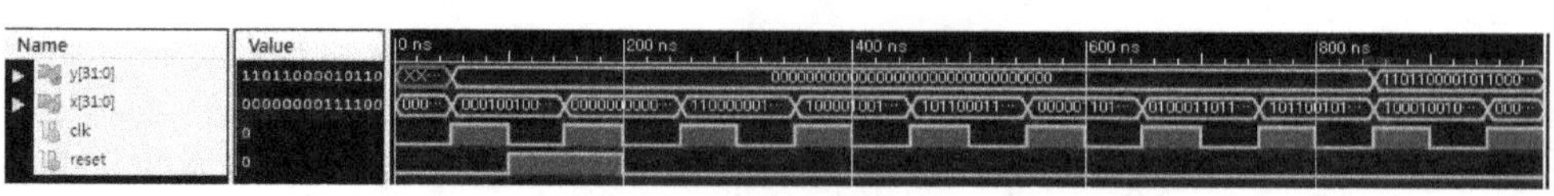

Figure 3.11 Simulation result

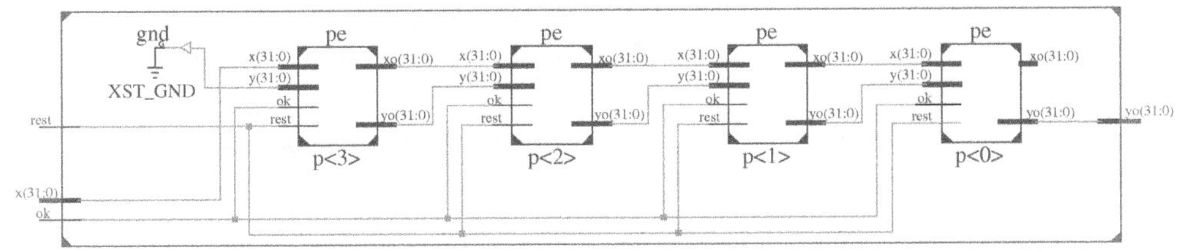

Figure 3.12 RTL schematic diagram after synthesis

The synthesis tool can provide a schematic diagram, as shown in Figure 3.12. The schematic describes connections of the four PE modules. An IDE usually provides functions for observing the design in detail. Electronic design automation (EDA) tools such as Altera Quartus tools and Xilinx ISE (or Vivado) provide a complete set of tools ranging from editing to FPGA programming.

Problems

3.1 [Neighborhood processor] Define the average with four-neighborhood and modify Listing 3.1 for the image average.

3.2 [Neighborhood processor] Integrate an image by modifying Listing 3.1 for the image average.

3.3 [Neighborhood processor] The code, Listing 3.1, is designed for a four-neighborhood system. Change the code for the eight-neighborhood system.

3.4 [Neighborhood processor] In Listing 3.1, the image is considered mono color. Expand the mono to the three channels, R, G, and B, all with the same word length.

3.5 [Viterbi processor] The purpose of the Viterbi forward probability is to find the ending of the shortest path. Write a code for finding the ending with the given $\{\alpha(N-1, j), \eta(j) | j \in [0, N_q - 1]\}$.

3.6 [Viterbi forward processor] The template, Listing 3.3, is designed for only three-neighbor. If the N_q nodes must be considered in comparing operation, the linear array is not possible due to enormous connections. In that case, serial processing is necessary. Write the code in HDL.

3.7 [Forward backward processor] The purpose of the forward algorithm is to compute the conditional probability that is used to solve the evaluation problem. Let the joint probability, $P(X|\Psi)$, where X is the Markov process and Ψ is the prior. Then, write a code for computing $P(X|\Psi)$ with `alpha`, which is obtained by Listing 3.5?

3.8 [RAM] In Listing 3.8, 1D array is used for storing image data (in the sense of word unit). Change the internal array, '`ram`,' to a 2D array.

3.9 [Array] In Listing 3.5, the signal input was used to carry initial weights. Instead, the weight can be loaded from an internal memory. Change the weight setting with a reg loading in the reset block.

3.10 [Array] In Listing 3.6, modify the Verilog codes `pe.v`, `network.v`, and `tb.v` so that the number of taps can be more general.

3.11 [Array] In Listing 3.5, for `pe.v`, the state coding is done in a 'binary scheme'. Change the state into a 'one-hot' scheme.

3.12 [Array] In Listing 3.5 to Listing 3.7, for `pe.v`, change the Moore machine into the Mealy machine with both binary and one-hot state representations.

3.13 [Array] In Listing 3.5 to Listing 3.7, for the module `network.v` used the 'communication list,' `t` and `s` are used to connect the ports of PEs. Instead of a connection list, use **`generate`** to obtain an equivalent network.

3.14 [Array] Design the other arrays in Figure 3.10 by modifying the following Verilog codes: `pe.v`, `network`, and `tb`.

3.15 [Array] Given the equation $y(t) = w_0x(t) + w_1x(t) + w_2x(t-2), t = 0, 1, \ldots,$ express a hardware algorithm that uses only a PE.

3.16 [Array] Given the equation $y(t) = w_0x(t) + w_2x(t-2)^2, t = 0, 1, \ldots,$ express a hardware algorithm that uses only a PE.

3.17 [Array] An IIR filter is given by $y(t) = \sum_k^p a_kx(t-k) + \sum_{l=1}^q b_ly(t-l)$. Design a machine.

3.18 [Array] For an image $I(x, y)$ $(x \in [0, N-1], y \in [0, M-1])$, the first-order forward difference is defined by $f(x, y) = I(x+1, y) - I(x, y)$. Design a machine for this operation.

References

Acceleware 2013 OpenCL Altera http://www.acceleware.com/opencl-altera-fpgas (accessed May 3, 2013).

Baker J 1979 Trainable grammars for speech recognition In *Speech communication papers presented at the 97th meeting of the Acoustical Society of America* (ed. Wolf JJ and Klatt DH), pp. 547–550 Acoustical Society of America.

Crow FC 1984 Summed-area tables for texture mapping *Computer Graphics (SIGGRAPH '84 Proceedings)*, pp. 207–212. Published as Computer Graphics (SIGGRAPH '84 Proceedings), volume 18, number 3.

Jeong H 1984 *Modeling and transformation of systolic network* Master's thesis Massachusetts Institute of Technology.

Kung H and Leiserson C 1980 Algorithms for VLSI processor arrays In *Introduction to VLSI Systems* (ed. Mead C and Conway L) Addison-Wesley Reading, MA pp. 271–291.

Lawrence R, Rabiner R, and Schafer R 2007 *Introduction to Digital Speech Processing*. Now Publishers Inc., Hanover, MA USA.

Leiserson C and Saxe J 1991 Retiming synchronous circuitry. *Algorithmica*, **6**(1), 5–35.

Manning C 2001 Probabilistic linguistics and probabilistic models of natural language processing NIPS 2001 Tutorial.

Petkovic N 1992 *Systolic Parallel Processing*. North Holland Publishing Co.

Rabiner L and Juang B 1993 *Fundamentals of Speech Recognition* Prentice Hall signal processing series. Prentice Hall.

Tapia E 2001 A note on the computation of high-dimensional integral images. *Pattern Recognition Letters* **32**(2), 197–201.

Viola P and Jones MJ 2011 Robust real time object detection *Workshop on Statistical and Computational Theories of Vision*.

Xilinx 2013 High level synthesis http://www.xilinx.com/training/dsp/high-level-synthesis-with-vivado-hls.htm (accessed May 3, 2013).

4

Verilog Vision Simulator

In designing a vision chip, testing is more than simply checking for the correct relationship between the actual output and the desired output, given the test vectors, as in the case of ordinary digital circuit design. The vision chip must deal with very large amounts of data and high data rates such as video frames, as well as various image formats such as bitmap, jpg, and tiff. The data rate in a stereo vision chip is expected to be two to three times higher than it is in an ordinary single video system. Moreover, the vision chip might be part of a large vision system that consists of various types of software and hardware. To build such a vision system, we have to interconnect two heterogeneous systems: vision software and a vision chip. Therefore, we have to move away from the conventional test bench concept to the more specialized concept of the *vision simulator*. This vision system will function as an interface to the chip and vision programs, in a similar fashion to open source computer vision (OpenCV). Generally, the simulator will perform a long sequence of operations: provide images to the chip, perform preprocessing, supply the intermediate preprocessed data to the chip, retrieve the result from the chip, perform post-processing, and provide the final output. In addition to simulation, the simulator by itself can be used as a research tool to develop vision algorithms. Thus, with a simulator, we can build a complete vision system comprising vision software and hardware.

In developing a vision simulator, we may choose one of two approaches. One approach is to use the Verilog system functions and tasks, provided in Verilog 2005 (IEEE 2005). As we learned in the previous chapter, the system tasks and functions are similar to those in C. We can use these functions to read images from files, apply preprocessing, feed the processed image to the chip, collect the results from the chip, and write the results to another file. Another approach is to use the Verilog Procedural Interface (VPI), in which Verilog code invokes C code, which then invokes the Verilog system tasks and functions, for image input and output, preprocessing, and post-processing. This method requires that packages be built both in Verilog and C, using libraries defined in VPI. Unfortunately, this approach is very challenging and appears impractical, compared to the tremendous investment required. Instead, it is more efficient to use the first approach, aided by the vision package, OpenCV (OpenCV 2013).

In this context, this chapter introduces two simulators: a Vision Simulator (VSIM) that is based on scan lines and another that is based on video frames. Both systems are fundamentally based on Verilog system tasks and functions and OpenCV. The processing element in VSIM is generally designed so that more detailed algorithms can be implemented on it. Among VSIMs, line-based VSIM (LVSIM) is designed for algorithms that process images line by line, as in DP. Frame-based VSIM (FVSIM) is more general; it allows neighborhood and iterative computations, as needed in relaxation and BP algorithms.

Architectures for Computer Vision: From Algorithm to Chip with Verilog, First Edition. Hong Jeong.

Companion Website: www.wiley.com/go/jeong

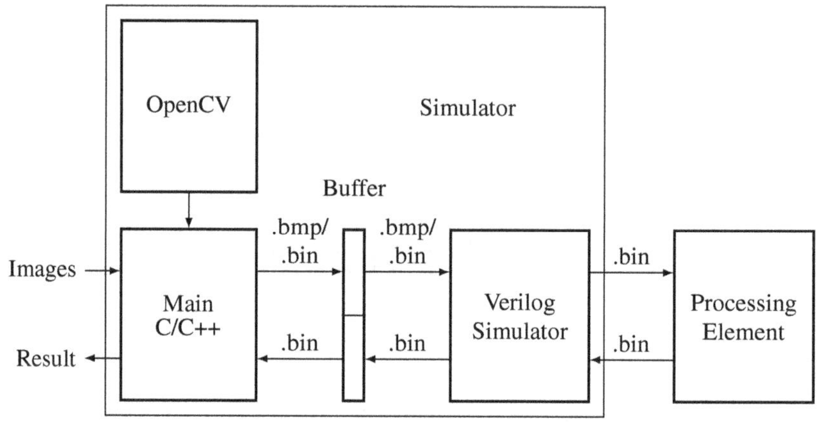

Figure 4.1 The structure of a vision simulator

4.1 Vision Simulator

In general, the simulator must contain the following three components: a main program in C/C++, a Verilog HDL simulator, and a processing element (Figure 4.1). The main program is a general image processing software written in a high-level language, the processing element is the target design for synthesis, and the Verilog HDL simulator is the interface between the main program and the processing element.

The main program is the front-end of the system, and as such receives a set of images, executes some vision algorithms, including preprocessing, and writes the intermediate result to a file, so that the Verilog simulator can access the intermediate result, process it, and store the result of processing in another part of the file. The main program then reads this result from the file, processes it further using vision algorithms, conducts post-processing, and outputs the final result. During the processing, the main program may use other vision packages, such as OpenCV. The OpenCV package represents an image by an object, `Mat`, and thereby manipulates it, using various vision processing operations. In its location between the main program and the processing element, the Verilog simulator reads information from the buffer file and supplies it to the processing element. At the end of processing, it reads the result from the processor and writes it back to the file. The processing element receives the raw image data from the Verilog simulator, processes it, and returns the result to the Verilog simulator. In this manner, the three components form a loop, consisting of forward and backward paths from the outside into the chip.

It is obvious that the programming paradigms of the three components are different: the main program is written in C/C++, the Verilog simulator is written in Verilog System tasks/functions, which may not be synthesized, and the processing element is written in Verilog HDL, which must be synthesized. To make components exchange data flawlessly without concern for their internal implementation, we must make the data format between any two interfacing systems the same. The input to the main program is a set of images, taken from still cameras or video cameras, which are encoded in various formats (Wikipedia 2013b). The format of the output from the main program is even more varied: data, feature maps, disparity maps, optical flow maps, other map types, and images. Between the main program and the Verilog simulator, the image must be coded in a common format, such as bitmap (i.e. a file with the .bmp extension) or raw image (i.e. a file with the .bin extension, signifying binary data). Between the Verilog simulator and the processing element, the data format must be raw (i.e. it should have a .bin extension).

In simple cases, the main program can be disregarded and the Verilog simulator alone used to manage the bitmap or raw image stored in the file. If image formats are a problem, OpenCV may not be necessary, because they can be converted to bitmap or raw image by dedicated image converters. In a sophisticated system, the main program can be used to connect the Verilog simulator and OpenCV, and transfer data between them, without relying on files. This scheme can be accomplished using the VPI in Verilog-2005 (also DPI in SystemVerilog), which links the high-level programming and Verilog (also SystemVerilog). A C program can be compiled with VPI constructs using `vpi_user.h` and called from the Verilog simulator as user defined procedures (UDPs). However, the programming complexity involved in building the complicated interface needed is not worth the time investment required. A more practical approach is to use a simple buffer (i.e. a file) between the main program and the Verilog simulator, as described above. The systems are loosely coupled but are very versatile in dealing with general cases. Under these assumptions, we develop the main program and the Verilog simulators, as well as a general form of processing element in the ensuing sections.

4.2 Image Format Conversion

Because several different programming environments must be linked, a common file format for exchanging the data in files is necessary. Two basic forms are used: raw format and bitmap format. (Let us use the file extension `.bin` for raw image files, and `.bmp` for bitmaps, as per convention.) The raw format is a 1D array of pixels in Verilog data format, obtained by rearranging the 2D image (Figure 4.2). In mathematical terms, an image is represented by an array, $I = \{I(x, y)|x \in [0, N-1], y \in [0, M-1]\}$ where each pixel is in the RGB color model, $I = \{(R, G, B)\}$, and in Verilog is represented by an array, '`reg [7:0] image [0:3*'N * 'M-1];`', where `'M` and `'N` are parameters representing row and column, respectively. For a pixel, the corresponding Verilog array is

$$\begin{cases} I_R(x, y) = \text{image } [3\text{Ny} + 3\text{x}], \\ I_G(x, y) = \text{image } [3\text{Ny} + 3\text{x} + 1], \\ I_B(x, y) = \text{image } [3\text{Ny} + 3\text{x} + 2]. \end{cases}$$

If the image is stored in a 2D Verilog array, '`reg [7:0] image [0:2][0:'N-1][0:'M-1];`', the mapping would be more natural. However, we prefer to use the 1D array representation because the coordinate transformation for this type of array is not very difficult. Furthermore, frequent image transfers between modules is involved, which necessitates a simple counter over more complicated counters.

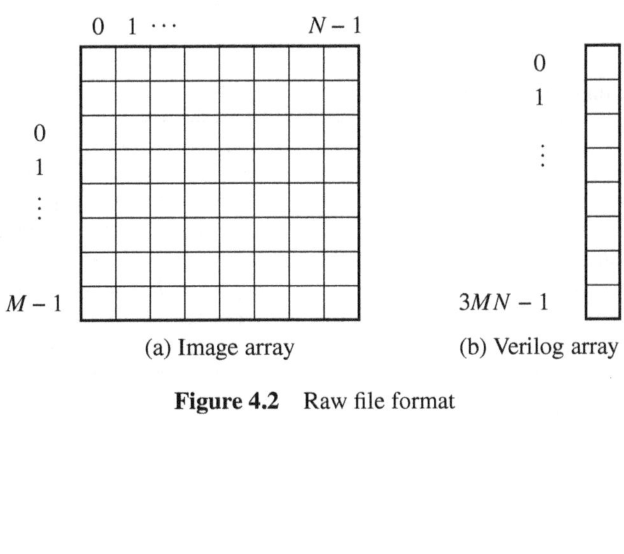

(a) Image array (b) Verilog array

Figure 4.2 Raw file format

Image processing also needs neighborhood computation. Between the image and the Verilog array, the relationship is

$$\begin{cases} I_R(x+a, y+b) = \text{image[3N(y+b) + 3(x+a)]}, \\ I_G(x+a, y+b) = \text{image[3N(y+b) + 3(x+a) + 1]}, \\ I_B(x+a, y+b) = \text{image[3N(y+b) + 3(x+a) + 2]}, \end{cases}$$

where (a, b) is the offset of the neighbor from the pixel (x, y). For a set of images, $I = \{I_1, I_2, \dots, I_T\}$, the raw map is a stack of the images '`reg [7:0] image [0: 3*'N*'M *'T-1].`'

For a pixel, `image[i]`, within an image, the neighborhoods are $(i+3, i-3, i+3N, i-3N)$ (i.e. east, west, south, north) for a four-neighborhood system and $(i+3, i+3N+3, i+3N, i+3N-3, i-3, i-3N-3, i-3N, i-3N+3)$ (i.e. east, southeast, south, southwest, west, northwest, north, northeast) for an eight-neighborhood system. In stereo matching or motion estimation, two or more images must be compared. For the neighborhoods $(i+3, i-3, i+3N, i-3N)$ in the first image, the corresponding pixels in the second image are $(3MN+i+3, 3MN+i-3, 3MN+i+3N, 3MN+i-3N)$ for a four-neighborhood system. For an eight-neighborhood system, the pixels, $(i+3, i+3N+3, i+3N, i+3N-3, i-3, i-3N-3, i-3N, i-3N+3)$, in the first image, correspond to the pixels, $(3MN+i+3, 3MN+i+3N+3, 3MN+i+3N, 3MN+i+3N-3, 3MN+i-3, 3MN+i-3N-3, 3MN+i-3N, 3MN+i-3N+3)$, in the second image. This relationship can be expanded to other neighborhood systems.

In addition to the raw format, we use the bitmap file format to facilitate the exchange of data between modules in the simulator. The bitmap image file format (Wikipedia 2013a) (a.k.a. BMP and DIB) is a raster graphics image file format used to store bitmap digital images, independently of the display device. The bitmap file format is capable of storing 2D digital images of arbitrary width, height, and resolution, both monochrome and color, in various color depths, and optionally with data compression, alpha channels, and color profiles. The values are stored in little-endian format. The general structure comprises fixed-size parts (headers) and variable-size parts appearing in a predetermined order (Table 4.1).

Although the format contains many parts describing every detail of the image, only the parts necessary for our needs are listed in the table. The offset is the address where the pixel array begins. Ordinarily, the *RGB* format is '8.8.8.0.0,' which means that the pixel array is a 24-bit RGB block, with each color represented by one byte. The order of the colors is B, R, G, from lowest to highest addresses. Normally the pixel order is upside-down with respect to the normal raster scan order, starting in the lower left corner, going from left to right, and then row by row from the bottom to the top of the image.

In calculating the variables, *padding* bytes (from zero to three), which are appended to the end of the rows in order to increase the length of the rows to a multiple of four bytes, must be considered. Therefore,

Table 4.1 Major components in the Bitmap format

Parameter	Value
File size	{image[5],image[4],image[3],image[2]}
Offset	{image[13],image[12],image[11],image[10]}
Width (pixels, no padding)	{image[21],image[20],image[19],image[18]}
Height (pixels, no padding)	{image[25],image[24],image[23],image[22]}
Bits per pixel	{image[31],image[30],image[29],image[28]}
Raw data size (padding)	{image[37],image[36],image[35],image[34]}

cf. Numbers in decimal. The notation, {`A,B`} means the concatenation, `AB`.

when the pixel array is loaded into memory, each row begins at a memory address that is a multiple of four. From the header information, we have to derive the parameters: row width, excluding padded bits, image size, and the number of padded bits, which sometimes may not be available in the header. The parameters can be derived using the following equations:

$$\begin{cases} (\text{Row width}) = (\text{Raw data size})/(\text{Height}), \\ (\text{Image size}) = (\text{Width}) \times (\text{Height}) \times (\text{Bits per pixel})/8, \\ (\text{Padding}) = (\text{Row width}) - (\text{Width}) \times (\text{Bits per pixel})/8. \end{cases}$$

The bitmap file is more useful than a file that is in the raw format because it can be viewed on a monitor. On the other hand, the raw format is required internally by modules that manipulate the raw array in image processing. Therefore, there has to be an interface for converting the bitmap to raw format and then reconstructing the raw image to bitmap file format. The former processing is required when the image processing is going to be applied, whereas the latter is required when the result is going to be observed. The header and the derived parameters are needed for such image conversions. In the vision simulator, the two conversions are major operations, which simulate the camera output and monitor display.

Let us build a module that converts file formats between BMP and BIN (binary). Although, there are many image converters and binary editors, the Verilog-based converter is especially necessary because it is the part of the vision simulator into which images are fed and which displays the resulting image format. Incidentally, through this design, we can understand both image formatting and Verilog coding. The internal function of the converter is illustrated in Figure 4.3. The input to the converter may be either of the two formats, bitmap or binary. Likewise, the output may be either of the two formats. If a bitmap file is converted to binary, the file must be stripped into header and binary, where only the binary part is output. If a binary file is converted to bitmap, the file must be transposed and an appropriate header synthesized, using the data in the Verilog header, and added. The key operation is the header extraction and synthesis, extraction of the binary, and pixel order inversion.

We divide the design into three parts: header, file reading, and file writing parts. The header specifies three pieces of information: The first piece of information is the conversion mode: bmp to bmp, bmp to bin, bin to bmp, and bin to bin, which is specified by the parameter `BMP_BIN`. The second piece of information defines the maximum size of the files. The third piece of information is the size of the bin file, which carries only the image intensities. This information is essential when the bin format is to be converted to bmp and bin formats.

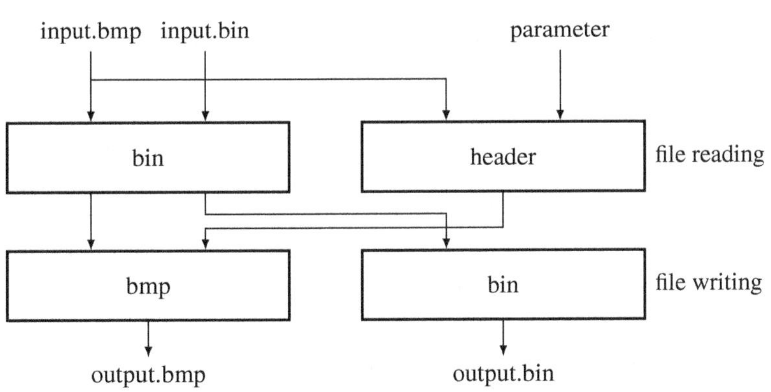

Figure 4.3 An image converter in Verilog

Listing 4.1 Converter: header and top module (1/3)

```
//converter mode
//00: bmp -> bmp, 01: bmp -> bin, 10: bin -> bmp, 11: bin -> bin
`define BMP_BIN  2'b10                               //default

//common to bmp and bin
`define BIN_ADDR   20                                //max  size 1 MB

//format for bin -> bmp, must be specified by the user
`define WIDTH    512                                 //width of bin
`define HEIGHT   512                                 //height of bin

//top module for instantiation
module converter;                                    //top module
  bmp_bin BMP_BIN ();                                //execute
endmodule
```

The first part (header) also contains an instantiation of the main module, `bmp_bin`. No signal, such as clock or reset, is necessary as this design is executed by the Verilog simulator, unencumbered by synthesis constraints.

The second part (file reading) is for reading bmp and bin files. This file reading part must provide two pieces of information: header and binary data. For the bmp file, the header and binary parts are all in a single file and thus must be extracted and stored. The header contains all the information about the image, such as width, height, and bits per pixel, as mentioned previously. The padding bits may or may not be provided in the header and must thus be computed and stored. The bitmap header is used when the converter converts the internally stored binary file into a bitmap file.

Listing 4.2 Converter: reading file (2/3)

```
module bmp_bin ();                                   //main converter
   //declaration
   reg [7:0] buffer [1:(1 << `BIN_ADDR)];            //[1:-] for $fread
   reg [7:0] image [0:(1 << `BIN_ADDR)];

   integer  load_file_id,save_file_id, c;            //file opening
   integer  i, j, k;                                 //variables
   reg [31:0] width,height,size,bpp,nop,padding,row_width,offset;
   reg [7:0] header [1:54];                          //bitmap header

   //Reading: bmp -> buffer -> image, header
   initial begin: READ_BMP                           //execute once
      if (`BMP_BIN == 2'b00 || `BMP_BIN == 01) begin //check mode
         load_file_id = $fopen(input.bmp,"rb");  //open a file
```

```
      c = $fread(buffer, load_file_id);            //read the file
      $fclose(load_file_id);                       //close the file
      if ( {buffer[2], buffer[1]} == 16'h4D42 ) begin //424D
         //image parameters for dealing with general bmp files
         size = {buffer[6],buffer[5],buffer[4],buffer[3]};
         offset ={buffer[14],buffer[13],buffer[12],buffer[11]};
         width = {buffer[22], buffer[21], buffer[20], buffer[19]};
         height = {buffer[26], buffer[25], buffer[24], buffer[23]};
         bpp = {buffer[30],buffer[29]};
         nop = {buffer[38],buffer[37],buffer[36],buffer[35]};
         row_width = nop / height;                 //row width (padding)
         padding = row_width - width * bpp / 8;    //padding

         //store header
         for ( i = 1; i <= offset; i = i + 1 ) begin
            header[i] = buffer[i];                 //store the header
         end

         //store the BIN image
         for ( i = 0; i < height; i = i + 1 ) begin
             //store BIN image
             for ( j = 0; j < (row_width - padding); j = j + 1 ) begin
               image[i* (row_width - padding) + j]
               = buffer[(height-1 - i)* row_width + j + offset + 1];
             end
         end
      end else $display ("Error: no bmp files.");
   end //if
end //initial

//Reading: bin -> image, header
initial begin: READ_BIN                            //execute once
   if ('BMP_BIN == 2'b10 || 'BMP_BIN == 11) begin //for the BIN map
      //check for the first enter
      load_file_id = $fopen(input.bin,"rb");       //1st file
      c = $fread(buffer, load_file_id);            //read file
      $fclose(load_file_id);
      for ( i = 0; i < 'HEIGHT; i = i + 1 ) begin
         //store BIN image
         for ( j = 0; j < 3 * 'WIDTH; j = j + 1 ) begin
            image[3 * i * 'WIDTH + j]
               = buffer[3 * i * 'WIDTH + j+1];
         end
      end
```

```
      //build header
      for (i = 1; i <= 54; i = i + 1) header[i] = 0; //store header
      //id
      {header[2], header[1]} = 16'h4D42;      //magic number

      //offset
      offset = 54;                            //offset
      header[14] = 8'h00; header[13] = 8'h00;
      header[12] = 8'b00; header[11] = 8'd 54;
      //DIB size                              //DIB size
      {header[18],header[17],header[16],header[15]} = 32'd 40;
      //width
      width = 'WIDTH;                         //width
      {header[22],header[21],header[20],header[19]} = 32'd 'WIDTH;

      //height
      height = 'HEIGHT;                       //height
      {header[26], header[25], header[24], header[23]}
         = 32'd 'HEIGHT;
      //Number of cplor planes
      {header[28],header[27]} = 16'd1;        //color planes
      //bits per pixel
      bpp = 24;                               //bits per pixel
      {header[30],header[29]} = 16'd 24;
      //padding
      case ((3 * 'WIDTH) % 4)                 //padded bits
         0: padding = 0;
         1: padding = 3;
         2: padding = 2;
         3: padding = 1;
      endcase
      //row_width
      row_width = 'WIDTH * 3 + padding;       //row width
      //nop
      nop = row_width * height;               //no of pixels
      {header[38],header[37],header[36],header[35]} = nop;
      //size
      size = offset + (3 * 'WIDTH + padding) * 'HEIGHT; //file size
      {header[6],header[5],header[4],header[3]} = size;
      //horizontal resolution
      {header[42],header[41],header[40],header[39]} = 32'h00000B13;
      //vertical resolution
      {header[46],header[45],header[44],header[43]} = 32'h00000B13;
   end//if
end //initial
```

The bin file has no image information and so this must be provided by the Verilog header file. In the reverse processing of the bitmap file, the header is composed from the various bitmap fields. The bitmap header is used when the converter converts the internally stored binary file into an external bitmap file. This processing is particularly needed in order to observe the output of the vision simulator, such as maps, disparity maps, and optical flow maps, as we shall see.

The third part of the converter writes the internally stored binary map, extracted or synthesized, to a binary file or a bmp file. For the bmp output, the internal binary file and the header must be used to synthesize a bmp file.

Listing 4.3 Converter: writing file (3/3)

```
//Writing: image, header -> bmp
initial begin: WRITE_BMP                              //execute once
   if ((`BMP_BIN == 2'b00) || (`BMP_BIN == 2'b10)) begin //ckeck mode
      save_file_id = $fopen(output.bmp, 'wb');        //open the file
      //write header first
      for ( i = 1; i <= offset; i = i + 1 ) begin
         $fwrite(save_file_id, '%c', header[i]); // write the header
      end

      //write image part
      for ( i=0; i< height; i=i+1 ) begin             //consider padding
         for ( j=0; j< (row_width - padding); j=j+1 ) begin
            $fwrite(save_file_id, '%c', image[(height-1 - i)
               *(row_width - padding) + j]);          //write image data
         end
         if (padding) begin                           //if no padding, skip
            for (k=0; k < padding; k=k+1)
               $fwrite(save_file_id,'%c',8'h00); // fill the padding
         end
      end //for

      //close the file
      $fclose(save_file_id);                          //close the file
   end //if
end //initial

//Writing: image -> bin
initial begin: WRITE_BIN                              //execute once
   if ((`BMP_BIN == 2'b01) || (`BMP_BIN == 2'b11)) begin //check mode
      save_file_id = $fopen(output.bin,"wb");         //open the file
      //write image part
      if (`BMP_BIN == 2'b01) begin
      for ( i = 0; i < 3 * width * height; i=i+1 ) begin //bmp
         $fwrite(save_file_id, "%c", image[i]);  //write image data
      end
```

```
        end else begin
            for ( i = 0; i < 3 * 'WIDTH * 'HEIGHT; i=i+1 ) begin //bin
                $fwrite(save_file_id, "%c", image[i]); //write image data
            end
        end

        //close the file
        $fclose(save_file_id);                          //close the file
    end //if
end //initial
endmodule
```

The header may be extracted or synthesized, as explained above. Further, the binary file may be extracted or directly inputted. The bin output does not require a header as it is just a file output of the internal binary data. In this case, image size header information is not used. This processing may be needed when the bin image is provided to other image processing software to conduct preprocessing or post-processing for the simulator.

One can easily verify the correctness of the converter by transforming twice – bmp to bin and then bin to bmp. To test the design, small size images may be needed because large size images require too much time, both for simulation and synthesis.

4.3 Line-based Vision Simulator Principle

The line-based vision simulator conducts processing on a line-by-line basis. To derive such a system, we first of all need to specify the computational scheme for dealing with a frame. Let us define basic quantities and order of computation, as depicted in Figure 4.4. A frame is an image plane, defined as $\mathcal{P} = \{(x,y)|x \in [0,N-1], y \in [0,M-1]\}$. The frame rate may be the conventional 30 fps (frames per second), but may be faster or slower, depending on the situation. Inside each frame, we define a strip (block, window, or lines), $S(j) = \{(x,j+b)|x \in [0,N-1], b \in [0,h-1]\}$, where $j \in [0,M-h]$. The strip moves downwards from $j = 0$ to $j = M - h$ and returns to the top of the image, and periodically

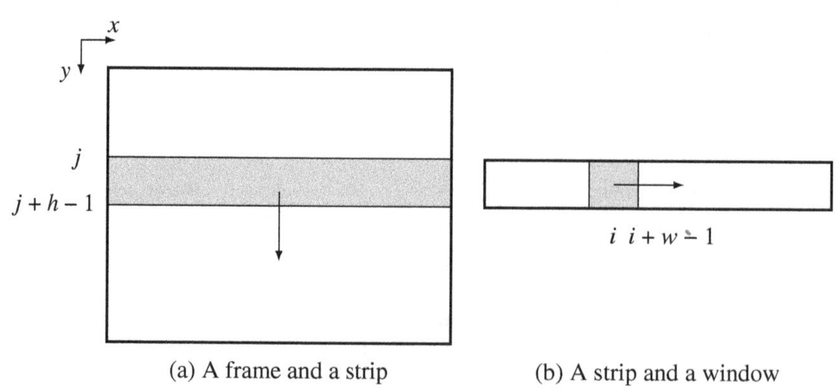

Figure 4.4 Frame, strip, and window

repeats this movement. In a one-pass algorithm, all computations must be completed during one scan. In a multi-pass algorithm, the computations must be repeated many times. The computational unit may be an entire strip or a smaller window (or block) in a strip. A window is defined by $w(i,j) = \{(i+a, j+b) | a \in [0, w-1], j \in [0, h-1]\}$, which moves to the right inside a strip. The computational unit may be the window – in which case all the pixels in the window are determined concurrently – or the pixels in the window – in which case all the pixels in the window are determined serially.

The overall structure of the vision simulator (i.e. the line-based vision simulation (LVSIM)) is shown in Figure 4.5. First of all, the target design is the processing element (PE), which is to be tested functionally and later synthesized for chip implementation. This processing element combines with other elements to construct the simulator. The simulator consists of three parts: a pair of image files, an input-output (IO) module, and one processor (PE) module. Generally, the images are a set of image pairs, captured from stereo cameras. However, for mono camera or motion estimation, only one set of images may be used.

In the forward pass, the file converter reads in two image files, converts them into binary files, and writes the results into the RAMs (IMAGE1 and IMAGE2). This action occurs repeatedly at predetermined intervals, which can be adjusted as needed. In the backward pass, the converter reads the RAM (RESULT) in the processing element, again periodically, and converts the contents to a BMP file. In this manner, a snapshot of the RAM contents can be obtained at desired intervals. The observation positions and intervals are all adjustable.

The processing element (PE) consists of three identical RAMs and a processor (PROC). Two of the three RAMs are used to capture the images from video cameras, in a real-time system. Depending on the given conditions on video input and RAMs (i.e. SRAM, SDRAM, etc.), the RAM module must be modified, using library modules, so that the image from the camera can be correctly delivered into the RAMs. For generality, this simulator uses conventional dual port synchronous RAM, instead of specialized RAM. The remaining RAM is used to store the processed result. The processor (PROC) is

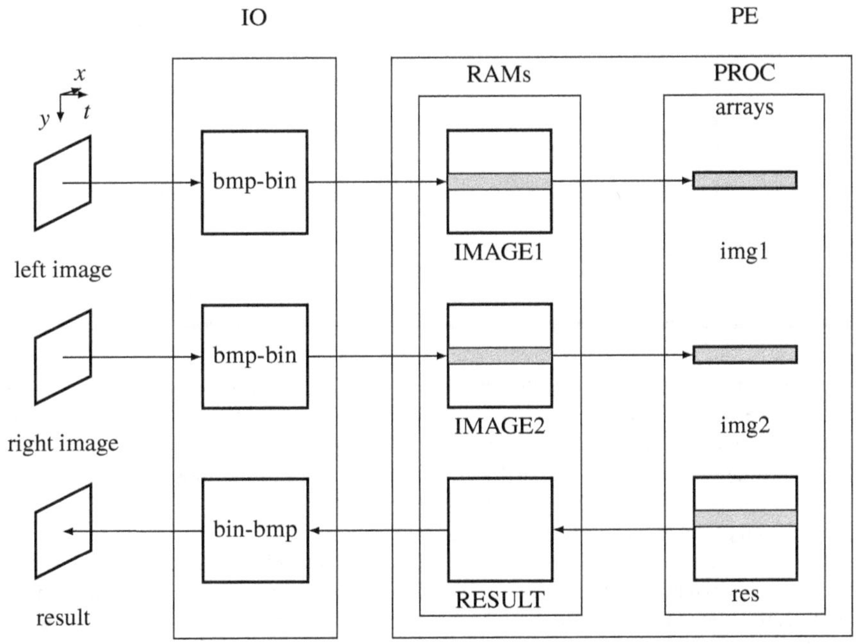

Figure 4.5 The structure of LVSIM

the main engine that actually executes the image processing algorithms. It takes a window of image from each RAM, stores the pair of image windows in two arrays, and uses them to update another array, which stores the temporary result. The windowed images are small but the resultant image is full. For a small application, the buffer, `res`, can also be made small like `img1` and `img2`. The intention is to compute line by line, in a raster scan manner. The size of the strip is defined by the parameters in the Verilog head file. We will build the processing element for DP-based algorithms based on this simulator in coming chapters.

4.4 LVSIM Top Module

Let us now actualize the simulator concepts in Verilog HDL codes. The overall system consists of two parts: a top module (`vsim.v`) for simulation and another top module (`pe.v`) for synthesis.

The first part is the top module of the simulator, containing all the components in Figure 4.5.

Listing 4.4 Top module for simulation: `vsim.v`

```
`define WIDTH      225                                    //image width
`define HEIGHT     188                                    //image height
`define ADDR_BITS  20                                     //max image size
`define LINES      50                                     //strip size

module vsim;                                              //vsim
   reg clock, reset;

   //instantiation
   pe PE (clock, reset);                                  //processing element
   io IO (clock, reset);                                  //file input output

   initial begin
      clock = 0;
      reset = 0; #30; reset = 1; #150; reset = 0;        //reset signal
   end
   always #50 clock =  ~clock;                            //clock generator
endmodule
```

The parameters specify all the information necessary for synthesis and simulation. The four parameters are the size of the image (`WIDTH` and `HEIGHT`), address bits (`ADDR_BITS`) for the RAMs to store the images, and the number of lines (`LINES`) for neighborhood processing. Other parameters are written in the simulation module, `vsim.v`. By default, the system is tuned to the most general case: stereo and motion. Other systems, such as mono camera, stereo, or motion, can be obtained by removing some of the resources, such as RAMs and internal buffers.

This module performs three tasks: instantiation of the processing element and the input-output element, generation of a reset signal, and generation of a common clock. The input-output element is for simulation and the processing element is for synthesis. Note that there is no port communication between the two modules. The input-output element, being a simulator, uses many unsynthesizable Verilog constructs, which provide powerful tools for simulation.

The processing element (`pe.v`) has the following structures:

Listing 4.5 Top module for synthesis: `pe.v`

```
module pe(input clock, reset);                      //processing element
   //variables: image ram
   wire ['ADDR_BITS - 1:0] i_raddr,                 //read addresses
      i_waddr1, i_waddr2,                           //write addresses
      r_raddr, r_waddr;                             //read RESULT
   wire [7:0] i_rdata1, i_rdata2,                   //read data
      i_wdata1, i_wdata2, r_wdata;                  //write data
   wire i_wen1, i_wen2, r_wen;                      //write enable

   //instantiation of synthesis modules
   //one processor and three RAMs
   ram IMAGE1  (clock, i_raddr, i_rdata1,
      i_waddr1, i_wdata1, i_wen1);                  //1st image RAM
   ram IMAGE2  (clock, i_raddr, i_rdata2,
      i_waddr2, i_wdata2, i_wen2);                  //2nd image RAM
   ram RESULT(clock, r_waddr, r_wdata, r_wen);      //result RAM
   processor PROC (clock, reset, i_raddr,           //processor
      r_waddr, i_rdata1, i_rdata2,
      r_wdata, r_wen);
endmodule
```

The purpose of this module is to create three RAMs (IMAGE1, IMAGE2, and RESULT) and a processor (PROC) and connect them, following the structure in Figure 4.5.

After synthesizing the processor (by Altera Quartus or Xilinx ISE), we can investigate the designed circuits in detail with the help of the schematic diagram. The top level view is depicted in Figure 4.6.

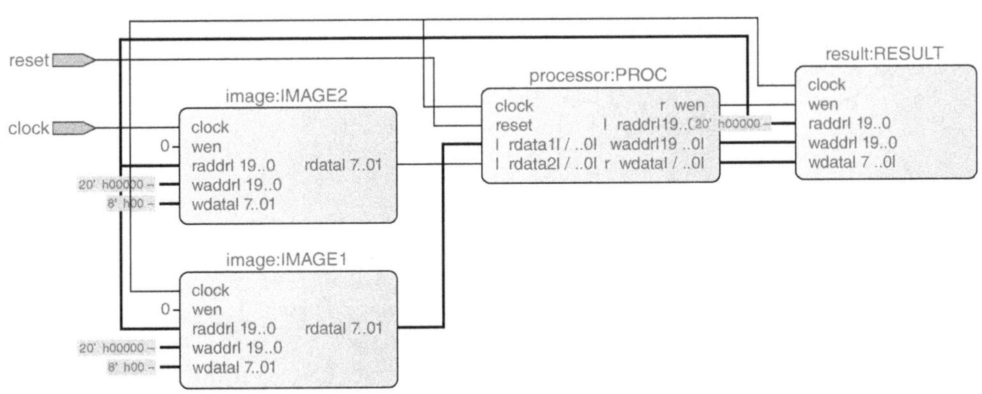

Figure 4.6 The top level schematic of the processing element

The three RAMs and the processor are connected via address bus, data bus, and write enable signals. Although all the possible lines are connected, the connections that are utilized depend on the algorithm running inside the processor. The input signals are just the clock and reset signals. The two RAMs (IMAGE1 and IMAGE2) must be linked to the video camera, via writing ports, in an actual system. (The processor only reads from the two image RAMs it does not write to them.)

The following sections address the substructures of the simulator: memories (IMAGE1, IMAGE2, and RESULT) and processor (PROC), in detail, with working codes.

4.5 LVSIM IO System

The simulator must supply data to the processor and display the data in the various parts, including inputs and outputs, dynamically. Unlike an ordinary test bench, the vision simulator must show us data by means of images. The input and output (IO) function is based on the image converter, as explained above, but is optimized for the simulator.

The function of this module can be explained using state diagrams (Figure 4.7). The interval at which the image RAMs are fed is based on the image processing algorithm. When a frame is completed, a new frame must be available in the RAM. This instance can be obtained from a variable in the processor. An $N \times M$ image frame is defined by $I = \{I(i,j)|i \in [0, M-1], j \in [0, N-1])\}$. In this frame, a window is defined by $W(i) = \{I(i+k,j)|k \in [0, m-1], j \in [0, N-1]\}$ and proceeds in the order, $i = 0, 1, \ldots, M-m+1$, where m is the number of lines in the window. When the window arrives, $W(M-m+1)$, it returns again to the top of the image, $W(0)$. At this point, a new image frame must be available in the RAM. In Figure 4.7(a), the process begins when the new frame signal is detected. First, the input image files are opened and read into buffers. Next, the contents in the buffers are classified into headers and binary images. The headers are used when the output from the processor is viewed as a bitmap. The binary data is then loaded into RAM, which completes the cycle.

The corresponding code reads as follows. The first part of the code is designed for loading the RAMs with binary images. In a real system, this section is replaced with video cameras that load the RAMs with binary images in effectively the same way.

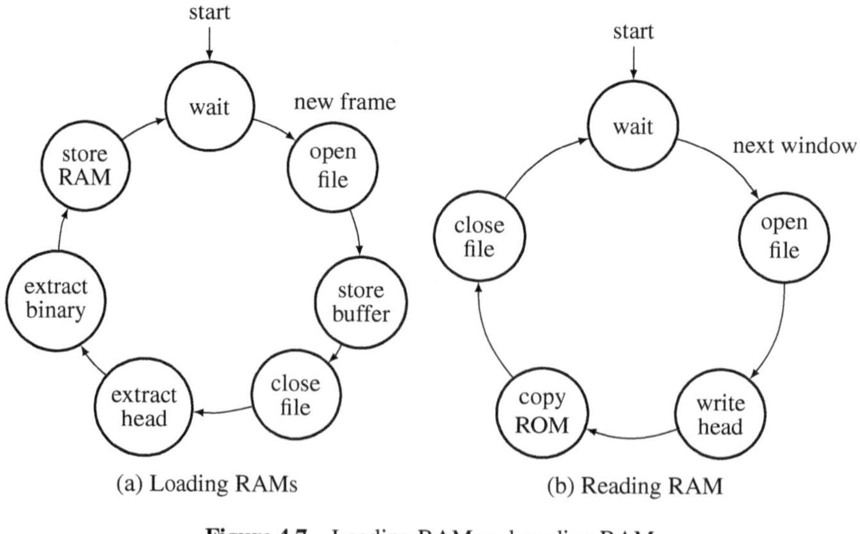

Figure 4.7 Loading RAM and reading RAM

Listing 4.6 IO system: io.v (1/2)

```
module io (input clock,reset);                         //read and write
   //declaration
   reg [7:0] buffer [1:(1 << 'ADDR_BITS)];             //1st buffer
   reg [7:0] buffer2 [1:(1 << 'ADDR_BITS)];            //2nd buffer
   integer load_file_id,save_file_id, c, count = 0; //file opening
   integer i, j, k;                                    //variables
   reg [31:0] width,height,size,bpp,nop,padding,row_width,offset;
   reg [7:0] header [1:54];                            //bitmap header

   //reading: bmp -> buffer -> image, header
   always @(PE.PROC.j) if (!PE.PROC.j) begin: READ //new frame
      //load two sequence of images
      case (count % 2)                                 //2: image sequence
         0: begin
            load_file_id = $fopen("inputl0.bmp","rb"); //1st image
            c = $fread(buffer, load_file_id);          //read the file
            $fclose(load_file_id);                     //close the file
            load_file_id = $fopen("inputr0.bmp","rb"); //2nd image
            c = $fread(buffer2, load_file_id);         //read the file
            $fclose(load_file_id);
            end
         1: begin
            load_file_id = $fopen("inputl1.bmp","rb"); //1st image
            c = $fread(buffer, load_file_id);          //read the file
            $fclose(load_file_id);                     //close the file
            load_file_id = $fopen("inputr1.bmp","rb"); //2nd image
            c = $fread(buffer2, load_file_id);         //read the file
            $fclose(load_file_id);
            end
    endcase

   //close the file
   if ( {buffer[2], buffer[1]} == 16'h4D42 ) begin          //424D
      //image parameters for dealing with general bmp files
      size = {buffer[6],buffer[5],buffer[4],buffer[3]};     //file size
      offset ={buffer[14],buffer[13],buffer[12],buffer[11]};
      width = {buffer[22], buffer[21], buffer[20], buffer[19]};
      height = {buffer[26], buffer[25], buffer[24], buffer[23]};
      bpp = {buffer[30],buffer[29]};                   //bits per pixel
      nop = {buffer[38],buffer[37],buffer[36],buffer[35]}; //pixels
      row_width = nop / height;                        //row width
      padding = row_width - width * bpp / 8;           //padding
```

```
        //store header
        for ( i = 1; i <= offset; i = i + 1 ) begin
            header[i] = buffer[i];              //store the header
        end
            //fill the RAMs for the two images
            for ( i = 0; i < height; i = i + 1 ) begin
               for ( j = 0; j < (row_width - padding); j = j + 1 ) begin
               PE.IMAGE1.ram[i* (row_width - padding) + j]
                  = buffer[(height-1 - i)* row_width + j + offset + 1];
               PE.IMAGE2.ram[i* (row_width - padding) + j]
                  = buffer2[(height-1 - i)* row_width + j + offset + 1];
               end
            end
            count = count + 1;
        end else $display ("Error: no bmp files.");
    end //always
```

The two 2D array buffers and the 1D array are provided for two files and a header. The process waits until a new frame is needed by the processor. (This happens when the strip returns to the top of the frame in Figure 4.4; that is, $S(j)$ becomes $S(0)$. All the computation must be finished before a new frame arrives.) Entering the loop, the process opens two files (one file in the case of mono processing) and stores them in two buffers. From the buffers, the headers and binaries are extracted and inverted in the correct row order. The header, which is common to both images, is stored for later use, and the binaries are loaded into the two RAMs. Thus, this action simulates video cameras feeding two RAMs. For each channel, the input images are a set of bitmap files, $I(0), I(1), \dots, I(n-1)$, for n number of images. The two channels read the image sequences, synchronize, and cycle through, as indicated by the counter. This part of the code can be easily modified for different scenarios: a still camera, a video camera, two still cameras, or two video cameras. The default setting is for two video cameras.

The second part of the code is designed for writing files using the data in the RAM, where the result is stored by the processor.

Listing 4.7 IO system: `io.v` (2/2)

```
    //writing: image, header -> bmp
    always @ (PE.PROC.j) begin: WRITE                 //new frame
       save_file_id = $fopen("output.bmp","wb");  //open the file
       //write header first
       for ( i = 1; i <= offset; i = i + 1 ) begin
          $fwrite(save_file_id, "%c", header[i]); //write the header
          //$display("header[%d] = %d",i, header[i]);
       end
```

```
        //write image part
        for ( i=0; i< height; i=i+1 ) begin         //consider padding
           for ( j=0; j< (row_width - padding); j=j+1 ) begin
              $fwrite(save_file_id, "%c", vsim.PE.RESULT.ram[(height-1 - i)
                    *(row_width - padding) + j]);  //monitoring position
           end
           if (padding) begin                       //no padding
              for (k=0; k < padding; k=k+1)
              $fwrite(save_file_id,"%c",8'h00);     //fill the padding
           end
        end //for

        //close the file
        $fclose(save_file_id);                      //close the file
        //$display("time = %t, read_write: write done.",$time);
    end //always
endmodule
```

The purpose of this code is to observe the result by reading the result RAM. A suitable instance for observation occurs at the point when the strip moves to the next position (in Figure 4.4, at the point when $S(j)$ changes to $S(j+1)$). The position of the observation is the result RAM, containing updated results. During the testing, it is very important to observe various places in the system. In such cases, the monitoring position can be set to the desired data in the processing element. The typical monitoring positions are the RAMs (IMG1 and IMG2) and the buffers (img1, img2, and res).

4.6 LVSIM RAM and Processor

The simulator needs three RAMs, two to capture the input images (IMAGE1 and IMAGE2) and one to preserve the results from the processor (RESULT). They are all the same type of RAMs, double-port synchronous RAMs.

Listing 4.8 RAM: `ram.v`

```
module ram(                                   //image ram
    input clock,
    input ['ADDR_BITS - 1:0] raddr,           //read address
    output reg [7:0] rdata,                   //read data
    input ['ADDR_BITS - 1:0] waddr,           //write address
    input [7:0] wdata,                        //write data
    input wen                                 //write enable
    );
```

```
    reg [7:0] ram [0:(2**'ADDR_BITS) - 1]; //array

    always @(posedge clock) begin
       if (wen)
          ram[waddr] <= wdata;             //write
          rdata <= ram[raddr];             //read
    end
endmodule
```

The output is not buffered, is thus available at all times, and needs no clock synchronization. The RAM design can be aided by the templates and IPs. In an actual system, SDRAMs may be used to capture the video signals. In such a case, IPs are required for designing DRAM controllers and PLLs.

The main part of the simulator is the processor, where all the data is processed. Conceptually, the operation is defined by

$$S(j) \leftarrow T(S_1(j), S_2(j), S(j)),$$

where $T(\cdot)$ denotes a transformation, representing an algorithm. Inputs $S_1(j)$ and $S_2(j)$ are strips of the image frames. Input $S(j)$ is the strip from the internal array and operates like a state memory (Figure 4.8). The registers (img1 and img2) storing the strips, $S_1(j)$ and $S_2(j)$, operate as caches and copy only the required portions of the external RAMs (IMAGE1 and IMAGE2). The array (res) is a full frame memory that stores the updated states and copies them back to the external RAM (RESULT) on a regular basis. This computational structure fundamentally realizes a state machine that updates its state based on its inputs and its previous state. The general computational structure opens up the possibility for iteration and neighborhood operations, $T(\cdot)$, which we will develop in subsequent chapters. Once the state, $S(j)$, is updated, the computation proceeds to the next strip, $S(j+1)$. If $S(j)$ hits the bottom of the frame, the computation advances to $S(0)$ in the next image frame.

To realize this concept in Verilog HDL, we need three always blocks: reading, writing, and processing (Figure 4.9). Activated by a semaphore (`do_load`), the reading block reads the external RAMs (IMAGE1

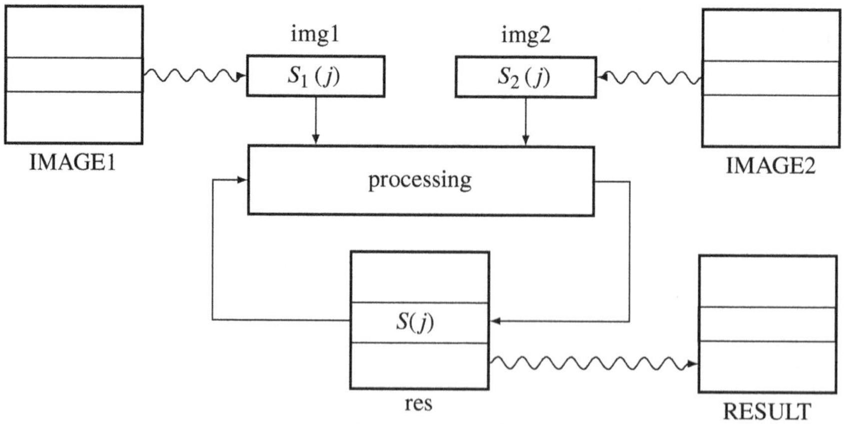

Figure 4.8 The operations in the processor

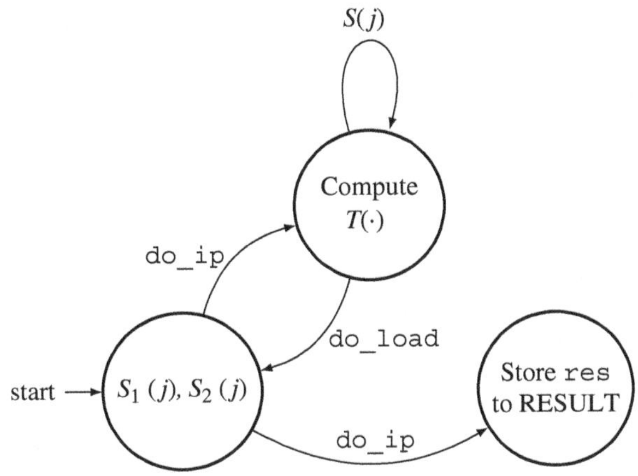

Figure 4.9 The always blocks for the processor

and IMAGE2) and builds $S_1(j)$ and $S_2(j)$ in the internal arrays (img1 and img2). It then activates the processing block by means of a semaphore (`do_ip`). The processing block computes a given algorithm on $S_1(j)$ and $S_2(j)$, to update $S(j)$ in the internal array (res). On completion, the process returns to the reading block from the processing block via a semaphore (`do_load`). It is not known in advance how much time the processing block may require, and so handshake control must be used for flexible control flow. On the writing side, the writing block writes the internal array (`res`) to the external RAM (RESULT). The two memories are the same in size and thus copying is simple. This copy operation is also relatively free from other blocks and can thus be assigned any time and interval. In the diagram, the writing action begins at the same time as the processing block begins processing.

This scheme is general because various algorithms can be plugged into the processing block, especially algorithms involving line-based processing. In any case, the purpose of the simulator is to provide a template for the processor by using other parts intact, or with minor modifications. Detailed coding for the processing block is possible only when an algorithm is determined. The time constraint is flexible and the computational resources, $S_1(j)$, $S_2(j)$ and $S(j)$, are enough for line-based algorithms.

The actual Verilog code is as follows.

Listing 4.9 Processor: `processor.v`

```
module processor(                                         //processor
   input clock, reset,
   output reg ['ADDR_BITS - 1:0] i_raddr, r_waddr,//address bus
   input [7:0] i_rdata1, i_rdata2,                        //data bus
   output reg [7:0] r_wdata,                              //data bus
   output reg r_wen                                       //write enable
   );

   //working array: window of images
   reg [7:0] img1  [0: 3* 'WIDTH * 'LINES - 1];  //1st image
   reg [7:0] img2  [0: 3* 'WIDTH * 'LINES - 1];  //2nd image
```

```
reg [7:0] res   [0: 3* `WIDTH * `HEIGHT - 1];  //result map

reg [`ADDR_BITS - 1:0] i, j, k, m, n, I;        //variables
reg [`ADDR_BITS - 1:0] idx, idx1;               //delay buffer
integer count;
reg do_load, do_ip, do_store;                   //switching processes

//get a block of the image: PE.IMAGE1 -> img1, PE.IMAGE2 -> img2
always @(posedge clock) begin: READ_img
   if (reset) begin
      k = 0;                                    //index in a strip
      j = 0;                                    //strip number
      idx = 0;                                  //address delay
      idx1 = 0;                                 //2nd address delay
      do_ip = 0;                                //semaphore
   end
   else if (do_load) begin                      //wait for input
      do_ip = 0;                                //deactivate processing
      if (j < `HEIGHT - `LINES + 1) begin       //for the strip[j]
         if (k < 3* `WIDTH * `LINES + 2) begin //+2 delay
            i_raddr = 3 * `WIDTH * j + k;       //read address
            img1[idx1] = i_rdata1;              //IMAGE1 -> img1
            img2[idx1] = i_rdata2;              //IMAGE2 -> img2
            idx1 = idx;                         //delay
            idx = k;                            //current pixel
            k = k + 1;                          //next strip
         end else begin
            do_ip = 1; k = 0; I = j;            //I for processing
            j = j + 1;                          //next strip
         end //else
      end else begin
         j = 0; k = 0;                          //image top S(0)
      end //else
   end //if
end //always

//store the result: res -> PE.RESULT
always @(posedge clock) begin: WRITE_res
   if (reset) begin r_wen <= 1; n <= 0;        //reset
   end
   else  begin                                  //res -> RESULT
      if (n < 3 * `WIDTH * `HEIGHT) begin       //a frame of result
         r_wdata <= res[n];                     //data
         r_waddr <= n;                          //address
         r_wen <= 1;                            //write enable
```

```
            n <= n + 1;                         //a pixel
         end
         else begin r_wen <= 1; n <= 0;         //write enable
         end
      end //else
   end //always

   //image processing: (img1, img2) -> res
   always @ (posedge clock) begin: PROCESSING
      if (reset) begin do_load = 1; do_store = 0; m = 0; end //reset
      else if (do_ip) begin                     //do image processing
         do_load = 0;                           //deactivate loading
         //wait for processing
         if (m < 3 * 'WIDTH * 'LINES) begin      //strip S(j)
            res[3 * 'WIDTH * I + m] = img1[m] - img2[m];
            m = m + 1;                          //next pixel
         end
         //end of major part
         else begin
            do_load = 1;                        //activate loading
            m = 0;                              //start new strip
         end
      end //else
   end //always
endmodule
```

The three always blocks appear in the following order: reading, writing, and processing. The reading block is active only when the processing block activates it by sending a semaphore (`do_load`). This block then begins by inhibiting the processing block using a semaphore (`do_ip`). Its major function is to provide new strips, $S_1(j)$ and $S_2(j)$, by copying the contents from the external memories to the internal registers. The loop count must be corrected by adding one or two more delays as '`if (k < 3* 'WIDTH * 'LINES + 2)`,' otherwise, the last one or two pieces of data may be ignored while they are being carried on the bus. The instances for moving to the next strip and next frame can be captured by the variables in this block. When the operations are finished, the reading block activates the processing block using a semaphore (`do_ip`). The processing block, when activated, begins by deactivating the reading block using a semaphore (`do_load`). This handshake must be carefully designed so that the semaphores are not driven by more than one always block. The writing block is activated at the same time as the processing block but can be modified to activate at any other time, for example when we want to observe the intermediate states.

4.7 Frame-based Vision Simulator Principle

The core concept of the line-based simulator is the internal cache memory, which stores only several lines of an image frame. There are many variations on this simulator. Among them, we may improve the strip so that it shifts downwards and skips more than one line. Another major improvement may

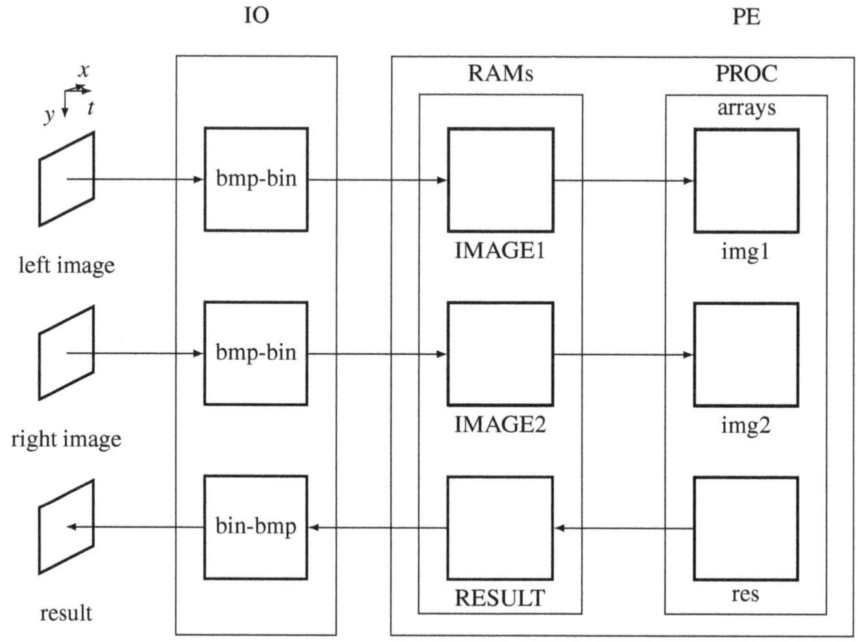

Figure 4.10 The structure of FVSIM

be to replace the fixed cache memory with barrel shifters, in which case each line of image would be read only once. The pitfall is that computing the coordinates in a strip would be rather complicated. The line-based simulator requires less internal memory and is thus faster in general. A suitable algorithm is DP, which computes line by line. The difficulty of this simulator is the neighborhood operation in the vertical direction. Because the scope is limited to small lines in the window, the pixels at the top and bottom of the strip cannot access the neighborhood pixels. If the neighborhood size is large, this problem gets even worse. Therefore, we would have to devise a very sophisticated scheme to resolve the start of the strip and the neighborhood pixels out of the window.

The other scheme is to use full frames instead of the small windows. The internal memory would increase in this case but would facilitate the most important algorithms: neighborhood operation and iteration. In fact, this scheme may be considered as the line-based scheme with a strip expanded to a full frame. In this scheme, computing addresses for the pixels is very simple. No scheme for keeping track of starting address, as in the line-based method, is required. This scheme is suitable for algorithms such as the relaxation and BP algorithms, and so will be used a lot in subsequent chapters.

The overall structure of the frame-based vision simulator (FVSIM) is illustrated in Figure 4.10. The big difference between it and the line-based simulator is the two internal arrays (img1 and img2), which are full frame-sized, in contrast to those of the line-based simulator. Here again, the target design is the processing element (PE), which includes RAMs (IMAGE1 and IMAGE2) and a processor (PE), as shown in the figure. Thus, all the RAMs are identical in type and size. In addition, the internal arrays are all the same in size. The structure is simple and so is the address calculation. The simulator consists of three parts: a set of image files, a file converter (IO), and one processor (PE) module. As before, the images are a set of image pairs, captured from stereo cameras, without loss of generality, and thus allows mono camera or motion estimation, with one channel of the input path being activated.

The IO is slightly modified so that the image can be read, and the result updated whenever the processor completes a whole frame. This scheme assumes a real-time system, in which the processor must complete the task for the current frame before the next frame arrives. This is in contrast to that of the line-based method, in which a complete processing is finished before a new line enters the internal arrays. Technically, this system needs more than one clock, one for the frame, one to read the frame into the array, and one for the processor – for consuming many clocks for each pixel. (PLL can be used to generate such clocks.) It depends on the actual algorithm to determine details of such clocks. For the observation, the contents of the RAM (RESULT) must be converted to a BMP file, on completion of each iteration.

In the following sections, we examine the components in this simulator.

4.8 FVSIM Top Module

Let us realize the frame-based simulator in Verilog HDL. Like the line-based simulator, the frame-based simulator consists of two parts: a top module (`vsim.v`) for simulation and a top module (`pe.v`) for synthesis.

The top module of the simulator contains all the modules in Figure 4.10: IO and PE. The code is as follows:

Listing 4.10 Top module for simulation: `vsim.v`

```
`define WIDTH      225                                  //image width
`define HEIGHT     188                                  //image height
`define ADDR_BITS  20                                   //max image size
`define ITER       0                                    //iteration no

module vsim;                                            //vsim
   reg clock, reset;

   //instantiation
   pe PE (clock, reset);                                //processing element
   io IO (clock, reset);                                //file input output

   initial begin
      clock = 0;
      reset = 0; #30; reset = 1; #150; reset = 0; //reset signal
   end
    always #50 clock =  ~clock;                         //clock generator
endmodule
```

At the beginning, the four parameters specify all the information necessary for synthesis and simulation. The big difference is the iteration parameter, instead of the line numbers that appear in the line-based simulator. For simplicity, all the word lengths for RAMs and arrays are set to one byte, which is common in RGB bit assignment. The simulator is made even more general, including neighborhood and iteration in stereo and motion. Similar to the line-based simulator, other applications, such as mono camera, stereo only, or motion only, can be achieved by removing a channel or resources, such as RAMs and internal buffers.

This module performs three tasks: instantiation of the processing element and the input-output element, generation of a reset signal, and generation of a common clock. The input-output element is for simulation, and the processing element is for synthesis. Note that there is no port communication between the two modules. The input-output element, being a simulator, uses many unsynthesizable Verilog constructs, which facilitates powerful tools for testing and monitoring.

The processing element is the same as in Listing 4.5 but is listed here again for completeness.

Listing 4.11 Top module for synthesis: `pe.v`

```
module pe(input clock, reset);                    //processing element
   //variables: image ram
   wire ['ADDR_BITS - 1:0] i_raddr,               //read addresses
      i_waddr1, i_waddr2,                         //write addresses
      r_raddr, r_waddr;                           //read RESULT
   wire [7:0] i_rdata1, i_rdata2, r_rdata,        //read data
      i_wdata1, i_wdata2, r_wdata;                //write data
   wire i_wen1, i_wen2, r_wen;                    //write enable

   //instantiation of synthesis modules
   //one processor and three RAMs
   ram IMAGE1  (clock, i_raddr, i_rdata1,
      i_waddr1, i_wdata1, i_wen1);                //1st image RAM
   ram IMAGE2  (clock, i_raddr, i_rdata2,
      i_waddr2, i_wdata2, i_wen2);                //2nd image RAM
   ram RESULT(clock, r_raddr, r_rdata,
      r_waddr, r_wdata, r_wen);                   //result RAM
   processor PROC (clock, reset, i_raddr,         //processor
      r_raddr, r_waddr,  i_rdata1, i_rdata2,
      r_rdata, r_wdata, r_wen);
endmodule
```

This module consists of three RAMs (IMAGE1, IMAGE2, and RESULT) and a processor (PROC), and connects them following the structure in Figure 4.10. Incidentally, the codes are maintained with simple statements as possible for easy understanding. At the time of synthesis, the codes must be elaborated so that all the wires are terminated with drivers and all the unused variables are removed. The schematic diagram of the FVSIM is similar to Figure 4.6.

The following sections explain the infrastructures of the simulator: memories (IMAGE1, IMAGE2, and RESULT) and processor (PROC), in detail, with working codes.

4.9 FVSIM IO System

The IO function module plays a very important role in the simulator. This module must supply data to the processor and display the data in the various parts, including inputs and outputs, dynamically. Because observation of the data is important, the vision simulator must show us data by means of images. This module is a slightly modified version of that in Figure 4.7.

The function of this module can be explained using state diagrams (Figure 4.11). The intervals at which the RAM is fed is based on the image processing algorithm. When a frame has been completed,

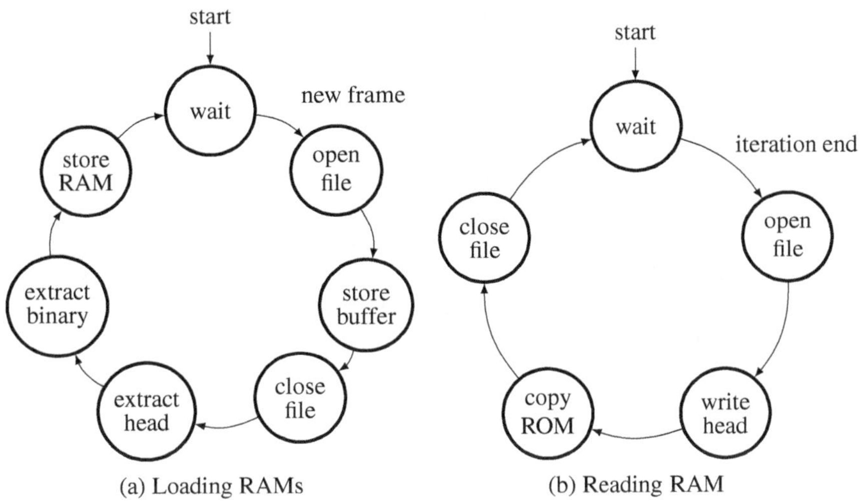

Figure 4.11 Loading RAM and reading RAM

a new frame must be available in the RAM. In the frame-based simulator, this instance can be easily captured by the semaphore (`do_load`). In Figure 4.7(a), the process begins when the new frame signal is detected. First, the input image files are opened and read into the buffers. The contents in the buffers are then classified into headers and binary images. The heads are used when the output from the processor is viewed as a bitmap. The binary data is then loaded into the RAM, which completes the cycle.

The corresponding code reads as follows. The first part of the code is designed for loading the RAMs with binary images. In a real system, this section is replaced with video cameras that load the RAMs with binary images in the same fashion.

Listing 4.12 IO system: `io.v` (1/2)

```
module io (input clock,reset);                     //read and write
   //declaration
   reg [7:0] buffer [1:(1 << 'ADDR_BITS)];         //1st buffer
   reg [7:0] buffer2 [1:(1 << 'ADDR_BITS)];        //2nd buffer
   integer load_file_id,save_file_id, c, count = 0;      //file opening
   integer  i, j, k;                               //variables
   reg [31:0] width,height,size,bpp,nop,padding,row_width,offset;
   reg [7:0] header [1:54];                        //bitmap header

   //reading: bmp -> buffer -> image, header
   always @(PE.PROC.j) if (!PE.PROC.do_load) begin: READ //new frame
      //load two sequence of images
      case (count % 2)                             //sequence length
         0: begin                                  //1st pair
            load_file_id = $fopen("input10.bmp","rb");    //1st image
            c = $fread(buffer, load_file_id);      //read the file
            $fclose(load_file_id);                 //close the file
```

```
         load_file_id = $fopen("inputr0.bmp","rb"); //2nd image
         c = $fread(buffer2, load_file_id);   //read the file
         $fclose(load_file_id);
         end
      1: begin                                //2nd pair
         load_file_id = $fopen("inputl1.bmp","rb"); //1st image
         c = $fread(buffer, load_file_id);    //read the file
         $fclose(load_file_id);               //close the file
         load_file_id = $fopen("inputr1.bmp","rb"); //2nd image
         c = $fread(buffer2, load_file_id);   //read the file
         $fclose(load_file_id);
      end
   endcase

   //close the file
   if ( {buffer[2], buffer[1]} == 16'h4D42 ) begin //424D
      //image parameters for dealing with general bmp files
      size = {buffer[6],buffer[5],buffer[4],buffer[3]}; //file size
      offset ={buffer[14],buffer[13],buffer[12],buffer[11]};
      width = {buffer[22], buffer[21], buffer[20], buffer[19]};
      height = {buffer[26], buffer[25], buffer[24], buffer[23]};
      bpp = {buffer[30],buffer[29]};          //bits per pixel
      nop = {buffer[38],buffer[37],buffer[36],buffer[35]}; //pixels
      row_width = nop / height;               //row width
      padding = row_width - width * bpp / 8;  //padding

      //store header
      for ( i = 1; i <= offset; i = i + 1 ) begin
         header[i] = buffer[i];               //store the header
      end

      //fill the RAMs for the two images
      for ( i = 0; i < height; i = i + 1 ) begin
         for ( j = 0; j < (row_width - padding); j = j + 1 ) begin
            PE.IMAGE1.ram[i* (row_width - padding) + j]
               = buffer[(height-1 - i)* row_width + j + offset + 1];
            PE.IMAGE2.ram[i* (row_width - padding) + j]
               = buffer2[(height-1 - i)* row_width + j + offset + 1];
         end
      end
      count = count + 1;
   end else $display ("Error: no bmp files.");
end //always
```

The two 2D array buffers and the 1D array are provided for two files and a header. The process waits until a new frame is needed by the processor. (This happens when the strip returns to the top of the frame in Figure 4.4, i.e. $S(j)$ becomes $S(0)$. All the computation must be finished before a new frame arrives.) Entering the loop, the process opens two files (one file in the case of mono processing) and stores them in the two buffers. From the buffers, the headers and binaries are extracted and inverted for the correct row order. The header, which is common to both images, is stored for later use and the binaries are loaded into the two RAMs. Thus, this action simulates video cameras feeding two RAMs. For each channel, the input images are a set of bitmap files, $I(0), I(1), \dots, I(n-1)$, for n number of images. The two channels read the image sequences, synchronize, and cycle through, as indicated by the counter. This part of the code can be easily modified for different scenarios: a still camera, a video camera, two still cameras, and two video cameras. The default is for two video cameras.

The second part of the code is designed for writing files using the data in the RAM, where the result is stored by the processor.

Listing 4.13 IO system: `io.v` (2/2)

```
   //writing: image, header -> bmp
   always @ (PE.PROC.iter) begin: WRITE              //new frame
      save_file_id = $fopen("output.bmp","wb");  //open the file
      //write header first
      for ( i = 1; i <= offset; i = i + 1 ) begin
         $fwrite(save_file_id, "%c", header[i]); //write the header
         //$display("header[%d] = %d",i,header[i]);
      end

      //write image part
      for ( i=0; i< height; i=i+1 ) begin          //consider padding
         for ( j=0; j< (row_width - padding); j=j+1 ) begin
            $fwrite(save_file_id, "%c", PE.RESULT.ram[(height-1 - i)
                  *(row_width - padding) + j]);  //monitoring position
         end
         if (padding) begin                         //no padding
            for (k=0; k < padding; k=k+1)
            $fwrite(save_file_id,"%c",8'h00);      //fill the padding
         end
      end //for

      //close the file
      $fclose(save_file_id);                        //close the file
      //$display("time = %t, read_write: write done.",$time);
   end //always
endmodule
```

The purpose of this code is to observe the result by reading the result RAM. A suitable instance for observation is at the point when the internal array (res) is transferred to the external RAM at the end of each iteration. The semaphore (`do_store`) indicates such an instance. However, the monitoring positions and time can easily be changed to other values.

4.10 FVSIM RAM and Processor

For completeness, we repeat the RAMs here. The simulator needs three RAMs, two to capture the input images (IMAGE1 and IMAGE2) and one to preserve the results from the processor (RESULT). However, they are all the same double-port synchronous RAMs.

Listing 4.14 RAM: `ram.v`

```
module ram(                                          //image ram
   input clock,
   input ['ADDR_BITS - 1:0] raddr,                   //read address
   output reg [7:0] rdata,                           //read data
   input ['ADDR_BITS - 1:0] waddr,                   //write address
   input [7:0] wdata,                                //write data
   input wen                                         //write enable
   );

   reg [7:0] ram [0:(2**'ADDR_BITS) - 1];            //array

   always @(posedge clock) begin
      if (wen)
         ram[waddr] <= wdata;                        //write
         rdata <= ram[raddr];                        //read
   end
endmodule
```

The RAM design can be aided by the templates and IPs. In an actual system, SDRAMs may be used to capture the video signals.

The major difference between this and the line-based method is the processor. Conceptually, the operation is defined by

$$S(t+1) \leftarrow T(I_1(t), I_2(t), S(t)),$$

where $T(\cdot)$ denotes a transformation, representing an algorithm. For each time t, the inputs, `I_1(t)`, `I_2(t)`, are the image inputs and `S(t)` is the buffer, which stores temporary results, operating as state memory (Figure 4.12). This computational structure is general and realizes a state machine, which updates its state based on its inputs and its previous state. The general computational structure opens up the possibility for iteration and neighborhood operations, $T(\cdot)$, which we will develop in subsequent

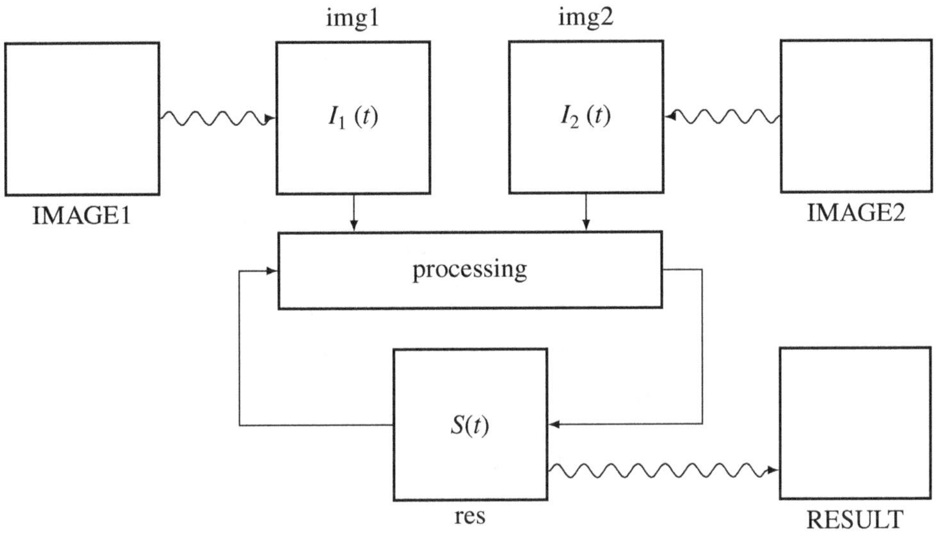

Figure 4.12 The operations in the processor

chapters. For a pixel, $p \in \mathcal{P}$, a set of neighbors is defined as $N(W(p))$. Thus, the neighborhood operation is defined by

$$S^{(k+1)} \leftarrow T(I_1(N(p)), I_2(N(p)), S^{(k)}(N(p)). \quad (4.1)$$

The architecture in Figure 4.12 is rather general and thus implies that this neighborhood operation is a special case. For concurrent operation, we may expand a pixel, $p \in \mathcal{P}$, into a window of pixels, $W(p)$. Consequently, the set of neighbors of the window is $N(W(p))$. In this case, the operation becomes

$$S^{(k+1)} \leftarrow T(I_1(N(W(p))), I_2(N(W(p))), S^{(k)}(N(W(p))). \quad (4.2)$$

We may expand this equation into iteration by introducing an iteration index, $k = 0, 1, \ldots, K - 1$

$$S^{k+1}(p) \leftarrow T(I_1(N(W(p))), I_2(N(W(p)), S^k(N(W(p)))). \quad (4.3)$$

To realize this concept in Verilog HDL, we need three `always` blocks: reading, writing, and processing (Figure 4.13) The reading block accesses the external RAMs (IMAGE1 and IMAGE2) and copies $S_1(j)$ and $S_2(j)$ into the internal arrays, img1 and img2. The reading block then activates the processing block, which computes a given algorithm on $S_1(j)$ and $S_2(j)$, to update $S(j)$ in the internal array (res). On completion, the process returns to the reading block from the processing block. It is not known in advance how much time the processing may consume and so semaphores must be exchanged for handshake control. On the writing side, the writing block writes the internal array (res) to the external RAM (RESULT). This action is relatively free from other processing and may need long intervals. In the diagram, the writing action begins at the same time as the processing block begins.

This scheme is general as various algorithms can be plugged into the processing block, especially algorithms involving neighborhood and iteration. The time constraint is flexible and the computational resources, $S_1(j)$, $S_2(j)$ and $S(j)$, are enough for such algorithms.

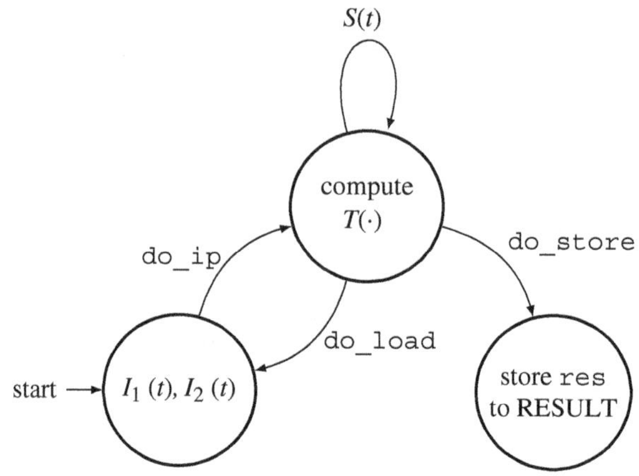

Figure 4.13 The always blocks for the processor

Let us consider the actual Verilog code. The code consists of three always blocks, appearing in the following order: reading, writing, and processing. The always block for reading is as follows:

Listing 4.15 Processor: `processor.v` (1/3)

```
module processor(                                    //processor
   input clock, reset,
   output reg ['ADDR_BITS - 1:0] i_raddr, r_waddr, //address bus
   input [7:0] i_rdata1, i_rdata2,                  //data bus
   output reg [7:0] r_wdata,                        //data bus
   output reg r_wen                                 //write enable
   );

   //working array
   reg [7:0] img1  [0: 3* 'WIDTH * 'HEIGHT - 1]; //1st image
   reg [7:0] img2  [0: 3* 'WIDTH * 'HEIGHT - 1]; //2nd image
   reg [7:0] res   [0: 3* 'WIDTH * 'HEIGHT - 1]; //result map

   reg ['ADDR_BITS - 1:0]  k, kk, n;                //variables
   reg ['ADDR_BITS - 1:0] idx, idx1;                //delay buffer
   reg do_load, do_store,  do_ip;                   //semaphores

   //neighborhood
   wire [7:0] im1 [0:8];                            //1st image: neighbor
   wire [7:0] im2 [0:8];                            //2nd image: neighbor
   wire [7:0] re [0:8];                             //result: neighbor
   reg ['ADDR_BITS - 1:0] x, y;                     //global counter
   reg [1:0] z;                                     //for x,y,z coordinates
```

```
wire ['ADDR_BITS-1:0] id1[0:8], id2[0:8];      //neighbor coordinates
genvar v, w;

//get image: PE.IMAGE1 -> img1, PE.IMAGE2 -> img2
always @(posedge clock) begin: READ_img
   if (reset) begin
      k = 0;                                   //index in a frame
      idx = 0;                                 //address delay
      idx1 = 0;                                //2nd address delay
   end
   else if (do_load && k < 3* 'WIDTH * 'HEIGHT + 2) begin
      do_ip = 0;                               //stop processor
      i_raddr = k;                             //read address
      img1[idx1] = i_rdata1;                   //load 1st image
      img2[idx1] = i_rdata2;                   //load 2nd image
      idx1 = idx;                              //delay
      idx = k;                                 //delay
      k = k + 1;                               //next pixel
   end else begin
      k = 0;                                   //first pixel
      do_ip = 1;                               //control to processor
   end
end //always
```

The reading block is active only when the processing block activates it by using the semaphore, `do_load`. This block then begins to inhibit the processing block using the semaphore, `do_ip`. The major operation is to provide a pair of new images, $I_1(t)$ and $I_2(t)$, by copying the contents from the external memories, `RAM1` and `RAM2`, to the internal registers, `img1` and `img2`. When the operation is finished, the reading block activates the processing block using the semaphore, `do_ip`. In return, the processing block, when activated, begins by deactivating the reading block using the semaphore, `do_load`. This handshake must be carefully designed so that the semaphores are not driven by more than one `always` block.

The writing block also does one-way processing, and continuously brings back the result to the external RAM. The writing block is activated at the same time as the reading block.

Listing 4.16 Processor: `processor.v` (2/3)

```
//store the result: res -> PE.RESULT
always @(posedge clock) begin: WRITE
   if (reset) begin
      r_wen <= 1;                              //write enable
      n <= 0;                                  //first pixel
   end
   else if (do_store) begin                    //wait for activation
      if (n < 3 * 'WIDTH * 'HEIGHT) begin
```

```
            r_wdata <= res[n];                          //load data
            r_waddr <= n;                               //load address
            n <= n + 1;                                 //next pixel
         end
         else n <= 0;                                   //first pixel
      end
   end //always
```

Therefore, the reading and writing blocks operate concurrently, without interfering with each other. The external RAM may be omitted and the resulting data can be put onto the pins, so that the data can be continuously obtained externally. It depends on the actual implementation of the RAMs and pins.

The main part of the processor consists of nested loops, with iteration outside and pixel visit in the inside loop. The always block is activated by the reading block via the semaphore, `do_ip`. In this manner, the `always` block may take as much time as needed to compute a frame, with neighborhood and iteration operations.

Listing 4.17 Processor: `processor.v` (3/3)

```
   //image processing: (img1, img2) -> res
   reg [7:0] iter;                                      //iteration variable
   always @ (posedge clock) begin: PROCESSOR
      if (reset) begin do_load = 1; do_store = 0;
         kk = 0;                                        //pixel position
         x = 0; y = 0; z = 0;                           //global address
         iter = 0;                                      //iteration no
      end
      else if (do_ip && iter < 'ITER) begin             //wait for activation
         do_load = 0; do_store = 1;                     //deactivate
         if (kk < 3 * 'WIDTH * 'HEIGHT) begin
            //main operation
             res[kk] =  (iter)? (res[kk] + im1[1]
                 + im1[3] + im1[5] + im1[7]) /5:0;

            //next local address
            kk = kk + 1;                                //pixel position

            //next global address
            if (z < 2) z = z + 1;                       //count z
            else if (x < 'WIDTH - 1) begin
               z = 0;  x = x + 1; end                   //count x
            else if (y < 'HEIGHT - 1) begin
               z = 0; x = 0;  y = y + 1; end            //count y
            else begin
               x = 0; y = 0; z = 0; end                 //reset (x,y,z)
         end
```

```
         else begin
            kk = 0;                                     //start pixel
            iter = iter + 1;                            //next iteration
            do_store = 1;                               //activate store
         end
      end //if
      else begin
         iter = 0;                                      //reset iteration
         do_load = 1;                                   //activate read
         do_store = 0; end                              //deactivate write
   end //always

   //building neighborhood
   assign id1[0] = kk;
   assign id1[1] = ((x > 0 ) && (x < 'WIDTH - 1)
      && (0 < y ) && (y <'HEIGHT - 1))? kk + 3 : kk;
   assign id1[2] = ((x > 0 ) && (x < 'WIDTH - 1)
      && (0 < y ) && (y <'HEIGHT - 1))? kk + 3 * 'WIDTH + 3 :kk;
   assign id1[3] = ((x > 0 ) && (x < 'WIDTH - 1)
      && (0 < y ) && (y <'HEIGHT - 1))? kk + 3 * 'WIDTH : kk;
   assign id1[4] = ((x > 0 ) && (x < 'WIDTH - 1)
      && (0 < y ) && (y <'HEIGHT - 1))? kk + 3 * 'WIDTH - 3 : kk;
   assign id1[5] = ((x > 0 ) && (x < 'WIDTH - 1)
      && (0 < y ) && (y <'HEIGHT - 1))? kk - 3 : kk;
   assign id1[6] = ((x > 0 ) && (x < 'WIDTH - 1)
      && (0 < y ) && (y <'HEIGHT - 1))? kk - 3 * 'WIDTH - 3 : kk;
   assign id1[7] = ((x > 0 ) && (x < 'WIDTH - 1)
      && (0 < y ) && (y <'HEIGHT - 1))? kk - 3 * 'WIDTH : kk;
   assign id1[8] = ((x > 0 ) && (x < 'WIDTH - 1)
      && (0 < y ) && (y <'HEIGHT - 1))? kk - 3 * 'WIDTH + 3 : kk;

   generate
      for (v = 0; v < 9; v = v + 1) begin: GEN_PE_ID //2nd image coords
         assign id2[v] = id1[v] + 3 * 'WIDTH * 'HEIGHT;
      end
   endgenerate

   //neighborhood values
   generate
      for (w = 0; w < 9; w = w + 1) begin: GEN_PE_IM
         assign im1[w] = img1[id1[w]];               //1st image neighbor
         assign im2[w] = img2[id2[w]];               //2nd image neighbor
         assign re[w] = res[id1[w]];                 //result image neighbor
      end
   endgenerate
endmodule
```

Each pixel must be accompanied by neighborhood pixels, in both images. In this code, the neighborhood calculations are achieved by combinational logic. The concept is as follows. The processor block chooses a pixel position to be computed next, which is represented by two equivalent coordinates, `kk` and `(x,y,z)`. The former is the pixel counter, while the latter is a set of counters for row, column, and RGB. This way of obtaining the pixel coordinates is efficient because it avoids division and multiplication. Otherwise, we would have to compute the coordinates as '$z = kk\%3, y = \lfloor kk/(3 \times \text{WIDTH}) \rfloor$,' and '$x = kk - 3 \times \text{WIDTH} \times y$.'

For each pixel, neighborhood indices are computed, with boundary conditions considered. If the neighborhood is out of the boundary, then its coordinates are set to those of the center pixel. In this way, all the neighbors beyond the boundary are set to the boundary values. However, this method can be modified using reflection, resulting in the outside pixels being reflections of the inside pixels. Any other definition of the boundary condition must appear around this code. The indices are converted to the actual values of the neighbors. In addition, the corresponding neighbors on the second image are computed, using the obtained neighbors of the first image. In actuality, the definition of the corresponding pixel depends on the application. In stereo matching and optical flow, the corresponding pixel is changing dynamically and the optimal one must be searched for. This template is simply set to zero disparity or optical flow. The neighborhood definition can be expanded, so that the range of the neighborhood is beyond just one pixel. In that case too, the logic is correct but the neighborhood arrays must be expanded appropriately.

Inside the always block in the processor, the operation can be defined by the neighbor pixels from the two images and the state register, to determine a new value for the state register. In an actual application, the neighborhood and the corresponding point must be fitted to the required values, in this standard template. Finally, this computational architecture is not just for the neighborhood and iterative computation. It is a general state machine and can therefore be used in more general vision applications.

4.11 OpenCV Interface

For more general vision processing, advanced packages such as OpenCV (Baggio *et al.* 2012; Bradski 2002; Bradski and Kaehler 2008; Laganiére 2011) can be used in conjunction with the target architecture. The problem is that there are two levels of barriers between Verilog and C++ (Stroustrup 2013). The first barrier is the communication between Verilog and C programs. One solution is to use a buffer file at the Verilog-C boundary to transfer images and data between the two systems, as indicated above.

Now that all other parts have been introduced in terms of VSIM, we can introduce the main program, which uses OpenCV.

Listing 4.18 OpenCV: `main`

```
#include <cv.h>
#include <highgui.h>
#include <conio.h>

void save_binary();                                  //save_binary function
void load_binary();                                  //load_binary function

int main()
{
    //choose save_binary or load_binary
```

```
    char ch;
    printf("Please enter what you want to do(1, 2).\n");
    printf("1) OpenCV -> Verilog\n2) Verilog -> OpenCV\n");
    ch = getch();
    putch(ch);
    printf(" is what you pressed\n");

    if (ch == "1"){                              //if 1 is pressed
       save_binary();                            //do save_binary function
    } else if (ch == "2"){                       //if 2 is pressed
       load_binary();                            //do load_binary function
    } else{
       printf("You pressed wrong number.");
    }
}
```

In the forward phase, the main program reads in an external file containing a set of image files, does some preprocessing with the help of OpenCV, and then writes the intermediate results to an output file, as a raw image, so that VSIM can access it. In the backward phase, the main program reads in the output file returned by the simulators, that is VSIM, does some post-processing, with the help of OpenCV, and writes the result to an output file. The advantage of using OpenCV is that the main program can access most of the image formats and convert them into the raw image and vice versa. The main program calls two procedures: one for reading in an image file into an image array and the other for writing an image array into an image file.

The reading procedure in the forward phase is as follows:

Listing 4.19 OpenCV: `load_binary`

```
void load_binary()
{
    char file_name[100] = "../image";             //binary file name
    char load_name[100] = "../image";             //original file name
    char save_name[100] = "../image";             //filtered file name

    FILE *file = fopen("../image/Output_data.dat", "rb"); //file open
    sprintf(load_name, "../image/load_image.bmp"); //original file name
    sprintf(save_name, "../image/save_image.bmp"); //filtered file name
    printf("Processing...\n");

    //original image structure
    IplImage* load_img = cvLoadImage(load_name, CV_LOAD_IMAGE_GRAYSCALE);
    int   height  = load_img->height;             //height
    int   width  = load_img->width;               //width
```

```
    int   widthstep = load_img->widthStep;          //width step
    uchar  *image  = new uchar[height*width];       //image data
    fread(image, sizeof(uchar), height*width, file); //file read
    //filtered image structure
    IplImage* save_img = cvCreateImage(cvSize(width, height),
       IPL_DEPTH_8U, 1);
    uchar  *data  = (uchar*)save_img->imageData;    //image data

    //copy image
    for (int i=0; i < height; i++){
       for (int j=0; j < width; j++){
          data[i*widthstep + j] = image[i*width + j];
       }
    }
    cvSaveImage(save_name, save_img);               //image save
    printf("Done.\n");
    fclose(file);                                   //file close
}
```

The properties of the images can be adjusted by various keys that are plugged into the arguments. Moreover, all the major parameters of the image are available.

The writing procedure in the backward phase is as follows:

Listing 4.20 OpenCV: `save_binary`

```
void save_binary()
{
    char load_name[100] = "../image";                   //image file name
    char file_name[100] = "../image";                   //binary file name

    FILE *file = fopen("../image/Input_data.dat", "wb"); //file open
    sprintf(load_name, "../image/load_image.bmp");      //image open
    printf("Processing...\n");

    //image structure
    IplImage* load_img = cvLoadImage(load_name, CV_LOAD_IMAGE_GRAYSCALE);

    int  height  = load_img->height;                    //height
    int  width   = load_img->width;                     //width
    int  widthstep = load_img->widthStep;               //widthstep
    uchar *data  = (uchar*)load_img->imageData;         //image data
    uchar *image  = new uchar[height*width];            //image data
```

```
    //copy image
    for (int i=0; i < height; i++){
        for (int j=0; j < width; j++){
            image[i*width + j] = data[i*widthstep + j];
        }
    }
    fwrite(image, sizeof(uchar), height*width, file); //file write
    printf("Done.\n");
    fclose(file);                                    //file close
}
```

The other forms of processing, such as preprocessing and post-processing, must work on the image array to generate a result as an output for either forward phase or backward phase.

To be efficient, an image processing system must comprise software and hardware systems, where the part of the algorithm characterized by serial computation with less computational complexity must be executed in software and the part characterized by parallel computation with huge computational complexity must be executed in hardware.

In this chapter, we developed two simulators, LVSIM and FVSIM, for the case of line-based and frame-based algorithms, respectively. The templates, LVSIM and FVSIM, can be expanded to the other variations. One possibility is to parallelize them by introducing nonblocking assignments. In such a case, the semaphores between always blocks must be carefully readjusted. The delay between the module and the RAM must also be considered. The other possibility is to merge the always blocks into one large finite state machine, so that the reading, writing, and processing operations are executed alternately.

In subsequent sections, we will use these simulators and focus on the processing elements. The goal is to design processing elements for the algorithms in the intermediate level vision, although some of the lower level vision is included during development. The final goal is the development of processors for stereo vision (possibly motion estimation). The purpose is not simply to derive all the codes for such systems but to introduce efficient ways of achieving our goals.

Problems

4.1 [Image conversion] Consider an $M \times N$ image array with RGB channels. How can you represent the image in Verilog data format? List the representations and compare and contrast their pros and cons.

4.2 [Image conversion] A bitmap contains a 225×188 image in an 8.8.8.0.0. format. What is the number of padding bytes in a row? What is the row width? What is the file size?

4.3 [Image conversion] Although the 1D Verilog array is useful for representing an image, sometimes it is required that the 3D coordinates (x, y, z) be retrieved from the array counter k. Let `[7:0] image [0: 3 * 'M * 'N - 1]` and `[7:0] image [0:1] [0:'M - 1][0:'N - 1]`. If the 1D counter k is successively incremented by one from `k=0` to `k=3 * 'M * 'N -1`, how can you compute the coordinates (x, y, z) in image$[z][x][y]$?

4.4 [Image conversion] The following code is used to read and write images in three steps. First, it reads in a file in bitmap format. Next, it extracts the header part and interprets it. Then, according to the header information, it extracts the raw image and stores it together with the header information. Finally, the stored header and the stored raw image are written to an external file.

Listing 4.21 Module: image_copy.v

```
module image_copy();
   integer load_file_id;                          //file ID for loading
   integer save_file_id;                          //file ID for saving
   integer height;                                //image height
   integer width;                                 //image width
   integer row_width;                             //image width step
   integer i, j;                                  //dummy indices
   reg [7:0] tmp [0:1000000];                     //temporary memory
   reg [7:0] image [0:1000000];                   //image memory

   initial begin
      //read a file
      load_file_id = $fopen("airplane.bmp", "rb"); //file ID for loading
      save_file_id = $fopen("save.bmp", "wb"); //file ID
      $fread(tmp, load_file_id);                  //read image

      //check bitmap id
      if ( {tmp[2], tmp[1]} == 16'h424D) begin //bitmap image id: 424D
         $display("It is a bmp file.");

         //retrieve height, width, and width step
         height = {tmp[26], tmp[25], tmp[24], tmp[23]}; //height
         width = {tmp[22], tmp[21], tmp[20], tmp[19]}; //width
         //width step (RGB + dummy 1 byte)
         row_width = 3*{tmp[22], tmp[21], tmp[20], tmp[19]}+1;

         //divide raw image data from image header section
         for ( i=0; i<height; i=i+1 ) begin
            for ( j=0; j<row_width; j=j+1 ) begin
               image[i*row_width + j] =
                  tmp[(height-1-i)*row_width+j+55]; //binary image
            end
         end

         //save image header
         for ( i=1; i<=54; i=i+1 ) begin
            $fwrite(save_file_id, "%c", tmp[i]); //write image header
         end

         //write image data
         for ( i=0; i<height; i=i+1 ) begin
```

```
            for ( j=0; j<row_width; j=j+1 ) begin
               $fwrite(save_file_id, "%c",
                  image[(height-1 - i)*row_width + j]);
            end
         end
      end
      else begin
         $display("It is not a bmp file.");
      end
      $fclose(load_file_id);
      $fclose(save_file_id);
   end //initial
endmodule
```

We would now like to enhance the code by splitting the module into two modules for reading and writing, and by building a top module that instantiates the two modules, then store the header and the raw image data in the top module by name reference.

4.5 [Image conversion] Let us enhance the code in the previous problem by introducing a new module, pe, which copies the raw image to another in the top module. The new module is dedicated to image processing and synthesis, while other modules are for simulation only. The current task of the processing element, pe, is just to copy one raw image into another.

4.6 [Simulator] In the simulator, only one place is observed in the code. How can you modify the code so that multiple places can be observed, possibly at different times?

4.7 [Simulator] Change the following code so that the statement is executed in each clock, instead of in one period.

```
always @ (posedge clock) begin
   if (trigger) begin
      for ( k = 0; k < 'CHANNEL * width * height; k = k + 1 ) begin
         result[k] = raw[k] - raw['CHANNEL * width * height + k];
      end
      trigger = 0;
   end
end //always
```

4.8 [Simulator] What is the problem with the line-based VSIM when computing neighborhood operations?

4.9 [Simulator] In FVSIM, the neighborhoods out of the boundary are all assigned boundary values. In Listing 4.15, kk represents the pixel count and (x, y, z) the pixel coordinates. In many applications, the pixels around the boundary must be arranged to be mirror symmetric. For such a case, modify the given code for the mirror symmetry.

4.10 [Simulator] In the `always` block, `READ_img`, in Listings 4.9 and 4.15, the data from RAM was assigned to the older address. What happens if the RAM output is buffered with a register?

4.11 [Simulator] In the `always` block, `READING`, in Listings 4.9 and 4.15, the data from RAM was assigned to the older address. What happens if the RAM output is buffered with a register?

4.12 [LVSIM] Modify LVSIM using nonblocking assignments so that all the statements work concurrently.

4.13 [FVSIM] Make the serial implementations of FVSIM concurrent by introducing nonblocking assignments.

4.14 [IO] In FSIM, the internal buffers, `img1`, `img2`, and `res`, are filled by reading the external RAMs, `RAM1`, `RAM2`, and `RES`. However, the memory contents can instead be loaded quickly by the IO circuit. This method is not synthesizable but useful for quick simulation. Change `io.v`.

References

Baggio DL, Emami SE, Escriva DM *et al.* 2012 *Mastering OpenCV with Practical Computer Vision Projects.* Packt Publishing.

Bradski GR 2002 OpenCV: Examples of use and new applications in stereo, recognition and tracking *Vision Interface*, p. 347.

Bradski GR and Kaehler A 2008 *Learning OpenCV.* O'Reilly Media, Inc.

IEEE 2005 *IEEE Standard for Verilog Hardware Description Language.* IEEE.

Laganiére R 2011 *OpenCV 2 Computer Vision Application Programming Cookbook.* O'Reilly Media, Inc.

OpenCV 2013 Home page http://opencv.org (accessed May 6, 2013).

Stroustrup B 2013 *The C++ Programming Language.* Pearson, Education, Inc.

Wikipedia 2013a BMP file format http://en.wikipedia.org/wiki/BMP_file_format (accessed Nov. 16, 2013).

Wikipedia 2013b Image file formats http://en.wikipedia.org/wiki/Image_format (accessed May 22, 2013).

Part Two
Vision Principles

5

Energy Function

Many of the computer vision problems at the low to intermediate levels can be considered to be labeling problems. Defined over the image plane, the labels form a function mapping that uniquely maps a set of pixels onto an attribute label. The quality of the labeling is signified with an energy function – a functional of the label function. Depending on the applications, energy functions have various different forms in their terms and relationships but have some common categories in their forms and solution methods. Finding correct representations for energy function and energy minimization methods (Heyden 2013; Szeliski *et al.* 2008) are key issues in vision problems.

Energy functions are found in many different domains, including optimization, Bayesian estimation, network flow (Ahuja *et al.* 1993; Cormen *et al.* 2001), and thermodynamics domains. In optimization domains, energy functions are known by various names, such as objective functions, loss functions, cost functions, and utility functions. The energy function used in thermodynamics is called (Helmholtz or Gibbs) free energy (Wikipedia 2013h) and equilibrium is the state in which the energy is at a minimum. In Bayesian estimation, the energy function is the likelihood of the ensemble probability, and the goal is often to determine the maximum a posteriori (MAP) estimate, the area where the energy is at a minimum. In a flow network, the energy is the maximum flow from the source to the sink and the purpose of graph cuts is to find the minimum cut to determine this energy. Regardless of the origin and the level of vision pathways, all the goals are to find the state in which the energy function is at a minimum. It is well known that the energy function in vision problems has the same structure, taking two common terms: data term (t-link in graph cuts terms (Boykov *et al.* 1998)) and smoothness term (n-link in graph cuts terms (Boykov *et al.* 1998)). The data term represents the likelihood, measuring the observation error between the measurement and the corresponding estimates. The smoothness term represents the prior, including the inherent statistical properties of the hidden states in nature.

Presently, the field of energy minimization is focused on the energy function model, which includes higher-order and irregular sets of partitions, and the inference methods that include linear programming relaxation (LPR), variations of *message passing*, and move-making algorithms in graph cuts (GC) (see (Kappes *et al.* 2013; Szeliski *et al.* 2008)).

This chapter relates how the concept of the energy equation evolves from the potential of MRF to the factor graph. In later chapters, the minimization of the energy function is studied in terms of the basic methods: relaxation (RE) machine, dynamic programming (DP) machine, belief propagation (BP) machine, and graph cuts (GC) machine.

Architectures for Computer Vision: From Algorithm to Chip with Verilog, First Edition. Hong Jeong.

Companion Website: www.wiley.com/go/jeong

5.1 Discrete Labeling Problem

In a labeling problem, we are given a set of objects, a set of labels for each object, a neighbor relation over the objects, and a constraint relation over labels of pairs (or n-tuples) of neighboring objects. The solution is an assignment of labels to each object in a manner that is consistent with respect to the constraint relation. The formal definition is as follows.

Definition 5.1 (Labeling problem) *Let $I = \{I(p)|p \in \mathcal{P}\}$ be an instance of an image, $\mathbf{x} = \{x(p)|p \in \mathcal{P}, x(p) \in \mathcal{L}\}$ be a labeling, where $\mathcal{L} = \{0, 1, \ldots, L-1\}$ is the labeling space of size L, and $N(\cdot)$ be a neighborhood. A data term $\phi : (x(p), I(p)) \mapsto \mathcal{R}$ and a smoothness $\psi : (x(p), x(q)) \mapsto \mathcal{R}$ for $p, q \in \mathcal{P}$. The energy function is then defined by*

$$E(\mathbf{x}) = \sum_{p \in \mathcal{P}} \phi(x(p)) + \sum_{p \in \mathcal{P}} \sum_{q \in N(p) \backslash p} \psi(x(p), x(q)). \tag{5.1}$$

Finally, the labeling problem is defined by

$$\mathbf{x}^* = \arg\min_{\mathbf{x}} E(\mathbf{x}). \tag{5.2}$$

Although the instance is confined to a single image, it may be generalized to a set of images of video streams. Two functions are defined in such a way that the data term depends on the label and the local instance, and the smoothness term depends on the local configuration of label distribution. The global cost is defined by the energy function, which is the sum of the data terms and the smoothness terms. All the functions are assumed to be bounded below.

This is one of the many definitions of the labeling problem, called *multiclass classification*. The more general definition is *multi-label classification* (Madjarov *et al.* 2012; Sorower 2010). The labeling problem is related to classification as well as the learning paradigm. According to the definition, the labeling problem becomes an optimization problem, given the energy function.

In the following, we justify the energy function by deriving it from the Markov random field (MRF) hypothesis and examine its meaning in more detail. Ensuing chapters will deal with the energy minimization directly in the paradigms: relaxation, dynamic programming, and message passing.

5.2 MRF Model

Let $\mathcal{P}$ be a plane with $N \times M$ lattice points. On this plane is defined an image, I, and the label, $X = \{x_p|p \in \mathcal{P}\}$, where $x \in \mathcal{L}$ for a label set $\mathcal{L}$. The image may be expanded to a set of images and the label to the *attributes* (or *descriptors*). The labeling problem is to find an optimal X given an image I. For stereo matching and motion estimation, the image is a pair of conjugate images and the attributes are the disparity (stereo matching) and optical flow (motion). To define the optimality, we have to define the label as random variables on the MRF plane and derive an optimal estimate of the distribution.

The problem formulation can be stated with the joint distribution $p(\mathbf{x}, I)$ and its marginal. We assume an MRF model in which the random variables are defined by their pairwise relationships. The concept is illustrated in Figure 5.1. The image plane is defined by the column and row coordinates, $\mathcal{P} = \{(x, y)|x \in [0, N-1], y \in [0, M-1]\}$. The relationship between the labels and the data is represented by a graph $G = (V, E, X)$, where the nodes are assigned random variables (i.e. labels) and the edges the joint probability. Each node is also connected to a single node that is assigned an image pixel. In later sections, this graph will be expanded to a more general graph, specifically, factor graph and hypergraph (Wikipedia 2013d).

Consequently, we now have a powerful representation scheme for the labeling in the form of a graph.

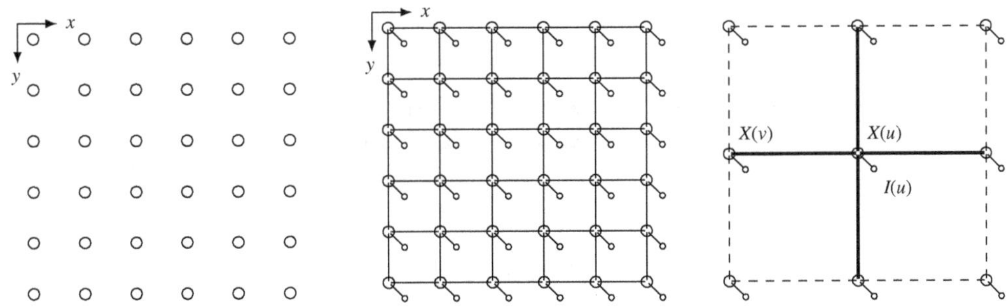

(a) image I (b) graph $G = (V, E)$ (c) neighborhood

Figure 5.1 MRF model of the image

Definition 5.2 (MRF Graph Model) *An MRF graph is a loopy undirected graph $G = (V, E, X)$, where the vertex (node) V consists of $\mathcal{P}$ and the edges E between neighbor vertices. Random variables X defined on the vertices are MRF. Dangling nodes, representing random variables I for representing image data, are attached to the pixel nodes.*

MRF is compactly characterized by four properties (Wikipedia 2013g): *context independence*, *pairwise Markov property*, *local Markov property*, and *global Markov property*. Let $\perp$ signify independence, $|$ signify the conditional, and $V \setminus \{i,j\}$ signify $V - \{i,j\}$. The context-independent property then has the following meaning:

$$X_i \perp I_j | I_i, \quad \forall j \in V \setminus i. \tag{5.3}$$

The pairwise Markov property means that any two unadjacent variables are conditionally independent, given that all other variables are conditionally independent.

$$X_i \perp X_j | X_{V \setminus \{i,j\}}, \quad \forall \{i,j\} \in V \text{ and } \{i,j\} \notin E. \tag{5.4}$$

The local Markov property states that a variable is conditionally independent of all other variables given its neighbors.

$$X_i \perp X_{V \setminus c(i)} | X_{N_i}, \quad \forall i \in V. \tag{5.5}$$

Here, N_i is the set of neighbors of i, excluding itself, and $c(i) = \{i\} \cup N_i$ is the *closed neighborhood* system of i. The global Markov property means that any two subsets of variables are conditionally independent given a separating subset, X_C.

$$X_A \perp X_B | X_C, \quad \forall A, B, C \subseteq V. \tag{5.6}$$

Here, any path from a node in A to a node in B must pass through C. In summary, the intention of these definitions is to limit the influence of a node just to its local neighborhood so that the joint distribution can be decomposed into many fragmented factors.

The next step is to define measurable quantities on the graph so that the labeling can be stated in terms of those quantities. Fortunately, there is an indispensable theorem that states that an MRF distribution

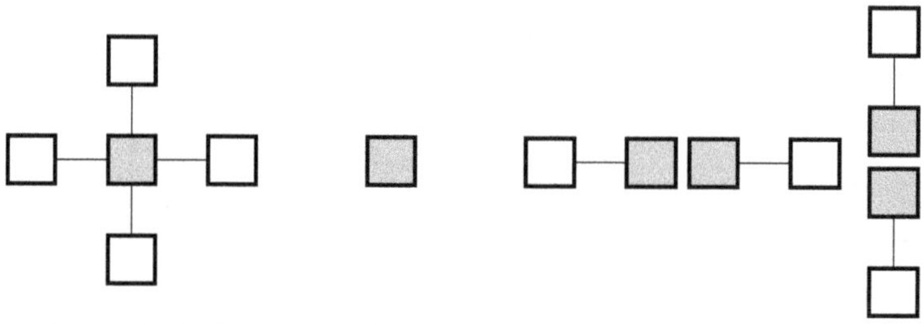

(a) four-neighborhood (b) singleton (c) doubletons

Figure 5.2 All types of cliques for a four-neighborhood system

can be modeled with a factorization – in particular, Gibbs distribution (Besag 1974; Clifford 1990; Hammersley and Clifford 1971). According to the Hammersley-Clifford theorem, we have

$$p(\mathbf{x}, I) = \frac{1}{Z}\exp\left\{-\sum_{c\in C}\psi_c(\mathbf{x})\right\} = \frac{1}{Z}\prod_{c\in C}p_c(\mathbf{x}), \tag{5.7}$$

where C is a set of *cliques*, ψ is a *clique potential*, and Z is a *partition function*. The clique is a set of nodes such that there is an edge between every pair of nodes that are members of the set. Therefore, the joint probability is the relationship between functions defined over cliques in the graphical model. Here, the joint distribution is expressed with the measurable quantities, potential and probability.

One of the simplest cases is the regular graph with four-neighborhood, in which two types of cliques are defined: singleton and doubleton. In Figure 5.2, all the cliques for the four-neighborhood system are illustrated. For the four-neighborhood system, the distribution becomes

$$\begin{aligned} p(\mathbf{x}, I) &= \frac{1}{Z}\exp\left\{-\left(\sum_{i\in\mathcal{P}}\phi(x_i, I_i) + \sum_{j\in\mathcal{N}_4(i)\setminus i}\psi(x_i, x_j)\right)\right\} \\ &= \frac{1}{Z}\prod_{i\in\mathcal{P}}p(x_i, I_i)\prod_{j\in\mathcal{N}_4(i)\setminus i}p(x_i, x_j), \end{aligned} \tag{5.8}$$

where $N_i \setminus i = N_i - \{i\}$. In this expression, $\phi(x_i, I_i)$ (equivalently $p(x_i, I_i)$) signifies the compatibility between a local observation (i.e. image) and the variable (i.e. label or attribute) and enforces a data constraint. The other term $\psi(x_i, x_j)$ (equivalently $p(x_i, x_j)$) signifies a compatibility between neighboring node labels enforcing the smoothness constraint.

Most of the vision problems at the low to intermediate levels lie in estimating the unknown variable X defined over the image plane, given the image I as an observation. The observation may signify an image, I, a pair of images, (I^l, I^r), or a sequence of images, $\{(I^l(t), I^r(t)|t = 0, 1, \ldots\}$. The variable X signifies some attribution map defined for each pixel or parts of pixels in the image, such as image, edge, disparity, optical flow, or class label. We use $\mathbf{x}$ for the realization of the random variable, X.

The system is weakly described by the *conditional*, $p(I|\mathbf{x})$, from which we can obtain the *maximum likelihood* (ML) estimate

$$\mathbf{x}^* = \max_{\mathbf{x}} p(I|\mathbf{x}). \tag{5.9}$$

The stronger description is the posterior. Bayes' rule gives

$$p(\mathbf{x}|I) = p(I|\mathbf{x})p(\mathbf{x})/p(I), \tag{5.10}$$

where $p(\mathbf{x}|I)$ is called *posterior* (*a posteriori*), $p(I|\mathbf{x})$ *conditional*, and $p(\mathbf{x})$ *prior* (*a priori*). One approach is to compute the maximum a posteriori (MAP): given I, estimate $\mathbf{x}$ such that

$$\mathbf{x}^* = \arg\max_{\mathbf{x}} p(\mathbf{x}|I) = \arg\max_{\mathbf{x}} p(I|\mathbf{x})p(\mathbf{x}). \tag{5.11}$$

A more practical approach is to compute the *marginalization*:

$$p(x_k) = \sum_{\mathbf{x}:(\mathbf{x})_k = x_k} p(\mathbf{x}|I). \tag{5.12}$$

The problem is that the complexity is exponential, which is impossible even for small problems. For instance, a problem with 100 pixels needs a search space of size 2^{99}. Fortunately, an efficient algorithm, called the belief propagation (BP) (Pearl 1982), has been introduced for such cases. Computing marginalization in an iterative manner, this method is known to be exact for Bayesian tree (i.e. BP) and approximate for loopy Bayesian networks (i.e. loopy belief propagation (LBP)).

Note that all the distributions are joint distributions. The terms usually consist of two different quantities, one that depends upon a particular problem (data term) and another that is commonplace in many vision problems (smoothness term). Exploring the one that depends on the particular problem is sometimes a major research concern. It is interesting that there exists a term that is commonplace in many problems. This term often appears as a smoothness, or regularization term, as will be seen.

5.3 Energy Function

From the Hammersley–Clifford theorem, the vision problem becomes a dual problem: random variable vs. energy and statistical estimation vs. functional optimization. In this context, we study the vision problem from the energy point of view. From (5.8), we obtain the posterior:

$$p(\mathbf{x}|I) = \frac{1}{Z}\exp\{-E(\mathbf{x})\}, \tag{5.13}$$

where the positive function $E(\mathbf{x})$ is called *energy*:

$$E(\mathbf{x}) = \sum_{i\in\mathcal{P}} \phi(x_i|I_i) + \sum_{i\in\mathcal{P}}\sum_{j\in N_i\setminus i} \psi(x_i, x_j). \tag{5.14}$$

Here, the terms, called *potential*, are related to the density by

$$\phi(x_i) = -\log p(x_i|I), \quad \psi(x_i, x_j) = -\log p(x_i, x_j), \tag{5.15}$$

where the context-independent condition is used for the singleton.

In information theory, the quantities ϕ and ψ are pieces of *information*. In computer vision, ϕ, is called the *data term* (or assignment cost) and ψ the *smoothness term* (or *prior term* or *separation cost*). The data term is a measure of the discrepancy between observed and estimated values. The measure of smoothness is a measure of the difference between neighboring pixels.

Because of the introduction of the energy function, obtaining a MAP estimate becomes an *energy minimization problem*.

$$\mathbf{x}^* = \arg\max_{\mathbf{x}} p(\mathbf{x}|I) \iff \mathbf{x}^* = \arg\min_{\mathbf{x}} E(\mathbf{x}). \tag{5.16}$$

This approach comprises two stages: determination of the energy function and choosing the appropriate optimization technique. To fully determine the energy function, we have to define the data term and the prior term. The two terms are specific to problems and conditions. The energy minimization in the second stage belongs to unconstrained optimization and has been investigated in many areas in the computer vision field.

Among others, four approaches that have been extensively studied are variational calculus (Courant and Hilbert 1953; Horn and Shunck 1981), DP (Amini *et al.* 1990; Bellman 1954), BP (Pearl 1982), and graph cuts (Greig *et al.* 1989). There is a package in OpenCV specifically for executing and testing such algorithms (Szeliski *et al.* 2006): iterated conditional modes (ICM), graph cuts, max-product belief propagation, and sequential tree-reweighted message passing (TRW-S). There is also a package, called *OpenGM* (Bazin *et al.* 2013), which wraps major energy models and inference techniques into a uniform software framework for reproducible benchmarking.

The development of vision algorithms may start from either (5.8) or (5.14). The energy function approach sometimes has advantages over the probabilistic approach in that it may be considered the more general concept. Even if its origin is the factorization, the energy can be enhanced by adding more constraints than can directly be interpreted in terms of probability. The resulting energy function sometimes becomes highly nonlinear and space-variant. Because of its importance, the energy function has to be formally defined.

Definition 5.3 (Energy Function) *For any given piece of data, $I = \{I(x,y) | (x,y) \in \mathcal{P}\}$, the energy function, $E(x)$, is a functional defined over $\mathcal{P}$ such that*

$$E(\mathbf{x}) = \sum_{i \in \mathcal{P}} \phi(x_i) + \sum_{i \in \mathcal{P}} \sum_{j \in N_i \backslash i} \psi(x_i, x_j).$$

- *The range is nonnegative real, $E : x \mapsto [0, \infty)$,*
- *$\mathbf{x}$ is a function satisfying $\mathbf{x} : (x,y) \in \mathcal{P} \mapsto \mathcal{R}$,*
- *$\phi(\cdot)$ is a data term satisfying $\phi(\cdot) : (x,y) \times I \mapsto \mathcal{R}$,*
- *$\psi(\cdot)$ is a prior term satisfying $\psi(p,q) : (p,q) \in \mathcal{P} \times \mathcal{P} \mapsto \mathcal{R}$.*

In this manner, we can seek the energy function, instead of undergoing the full derivation, considering all the possible constraints that may hold in the given problem. Moreover, by doing it this way, we can generalize the energy function so that it is more general than those derived from the Markov concept.

The smoothness term originated from the clique potential, which can be interpreted as some compatibility between neighboring pixels in terms of their values. As a term in an energy function, it can be viewed as a constraint, coupled with a Lagrange multiplier, which makes the constrained problem unconstrained, so that any minimization technique for global optimization can be applied. Applying a stricter constraint to the energy function results in the search space becoming smaller and the solution getting closer to the global solution.

5.4 Energy Function Models

Thus far, we have reviewed the traditional view of the energy function in terms of MRF, which is well documented (Szeliski *et al.* 2008). The concept of the energy function is emerging as a mainstay called *discrete energy minimization* in the computer vision domain (Kappes *et al.* 2013).

To integrate the classical and the state-of-the-art concepts, we view the energy function in three different tasks: energy model, inference scheme, and learning. The model deals with the definition of the energy function, the inference scheme deals with the general methods for energy minimization, and the learning addresses the problems of determining system parameters.

The energy model is being expanded to more general frameworks (Kappes *et al.* 2013): factor graph model, higher factors, larger irregular graphs, and a group of pixels instead of a single pixel. As such, the MRF in Definition 5.2 must be expanded to the factor graph (Kappes *et al.* 2013; Koller and Friedman 2009).

Definition 5.4 (MRF Factor Graph) *Define an MRF factor graph, $G = (U, V, X, \Theta)$, as a vertex weighted directed bipartite graph, where U is the* factor nodes, *V is the* variable nodes, $X = \{x_v | v \in V\}$ *is the MRF variables, and* $\Theta = \{\theta_u(\mathbf{x}_u) | \mathbf{x}_u = \{x_v | v \in N_u\}, u \in U\}$ *is the factors.*

Note that N_u is a set of variable nodes, which are connected to the factor node u.

According to the above definition, terms in the traditional MRF energy model are replaced with the functions of factors. The factor F defines every relationship in the general graph, including node-to-node (binary potential, smoothness term, or compatibility term) and node-to-data (unary potential, data term, or data fidelity), by its associated function sets. Thus, the representation becomes more general and explicit than the original MRF model, which is defined by an undirected graph.

There are several aspects of model G that explicitly characterize the target vision problem (Kappes *et al.* 2013) (e.g. stereo matching, motion estimation, and color segmentation) in terms of complexity and graph topology (Kappes *et al.* 2013). The number of possible labels is important since it is directly related to the feasibility of the algorithm. A larger dimension label space results in an increment of complexity in computation and memory. The properties of the graph, such as regularity and order, are also important cues for categorizing the model. The graph order is decided by the maximal degree among all factors in the graph. It directly indicates the complexity of interconnections between nodes in the graph. The regular graph assumption enables us to implement inference algorithms using massive computation methods that are preferred in VLSI, or other hardware-based algorithms. As the final aspect, we can consider the properties of the associated function (potential/energy function). This functional property affects the accuracy of the model and the feasibility of the corresponding inference algorithms. Energy functions based on high-order polynomials can describe a more complex vision environment, while optimizations on these functions are infeasible in many cases.

The general energy function on the factor graph model above is defined as

$$E(\mathbf{x}) = \sum_{f \in F} \psi_f(\mathbf{x}_{N_f}), \tag{5.17}$$

where N_f denotes neighborhood factors such as observation or other neighboring nodes in the MRF representation. Since this energy model can represent far more complex vision models (i.e. higher-order graphs or energy functions, and irregular graph representations) owing to its generality, we would like to confine our discussion to three major early vision applications: stereo matching, motion estimation, and image segmentation.

Because early vision labels depend on raw image observations rather than high-level information, the order of their factor graph model is at most two. Hence, we can consider only pairwise relationship to model the target problem. This fact simplifies the corresponding energy model, which only consists of data and smoothness terms. Moreover, most of the early vision algorithms are pixel-based, so we can assume that, except for the boundary points, the graphs are regular. Neighborhood systems for early vision applications are usually defined by four-neighbors because of the trade-off between performance and complexity. Nevertheless, there might be a more general representation beyond the factor graph, which includes complicated factors such as the *tripartite graph* (Memisevic 2013). The remaining issues on different applications are the label dimensions, additional parameters, and the functional properties of energy terms.

The detailed form of the energy model depends on the problem domains. In the following sections, we review only three domains: stereo matching, motion estimation, and segmentation. In the stereo matching domain, the goal is to recover hidden correspondences between pixels from different views. Therefore, the disparity value that defines the correspondences becomes the target label to infer. For basic observation, although a variety of cues are available, such as image color/intensity, gradient, or color segments, we consider image color/intensity as our primary consideration for simplicity.

5.5 Free Energy

All Bayesian inferences (Roweis and Ghahramani 1999) can be cast in terms of free energy minimization. When free energy is minimized with respect to internal states, the Kullback–Leibler divergence between the variational and posterior density over hidden states is minimized. This corresponds to approximate Bayesian inference when the form of the variational density is fixed, and exact Bayesian inference otherwise. Free energy minimization therefore provides a generic description of Bayesian inference and filtering (e.g. Kalman filtering).

The distance between the two distributions can be defined by the statistical divergence (Pardo 2005; Wikipedia 2013b). Among the many, the Kullback–Leibler (KL) divergence is frequently used for free energy computation. The KL divergence is a *premetric measure*, and its quantities can be interpreted via information theory. Thermodynamics analogy is possible but very limited because there are physical factors missing (specifically, pressure, volume, and temperature) from the statistical model. For a true pmf, $p(\mathbf{x})$, assume an approximate $\pi(\mathbf{x})$. The KL divergence is

$$\underbrace{D(\pi(\mathbf{x})||p(\mathbf{x}))}_{\textit{free energy}} = \sum_{\mathbf{x}} \pi(\mathbf{x}) \ln \frac{\pi(\mathbf{x})}{p(\mathbf{x})} = \underbrace{\left\{-\sum\nolimits_{\mathbf{x}} \pi(\mathbf{x}) \ln p(\mathbf{x})\right\}}_{\textit{energy}} - \underbrace{\left\{-\sum\nolimits_{\mathbf{x}} \pi(\mathbf{x}) \ln \pi(\mathbf{x})\right\}}_{\textit{entropy}\ S}.$$

The use of the true and approximate pmfs is opposed to the original order. The divergence consists of two terms – cross-entropy (or energy) and entropy. A specific example is that when the distribution is Gaussian, the entropy is unity. The entropy is the lower bound of the energy and the energy is the upper bound of the entropy. One can optimize either of the two terms, which are bounded below or above. The gap between the energy and entropy is the free energy that must be minimized for an optimal distribution, which is supposed to be in a state of equilibrium.

The general model of the system is Boltzmann's law $p(\mathbf{x}) = \frac{1}{Z}\exp\{-E(\mathbf{x})/kT\}$, where k is the Boltzmann constant and T is the temperature. We set $kT = 1$ if the temperature is constant or annealing is not considered.

$$\begin{aligned} D(\pi(\mathbf{x})||p(\mathbf{x})) &= \sum_{\mathbf{x}} \pi(\mathbf{x})E(\mathbf{x})/kT + \sum_{\mathbf{x}} \pi(\mathbf{x}) \ln \pi(\mathbf{x}) + \ln Z \\ &= E(\mathbf{x}) - S(\mathbf{x}) - F(\mathbf{x}), \end{aligned} \tag{5.18}$$

where $F(\mathbf{x}) = -\ln Z$ is the analogy of the Helmholtz free energy, which is defined as $-kT \ln Z$. Further, $S(\mathbf{x}) = -\sum_{\mathbf{x}} \pi(\mathbf{x}) \ln \pi(\mathbf{x})$ is the entropy and $E(\mathbf{x}) = \sum_{\mathbf{x}} \pi(\mathbf{x}) \ln E(\mathbf{x})$ is the internal energy. The approximate distribution is achieved by minimizing $E - S$, which is bounded below by the Helmholtz free energy.

Algorithms largely depend upon the models of the approximate distribution, $\pi(\mathbf{x})$. The mean field approximation models the joint pmf using the products of singletons:

$$\pi(\mathbf{x}) = \prod_{p \in \mathcal{P}} \pi(x_p) = \exp\left\{-\sum_{p} \phi(x_p)\right\}. \tag{5.19}$$

The pairwise MRF is

$$\pi(\mathbf{x}) = \frac{1}{Z}\exp\left\{-\sum_{p\in\mathcal{P}} \ln\phi_p(x_p) - \sum_{p,q\in\mathcal{P}} \ln\psi(x_p, x_q)\right\}. \tag{5.20}$$

The Bethe free energy is

$$\pi(\mathbf{x}) = \frac{\prod_{p,q} \pi(x_p, x_q)}{\prod_p \pi\left(x_p^{q_p-1}\right)}, \tag{5.21}$$

where q_p is the number of nodes neighboring node p (Pearl 1988). It is known that there is a close connection between the BP algorithm and the Bethe approximation: BP can only converge to a fixed point that is also a stationary point of the Bethe approximation to the free energy (Yedidia *et al.* 2005).

The free energy is related to the function of the biological system. Biological systems maintain their order by restricting themselves to a limited number of states and minimize a free energy function of their internal states, which entail beliefs about hidden states in their environment. The minimization of variational free energy is formally related to variational Bayesian methods and was originally introduced by Karl Friston, as active inference (Friston *et al.* 2006; Wikipedia 2013c).

5.6 Inference Schemes

Energy functions can model various quantities and interactions in computer vision applications. The only remaining task is to solve for a target quantity that minimizes its corresponding energy function, called the *inference*. Unfortunately, searching for the global optimal solutions for a discrete energy function is intrinsically an NP-hard problem owing to its combinatorial nature. Hence, there are innumerable works about the inference method from the perspective of discrete optimization. Traditional inference methods on discrete energy functions are based on various ideas from the area of optimization, such as variational calculus (VC), iterated conditional modes (ICM) (Besag 1986), simulated annealing (SA) (Kirkpatrick *et al.* 1983), and dynamic programming (DP) (Bertsekas 2007), to name a few. Further, there are numerous inference schemes that were successful in other areas, such as genetic programming (GP) (Banzhaf *et al.* 2001) and reinforcement learning (Sutton and Barto 1998).

Presently, the representative inference methods can be categorized as follows (Kappes *et al.* 2013): polyhedral and combinational methods, message passing methods, max-flow and move-making methods, and deep learning. The polyhedral and combinatorial methods are based on linear programming (LP) relaxation. In these methods, the original discrete optimization problem is represented by integer linear problems (ILP) that confine target solutions to finite-range integers in local polytope. Since this ILP is NP-hard, it is relaxed by several subproblems that can be solved by LP in polynomial time. There are two major methods in LP relaxation – the Cutting Plane (CP) method (Sontag *et al.* 2008) and the branch-and-bound (BB) method (Sun *et al.* 2012). Under tight bounding conditions, the solution from LP relaxation methods is guaranteed to be the global optimal solution. The message passing methods originated from the Belief Propagation (BP) (Pearl 1988) for acyclic graphs. The most popular message passing method in vision applications is loopy belief propagation (LBP) (Szeliski *et al.* 2008), which is an extension of the original BP to graphs with cycles. Although LBP has no confidence on optimality of the solution, it works well practically in many vision applications. At present, polyhedral methods are often reformulated by message passing algorithms, for example, the tree-reweighted algorithm (TRWS) (Kolmogorov 2006), its nonsequential version (TRBP) (Wainwright *et al.* 2005), and max-product linear programming (MPLP) algorithm (Globerson and Jaakkola 2007). In contrast to the case with LBP, the convergence of solutions is guaranteed with tight bounding conditions. Message passing algorithms are easily implemented and converted into parallel architecture. The max-flow and move-making methods are based on the graph cuts (GC) (Boykov and Kolmogorov 2004). This class includes QPBO (Rother *et al.* 2007), α- expansion ($\alpha - \beta$ swap) (Boykov *et al.* 2001), FastPD (Komodakis and Tziritas 2007), and α-FUSION (Fix *et al.* 2011). Deep learning is a newly emerging method (Bengio *et al.* 2013; Hinton 2007) among the current inference techniques.

A typical example of LP relaxation is as follows (Bazin *et al.* 2013). Let us consider the image planes, $(\mathcal{P}^l, \mathcal{P}^r)$, the images (I^l, I^r), and the feature descriptors, (F^l, F^r), where $F = \{f_i | i \in \mathcal{P}\}$. For the two images, an *assignment matrix*, $Z = \{z_{ij} | i \in \mathcal{P}^l\}$, where z is one if there is a match and zero otherwise, and the distance, $D = \{d(f_i, f_j) | i \in \mathcal{P}^l, j \in \mathcal{P}^r\}$, are defined. Additionally, let A_{ij} be the data associated with the input data pairs and θ be the model parameters between the data pairs, such as the fundamental matrix. The mixed integer optimization problem (MIOP) is defined as follows:

$$\begin{aligned} &\max \sum_{i \in \mathcal{P}^l, j \in \mathcal{P}^r} z_{ij}, \\ &s.t. \quad z_{ij} d(f_i, f_j) \leq z_{ij} T_a, \forall i \in \mathcal{P}^l, j \in \mathcal{P}^r \\ &z_{ij} |A_{ij}^T \theta| \leq z_{ij} T_g, |\theta|^2 = 1, z_{ij} \in \{0, 1\}, \\ &0 \leq \sum_{i \in \mathcal{P}^l} z_{ij} \leq 1, 0 \leq \sum_{j \in \mathcal{P}^r} z_{ij} \leq 1. \end{aligned} \tag{5.22}$$

Here, T_a and T_g are the parameters for the appearance and geometric terms.

This MIOP cannot be solved directly because of the nonlinear terms. Various methods can be used to convert the MIOP to LP relaxation. First, the bilinear terms, T_a and T_g, can be made linear (Chandraker and Kriegman 2008; Kahl *et al.* 2008; Olsson *et al.* 2009). Let $c = ab$, with $a \in [\underline{a}, \overline{a}]$ and $b \in [\underline{b}, \overline{b}]$, where $\underline{x} = \lfloor x \rfloor$ and $\overline{x} = \lceil x \rceil$. The bilinear term can then be relaxed by the convex and concave envelopes:

$$\begin{aligned} c &\geq \max(\underline{a}b + a\underline{b} - \underline{ab}, \overline{a}b + a\overline{b} - \overline{ab}), \\ c &\leq \min(\overline{a}b + a\underline{b} - \overline{a}\underline{b}, \underline{a}b + a\overline{b} - \underline{a}\overline{b}). \end{aligned} \tag{5.23}$$

The second technique is for the unknown bounds for θ. The branch-and-bound (BB) (Breuel 2003; Land and Doig 1960) is a general global optimization method that iteratively divides the search space into smaller ones and removes the spaces that contain poor solutions. If the lower bound for some space is greater than the upper bound for some other space, then the space may be safely discarded from the search. Using these methods, the MIOP can be converted to LP relaxation.

Another useful example of LP relaxation is MPLP (Globerson and Jaakkola 2007), which converts MAP problems in 2D MRF to MAP-LP relaxation problems. The original MAP problem is defined by energy functions comprising pairwise potentials,

$$E(x) = \sum_{i,j \in E} \psi_{ij}(x_i, x_j). \tag{5.24}$$

LP relaxation on the energy model begins from defining marginal distribution over variables in edge set E:

$$M_L(G) = \left\{ \mu \geq 0 | \sum_{x_i, x_j} \mu_{ij}(x_i, x_j) = 1 \right\}, \tag{5.25}$$

where M_L is the local marginal polytope satisfying $\sum_{x_i} \mu_{ij}(x_i, x_j) = \sum_{x_k} \mu_{jk}(x_j, x_k)$.

The resulting LP relaxation is given by

$$\max_{\mu \in M_L} \left\{ \sum_{i,j \in E} \sum_{x_i, x_j} \psi_{ij}(x_i, x_j) \mu_{ij}(x_i, x_j) \right\}. \tag{5.26}$$

The solution to this LP relaxation problem is the upper bound of the MAP solution satisfying

$$\max_{x} E(x) \leq \max_{\mu \in M_L} \left\{ \sum_{i,j \in E} \sum_{x_i, x_j} \psi_{ij}(x_i, x_j) \mu_{ij}(x_i, x_j) \right\}. \tag{5.27}$$

This is called edge consistent LP relaxation because marginals are constrained to be pairwise consistent. Given the LP relaxation of a MAP problem, a variety of ILP solving techniques can be applied, including CP or BB, to the primal or dual problem domain.

Solutions in the primal domain can be directly computed from standard LP algorithms for small problems. Unfortunately, most vision problems have a large solution scale, which makes primal solution practically infeasible. To tackle large problems, the dual problem of the original LP relaxation problem is widely used (Globerson and Jaakkola 2007; Kappes *et al.* 2012; Kolmogorov 2006; Komodakis and Paragios 2008; Sontag *et al.* 2008; Werner 2007) to provide the lower bound of the primal solution.

Neural networks are emerging with a new tool called *deep learning*, by which the layers are trained in two steps: pre-training and global training. Neural network studies are in many different directions (Bengio *et al.* 2013), such as probabilistic inference (i.e. restricted Boltzmann machine (RBM)), autoencoder framework, and manifold learning.

We will address the message-passing and the move-making methods in later chapters. In particular, we will focus on design for the relaxation, DP, and BP, which have the basic computational structures such as pipelining, iteration, and neighborhood computation.

5.7 Learning Methods

Before going further, let us consider the learning issues on the MRF model. Generally, an MRF system consists of a set of system parameters θ that defines its behavior under various conditions and environments. For example, we can easily consider the parametric model for observation noise. Under the Gaussian assumption, these parameters are the mean and variance of the noise. Further, for stereo applications, regularization weight is adjusted with respect to input image data to provide a more accurate matching result. The MRF model is, therefore, completely characterized by the distribution $p(\mathbf{x}|I, \theta)$, where θ is another hidden variable. Obtaining optimal system parameters for a given environment is a very important task in the labeling problem, and can be accomplished by a number of optimization approaches.

However, true observations on the label, $\mathbf{x}$, are not given in most vision problems. Therefore, supervised learning methods, which are relatively simpler than unsupervised methods, cannot be applied to recover an optimal parameter solution for a given system. To find the optimal system parameter for marginal likelihood $p(\mathbf{x}, I|\theta)$ under an unsupervised configuration, iterative labeling-estimation (Besag 1986; Bouman and Shapiro 1994; Kelly *et al.* 1988; Zhang 1992) alternate the labeling and estimation process while the other side is fixed. The expectation maximization (EM) algorithm (Dempster *et al.* 1977; McLachlan and Krishnan 1997) provides theoretical fundamentals and formalism for these iterative algorithms.

The purpose of the EM algorithm is to simultaneously search for the latent parameter θ and the label $\mathbf{x}$ that maximize the marginal distribution $p(\mathbf{x}, I|\theta)$. The optimization strategy of the EM algorithm is to divide the original optimization problem into two steps: E-step (expectation) and M-step (maximization).

In the E-step, the inference on the label is tried while fixing the parameters:

$$p(\mathbf{x}|I,\theta) = \frac{1}{Z}p(I|\mathbf{x},\theta)p(\mathbf{x}|\theta), \tag{5.28}$$

$$\mathbf{x}^* = \arg\max_{\mathbf{x}} p(\mathbf{x}|I,\theta)). \tag{5.29}$$

During this process, the conditional distribution given the image observation and fixed parameter estimates is maximized by latent label data $\mathbf{x}$, to provide expectation of target marginal likelihood $p(\mathbf{x}, I|\theta)$.

In the M-step, learning is achieved by maximizing previously computed expectations along the parameter space.

$$\theta^* = \arg\max_{\theta} E(p(\mathbf{x}, I|\theta)) = \arg\max_{\theta} \sum_{\mathbf{x}} p(\mathbf{x}, I|\theta)p(\mathbf{x}|I,\theta). \tag{5.30}$$

The E-step and M-step are iterated until the resulting parameters are converged. Final parameters are maximum likelihood solutions for the marginal distribution.

In addition to the EM framework, there are a number of works that cope with the MRF parameter estimation problem, such as iterative conditional estimation (ICE) (Giordana and Pieczynski 1997), least square estimation (Borges 1999; Derin and Elliott 1987), Markov chain Monte Carlo (MCMC) (Descombes *et al.* 1999), simulated annealing (Lakshmanan and Derin 1989), and other artificial intelligence algorithms (Yu 2012). In stereo contexts, empirical decision on parameters were popular since including the parameter learning process makes a problem more complex. Recently, a number of works related to learning MRF for stereo matching have been presented (Cheng and Caelli 2007; Huq *et al.* 2008; Trinh and McAllester 2009; Zhang and Seitz 2007). In NN frameworks, the learning of deep architectures is actively underway for both representation and parameters (Bengio *et al.* 2013).

5.8 Structure of the Energy Function

Although the energy function is rooted in MRF factorization, algorithms dealing with advanced problems often start directly from energy functions that are far more sophisticated than can be interpreted as graphical models. The original labeling problem, which was interpreted as an estimation problem in probability, becomes a matching problem, which is interpreted as an optimization problem in the energy function.

Basic categorization data and smoothness terms are too simple for many problems. In general, the two terms can be divided into more detailed terms. Let us now return to the posterior:

$$p(\mathbf{x}|I) = p(\mathbf{x})p(\mathbf{x}|I)/p(I). \tag{5.31}$$

The prior and the conditional terms are the origins of the smoothness and data terms. In many cases, the variables can be factorized and partitioned into regular or irregular sizes:

$$p(\mathbf{x}|I) = \prod_i p(\mathbf{x}_i) \prod_j p(I|\mathbf{x}_j), \tag{5.32}$$

which results in the energy equation:

$$E(\mathbf{x}) = \sum_j E(\mathbf{x}_j|I) + \sum_i E(\mathbf{x}_i). \tag{5.33}$$

The first term, collectively called the data term (or appearance model), actually consists of many heterogeneous terms. Analogously, the second term, collectively called the smoothness term (or geometrical constraint), actually denotes many heterogeneous terms representing geometric properties between partitions.

It is possible that in the future the structure of the energy function will become more sophisticated, revealing properties that are common and general but not yet discovered. For example, in (Choi *et al.* 2013), the data term is divided into the target observation and the feature observations terms. The smoothness term is divided into the camera, target, and geometric feature terms. Another example is that presented by Torresani (Torresani *et al.* 2013), in which the energy function, consisting of appearance, occlusion, geometry, and coherence terms, is interpreted as a graph-matching problem:

$$E(x) = E^a(x) + E^o(x) + E^g(x) + E^c(x), \tag{5.34}$$

where the weights are included inside the terms. The appearance and the geometry terms are the generalizations of the data and the smoothness terms. The occlusion terms are introduced for indeterminate positions and the coherence terms are introduced for the collective values of the neighborhoods.

Although roughly stated with data and smoothness terms, the detailed form of (5.33) depends upon the problems. In image restoration, it may depend on only one image but in motion or stereo vision it may depend on more than one image. The data term may have the form

$$\phi(x_i|I_i) = \|\hat{I}(x_i) - I_i\|, \tag{5.35}$$

where $\hat{I}$ is an estimation of the input data I_i by the variable x_i). The distance function is a measure between the true and estimated data.

Unlike the data term, the smoothness term is rather general. Nevertheless, there are many variations on its forms and usage. Returning to the derivation, the smoothness term originated from the joint distribution $p(x_i, x_j)$, meaning some homogeneity in doubletons:

$$p(\mathbf{x}_p, \mathbf{x}_q) = \frac{1}{Z}\exp\{-\psi(p,q)\}. \tag{5.36}$$

In images, the prior of doubletons is related to the smoothness of the surface, which is often modeled as a smoothness measure using the differential.

The smoothness measure often uses the $L_p - norm$, especially with $p = 1$ or $p = 2$. Among the measures, L_1 is the baseline measure in compressed sensing (Candes and Wakin 2008; Candès *et al.* 2006; Donoho 2006). In other applications, L_2 is often used because of its differentiability. Various models exist (Xu *et al.* 2012): linear model or quadratic model, truncated quadratic, Potts model, generalized Potts model, Charbonnier (Bruhn *et al.* 2005) and Lorentzian (Black and Anandan 1996).

Let $x = x_p - x_q$. Then, the possible measures are as follows:

$$\begin{cases} L_p: & \psi(x) = \|x\|_p, \\ TruncatedL_p: & \psi(x) = \min\{\|x\|_p, T_h\}, \\ Potts: & \psi(x) = 1 - \delta(x), \\ ApproximatePotts: & \psi(x) = 0 \text{ if } \|x\|_p < \Delta, T_h \text{ if } \|x\|_p > \Delta, \\ Charbonnier: & \sqrt{x^2 + \epsilon^2}, \\ Lorentzian: & \log(1 + \frac{x^2}{2\sigma^2}). \end{cases} \tag{5.37}$$

Here, $\delta(\cdot)$ is a Kronecker delta and $\epsilon, \sigma, \gamma, T_h > 0$ are parameters. The smoothness functions are illustrated in Figure 5.3.

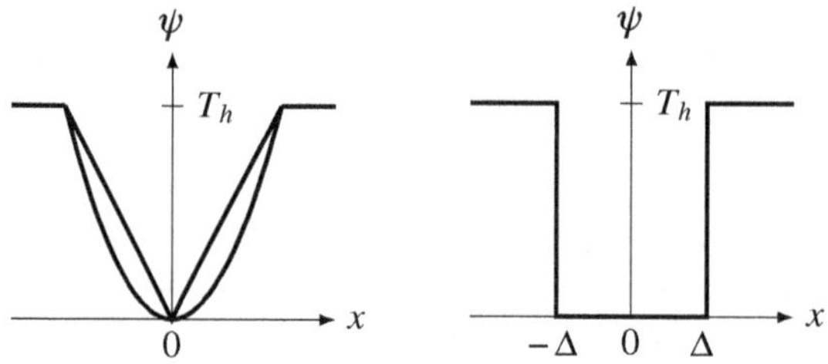

Figure 5.3 Graphs for the prior functions (T_h, Δ: threshold)

The smoothness term can be made anisotropic so that different smoothness may be applied to different directions in accordance with the local conditions. The quadratic measure can be written as

$$E(\mathbf{x}) = \int_{\Omega} \psi(\|\nabla \mathbf{x}(x, y)\|^2) dxdy. \tag{5.38}$$

If $\psi(\cdot)$ is in a certain form, $\nabla E(\cdot)$ becomes an anisotropic diffusion function:

$$\frac{\partial \mathbf{x}}{\partial t} = div(D(x, y, t)\nabla f). \tag{5.39}$$

The anisotropic diffusion term performs well in preserving boundaries while smoothing the surfaces. As was proved in (Wikipedia 2013a), it can be shown that the energy equation and the diffusion are related by

$$\psi'(x, y) = D(x, y). \tag{5.40}$$

As we will see, because of this property, the Euler–Lagrange equation of the energy equation contains the anisotropic diffusion term. In other optimization methods that directly minimize the energy function, the prior must be satisfied with the condition in Equation (5.40).

The smoothness term is related to the distance measures, which are numerous in definition, including methods such as earth mover's distance (EMD) (Rubner *et al.* 1997 2000), Bhattacharyya coefficients (Bhattacharyya 1946; Comaniciu *et al.* 2003), and β-divergence (Cichocki *et al.* 2006). However, the practical design prefers less computation and simpler circuits, as typified by the Potts model and the linear truncated function (see the problems at the end of this chapter).

5.9 Basic Energy Functions

Let us begin with the energy function in Definition 5.1. The data term is problem dependent but the smoothness term is more general in many problems. This term is naturally involved with differentials. In this model, the neighborhood operation is replaced with differentials. If we consider up to the second-order derivative, the energy function becomes

$$E(f) = \sum_{(x,y)\in P} \left\{ \phi(f) + \lambda|\nabla f|^2 + \mu|\nabla^2 f|^2 \right\}, \tag{5.41}$$

where λ and μ are the Lagrange multipliers. The smoothness term contains a gradient and a Laplacian, which measure the roughness up to the second order derivative. A more advanced model may be

$$E(f) = \sum_{(x,y)\in\mathcal{P}} \{\phi(f) + \eta(x,y)[\lambda|\nabla f|^2 + \mu|\nabla^2 f|^2]\}, \tag{5.42}$$

where $\eta(x, y)$ is a switch function indicating possible discontinuities, such as occlusion or object boundary. Inclusion of such a nonlinear factor may require very different methods to find a solution.

The differentiation must be preceded by a smoothing operation, such as Gaussian filter. The combined smoothing and differentiation can be considered as filtering with Gaussian differentials. This concept can give us the meaning of the properties of the smoothness term. It is easy to get

$$\nabla G = -\left(\frac{x}{s}, \frac{y}{t}\right)^T G(x, y, s, t), \quad \nabla^2 G = \frac{(x^2 - s^2)(y^2 - t^2)}{s^4 t^4} G^2(x, y, s, t). \tag{5.43}$$

The shape of the responses is illustrated in Figure 5.4. The Gaussian is considered anisotropic, $s \neq t$, to observe more intuition of the smoothing effects. The first row shows the first derivative G_x and G_x/G. G_x detects variations in the x-axis and G_y detects variations in the y-axis. The second row shows the ∇G and $\nabla^2 G/G$. This operator detects the zero crossing (ZC), signifying possible edges. It is well-known that the Laplacian is related with retinal response on edges and approximated with DOG (Marr and Hildreth 1980).

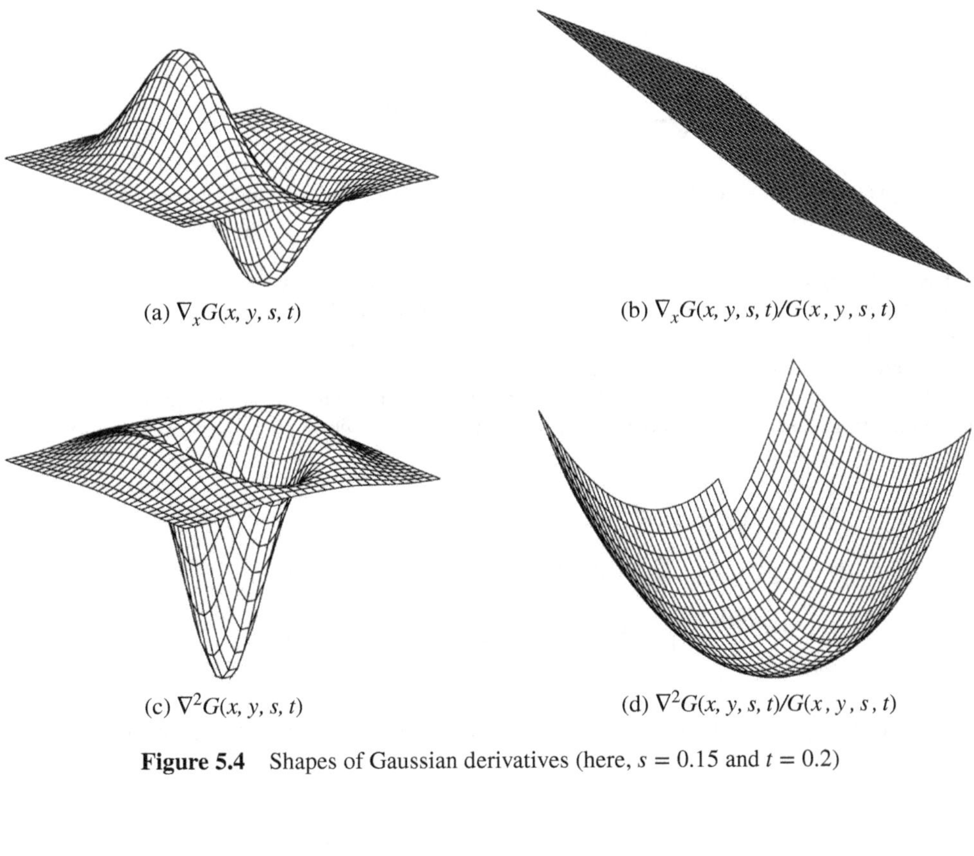

(a) $\nabla_x G(x, y, s, t)$ (b) $\nabla_x G(x, y, s, t)/G(x, y, s, t)$

(c) $\nabla^2 G(x, y, s, t)$ (d) $\nabla^2 G(x, y, s, t)/G(x, y, s, t)$

Figure 5.4 Shapes of Gaussian derivatives (here, $s = 0.15$ and $t = 0.2$)

The energy function can specify various vision modules. However, a problem exists because it has no unique representation for a given module, since different applications may emphasize different aspects of the data and smoothness terms. However, there exist several fundamental forms, in which the terms appear to be essential, even if some delicate features are missing. Among the vision modules, some representative problems are image restoration, stereo vision, and motion estimation.

The goal of image restoration is to recover an original image from a corrupted one by removing as much of the effects of noise as possible. Here is a challenge: for a given $I(x, y)$, restore the estimated image $f(x, y)$. The energy function is defined as

$$E(f) = \sum_{(x,y)\in\mathcal{P}} (I(x, y) - f(x, y))^2 + \lambda \sum_{(x,y)\in\mathcal{P}} |\nabla f|^2. \tag{5.44}$$

Here, λ is introduced as a Lagrange multiplier that adjusts the weight of the two terms.

Stereo vision is one of the major applications of the MRF model. To facilitate a concise description, we assume that the stereo vision system has perfectly calibrated binocular cameras, and that the disparity map is left-referenced. The goal is to estimate a dense disparity map $D(x, y)$ between two input images $I_L(x, y), I_r(x, y)$, which can be easily represented as the 2D labeling problem in the image plane. Fundamentally, the entire energy function to be minimized is defined as

$$\begin{aligned}
E^r(D) &= E_d(D_p) + \lambda E_s(D_p, D_\mathbf{q}) = \sum_{(x,y)\in\mathcal{P}} \|I^r(x, y) - I^l(x + d(x, y), y)\|^2 \\
&\quad + \lambda \sum_{(x,y)\in\mathcal{P}} \sum_{(x',y')\in N_{xy}} \min(\|d(x, y) - d(x', y')\|, T_s), \\
E^l(D) &= E_d(D_p) + \lambda E_s(D_p, D_\mathbf{q}) = \sum_{(x,y)\in\mathcal{P}} \|I^l(x, y) - I^r(x + d(x, y), y)\|^2 \\
&\quad + \lambda \sum_{(x,y)\in\mathcal{P}} \sum_{(x',y')\in N_{xy}} \min(\|d(x, y) - d(x', y')\|, T_s),
\end{aligned} \tag{5.45}$$

where T_s is the threshold for truncation. The singleton $E_d(D_p)$ usually includes photo-consistency constraints between the left and right images. The doubleton $E_s(D_p, D_q)$ is the smoothness term (see the problems at the end of this chapter).

The goal of motion estimation is to estimate the motion vector between two consecutive image frames in a video sequence. Hence, the input is two images, $I_t(x, y)$ and $I_{t+1}(x, y)$, and the target attribute is a 2D array of motion vectors $\mathbf{V} = \{[u(x, y), v(x, y)]^T | (x, y) \in \mathcal{P}\}$. Because the two corresponding pixels in adjacent frames can be warped forward and backward with respect to the motion vector value of a particular position in reference view, the motion estimation problem can intuitively be considered an extension of the stereo vision problem. Generally, an energy function for motion estimation is defined as

$$\begin{aligned}
E(\mathbf{V}) &= E_d(V_p) + \lambda E_s(V_p, V_q) \\
&= \sum_{(x,y)\in\mathcal{P}} \|I_t(x, y) - I_{t+1}(x + u(x, y), y + v(x, y))\|^2 \\
&\quad + \lambda \sum_{(x,y)\in\mathcal{P}} \sum_{(x',y')\in N_{xy}} \min(\|\psi(x, y) - \psi(x', y')\|^2, T_m).
\end{aligned} \tag{5.46}$$

The format is very similar to that of the stereo case; in fact, disparity is changed into a motion vector quantity. Truncated quadratic form is preferred in motion estimation problems.

In later chapters, we will design the circuits for stereo matching, modifying the energy function to more appropriate forms for practical implementation.

Problems

5.1 [Labeling] For an image with $M \times N$ 8-bit pixels, how many labels may exist? For $M = N = 100$, what is the total number of labels?

5.2 [Labeling] For the previous search space, a computer algorithm is going to search for an optimal solution. If 1ns is needed to test a label, how long will it take to inspect all the space?

5.3 [Inference] Check the relationship in Equation (5.23).

5.4 [Inference] In Equation (5.23), the ordinary bound is $\underline{ab} \le ab \le \overline{ab}$. The new lower and upper bounds must be better than the ordinary bound. How much better are the new bounds than the ordinary ones?

5.5 [Structure] Some algorithms such as Bayesian estimates, simulated annealing, and graph cuts, are driven by various probability distribution functions, such as uniform, Gaussian, Laplacian, and Gibbs distributions. There are numerous pseudorandom number generators (PRNG) (refer to the lists in (Wikipedia 2013f). The uniform distribution is a versatile distribution that can be used to derive other distributions. One of the simplest uniform distributions is the linear feedback shift register (LFSR) (Wikipedia 2013e), a shift register whose input bit is a linear function of its previous state. There are versions for Fibonacci, Galois, and maximal-length. Design a 20-bit maximal-length LFSR using the table in (Koopman 2013).

5.6 [Structure] Design a PRGN that generates ones with a probability of $1/2^n$, where n is a positive integer.

5.7 [Structure] In some applications, such as simulated annealing and graph cuts, we randomly select samples in a window, say a 10×10 window. Design such a circuit with the LFSR.

5.8 [Structure] Among the loss (error) functions, design a truncated linear function.

5.9 [Structure] Among the loss (error) functions, design a Potts model in Verilog HDL.

5.10 [Basic Energy] Equation (5.45) is defined for the right image plane as a reference. Write the same form for the left image plane.

References

Ahuja RK, Magnanti TL, and Orlin JB 1993 *Network Flows: Theory, Algorithms, and Applications*. Prentice Hall.

Amini AA, Weymouth TE, and Jain RC 1990 Using dynamic programming for solving variational problems in vision. *IEEE Trans. Pattern Anal. Mach. Intell.* **12**(9), 855–867.

Banzhaf W, Nordin P, Keller RE, and Francone FD 2001 *Genetic Programming – An Introduction; On the Automatic Evolution of Computer Programs and its Applications* third edn. Morgan Kaufmann, dpunkt.verlag.

Bazin J, Li H, Kweon IS, Demonceaux C, Vasseur P, and Ikeuchi K 2013 A branch-and-bound approach to correspondence and grouping problems. *IEEE Trans. Pattern Anal. Mach. Intell.* **35**(7), 1565–1576.

Bellman R 1954 The theory of dynamic programming. *Bulletin of the American Mathematical Society* **60**, 503–516.

Bengio Y, Courville AC, and Vincent P 2013 Representation learning: a review and new perspectives. *IEEE Trans. Pattern Anal. Mach. Intell.* **35**(8), 1798–1828.

Bertsekas DP 2007 *Dynamic Programming and Optimal Control* vol. 1,2. Athena Scientific.

Besag J 1974 Spatial interaction and the statistical analysis of lattice systems. *Journal of the Royal Statistical Society, Series B* **36**, 192–236.

Besag J 1986 On the statistical analysis of dirty pictures. *Journal Royal Statistical Society* **B-48**(3), 259–302.

Bhattacharyya A 1946 On a measure of divergence between two multinomial populations. *The Indian Journal of Statistics (1933–1960)* **7**(4), 401–406.

Black MJ and Anandan P 1996 The robust estimation of multiple motions: Parametric and piecewise-smooth flow fields. *Computer Vision and Image Understanding* **63**(1), 75–104.

Borges CF 1999 On the estimation of Markov random field parameters. *IEEE Trans. Pattern Anal. Mach. Intell.* **21**(3), 216–224.

Bouman C and Shapiro M 1994 A multiscale random field model for Bayesian segmentation. *IEEE Trans. Pattern Anal. Mach. Intell.* **3**(2), 162–177.

Boykov Y and Kolmogorov V 2004 An experimental comparison of min-cut/max-flow algorithms for energy minimization in vision. *IEEE Trans. Pattern Anal. Mach. Intell.* **26**(9), 1124–1137.

Boykov Y, Veksler O, and Zabih R 1998 Markov random fields with efficient approximations *International Conference on Computer Vision and Pattern Recognition (CVPR)*.

Boykov Y, Veksler O, and Zabih R 2001 Fast approximate energy minimization via graph cuts. *IEEE Trans. Pattern Anal. Mach. Intell.* **23**(11), 1222–1239.

Breuel TM 2003 Implementation techniques for geometric Branch-and-Bound matching methods. *Computer Vision and Image Understanding* **90**(3), 258–294.

Bruhn A, Weickert J, and Schnorr C 2005 Lucas/Kanade meets Horn/Schunck: Combining local and global optic flow methods. *International Journal of Computer Vision* **61**(3), 211–231.

Candes E and Wakin M 2008 An introduction to compressive sampling. *IEEE Signal Processing Magazine* **25**(2), 21–30.

Candès EJ, Romberg JK, and Tao T 2006 Stable signal recovery from incomplete and inaccurate measurements. *Comm. Pure Appl. Math.* **59**(8), 1207–1223.

Chandraker M and Kriegman DJ 2008 Globally optimal bilinear programming for computer vision applications *CVPR*, pp. 1–8.

Cheng L and Caelli T 2007 Bayesian stereo matching. *Computer Vision and Image Understanding* **106**(1), 85–96.

Choi W, Pantofaru C, and Savarese S 2013 A general framework for tracking multiple people from a moving camera. *IEEE Trans. Pattern Anal. Mach. Intell.* **35**(7), 1577–1591.

Cichocki A, Zdunek R, and Amari Si 2006 Csiszar divergences for non-negative matrix factorization: Family of new algorithms *Independent Component Analysis and Blind Signal Separation* Springer pp. 32–39.

Clifford P 1990 Markov random fields in statistics In *Disorder in Physical Systems. A Volume in Honour of John M. Hammersley* (ed. Grimmett GR and Welsh DJA), pp. 19–32. Clarendon Press, Oxford.

Comaniciu D, Ramesh V, and Meer P 2003 Kernel-based object tracking. *IEEE Trans. Pattern Anal. Mach. Intell.* **25**(5), 564–577.

Cormen T, Rivest CLR, and Stein C 2001 *Introduction to Algorithms* second edn. The MIT Press.

Courant R and Hilbert D 1953 *Methods of Mathematical Physics*, vol. 1. Interscience Press.

Dempster A, Laird N, and Rubin D 1977 Maximum likelihood from incomplete data via the em algorithm. *Journal of the Royal Statistical Society, Series B* **39**, 1–38.

Derin H and Elliott H 1987 Modeling and segmentation of noisy and textured images using Gibbs random fields. *IEEE Trans. Pattern Anal. Mach. Intell.* **9**(1), 39–55.

Descombes X, Morris RD, Zerubia J, and Berthod M 1999 Estimation of Markov random field prior parameters using Markov chain Monte Carlo maximum likelihood. *IEEE Trans. Image Processing* **8**(7), 954–963.

Donoho D 2006 Compressed sensing. *IEEE Trans. Information Theory* **52**(4), 1289–1306.

Fix A, Gruber A, Boros E, and Zabih R 2011 A graph cut algorithm for higher-order Markov random fields In *ICCV* (ed. Metaxas DN, Quan L, Sanfeliu A, and Gool LJV), pp. 1020–1027. IEEE.

Friston K, Kilner J, and Harrison L 2006 A free energy principle for the brain. *J Physiol Paris.* **100**(1-3), 70–87.

Giordana N and Pieczynski W 1997 Estimation of generalized multisensor hidden Markov Chain and unsupervised image segmentation. *IEEE Trans. Pattern Anal. Mach. Intell.* **19**(5), 465–475.

Globerson A and Jaakkola T 2007 Fixing max-product: Convergent message passing algorithms for MAP LP-relaxations In *NIPS* (ed. Platt JC, Koller D, Singer Y, and Roweis ST). Curran Associates, Inc.

Greig D, Porteous B, and Seheult A 1989 Exact maximum a posteriori estimation for binary images. *Journal of the Royal Statistical Society Series B* **51**, 271–279.

Hammersley J and Clifford P 1971 Markov fields on finite graphs and lattices Unpublished note.

Heyden A 2013 Energy minimization methods in computer vision and pattern recognition *9th International Conference, EMMCVPR 2013* CVPR.

Hinton GE 2007 Learning multiple layers of representation. *Trends in Cognitive Science* **11**(10), 428–434.

Horn B and Shunck B 1981 Determining optical flow. *Artificial Intelligence* **17**(1-3), 185–203.

Huq S, Koschan A, Abidi B, and Abidi M 2008 Efficient BP stereo with automatic parameter estimation *15th IEEE International Conference on Image Processing*, pp. 301–304.

Kahl F, Agarwal S, Chandraker MK, Kriegman DJ, and Belongie S 2008 Practical global optimization for multiview geometry. *International Journal of Computer Vision* **79**(3), xx–yy.

Kappes JH, Andres B, Hamprecht FA, Schnorr C, Nowozin S, Batra D, Kim S, Kausler BX, Lellmann J, Komodakis N, and Rother C 2013 A comparative study of modern inference techniques for discrete energy minimization problems *EMMCVPR 2013*.

Kappes JH, Savchynskyy B, and Schnorr C 2012 A bundle approach to efficient MAP-inference by Lagrangian relaxation *CVPR*, pp. 1688–1695.

Kelly PA, Derin H, and Hartt KD 1988 Adaptive segmentation of speckled images using a hierarchical random field model. *IEEE Trans. Acoustic, Speech and Signal Processing* **36**, 1628–1641.

Kirkpatrick S, Jr. DG, and Vecchi MP 1983 Optimization by simmulated annealing. *Science* **220**(4598), 671–680.

Koller D and Friedman N 2009 *Probabilistic Graphical Models: Principles and Techniques*. MIT Press.

Kolmogorov V 2006 Convergent Tree-reweighted message passing for energy minimization. *IEEE Trans. Pattern Anal. Mach. Intell.* **28**(10), 1568–1583.

Komodakis N and Paragios N 2008 Beyond loose lp- relaxations: Optimizing MRFs by repairing cycles *ECCV*.

Komodakis N and Tziritas G 2007 Approximate labeling via graph cuts based on linear programming. *IEEE Trans. Pattern Anal. Mach. Intell.* **29**(8), 1436–1453.

Koopman P 2013 Maximal length lfsr feedback terms http://www.ece.cmu.edu/~koopman/lfsr/index.html (accessed Dec. 15, 2013).

Lakshmanan S and Derin H 1989 Simultaneous parameter estimation and segmentation of Gibbs random fields using simulated annealing. *IEEE Trans. Pattern Anal. Mach. Intell.* **11**(8), 799–813.

Land AH and Doig AG 1960 An automatic method of solving discrete programming problems. *Econometrica: Journal of the Econometric Society* **28**, 497–520.

Madjarov G, Kocev D, Gjorgjevikj D, and Džeroski S 2012 An extensive experimental comparison of methods for multi-label learning. *Pattern Recognition* **45**(9), 3084–3104.

Marr D and Hildreth E 1980 Theory of edge detection. *Proceedings of the Royal Society of London. Series B. Biological Sciences* **207**(1167), 187–217.

McLachlan GJ and Krishnan T 1997 *The EM Algorithms and Extensions*. John Wiley & Sons, Inc.

Memisevic R 2013 Learning to relate images. *IEEE Trans. Pattern Anal. Mach. Intell.* **35**(8), 1829–1846.

Olsson C, Kahl F, and Oskarsson M 2009 Branch-and-bound methods for euclidean registration problems. *IEEE Trans. Pattern Anal. Mach. Intell.* **31**(5), 783–794.

Pardo L 2005 *Statistical Inference Based on Divergence Measures*. CRC Press.

Pearl J 1982 Reverend Bayes on inference engines: A distributed hierarchical approach In *AAAI* (ed. Waltz D), pp. 133–136. AAAI Press.

Pearl J 1988 *Probabilistic Reasoning in Intelligent Systems: Networks of Plausible Inference*. Morgan Kaufmann, San Francisco, CA.

Rother C, Kolmogorov V, Lempitsky V, and Szummer M 2007 Optimizing binary MRFs via extended roof duality *Computer Vision and Pattern Recognition, 2007. CVPR'07. IEEE Conference on*, pp. 1–8 IEEE.

Roweis S and Ghahramani Z 1999 A unifying review of linear Gaussian models. *Neural computation* **11**(2), 305–345.

Rubner Y, Guibas LJ, and Tomasi C 1997 The earth mover's distance, multi-dimensional scaling, and color-based image retrieval *Image Understanding Workshop*, pp. 661–668.

Rubner Y, Tomasi C, and Guibas LJ 2000 The Earth Mover's Distance as a metric for image retrieval. *International Journal of Computer Vision* **40**(2), 99–121.

Sontag D, Meltzer T, Globerson A, Weiss Y, and Jaakkola T 2008 Tightening LP relaxations for MAP using message-passing *UAI*.

Sorower MS 2010 A literature survey on algorithms for multi-label learning. Technical report, Technical report, Oregon State University, Corvallis, OR, USA (December 2010).

Sun M, Telaprolu M, Lee H, and Savarese S 2012 Efficient and exact MAP-MRF inference using branch and bound *AISTATS*, pp. 1134–1142.

Sutton RS and Barto AG 1998 *Reinforcement Learning: An Introduction*. The MIT Press, Cambridge, MA.

Szeliski R, Zabih R, Scharstein D, Veksler O, V K, Agarwala A, Tappen M, and Rother C 2006 A comparative study of energy minimization methods for Markov random fields *Ninth European Conference on Computer Vision*, vol. 2, pp. 16–29 ECCV.

Szeliski RS, Zabih R, Scharstein D, Veksler OA, Kolmogorov V, Agarwala A, Tappen M, and Rother C 2008 A comparative study of energy minimization methods for Markov random fields with smoothness-based priors. *IEEE Trans. Pattern Anal. Mach. Intell.* **30**(6), 1068–1080.

Torresani L, Kolmogorov V, and Rother C 2013 A dual decomposition approach to feature correspondence. *IEEE Trans. Pattern Anal. Mach. Intell.* **35**(2), 259–271.

Trinh H and McAllester D 2009 Unsupervised learning of stereo vision with monocular cues *BMVC*.

Wainwright MJ, Jaakkola TS, and Willsky AS 2005 Map estimation via agreement on trees: Message-passing and linear programming. *IEEE Trans. Information Theory* **51**(11), 3697–3717.

Werner T 2007 A linear programming approach to max-sum problem : A review. *IEEE Trans. Pattern Anal. Mach. Intell.* **29**, 1165–1179.

Wikipedia 2013a Anisotropic diffusion http://en.wikipedia.org/wiki/Anisotropic_diffusion (accessed Sept. 30, 2013).

Wikipedia 2013b Divergence http://en.wikipedia.org/wiki/Divergence_(statistics) (accessed Nov. 24, 2013).

Wikipedia 2013c Free energy principle http://en.wikipedia.org/wiki/Active_inference (accessed on Dec. 17, 2013).

Wikipedia 2013d Hypergraph http://en.wikipedia.org/wiki/Hypergraph (accessed Sept. 24, 2013).

Wikipedia 2013e Linear Feedback Shift Register http://en.wikipedia.org/wiki/LFSR (accessed Sept. 30, 2013).

Wikipedia 2013f List of random number generators http://en.wikipedia.org/wiki/List_of_random_number_generators (accessed Sept. 30, 2013).

Wikipedia 2013g Markov random field http://en.wikipedia.org/wiki/Markov_random_field (accessed Sept. 24, 2013).

Wikipedia 2013h Thermodynamic free energy http://en.wikipedia.org/wiki/Thermodynamic_free_energy (accessed Sept. 24, 2013).

Xu L, Jia J, and Matsushita Y 2012 Motion detail preserving optical flow estimation. *IEEE Trans. Pattern Anal. Mach. Intell.* **34**(9), 1744–1757.

Yedidia JS, Freeman WT, and Weiss Y 2005 Constructing free-energy approximations and generalized Belief Propagation algorithms. *IEEE Trans. Information Theory* **51**(7), 2282–2312.

Yu Y 2012 Estimation of Markov random field parameters using ant colony optimization for continuous domains *2012 Spring Congress on Engineering and Technology*, pp. 1–4.

Zhang J 1992 The Mean Field Theory in EM procedures for Markov random fields. *IEEE Trans. Image Processing* **40**(10), 2570–2583.

Zhang L and Seitz SM 2007 Estimating optimal parameters for MRF stereo from a single image pair. *IEEE Trans. Pattern Anal. Mach. Intell.* **29**(2), 331–342.

6

Stereo Vision

Binocular stereo vision is one of the major vision modules by which one can induce the depth of the surface shape and the volume information of the objects. Created by a pair of cameras, a conjugate pair of images contains the depth information by means of disparity. Binocular vision naturally expands to other vision, such as trinocular or multi-view vision (Faugeras 1993; Faugeras and Luong 2004; Hartley and Zisserman 2004).

Stereo vision deals with the three major problems: correspondence geometry, camera geometry, and scene geometry. Of these, stereo matching deals with the correspondence geometry and remains the major research area. It can be classified into various categories according to the features, measures, inference methods, and learning methods. A comprehensive survey of recent progress on stereo matching is presented by (Scharstein and Szeliski 2002) for algorithms, and by (Tippetts *et al.* 2013) for realizations. Also, they have provided a benchmark for quantitative evaluation of existing stereo matching algorithms.

This chapter introduces some fundamental concepts of stereo vision problems and stereo matching. Instead of reviewing all the extensive stereo matching algorithms and realizations, we focus instead on the fundamental constructs of the energy function, classified as appearance model and geometric constraints. The models and constraints are examined in five categories: space, time, frequency, discrete space, and other vision module. Stereo matching, as other vision problems, is inherently ill-posed, and thus needs the best possible natural constraints. Unfortunately, all the constraints are not sufficient and necessary conditions but are always accompanied by exceptional cases. This is why the study of natural constraints must be emphasized compared to others. The actual algorithm uses constraints, features, measures in energy function and optimization methods and parameter estimation methods in a variety of ways.

The contents are not intended to be complete in their scope and depths but intended to be a good preparation for the topics in subsequent chapters. In particular, a baseline form of energy function is expressed, which will be used in later chapters for the study of computational structure and circuit design.

6.1 Camera Systems

Projective geometry (Faugeras 1993; Faugeras and Luong 2004; Hartley and Zisserman 2004) is one of the three components of the image formation process, along with the illumination and reflectance properties. Since stereo and motion deal with images and videos, knowing the optical environment is important to describe various vision quantities mathematically. First, we must know the mechanism of projection from object to image plane. Next, the relationship between world coordinates and image coordinates must be specified in detail.

Architectures for Computer Vision: From Algorithm to Chip with Verilog, First Edition. Hong Jeong.

Companion Website: www.wiley.com/go/jeong

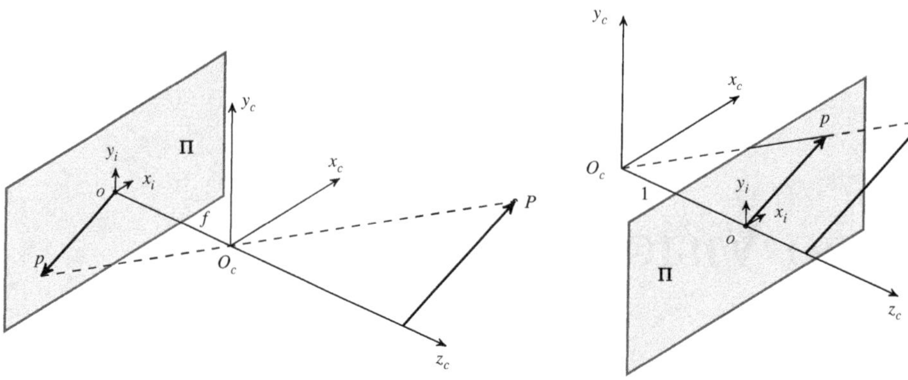

(a) Pinhole camera (b) Normalized camera

Figure 6.1 Two camera systems: pinhole and normalized cameras

In a *perspective model* (or *pinhole model*) camera, the image plane is positioned behind the lens center, in inverted direction. (Figure 6.1(a).) The camera coordinates are denoted by O_c, which is called the *center of projection* (or *optical center*). An image plane $\mathbf{\Pi}$ is positioned at a distance f, which is called *focal length*. Here, the center of the image, o, is the origin of the image coordinates. A point P in the 3-space is projected, through O_c, on the image plane $\mathbf{\Pi}$, forming an image p in an inverted and scaled shape.

The inverted image is inconvenient and thus often represented in a different scheme, in which the image is positioned in the same direction as the object. The scheme is to consider a virtual image plane that is located before the lens so that the coordinates of camera and image are overlapped in the depth direction. This scheme, especially with $f = 1$, is called *normalized camera* (Figure 6.1(b)). The fronto-parallel plane $\mathbf{\Pi}$ at the focal length, f, in front of the x_cy_c-plane is called the *virtual image plane*. The *principal plane* is the plane that includes the optical center. The *principal point*, o, is where the *principal axis* z_c and the plane $\mathbf{\Pi}$ coincide. We often use the normalized camera, unless otherwise stated.

In *Cartesian coordinates*, a point $\tilde{\mathbf{x}}_c = (x_c, y_c, z_c)^T$ is projected to the point $\tilde{\mathbf{x}}_i = (x_i, y_i)^T$, satisfying

$$x_i = \frac{f}{z_c}x_c, \quad y_i = \frac{f}{z_c}y_c, \tag{6.1}$$

which means that the system is perspective.

In projective geometry, using *homogeneous coordinates* is essential, because it makes perspective projection a linear transformation. In 2D space, a point $\tilde{\mathbf{x}} = (x, y)$ in inhomogeneous system (Cartesian, $\mathbb{E}^2$) is represented by $\mathbf{x} = [x, y, 1]$ in homogeneous system ($\mathbb{P}^2$). Inversely, a point $\mathbf{x} = [x, y, w]$ in homogeneous system is represented by $\tilde{\mathbf{x}} = (x/w, y/w)$ if $w \neq 0$. (For simplicity, sometimes we use row vector instead of column vector.) In short, $[x, y, w] \equiv (x/w, y/w)$ if $w \neq 0$. In 3D space, a point $\tilde{\mathbf{x}} = (x, y, z)$ in inhomogeneous system ($\mathbb{E}^3$) is represented by $\mathbf{x} = [x, y, z, 1]$ in homogeneous system ($\mathbb{P}^3$). Inversely, a point $\mathbf{x} = [x, y, z, w]$ in homogeneous system is represented by $\tilde{\mathbf{x}} = (x/w, y/w, z/w)$ if $w \neq 0$. In short, $[x, y, z, w] \equiv (x/w, y/w, z/w)$ if $\neq 0$.

The algebraic properties are summarized as follows. For vector addition, $[x, y, z] + [a, b, c] = [za + xc, zb + yc, zc]$. For scalar multiplication, $a[x, y, z] = [ax, ay, z]$, where $a \neq 0$. For linear combination, $\alpha[x, y, z] + \beta[a, b, c] = [z\beta\alpha + \alpha xc, z\beta b + \alpha yc, zc]$. For derivative, $d[x, y, w] = [dx, dy, w]$.

In geometric interpretation, $\mathbb{E}^2$ is spanned by $(1, 0)$ and $(0, 1)$, but $\mathbb{P}^2$ is spanned by $[1, 0, 1]$, $[0, 1, 1]$, and the *ideals*: $\mathbf{x}_\infty = [1, 0, 0]$ and $\mathbf{y}_\infty = [0, 1, 0]$, called *point at infinity*, and $\mathbf{l}_\infty = [0, 0, 1]$, called *line at infinity*. However, $[0, 0, 0]^T$ does not represent any point. Excluding $[0, 0, 0, 0]$, $\mathbb{P}^3$ consists of the bases $([1, 0, 0, 1], [0, 1, 0, 1], [0, 0, 1, 1])$, the ideals $(x_\infty, y_\infty, z_\infty, \pi_\infty)$. The same concept can be expanded to $\mathbb{E}^3$ and $\mathbb{P}^3$ and further higher dimension. (For further information on projective geometry, refer to (Faugeras and Luong 2004; Hartley and Zisserman 2004).)

According to the homogeneous coordinates, Equation (6.1) becomes

$$\begin{pmatrix} x_i \\ y_i \end{pmatrix} \equiv \begin{bmatrix} fx_c \\ fy_c \\ z_c \end{bmatrix}. \tag{6.2}$$

In the following, the notations of row and column vectors and of the coordinates are used interchangeably and the actual meaning must be clear from the context.

6.2 Camera Matrices

A discrete image is often modeled as an array of $N \times M$ pixels: $I = \{I(x, y)|x \in [0, N-1], y \in [M-1]\}$, where the origin of the image is the north-west corner of the array, like a matrix. Conceptually, such a discrete image is obtained from a continuous image, $I(x, y), x \in [-a, a], y \in [-b, b]$, where a and b are image sizes. Therefore, the two formats are related, with coordinate transformation such as translation and scale change. Moreover, the camera image must be related to world coordinates, for the camera is positioned and oriented in 3-space. Besides, the object itself has coordinates. Considering all these together, we will need the five coordinates system: (x, y) for the *pixel coordinates*, (x_c, y_c) for the *image coordinates*, (x_c, y_c, z_c) for the *camera coordinates*, (x_o, y_o) for the *object coordinates*, and (X, Y, Z) for the *world coordinates*. In Figure 6.2, the five coordinates systems are represented by the origins and the projected points. In this optical alignment, P is observed as (X, Y, Z) in world coordinates, (x_o, y_o, z_o) in object coordinates system, (x_c, y_c, z_c) in camera coordinates system, (x_c, y_c) in image coordinates system, and (x, y) in pixel coordinates system.

The coordinates transformation from world to pixel plane can be described by linear mapping, provided that homogeneous coordinates are adopted. The mapping consists of the four stages: from object to world, world to camera, camera to image, and image to pixel image. (The object coordinates are ignored for simplicity.) The mapping from world to camera is an *orthographic projection* in 3D that can be specified by the rotation matrix $R_{3\times3}$ and the translation vector $\mathbf{t}_{3\times1}$. The mapping from camera to image is a *perspective projection*, which is specified by the focal length f. The mapping from image to pixel is a mapping specified by the translation (o_x, o_y) in pixels and scaling by the effective size of the pixel, (s_x, s_y), in the horizontal and vertical direction, respectively. As such, an image point, (x, y), can be related to the object point, (X, Y, Z), in the world coordinates in the following way. To differentiate between homogeneous and inhomogeneous coordinates, let

$$\mathbf{X} = (X, Y, Z, 1)^T, \tilde{\mathbf{X}} = (X, Y, Z)^T, \mathbf{x} = (x, y, 1)^T, \tilde{\mathbf{x}} = (x, y)^T. \tag{6.3}$$

In general, the world and camera coordinates have the relationship, which is described by rotation R and translation $\mathbf{t}$. In homogeneous coordinates systems, the relationship is linear, $\mathbf{x}_c = [R|\mathbf{t}]\mathbf{X}$:

$$\begin{bmatrix} x_c \\ y_c \\ z_c \\ 1 \end{bmatrix} = \begin{bmatrix} R & \mathbf{t} \\ 0 & 1 \end{bmatrix}_{4\times4} \begin{bmatrix} X \\ Y \\ Z \\ 1 \end{bmatrix}. \tag{6.4}$$

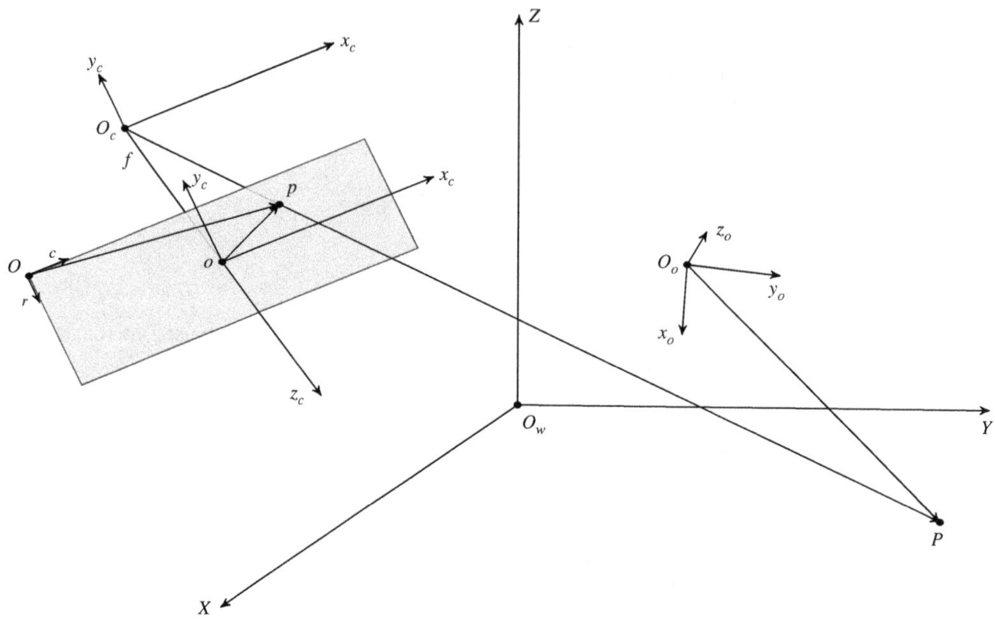

Figure 6.2 Coordinates systems: pixel (O), image (o), camera (O_C), object (O_o), and world coordinates (O_w)

The projection from camera to image coordinates is described by perspective transformation: $\mathbf{x}_i = diag(1, 1, 1/f)[I|0]\mathbf{x}_c$:

$$\begin{bmatrix} x_i \\ y_i \\ w_i \end{bmatrix} = \begin{bmatrix} 1 & 0 & 0 \\ 0 & 1 & 0 \\ 0 & 0 & 1/f \end{bmatrix}_{3\times3} \begin{bmatrix} 1 & 0 & 0 & 0 \\ 0 & 1 & 0 & 0 \\ 0 & 0 & 1 & 0 \end{bmatrix}_{3\times4} \begin{bmatrix} x_c \\ y_c \\ z_c \\ 1 \end{bmatrix}, \tag{6.5}$$

where the dimension is reduced and the scale is reduced by the focal length f. The mapping from image $\mathbf{x}_i$ to pixel $\mathbf{x}$ is expressed by

$$\begin{bmatrix} x \\ y \\ w \end{bmatrix} = \begin{bmatrix} s_x & 0 & 0 \\ 0 & s_y & 0 \\ 0 & 0 & 1 \end{bmatrix} \begin{bmatrix} 1 & 0 & o_x \\ 0 & 1 & o_y \\ 0 & 0 & 1 \end{bmatrix} \begin{bmatrix} x_i \\ y_i \\ z_i \end{bmatrix}, \tag{6.6}$$

where (s_x, s_y) are scale factors (isotropic if equal and anisotropic if unequal), and (o_x, o_y) is the offset between image and pixel planes.

The overall combination of Equations (6.4), (6.5) and (6.6) becomes

$$\begin{bmatrix} x \\ y \\ w \end{bmatrix} = \begin{bmatrix} s_x & 0 & 0 \\ 0 & s_y & 0 \\ 0 & 0 & 1 \end{bmatrix} \begin{bmatrix} 1 & 0 & o_x \\ 0 & 1 & o_y \\ 0 & 0 & 1 \end{bmatrix} \begin{bmatrix} 1 & 0 & 0 \\ 0 & 1 & 0 \\ 0 & 0 & 1/f \end{bmatrix} \begin{bmatrix} 1 & 0 & 0 & 0 \\ 0 & 1 & 0 & 0 \\ 0 & 0 & 1 & 0 \end{bmatrix} \begin{bmatrix} R & \mathbf{t} \\ 0 & 1 \end{bmatrix} \begin{bmatrix} X \\ Y \\ Z \\ 1 \end{bmatrix}. \tag{6.7}$$

We represent this by

$$\mathbf{x} = C\mathbf{X} = KC_0 \begin{bmatrix} R & \mathbf{t} \\ 0 & 1 \end{bmatrix} = K_{3\times 3}[R|\mathbf{t}]_{3\times 4}\mathbf{X}, \tag{6.8}$$

where C, C_0, and K are respectively called the *camera matrix*, *canonical form*, and *calibration matrix*. The calibration matrix has the form:

$$K = \begin{bmatrix} s_x & 0 & 0 \\ 0 & s_y & 0 \\ 0 & 0 & 1 \end{bmatrix} \begin{bmatrix} 1 & 0 & o_x \\ 0 & 1 & o_y \\ 0 & 0 & 1 \end{bmatrix} \begin{bmatrix} f & 0 & 0 \\ 0 & f & 0 \\ 0 & 0 & 1 \end{bmatrix}$$

$$= \begin{bmatrix} fs_x & 0 & s_x o_x \\ 0 & fs_y & s_y o_y \\ 0 & 0 & 1 \end{bmatrix} = \begin{bmatrix} \alpha & \gamma & u_0 \\ 0 & \beta & v_0 \\ 0 & 0 & 1 \end{bmatrix}. \tag{6.9}$$

Here, α and β denote focal length in terms with pixels, γ (often zero) denotes skew coefficient.

The *normalized camera matrix* C_N is defined by

$$C_N = K^{-1}C = [R|\mathbf{t}]_{3\times 4}. \tag{6.10}$$

This is equivalent to the camera in which the focal length is unity, the origin is centered on the image, and the scale is unity. Thus the intrinsic parameters are removed and only the extrinsic parameters are retained. This camera is often the starting point when only the extrinsic parameters must be considered.

Conceptually, the camera matrix consists of three vanishing points and the projection of world origin:

$$C = \begin{bmatrix} \mathbf{v}_x & \mathbf{v}_y & \mathbf{v}_z & \mathbf{o}_w \end{bmatrix}. \tag{6.11}$$

Let $\mathbf{x}_\infty = [1, 0, 0, 0]^T$, $\mathbf{y}_\infty = [0, 1, 0, 0]^T$, and $\mathbf{z}_\infty = [0, 0, 1, 0]^T$ be ideals and $\mathbf{O} = [0, 0, 0, 1]^T$ be the world origin. Then, we have

$$\mathbf{v}_x = C\mathbf{x}_\infty, \quad \mathbf{v}_y = C\mathbf{y}_\infty, \quad \mathbf{v}_z = C\mathbf{z}_\infty, \quad \mathbf{o} = C\mathbf{O}, \tag{6.12}$$

where the first three vectors represent respectively the x, y, and z vanishing points and the last represents the projection of the world origin.

In general, the image plane may be transformed from 2D to 2D, so-called *homography*: $\mathbf{x} = H\mathbf{x}'$ with $\mathbf{x}' = C\mathbf{X}$. Then, the general expression is $\mathbf{x} = HC\mathbf{X}$ and thus the general camera matrix C' is the product of homography and camera matrix:

$$C' = HC_N. \tag{6.13}$$

The camera matrix expresses the 3D to 2D transformation including rotation, translation, perspective, scaling (isotropic or anisotropic), and offset. The homography expresses the 2D to 2D transformation, meaning 2D rotation, 2D translation, 2D perspective, and 2D scaling (isotropic or anisotropic).

Excluding homography, the overall system can be described by $(K, R, \mathbf{t})$. In particular, the parameters in $(R, \mathbf{t})$ called *extrinsic parameters* and consist of six parameters. The parameters in K is called *intrinsic parameters* and consists of five parameters. As a result, the system consists of a total of 11 parameters.

6.3 Camera Calibration

Determining the parameters given the image and scene points is called *camera calibration*. Among many, the three major approaches are: direct linear transformation (DLT) method (Dubrofsky 2007; Hartley and Zisserman 2004), Roger Y. Tsai algorithm (Tsai 1987), and Zhang's method (Zhang 2000).

The DLT supposes that $\{(x_k, y_k), (X_k, Y_k, Z_k)|k \in [1, K]\}$ is the set of 2D-3D pairs. From Equation (6.8),

$$x_k = \frac{c_{00}X_k + c_{01}Y_k + c_{02}Z_k + c_{03}}{c_{20}X_k + c_{21}Y_k + c_{22}Z_k + 1},$$

$$y_k = \frac{c_{10}X_k + c_{11}Y_k + c_{12}Z_k + c_{13}}{c_{20}X_k + c_{21}Y_k + c_{22}Z_k + 1}. \tag{6.14}$$

This equation becomes

$$x_k(c_{20}X_k + c_{21}Y_k + c_{22}Z_k + 1) = c_{00}X_k + c_{01}Y_k + c_{02}Z_k + c_{03},$$

$$y_k(c_{20}X_k + c_{21}Y_k + c_{22}Z_k + 1) = c_{10}X_k + c_{11}Y_k + c_{12}Z_k + c_{13}, \tag{6.15}$$

which can be solved by linear regression methods such as least squares or pseudo-inverse. Since 11 parameters are unknown and two equations are available per point, six points are sufficient, though more points may be better for making the system over-determined.

The parameters can be determined by solving nonlinear equations (Tsai 1987). The 2D coordinates are just a nonlinear function of its 3D coordinates, expressed with camera parameters:

$$x_k = f(X_k, Y_k, Z_k|K, R, T),$$

$$y_k = g(X_k, Y_k, Z_k|K, R, T), \tag{6.16}$$

where f and g are the nonlinear functions, derived from Equation (6.8). Consider that we are given N points in each of M images: $\{(x_i^j, y_i^j)|i \in [1, N], j \in [1, M]\}$. The parameters can be estimated by the nonlinear optimization:

$$\sum_{j=1}^{M}\sum_{i=1}^{N}(x_i^j - f(X_i, Y_i, Z_i|K, R, T))^2 + (y_i^j - g(X_i, Y_i, Z_i|K, R, T))^2. \tag{6.17}$$

Once we have recovered the numerical form of the camera matrix, we still have to separate out the intrinsic and extrinsic parameters. This problem is not an estimation problem but a matrix decomposition such as SVD. The parameters can also be obtained by using the homography method (Zhang 2000). Suppose the corresponding pairs are $\mathbf{x}$ and $\mathbf{X}$.

$$\mathbf{x} = K[R|\mathbf{t}]\mathbf{X}. \tag{6.18}$$

Let $Z = 0$, then

$$\begin{bmatrix} x \\ y \\ 1 \end{bmatrix} = K[\,\mathbf{r}_1 \quad \mathbf{r}_2 \quad \mathbf{r}_3 \quad \mathbf{t}\,] \begin{bmatrix} X \\ Y \\ Z \\ 1 \end{bmatrix} = K[\,\mathbf{r}_1 \quad \mathbf{r}_2 \quad \mathbf{t}\,] \begin{bmatrix} X \\ Y \\ 1 \end{bmatrix}. \tag{6.19}$$

Therefore, the homography is $H = K[\mathbf{r}_1, \mathbf{r}_2, \mathbf{t}]$, which can be estimated by the given N corresponding pairs:

$$H = \arg\min_H \sum_{i=1}^{N} \|\mathbf{x}_i - H\mathbf{X}_i\|^2. \tag{6.20}$$

Given the homography, $H = [\mathbf{h}_1, \mathbf{h}_2, \mathbf{h}_3]$, we can compute the intrinsic parameters by solving

$$[\,\mathbf{h}_1 \quad \mathbf{h}_2 \quad \mathbf{h}_3\,] = \lambda K[\,\mathbf{r}_1 \quad \mathbf{r}_2 \quad \mathbf{t}\,], \tag{6.21}$$

where λ is a scale factor. Since the rotation matrix R is orthonormal, $\mathbf{r}_1$ and $\mathbf{r}_2$ in Equation (6.21) satisfy

$$\mathbf{r}_1^T\mathbf{r}_2 = \mathbf{h}_1^T K^{-T} K^{-1} \mathbf{h}_2 = 0. \tag{6.22}$$

Let $B = K^{-T}K^{-1}$, then from Equation (6.18), B becomes

$$B = \begin{bmatrix} \frac{1}{\alpha^2} & -\frac{\gamma}{\alpha^2\beta} & \frac{v_0\gamma - u_0\beta}{\alpha^2\beta} \\ -\frac{\gamma}{\alpha^2\beta} & \frac{\gamma^2}{\alpha^2\beta^2} + \frac{1}{\beta^2} & -\frac{\gamma(v_0\gamma - u_0\beta)}{\alpha^2\beta^2} - \frac{v_0}{\beta^2} \\ \frac{v_0\gamma - u_0\beta}{\alpha^2\beta} & -\frac{\gamma(v_0\gamma - u_0\beta)}{\alpha^2\beta^2} - \frac{v_0}{\beta^2} & \frac{(v_0\gamma - u_0\beta)^2}{\alpha^2\beta^2} + \frac{v_0}{\beta^2} + 1 \end{bmatrix}. \tag{6.23}$$

Now let's simplify Equation (6.21) by vector products. Since B is symmetric, we can represent it by the upper diagonal elements, $\mathbf{b} = [B_{11}, B_{12}, B_{22}, B_{13}, B_{23}, B_{33}]^T$. For H, define $\mathbf{h} = [h_{11}h_{21}, h_{11}h_{22} + h_{12}h_{21}, h_{12}h_{22}, h_{13}h_{21} + h_{11}h_{23}, h_{13}h_{22} + h_{12}h_{23}]^T$. Then, Equation (6.22) becomes

$$\mathbf{h}^T\mathbf{b} = 0. \tag{6.24}$$

From this, we obtain the following variables first,

$$\begin{aligned} v_0 &= (B_{12}B_{13} - B_{11}B_{23}) / \left(B_{11}B_{22} - B_{12}^2\right), \\ \lambda &= B_{33} - \left[B_{13}^2 + v_0(B_{12}B_{13} - B_{11}B_{23})\right] / B_{11}, \end{aligned} \tag{6.25}$$

then the remaining parameters,

$$\alpha = \sqrt{\lambda / B_{11}}, \quad \gamma = -B_{12}\alpha^2/\lambda, \quad u_0 = \gamma v_0/\beta - B_{13}\alpha^2/\lambda. \tag{6.26}$$

Next, let's solve for the extrinsic parameters. From Equation (6.21),

$$\mathbf{r}_1 = \lambda K^{-1}\mathbf{h}_1, \mathbf{r}_2 = \lambda K^{-1}\mathbf{h}_2, \mathbf{r}_3 = \mathbf{r} \times \mathbf{r}_2, \mathbf{t} = \lambda K^{-1}\mathbf{h}_3. \tag{6.27}$$

Besides, we may need more parameters, such as radial distortion (de Villiers *et al.* 2010; Weng *et al.* 1992). Let (x, y) and (x', y') be ideal and real image coordinates. Let (x, y) be ideal normalized image coordinates and (x', y') be real normalized image coordinates. Then, we have

$$\begin{aligned} x' &= x + x\left[k_1(x^2+y^2) + k_2(x^2+y^2)^2\right], \\ y' &= y + y\left[k_1(x^2+y^2) + k_2(x^2+y^2)^2\right], \end{aligned} \tag{6.28}$$

where k_1 and k_2 are distortion parameters. In the pixel domain, (u, v) is the ideal pixel image coordinates and (u', v') is real observed image coordinates. Then,

$$\begin{aligned} u' &= u + (u - u_0)\left[k_1(x^2+y^2) + k_2(x^2+y^2)^2\right], \\ v' &= v + (v - v_0)\left[k_1(x^2+y^2) + k_2(x^2+y^2)^2\right]. \end{aligned} \tag{6.29}$$

This equation can be represented by $D\mathbf{k} = \mathbf{d}$, or

$$\begin{bmatrix} (u-u_0)(x^2+y^2) & (u-u_0)(x^2+y^2)^2 \\ (v-v_0(x^2+y^2) & (v-v_0)(x^2+y^2)^2 \end{bmatrix} \begin{bmatrix} k_1 \\ k_2 \end{bmatrix} = \begin{bmatrix} u'-u \\ v'-v \end{bmatrix}. \tag{6.30}$$

The pseudo-inverse is $\mathbf{k} = (D^T D)^{-1} D^T \mathbf{d}$. If we are given M images with N points each, we can solve this by linear least squares estimation (LLSE). Combining the homography and the distortions, we have the complete LLSE:

$$\sum_{i=1}^{N} \sum_{j=1}^{M} \|\mathbf{x}_{ij} - \hat{x}(A, k_1, k_2, R_i, t_i, \mathbf{X}_j)\|^2, \tag{6.31}$$

where $\hat{x}$ means the projective transform with the intrinsic and extrinsic parameters.

There has been extensive research on camera calibration (Brahmachari and Sarkar 2013; Chin *et al.* 2009; Hartley and Li 2012; Ni *et al.* 2009; Rozenfeld and Shimshoni 2005; Zheng *et al.* 2011). OpenCV (OpenCV 2013) contains standard camera calibration programs that find intrinsic and extrinsic parameters, together with distortions.

6.4 Correspondence Geometry

If more than two cameras are used to capture the same scene, there exist some constraints for the points in the same image and for the corresponding points in different images. Such constraints play key roles in restoring three-dimensional information.

In stereo vision, the major problems are classified into these three: correspondence geometry, camera geometry, and scene geometry. The correspondence problem is to study the topic: given an image point

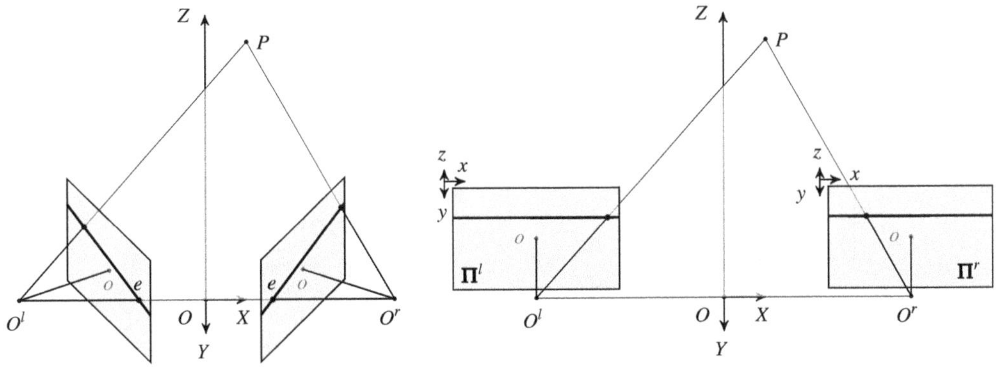

(a) Convergent system (b) Rectified system

Figure 6.3 Stereo camera systems: convergent and rectified systems

in the first view, how does it constrain the corresponding point in the second view? The camera geometry is the problem: given a set of corresponding points, what are the cameras matrices for the two views? The scene geometry is the problem: given corresponding image points and cameras matrices, what is the position of the point in 3D? To answer such problems, we have to understand the geometry of the stereo system.

The binocular vision system consists of two cameras aligned as in Figure 6.3(a). The points, O^l and O^r, are respectively the projection centers of the left and right cameras. The common focal length is f. In this alignment, a point P forms a plane PO^lO^r, which is called the *epiplane*. The lines on the images, called *epipolar lines*, are the projection of the *pencil* of planes passing through the optical centers. Therefore, $\mathbf{l}^l = PO^lO^r \cap \mathbf{\Pi}^l$ and $\mathbf{l}^r = PO^lO^r \cap \mathbf{\Pi}^r$. The point $\mathbf{e}$, called the *epipole*, is where the projection center of the other camera is mapped on the image plane. Therefore, $\mathbf{e}_l = \overline{O^lO^r} \cap \mathbf{\Pi}^l$ and $\mathbf{e}_r = \overline{O^lO^r} \cap \mathbf{\Pi}^r$.

If the camera system is aligned in such a way that two optical axes are parallel, the system looks like Figure 6.3(b). The images in this system are called *rectified images*, which are often the starting point of the stereo matching. The image planes are coplanar and the epipolar lines are collinear and thus the search for matching points becomes a one-dimensional search problem. The rectification process is to convert the convergent system to the rectified system by coordinate transformations.

Let's observe how different points in 3-space generate different epipolar lines in the image convergent and rectified planes. Figure 6.4 shows the epipolar lines generated by the points at different heights. In the rectified image, the epipolar lines are always parallel and the epipole is at infinity at the same height, $\mathbf{e}^l = \mathbf{e}^r = \infty$. Furthermore, the row of an epipolar line is the same as the y-axis of the camera image. In such a rectified system, a 3-space point appears on both epipolar lines which are in the same epiplane. On the other hand, in a convergent system, all the epipolar lines pass through an epipole, $\mathbf{e}$, forming a set of rays. In this system, too, an object point appears on the corresponding epipolar lines in both images.

Let's derive the relationship between corresponding points (Figure 6.5). In this figure, $\mathbf{p}_l$ and $\mathbf{p}_r$ are a conjugate pair, $\mathbf{l}_l$ and $\mathbf{l}_r$ are epipolar lines, and $\mathbf{e}_l$ and $\mathbf{e}_r$ are epipoles. A point P is observed as $\mathbf{P}_l$ and $\mathbf{P}_r$ on the left and right cameras and $\mathbf{p}_l$ and $\mathbf{p}_r$ on the left and right images, respectively. The object point and the image point are all related by

$$\mathbf{p}_l = \frac{f}{Z_l}\mathbf{P}_l, \quad \mathbf{p}_r = \frac{f}{Z_r}\mathbf{P}_r. \tag{6.32}$$

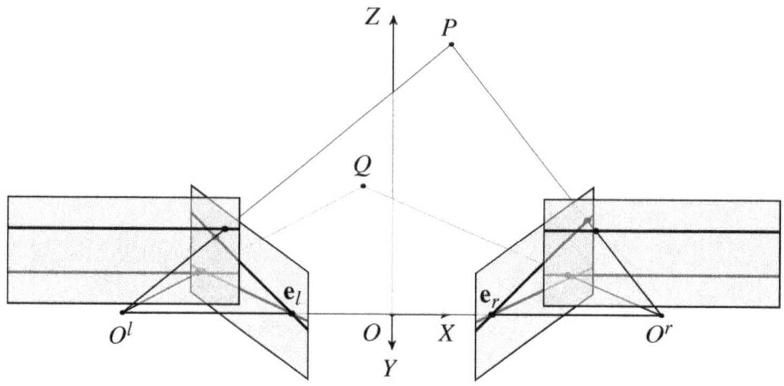

Figure 6.4 Epiplanes, epipolar lines, and epipoles for two points

If the right system is translated and rotated with respect to the left system by the rotation matrix R and translation vector $\mathbf{t} = (t_x, t_y, t_z)^T$, then the vector on the left system is observed in the right system as

$$\mathbf{P}_r = R(\mathbf{P}_l - \mathbf{t}). \tag{6.33}$$

Since the three vectors, $\mathbf{P}_l - \mathbf{t}$, $\mathbf{t}$, and $\mathbf{P}_l$, are all on the same epiplane, the following relationship must hold:

$$(\mathbf{P}_l - \mathbf{t})^T \mathbf{t} \times \mathbf{P}_l = 0. \tag{6.34}$$

Since $R^T R = I$,

$$(\mathbf{P}_l - \mathbf{t})^T R^T R \mathbf{t} \times \mathbf{P}_l = 0. \tag{6.35}$$

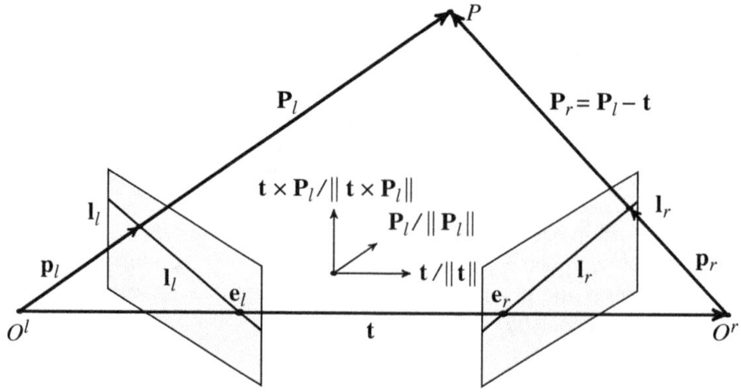

Figure 6.5 The geometry of two camera system

Combining the front two factors into one, we have

$$(R(\mathbf{P}_l - \mathbf{t}))^T R\mathbf{t} \times \mathbf{P}_l = 0, \tag{6.36}$$

which with Equation (6.33) becomes

$$\mathbf{P}_r^T R\mathbf{t} \times \mathbf{P}_l = 0. \tag{6.37}$$

Substituting Equation (6.32) into (6.37) yields

$$\mathbf{p}_r^T E\mathbf{p}_l = 0, \quad \text{where } E = R[\mathbf{t}]_\times, \quad [\mathbf{t}]_\times \triangleq \begin{bmatrix} 0 & -t_z & t_y \\ t_z & 0 & -t_x \\ -t_y & t_x & 0 \end{bmatrix}, \tag{6.38}$$

where $[\mathbf{t}]_\times$ is a skew symmetric matrix representing the cross product-conversion to matrix representation of the cross product with $\mathbf{t}$. (We sometimes use T instead of $[\mathbf{t}]_\times$.) That is, for two vectors $\mathbf{a}$ and $\mathbf{b}$, the cross product becomes $\mathbf{a} \times \mathbf{b} = [\mathbf{a}]_\times \mathbf{b}$. The relationship, called *essential matrix* E, was first derived by (Longuet-Higgins 1981). Conceptually, this equation means that in camera images the corresponding points must be on the same epipolar line. For a pair of conjugate points, (x_l, y_l) and (x_r, y_r), in the image plane, this equation specifies that $y_l = y_r$ but doesn't specify the relation between x_l and x_r.

The essential matrix encodes information on the extrinsic parameters only. The essential matrix explains that the conjugates pair, $\mathbf{p}_l$ and $\mathbf{p}_r$, is on the epipolar lines, $\mathbf{l}_l = E^T\mathbf{p}_r$ and $\mathbf{l}_r = E\mathbf{p}_l$, we have $\mathbf{p}_r^T\mathbf{l}_r = 0$ and $\mathbf{l}_l^T\mathbf{p}_l = 0$. Since $\mathbf{p}_r^T E\mathbf{e}_l = 0$ and $\mathbf{e}_r^T F\mathbf{p}_l = 0$ hold for all $\mathbf{p}_r$ and $\mathbf{p}_l$, respectively, $E\mathbf{e}_l = 0$ and $E^T\mathbf{e}_r = 0$. It has rank 2 since R is full rank but $[t]_\times$ is rank 2. Its two nonsingular values are equal. The degree of freedom is 5. The essential matrix can be decomposed into the product of epipole and homography. Let

$$\mathbf{p}_r = H\mathbf{p}_l, \tag{6.39}$$

with the homography, H. Then, we get

$$\begin{aligned} \mathbf{l}_r &= E\mathbf{p}_l \\ &= [\mathbf{e}_r]_\times \mathbf{p}_r = [\mathbf{e}_r]_\times H\mathbf{p}_l. \end{aligned} \tag{6.40}$$

Repeating for the epipolar line on the left image plane, we have

$$E = [\mathbf{e}_r]_\times H, \quad E^T = [\mathbf{e}_l]_\times H^{-1}. \tag{6.41}$$

(See the problems at the end of this chapter.)

Suppose that $\mathbf{p} = [u, v, 1]^T$ and $\mathbf{p}' = [u', v', 1]^T$ are a corresponding pair. For $N \geq 8$ points, the essential matrix can be obtained by

$$E^\star = \arg\min_E \sum_{k=1}^N \mathbf{p}^T E\mathbf{p}', \quad s.t. \quad \|E\|^2 = 1. \tag{6.42}$$

This can be transformed to the linear least squares estimation (LLSE). For the points and essential matrix, define the vectors: $\mathbf{x} = (uu', uv', u, vu', vv', v, u', v', 1)^T$ and $\mathbf{e} = (e_{11}, e_{12}, e_{13}, e_{21}, e_{22}, e_{23}, e_{31}, e_{32}, 1)^T$.

Then, Equation (6.38) becomes $\mathbf{x}^T\mathbf{e} = 0$. For $N \geq 8$ points, define $X = (\mathbf{x}_1, \ldots, \mathbf{x}_N)$. Then, the essential matrix can be estimated by

$$E = \arg\min_{\mathbf{e}} \|X^T\mathbf{e}\|^2. \tag{6.43}$$

In this formula, the solution is the eigenvector associated with the smallest eigenvalue of $\mathbf{e}^T\mathbf{e}$.

For the uncalibrated camera, this equation must be expressed in terms with the conjugate points in the pixel planes. Since the mapping from camera image to the pixel plane can be specified by a shifted, rotated, and scaled transformation by the calibration matrix K, the image point $\mathbf{p}$ and the pixel coordinates $\mathbf{q}$ are related by

$$\mathbf{q}_l = K_l\mathbf{p}_l, \quad \mathbf{q}_r = K_r\mathbf{p}_r. \tag{6.44}$$

Putting this into Equation (6.38) yields

$$\mathbf{q}_r^T F\mathbf{q}_l = 0, \quad \text{where } F = K_r^{-1}EK_l^{-1}. \tag{6.45}$$

This relation, called the *fundamental matrix*, was first derived by Luong (Faugeras *et al.* 1992; Luong and Faugeras 1996). Conceptually, this relationship means that in pixel images the corresponding points must be located on the corresponding epipolar lines. Likewise the essential matrix, for a pair of conjugate points, (x_l, y_l) and (x_r, y_r), in the pixel plane, this equation specifies that $y_l = y_r$ but doesn't specify the relation between x_l and x_r. (See the problems at the end of this chapter.)

As opposed to the essential matrix, the fundamental matrix expresses some important properties of the uncalibrated camera system. The fundamental matrix encodes information both the intrinsic and extrinsic parameters. It has rank 2 due to E. It has seven degrees of freedom also up to scale. The lines $F\mathbf{q}_l$ and $F^T\mathbf{q}_r$ represent the epipolar lines associated with $\mathbf{p}_l$ and $\mathbf{p}_r$, respectively. Also, the epipoles are null points, satisfying $F\mathbf{e}_l = 0$ and $F^T\mathbf{e}_r = 0$.

6.5 Camera Geometry

The eight-point algorithm (Chojnacki and Brooks 2007; Hartley 1997; Longuet-Higgins 1981) is to determine the parameters with the known eight conjugate pairs. Suppose that $\mathbf{q} = (u, v)$ and $\mathbf{q}' = (u'v')$ are a corresponding pair. For $N \geq 8$ points, the fundamental matrix can be obtained by

$$F = \arg\min_{F} \sum_{k=1}^{N} \mathbf{q}^T F\mathbf{q}', \quad s.t. \|F\|^2 = 1. \tag{6.46}$$

This can be transformed to the linear least squares estimation (LLSE). For the points and essential matrix, define the vectors: $\mathbf{x} = (uu', uv', u, vu', vv', v, u', v', 1)^T$ and $\mathbf{f} = (f_{11}, f_{12}, f_{13}, f_{21}, f_{22}, f_{23}, f_{31}, f_{32}, 1)^T$. Then, Equation (6.38) becomes $\mathbf{x}^T\mathbf{f} = 0$. For $N \geq 8$ points, define $X = (\mathbf{x}_1, \ldots, \mathbf{x}_N)$. Then, the fundamental matrix can be estimated by

$$F^{\star} = \arg\min_{\mathbf{f}} \|X^T\mathbf{f}\|^2. \tag{6.47}$$

In this formula, the solution is the eigenvector associated with the smallest eigenvalue of $\mathbf{f}^T\mathbf{f}$.

For a full description of the perspective projection and the relationship between cameras, all the matrices (i.e. C, E and finally R and $[t_x]$) must be recovered, starting from F. From the recovered F, we can compute the singular value decomposition (SVD):

$$F = U\Sigma V, \quad \Sigma = diag(\sigma_1, \sigma_2, \sigma_3), \tag{6.48}$$

where U and V are lower and upper triangular matrices, respectively. We project the fundamental matrix onto the essential manifold:

$$F = U\Sigma' V^T, \quad \Sigma' = diag(\sigma_1, \sigma_2, 0). \tag{6.49}$$

The SVD of F contains the information on epipoles. The epipole $\mathbf{e}$ is a null vector, satisfying $F\mathbf{e}_l = 0$. Therefore, the epipole is the column of V^T corresponding to the null singular value, $V^T = (\mathbf{v}_1, \mathbf{v}_2, \mathbf{e}_l)$. Similarly, $\mathbf{e}_r$ satisfies $F^T\mathbf{e}_r = 0$ and thus the column of U^T corresponding to the null singular value, $U^T = (\mathbf{u}_1, \mathbf{u}_2, \mathbf{e}_r)$.

From the fundamental matrix, we obtain the essential matrix,

$$E = Udiag(\sigma, \sigma, 0)V^T, \tag{6.50}$$

where $\sigma = (\sigma_1 + \sigma_2)/2$. The obtained essential matrix minimizes the Frobenius distance $\|E - F\|^2$.

Once the essential matrix is obtained, the other matrices, $E = TR$, can be recovered by SVD (Hartley and Zisserman 2004):

$$E = U\Sigma V^T, \tag{6.51}$$

where $\Sigma = diag(1, 1, 0)$. Let's define the skew symmetric matrix, $W^{-1} = W^T$:

$$W = \begin{bmatrix} 0 & -1 & 0 \\ 1 & 0 & 0 \\ 0 & 0 & 1 \end{bmatrix}, \quad W^T = \begin{bmatrix} 0 & 1 & 0 \\ -1 & 0 & 0 \\ 0 & 0 & 1 \end{bmatrix}. \tag{6.52}$$

Then, there are two solutions:

$$\begin{aligned} (T_1, R_1) &= (VW\Sigma V^T, UWV^T), \\ (T_2, R_2) &= (VW^T\Sigma V^T, UW^T V^T). \end{aligned} \tag{6.53}$$

6.6 Scene Geometry

The scene geometry problem is to find $\mathbf{X}$, given E and the corresponding pair, $\mathbf{x}_l$ and $\mathbf{x}_r$. According to (Longuet-Higgins 1981), this problem can be solved as follows.

Let $R = (\mathbf{r}_1^T, \mathbf{r}_2^T, \mathbf{r}_3^T)^T$. For simplicity, consider that the world coordinates and the left camera coordinates coincide. The camera systems are normalized, with the essential matrix $(R|\mathbf{t})$ and the corresponding pair is given by $\tilde{\mathbf{x}}_l$ and $\tilde{\mathbf{x}}_r$. Between the recovered scene points, $\tilde{\mathbf{X}}_1$ and $\tilde{\mathbf{X}}_r$, the following relationship holds:

$$\tilde{\mathbf{X}}_r = R(\tilde{\mathbf{X}}_l - \mathbf{t}). \tag{6.54}$$

The components are

$$X_r = \mathbf{r}_1(\tilde{\mathbf{X}}_l - \mathbf{t}), \quad Y_r = \mathbf{r}_2(\tilde{\mathbf{X}}_l - \mathbf{t}), \quad Z_r = \mathbf{r}_3(\tilde{\mathbf{X}}_l - \mathbf{t}). \tag{6.55}$$

Then, the image coordinates are $\mathbf{x}_r = K\tilde{\mathbf{X}}_r$:

$$x_r = \frac{X_r}{Z_r} = \frac{X_r/Z_l}{Z_r/Z_l} = \frac{\mathbf{r}_1(\mathbf{x}_l - \mathbf{t}/Z_l)}{\mathbf{r}_3(\mathbf{x}_l - \mathbf{t}/Z_l)}, \quad y_r = \frac{Y_r}{Z_r} = \frac{Y_r/Z_l}{Z_r/Z_l} = \frac{\mathbf{r}_2(\mathbf{x}_l - \mathbf{t}/Z_l)}{\mathbf{r}_3(\mathbf{x}_l - \mathbf{t}/Z_l)}. \tag{6.56}$$

From this, we get one element of the 3D coordinates:

$$Z_l = f\frac{(\mathbf{r}_1 - x_r\mathbf{r}_3)\mathbf{t}}{(\mathbf{r}_1 - x_r\mathbf{r}_3)\mathbf{x}_l}, \quad Z_l = f\frac{(\mathbf{r}_1 - y_r\mathbf{r}_3)\mathbf{t}}{(\mathbf{r}_1 - y_r\mathbf{r}_3)\mathbf{x}_l}. \tag{6.57}$$

Here, the scale factor f is restored. As a last step, the remaining element can be recovered by

$$\begin{bmatrix} X_l \\ Y_l \end{bmatrix} = Z_l \begin{bmatrix} x_l \\ y_l \end{bmatrix}. \tag{6.58}$$

Therefore, $\tilde{\mathbf{X}}$ is recovered from $\tilde{\mathbf{x}}_l$ and $\tilde{\mathbf{x}}_r$, with the help of $(R|\mathbf{t})$). Due to the inaccurate corresponding pair, Z_l in Equation (6.57) may not be the same. In actual algorithm, the estimation error must be minimized for more than one corresponding pairs.

There is a common case, where the camera is positioned at $(B, 0, 0)$, tilted with θ with respect to the baseline. The two cameras are focused at the point C, called the *subject distance*. In this common case, we have the explicit solution for the 3D position (Figure 6.6). The right camera is shifted by $\mathbf{t} = (B, 0, 0)$ and rotated by

$$R = \begin{bmatrix} \sin\theta & 0 & -\cos\theta \\ 0 & 1 & 0 \\ \cos\theta & 0 & \sin\theta \end{bmatrix}, \quad \mathbf{t} = (B, 0, 0)^T, \tag{6.59}$$

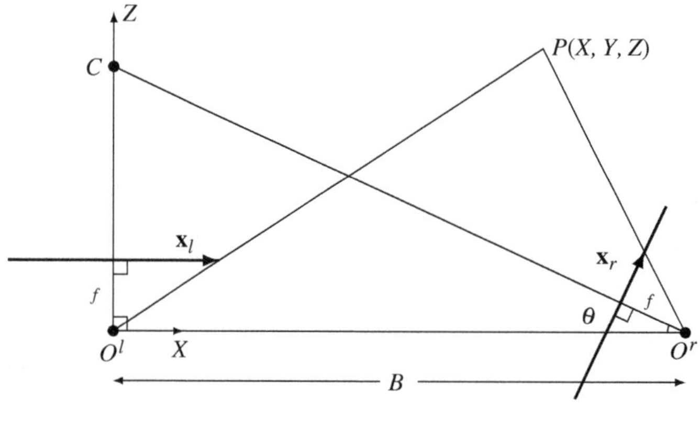

Figure 6.6 Cameras on the same plane: world and left camera coordinates coincide. The cameras are focused at the common point C (f: focal length and B: baseline.)

where θ is the angle between the optical axis and the baseline. In that case, Equation (6.58) is reduced to

$$X_l = x_l \frac{f(\sin\theta - x_r\cos\theta)B}{x_l(\sin\theta - x_r\cos\theta) - (\cos\theta + x_r\sin\theta)},$$
$$Y_l = y_l \frac{f(\sin\theta - x_r\cos\theta)B}{x_l(\sin\theta - x_r\cos\theta) - (\cos\theta + x_r\sin\theta)},$$
$$Z_l = \frac{f(\sin\theta - x_r\cos\theta)B}{x_l(\sin\theta - x_r\cos\theta) - (\cos\theta + x_r\sin\theta)}. \quad (6.60)$$

6.7 Rectification

In convergent systems, finding corresponding points is a 2D search problem because the epipolar lines are radiating lines on the plane. Rectification is a warping process via perspective transformation so that epipolar lines are horizontal. In a rectified system, the problem is a 1D search problem because the epipolar lines are all horizontally parallel. As such most stereo matching algorithms start with the premise: epipolar lines in the rectified system.

To see the relationship between the two systems, look at Figure 6.7. In this system, a set of points, $\{P, O^l, O^r\}$, constructs an epiplane, PO^lO^r, which intersect the planes of the convergent systems, producing epipolar lines in slanted directions. The rectified system can be achieved by rotating the convergent system around the projection center maintaining the focal length unchanged. The condition for the rotation matrix R is that in the rotated planes the epipolar lines should be collinear.

Let $\mathbf{x}_r^T F \mathbf{x}_l = 0$. The problem is to find homographies H_l and H_r such that $\mathbf{y}_l = H_l\mathbf{x}_l$ and $\mathbf{y}_r = H_r\mathbf{x}_r$, which satisfies $\mathbf{y}_r^T F' \mathbf{y}_l = 0$. Solving this, we obtain

$$F'H^{-T}FH^{-1} = \begin{bmatrix} 0 & 0 & 0 \\ 0 & 0 & -1 \\ 0 & 1 & 0 \end{bmatrix}, \quad (6.61)$$

for the parallel camera.

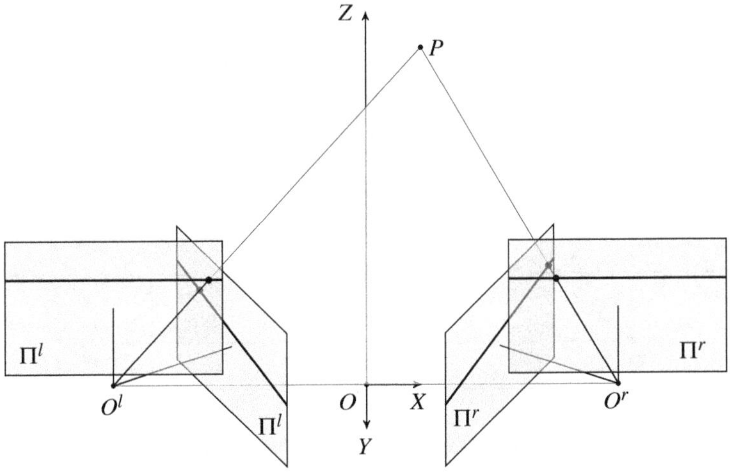

Figure 6.7 Two camera systems: rectified and convergent cameras

There are basically three algorithms for image rectification: planar rectification (Fusiello *et al.* 2000; Trucco and Verri 1998), cylindrical rectification (Oram 2001), and polar rectification (Pollefeys *et al.* 1999). Planar rectification is as follows.

Assume that the system is normalized and the extrinsic parameters $[R|\mathbf{t}]$ are given. The first step is to rotate the left image plane so that the epipole goes to infinity along the horizontal line. Since the rotation matrix is orthonormal, only one vector can be specified and thereby we can derive the other two. The starting vector is conveniently decided by the epipole which is a foreshortened vector of the translation $\mathbf{t}$ between two camera coordinates. Thus, let the first vector, $\mathbf{u} = \mathbf{t}/\|\mathbf{t}\|$. The other two vectors can be built as follows:

$$R^T_{rect} = \left[\mathbf{u}, \mathbf{u}_\perp, \mathbf{u} \times \mathbf{u}_\perp\right], \tag{6.62}$$

where $\mathbf{u}_\perp$ must satisfy $\mathbf{u} \times \mathbf{u}_\perp$ and the z-axis. Set the rotation matrices $R_l = R_{rect}$ and $R_r = RR_{rect}$ for the left and right cameras. Once R_l and R_r are obtained, the points, $\mathbf{q}$, in the rectified system can be obtained from the points, $\mathbf{p}$, in the convergent system, according to

$$\mathbf{q}_l = \frac{f}{z_l} R_l \mathbf{p}_l, \quad \mathbf{q}_r = \frac{f}{z_r} R_r \mathbf{p}_r, \tag{6.63}$$

where $\mathbf{p}_l = (x_l, y_l, z_l)^T$ and $\mathbf{p}_r = (x_r, y_r, z_r)^T$. As a consequence of rectification, the epipoles are all located at infinity $\mathbf{e}^l = \mathbf{e}^r = \infty$ and the epipolar lines are collinear $\mathbf{l}^l \times \mathbf{l}^r = 0$.

After the transformation, the resulting image must be resampled and interpolated to compensate for the irregular empty pixels. (For further methods, refer to (Kang and Ho 2011; Loop and Zhang 1999; Miraldo and Araújo 2013; OpenCV 2013; Zhang 2000).)

The rectified system is a special case, shown in Figure 6.6. The right camera is positioned at $(B, 0, 0)$, in parallel with the left camera. This is the most common framework for a rectified system (Figure 6.8). The right camera is shifted by $\mathbf{t} = (B, 0, 0)$ and thus $\theta = \pi/2$ in Equation (6.60).

$$X_l = x_l \frac{fB}{x_l - x_r}, \quad Y_l = y_l \frac{fB}{x_l - x_r}, \quad Z_l = \frac{fB}{x_l - x_r}. \tag{6.64}$$

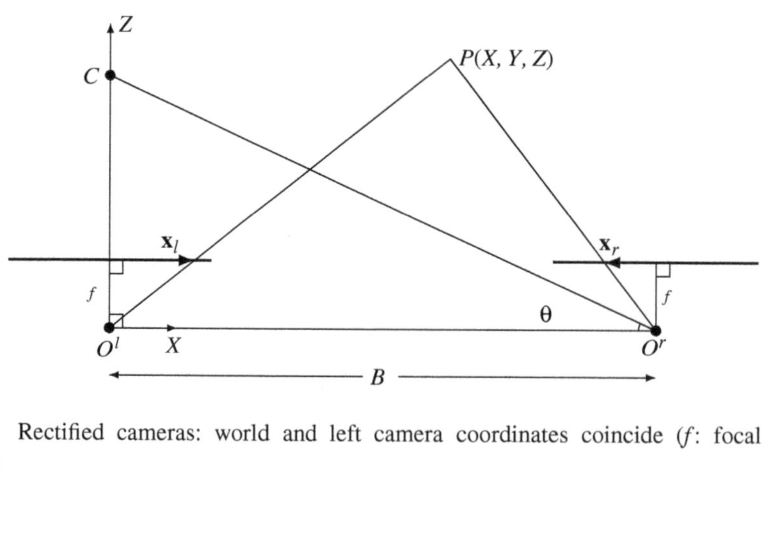

Figure 6.8 Rectified cameras: world and left camera coordinates coincide (f: focal length and B: baseline)

As a consequence of rectification, we have derived Equation (6.64). This standard configuration is called the *epipolar plane model*. In this alignment, a point P is projected on (x^l, y^l) for the left image and (x^r, y^r) for the right image. The two image points are collectively called *corresponding points*.

The Equations (6.64) can be conveniently described by the common variable,

$$d = x_l - x_r, \tag{6.65}$$

which is called *disparity*. It satisfies always $d \geq 0$ and configures the 3D positions by

$$X_l = x_l\frac{fB}{d}, \quad Y_l = y_l\frac{fB}{d}, \quad Z_l = \frac{fB}{d}. \tag{6.66}$$

Unlike in the rectified system, the depth is not a simple function of the disparity.

In Equation (6.66), the importance of disparity is self-evident; depth estimation becomes the disparity estimation problem. In this optical arrangement, $x^l \geq x^r \geq 0$. When we estimate the disparity, so-called *stereo matching*, one of the two image coordinates must be chosen as a reference. To distinguish the two cases, we define the *left* and *right disparities*:

$$d^l \triangleq d(x^l) = x^l - x^r, \quad d^r \triangleq d(x^r) = x^l - x^r. \tag{6.67}$$

Here, $d \geq 0$, regardless of the reference systems. Since the mapping between the conjugate pairs is not a one-to-one mapping due to occlusion, the two quantities, d^l and d^r, are not generally the same. Knowing both d^l and d^r may help to determine the occluding area.

As a special case, if the world coordinates are located between the two cameras, we get

$$(X, Y, Z) = \left(B\left(\frac{x_l}{d} - \frac{1}{2}\right), \frac{B}{d}y, \frac{f}{d}B\right) = \left(B\left(\frac{x_r}{d} + \frac{1}{2}\right), \frac{B}{d}y, \frac{f}{d}B\right). \tag{6.68}$$

If the world coordinates coincide with the left camera coordinates, the 3D position is

$$(X, Y, Z) = \left(\frac{B}{d}x_l, \frac{B}{d}y, \frac{f}{d}B\right) = \left(\frac{B}{d}x_r + B, \frac{B}{d}y, \frac{f}{d}B\right). \tag{6.69}$$

6.8 Appearance Models

In a simple rectified system, 3-D positions can be recovered by the disparity in Equation (6.66). Otherwise, the scene geometry can be recovered by the conjugate pairs as mentioned previously. Therefore, the remaining problem is to find the conjugate pairs, so-called *correspondence problem*, and represent them with the disparity map. The constraint is that the conjugate pairs are on the epipolar line, as specified by the fundamental matrix. Stereo matching is the method for solving the correspondence problem.

To fulfill this goal, we need some measures to decide the features, distance measures, inference method, and learning method. The feature is a representation of the matching pixels and generalized from local to global descriptors. The candidate pairs are compared with the distance measures or other correlation measures. The matching error is represented by a constrained optimization problem, which can be resolved by many inference methods. Finally, all the parameters included in the optimization problem are often estimated by learning methods. Owing to the diversity of stereo matching, some taxonomy has been tried so far (Scharstein and Szeliski 2002).

Numerous techniques and algorithms have been introduced for solving the constrained and unconstrained optimization of the stereo matching problem. However, there is still uncertainty of the bound of performance and the ground-truth solutions. The problem is not the technique for solving the problem but it seems to reside in the uncertainty in the modeling and the constraints for solving the ill-posed problem. In this context, instead of reviewing the vast methods, we focus on the more fundamental principles, called constraints, as they are close to the nature and building blocks of the optimization problem. The constraints together become the energy function, consisting of the data term D and the smoothness term V with the Lagrange multiplier:

$$E(d) = D(d) + \lambda V(d). \tag{6.70}$$

Here, the disparity on the image plane is represented collectively by the disparity map. Depending on the reference coordinates, the disparity can be defined as left, right, or center disparity. As mentioned in Chapter 5, the general form consists of the appearance and geometric constraints, which will be addressed in this and following sections.

As an example, the stereo images consist of a pair of left and right images (Middlebury 2013), as shown in Figure 6.9. The first two images are the left and right images. The next two images are the ground-truth disparity maps. The brightness shows the depth and the black segments show the pixels where the depth information is unavailable due to the sensor limitation. The ground truth is not the

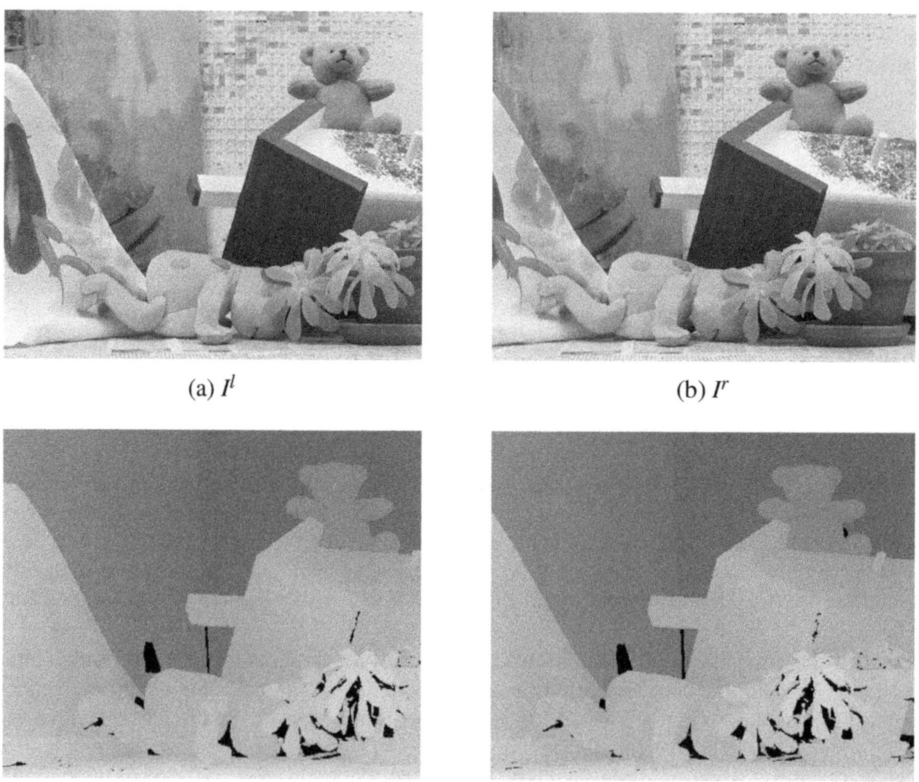

(a) I^l (b) I^r

(c) d^l: ground-truth (d) d^r: ground-truth

Figure 6.9 The stereo images and the ground-truth disparity map baseline of the disparity map but a reference, because a lot of the state-of-the-art algorithms, such as message passing, move-making, or LPR-based algorithms, tend to beat the ground truth.

The appearance model can be interpreted in many different ways: conservation laws, assignment error, observation error, unary potential, etc. Whatever the interpretation, the appearance model appears as a data term, relating the image and the putative disparity. One of the most prevailing laws is the *photometric constraints* (or intensity conservation or brightness conservation) of the corresponding points, which posits that the intensity of the same object is invariant in different views, assuming that they are spatially and temporally differentiable. This assumption results in the two equations:

$$I^l(x,y) = I^r(x + d^l(x,y), y), \quad I^r(x,y) = I^l(x + d^r(x,y), y). \tag{6.71}$$

For large variations of the disparity range, any series expansion of this function is inappropriate, unlike the series expansion that is possible for optical flow.

The two disparities are not always the same in general environment, because the disparities can be viewed as two different mappings. That is, d^l: $(x,y) \mapsto (x + d^l(x,y), y)$ and d^r: $(x,y) \mapsto (x + d^r(x,y), y)$. The error variance of the disparity is also increasingly deteriorated as the matching point approaches the boundary. For the right disparity, the mapping ranges is $x^r \in [0, N-1] \mapsto x^l \in [x^r, N-1]$, and for the left disparity, the mapping range is $x^l \in [0, N-1] \mapsto x^r \in [0, x^l]$. It is natural that the uncertainty of the disparity increases as the point approaches the boundary (right boundary for the right disparity and left boundary for the left disparity). On the other hand, the uncertainty is minimal on the other end of the boundary (left boundary for the right disparity and right boundary for the left disparity).

6.9 Fundamental Constraints

Unlike the epipolar hypothesis, other constraints are not always true. Although the brightness conservation is the natural choice of data term in the energy function, the problem is ill-posed in nature and thus needs more constraints to limit the search space. The geometric constraints fill such gaps, revealing the natural properties of the 3D geometry because a priori knowledge is possible. Because objects interact in time and space, there exist numerous geometric constraints. Let us examine the constraints, classified as space, time, frequency, segment, and 3D-based constraints.

Among the disparity-based constraints, the most fundamental constraint is the *smoothness constraint*, which means that the disparity of the neighboring pixels on an object surface must be as smooth (differentiable) as possible since the object surface is generally smooth. The smoothness measure assumes that if the surface is smooth, so do the disparity values:

$$\nabla Z(p) \longrightarrow \nabla d(p) = 0. \tag{6.72}$$

This premise is also very difficult to justify, because the disparity is the result of two different views for the same surface and thus the slope and the boundaries may affect the disparity in a very complicated manner. The are many variations of this form in terms of the derivative order, neighborhood size, and truncated values. Among many others, the linear truncation and Pott's model are the most popular methods. This constraint holds only when the neighbors are on the same surface but not across the boundary. Enforcing this constraint tends to make the boundary smooth, losing the sharp transition, even when sophisticated surface fitting methods (i.e. membrane or thin plate) are adopted. To achieve anisotropic diffusion, these constraints must be supported by the estimation of surface, boundary, and occlusion.

Another constraint is the *occlusion*, an invisible part of the scene for one of the two cameras. Examples are shown in Figure 6.10. The disparity maps contain occluding regions, particularly around object

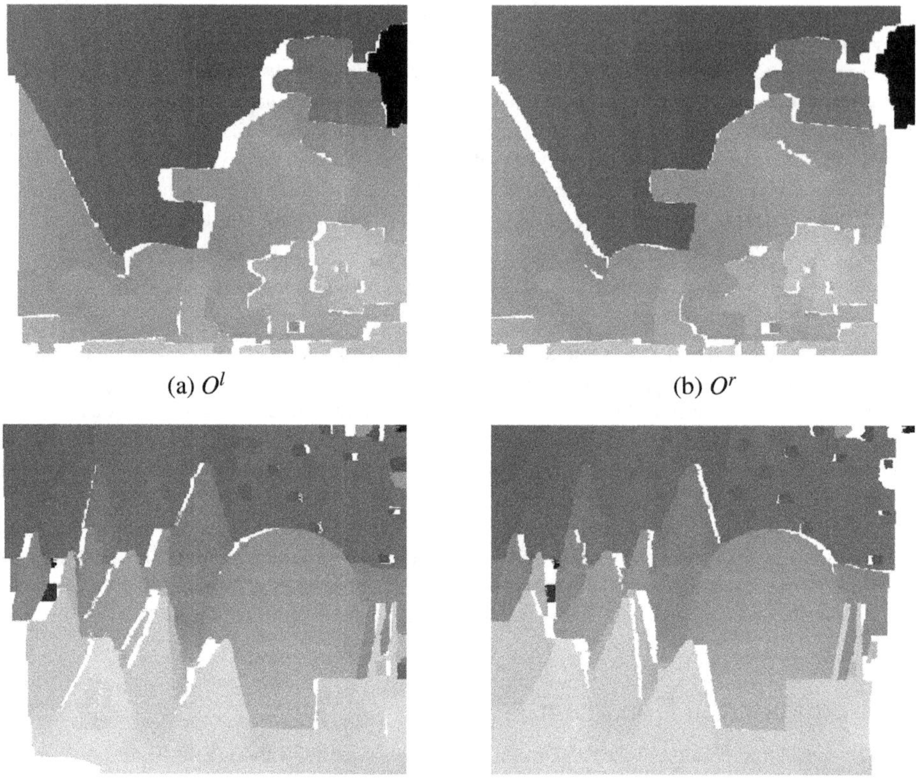

(a) O^l (b) O^r

(c) O^l (d) O^r

Figure 6.10 The occluding regions of the Teddy and Cones images

boundaries. Each disparity map, left or right, has its own occluding regions. Also, the occluding regions tend to be sparse and difficult to detect for small objects.

Knowing the occluding region can help the stereo matching drastically, because the smoothness can be suppressed in those areas, resulting in sharp boundaries and preventing smearing between adjacent regions. However, determining the occluding areas is a difficult problem, particularly when only one type of disparity map is available (Min and Sohn 2008; Tola *et al.* 2010; Zitnick and Kanade 2000).

Let $O(p)$ represent an indicator function for the occlusion at $p \in \mathcal{P}$. One way to define occlusion is to check the one-to-one correspondence (Bleyer and Gelautz 2007; Kolmogorov 2005; Lin and Tomasi 2003). We can classify the pixels into two classes: consistent (one-to-one mapping) and occlusion (many-to-one mapping). For d^l: $p \in \mathcal{P}^l \mapsto q \in \mathcal{P}^r$ and d^r: $p \in \mathcal{P}^r \mapsto q \in \mathcal{P}^l$, we define

$$O^l(p) = \begin{cases} 1, & d^l(p) \neq d^r(p - d^l(p)), \\ 0, & \text{otherwise.} \end{cases} \tag{6.73}$$

$$O^r(p) = \begin{cases} 1, & d^r(p) \neq d^l(p + d^r(p)), \\ 0, & \text{otherwise.} \end{cases} \tag{6.74}$$

The *left/right occlusion map* is an $M \times N$ binary image which is the collection of such sites. This constraint is also not strict, due to the slanted surfaces (Bleyer *et al.* 2010; Ogale and Aloimonos 2004; Sun *et al.* 2005). The occlusion can also be defined by (Woodford *et al.* 2009)

$$O^k(p) = \begin{cases} 1, & \exists q : p - d(p) = q - d(q) \cup d(p) < d(q)), \quad p, q \in \mathcal{P}^k, \\ 0, & \text{otherwise}, \end{cases} \tag{6.75}$$

where $k \in \{l, r\}$.

The possible preservation of order might be a strong constraint in stereo matching. The distribution of disparities between neighbor pixels may be arbitrary in principle, but the order of pixels tends to be preserved in both image and disparity map. To see this, consider two consecutive pixels, x^l and $x^l + 1$, which have disparities, $d^l(x^l)$ and $d^l(x^l + 1)$, respectively. The corresponding pixels are $x^r = x^l + d^l(x^l)$ and $x^r = x^l + 1 + d^l(x^l + 1)$, respectively. Since $x^l < x^l + 1$, it is natural that $x^l + d^l(x^l) \leq x^l + 1 + d^l(x^l + 1)$. From this thought, we can conclude that

$$\begin{cases} 0 \leq d^l(x^l) \leq 1 + d^l(x^l + 1), \\ 0 \leq d^r(x^r) \leq 1 + d^r(x^r + 1). \end{cases} \tag{6.76}$$

Unfortunately, this is a rough guide and not true even for smooth surfaces, where the order may not be preserved (Forsyth and Ponce 2003). The actual surface may be more than simple smoothness but very complicated, with many singular points.

Likewise the smoothness constraint, this constraint is also not strict. Around some narrow objects the background points may be viewed in reverse order. For a strong constraint on the local orders, *angular embedding* (Yu 2012) might be a potentially strong method.

6.10 Segment Constraints

The segmented image itself implies a certain kind of disparity information (Bleyer and Gelautz 2007; Deng *et al.* 2005; Hong and Chen 2008; Tao *et al.* 2001; Zitnick *et al.* 2004). Image segmentation turns the original image into several compact regions, called segments, where each of them consists of homogeneous pixels in image color, intensity, texture, or surface orientation. A segment provides primitive information, such as object color, size, location, or boundary. As such, segments possess potentially useful constraints for stereo matching in terms with boundary and surface. Furthermore, other vision modules, lower and higher levels, may help to provide information on the boundary and region, as a means of module integration.

It is conjectured that for a given segment, the variation of disparity is small. Let $S(p)$ denote the segment label for p. Then, within the segment, the following holds:

$$\nabla S(p) = 0 \longrightarrow \nabla d(p) = 0. \tag{6.77}$$

This constraint is similar to Equation (6.72) but is related with a lot of attributes other than the depth. Unfortunately, this conjecture may not be true in general. The same surface may be segmented into different segments due to brightness, color, and texture discontinuities.

The first useful clue obtained from the segment is the boundary constraint. Although not strict, there exist some correlations between boundaries of the segments, objects, and disparities. It is often the case that boundaries of segments coincide with boundaries of objects and thus the disparity boundaries. The segment boundary affects the disparity boundary, as a modified version of smoothness constraint:

$$\nabla S(p) \neq 0 \longrightarrow \nabla d(p) \neq 0. \tag{6.78}$$

This constraint can also be used in either the left or right disparity, depending which image plane is used as reference.

Next comes the planar constraint, which focuses on the surfaces instead of the boundary. The underlying concept is that there exist some correlations between segment surface, object surface, and disparity surface. The idea is to fit the segment with surface model and match with that of the disparity. Given the surface model, $f(S(p))$, the problem is to match to that of the disparity:

$$d(p) = f(S(p)). \tag{6.79}$$

This can be embedded into the energy function as an integration of local neighborhood error. In actual algorithms, the region is over-segmented, fitted, and merged into larger ones to make the disparity representation more compact.

So far, we have considered the information which is available from the given images and videos. Besides this intrinsic information, a lot of extrinsic information may be available through internet image repositories or web videos, as evidenced by the Big Data research. In such places, videos and images are usually tagged with a lot of information such as place, time, person, objects, and so on. In addition, algorithms for representation and extraction algorithms on person, object, or action provide multimodal information for the constraints on object and connectivity.

6.11 Constraints in Discrete Space

The ultimate goal of the stereo matching is to interpret the geometry of the objects in 3D space, by measuring the relative depths of the surfaces and their occluding relationship. This scene-centered view naturally assumes the conjecture – continuous space. There is another dual concept, namely view-centered. When viewed in the digital image, the scene is observed only in the two properties: discrete in space, time, and intensities. Since the image is defined only on a discrete plane, space must also be considered discrete or quantized from the beginning. Spaces that are not observed cannot be recovered in principle and thus must be excluded from consideration. This concept may limit the the search space to the observable space only, a discrete space. In this manner, the search space becomes very compact and faithful to the measurement.

Look at Figure 6.11(a), which depicts image pixels and rays within a *field of view* (FOV), that is defined by an optical system. In this figure, observable space is defined by a set of rays passing through the optical center O and image pixels. Positions that are not located on the rays are not observable or partially integrated into the rays via imaging system. For an image with N pixels width, only N rays can be observed. However, the ray is continuous and all the points on it is observable.

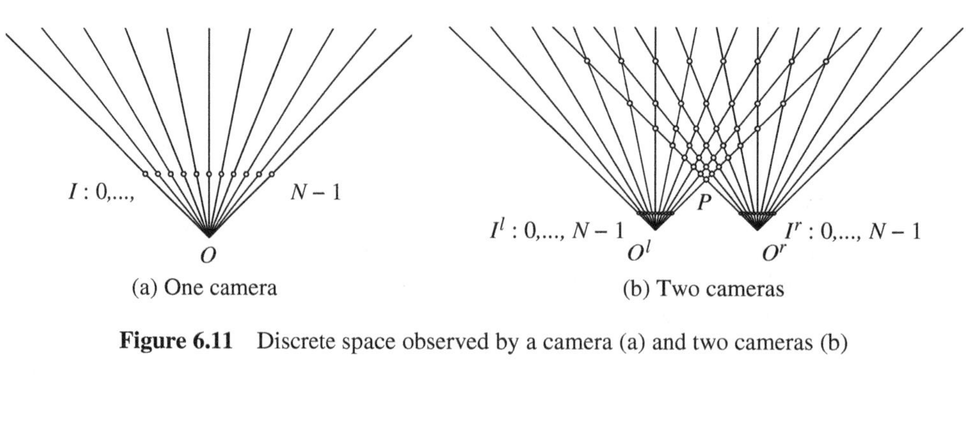

Figure 6.11 Discrete space observed by a camera (a) and two cameras (b)

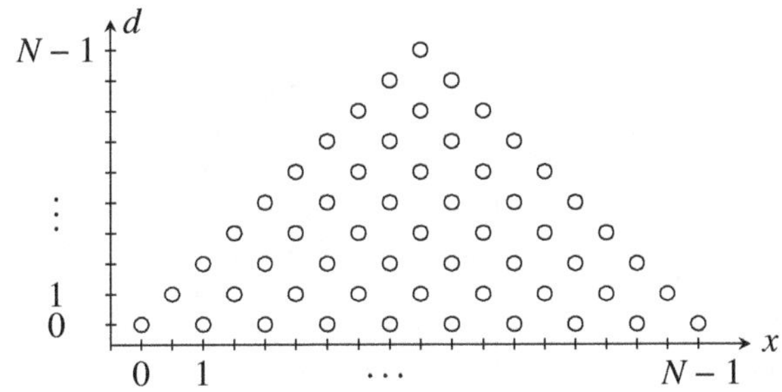

Figure 6.12 The observable space is a discrete triangle. The point at infinity is mapped to the zero disparity

If two cameras are introduced, as shown in Figure 6.11(b), the observable space becomes even smaller because the space consists of the set of intersecting points of the two rays. Now, only the discrete points on a ray are observable and thus the observable space is a discrete cone. The point, P, indicates the nearest position, where the disparity is maximal, $D_{max} = N - 1$. The point at infinity, that is the vanishing point, is where the parallel rays meet ultimately. In between the two extreme points, *iso-disparity* lines are formed, where the points are located in the same distance from the optical center.

The key point in this observation is that the observable space is a triangle region (or cone) which consists of intersecting points. From Figure 6.11(b), the observable space is extracted, rescaled, and illustrated in Figure 6.12. Represented on the left is the disparity level, which is equally spaced for convenience. The pixels are located along the horizontal line. The importance of this representation is that the stereo matching can be reduced to a search problem in a discrete triangular region.

In a *trinocular* stereo vision system, a third camera is introduced between the two cameras (An *et al.* 2004; Ueshiba 2006). Being rectified, all the three optical axis are parallel and all the three image planes are coplanar as shown in Figure 6.13. In general, more than one camera system is called *multiple view system* and described by *multiple view geometry* (Faugeras and Luong 2004; Hartley and Zisserman 2004). In a multiple view synthesis system, the extra positions between the left and right cameras are considered as positions for virtual images (Karsten *et al.* 2009; Scharstein 1999; Tian *et al.* 2009). In a

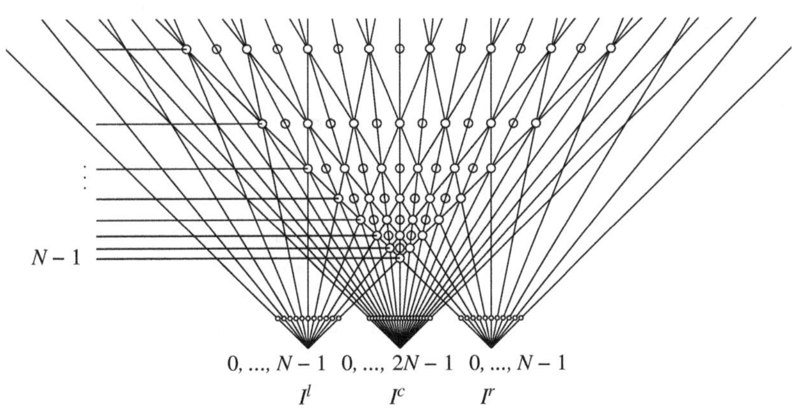

Figure 6.13 Coordinate systems: left (o^l), right (o^r) and center reference (o^c)

binocular vision system, the intermediate position can be considered as a new coordinate to represent the left and right disparities.

Let's represent the the new coordinates by o^c. The advantage of the new coordinates is that the left and right disparities can be represented in the same coordinates, as a *cyclopean view* (Julesz 1971; Wolfe *et al.* 2006). A complete description of disparity needs two quantities (d^l, d^r). However, this description is possible with a single view, o^c. Besides the convenience of representation, the new coordinates let us observe the occluding points. The filled circles are visible commonly by the three coordinates systems. In the left or right system, only one point along the ray is observable. Other points behind the observed point are occluded. However, in the new coordinates, all such occluding points are also visible. The places with empty circles are unobservable by any of the cameras but useful to represent the virtual positions. However, the new representation needs higher resolution than the image: $x^c \in [0, 2N - 1]$.

The whole effort for coordinates system is to describe the disparity as a function. As disparity is involved with more than one images, reference coordinates are not unique. For binocular stereo, the disparity is represented either by d^l or d^r. Having introduced a third coordinate, the disparity can be represented by d^c. Let the three coordinates be *left (reference) coordinates*, *right (reference) coordinates*, and *center (reference) coordinates* (aka *cyclopean coordinates* (Belhumeur 1996; Marr and Poggio 1979)). As the number of cameras is increased, the search space becomes sparser but keeps its triangular shape.

Now, let us examine the search spaces, represented in the three coordinates systems, in terms of disparity computation (Figure 6.14). In the search spaces, the nodes are represented by

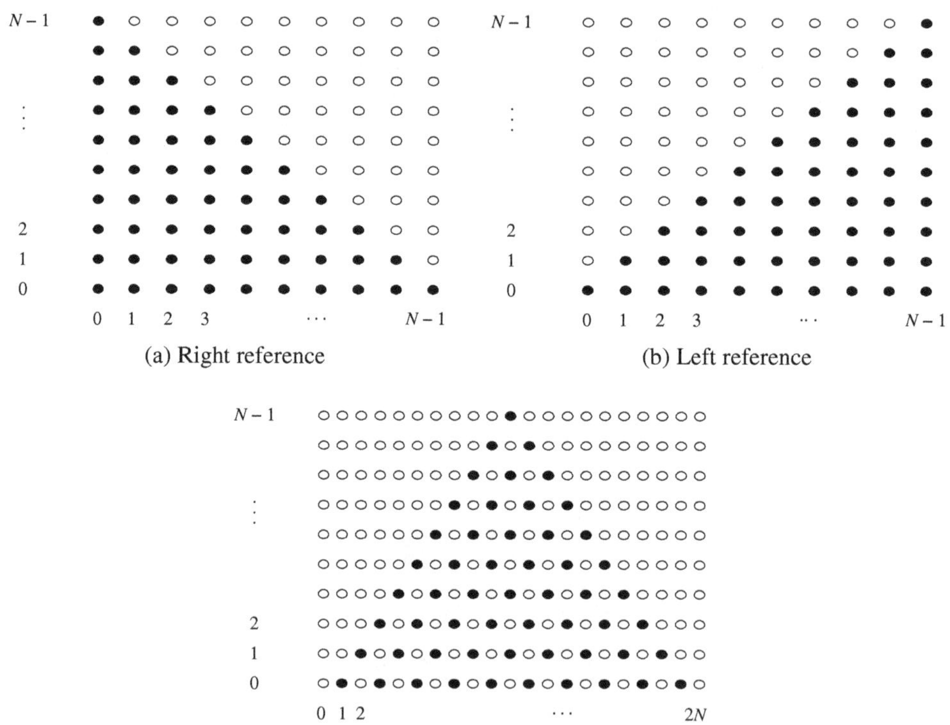

Figure 6.14 Search spaces for disparity (horizontal: pixel and vertical: disparity)

$\{(x^r, d^r)|x^r \in [0, N-1], d^r \in [0, N-1]\}$, $\{(x^l, d^l)|x^l \in [0, N-1], d^l \in [0, N-1]\}$, and $\{(x^c, d^c)|x^c \in [0, 2N-1], d^c \in [0, N-1]\}$. At first observation, the node types are not all the same, classified as *matching*, *occluding*, and *virtual*. As the name represents, the matching nodes, as denoted by the filled circles, are the places that one or two cameras can observe. Likewise, the occluding nodes, as represented by the empty circles in the left and right systems, are the places which cannot be observed by two cameras simultaneously. The empty nodes in the center reference system, the so-called virtual nodes, are different from the occluding nodes, because they are introduced to fill the spaces in a regular manner.

In the second observation, the search space is characterized by triangular distribution of matching nodes. This means that, for the right disparity, the number of candidate matching points becomes less as we move to the right boundary. The reverse is true for the left disparity. For the center reference, the uncertainty increases at both ends. This property naturally affects the disparity map, with blurred values around image boundaries.

The legal disparity is interpreted here as a connected path from one side to the other side, which represents the dissection of the object surface in some transformed way. Assigning penalties and constraints on the possible paths, the stereo matching becomes the shortest paths problem. For the left and right systems, the path should be positioned in the matching nodes area, because the occluding region is unobserved. However, in the center reference system, the shortest path may pass through the empty nodes, because they are not actually occluding points but virtual points, to make the search path smooth if required.

Choosing matching nodes must be based on observations, I^l and I^r as well as the smoothness between neighbor nodes. Analogously, choosing virtual nodes must be based on some prior, such as smoothness constraints. The appearance model and the geometric constraints play roles in defining good paths in these spaces.

Since the the three coordinates represent the same scene, there exist relationships between the coordinates systems. Suppose that (x^l, x^r, x^c) are the corresponding points with the disparities, (d^l, d^r, d^c). Then, the center disparity and the corresponding points are related as follows:

$$\begin{aligned} &d^c(x^c) \mapsto x^l = \frac{1}{2}(x^c + d^c - 1),\ x^r = \frac{1}{2}(x^c - d^c - 1),\ \forall (x^c + d^c = odd), \\ &(x^l, x^r) \mapsto x^c = x^l + x^r + 1,\ d^c = x^l - x^r,\ \forall (x^l, x^r). \end{aligned} \tag{6.80}$$

First, if $x^c + d^c = odd$, the disparity $d^c(x^c)$ specifies the conjugate pair, $(I^l(\frac{1}{2}(i + d^c - 1)), I^r(\frac{1}{2}(i - d^c - 1)))$. For $i + d^c = even$, the node has no corresponding image pixels. Second, the conjugate pair, $(I^l(x^l), I^r(x^r))$, specifies the disparity, $d^c(x^l + x^r + 1) = x^l - x^r$.

Similarly, the left and right disparities have the following relationships.

$$\begin{cases} d^l(x^l) \mapsto x^c = 2x^l - d^l + 1, & d^r(x^r) \mapsto x^c = 2x^r + d^r + 1, \\ d^l(x^l) \mapsto x^r = x^l - d^l, & d^r(x^r) \mapsto x^l = x^r + d^r, \\ (x^l, x^r) \mapsto d^l(x^l) = x^l - x^r, & d^r(x^r) = x^l - x^r. \end{cases} \tag{6.81}$$

By these equations, disparities in one coordinates system can be transformed into another coordinate system. Moreover, the equations naturally represent the geometric constraints of the disparities and corresponding points in stereo matching. Assuming multiple views and discrete observations, we obtain a lot of constraints that must be satisfied by the legal disparities.

6.12 Constraints in Frequency Space

So far we have studied disparity as a warping function in the space domain. The notion of spatial warping can be expanded to the spectral domain, regarded as a phase warping in the spectral domain (Candocia and Adjouadi 1997; Fookes *et al.* 2004; Lucey *et al.* 2013; Sheu and Wu 1995). This view can be expanded to the space-time space, often called the space-time cube, and frequency representation of both space and time.

As a similar vision module, motion is known to have a certain conservation law in the frequency domain (Fleet and Jepson 1990, 1993; Gautama and van Hulle 2002). However, the same is not true in stereo vision. The major reason is that the optical flows can be modeled as differentials but the disparity cannot be modeled in that way. Any linear approximation of the photometric conservation laws is over-simplification. Nevertheless, the disparity, as a warping function, has certain properties in the spectral domain.

Let's consider two line images $g(x)$ and $h(x)$, and a disparity function, $\phi(x) = x + d(x)$. Then, the target function can be regarded as a composite function: $h(x) = g(\phi(x))$. The goal of stereo matching is interpreted as finding the warping function for the given $g(\cdot)$ and $h(\cdot)$. In this case, the reference coordinates is the left image and thus the left disparity is obtained. Changing the role of the two images, we can obtain the other type of disparity, the right disparity.

To proceed further, let's first investigate the properties of the warping function in the spectral domain. In discrete space, the functions are represented by vectors.

$$\begin{cases} \mathbf{g} = (g(0), \dots, g(N-1))^T, \\ \mathbf{h} = (h(0), \dots, h(N-1))^T, \\ \phi = (\phi(0), \dots, \phi(N-1))^T. \end{cases} \tag{6.82}$$

Let G and H be the DFTs s of $\mathbf{g}$ and $\mathbf{h}$, respectively. Then, the image vectors have the forms:

$$G = W\mathbf{g}, \quad H = W\mathbf{h}, \tag{6.83}$$

where W is the DFT matrix:

$$W = \{w_{k,l} | k, l \in [0, N-1]\}, w_{i,j} = \exp\{-2\pi jkl\}. \tag{6.84}$$

Then, the composite function, $h(x)$, can be represented as

$$h(x) = g(\phi(x)) = \frac{1}{N} \sum_{l=0}^{N-1} exp\{j2\pi l\phi(x)/N\} G(l). \tag{6.85}$$

Taking the DFT of $h(x)$, we have

$$H(k) = \frac{1}{N} \sum_{x=0}^{N-1} \sum_{l=0}^{N-1} G(l) e^{j2\pi l\phi(x)/N} e^{-j2\pi kx/N}. \tag{6.86}$$

Next, let us switch the order of integration. Then, we get

$$H(k) = \frac{1}{N} \sum_{l=0}^{N-1} G(l) \sum_{x=0}^{N-1} e^{j2\pi l\phi(x)/N} e^{-j2\pi kx/N}. \tag{6.87}$$

Noticing that the inner integral is independent of G, we give it its own name, $P(k,l)$ (Bergner *et al.* 2006),

$$P(k,l) \triangleq \frac{1}{N}\sum_{x=0}^{N-1} e^{j2\pi(l\phi(x)-kx)/N}, \tag{6.88}$$

and call it the *spectral warping function* (SWF). Substituting Equation (6.88) into (6.87) yields

$$H(k) = \sum_{l=0}^{N-1} P(k,l)G(l). \tag{6.89}$$

In vector notation, this equation becomes

$$H = PG, \tag{6.90}$$

where $P = \{p_{k,l}\}$.

Now, all the important properties of the disparity are included in SWF. Note that $P(k,l)$ is point-symmetric:

$$P(k,l) = P^*(-k,-l). \tag{6.91}$$

The kernel P is independent of the properties of g and solely depends on ϕ. Also, it can be interpreted as a map telling how a certain frequency component of G is mapped to a frequency in the target spectrum of H.

Figure 6.15 depicts intensity and warping functions and their spectral warping matrix $P(k,l)$ for the test stereo dataset. The graphs on the second row contain the intensity function $f(x)$ of the reference frame and the warping function $\phi(x)$ along the indicated scan line, respectively. The plot in the last row shows profiles of the corresponding kernel maps. Equation (6.90) means that $G(l)$ is integrated along the column k of the kernel map to produce $H(k)$. If the warping is constant, the kernel map is also uniform. Otherwise, the input spectrum is modulated by the kernel to produce the resulting spectrum.

The spectral warping function can be factorized further. Consider the $N \times N$ matrices:

$$\begin{cases} W &= \{w_{k,x}\} = \{e^{-2\pi jkx/N}\}, \\ S &= \{s_{x,l}\} = \{s_{x,l} = \frac{1}{N}e^{2\pi jl\phi(x)/N}\}. \end{cases} \tag{6.92}$$

Then, Equation (6.88) becomes

$$P = WS. \tag{6.93}$$

Because of this, Equation (6.90) is decomposed into the factorization:

$$H = WSG. \tag{6.94}$$

In this expression, the disparity is decomposed into the position and value, represented by the two phasor matrices, W and S. The two phasors are the unit vectors positioned in a unit circle. The constraints for the disparity appear as the phasor magnitude and ordering in the spectral domain.

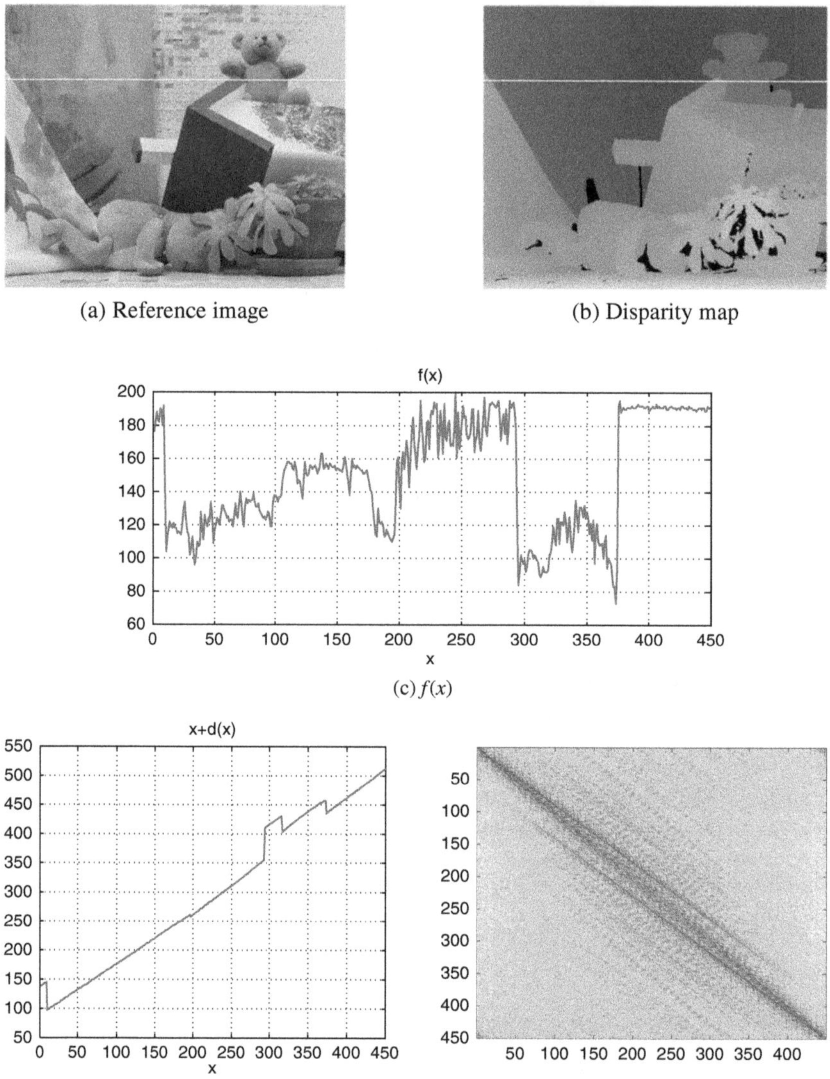

(a) Reference image (b) Disparity map

(c) $f(x)$

(d) $\phi(x)$ (e) $P(k, l)$

Figure 6.15 Profile, disparity, and SWP for the scan line

The matrix S is orthogonal:

$$SS^* = I/N, \tag{6.95}$$

though it is not unitary due to the asymmetric definition of DFT. Containing the disparity as phasor, S is the variable to be recovered. In the spectrum, information on disparity is encoded in the phasor position and their order. Like angle modulation, the noise on disparity tends to affect the phasor amplitude rather than its phase. (See the problems at the end of this chapter.)

6.13 Basic Energy Functions

We have observed that the central problem of depth estimation is the stereo matching that searches for an optimal disparity. The major mechanism for disparity is the photometric constraint, Equation (6.71), which defines the brightness invariance between a pair of corresponding points. However, the disparity cannot be determined uniquely because it is not one-to-one mapping. To narrow down the vast search space, various constraints are introduced.

In the energy representation, the photometric constraint plays a major role and the other constraints play a role of limiting the search space.

$$\begin{aligned} E^r(D) = & \sum_{(x,y)\in\mathcal{P}} \|I^r(x,y) - I^l(x+d(x,y),y)\|^2 \\ & + \lambda \sum_{(x,y)\in\mathcal{P}} \sum_{(x',y')\in\mathcal{N}(x,y)} \min(\|d(x,y) - d(x',y')\|, T_s), \\ E^l(D) = & \sum_{(x,y)\in\mathcal{P}} \|I^l(x,y) - I^r(x-d(x,y),y)\|^2 \\ & + \lambda \sum_{(x,y)\in\mathcal{P}} \sum_{(x',y')\in\mathcal{N}(x,y)} \min(\|d(x,y) - d(x',y')\|, T_s), \end{aligned} \tag{6.96}$$

where λ is the Lagrange multiplier and T_s is the threshold. The first term comes from the photometric constraint, Equation (6.71), and is defined along the epipolar line. The second term comes from the smoothness constraint, Equation (6.72), and is defined over local neighborhood. The parameter, λ, is a Lagrange multiplier, which makes the problem unconstrained minimization. To detect the occlusion, both the left and right disparities must be obtained, as discussed in Equation (6.74).

There is a third viewpoint, the center referenced system, where the energy function can be defined, with the help of Equation (6.80),

$$\begin{aligned} E(D) = & \sum_{y=0}^{M-1} \sum_{\substack{x=1 \\ x+d(x)=\text{odd}}}^{2N-1} \|I^l((x+d(x)-1)/2) - I^r((x-d(x)-1)/2)\|^2 \\ & + \sum_{y=0}^{M-1} \lambda \sum_{\substack{x=0 \\ x+d(x)=\text{even}}}^{2N} \|\nabla d\|^2. \end{aligned} \tag{6.97}$$

Note that $x^c \in [0, 2N]$, while $x^l, x^r \in [0, N-1]$, due to Equations (6.80) and (6.81).

Although defined on the image plane, the energy function can be alternatively defined for an epipolar line. The DP algorithm can manage one line at a time but other algorithms, such as relaxation, BP, and GC, can manage globally the entire image plane or part of it.

Equations (6.96) and (6.97) are the most basic forms of stereo matching. Various alternative representations may be derived by combining appearance and geometric constraints, features, and measures. The additional constraints may be directional smoothness and occlusion indicator which turns and off the smoothness term. Unless otherwise stated, these basic forms will be used as baseline equations for circuit design, though some modifications may be inevitable.

Problems

6.1 [Correspondence] Using Equation (6.45), show that the epipolar line is collinear and that the corresponding points are located on it.

6.2 [Correspondence] Derive $E^T = [\mathbf{e}_l]_\times H^{-1}$ in Equation (6.41).

6.3 [Correspondence] For parallel optics, derive the essential matrix. Check for the essential matrix equation.

6.4 [Correspondence] For parallel cameras, derive the fundamental matrix and check for the fundamental matrix equation. What is the epipole?

6.5 [Correspondence] What does the fundamental matrix mean in the rectified system?

6.6 [Rectification] In Equation (6.62), derive the three component of R_{rect}. Check for the parallel camera system.

6.7 [Rectification] Consider a rectified system. In reference to the world coordinates, the cameras are located at $(-B/2, 0, 0)^T$ and $(B/2, 0, 0)^T$ and the principal points are defined at $(-B/2, 0, f)^T$ and $(B/2, 0, f)^T$, where f is the focal length and B is the baseline between the two camera centers. If the disparity is defined as $d = x_l - x_r$, what is the position of the object, (X, Y, Z)?

6.8 [Rectification] Repeat the previous problem, when the world coordinates coincide with the left camera and the right camera.

6.9 [Rectification] For the rectified system, with baseline B and focal length f, derive the camera and fundamental matrices.

6.10 [Spectrum] Solve Equation (6.94) for S using pseudo-inverse and discuss the properties.

References

An L, Jia Y, Wang J, Zhang X, and Li M 2004 An efficient rectification method for trinocular stereovision. *Pattern Recognition, 2004. ICPR 2004. Proceedings of the 17th International Conference on*, vol. 4, pp. 56–59 IEEE.

Belhumeur PN 1996 A Bayesian approach to binocular steropsis. *International Journal of Computer Vision* **19**(3), 237–260.

Bergner S, Muler T, Weiskopf D, and Muraki D 2006 A spectral analysis of function composition and its implications for sampling in direct volume visualization. *IEEE Trans. Vis. Comput. Graph.* **12**(5), 1353–1360.

Bleyer M and Gelautz M 2007 Graph-cut-based stereo matching using image segmentation with symmetrical treatment of occlusions. *Signal Processing: Image Communication* **22**(2), 127–143.

Bleyer M, Rother C, and Kohli P 2010 Surface stereo with soft segmentation. *Computer Vision and Pattern Recognition (CVPR), 2010 IEEE Conference on*, pp. 1570–1577 IEEE.

Brahmachari AS and Sarkar S 2013 Hop-diffusion Monte Carlo for epipolar geometry estimation between very wide-baseline images. *IEEE Trans. Pattern Anal. Mach. Intell.* **35**(3), 755–762.

Candocia F and Adjouadi M 1997 A similarity measure for stereo feature matching. *IEEE Trans. Image Processing* **6**(10), 1460–1464.

Chin TJ, Wang H, and Suter D 2009 Robust fitting of multiple structures: The statistical learning approach. *ICCV*, pp. 413–420 IEEE.

Chojnacki W and Brooks MJ 2007 On the consistency of the normalized eight-point algorithm. *Journal of Mathematical Imaging and Vision* **28**(1), 19–27.

de Villiers JP, Leuschner FW, and Geldenhuys R 2010 Modeling of radial asymmetry in lens distortion facilitated by modern optimization techniques. *IS&T/SPIE Electronic Imaging*, pp. 75390J–75390J International Society for Optics and Photonics.

Deng Y, Yang Q, Lin X, and Tang X 2005 A symmetric patch-based correspondence model for occlusion handling. *Computer Vision, 2005. ICCV 2005. Tenth IEEE International Conference on*, vol. 2, pp. 1316–1322 IEEE.

Dubrofsky E 2007 *Homography estimation* Master's thesis Carleton University.

Faugeras O 1993 *Three-Dimensional Computer Vision: A Geometric Viewpoint*. MIT Press, Cambridge, Massachusetts.

Faugeras O and Luong Q 2004 *The Geometry of Multiple Images: The Laws That Govern the Formation of Multiple Images of a Scene and Some of Their Applications*. MIT Press.

Faugeras O, Luong Q, and Maybank S 1992 Camera self-calibration: Theory and experiments. *ECCV*, pp. 321–334.

Fleet DJ and Jepson AD 1990 Computation of component image velocity from local phase information. *International Journal of Computer Vision* **5**(1), 77–104.

Fleet DJ and Jepson AD 1993 Stability of phase information. *IEEE Trans. Pattern Anal. Mach. Intell.* **15**(12), 1253–1268.

Fookes C, Maeder A, Sridharan S, and Cook J 2004 Multi-spectral stereo image matching using mutual information. *3D Data Processing, Visualization and Transmission, 2004. 3DPVT. Proceedings. 2nd International Symposium on*, pp. 961–968 IEEE.

Forsyth D and Ponce J 2003 *Computer Vision: A Modern Approach*. Prentice Hall.

Fusiello A, Trucco E, and Verri A 2000 A compact algorithm for rectification of stereo pairs. *Machine Vision Application* **12**(1), 16–22.

Gautama T and van Hulle MM 2002 A phase-based approach to the estimation of the optical flow field using spatial filtering. *IEEE Trans. Neural Networks* **13**(5), 1127–1136.

Hartley R and Li H 2012 An efficient hidden variable approach to minimal-case camera motion estimation. *IEEE Trans. Pattern Anal. Mach. Intell.* **34**(12), 2303–2314.

Hartley R and Zisserman A 2004 *Multiple View Geometry in Computer Vision*. Cambridge University Press.

Hartley RI 1997 In defense of the eight-point algorithm. *IEEE Trans. Pattern Anal. Mach. Intell.* **19**(6), 580–593.

Hong L and Chen GQ 2008 Segment based image matching method and system. US Patent 7,330,593.

Julesz B 1971 *Foundations of Cyclopean Perception*. University of Chicago Press.

Kang YS and Ho YS 2011 An efficient image rectification method for parallel multi-camera arrangement. *Consumer Electronics, IEEE Transactions on* **57**(3), 1041–1048.

Karsten M, Aljoscha S, Kristina D, Philipp M, Peter K, Thomas W *et al.* 2009 View synthesis for advanced 3D video systems. *EURASIP Journal on Image and Video Processing* **2008**, 1–11.

Kolmogorov V 2005 *Graph Cut Algorithms for Binocular Stereo with Occlusions*. Springer-Verlag.

Lin MH and Tomasi C 2003 Surfaces with occlusions from layered stereo. *Computer Vision and Pattern Recognition, 2003. Proceedings. 2003 IEEE Computer Society Conference on*, vol. 1, pp. I–710 IEEE.

Longuet-Higgins HC 1981 A computer algorithm for reconstructing a scene from two projections. *Nature* **293**(5828), 133–135.

Loop C and Zhang Z 1999 Computing rectifying homographies for stereo vision. *Computer Vision and Pattern Recognition, 1999. IEEE Computer Society Conference on.*, vol. 1 IEEE.

Lucey S, Ashrat RNN, and Sridharan S 2013 Fourier Lukas-Kanade algorithm. *IEEE Trans. Pattern Anal. Mach. Intell.* **35**(6), 1383–1396.

Luong Q and Faugeras O 1996 The fundamental matrix: Theory, algorithms, and stability analysis. *International Journal of Computer Vision* **17**(1), 43–75.

Marr D and Poggio T 1979 A computational theory of human stereo vision. *jChemPhys* **21**(6), 1087–1092.

Middlebury U 2013 Middlebury stereo home page http://vision.middlebury.edu/stereo (accessed Sept. 4, 2013).

Min D and Sohn K 2008 Cost aggregation and occlusion handling with WLS in stereo matching. *IEEE Trans. Image Processing* **17**(8), 1431–1442.

Miraldo P and Araújo H 2013 Calibration of smooth camera models. *IEEE Trans. Pattern Anal. Mach. Intell.* **35**(9), 2091–2103.

Ni K, Jin H, and Dellaert F 2009 Groupsac: Efficient consensus in the presence of groupings. *ICCV*, pp. 2193–2200. IEEE.

Ogale AS and Aloimonos Y 2004 Stereo correspondence with slanted surfaces: Critical implications of horizontal slant. *Computer Vision and Pattern Recognition, 2004. CVPR 2004. Proceedings of the 2004 IEEE Computer Society Conference on*, vol. 1, pp. I–568 IEEE.

OpenCV 2013 Camera calibration and 3D reconstruction http://docs.opencv.org/master/modules/calib3d/doc/-camera_calibration_and_3d_reconstruction.html?highlight=bouguet (accessed Oct. 11, 2013).

Oram D 2001 Rectification for any epipolar geometry. *BMVC*, p. Session 7: Geometry and Structure.

Pollefeys M, Koch R, and Van Gool L 1999 A simple and efficient rectification method for general motion. *Computer Vision, 1999. The Proceedings of the Seventh IEEE International Conference on*, vol. 1, pp. 496–501 IEEE.

Rozenfeld S and Shimshoni I 2005 The modified pbM-estimator method and a runtime analysis technique for the RANSAC family. *CVPR*, pp. I: 1113–1120.

Scharstein D 1999 *View Synthesis using Stereo Vision*. Springer-Verlag.

Scharstein D and Szeliski R 2002 A taxonomy and evaluation of dense two-frame stereo correspondence algorithms. *International Journal of Computer Vision* **47**(1–3), 7–42.

Sheu HT and Wu MF 1995 Fourier descriptor based technique for reconstructing 3D contours from stereo images. *IEE Proceedings-Vision, Image and Signal Processing* **142**(2), 95–104.

Sun J, Li Y, Kang SB, and Shum HY 2005 Symmetric stereo matching for occlusion handling. *Computer Vision and Pattern Recognition, 2005. CVPR 2005. IEEE Computer Society Conference on*, vol. 2, pp. 399–406 IEEE.

Tao H, Sawhney HS, and Kumar R 2001 A global matching framework for stereo computation. *Computer Vision, 2001. ICCV 2001. Proceedings. Eighth IEEE International Conference on*, vol. 1, pp. 532–539 IEEE.

Tian D, Lai PL, Lopez P, and Gomila C 2009 View synthesis techniques for 3D video. *SPIE Optical Engineering+ Applications*, pp. 74430T–74430T International Society for Optics and Photonics.

Tippetts BJ, Lee DJ, Lillywhite K and Archibald J 2013 Review of stereo vision algorithms and their suitability for resource-limited systems http://link.springer.com/article/10.1007%2Fs11554-012-0313-2 Sept. 4, 2013).

Tola E, Lepetit V, and Fua P 2010 Daisy: An efficient dense descriptor applied to wide-baseline stereo. *IEEE Trans. Pattern Anal. Mach. Intell.* **32**(5), 815–830.

Trucco E and Verri A 1998 *Introductory Techniques for 3-D Computer Vision*. Prentice Hall.

Tsai R 1987 A versatile camera calibration technique for high-accuracy 3D machine vision metrology using off-the-shelf tv cameras and lenses. *Robotics and Automation, IEEE Journal of* **3**(4), 323–344.

Ueshiba T 2006 An efficient implementation technique of bidirectional matching for real-time trinocular stereo vision. *Pattern Recognition, 2006. ICPR 2006. 18th International Conference on*, vol. 1, pp. 1076–1079 IEEE.

Weng J, Cohen P, and Herniou M 1992 Camera calibration with distortion models and accuracy evaluation. *IEEE Trans. Pattern Anal. Mach. Intell.* **14**(10), 965–980.

Wolfe JM, Kluender KR, Levi DM, Bartoshuk LM, Herz RS, Klatzky RL, and Lederman SJ 2006 *Sensation & Perception*. Sinauer Associates Sunderland, MA.

Woodford O, Torr P, Reid I, and Fitzgibbon A 2009 Global stereo reconstruction under second-order smoothness priors. *IEEE Trans. Pattern Anal. Mach. Intell.* **31**(12), 2115–2128.

Yu Y 2012 Estimation of Markov random field parameters using ant colony optimization for continuous domains. *2012 Spring Congress on Engineering and Technology*, pp. 1–4.

Zhang Z 2000 A flexible new technique for camera calibration. *IEEE Trans. Pattern Anal. Mach. Intell.* **22**(11), 1330–1334.

Zheng Y, Sugimoto S, and Okutomi M 2011 A Branch and Contract algorithm for globally optimal fundamental matrix estimation. *CVPR*, pp. 2953–2960 IEEE.

Zitnick CL and Kanade T 2000 A cooperative algorithm for stereo matching and occlusion detection. *IEEE Trans. Pattern Anal. Mach. Intell.* **22**(7), 675–684.

Zitnick CL, Kang SB, Uyttendaele M, Winder S, and Szeliski R 2004 High-quality video view interpolation using a layered representation. *ACM Transactions on Graphics (TOG)*, vol. 23, pp. 600–608 ACM.

7

Motion and Vision Modules

This chapter introduces some of the issues associated with vision modules and their integration. For the issue of motion, we first review the geometry of the 3D and 2D motion fields. We also review the basics of structure from motion, and then focus on optical flow, in which we examine various constraints in a more fundamental manner and review basic energy minimization. The contents are not intended to be complete in scope and depth, as the aim is to lay the groundwork for the topics in subsequent chapters. For a more comprehensive treatment of motion, please refer to books on multiple view geometry (Faugeras and Luong 2004; Hartley and Zisserman 2004), reviews of optical flow (Baker *et al.* 2011; Barron *et al.* 1994; Fleet and Weiss 2006; McCane *et al.* 2001), and scene flow (Cech *et al.* 2011; Huguet and Devernay 2007; Vedula *et al.* 2005). In addition, a web site dealing with optical flow is also available (Middlebury 2013).

Like binocular stereo vision, motion vision is one of the major vision modules by which we can induce motion information in addition to the depth of the surface shape and the volume information of objects. Created by a camera, the successive frames of images contain depth information by means of optical flow. The relative velocity between the scene motion and the egomotion appears as the motion field, when it is projected onto the image plane. The optical flow refers to the apparent velocity of the motion velocity when viewed with the eyes.

The problem of motion is that of how to recover the 3D structure or the pose for a rigid or non-rigid body and moving camera (egomotion). Unlike stereo vision, motion estimation is involved with multidimensional search, camera motion, and rigid or non-rigid body. For the rigid body, structure from motion (SfM) (Ullman 1979) and for the non-rigid body, *scene flow* (Vedula *et al.* 2005), have been developed. The natural method is to estimate the motion field from the image features directly. The other method is to estimate a dense intermediate variable, called *optical flow*, from the images and then use it to estimate the scene flow.

The second part of this chapter introduces the integration of vision modules, which is by no means complete but it may give rise to some interesting research questions. There are numerous approaches to model fusion, especially stereo and motion (Li and Sclaroff 2008; Liu and Philomin 2009; Pons *et al.* 2007; Wedel *et al.* 2011, 2008b; Zhang *et al.* 2003). The general approach is to build each module, obtain the results, and combine the results via energy minimization or boosting techniques. Instead we focus on the relationships between some of the major vision modules, bypassing the final motion and structure variables. This approach gives us an intuitive look into the opto-geometrical relationships between vision variables and stronger combined constraints than individual constraints. This chapter concludes with a

Architectures for Computer Vision: From Algorithm to Chip with Verilog, First Edition. Hong Jeong.

Companion Website: www.wiley.com/go/jeong

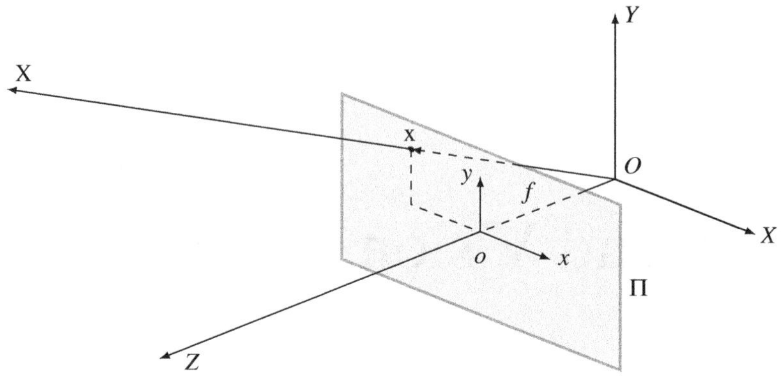

Figure 7.1 A 3D space O and image plane Π ($\mathbf{X}$ and $\mathbf{x}$ are the object position and image, respectively)

set of ordinary differential equations that directly link the 2D variables – namely, disparity, optical flow, blur diameter, and surface normal.

7.1 3D Motion

Visual motion provides three types of information: camera motion, dynamics of the moving objects, and the spatial layout of the scene. To begin with, we consider a 3D space, in which the image plane Π and an object $\mathbf{X}$ are defined (Figure 7.1). The world coordinates and the image coordinates are defined by the origins O and o, respectively. The image plane is positioned at $(0, 0, f)$ in this space, where f is the focal length. The vector $\mathbf{X}$ is projected onto $\mathbf{x}$ in the image plane. When $\mathbf{X}$ moves, $\mathbf{x}$ does so also in the 2D plane. There is a geometrical relationship between the object motion and the observed velocities. The relationships can be represented in various forms: component, vector, and matrix. In a more general setting, both objects and camera may move, resulting in relative velocities.

In a perspective projection, if a point $\mathbf{X} = (X, Y, Z)^T$ in 3D space is mapped to a point $\mathbf{x} = (x, y, f)^T$ in 2D space, the image position is represented by

$$\begin{cases} x = f\frac{X}{Z}, \\ y = f\frac{Y}{Z}, \end{cases} \quad \text{or} \quad \begin{bmatrix} x \\ y \end{bmatrix} = \begin{bmatrix} f & 0 & 0 \\ 0 & f & 0 \end{bmatrix} \frac{1}{Z} \begin{bmatrix} X \\ Y \\ Z \end{bmatrix}. \tag{7.1}$$

This is the relationship of the absolute positions (x, y) and (X, Y, Z) in the two spaces. The relationship between differentials $\dot{\mathbf{x}}$ and $\dot{\mathbf{X}}$ in the two spaces is sometimes needed.

$$\begin{cases} \dot{x} = f\frac{\dot{X}}{Z} - x\frac{\dot{Z}}{Z}, \\ \dot{y} = f\frac{\dot{Y}}{Z} - y\frac{\dot{Z}}{Z}, \end{cases} \quad \text{or} \quad \begin{bmatrix} \dot{x} \\ \dot{y} \end{bmatrix} = \begin{bmatrix} f & 0 & -x \\ 0 & f & -y \end{bmatrix} \frac{1}{Z} \begin{bmatrix} \dot{X} \\ \dot{Y} \\ \dot{Z} \end{bmatrix}. \tag{7.2}$$

Note that different matrices are used in transforming the position and velocity from 3D to 2D. In general, the relationship of the coordinates as well as their differentials is nonlinear. Higher-order differentials are involved with even more nonlinear representation.

If the 3D position moves with $\dot{\mathbf{X}} = (U, V, W)^T$, the observed velocity $\dot{\mathbf{x}} = (u, v, 0)^T$ becomes

$$\begin{cases} u = f\frac{U}{Z} - x\frac{W}{Z}, \\ v = f\frac{V}{Z} - y\frac{W}{Z}, \end{cases} \quad \text{or} \quad \begin{bmatrix} u \\ v \end{bmatrix} = \begin{bmatrix} f & 0 & -x \\ 0 & f & -y \end{bmatrix} \frac{1}{Z} \begin{bmatrix} U \\ V \\ W \end{bmatrix}. \tag{7.3}$$

If the object is rigid, the motions of the points on the object surface are all dependent. Otherwise, if the object is non-rigid (Vedula *et al.* 2005), the object points are all independent in their motion. To deal with a non-rigid body, we need a dense three-dimensional vector field defined for every point on every surface in the scene.

For a rigid body's motion, we define the translational and rotational velocities by $\mathbf{t} = (t_x, t_y, t_z)^T$ and $\boldsymbol{\omega} = (\omega_x, \omega_y, \omega_z)^T$. In the world coordinate system, the composite velocity of the object is

$$\dot{\mathbf{X}} = \mathbf{t} + \boldsymbol{\omega} \times \mathbf{X}. \tag{7.4}$$

In matrix form, the motion vector becomes

$$\dot{\mathbf{X}} = \mathbf{t} - [\mathbf{X}]_\times \boldsymbol{\omega} = \mathbf{t} + \begin{bmatrix} I & -[\mathbf{X}]_\times \end{bmatrix} \begin{bmatrix} \mathbf{t} \\ \boldsymbol{\omega} \end{bmatrix}, \tag{7.5}$$

which, in component form, is

$$\begin{cases} U = t_x + \omega_y Z - \omega_z Y, \\ V = t_y + \omega_z X - \omega_x Z, \\ W = t_z + \omega_x Y - \omega_y X. \end{cases} \quad \text{or} \quad \begin{bmatrix} U \\ V \\ W \end{bmatrix} = \begin{bmatrix} 1 & 0 & 0 & 0 & Z & -Y \\ 0 & 1 & 0 & -Z & 0 & X \\ 0 & 0 & 1 & Y & -X & 0 \end{bmatrix} \begin{bmatrix} \mathbf{t} \\ \boldsymbol{\omega} \end{bmatrix}. \tag{7.6}$$

Combining Equations (7.3) and (7.6), we get

$$\begin{cases} u = \frac{ft_x - xt_z}{Z} - \frac{\omega_x xy}{f} + \omega_y \left(\frac{x^2}{f} + f \right) - \omega_z y, \\ v = \frac{ft_y - yt_z}{Z} - \omega_x \left(\frac{y^2}{f} + f \right) + \frac{\omega_y xy}{f} + \omega_z x. \end{cases} \tag{7.7}$$

The matrix representation is $\dot{\mathbf{x}} = H\dot{\mathbf{X}}$:

$$\begin{bmatrix} u \\ v \end{bmatrix} = \begin{bmatrix} f & 0 & -x \\ 0 & f & -y \end{bmatrix} \frac{1}{Z} \begin{bmatrix} 1 & 0 & 0 & 0 & Z & -Y \\ 0 & 1 & 0 & -Z & 0 & X \\ 0 & 0 & 1 & Y & -X & 0 \end{bmatrix} \begin{bmatrix} \mathbf{t} \\ \boldsymbol{\omega} \end{bmatrix} \tag{7.8}$$

and the vector form is

$$\dot{\mathbf{x}} = \frac{\hat{\mathbf{z}} \times (\mathbf{t} \times \mathbf{x})}{\mathbf{X} \cdot \hat{\mathbf{z}}} + \{\hat{\mathbf{z}} \times (\mathbf{x} \times (\boldsymbol{\omega} \times \mathbf{x}))\}. \tag{7.9}$$

The motion flow comprises translational and rotational components (Figure 7.2). This figure shows two cases of pure translation, a case of pure rotation, and one of composite motion.

Let's represent the composite motion vector by

$$\dot{\mathbf{x}} = \dot{\mathbf{x}}_{tr} + \dot{\mathbf{x}}_{rot}. \tag{7.10}$$

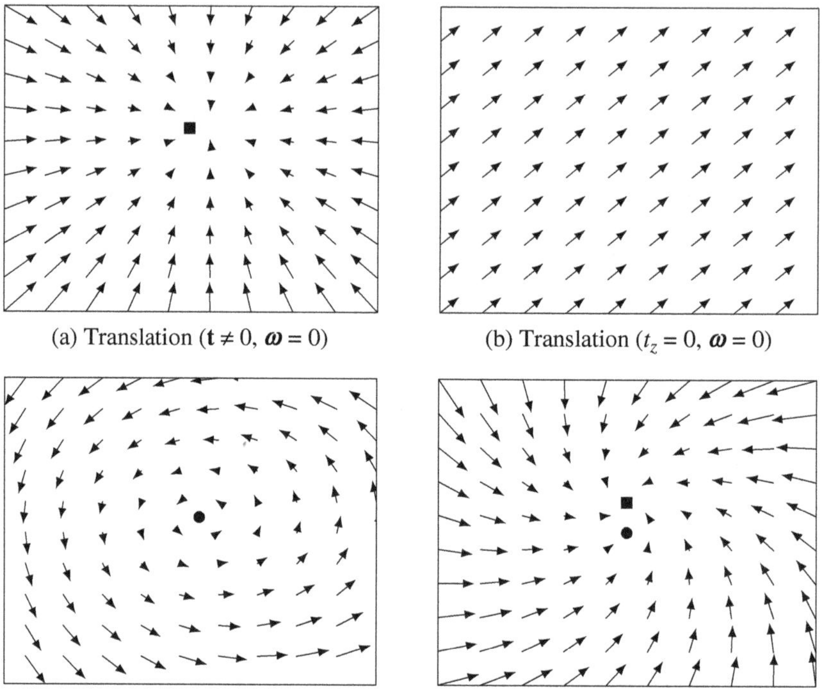

(a) Translation ($\mathbf{t} \neq 0$, $\boldsymbol{\omega} = 0$) (b) Translation ($t_z = 0$, $\boldsymbol{\omega} = 0$)

(c) Rotation ($\mathbf{t} = 0$, $\boldsymbol{\omega} \neq 0$) (d) Composite motion ($\mathbf{t}$, $\boldsymbol{\omega} \neq 0$)

Figure 7.2 Motion fields (FOC, FOE, and AOR are denoted with marks. $f = 1$ and $Z = 10$)

The first term is a translation component, known up to a scale factor Z, that is $\mathbf{t}/Z$. The second term is a rotational component, which is independent of the depth, Z. If $t_z \neq 0$, the translational flow field is

$$u_{tr} = (x_0 - x)\frac{t_z}{Z}, \quad v_{tr} = (y_0 - y)\frac{t_z}{Z}, \quad \text{if } t_z \neq 0, \tag{7.11}$$

where $(x_0, y_0) = (ft_x/t_z, ft_y/t_z)$ is the *focus of expansion* (FOE) (or *focus of contraction* (FOC)), which is the fixed point of the translational flow field. The translation vector is also related to the *time to collision*:

$$T = (x_0 - x)/u_{tr} = (y_0 - y)/v_{tr}, \tag{7.12}$$

which is equivalent to Z/t_z.

The motion field is radial with all the vectors pointing towards or away from a single point. The length of the motion field is inversely proportional to the depth. It is also directly proportional to the distance to the FOE. If $t_z = 0$, the translational field is

$$u = f\frac{t_x}{Z}, \quad v = f\frac{t_y}{Z}. \tag{7.13}$$

All motion field vectors are parallel to each other and inversely proportional to depth.

If $\omega_z \neq 0$, the rotational flow field is

$$u_{rot} = -\frac{\omega_x xy}{f} + \omega_y \left(\frac{x^2}{f} + f\right) - \omega_z y, \quad v_{rot} = -\omega_x \left(\frac{y^2}{f} + f\right) + \frac{\omega_y xy}{f} + \omega_z x, \tag{7.14}$$

which is centered at a fixed point, $(f\omega_x/\omega_z, f\omega_y/\omega_z)$, called an *axis of rotation* (AOR).

Thus far, we have considered a point motion. In many cases, the moving objects may be modeled by a moving plane. Let us consider such a plane, $\mathbf{X} = (X, Y, Z)^T$, which has the normal vector $\mathbf{n} = (n_x, n_y, n_z)^T$ and a distance d from the origin. Then, $\mathbf{n}^T \cdot \mathbf{X} = d$. Substituting the image point, $\mathbf{x} = f\mathbf{X}/Z$, we obtain

$$Z = \frac{fd}{n_x x + n_y y + n_z f}. \tag{7.15}$$

Putting this into Equation (7.7), we have the motion field equation:

$$\begin{cases} u = \frac{1}{fd}\left(a_1 x^2 + a_2 xy + a_3 fx + a_4 fy + a_5 f^2\right), \\ v = \frac{1}{fd}\left(a_1 xy + a_2 y^2 + a_6 fy + a_7 fx + a_8 f^2\right), \end{cases} \tag{7.16}$$

where

$$a_1 = -d\omega_y - t_z n_x, a_2 = d\omega_x - t_z n_y, a_3 = -t_z n_z + t_x n_x, a_4 = d\omega_z + t_x n_y,$$
$$a_5 = -d\omega_y + t_x n_z, a_6 = -t_z n_z + t_y n_y, a_7 = -d\omega_z + t_y n_x, a_8 = d\omega_x + t_y n_z.$$

The motion field is the second-order polynomials, where the coefficients are the functions of $(\mathbf{n}, d, \mathbf{t}, \boldsymbol{\omega})$. That is, the motion field of a planar surface is a quadratic function in the image.

7.2 Direct Motion Estimation

Direct motion estimation is used to recover the 3D motion from the observed image features, without relying on the intermediate variable, *optical flow*. Because the concept is very intuitive, let us first review this method.

From the outset, we assume the brightness constancy constraint, which will be treated in detail in Section 7.5:

$$-\frac{dI}{dt} = [I_x \quad I_y]\begin{bmatrix} u \\ v \end{bmatrix}. \tag{7.17}$$

Combining Equations (7.8) and (7.17), we get

$$-\frac{dI}{dt} = [I_x \quad I_y]\begin{bmatrix} f & 0 & -x \\ 0 & f & -y \end{bmatrix}\frac{1}{Z}\begin{bmatrix} 1 & 0 & 0 & 0 & Z & -Y \\ 0 & 1 & 0 & -Z & 0 & X \\ 0 & 0 & 1 & Y & -X & 0 \end{bmatrix}\begin{bmatrix} \mathbf{t} \\ \boldsymbol{\omega} \end{bmatrix}. \tag{7.18}$$

We can reduce the variables in this equation by using Equation (7.1):

$$-\frac{dI}{dt} = [I_x \quad I_y]\begin{bmatrix} f & 0 & -x \\ 0 & f & -y \end{bmatrix}\frac{1}{Z}\begin{bmatrix} 1 & 0 & 0 & 0 & Z & -yZ/f \\ 0 & 1 & 0 & -Z & 0 & xZ/f \\ 0 & 0 & 1 & yZ/f & -xZ/f & 0 \end{bmatrix}\begin{bmatrix} \mathbf{t} \\ \boldsymbol{\omega} \end{bmatrix}. \tag{7.19}$$

We have one equation for each pixel, which contains seven variables, $(Z, \mathbf{t}, \boldsymbol{\omega})$. There are algorithms that solve this problem, by modeling Z in parameters (Black and Yacoob 1995; Negahdaripour and Horn 1985).

In real-time stereo (Harville *et al.* 1999), the depth can be measured directly. The depth constraint can then be derived and combined with the brightness constraint. The direct depth method uses the depth data, Z, to model the depth as

$$Z(x, y, t) = Z(x + u, y + v, t + 1) - W, \tag{7.20}$$

which gives the depth constraint,

$$Z_x u + Z_y v + Z_t - W = 0. \tag{7.21}$$

Note that the constraint is similar to that of brightness. We can derive

$$-Z_t = \frac{1}{Z}\left[fZ_x \quad fZ_y - (Z + xZ_x + yZ_y)\right]\begin{bmatrix} U \\ V \\ W \end{bmatrix}. \tag{7.22}$$

Similarly, for the brightness constraint, we obtain

$$-I_t = \left[fI_x \quad fI_y \quad -(xI_x + yI_y)\right]\begin{bmatrix} U \\ V \\ W \end{bmatrix}. \tag{7.23}$$

Combining Equations (7.22) and (7.23), we get

$$\begin{bmatrix} -I_t \\ -Z_t \end{bmatrix} = \begin{bmatrix} fI_x & fI_y & -(xI_x + yI_y) \\ fZ_x & yZ_y & -(Z + xZ_x + yZ_y) \end{bmatrix}\frac{1}{Z}\begin{bmatrix} U \\ V \\ W \end{bmatrix}. \tag{7.24}$$

Finally, we have

$$\begin{bmatrix} -\frac{dI}{dt} \\ -\frac{dZ}{dt} \end{bmatrix} = \begin{bmatrix} fI_x & fI_y & -(xI_x + yI_y) \\ fZ_x & yZ_y & -(Z + xZ_x + yZ_y) \end{bmatrix}\frac{1}{Z}\begin{bmatrix} 1 & 0 & 0 & 0 & Z & -yZ/f \\ 0 & 1 & 0 & -Z & 0 & xZ/f \\ 0 & 0 & 1 & yZ/f & -xZ/f & 0 \end{bmatrix}\begin{bmatrix} \mathbf{t} \\ \boldsymbol{\omega} \end{bmatrix}. \tag{7.25}$$

If $\nabla_t I$ and $\nabla_t Z$ are available, we can solve this equation for $(\mathbf{t}, \boldsymbol{\omega})$.

7.3 Structure from Optical Flow

The other approach is to recover the motion $(\mathbf{t}, \boldsymbol{\omega})$ from the given *optical flow*, (u, v). First, let us estimate $\mathbf{t}$ from the optical flow. One of the methods is to minimize the energy:

$$E(\mathbf{t}, Z) = \int \left(u - \frac{ft_x - xt_z}{Z}\right)^2 + \left(v - \frac{ft_y - yt_z}{Z}\right)^2 dxdy. \tag{7.26}$$

If we define $a = ft_x - xt_z$ and $b = ft_y - yt_z$, the energy function has the form $\langle (u, v), \frac{1}{Z}(a, b)\rangle$. We first minimize the sum of least squares with respect to the depth, obtaining $Z = (a^2 + b^2)/(au + bv)$. Inserting Z into the energy equation, we have

$$E(\mathbf{t}) = \int \frac{av - bu}{a^2 + b^2} dxdy. \tag{7.27}$$

If we differentiate this function in terms of t_x, t_y, and t_z, we obtain

$$\int (ft_y - yt_z)Fdxdy = 0, \int (ft_x - xt_z)Fdxdy = 0, \int (yt_x - xt_y)Fdxdy = 0, \tag{7.28}$$

where $F = (av - bu)/(a^2 + b^2)$. The three equations are linearly dependent and difficult to solve.

Therefore, we define a different norm instead:

$$E(\mathbf{t}, Z) = \int \left\{ \left(u - \frac{ft_x - xt_z}{Z}\right)^2 + \left(v - \frac{ft_y - yt_z}{Z}\right)^2 \right\}(a^2 + b^2)dxdy. \tag{7.29}$$

If we differentiate the function with respect to Z, we get the same $Z = (a^2 + b^2)/(au + bv)$, but have a simpler energy function,

$$E(\mathbf{t}) = \int (av - bu)^2 dxdy. \tag{7.30}$$

Differentiating this function with respect to the variables, we have

$$\begin{bmatrix} a & d & f \\ d & b & e \\ f & e & c \end{bmatrix} \mathbf{t} = 0, \quad \|\mathbf{t}\| = 1, \tag{7.31}$$

where

$$a = \int v^2 dxdy, b = \int u^2 dxdy, c = \int (yu - xv)dxdy, d = \int uvdxdy,$$

$$e = \int u(yu - xv)dxdy, f = \int v(yu - xv)dxdy.$$

The solution is a singular vector that has the smallest singular value.

For the rotational case, we define

$$E(\mathbf{t}) = \int (u - u_{rot})^2 + (v - v_{rot})^2 dxdy. \tag{7.32}$$

Differentiating with $(\omega_x, \omega_y, \omega_z)$, we have

$$\begin{bmatrix} xy & f - x^2 & y \\ f + y^2 & -xy & -x \end{bmatrix} \begin{bmatrix} \omega_x \\ \omega_y \\ \omega_z \end{bmatrix} = \begin{bmatrix} u \\ v \end{bmatrix}. \tag{7.33}$$

This can also be solved by LMS or pseudo-inverse.

When the motion field contains both translational and rotational components, we can define the metric:

$$E(\mathbf{t},\boldsymbol{\omega}) = \int \left\{ \begin{bmatrix} u - u_{rot} \\ v - v_{rot} \end{bmatrix} \cdot \begin{bmatrix} -v_{tr} \\ u_{tr} \end{bmatrix} \right\}^2 dxdy, \tag{7.34}$$

or, in vector form,

$$\int ((\mathbf{t} \times \mathbf{x})(\dot{\mathbf{x}} - \omega \times \mathbf{x}))^2 d\mathbf{x}. \tag{7.35}$$

The motion parallax can be assumed because the difference in motion between two very close points does not depend on rotation. This information can be used at depth discontinuities to obtain the direction of translation. For two points,

$$\Delta u_{tr} = u_1 - u_2 = (x - x_0)\left(\frac{1}{Z_1} - \frac{1}{Z_2}\right), \tag{7.36}$$

$$\Delta v_{tr} = v_1 - v_2 = (y - y_0)\left(\frac{1}{Z_1} - \frac{1}{Z_2}\right). \tag{7.37}$$

Therefore,

$$\frac{\Delta v}{\Delta u} = \frac{y - y_0}{x - x_0}. \tag{7.38}$$

On the other hand, vector components that are perpendicular to the translational component are due to the rotation.

$$\mathbf{u}_{tr}^{\perp} = \frac{(y - y_0, x - x_0)^T}{\|(y - y_0, x - x_0)\|}, \tag{7.39}$$

taking

$$\mathbf{u} \cdot \mathbf{u}^{\perp} = \frac{1}{(y - y_0, x - x_0)}(y - y_0)u_{rot} - (x - x_0)v_{rot}. \tag{7.40}$$

One of the motion estimation methods is to decompose the motion flow into translational and rotational components. Translational flow field is radial (all vectors emanate from – or pour into – one point), whereas rotational flow field is quadratic in image coordinates. Either search in the space of rotations: remaining flow field should be translational. Translational flow field is evaluated by minimizing deviation from the radial field:

$$(-v, u) \cdot (x - x_0, y - y_0) = 0, \tag{7.41}$$

or search in the space of the directions of translation: vectors perpendicular to translation are due to rotation only. Refer to (Burger and Bhanu 1990; Heeger and Jepson 1992; Nelson and Aloimonos 1988; Prazdny 1981).

The other line of research is to use the parametric model for the motion field (Higgins and Prazdny 1980; Waxman 1987). In this approach, the flow is linear in the motion parameters (quadratic or higher order in the image coordinates) and thereby the parametric model for local surface patches (planes or quadrics) solves locally for motion parameters and structure.

7.4 Factorization Method

Given a set of feature tracks, the factorization method estimates the 3D structure and 3D (camera) motion by SVD (Tomasi and Kanade 1992a), using an assumption of orthographic projection.

A general affine camera is represented by the combination of the orthographic projection and the affine transformation of the image:

$$\mathbf{x} = A\mathbf{X} + \mathbf{b}, \quad \text{or} \quad \begin{bmatrix} x \\ y \end{bmatrix} = \begin{bmatrix} a_{11} & a_{12} & a_{13} \\ a_{21} & a_{22} & a_{23} \end{bmatrix} \begin{bmatrix} X \\ Y \\ Z \end{bmatrix} + \begin{bmatrix} b_1 \\ b_2 \end{bmatrix}, \tag{7.42}$$

where A is the projection matrix and b is the translation vector. Let $\{\mathbf{x}_{ij} | i \in [1,m], j \in [1,n]\}$ be the images of the fixed 3D points, $\{\mathbf{X}_j | j \in [1,n]\}$, with m cameras. Considering the affine transformation, the projection is represented by

$$\mathbf{x}_{ij} = A_i\mathbf{X}_j + \mathbf{b}_i, \quad i \in [1,m], j \in [1,n]. \tag{7.43}$$

The problem is to determine m projection matrices A, m vectors $\mathbf{b}$, and n points $\mathbf{X}$, given the mn points $\mathbf{x}$. For the reconstruction, we have $2mn$ known variables, $8m + 3n - 12$ unknowns, and 12 degrees of freedom for the affine transformation:

$$2mn \geq 8m + 3n - 12. \tag{7.44}$$

This equation gives $m \geq 2$ and $n \geq 4$ in ideal cases. Generally, we need more than four corresponding points:

Let us subtract the centroid of the image points:

$$\begin{aligned} \mathbf{x}_{ij} - \frac{1}{n} \sum_{j \in [1,n]} \mathbf{x}_{ij} &= (A_i\mathbf{X}_j + \mathbf{b}_i) - \frac{1}{n} \sum_{j \in [1,n]} (A_i\mathbf{X}_j + \mathbf{b}_i) \\ &= A_i \left\{ \mathbf{X}_j - \frac{1}{n} \sum_{j \in [1,n]} \mathbf{X}_j \right\}, \quad i \in [1,m]. \end{aligned} \tag{7.45}$$

We have also the 3D points, subtracted with the centroids. For simplicity, we assume that the origin of the camera and the world coordinate systems are all defined at the centroid of the image points and 3D points:

$$\mathbf{x}_{ij} = A_i\mathbf{X}_j, \quad i \in [1,m], j \in [1,n]. \tag{7.46}$$

We build a matrix equation, $H = AX$:

$$H = \begin{bmatrix} \mathbf{x}_{11} & \mathbf{x}_{12} & \cdots & \mathbf{x}_{1n} \\ \mathbf{x}_{21} & \mathbf{x}_{22} & \cdots & \mathbf{x}_{2n} \\ & & & \\ \mathbf{x}_{11} & \mathbf{x}_{12} & \cdots & \mathbf{x}_{1n} \end{bmatrix} = \begin{bmatrix} A_1 \\ A_2 \\ \vdots \\ A_m \end{bmatrix} [\mathbf{X}_1 \quad \mathbf{X}_2 \quad \cdots \quad \mathbf{X}_n]. \tag{7.47}$$

Here, H is the $2m \times n$ measurement matrix, A is the $2m \times 3$ motion matrix, and X is the $3 \times n$ structure matrix. Note that the measurement matrix only has rank 3.

The problem becomes one of computing

$$(A^*, X^*) = \arg\min_{A,X} |H - AX|^2. \tag{7.48}$$

The usual approach is to decompose the measurement matrix into two matrices with rank 3. First, we use the SVD,

$$H = U\Lambda' V, \tag{7.49}$$

where Λ' is a diagonal matrix that has the eigenvalues sorted along the diagonal. Then, take the first three largest eiegenvalues, $\lambda_1 \geq \lambda_2 \geq \lambda_3$, of Λ' and build the diagonal matrix:

$$\Lambda = diag(\lambda_1, \lambda_2, \lambda_3). \tag{7.50}$$

The solution is

$$A = U\Lambda^{1/2}, X = \Lambda^{1/2}V. \tag{7.51}$$

The decomposition is not unique, since

$$H = AGG^{-1}X, \tag{7.52}$$

where G is any 3×3 invertible matrix. To remove this uncertainty, we use the constraint that the image axes are perpendicular and unity. For each camera, $A_i = (\mathbf{a}_{i1}, \mathbf{a}_{i2})^T$, find F_i that satisfies

$$\mathbf{a}_{i1}^T F\mathbf{a}_{i1} = 1 \quad \mathbf{a}_{i2}^T F\mathbf{a}_{i2} = 1, \quad \mathbf{a}_{i1}^T F\mathbf{a}_{i2} = 0. \tag{7.53}$$

This gives us a large set of equations for the entries in matrix F. Using Cholesky decomposition, we have $F = GG^T$. The solution is then

$$A_i \leftarrow A_i G, \quad X_i \leftarrow G^{-1}X_i, \quad i \in [1, m]. \tag{7.54}$$

There are numerous variations of the factorization methods: orthographic (Tomasi and Kanade 1992b), weak perspective (Tomasi and Weinshall 1993), para-perspective (Poelman and Kanade 1994, 1997), sequential factorization (Morita and Kanade 1997), perspective (Sturm and Triggs 1996), factorization with uncertainty (Anandan and Irani 2002), element-wise factorization (Dai *et al.* 2013), online factorization (Kennedy *et al.* 2013), and affine factorization (Wang *et al.* 2013).

7.5 Constraints on the Data Term

Thus far, we have reviewed some issues associated with estimating 3D motion and structures, directly or indirectly, from images. The optical flow is an intermediate variable that behaves like a latent variable in 3D reconstruction. Unlike the 3D quantities, the optical flow is defined on the 2D image and is related to the correspondence problem in two or more image sequences. In this problem, the constraints are the most crucial, together with minimization method, for resolving the uncertainties originating from the ill-posed nature.

To estimate optical flow, we usually build an energy function that consists of data and smoothness terms:

$$E(\mathbf{v}) = \sum_{p \in \mathcal{P}} \phi(\mathbf{v}(p)) + \sum_{p,q \in \mathcal{N}} \psi_{pq}(\mathbf{v}(p), \mathbf{v}(q)). \tag{7.55}$$

Here, the variable is the optical flow, $\mathbf{v}$. The data term builds a relationship between the data and the estimated variable. The smoothness function states the relationship between neighborhoods in terms

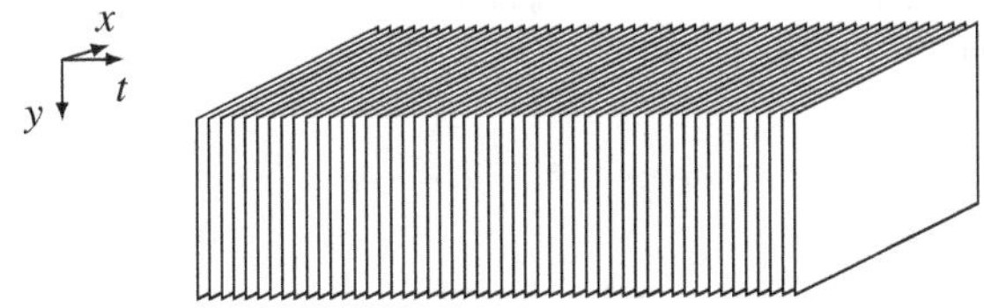

Figure 7.3 A motion cube ($\{I(x,y,t)|x,y \in \mathcal{P}, t = 0, 1, \ldots\}$)

of the optical flow. From a physical point of view, the data term is related to the conservation law of brightness or the differential of brightness in time and space. The smoothness term is related with the spatial variation of the estimated variables. The constraint is local in the data term but global in the smoothness term.

The optical flow problem consists of building the energy function, which is a cost function of the variables, and solving it using the optimization method, which is a general optimization technique tailored to the problem. Therefore, the performance to a large extent depends on how the energy function models the problem with efficient constraints. The multitude of algorithms in optical flow largely depends on the diversity of the constraints and the method of optimization. In this section, we review some representative local and global constraints. For an extensive review on optical flow, see (Raudies 2013; Wikipedia 2013b). Let us review in detail the constraints on the data term first.

The starting point of the constraints on the data term is the *brightness constancy* (BC). The motion analysis needs a stack of video frames, which can be represented as depicted in Figure 7.3. A video signal can be viewed as a stack of images in the direction of the time domain. In the spatiotemporal space, called the *motion cube*, objects are considered to move in the x-y plane as well as in the t direction. The constraint on motion is the relationship between successive image frames, $\{I(x,y,t)|t = 0, 1, \ldots\}$. For the stereo-motion system, the data sequence is the image pairs, $\{(I^l(x,y), I^r(x,y)|x,y \in \mathcal{P}, t = 0, 1, \ldots\}$. In this spatiotemporal space, many new features can be defined (Freeman and Adelson 1991; Sizintsev and Wildes 2012).

The optical flow is a generalization of the disparity from 1D to 2D. Therefore, the constraints must also be generalized. As with binocular vision, the corresponding points must have the same intensity, called the *photometric constraint*. When the optical flow is (u, v), the two points must be equally bright, unless some special illumination is involved. The brightness conservation equation (or *image constraint equation*) (Fennema and Thompson 1979) is

$$I(x,y,t) - I(x+u, y+v, t+1) = 0, \tag{7.56}$$

where the time is normalized to the sampling interval. This is the *brightness constancy* (BC).

The residual is defined by

$$\delta = I(x+u, y+v, t+1) - I(x,y,t), \tag{7.57}$$

which is a generalization of Equation (6.71). This measure assumes that the illumination is constant within the sampling time, and holds even for large variations of optical flow. Because this measure holds for a pixel, it causes the *aperture problem* to arise. For a pair of pixels, we have one equation with two variables, and thus obtain one vector: the normal. To remove the uncertainty, we build the energy function by integrating the local measure and constraints over the image plane.

The next constraint is the linearized brightness constancy. If the variation in optical flow is small, the BC can be approximated by the Taylor series,

$$I(x+u, y+v, t+1) = \frac{\partial}{\partial x}I + \frac{\partial}{\partial y}I + \frac{\partial}{\partial t}I + O(u, v), \tag{7.58}$$

where $O(u, v)$ is the higher-order terms. Taking the first-order Taylor series, we obtain the optical flow constraint equation (OFCE) (Horn and Shunck 1981),

$$I_x u + I_y v + \frac{\partial I}{\partial t} = 0, \quad \text{or} \quad \nabla I^T \mathbf{v} = -I_t, \quad \text{or} \quad (\nabla_t I)^T \begin{bmatrix} u \\ v \\ 1 \end{bmatrix} = 0, \tag{7.59}$$

where, $\mathbf{v} = (u, v)^T$ is the motion vector and $\nabla_t = (\partial_x, \partial_y, \partial_t)^T$ is the gradient operator. We simply call this the *linearized brightness constancy* (LBC). We define the residual by

$$\delta = \underbrace{\begin{bmatrix} I_x & I_y & I_t \end{bmatrix}}_{(\nabla_t I)^T} \begin{bmatrix} u \\ v \\ 1 \end{bmatrix}. \tag{7.60}$$

Although this measure is defined for a small variable, it inherits all the properties of the BC.

Two variables in one equation signify that the equation is under-determined. Using the Moore-Penrose pseudo-inverse, we have $\mathbf{v}^{\perp} = -I_t \nabla I / |\nabla I|^2$. This is just a row-space vector and all the null-space vectors are missing. Any vector having the form $\mathbf{v} = \mathbf{v}^{\perp} + \mathbf{v}^{\parallel}$ satisfies the equation, where $\hat{\mathbf{v}}^{\parallel}$ is the unit null-space vector and $\lambda \in \mathcal{R}$. This can be interpreted geometrically as follows. In (u, v) space, the equation represents a line. For all vectors on this line $\mathbf{v}^{\perp}$ is unique. In the (u, v) plane, the photometric constraint is represented by a straight line (Figure 7.4). Only a normal vector, $\mathbf{v}$, can be estimated with the given photometric constraint. This phenomenon is often called the *aperture problem*. Viewing in a small window, we can estimate only the normal component of the motion field. This uncertainty can be resolved by constraint propagation between neighborhoods. Hence, the energy function must be an integration of the residuals over the entire image plane.

Even this normal vector cannot be estimated immediately. To see this, consider one-dimensional motion as in depicted Figure 7.5. Assume that an object moves from $I(x, t)$ to $I(x, t+1)$. To determine the vector $\mathbf{v}$, we need a normal vector and a gradient vector. $\mathbf{v}_0$ is obtained at the first iteration. Starting

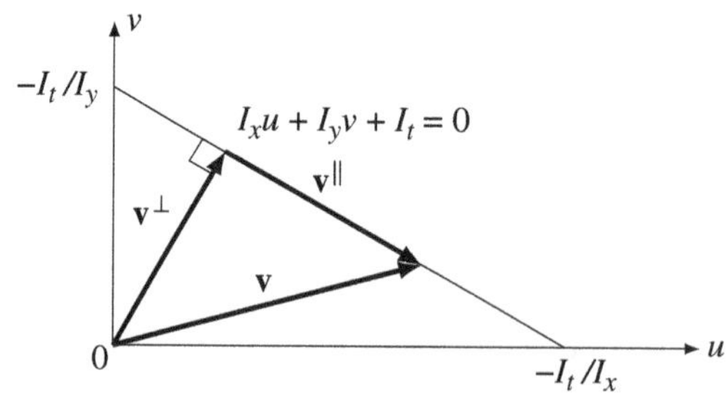

Figure 7.4 Given the photometric constraint, only the normal vector, $\mathbf{v}^{\perp}$, of the true vector, $\mathbf{v}$, can be estimated: $\mathbf{v}^{\parallel}$ for null vector (The unit null vector: $\hat{\mathbf{v}}^{\parallel} = \frac{1}{I_x^2 + I_y^2}(-I_y, I_x)^T$.)

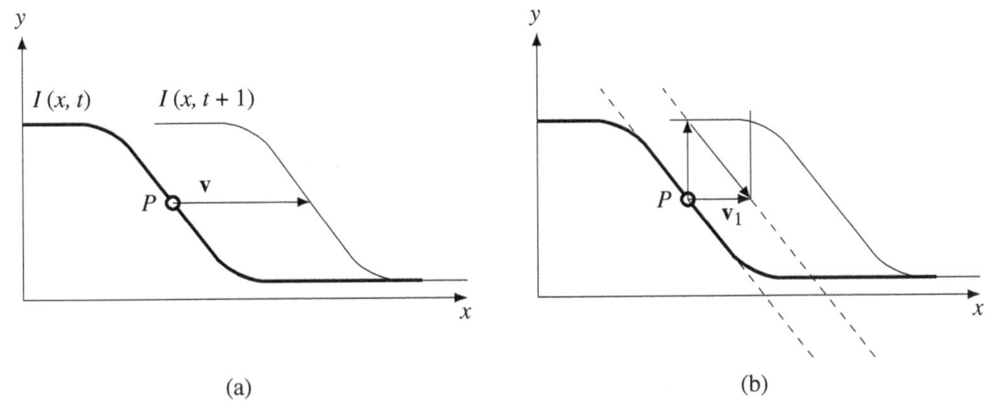

Figure 7.5 Meaning of the photometric constraint: $\nabla I^T \mathbf{v} = -I_t$

from this intermediate position, the next vector can be obtained. The same process can be repeated until the vector arrives near the second curve, $I(x, t+1)$. In math expressions, we have

$$\begin{aligned} \mathbf{v}_0(\mathbf{x}) &= -(\nabla I \nabla I^T)^+ \nabla I(\mathbf{x}, t)(I(\mathbf{x}, t+1) - I(\mathbf{x}, t)), \\ \mathbf{v}_k(\mathbf{x}) &= -(\nabla I \nabla I^T)^+ \nabla I(\mathbf{x}, t)(I(\mathbf{x} + \mathbf{v}_{k-1}, t+1) - I(\mathbf{x}, t)), k = 1, 2, \ldots, T, \end{aligned} \tag{7.61}$$

where T is the termination time when the difference $(I(\mathbf{x} + \mathbf{v}_{k-1}, t+1) - I(\mathbf{x}, t))$ is within a small termination condition. The convergence can be enhanced if we use the higher terms in the Taylor series of $I(x + u, y + v, t + 1)$. This iterative approach is used in (Lucas and Kanade 1981).

We can use a local average to expand the LBC to the gradient structure tensor. Multiplying $\nabla_t I$ on both sides of Equation (7.59), we obtain

$$\nabla_t I (\nabla_t I)^T \begin{bmatrix} u \\ v \\ 1 \end{bmatrix} = 0. \tag{7.62}$$

The 2×2 upper-left submatrix is the Harris operator (Harris and Stephens 1988). If we further apply Gaussian filtering to a small neighborhood, the equation becomes

$$\begin{bmatrix} \sum w_p I_x^2(p) & \sum w_p I_x(p) I_y(p) & \sum w_p I_x(p) I_t(p) \\ \sum w_p I_y(p) I_x(p) & \sum w_p I_y^2(p) & \sum w_p I_y(p) I_t(p) \\ \sum I_t(p) I_x(p) & \sum w_p I_t(p) I_y(p) & \sum I_t^2(p) \end{bmatrix} \begin{bmatrix} u \\ v \\ 1 \end{bmatrix} = 0, \tag{7.63}$$

where $\{w_p | p \in \mathcal{N}_{xy}\}$ is a template of the Gaussian filter. The matrix is called a *motion tensor* (or *structure tensor*). This equation is represented by

$$\begin{bmatrix} \sum w_p I_x^2(p) & \sum w_p I_x(p) I_y(p) \\ \sum w_p I_y(p) I_x(p) & \sum w_p I_y^2(p) \end{bmatrix} \begin{bmatrix} u \\ v \end{bmatrix} = - \begin{bmatrix} \sum w_p I_x(p) I_t(p) \\ \sum w_p I_y(p) I_t(p) \end{bmatrix}. \tag{7.64}$$

This constraint is used in (Lucas and Kanade 1981).

The brightness constancy is not always true. If the background illumination is graded, $\nabla I \neq 0$, it fails. In such a case, we may use the *gradient brightness constancy* (GBC):

$$\nabla I(x+u, y+v, t+1) - \nabla I(u, v, t) = 0. \tag{7.65}$$

This constraint also may fail for large changes in background illumination.

Several methods exist that assume that higher-order derivatives are conserved (Nagel 1987; Simoncelli 1993; Uras *et al.* 1989). The constraint is expressed as

$$uI_{xx} + vI_{xy} + I_{xt} = 0, \quad uI_{xy} + vI_{yy} + I_{yt} = 0. \tag{7.66}$$

Because of the higher-order derivatives, this method tends to be fragile to noise and may lose the information about the first-order deformation. We may also build matrices similar to the structure matrix, by taking local Gaussian filtering.

In a more general environment, the local features can be expanded to the local descriptors (Bay *et al.* 2006; Calonder *et al.* 2010; Lowe 2004; Tola *et al.* 2010), which provide robust and accurate correspondences between images under noisy environments. The correspondence based on the descriptors acts as a concrete matching cue in scenarios with large brightness changes, large motion of small objects, and affine distortions between frames. Define $\rho(x, y)$ to be the matching score for the two descriptors in the current frame and their corresponding descriptors in the next frame, respectively. The descriptor matching term can then be defined as

$$\delta(x, y)\rho(x, y)\|\mathbf{v} - \tilde{\mathbf{v}}\|_2^2 = 0, \tag{7.67}$$

where $\delta(x, y)$ is the indicator variable that is activated when the descriptor is located at (x, y) and $\tilde{\mathbf{v}}$ is the correspondence vector from descriptor matching.

Similarly to the brightness, we can define phase constancy for the phase. In the frequency domain, the motion reveals a certain conservation law – conservation of phase in each bandpass channel (Fleet and Jepson 1990, 1993; Gautama and van Hulle 2002). Given a complex-valued bandpass channel, $r(x, y, t)$, with phase $\phi(x, y, t)$, the conservations law is stated as

$$\phi(x, y, t) = \phi(x+u, y+v, t+1), \tag{7.68}$$

which is similar to the brightness constancy. We call this the *phase constancy* (PC). In the first-order Taylor series, this becomes

$$\phi_x u + \phi_y v + \phi_t = 0, \tag{7.69}$$

or in vector notation,

$$\nabla\phi(\mathbf{x}, t)^T \mathbf{v} + \phi_t(\mathbf{x}, t) = 0. \tag{7.70}$$

The difficulty is that phase is a multifunction, only uniquely defined on intervals of width 2π, so explicit differentiation is difficult. Instead, the phase derivative is replaced with amplitude derivative (Fleet 1992; Fleet and Jepson 1990):

$$\phi_x(\mathbf{x}, t) = \frac{Im[r_x(\mathbf{x}, t)r^*(\mathbf{x}, t)]}{|r(\mathbf{x}, t)|^2}, \quad \phi_t(\mathbf{x}, t) = \arg[r(\mathbf{x}, t+1)r^*(\mathbf{x}, t)]. \tag{7.71}$$

The phase is amplitude invariant and thus is quite robust to illumination but fragile near occlusion boundaries and fine-scale objects.

7.6 Continuity Equation

One of the universal laws in physics is that of conservation, which is represented by the continuity equation. In computer vision, the brightness, gradient brightness, and phase are the quantities preserved even in space and time variations. If $I\mathbf{v}$ is regarded as a flux, the LBC can be represented by the mass continuity equation:

$$\frac{\partial}{\partial t} I + \nabla \cdot (I\mathbf{v}) = 0, \quad \nabla \mathbf{v} = 0, \tag{7.72}$$

where $\nabla\cdot$ is divergence. Note that the vector is constrained to $\nabla \mathbf{v} = 0$, which means the smoothness constraint, as we will see shortly. In an analogy to fluid dynamics, $\nabla \cdot \mathbf{v} = 0$ means that the divergence of the velocity field is zero everywhere, indicating that the local volume dilation rate is zero. If we consider $\nabla I\mathbf{v}$ as a flux, the GBC becomes

$$\frac{\partial}{\partial t} \nabla I + \nabla \cdot (\mathbf{v}^T \nabla I) = 0, \quad \nabla \mathbf{v} = 0. \tag{7.73}$$

The same continuity equation can be applied to the phase. For the phase, we may consider $\phi\mathbf{v}$ as a flux. The LPC then becomes

$$\frac{\partial}{\partial t} \phi + \nabla \cdot (\phi\mathbf{v}) = 0, \quad \nabla \mathbf{v} = 0. \tag{7.74}$$

Similarly, for the GPC, the continuity equation becomes

$$\frac{\partial}{\partial t} \nabla \phi + \nabla \cdot (\mathbf{v}^T \nabla \phi) = 0, \quad \nabla \mathbf{v} = 0. \tag{7.75}$$

The LBC can be represented by

$$(\nabla_t I)^T \mathbf{v} = 0, \tag{7.76}$$

where $\nabla_t = (\partial/\partial x, \partial/\partial y, \partial/\partial t)^T$. Multiplying ∇_t on both sides and convolving with Gaussian filter, we have

$$G * \nabla_t I (\nabla_t I)^T \mathbf{v} = 0. \tag{7.77}$$

The resulting matrix is the structure matrix. This derivation can also be applied to the other variables.

It appears that the various models on the data terms are related to the continuity equation. Moreover, the continuity equations are naturally expanded to color systems such as RGB or HSV. For a detailed review of continuity, refer to (Raudies 2013).

7.7 The Prior Term

In addition to the data term, the prior term in an energy equation is related to various constraints associated with motion mechanics and geometry. These constraints are free from the data but dependent on the nature of the variables in a wider range than the local points. In optimization view, the prior term behaves as a regularizer. The constraints can be classified into isotropic and anisotropic regularizers. The isotropic regularizer applies the constraint uniformly over the image regardless of the object or motion boundary. The anisotropic regularizer, on the other hand, determines the weights and directions depending on the local context.

Let us first review the isotropic smoothness constraints. One of the important constraints on optical flow is the spatial continuity of the optical flow on the surface. The simplest way to represent the spatial smoothness of flow vectors is to favor the following first-order derivatives:

$$\nabla \mathbf{v} = 0, \tag{7.78}$$

which is the generalization of the disparity from one dimension to two dimensions. The continuity equations assume this constraint.

In the construction of the smoothness energy function from the first-order constraint defined above, a variety of penalty functions are utilized to accurately model the characteristics of flow vectors under complex situations. The energy function based on L_2 norm is

$$\|\nabla \mathbf{v}\|_2 = \left(\frac{\partial u}{\partial x}\right)^2 + \left(\frac{\partial u}{\partial y}\right)^2 + \left(\frac{\partial v}{\partial x}\right)^2 + \left(\frac{\partial v}{\partial y}\right)^2. \tag{7.79}$$

The energy function based on L_1 is

$$\|\nabla \mathbf{v}\}_1 = \left|\frac{\partial u}{\partial x} + \frac{\partial u}{\partial y} + \frac{\partial v}{\partial x} + \frac{\partial v}{\partial y}\right| \text{ or } \|\nabla \mathbf{v}\|_1 = \left|\frac{\partial u}{\partial x}\right| + \left|\frac{\partial u}{\partial y}\right| + \left|\frac{\partial v}{\partial x}\right| + \left|\frac{\partial v}{\partial y}\right|. \tag{7.80}$$

The prior can be classified into homogeneous and inhomogeneous regularizer. The inhomogeneous regularizers are further classified into image-driven or flow-driven and isotropic or anisotropic (Raudies 2013). The above regularizers are homogeneous according to this classification.

An *image-driven isotropic regularizer* varies smoothness depending on the image context:

$$\psi(\mathbf{v}) = \rho(\|\nabla I\|_2^2)\|\nabla \mathbf{v}\|_2^2, \quad \rho(x) = \left(1 + \frac{x^2}{\sigma^2}\right), \tag{7.81}$$

where σ is a parameter. The regularization becomes strong around image discontinuity and weak at the uniform region. There is no directional preference, depending on edge direction (Alvarez *et al.* 1999).

An *image-driven anisotropic regularizer* changes smoothness asymmetrically depending on the image context:

$$\psi(\mathbf{v}) = \nabla u \Lambda (\nabla u)^T + \nabla v \Lambda (\nabla v)^T, \Lambda = \frac{1}{|\nabla I|_2^2 + \kappa}\begin{bmatrix} (\partial_y)^2 + \kappa^2 & -\partial_x I \partial_y I \\ -\partial_x I \partial_y I & (\partial_x I)^2 + \kappa^2 \end{bmatrix}, \tag{7.82}$$

where κ is a constant. The smoothing becomes weak at the boundary and strong at the homogeneous region. The smoothing also applies only along the boundary, and not across it.

A *flow-driven isotropic regularizer* controls the smoothness according to the flow of vectors. The following measure uses a convex function of the vector (Bruhn *et al.* 2006):

$$\psi(\mathbf{v}) = \rho(\|\nabla u\|_2^2 + \|\nabla v\|_2^2), \quad \rho(x) = \sqrt{s + \kappa}, \tag{7.83}$$

where κ is a constant.

A *flow-driven anisotropic regularizer* defines the smoothness anisotropically depending on the vector flow (Weickert and Schnorr 2001):

$$\psi(\mathbf{v}) = tr\{\rho((\nabla u)^T \nabla u + (\nabla v)^T \nabla v)\}, \quad \rho(x) = \sqrt{x + \kappa}, \tag{7.84}$$

where κ is a constant and tr means trace. See (Raudies 2013) for more details on regularizers.

The *motion occlusion* is the generalization of the disparity occlusion. When an object moves with $\mathbf{v}$, there appear two undetermined regions to the front, mid, and rear regions of the object. Let an object A move from $A(t) \subset \mathcal{P}$ to $A(t+1) \subset \mathcal{P}$. The front occluding region $A(t-1) - A(t)$ then appears in $I(t)$, the rear occluding region $A(t) - A(t+1)$ appears in $I(t)$, and the middle occluding area is the overlapped region, $A(t) \cup A(t+1)$, which exists in both images. The occluding regions – front and rear regions – are the uncertain regions where the optical flow cannot be defined. Detecting the regions is a crucial task in optical flow computation.

The occluding region is principally where the optical flow is not defined. However, the occluding region is defined only when the optical flow is assumed. Therefore, most algorithms define an occluding indicator that is a function of optical flow and use it to switch the smoothness term, so that the smoothness term is validated only in the non-occluding region.

Let $\rho(\mathbf{x}, t)$ be an occlusion indicator (or detector). The occlusion can be detected by the squared image residue (Xiao *et al.* 2006):

$$\rho(\mathbf{x}, t) = \begin{cases} 0, & (I(\mathbf{x}, t) - I(\mathbf{x} + \mathbf{v}, t+1))^2 > \epsilon, \\ 1, & otherwise, \end{cases} \tag{7.85}$$

where ϵ is a threshold to detect the occlusion. If $\rho = 0$, the pixel is occluded and if $\rho = 1$, the pixel is visible in both images. To make the occlusion indicator, it can be approximated by

$$\rho(\mathbf{x}, t) = \frac{1}{2} + \frac{1}{\pi} \tan^{-1}((I(\mathbf{v}, t) - I(\mathbf{x} + \mathbf{v}, t+1))^2 - \epsilon). \tag{7.86}$$

The optical flow vector can be used to detect occlusions (Sand and Teller 2008; Sand 2006):

$$\rho(\mathbf{x}, t) = |\nabla \cdot \mathbf{v}|. \tag{7.87}$$

The edges and corners in the spatiotemporal domain correspond to the occluded pixels. These points of interest are detected using the minimum eigenvalue of the gradient structure tensor (Feldman and Weinshall 2006, 2008):

$$\rho(\mathbf{x}, t) = \lambda_{min}\{G(\mathbf{x}, \sigma) * (\nabla I(\mathbf{x}, t) \nabla I(\mathbf{x}, t))\}, \tag{7.88}$$

where the operators $*$ and G represent convolution and Gaussian kernel, respectively. The operator is invariant to the translation and rotation. The region with higher values of λ tends to be the outline of the object. This operator can be modified to the velocity-adapted occlusion detector (Feldman and Weinshall 2006, 2008):

$$\rho(\mathbf{x}, t) = \frac{det(G)}{G^*}, \tag{7.89}$$

where G denotes the 2×2 upper-left submatrix of the gradient structure tensor.

The Frobenius norm of the gradient of the optical flow field can be used to capture the motion discontinuity (Sargin *et al.* 2009):

$$\rho(\mathbf{x}, t) = \|\nabla \mathbf{v}(\mathbf{x})\|_F, \tag{7.90}$$

which is helpful to detect occlusion.

The occlusion indicator is usually utilized in controlling the prior term:

$$E(\mathbf{v}) = \sum_{p\in\mathcal{P}} \phi(\mathbf{v}(p)) + \rho(\mathbf{x}, t) \sum_{p,q\in\mathcal{N}} \psi_{pq}(\mathbf{v}(p), \mathbf{v}(q)). \tag{7.91}$$

Around the occlusion, only the data term operates, the smoothness term is ignored. As a result, the occlusion region is undetermined but the boundaries are accurately preserved.

Another strong constraint for the smoothness term is based on the parametric motion model. The global motion model (Altunbasak *et al.* 1998; Cremers and Soatto 2005; Odobez and Bouthemy 1995) offers more constrained solutions than smoothness, such as the Horn–Schunck method. It also involves integration over a larger area than a translation-only model can accommodate, such as the Lukas-Kanade method. More specifically, we suppose

$$E(\mathbf{a}) = \sum (I(T(\mathbf{x}, \mathbf{a})) - I_0(\mathbf{x}))^2, \tag{7.92}$$

where $T(\cdot)$ is a transformation in 2D or 3D, with parameters $\mathbf{a}$. The possible models are 2D and 3D motion models. The 2D models include translation, affine, quadratic, and homography. The 3D model includes camera motion, homography with epipole, and plane with parallax (Adiv 1985; Hanna 1991; Nir *et al.* 2008; Valgaerts *et al.* 2008; Wedel *et al.* 2008a, 2009).

A quadratic model for the 2D motion is parameterized by

$$\begin{cases} u = a_1 + a_2x + a_3y + a_7x^2 + a_8xy, \\ v = a_4 + a_5x + a_6y + a_7xy + a_8y^2. \end{cases} \tag{7.93}$$

In the projective model, the parameters are

$$u = \frac{a_1 + a_2x + a_3y}{a_7 + a_8x + a_9y} - x, \quad v = \frac{a_4 + a_5x + a_6y}{a_7 + a_8x + a_9y} - y. \tag{7.94}$$

In the 3D motion model, the instantaneous camera motion method assumes the global parameters, $\boldsymbol{\omega}$ and $\mathbf{t}$, together with the local parameter, $Z(x, y)$. The motion vector is

$$\begin{cases} u = -xy\omega_x + (1 + x^2)\omega_y - y\omega_z + (t_x - xt_z)/Z, \\ v = -(1 + y^2)\omega_x + xy\omega_y - x\omega_z + (t_y - xt_z)/Z. \end{cases} \tag{7.95}$$

The model for homography and epipole uses the global parameters, $a_1, \ldots, a_9, t_1, \ldots, t_3$ and the local parameters: $\gamma(x, y)$.

$$u = \frac{a_1x + a_2y + a_3 + \gamma t_1}{a_7x + a_8y + a_9 + \gamma t_3} - x, \quad v = \frac{a_4x + a_5y + a_6 + \gamma t_1}{a_7x + a_8y + a_9 + \gamma t_3} - x. \tag{7.96}$$

There is a method that uses residual planar parallel motion, that also uses the global parameters: a_1, a_2, a_3 and the local parameter $\gamma(x, y)$.

$$u = \frac{\gamma}{1+\gamma a_3}(a_3 x - a_1), \quad v = \frac{\gamma}{1+\gamma a_3}(a_3 y - a_2). \tag{7.97}$$

In addition to constraints, special features have been developed for motion estimation. In space-time, the feature can be either intensity variation (Sizintsev and Wildes 2012) or texture (Derpanis and Wildes 2012), quadric elements (Granlund and Knutssen 1995) or Grammian (Shechtman and Irani 2007). The quantities can be a response from the local filter responses such as Gaussian–Hilbert (Freeman and Adelson 1991), Gabor, and log-normal. For example, Sizintsev *et al.* proposed *Stequel* as a quadric weighted by the Gaussian-Hilbert response in icosahedron directions (Jenkins and Tsotsos 1986; Sizintsev and Wildes 2012).

7.8 Energy Minimization

We have reviewed various constraints on the data and prior terms. The energy function consists of both these terms. Therefore there are numerous variations on combinations of the data and smoothness terms. In minimizing the energy function, many optimization methods can be utilized, including baseline methods such as those of Horn and Shunck (Horn and Shunck 1981) and Lukas and Kanade (Lucas and Kanade 1981). Horn's method advocates the LBC and smoothness regularization for the energy function and the variational method for energy minimization. On the other hand, Lukas–Kanade's method uses the gradient structure tensor for the energy function and the LMS method for energy minimization.

A general solution based on the variational method is given by (Horn and Shunck 1981). The energy function is the combination of the LBC and the smoothness function with gradient magnitude:

$$E(u, v) = \sum_{(x,y)\in\mathcal{P}} (I_x u + I_y v + I_t)^2 + \lambda \sum_{v\in\mathcal{N}(u)} |\nabla(u, v)^T|^2. \tag{7.98}$$

Let $E = \int F(u, v, u_x, u_y, v_x, v_y)dxdy$ and derive the Euler–Lagrange equations,

$$F_u - \partial_x F_{u_x} - \partial_y F_{u_y} = 0, \quad F_v - \partial_x F_{v_x} - \partial_y F_{v_y} = 0. \tag{7.99}$$

Inserting F, this becomes

$$I_x(I_x u + I_y v + I_t) - \lambda\nabla^2 u = 0, \quad I_y(I_x u + I_y v + I_t) - \lambda\nabla^2 v = 0. \tag{7.100}$$

Let the local average

$$\bar{u}(x, y) = \sum w_{(k,l)\in\mathcal{N}(x,y)} u(x - k, y - l) \tag{7.101}$$

and the Laplacian

$$\nabla^2 = \bar{u}(x, y) - u(x, y). \tag{7.102}$$

Then, the equations become

$$(I_x^2 + \lambda)u + I_x I_y v = \lambda\bar{u} - I_x I_t, \quad I_x I_y u + (I_y^2 + \lambda)v = \lambda\bar{v} - I_y I_t. \tag{7.103}$$

Solving this, and taking iterative forms, we have the equations,

$$\begin{cases} u^{(k+1)} = \bar{u}^{(k)} - \frac{I_x(I_x\bar{u}^{(k)}+I_y\bar{v}^{(k)}+I_t)}{\lambda+I_x^2+I_y^2}, \\ v^{(k+1)} = \bar{v}^{(k)} - \frac{I_y(I_x\bar{u}^{(k)}+I_y\bar{v}^{(k)}+I_t)}{\lambda+I_x^2+I_y^2}. \end{cases} \tag{7.104}$$

The computational structure is suitable for the Gauss–Seidel or Jacobi methods. This can be efficiently realized with the relaxation, DP, and BP architectures, introduced in Chapters 8 through 10.

The other general solution based on LMS is given by (Lucas and Kanade 1981), which uses the gradient structure tensor. For a point, Equation (7.59) becomes

$$\nabla I^T \mathbf{v} = -\left[I_t(x,y) \right]. \tag{7.105}$$

The pseudo-inverse is

$$\mathbf{v} = -\frac{\nabla I}{\|\nabla I\|^2} I_t(x,y). \tag{7.106}$$

For a point, we have one equation and two variables. The solution is the normal flow, $\mathbf{v}^{\perp}$, as observed in the aperture problem.

To get more equations for a pixel, impose additional constraints by assuming that the flow field is smooth locally, and thus the neighbors have the same optical flow. Consequently, we obtain, $A\mathbf{v} = -\mathbf{I}_t$:

$$\begin{bmatrix} I_x(x_1,y_1) & I_y(x_1,y_1) \\ \vdots & \vdots \\ I_x(x_n,y_n) & I_y(x_n,y_n) \end{bmatrix} \begin{bmatrix} u \\ v \end{bmatrix} = - \begin{bmatrix} I_t(x_1,y_1) \\ \vdots \\ I_t(x_n,y_n) \end{bmatrix}. \tag{7.107}$$

Usually, A is a local weighted sum of intensity with a Gaussian function. This can be represented by the Gaussian kernel, $W = \{w_{ij} | i,j \in [1,n]\}$:

$$A^T W A \mathbf{v} = -A^T W \mathbf{I}_t. \tag{7.108}$$

In component form, this is

$$\begin{bmatrix} \sum_k w_k I_x^2 & \sum_k w_k I_x I_y \\ \sum_k w_k I_x I_y & \sum_k w_k I_y^2 \end{bmatrix} \begin{bmatrix} u \\ v \end{bmatrix} = - \begin{bmatrix} \sum_k w_k I_x(x_k,y_k) I_t(x_k,y_k) \\ \sum_k w_k I_y(x_k,y_k) I_t(x_k,y_k) \end{bmatrix}. \tag{7.109}$$

This system is over-determined and thus can be solved by LLSE. If $A^T W A$ is invertible, we have

$$\mathbf{v} = -(A^T W A)^{-1} A^T W \mathbf{I}_t. \tag{7.110}$$

In general, the brightness constancy is not satisfied, the motion is not small, a point does not move like its neighbors, and thus, the LMS method is not satisfactory. The enhanced method is the iterative Lukas–Kanade method (Kanade 1987; Lucas and Kanade 1981).

7.9 Binocular Motion

When objects are observed with a stereo camera, the image frames contain both stereo and motion information, for example disparity and optical flow. Let us consider the case depicted in Figure 7.6, in which the origins O_l and O_r are, respectively, the projective centers of the left and right images, I_t^l and I_t^r; the image planes are coplanar and the optical axes are parallel, separated by a baseline B. In this setting, a point $\mathbf{P} = (X, Y, Z)^T$ moving from P to Q is projected onto the two image planes as $\mathbf{p}_l = (x_l, y_l)^T$ and $\mathbf{p}_r = (x_r, y_r)^T$. This alignment is parallel optics, and the epipolar lines, on which corresponding points are located, are the same for both images.

Two images of the same size, $M \times N$, are captured at constant intervals in time t. In 3-space, the point $\mathbf{P}$ is generally moving with a velocity $\mathbf{V} = (U, V, W)^T$, where (U, V, W) describes the translation components. Accordingly, the two projected points also move on the image planes with the optical flows, $\mathbf{v}_l = (u^l, v^l)$ and $\mathbf{v}_r = (u^r, v^r)$. Furthermore, the two projected points are separated with the disparity, d, on both image planes. (Incidentally, the rotational movement is omitted to make the problem simple.) If the sampling rate is fast enough or, equivalently, the rotation is slow enough, this assumption is correct even for the general case.

From Equation (7.7), we have

$$\begin{cases} (u^l, v^l) = \frac{f}{Z}(U, V) - f\frac{W}{Z^2}(X, Y), \\ (u^r, v^r) = \frac{f}{Z}(U, V) - f\frac{W}{Z^2}(X - B, Y). \end{cases} \tag{7.111}$$

Likewise, the disparity–depth relation becomes

$$d = \frac{fB}{Z}. \tag{7.112}$$

Taking the time derivative of both sides, we obtain

$$\dot{d} = -\frac{fBW}{Z^2}. \tag{7.113}$$

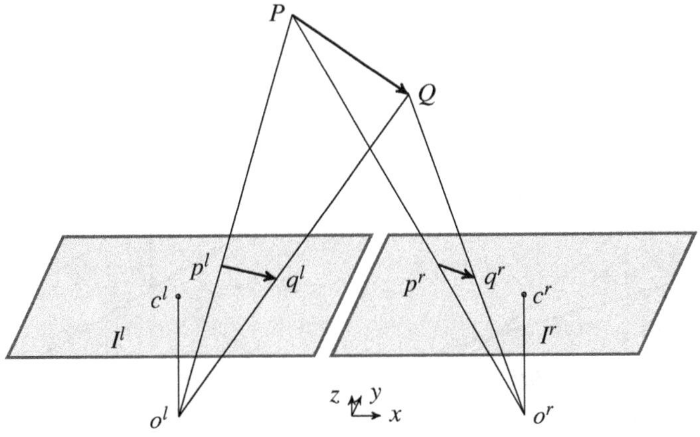

Figure 7.6 Projection of moving object

Substituting Equation (7.113) into Equation (7.111) yields the equation

$$u^r - u^l = \dot{d}, \quad v^l - v^r = 0. \tag{7.114}$$

The first equation specifies that the difference between the two optical flows is identical to the difference between the two disparities. The second equation is due to the epipolar assumption: the corresponding points are on the same epipolar line whenever the point moves. This equation means that there are five variables in two equations and explains the relationship between disparity and optical flow, bypassing the 3D positions and velocity.

The combination of motion and stereo can be explained by the two frames of stereo images, $\{I^l(x, y, t), I^r(x, y, t), I^l(x, y, t+1), I^r(x, y, t+1)\}$. In this system, we assume that $d(x, y, t) = d_0(x, y, t)$ is known. Then, for the unknowns, $(\mathbf{v}^l, \mathbf{v}^r, d)$, the following constraints hold:

$$\begin{cases} I^l(x,y,t) = I^r(x+d_0,y,t), & I^l(x,y,t+1) = I^r(x+d,y,t+1), \\ u^r - u^l = \dot{d}, & v^l - v^r = 0, \\ M2: I^r_x u^r + I^r_y v^r + I^r_t = 0, & M3: I^l_x u^l + I^l_y v^l + I^l_t = 0. \end{cases} \tag{7.115}$$

The first two equations are the brightness constraints for the stereo matching. The next two constraints are the relationships between disparity and optical flow. The last two equations are the linearized brightness constraints for the optical flow. For the four points, we have four equations and five variables.

The constraint equations are drawn in Figure 7.7. Unlike Figure 7.4, two lines characterize the (u, v) plane. The equation, $v^l - v^r = 0$, appears as a vertical line in this graph and the resulting crossing points define (u^l, u^r). However, the position of the vertical line is defined by $\dot{d}$, the vertical separation between the two lines. Hence, if $\dot{d}$ is decided, via stereo matching, $\mathbf{v}^l$ and $\mathbf{v}^r$ are all determined uniquely. Since there is no other constraint on the two lines except a negative slope, degenerate cases exist. The typical case is when the two lines are parallel to each other. In this case, even though the separation $\dot{d}$ is known, no single $v^l = v^r$ is defined. The degenerate case occurs when the slopes of the two lines are the same: $I^l_y/I^l_x = I^r_y/I^r_x$. The worst case occurs when the two lines are overlapping, that is $I^l_x = I^r_x$ and $I^l_y = I^r_y$. We may solve this problem by the variational method or the LMS method (Jeong *et al.* 2012).

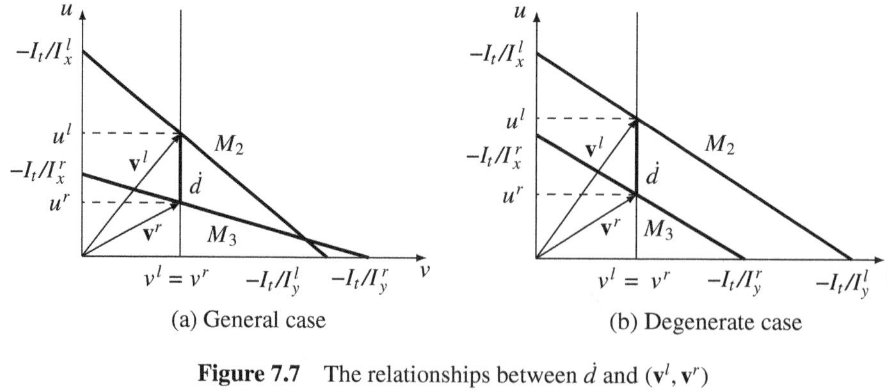

Figure 7.7 The relationships between $\dot{d}$ and $(\mathbf{v}^l, \mathbf{v}^r)$

7.10 Segmentation Prior

The determination of disparity and optical flow is generally aided by image segmentation. This concept can be generalized to the segmentation, which involves many attributes of the image. The segmentation, whether it is defined for regions or edges, is usually the final goal of the early vision. Using this method, regions classified as having the same label tend to be assigned with the same disparity or optical flow. This segment-based constraint, if available, can help the smoothness constraint to retain the sharp boundaries. The reason is that the pixels defined inside the segments or contours are similar with respect to some characteristic but the pixels in adjacent regions or across contours are significantly different with respect to the same characteristics. The result of segmentation can be easily integrated into the energy functions in higher level vision, in the form of constraint terms or initial values of the labeling. However, the segment characteristics such as brightness, color, texture, and edges and the high level characteristics such as surface orientation, disparity, optical flow, or object class may not always coincide. Some of the typical methods are thresholding, edge detection, histogram, compression-based, region growing, clustering, split-and-merge, model-based method, graph partitioning, and multi-scale methods.

One of the practical segmentation methods is *soft matting* (Levin *et al.* 2007, 2008, 2011; Shi and Malik 2000; Sun *et al.* 2010), which can be easily ported to the disparity and optical flow. In this method, the *matting Laplacian matrix* (Levin *et al.* 2008) is

$$L_k = \sum_{(i,j)\in N_k} \left(\delta_{ij} - \frac{1}{|N_k|} \left(1 + (I_i - \mu_k)^T \left(\Sigma_k + \frac{\epsilon}{|N_k|} \right)^{-1} (I_j - \mu_k) \right) \right), \tag{7.116}$$

where I_i and I_j are the colors of the input image at pixels i and j, δ_{ij} is the Kronecker delta, μ_k and Σ_k are the mean and covariance matrix of the colors in window N_k, I_3 is a 3×3 identity matrix, ϵ is a regularization parameter, and $|N_k|$ is the number of pixels in window N_k.

We can consider the Laplacian matrix as a quadratic approximation of exponential form:

$$L_k = \sum_{k|(i,j)\in N_k} \left(\delta_{ij} - \frac{1}{|N_k|} \exp \left[(I_i - \mu_k)^T \left(\Sigma_k + \frac{\epsilon}{|N_k|} \right)^{-1} (I_j - \mu_k) \right] \right). \tag{7.117}$$

Furthermore, omitting the ϵ term and generalizing the correlation term yields

$$L_k = \sum_{k|(i,j)\in N_k} \left(\delta_{ij} - \frac{1}{|N_k|} \exp -(I_i - I_j)^T \Sigma_k^{-1} (I_i - I_j) \right). \tag{7.118}$$

The segmentation result using L_k can be added to the smoothness constraint in the energy equation, so that the same segment may be assigned with the same labels.

7.11 Blur Diameter

Thus far, we have examined stereo vision and motion estimation, estimating depth, motion, structure, and camera pose. Now we examine some of other modalities in vision that are associated with depth estimation. The intrinsic parameters explain the pixels, focal length, and possibly the lens distortion. What is missing is the effect of real aperture, which generates unequal sharpness, called *blurring*, across the image plane. At one end, this unequal focusing is regarded as undesirable and must be rectified by inverse filtering. At the other end, except for artistic effect such as portrait photographing, the defocusing is considered as an encoding process of depth information, such that the degree of blur is in proportion to the depth. The amount of blur can be represented by the blur diameter of the PSF. Like the disparity or optical flow, the blur diameter can be estimated and used for depth computation.

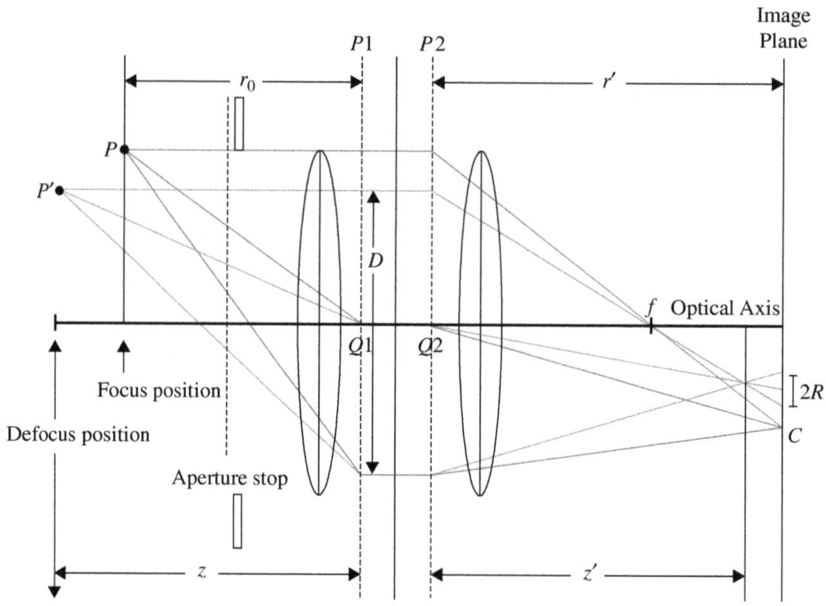

Figure 7.8 The camera optics with thin convex lens

Suppose that there is a typical lens system, such as that drawn in Figure 7.8, which is called a *thin lens system*. In this figure, $P1$ and $P2$ are the *principal planes*, and $Q1$ and $Q2$ are the *principal points*. A lens with focal length f is focused on a scene point P at a *subject distance* r_0, and this focused point is mapped to r' on the image plane. A point other than the subject distance is mapped to z' and thus defocused, as indicated by the blur diameter $2R$.

For a point, P, this system satisfies

$$\frac{1}{r_0} + \frac{1}{r'} = \frac{1}{f}. \tag{7.119}$$

For a point, P, the defocused image satisfies

$$\frac{1}{z} + \frac{1}{z'} = \frac{1}{f}. \tag{7.120}$$

These equations express the fact that a point between the lens and P is focused in front of the image plane, whereas a point behind P is focused behind the image plane. In either case, the projected image will appear as a spot with radius R of the *circle of confusion* (or *blur circle*), on the image plane.

Comparing the two triangles, one on either side of f, we can derive a relationship between the blur radius R and the distance z':

$$\frac{R}{D} = \frac{r' - z'}{z'}. \tag{7.121}$$

Using r' in Equation (7.119) and z' in Equation (7.120), we have

$$R = \frac{Dr_0 f}{r_0 - f}\left(\frac{1}{r_0} - \frac{1}{Z}\right). \tag{7.122}$$

For the case where $r_0 \gg f$ and $|z - r_0|$ are not negligible, Equation (7.122) becomes

$$R \cong fD\left(\frac{1}{r_0} - \frac{1}{Z}\right). \tag{7.123}$$

Once R is known, we can obtain the object distance from the blur disk:

$$Z = f\left(\frac{f}{r_0} - \frac{R}{D}\right)^{-1}. \tag{7.124}$$

We have observed that, like disparity and optical flow, the *blur diameter* is another measure that can be obtained from images. If the imaging system consists of compound lenses, the blur–depth relationship becomes a complicated nonlinear system, although the depth is still related with the blur diameter. Blur estimation has been studied in areas such as depth from focus (DfF) (Grossmann 1987; Jing and Yeung 2012) and depth from defocus (DfD) (Li *et al.* 2013; Subbarao and Surya 1994).

7.12 Blur Diameter and Disparity

Similar to disparity and optical flow giving measures on depth, the blur diameter provides the same measure of depth. It would therefore be useful if the three quantities could be linked in such a way that the common depth quantity is eliminated and the variables are linked directly. In this light, let us first consider linking disparity and blur diameter (Ito *et al.* 2010; Schechner and Kiryati 2000; Subbarao *et al.* 1997).

If we substitute $Z = fB/d$ into (7.124) to remove Z, we obtain

$$\frac{d}{B} + \frac{R}{D} = 1 - \frac{f}{r'}. \tag{7.125}$$

This equation links disparity and blur diameter directly, without intervention of the depth, and has the following properties. In a normalized system, this equation has the form $\hat{d} + \hat{R} = 1 - \hat{f}$, where the three quantities, $\hat{d}$, $\hat{R}$, and $\hat{f}$, are the normalized values with respect to the baseline, lens diameter, and the image plane distance, respectively. The variables are the disparity and the blur diameter. The two variables have opposite properties in terms of addition: if one decreases, the other increases equivalently, maintaining the total sum at a constant.

It is convenient to generalize R so that it can be either positive or negative depending on the distance $r' - z'$. Substituting Z for r_0 in Equation (6.66) yields

$$r_0 = \frac{r'B}{d_0}. \tag{7.126}$$

With this and Equation (7.122), we obtain

$$\begin{cases} R > 0, & d < d_0, \\ R = 0, & d = d_0, \\ R < 0, & d > d_0. \end{cases} \tag{7.127}$$

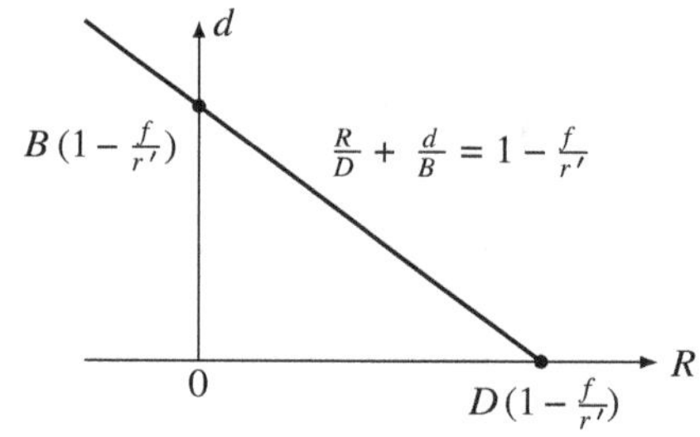

Figure 7.9 The d–R curve

The d–R curve is drawn in Figure 7.9. Here, the x-intercept is the position where the object is at infinity and the y-intercept is the position where the object is focused. The negative diameter means that the object is focused behind the image plane.

This relationship can be used as a constraint for determining disparity, given blur diameter:

$$\psi_p(d) = \left(d - 1 - \frac{f}{r'} - \frac{B}{D}R\right)^2. \tag{7.128}$$

Note that this constraint holds for a pixel, similar to the data term.

7.13 Surface Normal and Disparity

In other vision modules such as shading, texture, and silhouette, the major estimated quantity is the *surface normal*. Considering the depth $(x, y, Z(x, y))$, we have the surface normal (Horn 1986):

$$\mathbf{n} = \frac{1}{\sqrt{1 + p^2 + q^2}}[-p, -q, 1]^T, \tag{7.129}$$

where (p, q) is the gradient,

$$p = \frac{\partial Z}{\partial x}, \quad q = \frac{\partial Z}{\partial y}. \tag{7.130}$$

The surface normal can be represented by a more versatile vector, called *stereographic projection* (Horn 1986).

If a surface is sloped, the slope affects both the surface normal and the disparity (Figure 7.10). At (x^l, y^l), the surface depth is $Z(x, y)$ and the disparity is $d(x^l, y^l)$. At $(x^l + \Delta x^l, y^l + \Delta y^l)$, the depth changes by ΔZ and the disparity changes by Δd. If the surface is fronto-parallel, the depth and the disparity are both constant.

To obtain the relationship between the disparity and the surface slope, we substitute Equation (6.66) into Equation (7.130) and obtain

$$p = -\frac{fB}{d^2}\frac{\partial d}{\partial x}, \quad q = -\frac{fB}{d^2}\frac{\partial d}{\partial y}, \tag{7.131}$$

which is, in fact, $p = fB\partial_x d^{-1}$ and $q = fB\partial_y d^{-1}$. Here, the normal vector and the disparity are all defined in the image coordinates. These identities represent the direct relationship between the disparity and the

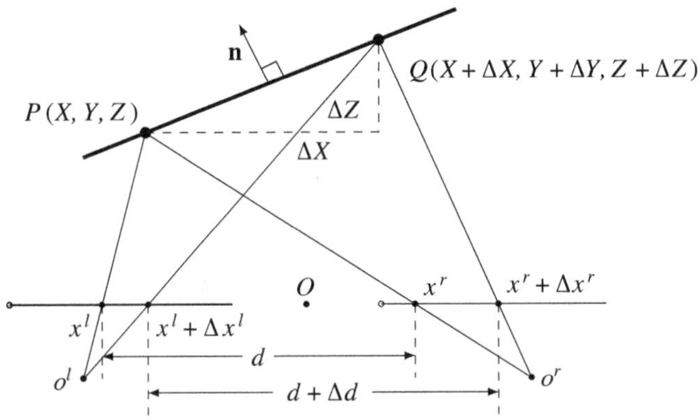

Figure 7.10 The relationship between disparity and surface normal (**n**: surface normal and d: disparity)

surface orientation, all in the image plane. If (p, q) is given, these equations can be used as constraints in stereo matching (and vice versa):

$$\psi_{x,y,x',y'}(d(x,y), d(x',y')) = \left(p + \frac{fB}{d^2}(d(x,y) - d(x',y))\right)^2 + \left(q + \frac{fB}{d^2}(d(x,y) - d(x,y'))\right)^2, \quad \forall (x',y') \in \mathcal{N}_{xy}. \tag{7.132}$$

Here the distance between neighbors is assumed to be unity.

The surface normal is often estimated with a surface model. If the surface is planar, $Z(x,y) = ax + by + c$, we have the constraints, $d_x = -d^2a/fB, d_y = -d^2b/fB$. As a special case, if the surface is a fronto-parallel plane, the disparity is constant. For a quadratic model of the surface, $Z(x,y) = ax^2 + by^2 + cxy + d$, the disparity becomes $d_x = ax + cy, d_y = by + cx$.

If $(p, q) \neq 0$, these equations can be further combined into one:

$$q\frac{\partial d}{\partial x} = p\frac{\partial d}{\partial y}. \tag{7.133}$$

This equation means that the two normals, $\mathbf{n} = (-p, -q, 1)^T$ and $\mathbf{d} = (-d_x, -d_y, 1)^T$, exist in the same vertical plane, that is $(\mathbf{d} \times \mathbf{n}) \cdot \hat{\mathbf{Z}} = 0$. This equation can also be used as a constraint to the smoothness terms.

7.14 Surface Normal and Blur Diameter

We may link the blur diameter and the surface normal. This can be achieved by substituting Equation (7.124) into Equation (7.130). The result is

$$p = \frac{f}{\left(\frac{f}{r_0} - \frac{R}{D}\right)^2}\frac{\partial R/D}{\partial x}, \quad q = \frac{f}{\left(\frac{f}{r_0} - \frac{R}{D}\right)^2}\frac{\partial R/D}{\partial y}. \tag{7.134}$$

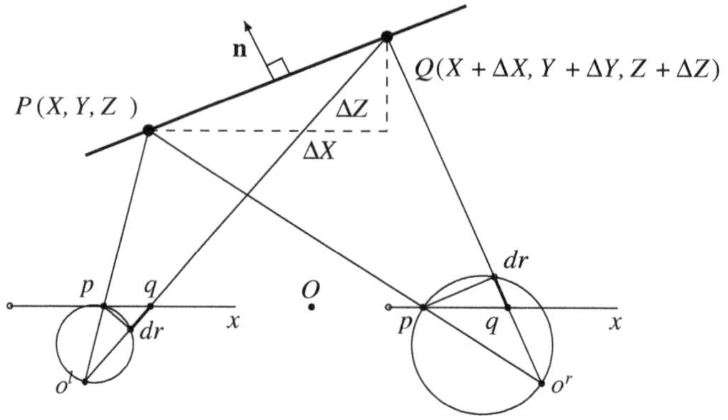

Figure 7.11 The relationship between surface normal and blur diameter (**n**: surface normal)

These equations directly link the surface normal to the blur diameter. They can be combined to give

$$qR_x = pR_y. \tag{7.135}$$

This equation means that the two normals, $\mathbf{n} = (-p, -q, 1)^T$ and $\mathbf{d} = (-R_x, -R_y, 1)^T$, exist in the same vertical plane, that is $(\mathbf{R} \times \mathbf{n}) \cdot \hat{\mathbf{Z}} = 0$.

The relationship of the surface normal to the blur diameter is illustrated in Figure 7.11. On the left image, the slope ΔZ appears as a prolonged dr, which affects the degree of blur.

For a stereo system, the surface slope influences the blur diameter on both images, as shown in the figure. On the right image, the slope appears as a shortened dr and is represented in Equation (7.124). Unlike other measures, the blur diameters are defined separately in the two images. This results in another relationship: blur difference in two images. This means that more than two modules can be described. In this particular case, disparity, surface normal, and blur diameters are involved.

To obtain the relationship between the blur diameter and the disparity, we insert Equation (7.131) into (7.134) to get

$$\frac{\partial R}{\partial x}\frac{\partial d}{\partial y} = \frac{\partial R}{\partial y}\frac{\partial d}{\partial x}. \tag{7.136}$$

For the functions, $R(x, y)$ and $d(x, y)$, this equation means that the two normals, $\mathbf{R} = (-R_x, -R_y, 1)^T$ and $\mathbf{d} = (-d_x, -d_y, 1)^T$, exist in the same vertical plane: $(\mathbf{R} \times \mathbf{d}) \cdot \hat{\mathbf{Z}} = 0$. We have two sets of equations, Equations (7.125) and (7.136). In one equation, the variables are directly related in a linear equation, and in the other the variables are related in the ratio of differentials.

7.15 Links between Vision Modules

There are vision modules for depth estimation such as depth from defocus (DfD), shape from shading (SfS) (Harrison and Joseph 2012), shape from texture (SfT), shape from contour or silhouette (SfC), as well as stereo vision and motion vision. Integration of vision modules can be achieved by combining them in an energy equation and minimizing it to achieve the best depth. The other approach is to treat the vision modules as weak classifiers and build a combined classifier with boosting methods. It is

Table 7.1 The 2D and 3D quantities

Measures		Depth	Velocity
Disparity	d	$Z = f\frac{B}{d}$	
Optical flow	(u, v)		$U = \frac{uZ + xW}{f}, V = \frac{vZ + yW}{f}$
Surface normal	(p, q)	$p = \frac{\partial Z}{\partial x}, q = \frac{\partial Z}{\partial y}$	
Blur diameter	R	$Z = f\left(\frac{f}{r_0} - \frac{R}{D}\right)^{-1}$	

cf. f: focal length, B: baseline, D: lens diameter, r_0: subject distance, and r': image distance.

evident that this integration is limited since the interacting mechanisms between modules are ignored. Eventually, one must look into the tighter relationships between variables defined in different modules.

Thus far, we have examined the constructs for depth estimation: disparity, optical flow, blur diameter, and surface orientation. The relationship between the 2D and 3D variables are summarized in Table 7.1.

The 2D quantities are obtained by various vision modules, as stated. Given the 2D quantities, the 3D variables (depth and velocity) can be obtained using the formula in the table. In this formula, we assume the simplest models possible to avoid complexity. In stereo vision, the epipolar rectified system is assumed. For a convergent system, the 3D quantities must be transformed with the projective matrix, which were used in the rectification process. In addition, the aperture system is assumed to be the thin lens system. The disparity and blur diameter give depth in absolute values whereas the surface normal gives only the orientation of the surface. In velocity computation, the quasi-orthographic projection and the small velocity in the Z direction are assumed, and the rotational velocity ignored. For a more general system, we have to replace the equations with more accurate ones.

To remove the 3D variables, the 2D variables can be combined in various ways. The resulting equation gives the direct relationship between the 2D variables, bypassing the 3D variables. Table 7.2 summarizes the relationships between the 2D variables.

The upper triangle is filled with the ordinary equations and the lower triangle is filled with differential equations. Among others, the disparity–normal relationship has the significant meaning that it links the

Table 7.2 The relationships between 2D variables

	d	(u, v)	(p, q)	R
d	–	$\begin{cases} \dot{d} = u^r - u^l \\ v^l = v^r \end{cases}$	$\begin{cases} p = -\frac{fB}{d^2}d_x \\ q = -\frac{fB}{d^2}d_y \end{cases}$	$\frac{d}{B} + \frac{R}{D} = 1 - \frac{f}{r'}$
(u, v)	–	–	–	–
(p, q)	$qd_x = pd_y$	–	–	$\begin{cases} p = \frac{f}{\left(\frac{f/D}{r_0} - \frac{R}{D}\right)^2}R_x \\ q = \frac{f}{\left(\frac{f/D}{r_0} - \frac{R}{D}\right)^2}R_y \end{cases}$
R	$R_xd_y = R_yd_x$	–	$qR_x = pR_y$	–

cf. (p, q): the surface gradient, (d_x, d_y): the disparity gradient, and (R_x, R_y): the gradient of blur diameter.

stereo with other modules that provide surface orientation, such as shading, texture, and contour. This table is complete in the sense that the relationships for the optical flow–surface normal and optical flow–blur cannot be obtained without introducing the 3D variables. Because the optical flow is related to (U, V, W) in addition to Z, the blur or surface normal cannot remove all of these four variables. The common properties of the three normals for $Z(x, y)$, $d(x, y)$, and $R(x, y)$ are all positioned in the same vertical plane.

The equations in Table 7.2 are defined between two vision variables. It is possible that three or more variables are linked together. One set of equations is

$$p = -\frac{f/B}{\left(1 - \frac{f}{r'} - \frac{R}{D}\right)^2} d_x, \quad q = -\frac{f/B}{\left(1 - \frac{f}{r'} - \frac{R}{D}\right)^2} d_y. \tag{7.137}$$

The other set of equations is

$$p = \frac{f}{\left(\frac{f}{r_0 D} - 1 + \frac{f}{r'} + \frac{d}{B}\right)^2} R_x, \quad q = \frac{f}{\left(\frac{f}{r_0 D} - 1 + \frac{f}{r'} + \frac{d}{B}\right)^2} R_y. \tag{7.138}$$

In these equations, the optical flow is missing (see the problems at the end of this chapter). If the optical flow is included also, Equations (7.137) and (7.138) become one or more integro-differential equations, such as

$$f(\mathbf{v}^l, \mathbf{v}^r, d_x, d_y, d_t, p, q, R_x, R_y) = 0, \tag{7.139}$$

which we call the *fundamental equation* (FE). The equations in Table 7.2 and Equations (7.137) and (7.138) are all special cases of this integrated equation.

Thinking about interaction between two or more vision modules might give insight into understanding human visual perception. As remarked in Chapter 5, the vision problem can be considered as the minimization of the free energy. If the vision modules work simultaneously, the free energy is composed of FE, together with the ordinary data term and the smoothness term. There is evidence that the human visual system is organized in a systematic manner, such as modules and hierarchy (Bear *et al.* 2007; Purves 2008; Hubel 1988). It is now necessary to investigate the relationships between vision modules, instead of treating them as independent modules, and integrating them afterward to obtain the best common variables, such as structures and poses. The constraints for the linked variables are much stronger than the constraints when the modules are treated independently and integrated only for their results. Beyond vision, there is the area of multisensory integration (Wikipedia 2013a), in which multimodal integration is studied, so that the information from the different sensory modalities, such as sight, sound, touch, smell, self-motion, and taste, may be integrated.

Problems

7.1 [3D motion] An airplane at height L is moving with constant velocity v towards the image plane. Derive a formula that determines the time to collision by observing the projected image. Use the focal length f for the camera.

7.2 [3D motion] Prove the following. If another plane has the direction, $\mathbf{n} = \mathbf{t}/|\mathbf{t}|$, and rotates in $\boldsymbol{\omega} + \mathbf{n} \times \mathbf{t}$, then the two planes have the same motion field.

7.3 [Direct motion] Derive Equation (7.22).

7.4 [Binocular motion] Expand Equation (7.114) to the general case where the system is not rectified but the motion is still translational.

7.5 [Surface normal and blur diameter] Prove that **n** and $(-d_x, -d_y, 1)$ are in the same vertical plane.

7.6 [Blur diameter and disparity] Prove that the two vectors, $(-R_x, -R_y, 1)^T$ and $(-d_x, -d_y, 1)^T$, are in the same vertical plane.

7.7 [Vision modules] Using Equation (7.131), derive an equation that holds for the three 2D variables: surface normal, disparity, and blur diameter.

7.8 [Vision modules] Using Equation (7.134), derive an equation that holds for the three 2D variables: surface normal, disparity, and blur diameter.

7.9 [Vision modules] Derive an equation containing all three variables: disparity, surface normal, and blur diameter.

7.10 [Vision modules] How can the optical flow be linked to the other 2D variables?

References

Adiv G 1985 Determining three-dimensional motion and structure from optical flow generated by several moving objects. *IEEE Trans. Pattern Anal. Mach. Intell.* **7**(4), 384–401.

Altunbasak Y, Eren PE, and Tekalp AM 1998 Region-based parametric motion segmentation using color information. *Graphical models and image processing* **60**(1), 13–23.

Alvarez L, Esclarin J, Lefebure M, and Sanchez J 1999 A PDE model for computing the optical flow *Proc. XVI congreso de ecuaciones diferenciales y aplicaciones*, pp. 1349–1356.

Anandan P and Irani M 2002 Factorization with uncertainty. *International Journal of Computer Vision* **49**(2-3), 101–116.

Baker S, Scharstein D, Lewis JP, Roth S, Black MJ, and Szeliski R 2011 A database and evaluation methodology for optical flow. *International Journal of Computer Vision* **92**(1), 1–31.

Barron JL, Fleet DJ, and Beauchemin SS 1994 Performance of optical flow techniques. *International Journal of Computer Vision* **12**(1), 43–77.

Bay H, Tuytelaars T, and Van Gool L 2006 SURF: Speeded up robust features*Computer Vision–ECCV 2006* Springer pp. 404–417.

Bear M, Conners B, and Paradiso M 2007 *Neuroscience: Exploring the Brain* third edn. Williams & Wilkins, Baltimore.

Black MJ and Yacoob Y 1995 Tracking and recognizing rigid and non-rigid facial motions using local parametric models of image motion *Computer Vision, 1995. Proceedings, Fifth International Conference on*, pp. 374–381IEEE.

Bruhn A, Weickert J, Kohlberger T, and Schnorr C 2006 A multigrid platform for real-time motion computation with discontinuity-preserving variational methods. *International Journal of Computer Vision* **70**(3), 257–277.

Burger W and Bhanu B 1990 Qualitative understanding of scene dynamics for mobile robots. *International Journal of Robotics Research* **9**(6), 74–90.

Calonder M, Lepetit V, Strecha C, and Fua P 2010 Brief: Binary robust independent elementary features *Computer Vision–ECCV 2010* Springer pp. 778–792.

Cech J, Sanchez-Riera J, and Horaud R 2011 Scene flow estimation by growing correspondence seeds *Computer Vision and Pattern Recognition (CVPR), 2011 IEEE Conference on*, pp. 3129–3136IEEE.

Cremers D and Soatto S 2005 Motion competition: A variational approach to piecewise parametric motion segmentation. *International Journal of Computer Vision* **62**(3), 249–265.

Dai Y, Li H, and He M 2013 Projective multiview structure and motion from element-wise factorization. *IEEE Trans. Pattern Anal. Mach. Intell.* **35**(9), 2238–2251.

Derpanis K and Wildes R 2012 Spacetime texture representation and recognition based on a spatiotemporal orientation analysis. *IEEE Trans. Pattern Anal. Mach. Intell.* **34**(6), 1193–1205.

(ed. Purves D) 2008 *Neuroscience* fourth edn. Sinaur Associates.

Faugeras O and Luong Q 2004 *The Geometry of Multiple Images: The Laws That Govern the Formation of Multiple Images of a Scene and Some of Their Applications*. MIT Press.

Feldman D and Weinshall D 2006 Motion segmentation using an occlusion detector *Workshop on Dynamical Vision*, pp. 34–47.

Feldman D and Weinshall D 2008 Motion segmentation and depth ordering using an occlusion detector. *IEEE Trans. Pattern Anal. Mach. Intell.* **30**(7), 1171–1185.

Fennema C and Thompson W 1979 Velocity determination in scenes containing several moving objects. *Computer Graphics and Image Processing* **9**(9), 301–315.

Fleet D and Weiss Y 2006 Optical flow estimation *Handbook of Mathematical Models in Computer Vision* Springer pp. 237–257.

Fleet DJ 1992 *Measurement of Image Velocity*. Kluwer.

Fleet DJ and Jepson AD 1990 Computation of component image velocity from local phase information. *International Journal of Computer Vision* **5**(1), 77–104.

Fleet DJ and Jepson AD 1993 Stability of phase information. *IEEE Trans. Pattern Anal. Mach. Intell.* **15**(12), 1253–1268.

Freeman WT and Adelson EH 1991 The design and use of steerable filters. *IEEE Trans. Pattern Anal. Mach. Intell.* **13**(9), 891–906.

Gautama T and van Hulle MM 2002 A phase-based approach to the estimation of the optical flow field using spatial filtering. *IEEE Trans. Neural Networks* **13**(5), 1127–1136.

Granlund G and Knutssen H 1995 *Signal Processing for Computer Vision*. Kluwer.

Grossmann P 1987 Depth from focus. *Pattern Recognition Letters* **5**(1), 63–69.

Hanna K 1991 Direct multi-resolution estimation of ego-motion and structure from motion *Visual Motion, 1991, Proceedings of the IEEE Workshop on*, pp. 156–162.

Harris C and Stephens MJ 1988 A combined corner and edge detector *Alvey Conference*, pp. 147–152.

Harrison AP and Joseph D 2012 Maximum likelihood estimation of depth maps using photometric stereo. *IEEE Trans. Pattern Anal. Mach. Intell.* **34**(7), 1368–1380.

Hartley R and Zisserman A 2004 *Multiple View Geometry in Computer Vision*. Cambridge University Press.

Harville M, Rahimi A, Darrell T, Gordon G, and Woodfill J 1999 3D pose tracking with linear depth and brightness constraints *Computer Vision, 1999. The Proceedings of the Seventh IEEE International Conference on*, vol. 1, pp. 206–213 IEEE.

Heeger DJ and Jepson AD 1992 Subspace methods for recovering rigid motion I: Algorithms and implementation. *International Journal of Computer Vision* **7**(2), 95–117.

Higgins HCL and Prazdny K 1980 The interpretation of a moving retinal image. *Proceedings of Royal Society of London* **B-208**, 385–397.

Horn B and Shunck B 1981 Determining optical flow. *Artificial Intelligence* **17**(1-3), 185–203.

Horn BKP 1986 *Robot Vision*. MIT Press, Cambridge, Massachusetts.

Hubel D 1988 *Eye, Brain, and Vision*. W H Freeman & Co, http://hubel.med.harvard.edu/index.html.

Huguet F and Devernay F 2007 A variational method for scene flow estimation from stereo sequences *Computer Vision, 2007. ICCV 2007. IEEE 11th International Conference on*, pp. 1–7IEEE.

Ito M, Takada Y, and Hamamoto T 2010 Distance and relative speed estimation of binocular camera images based on defocus and disparity information *PCS*, pp. 278–281. IEEE.

Jenkins M and Tsotsos J 1986 Applying temporal constraints to the dynamic stereo problem. *Journal of Computer Vision, Graphics, and Image Processing* **3358**, 16–32.

Jeong H, Yan S, and Han SH 2012 Integrating stereo disparity and optical flow by closely-coupled method. *Journal of Pattern Recognition Research* **7**(1), 175–187.

Jing BZ and Yeung DS 2012 Recovering depth from images using adaptive depth from focus *ICMLC*, pp. 1205–1211. IEEE.

Kanade T 1987 *Three-Dimensional Machine Vision*. Kluwer.

Kennedy R, Balzano L, Wright SJ, and Taylor CJ 2013 Online algorithms for factorization-based structure from motion. *CoRR* **abs/1309.6964**, on revision.

Levin A, Fergus R, Frédo D, and Freeman W 2007 Image and depth from a conventional camera with a coded aperture *ACM SIGGRAPH 2007 papers* SIGGRAPH '07. ACM, New York, NY, USA.

Levin A, Lischinski D, and Weiss Y 2008 A closed-form solution to natural image matting. *IEEE Trans. Pattern Anal. Mach. Intell.* **30**(2), 228–242.

Levin A, Weiss Y, Durand F, and Freeman WT 2011 Understanding blind deconvolution algorithms. *IEEE Trans. Pattern Anal. Mach. Intell.* **33**(12), 2354–2367.

Li C, Su S, Matsushita Y, Zhou K, and Lin S 2013 Bayesian depth-from-defocus with shading constraints *CVPR*, pp. 217–224. IEEE.

Li R and Sclaroff S 2008 Multi-scale 3D scene flow from binocular stereo sequences. *Computer vision and image understanding* **110**(1), 75–90.

Liu F and Philomin V 2009 Disparity estimation in stereo sequences using scene flow. *BMVC*, vol. 1, p. 2.

Lowe D 2004 Distinctive image features from scale-invariant keypoints. *International Journal of Computer Vision* **60**(2), 91–110.

Lucas BD and Kanade T 1981 An iterative image registration technique with an application to stereo vision. *Image Understanding Workshop*, pp. 121–130.

McCane B, Novins K, Crannitch D, and Galvin B 2001 On benchmarking optical flow. *Computer Vision and Image Understanding* **84**(1), 126–143.

Middlebury 2013 Middlebury optical flow home page http://vision.middlebury.edu/flow/ (accessed Dec. 23, 2013).

Morita T and Kanade T 1997 A sequential factorization method for recovering shape and motion from image streams. *IEEE Trans. Pattern Anal. Mach. Intell.* **19**(8), 858–867.

Nagel HH 1987 On the estimation of optical flow: Relations between different approaches and some new results. *Artificial Intelligence* **33**, 299–324.

Negahdaripour S and Horn BK 1985 Determining 3D motion of planar objects from image brightness patterns. *IJCAI*, pp. 898–901.

Nelson RC and Aloimonos Y 1988 Finding motion parameters from spherical flow fields (or the advantages of having eyes in the back of your head). *Biological Cybernetics* **58**, 261–273.

Nir T, Bruckstein AM, and Kimmel R 2008 Over-parameterized variational optical flow. *International Journal of Computer Vision* **76**(2), 205–216.

Odobez JM and Bouthemy P 1995 Robust multiresolution estimation of parametric motion models. *Journal of visual communication and image representation* **6**(4), 348–365.

Poelman CJ and Kanade T 1994 A paraperspective factorization method for shape and motion recovery. *Lecture Notes in Computer Science* **800**, 97–110.

Poelman CJ and Kanade T 1997 A paraperspective factorization method for shape and motion recovery. *IEEE Trans. Pattern Anal. Mach. Intell.* **19**(3), 206–218.

Pons JP, Keriven R, and Faugeras O 2007 Multi-view stereo reconstruction and scene flow estimation with a global image-based matching swith. *International Journal of Computer Vision* **72**(2), 179–193.

Prazdny K 1981 Determining the instantaneous direction of motion from optical flow generated by a curvilinearly moving observer *Image Understanding Workshop*, pp. 14–21.

Raudies F 2013 Optic flow http://www.scholarpedia.org/article/Optic_flow (accessed on Dec. 8, 2013).

Sand P and Teller S 2008 Particle video: Long-range motion estimation using point trajectories. *International Journal of Computer Vision* **80**(1), xx–yy.

Sand PPM 2006 *Long-range Video Motion Estimation Using Point Trajectories* PhD thesis MIT, Dept. of Electrical Engineering and Computer Science.

Sargin ME, Bertelli L, Manjunath BS, and Rose K 2009 Probabilistic occlusion boundary detection on spatio-temporal lattices *ICCV*, pp. 560–567. IEEE.

Schechner YY and Kiryati N 2000 Depth from defocus vs. stereo: How different really are they?. *International Journal of Computer Vision* **39**(2), 141–162.

Shechtman E and Irani M 2007 Space-time behavior-based correlation-or-how to tell if two underlying motion fields are similar without computing them?. *IEEE Trans. Pattern Anal. Mach. Intell.* **29**(11), 2045–56.

Shi J and Malik J 2000 Normalized cuts and image segmentation. *IEEE Trans. Pattern Anal. Mach. Intell.* **22**(8), 888–905.

Simoncelli EP 1993 Distributed analysis and representation of visual motion *Ph.D.*

Sizintsev M and Wildes R 2012 Spatiotemporal stereo and scene flow via stequel matching. *IEEE Trans. Pattern Anal. Mach. Intell.* **34**(6), 1206–1219.

Sturm PF and Triggs B 1996 A factorization based algorithm for multi-image projective structure and motion *ECCV*, pp. II:709–720.

Subbarao M and Surya G 1994 Depth from defocus: A spatial domain approach. *International Journal of Computer Vision* **13**(3), 271–294.

Subbarao M, Yuan T, and Tyan J 1997 Integration of defocus and focus analysis with stereo for 3D shape recovery*In Proc. SPIE Three Dimensional Imaging and Laser-Based Systems for Metrology and Inspection iii*, vol. 3204, pp. 11–23.

Sun J, He K, and Tang X 2010 Single image haze removal using dark channel priors. US Patent App. 12/697,575.

Tola E, Lepetit V, and Fua P 2010 Daisy: An efficient dense descriptor applied to wide-baseline stereo. *IEEE Trans. Pattern Anal. Mach. Intell.* **32**(5), 815–830.

Tomasi C and Kanade T 1992a The factorization method for the recovery of shape and motion from image streams *Image Understanding Workshop*, pp. 459–472.

Tomasi C and Kanade T 1992b Shape and motion from image streams under orthography: a factorization method. *International Journal of Computer Vision* **9**, 137–154.

Tomasi C and Weinshall D 1993 Linear and incremental acquisition of invariant shape models from image sequences *ICCV*, pp. 675–682.

Ullman S 1979 *The Interpretation of Visual Motion*. MIT Press.

Uras S, Girosi F, Verri A, and Torre V 1989 A computational approach to motion perception. *Biological Cybernetics* **60**, 79–87.

Valgaerts L, Bruhn A, and Weickert J 2008 *A Variational Model for the Joint Recovery of the Fundamental Matrix and the Optical Flow* vol. 5096 of *Lecture Notes in Computer Science*. Springer Berlin Heidelberg.

Vedula S, Rander P, Collins R, and Kanade T 2005 Three-dimensional scene flow. *IEEE Trans. Pattern Anal. Mach. Intell.* **27**(3), 475–480.

Wang G, Zelek JS, Wu QMJ, and Bajcsy R 2013 Robust rank-4 affine factorization for structure from motion *WACV*, pp. 180–185. IEEE Computer Society.

Waxman AM 1987 An image flow paradigm *RCV87*, pp. 145–168.

Wedel A, Brox T, Vaudrey T, Rabe C, Franke U, and Cremers D 2011 Stereoscopic scene flow computation for 3D motion understanding. *International Journal of Computer Vision* **95**(1), 29–51.

Wedel A, Pock T, Braun J, Franke U, and Cremers D 2008a Duality TV-L1 flow with fundamental matrix prior *Image and Vision Computing New Zealand, 2008. IVCNZ 2008. 23rd International Conference*, pp. 1–6.

Wedel A, Pock T, Zach C, Bischof H, and Cremers D 2009 *An Improved Algorithm for TV-L1 Optical Flow* vol. 5604 of *Lecture Notes in Computer Science*. Springer Berlin Heidelberg.

Wedel A, Rabe C, Vaudrey T, Brox T, Franke U, and Cremers D 2008b *Efficient Dense Scene Flow from Sparse or Dense Stereo Data*. Springer.

Weickert J and Schnorr C 2001 A theoretical framework for convex regularizers in PDE-based computation of image motion. *International Journal of Computer Vision* **45**(3), 245–264.

Wikipedia 2013a Multisensory integration http://en.wikipedia.org/wiki/Multisensory_integration (accessed Nov. 2, 2013).

Wikipedia 2013b Optical flow http://en.wikipedia.org/wiki/Optic_flow (accessed on Dec. 8, 2013).

Xiao JJ, Cheng H, Sawhney HS, Rao C, and Isnardi M 2006 Bilateral filtering-based optical flow estimation with occlusion detection *ECCV*, pp. I: 211–224.

Zhang L, Curless B, and Seitz SM 2003 Spacetime stereo: Shape recovery for dynamic scenes *Computer Vision and Pattern Recognition, 2003. Proceedings. 2003 IEEE Computer Society Conference on*, vol. 2, pp. II–367 IEEE.

Part Three
Vision Architectures

8

Relaxation for Energy Minimization

This chapter introduces the relaxation equation and architecture, one of the basic computing methods in energy minimization: relaxation, dynamic programming, message passing, graph cuts, and linear programming relaxation (LPR).

Early to intermediate vision has a common computation structure. One structure has the attributes to be computed defined on the pixels or a group of pixels. Another structure has the attribute in a pixel correlated with its neighbor values, as often modeled by MRF. Yet another structure has the attributes being obtainable by iteration, relaxing intermediate values, and reusing them for a better solution in a recursive way. We examine a computation structure that combines all these together in terms of representation and architecture.

First, we represent the relaxation equation in time and space in terms of its common structures – iteration, neighborhood computation, and concurrency – and thereby observe how the general computational architectures, Gauss–Seidel and Jacobi methods, can be combined and the numerous architectural variations that can be positioned between the two ends of the spectrum.

Next, we represent the relaxation in a graph, which is the product space of the image plane and iteration. The computation can be viewed in different ways, such as edge connections and spanning orders, in the graph. Deforming the graph in an affine manner, we obtain a new graph in which the connections enable different spanning orders. As a result of the graphical representations, we obtain three basic computational structures – the Gauss–Seidel–Jacob (GSJ) method, the *diagonal method*, and the *vertical method*. As regards computation order, the GSJ method completes the plane and advances to the next layer, but the diagonal and vertical methods operate in reverse. In terms of memory, the GSJ method requires RAM, whereas the diagonal and vertical methods require queues. Finally, we define hardware algorithms that are close to Verilog design, called *RE* and *FRE* machines, for the GSJ and vertical methods.

The later part of this chapter deals with the relaxation equation, an equation that is typical in computer vision. Starting from the energy equation, this chapter outlines how to derive the relaxation equation, following variational calculus, discretization, and iteration formation. Incidentally, isotropic and anisotropic diffusion are explained as common smoothness terms.

The RE and FRE machines and the relaxation equation form the bases of machine design in Chapter 11.

Architectures for Computer Vision: From Algorithm to Chip with Verilog, First Edition. Hong Jeong.

Companion Website: www.wiley.com/go/jeong

8.1 Euler–Lagrange Equation of the Energy Function

Relaxation labeling is a numerical method for solving the discrete labeling in Definition 5.1. In this approach, we are concerned with the decomposition of a complex computation into a network of simple local computations and the use of context in resolving ambiguities. As a result, the algorithm becomes parallel, with each process making use of the context to assist in labeling decisions. Relaxation operations were originally introduced to solve systems of linear equations. In relaxation labeling, the relaxation operations are extended, the solutions involve symbols rather than functions, and weights are attached to labels, which do not necessarily have a natural ordering.

Let us begin with the energy function in Definition 5.1:

$$E(f) = \sum_{(x,y)\in\mathcal{P}} \left\{ \phi(f(x,y)) + \lambda \sum_{(x',y')\in N(x,y)\backslash(x,y)} \psi(f(x,y), f(x',y')) \right\}, \tag{8.1}$$

where λ is the Lagrange multiplier. The overall energy comprises a functional:

$$E(f) = \sum_{(x,y)\in\mathcal{P}} F(f, f_x, f_y, f_{xx}, f_{yy}, f_{xy}, g), \tag{8.2}$$

where F includes the data and prior terms:

$$F(f, f_x, f_y, f_{xx}, f_{yy}, f_{xy}, g) = \phi(f) + \lambda g(x,y) \sum_{(x',y')\in N(x,y)\backslash(x,y)} \psi(f(x,y), f(x',y')). \tag{8.3}$$

The energy model may be enhanced by introducing a switch function multiplied to the second term, as in the case of occlusion modeling. The switch function can be modeled as a binary indicator or, more generally, as a differentiable function such as a sigmoid. Depending on the switch function, the ensuing derivation is rather different.

Minimizing the energy by using function f leads to the Euler–Lagrange equation (Courant and Hilbert 1953; Horn 1986; Wikipedia 2013b): The problem is the Euler–Lagrange equation with two functions and two variables:

$$F_f - \partial_x F_{f_x} - \partial_y F_{f_y} + \partial_{xx} F_{f_{xx}} + \partial_{yy} F_{f_{yy}} = 0, \quad F_g = 0. \tag{8.4}$$

In other cases in which the number of variables is greater than one, the number of Euler equations is also greater than one. To continue, we have to specify $F(\cdot)$ further. The second term in Equation 8.1 signifies local variation, which is often modeled using differentials. Considering second-order derivatives, we get

$$F(f, f_x, f_y, f_{xx}, f_{yy}, f_{xy}, g) = \phi(f) + \lambda|\nabla f|^2 + \mu|\nabla^2 f|^2. \tag{8.5}$$

This assumption is a simple example. There are many variations in which the smoothness term is models, which prelude the use of simple differentials. In most cases, problems occur when the range of variables is too wide to be approximated by Taylor series and/or the term is nonlinear because of some multiplied factors, such as occlusion terms. In addition, the measure can be other than the Euclidean metric, which makes the differential difficult. For such a case, the basic form of the relaxation equation is in fact often modified directly without undergoing the derivation process.

Substituting Equation (8.5) into Equation (8.4) yields

$$\lambda\nabla^2 f - \mu\nabla^2\nabla^2 f = \phi_f. \tag{8.6}$$

The Laplacian, ∇^2, is related to the diffusion equation, $\nabla^2 = -\frac{d}{dt}f$, in thermal physics. The biharmonic operator (Polyanin and Zaitsev 2012), is related to the biharmonic equation $\nabla^2\nabla^2 f = 0$ in continuum mechanics.

The equations contain two major terms: Laplacian (Ursell 2007) and biharmonic operators (Polyanin and Zaitsev 2012):

$$\nabla^2 = \frac{\partial^2}{\partial x^2} + \frac{\partial^2}{\partial y^2}, \quad \nabla^2\nabla^2 = \frac{\partial^4}{\partial x^4} + 2\frac{\partial^4}{\partial x^2 \partial y^2} + \frac{\partial^4}{\partial y^4}. \tag{8.7}$$

The Euler equation for the general energy equation is compound because of the diffusion and biharmonic operators. In practical applications, only one of the two operators is adopted.

In its simplest form, the diffusion term is isotropic but in many cases, it becomes an anisotropic operator. Such cases arise when we deal with directive smoothing or determine local variations adaptively. For example, in edge preserving filtering, the smoothing must be differentiated from uniform and boundary regions. Anisotropic diffusion is made possible by introducing a nonlinear diffusion coefficient between the derivatives (Perona and Malik 1990):

Let us examine the properties of the Laplacian and biharmonic operators. The Euler–Lagrangian equation can be considered a filtering process of f, driven by the observed signal ϕ_f. The signal f is often smoothed by the Gaussian filter, allowing the linear filter to function as a Gaussian filter. The equation consists of two major terms: diffusion and biharmonic terms. The net result is the combination of the two filters and thus it is necessary to observe the homogeneous solution.

The Gaussian derivatives are conveniently represented by the Hermite polynomials (Wikipedia 2013d):

$$\frac{\partial^n G(x,\sigma)}{\partial x^n} = (-1)^n \frac{1}{(\sigma\sqrt{2})^n} H_n\left(\frac{x}{\sigma\sqrt{2}} G(x,\sigma)\right). \tag{8.8}$$

Then, up to fourth order, $\partial_x^n G(x,\sigma)/G(x,\sigma)$ becomes

$$1, -\frac{x}{\sigma^2}, \frac{x^2-\sigma^2}{\sigma^4}, -\frac{x^3-3x\sigma^2}{\sigma^6}, \frac{x^4-6x^2\sigma^4+3\sigma^2}{\sigma^8}. \tag{8.9}$$

It is also well known that the Laplacian can be approximated by a DOG filter (Marr and Hildreth 1980). This property has been generalized to higher-order derivatives, with the proposal that the higher-order Gaussian filters can be constructed by linear summation of lower-order filters (De Ma and Li 1998; Ghosh *et al.* 2004).

The 2D Gaussian filter is represented by $G(x, y, s, t)$, where s and t may be different for an anisotropic system:

$$G(x,y,s,t) = G(x,s)G(y,t) = \frac{1}{2\pi st} e^{-(x^2/2s^2 + y^2/2t^2)}. \tag{8.10}$$

Using the separability property and the Hermite series, we can derive higher-order 2D filters. In particular, the second order is

$$\nabla^2 G(x,y,s,t) = \left(\frac{x^2-s^2}{s^4} + \frac{y^2-t^2}{t^4}\right) G(x,y,s,t), \tag{8.11}$$

which is well-known as LoG and often approximated by DOG (Marr and Hildreth 1980). The biharmonic filter is the fourth-order Gaussian:

$$\frac{\nabla^2 \cdot \nabla^2 G(x,y,\sigma)}{G(x,y,\sigma)} = \frac{2\pi}{\sigma^6}\{\sigma^4 + 3\sigma^4(x+y) - \sigma^2(x^2+y^2) - \sigma^2(x^3+y^3) + x^2y^2\}. \tag{8.12}$$

The filters are compared in Figure 8.1. The first row shows the Laplacian: $\nabla^2 G$ and $\nabla^2 G/G$. The second row shows the biharmonic: $\nabla^2 \cdot \nabla^2 G$ and $\nabla^2 \cdot \nabla^2 G/G$. The third row shows the composite filter: $(\nabla^2 + \nabla^2 \cdot \nabla^2)G$ and $(\nabla^2 + \nabla^2 \cdot \nabla^2)G/G$.

From another viewpoint, the diffusion operator in Equation (8.6) can be interpreted as a heat equation and thereby modeled in many different ways. The simple interpretation is the *isotropic diffusion*:

$$\frac{\partial f}{\partial t} = D\nabla^2 f, \tag{8.13}$$

where D is a scalar called the *diffusion coefficient*. The solution of this equation is Gaussian (see the problems at the end of this chapter). The next level of the diffusion equation is *anisotropic diffusion*, in which the diffusion coefficient depends upon the coordinates:

$$\frac{\partial f}{\partial t} = \nabla \cdot (D(x,y,f)\nabla f) = D\nabla^2 f + \nabla D \cdot \nabla f, \tag{8.14}$$

where '$\nabla\cdot$' is the divergence operator. An even more general representation is the *tensor diffusion*, in which the scalar diffusion is extended to the diffusion tensor – a positive semi-definite symmetric matrix:

$$\frac{\partial f}{\partial t} = \nabla \cdot (D(x,y,f)\nabla f) = \sum_{i=1}^{2}\sum_{j=1}^{2} \frac{\partial}{\partial x_i}\left[D_{ij}(x,y,f)\frac{\partial f(x,y,t)}{\partial x_j}\right]. \tag{8.15}$$

In image processing, the research on nonlinear diffusion is rooted in the following equation (Perona and Malik 1990):

$$\frac{\partial f}{\partial t} = \nabla \cdot \left(\frac{\nabla f}{|\nabla f|^2 + \lambda^2}\right), \tag{8.16}$$

where λ is a parameter. Such cases occur when we deal with directive smoothing or determine local variations adaptively. For example, in edge preserving filtering, the smoothing must be differentiated from the uniform region and the boundary region. Among the many, some examples are $\partial f/\partial t = \nabla \cdot (|\nabla f|^{-1}\nabla f)$ (Rudin *et al.* 1992), $\partial f/\partial t = |\nabla f||k * \nabla f|\nabla \cdot (|\nabla f|^{-1}\nabla f)$ (Alvarez *et al.* 1992), and $\partial f/\partial t = \nabla \cdot (\sqrt{1+|\nabla f|^2}\nabla f)$ (Sochen *et al.* 1998). Presently, the diffusion equation has been extended significantly, up to the *generalized heat equation*:

$$\frac{\partial f}{\partial t} = F(D(x,y,t), \nabla^2 f(x,y,t), \nabla f(x,y,t), f(x,y,t)), \tag{8.17}$$

where $F(\cdot)$ denotes a function (see (ter Haar Romeny 1994; Weickert 2008) for the surveys). If the problem is given by this heat equation, instead of the energy equation, the stage of obtaining the Euler equation is not needed. The relaxation equation is obtained directly by discretizing this equation:

$$f^{(t+1)} = f^{(t)} + F(D(x,y,t), \nabla^2 f^{(t)}(x,y,t), \nabla f^{(t)}(x,y,t), f^{(t)}(x,y,t)). \tag{8.18}$$

For numerical computation, the terms on the right must be discretized accordingly.

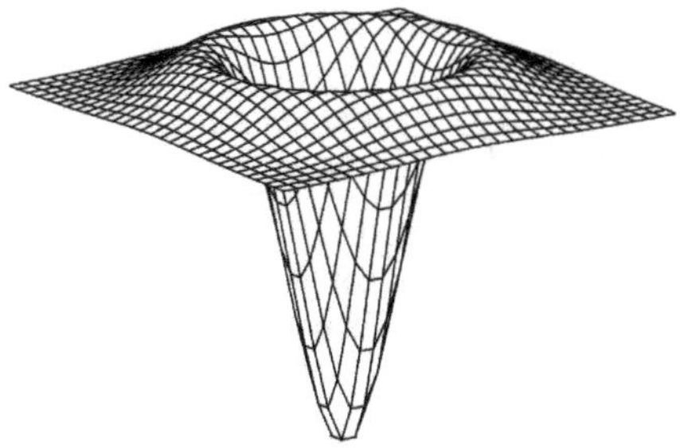

(a) $\nabla^2 G(x, y, s, t)$

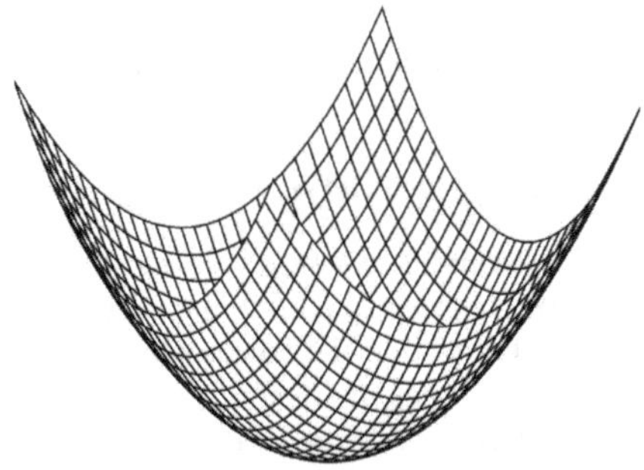

(b) $\nabla^2 G(x, y, s, t)/G(x, y, s, t)$

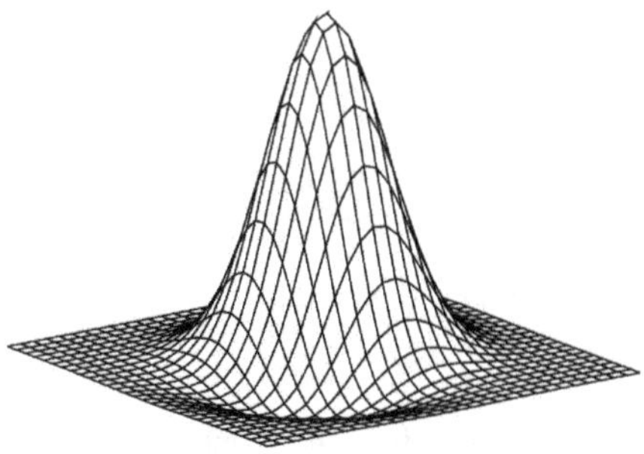

(c) $\nabla^2 \bullet \nabla^2 G(x, y, s, s)$

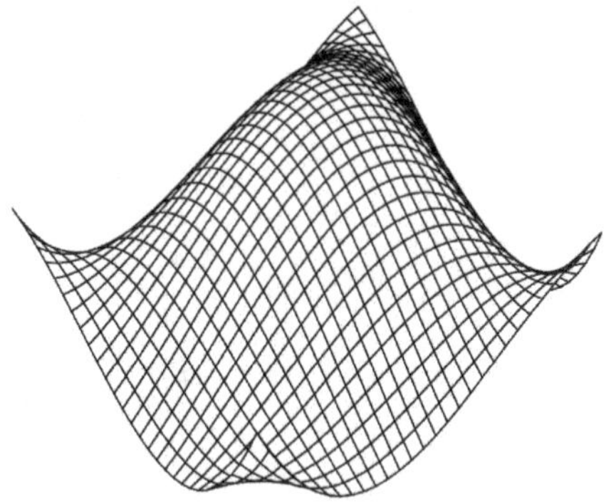

(d) $\nabla^2 \bullet \nabla^2 G(x, y, s, s)/G(x, y, s, s)$

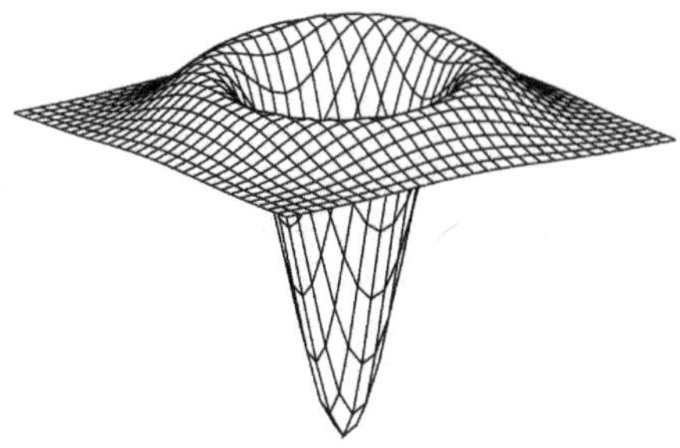

(e) $(\nabla^2 + \lambda \nabla^2 \bullet \nabla^2)G$

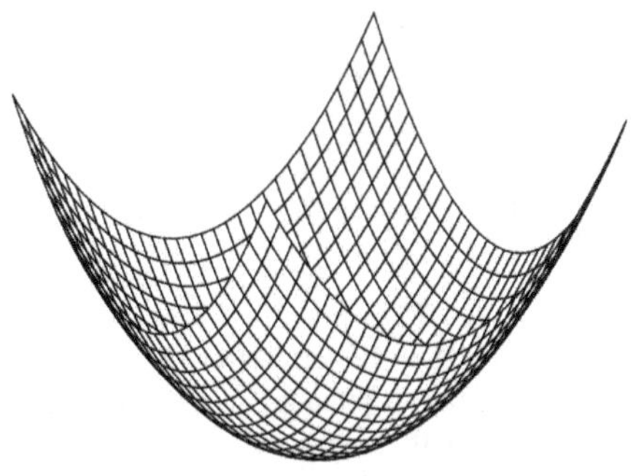

(f) $(\nabla^2 + \lambda \nabla^2 \bullet \nabla^2)G/G$

Figure 8.1 Shapes of Gaussian derivatives ($s = 0.15$, $t = 0.15$, and $\lambda = 20$)

Including anisotropic tensor and the biharmonic operator, the Euler–Lagrange equation becomes

$$\lambda \nabla \cdot (D\nabla f) - \mu \nabla^2 \nabla^2 f = \phi_f. \tag{8.19}$$

In a simple but practical case, the Euler–Lagrange equation is often modeled by

$$\lambda \nabla^2 f = \phi_f. \tag{8.20}$$

Meaningful interpretation is possible if the data term satisfies certain conditions (Ursell 2007).

As a result, we have various levels of Euler–Lagrange equations: Equations (8.6), (8.19), and (8.20). The equations further depend on the diffusion model and the nonlinear term by $g(\cdot)$.

8.2 Discrete Diffusion and Biharminic Operators

The Euler–Lagrange equations are completed only when the data term ϕ_f is known. Even so, it is very difficult to obtain an explicit solution. A practical approach is the numerical computation on the relaxation equations. To arrive at the relaxation equation, we need to discretize the Euler–Lagrange equation and then convert it into iterative form, while considering possible convergence. We then have to concentrate on the two terms: diffusion and biharmonic.

To begin with, we need to obtain kernels for the basic differentials. Let us represent the n-th-order differential $\partial^n/\partial x^n$ by the forward (Δ^n), and backward (∇^n) and central (δ^n) difference operators (Wikipedia 2013c), which are

$$\Delta^n[f](x) = \sum_{i=0}^{n}(-1)^i\binom{n}{i}f(x+(n-i)),$$

$$\nabla^n[f](x) = \sum_{i=0}^{n}(-1)^i\binom{n}{i}f(x-i),$$

$$\delta^n[f](x) = \sum_{i=0}^{n}(-1)^i\binom{n}{i}f\left(x+\left(\frac{n}{2}-i\right)\right). \tag{8.21}$$

It is practical to use 3×3 templates for the differences in image processing. The templates for the second derivatives can be obtained by multiplying the first-order templates twice. In this case, the forward and backward templates are alternately multiplied to obtain efficient templates. In general, to make the higher-order difference kernel symmetric about a center point, the forward, backward, and central differences are mixed alternately. Some of the frequently used kernels are

$$\begin{cases} \Delta_x f(x,y) = f(x+1,y) - f(x,y), & \nabla_x f(x,y) = f(x,y) - f(x-1,y), \\ \Delta_y f(x,y) = f(x,y+1) - f(x,y), & \nabla_y f(x,y) = f(x,y) - f(x,y-1), \\ \delta_x f(x,y) = \frac{1}{2}(f(x+1,y) - f(x-1,y)), & \delta_y f(x,y) = \frac{1}{2}(f(x,y+1) - f(x,y-1)). \end{cases}$$

Let us now return to Equation (8.6) to discretize the diffusion and biharmonic operators. The Laplacian operator can be approximated in many different ways (Wikipedia 2013a). The discrete Laplacian is often approximated by the five-point stencil:

$$\nabla^2 f = f(x+1,y) + f(x-1,y) + f(x,y+1) + f(x,y-1) - 4f(x,y). \tag{8.22}$$

The anisotropic diffusion operator in Equation (8.14) is approximated by

$$\nabla \cdot (D(x,y,t)\nabla f) = \frac{1}{2}\sum_{i,j\in\{-1,1\}}(D(x+i,y+j) + D(x,y))(f(x+i,y+j) - f(x,y)). \tag{8.23}$$

The derivation is all based on four neighbors and typical stencils among many.

Similarly, the biharmonic operator can be discretized in many different ways (Chen *et al.* 2008). The standard stencil is the 13-point biharmonic operator that is obtained by applying the five-point diffusion operator twice.

$$\begin{aligned}\nabla^4 f = 2\{&20f(x,y) - 8[f(x+1,y) + f(x-1,y) + f(x,y+1) + f(x,y-1)]\\ &+ 2[f(x+1,y+1) + f(x-1,y+1) + f(x-1,y-1) + f(x+1,y-1)]\\ &+ [f(x+2,y) + f(x-2,y) + f(x,y+2) + f(x,y-2)]\}.\end{aligned} \tag{8.24}$$

There are a lot of issues surrounding modifying the kernel to compensate for errors on grid points near the boundary (Glowinski and Pironneau 1979).

8.3 SOR Equation

In the final stage, we have to convert the difference equation into SOR. The general concept of successive over relaxation (SOR) is as follows. If $T(\cdot)$ is a contraction mapping,

$$f(x,y) = T(f(x,y)), \tag{8.25}$$

then the corresponding SOR (Young 1950) can be obtained by

$$f^{(t+1)}(x,y) = (1-\omega)f^{(t)} + \omega T(f^{(t)}(x,y)), \tag{8.26}$$

where ω is the relaxation parameter. The system is under-relaxation if $\omega < 1$ and over-relaxation if $1 < \omega < 2$.

For Equation (8.20), we get the relaxation equation,

$$f^{(t+1)}(x,y) = (1-\omega)f^{(t)}(x,y) + \omega\left(\bar{f}^{(t)}(x,y) - \frac{1}{4}\phi_f^{(t)}(x,y)\right), \quad \forall (x,y) \in \mathcal{P}, \tag{8.27}$$

where $\bar{f}$ denotes the four-neighbor average. The convergence speed can be adjusted by ω. Similarly, for Equation (8.6), we have

$$\begin{aligned}f^{(t+1)}(x,y) = (1-\omega)f^{(t)}(x,y) + \omega\Big\{&\bar{f}(x,y) - \frac{\mu}{2\lambda}[20f(x,y)\\ &- 8[f(x+1,y) + f(x-1,y) + f(x,y+1) + f(x,y-1)]\\ &+ 2[f(x+1,y+1) + f(x-1,y+1) + f(x-1,y-1) + f(x+1,y-1)]\\ &+ [f(x+2,y) + f(x-2,y) + f(x,y+2) + f(x,y-2)]] - \frac{1}{4\lambda}\phi_f(x,y)\Big\}.\end{aligned} \tag{8.28}$$

The parameters, λ, μ, and ω, play important roles in system stability. Actually, there is no unique way of deriving the SOR. Some may even lead to the system becoming unstable. The system can be more complicated if anisotropic diffusion and the enhanced biharmonic stencils are utilized. The complete expression is possible only when the data term ϕ_f is known. If $\phi = (T(f) - I)^2$, we get $\phi_f = 2(T(f) - I)T_f$, which further reduces to $\phi_f = 2(f - I)$ if $T(f) = f$. If ϕ is known, the terms can be better modified, with the terms and relaxation parameter readjusted.

Equations (8.27) and (8.28) are typical in image processing, although the details may vary depending on the problems. If the data term is available, we can elaborate the equation by adding more terms and modifying the links between the terms by adding switching factors, which are otherwise difficult in the original energy function. In the next chapter, we derive this type of expression in stereo matching and thereby design appropriate relaxation machines.

8.4 Relaxation Equation

Thus far, we have derived a relaxation equation from a basic energy function. We will now expand the expression to a more general case. There are two types of relaxations in mathematical optimization: modeling strategy and iterative method. Relaxation as an iterative method solves a problem by generating a sequence of improved approximate solutions for the given problem until it reaches a termination condition, usually defined by convergent criteria. Relaxation as a modeling strategy solves a problem by converting the given difficult problem to an approximate one, relaxing the cost functions and constraints. The two methods are widely used in vision computation, as successive over-relaxation (SOR) for solving differential and nonlinear equations and as LPR for solving integer programming. In this chapter, we deal with the computational structure of iterative relaxation.

Relaxation is one of the most classical algorithms in computer vision that use iteration and neighborhood computation (Glazer 1984; Hinton 2007; Kittler and Illingworth 1985; Kittler *et al.* 1993; Terzopoulos 1986). This algorithm is a natural choice in solving many vision problems, because it is related with the operations: energy minimization, discretization, iterative computation, neighborhood computation.

In image processing, relaxation research is largely rooted in (Hummel and Zucker 1983). After a long evolution, relaxation has evolved up to message passing (Pearl 1982) and graph cut (Boykov *et al.* 1998). Beside the principles, there are also works on relaxation architectures pursuing parallelism (Gu and Wang 1992; Kamada *et al.* 1988; Mori *et al.* 1995; Wang *et al.* 1987) and hierarchical structures (Cohen and Cooper 1987; Hayes 1980; Miranker 1979).

From a computational point of view, relaxation algorithms can be characterized by the following factors: transformation, neighborhood topology, concurrent processing, initial and boundary conditions, computation order, and scale. The objective of the algorithm is to update the center pixel by concurrently mapping neighborhood values, following initialization, boundary condition, and computation order. Let us examine the factors individually below.

First, consider the transformation that maps the input state to a new state. For a point, $p \in \mathcal{P}$, define a function f that maps the point to a vector, $f : p \in \mathcal{P} \mapsto \mathcal{R}^K$, where K means K-dimensional. In addition, define a function T that maps a neighborhood to its center node, $T : N(p) \mapsto p$, where $N(p)$ denotes the neighborhood of p, including itself. We can then define the relaxation equation by

$$f^{(t+1)}(p) = T^{(t)}(I(p), f^{(t)}(N(p))), \quad n = 0, 1, \ldots, T - 1. \tag{8.29}$$

Here, t denotes time up to the maximum T. Usually, the iteration is continued until convergence but in practice it is terminated in a predefined time. The operation becomes a point-operation or neighborhood operation, depending on the neighborhood size. The mapping from neighbors to the center point is represented by a function and its parameters, which can be time-varying or time-invariant, fixed or variable connections, or linear or nonlinear.

For a linear time-invariant system, we get an IIR filter:

$$f^{(t+1)}(p) = \sum_{q \in N(p)} T(p, q) f^{(t)}(q) + TI(p), \tag{8.30}$$

and for a linear time and shift invariant system, we get an FIR filter:

$$f^{(t+1)}(p) = \sum_{q \in N(p) \setminus p} T(|p - q|) f^{(t)}(q) + TI(p). \tag{8.31}$$

The operation can be as simple as the momentums: arithmetic mean, geometric mean, harmonic mean, contraharmonic mean, and the statistical momentum: median, max, min, midpoint, alpha-trimmed mean

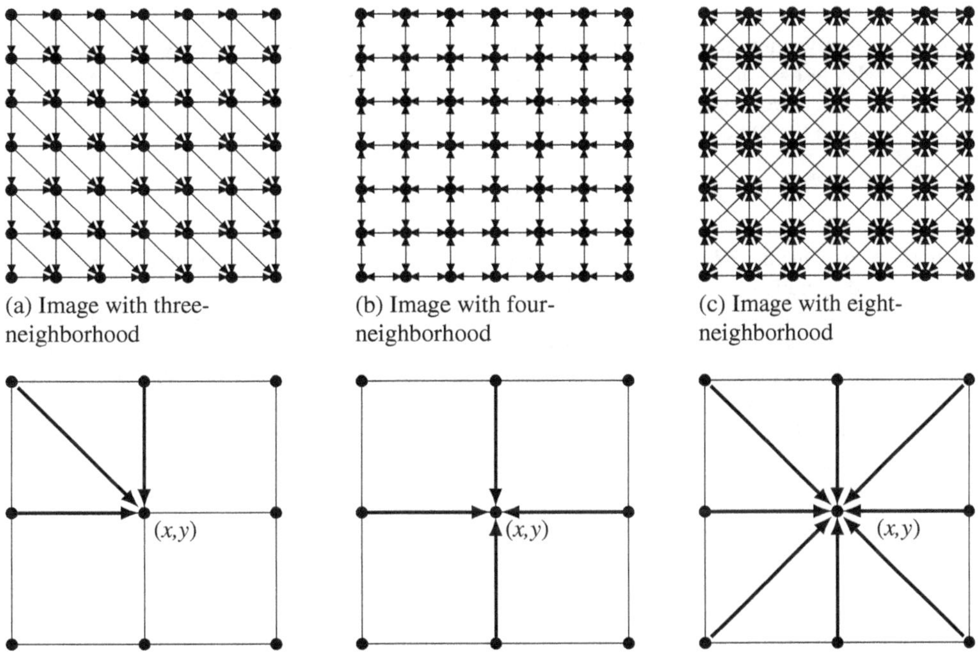

(a) Image with three-neighborhood (b) Image with four-neighborhood (c) Image with eight-neighborhood

(d) three-neighborhood (e) four-neighborhood (f) eight-neighborhood

Figure 8.2 Neighborhood systems: (a)–(c) for images and (d)–(f) for neighborhoods

(Gonzalez *et al.* 2009), morphological operations, Nagao-Matsuyama filter (Nagao and Matsuyama 2013) and as complicated as message passing and graph cuts.

Relaxation is also characterized by neighborhood topology, which means a set of neighbor nodes and the connection to the center node. It may be variable or fixed in both time and space. Typical neighborhood systems are depicted in Figure 8.2. The three image planes, with different neighborhood connections, are shown at the top of the figure. The arrows signify influence between neighborhoods as opposed to physical connections. Below these images are the neighborhood definitions, consisting of a center pixel and neighbor pixels. In the three-neighborhood system, a node is connected to three neighbor nodes. Similarly, in four- and eight-neighborhood systems, a center pixel is connected to four or eight neighbors. Let us denote the neighborhood system by N_3, N_4, and N_8. The three neighborhood systems are the simplest models of MRF, that is first-order Markov field. The rarest among them is the three-neighbor system such as summed area table (SAT) (Crow 1984) (see problems).

More specifically, the neighborhood systems are as follows:

$$\begin{aligned}
N_3(x,y) &= \{(x,y),(x-1,y-1),(x,y-1),(x-1,y)\},\\
N_4(x,y) &= \{(x,y),(x+1,y),(x-1,y),(x,y-1),(x,y+1)\},\\
N_8(x,y) &= \{(x,y),(x+1,y),(x+1,y-1),(x,y+1),(x-1,y-1),\\
&\quad (x-1,y),(x-1,y+1),(x,y-1),(x+1,y+1)\}.
\end{aligned} \tag{8.32}$$

In some cases, typically BP, it is convenient to represent neighbors relative to the center node: c(enter), e(ast), w(est), s(outh), n(orth), ne (north-east), se (south-east), sw (south-west), and nw (north-west), or using numbers clockwise from one to four: $N_4(p) = \{p, e(p), w(p), s(p), n(p)\}$ or $N_4 = \{1, 2, 3, 4\}$.

Relaxation is also realized in parallel if possible. To achieve concurrent operations, we expand the center pixel to a window (or block) of pixels. The operation can then be executed window by window, with the nodes in the window all being maintained concurrently. Let $A(p)$ denote a window around p and $N(A(p))$ the set of neighbors in $A(p)$: $N(A(p)) = \{r | r \in N(q), q \in A(p)\}$. For such a window-based system, Equation (8.29) becomes

$$f^{(t+1)}(A(x,y)) = T(I(A(x,y)), f^{(t)}(N(A(x,y)))), \quad t \in [0, T-1]. \tag{8.33}$$

In short, let us call this *RE* (Relaxation Equation). This is a general representation for the features: neighborhood operation, iterative computation, and parallel processing.

Relaxation algorithms are also characterized by initial and boundary conditions. For the initial condition, the initial value is normally $f^{(0)}(p) = I(p), p \in \mathcal{P}$. For the boundary condition, the neighbor may not be completely inside the image, provided that the center point is near the image boundary. For brevity, let $N(\mathcal{P}) = \{q | q \in N(p), p \in \mathcal{P}\}$. There are two methods: global and local methods. In the global method, an additional step is needed for boundary management, along with the main computation. The *border shrink method* deals with those points whose neighbors are all in the image plane:

$$f^{(t+1)}(p) = T^{(t)}(I(p), f^{(t)}(N(p))), \quad \forall p \in \{p | N(p) \in \mathcal{P}\}. \tag{8.34}$$

The result is a smaller area by the neighborhood size: $\{p | N(p) \in \mathcal{P}, p \in \mathcal{P}\}$. The *zero padding method* pads zeros in the exterior points.

$$\begin{aligned} &f^{(t)}(q) = 0, \quad \forall q \in N(\mathcal{P}) \setminus \mathcal{P}, \\ &f^{(t+1)}(p) = T^{(t)}(I(p), \quad f^{(t)}(N(p))), \quad \forall p \in \mathcal{P}. \end{aligned} \tag{8.35}$$

The result is the same size as the image but it is influenced by the sudden changes of the image across the boundary. The other method is the *border expansion method* that pads the exterior using the nearby boundary values.

$$\begin{aligned} &f^{(t)}(q) = f^{(t)}(\arg\min_{r \in \mathcal{P}} |r - q|), \quad \forall q \in N(\mathcal{P}) \setminus \mathcal{P}, \\ &f^{(t+1)}(p) = T^{(t)}(I(p), \quad f^{(t)}(N(p))), \quad \forall p \in \mathcal{P}. \end{aligned} \tag{8.36}$$

The boundary effect is less severe than the zero padding. The *mirror expansion method* fills the exterior points using the mirror image at the image boundary.

$$\begin{aligned} &f^{(t)}(q) = f^{(t)}(2(\arg\min_{p \in \mathcal{P}} |p - q|) - q), \quad \forall q \in N(\mathcal{P}) \setminus \mathcal{P}, \\ &f^{(t+1)}(p) = T^{(t)}(I(p), \quad f^{(t)}(N(p))), \quad \forall p \in \mathcal{P}. \end{aligned} \tag{8.37}$$

The result is less sensitive to local variations at the image boundary than other methods.

In the local method, the boundary is treated in each node locally on the fly. During the computation, each processor checks itself to determine whether it needs exterior values; if the answer is yes, it generates the exterior value, otherwise it continues. In this local method, additional logic is needed by the processors to check its position and generate the exterior values. For the border shrink method, each node executes the following:

$$\text{if } p \in \{p | N(p) \in \mathcal{P}\}, \text{ then } f^{(t+1)}(p) = T^{(t)}(I(p), f^{(t)}(N(p))). \tag{8.38}$$

The zero padding method is realized by the conditional execution:

$$\begin{aligned} &\text{if } q \notin N(\mathcal{P}) \setminus \mathcal{P} \quad \forall q \in N(p), \text{ then } f^{(t)}(q) = 0, \\ &f^{(t+1)}(p) = T^{(t)}(I(p), \quad f^{(t)}(N(p))), \quad \forall p \in \mathcal{P}. \end{aligned} \tag{8.39}$$

The border expansion method executes the relaxation in the following way:

$$\begin{aligned} &\text{if } q \notin N(\mathcal{P}) \quad \forall q \in N(p), \text{ then } f^{(t)}(q) = f^{(t)}(\arg\min_{r \in \mathcal{P}} |r - q|), \\ &f^{(t+1)}(p) = T^{(t)}(I(p), \quad f^{(t)}(N(p))), \quad \forall p \in \mathcal{P}. \end{aligned} \tag{8.40}$$

Finally, the mirror expansion method executes locally:

$$\begin{aligned} &\text{if } q \notin N(\mathcal{P}) \quad \forall q \in N(p), \text{ then } f^{(t)}(q) = f^{(t)}(2(\arg\min_{p \in \mathcal{P}} |p - q|) - q), \\ &f^{(t+1)}(p) = T^{(t)}(I(p), \quad f^{(t)}(N(p))), \quad \forall p \in \mathcal{P}. \end{aligned} \tag{8.41}$$

The two methods have clear advantages and disadvantages. The local method is generally better for hardware design, for accessing exterior points with additional indexes, and for managing large memory with expanded boundaries, which are generally disadvantages in circuit design.

Relaxation algorithms are characterized by their order of computation. Let the image plane be $\mathcal{P}$ and the iteration $\mathcal{T} = [0, T-1]$. A relaxation can be viewed as a process of visiting all the nodes in $V = \mathcal{P} \times \mathcal{T}$ in some proper order. For brevity, let $(a(b(c))|A)$ represent a loop operation, where c changes most rapidly, a changes the slowest, and A represents block (window) processing.

The orders, $(1(x(y)))$ or $(1(y(x)))$, are one-pass algorithms, which are most desirable, at least for the elapsed time. This class of algorithms includes one-pass labeling and SUM. Represented by $(2(x(y)))$ or $(2(y(x)))$, two-pass algorithms determine the solution using two passes. In general, $(t(x(y)))$ denotes a multi-pass algorithm, such as labeling, segmentation, morphology, filtering, connected-component, relaxation, BP, and GC, to name a few.

One of the most important multi-pass algorithms is the Gauss–Seidel method:

$$f^{(t+1)}(x,y) = T(I(x,y), f^{(t)}(x,y), f^{(t+1)}(x-1,y), f^{(t+1)}(x,y-1), f^{(t)}(x+1,y), f^{(t)}(x,y+1)), \quad (t(y(x))). \tag{8.42}$$

The proceeding order is the most usual scan, that is a raster scan. The neighbors are the most recently used (MRU) nodes. In contrast to raster scan, $(t(x,y))$ means that an entire image plane is updated concurrently, as in the Jacobi method.

$$f^{(t+1)}(x,y) = T(I(x,y), f^{(t)}(x,y), f^{(t+)}(x-1,y), f^{(t)}(x,y-1), f^{(t)}(x+1,y), f^{(t)}(x,y+1)), \quad (t(x,y)). \tag{8.43}$$

Equation (8.33) includes Gauss–Seidel and Jacobi methods (Golub and Van Loan 1996; Press *et al.* 2007) as special cases. If the window size is a pixel, it reduces to Gauss–Seidel and if $A = \mathcal{P}$, it becomes the Jacobi method. The two methods are on opposite ends of the relaxation algorithms spectrum. In summary, a complete expression of relaxation must be constructed using Equation (8.33), mapping, concurrent processing, initial and boundary policy, neighborhood definition, and updation order.

A very different scheme is possible using $(x(y(t)))$ or $(y(x(t)))$, which means that the computation proceeds in iteration axis first, then in the column (row) direction, and then the row (column) direction.

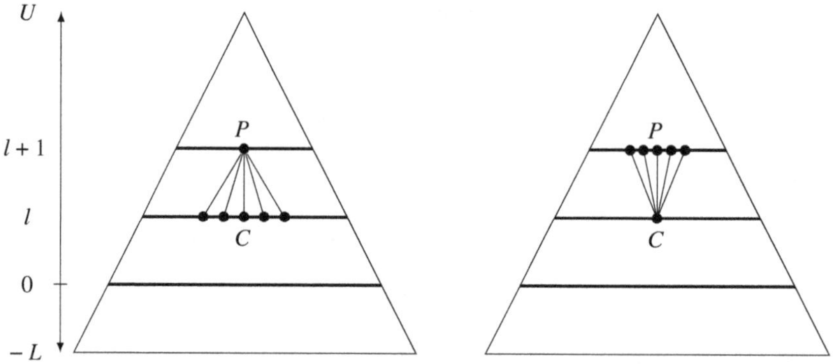

Figure 8.3 Pyramid hierarchy: (a) children and (b) parent

To deal with all these methods in a coherent way, we first consider an efficient method for representing the computational space in the following section.

Finally, vision problems often involve multi-scale (or multi-resolution) problems. One of the approaches to the scale is using pyramidal hierarchy, in which the bottom and top levels indicate fine and coarse scales. This computational hierarchy is efficiently realized using the multigrid method (Heath 2002; Terzopoulos 1986; Wesseling 1992), which primarily performs smoothing, down-sampling, and interpolation. Pyramid algorithms are widely used in image representation and processing (Burt 1984; Jolion and Rosenfeld 1994; Kim *et al.* 2013; Lindeberg 1993).

Suppose that a pyramid has levels $l \in [-L, U]$, where L and U are nonnegative integers representing, respectively, subpixel and coarse scales (Figure 8.3). The connection of the pyramid is the parent node P at the upper level and the children nodes C in the lower level. There are two types of pyramids: nonoverlapping and overlapping. For nonoverlapping pyramids, we define the nodes and connections such that for $l \in [-L, U]$, $(x, y, l) \in 2^{-l}\mathcal{P}$, $S(x, y, l) = \{(2x, 2y), (2x + 1, 2y), (2x, 2y + 1), (2x + 1, 2y + 1)\}$, and $P(x, y, l) = \{(\lfloor x/2 \rfloor, \lfloor y/2 \rfloor)\}$. For overlapping pyramids, we define the nodes and connections such that for $l \in [-L, U]$, $(x, y, l) \in 4^{-l}\mathcal{P}$, the candidate children are $S(x, y, l) = \{(2x + i, 2y + j) | i, j \in \{-1, 0, 1, 2\}\}$, and the parents are $P(x, y, l) = \{(x + i)/2, (y + j)/2 | i, j \in \{-1, 1\}\}$.

As inputs to the pyramid, the images are usually provided in image pyramid filtered using kernels such as Gaussian, Laplacian, and binomial coefficients. In a Gaussian pyramid, the image in each level I^l is built by smoothing the adjacent level image with Gaussian kernel $G(x, y)$ and down-sampling ($\downarrow$) or up-sampling ($\uparrow$):

$$I^l(x, y) = \begin{cases} I(x, y), & l = 0, \\ [I^{l-1}(x, y) * G(x, y)] \downarrow, & l \in [1, U], \\ [I^{l+1}(x, y) \uparrow * \, G(x, y)], & l \in [-L, -1]. \end{cases} \tag{8.44}$$

The control flow of the pyramid is also described by the upward and downward streams. In both directions, node operations are the same but the initialization is different. Depending on the directions, the node must be initialized by the average of the parent or the children.

$$f^{(0)}(x, y, l) \leftarrow \begin{cases} \frac{1}{|P|} \sum_{p \in P(x,y,l)} f^{(T-1)}(p), & \text{downward}, \\ \frac{1}{|S|} \sum_{p \in S(x,y,l)} f^{(T-1)}(p), & \text{upward}, \end{cases} \tag{8.45}$$

where $|P|$ and $|S|$ are, respectively, the sizes of the parent and child.

In accordance with the conventions, the relaxation equation becomes

$$f^{(t+1)}(A(x,y,l)) = T(I^l(A(x,y,l)), f^{(t)}(N(A(x,y,l)))), \quad t \in [0, T-1], (x,y) \in 2^{-l}\mathcal{P}, l \in [-L, U]. \tag{8.46}$$

For a full description of relaxation, we have to specify all the factors as explained in an algorithmic form. Since the upward and downward control depends on application, we may have to write the downward algorithm only.

Algorithm 8.1 (Relaxation) *Given I, compute the following.*

- *Input: image pyramid* $\{I^l | l \in [-L, U]\}$.
- *Output:* $f^{(T-1)}(A(x,y,-L)), \quad \forall(x,y) \in \mathcal{P}$.
- *Window:* $A(x,y) = \{(x+i, y+j) | i \in [0, n-1], j \in [0, m-1]\}$.
- *Boundary: global or local methods.*

1. *for* $l = U, U-1, \ldots, -L$,
2. *for* $t = 0, 1, \ldots, T-1$ *and* $\forall(x,y) \in 2^{-l}\mathcal{P}$,
   (a) *if* $l = U$ *and* $t = 0$, $f(x,y,l) \leftarrow 0$,
   (b) *else if* $t = 0$, $f(x,y,l) \leftarrow \frac{1}{|P|} \sum_{p \in P(x,y,l)} f(p)$,
   (c) *else* $f(A(x,y,l)) \leftarrow T(I^l(A(x,y,l)), f(N(A(x,y,l))))$.

We have now arrived at the final expression that includes all the major factors of relaxation: transformation, neighborhood, window, initialization, boundary condition, and scale. Even if the hierarchy has been considered, the major operation is the iterative updation, which is the same regardless of the level. Therefore, in the following section, we concentrate on the operation in a fixed level, as described by Equation (8.33) instead of Equation (8.46), unless otherwise stated.

8.5 Relaxation Graph

Computing RE can be viewed as determining all the nodes $V = \{(x,y,t) | (x,y) \in \mathcal{P}, t \in \mathcal{T}\}$ in systematic order. The space of the nodes can be considered as a stack of $\mathcal{P}$ planes numbered upwards with $\mathcal{T}$.

The concept is illustrated in Figure 8.4. The bottom layer represents an image plane while the top layer represents a result plane. In the side views, the vertical and diagonal edges represent the neighborhood

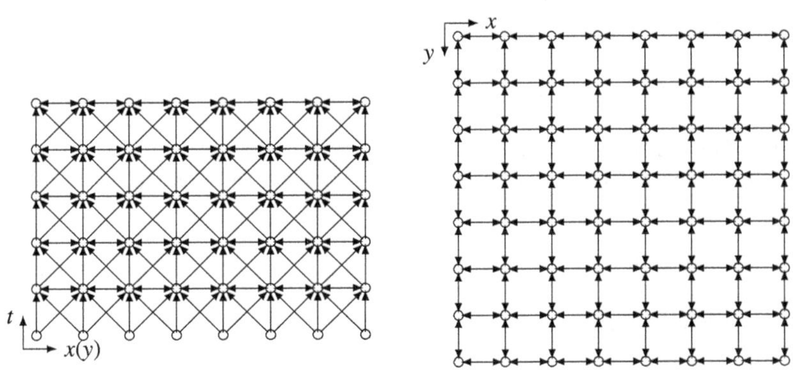

(a) $t - x(y)$ plane (b) $x - y$ plane

Figure 8.4 A graph $G = (V, E, F)$ for relaxation (N_4 system is shown) connections from lower level to higher level. In the top view, the edges look like an ordinary four-neighborhood but they mean connections between successive layers. In this graph, we can view the RE as a method by which we determine nodes, one by one or window by window, from one layer to another layer in the upward direction. The top layer signifies the end of the iteration, and contains the final result.

This concept is formally defined as a graph $G = (V, E, F)$.

Definition 8.1 (Relaxation graph) *A relaxation graph $G = (V, E, F)$ is a graph consisting of the nodes $V = \{(x, y, t)|(x, y) \in \mathcal{P}, t \in \mathcal{T}\}$ and the edges are defined in the neighborhood $N(x, y, t)$ and connected bidirectionally in the same layer and unidirectionally from lower to upper layer. A node $v \in V$ is assigned with a value $F(v) \in \mathcal{R}$. Especially, at the bottom plane, $F(x, y, 0) \leftarrow I(x, y)$ and at the top layer $F(x, y, T-1)$, the result is stored.*

In the graph, the nodes on the bottom and top layers are special in that one is input and the other is output. Apart from this, all the other nodes are identical in their operation and connection.

Nodes on the same layer are connected bidirectionally, whereas nodes that are between two layers are connected unidirectionally. The connection is based on the neighborhood system: N_3, N_4, or N_8. In this graph, the neighbor nodes are as follows:

$$N(x, y, t) = \{(x + i, y + j, t + k)|i, j \in \{-1, 1\}, t \in \{0, -1\}\}. \tag{8.47}$$

Nodes in N_4 and N_8 are part of this node set.

In this graph, the computational order is not unique. For t, there is only one direction: increasing the order. However, x and y can proceed forward and backward. Consequently, there is a total of 24 possible methods. Gauss–Seidel and Jacobi are only two special cases, having the orders $(t(y(x)))$ and $(t(x, y))$.

Among the many methods, only six are practical (Figure 8.5). The figure illustrates only the $t - y$ section of V. It also shows the center node, neighbor connection, storage, and proceeding direction. This figure contains six basic orders of computation. Each row represents computing directions and each column represents neighborhood connections: Gauss–Seidel or Jacobi connections. Common to all the computing orders, the computation starts from the bottom layer, where the nodes are initialized by the input image and ends at the top layer, where the nodes contain the final result. In between, the nodes are updated, using the values in the neighbor nodes, which have already been visited and determined in the previous stage. The stored values and proper order facilitate recursive computation in the six cases. It is obvious that there are three different orders of computation: Gauss–Seidel–Jacobi, diagonal, and vertical methods. Let us examine the methods in more detail.

As the first figure shows, Gauss–Seidel, which has computation order $(t(y(x)))$, is one possibility. The neighbor connection is defined by

$$N(x, y, t) = \{(x, y-1, t), (x-1, y, t), (x, y, t-1), (x+1, y, t-1), (x, y+1, t-1)\}, \tag{8.48}$$

where two neighbors are on the same layer and the other three are in the lower layer. The required storage is $O(MN)$. The second method is Jacobi, which has computation order $(t(x, y))$. The neighbors are defined as

$$N(x, y, t) = \{(x, y-1, t-1), (x-1, y, t-1), (x, y, t-1), (x+1, y, t-1), (x, y+1, t-1)\}, \tag{8.49}$$

where all the neighbors belong to the lower layer. This method needs $O(2MN)$ storage, for lower and upper layers.

Counterintuitively, the diagonal direction is possible for both Gauss–Seidel and Jacobi connections, as shown in the second row. The diagonal computation of the Gauss–Seidel connection is represented

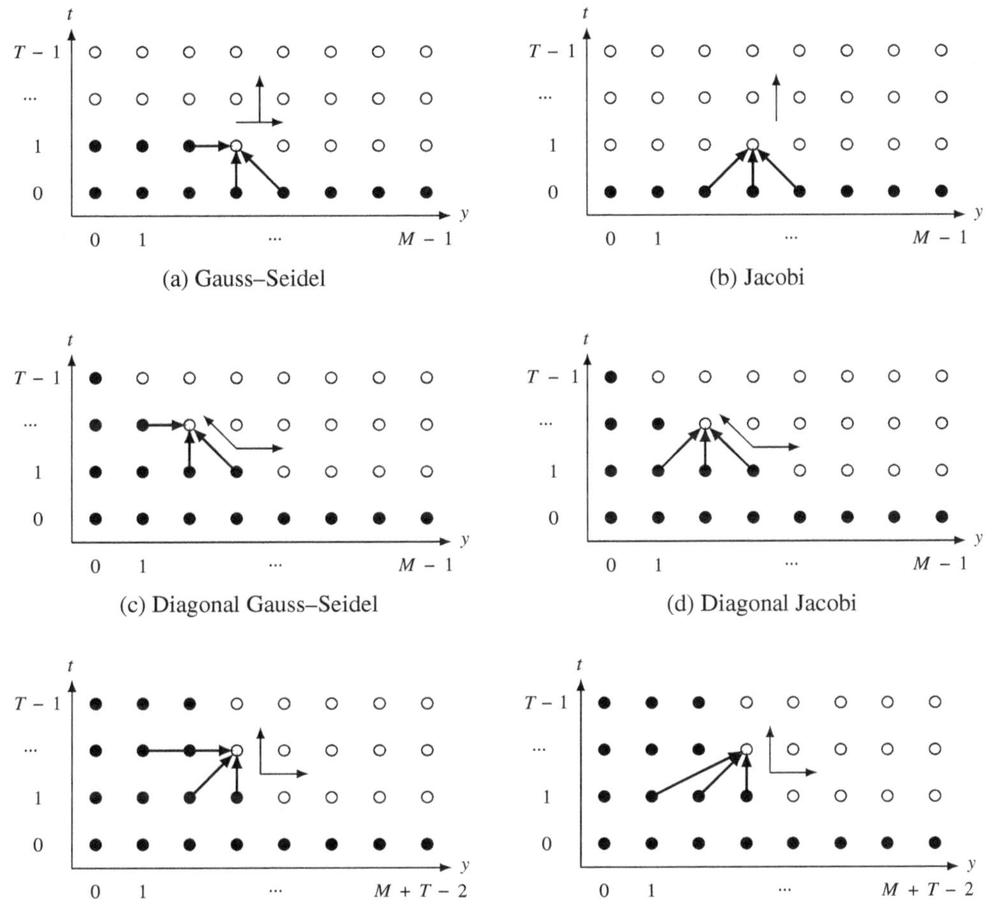

(a) Gauss–Seidel (b) Jacobi

(c) Diagonal Gauss–Seidel (d) Diagonal Jacobi

(e) Vertical Gauss–Seidel (f) Vertical Jacobi

Figure 8.5 Basic methods of computation order

by $(y - t(t(x)))$. The dual method $(x - t(t(y)))$ is also possible. The required storage is $O(NT)$. Similarly, the Jacobi connection can also be computed diagonally, with $(y - t(t(x)))$ (or $(x - t(t(y)))$) order and $O(NT)$ storage.

The shifted graph and connections are depicted on the third row. Instead of the original graph and diagonal direction, we may shift the graph so that the current node refers to those nodes whose index does not exceed that of the current node. In this manner, the diagonal computation can be converted to vertical direction for both Gauss–Seidel and Jacobi connections. The computation order is $(y(x(t)))$ or $(x(y(t)))$ and the storage is $O(2NT)$.

The vertical computation is more than simplifying the diagonal computation. It actually contains three more variants: y, x, and x-y shifts. Shifting in the y-axis, as shown in the figure, results in vertical movement in the y-t plane. Likewise, shifting in the x-axis results in vertical movement in the x-t direction. There is a third transformation, in which the original graph is shifted in both the x and y directions. The result is diagonal movement in both the x-t and y-t planes. As a consequence, we will deal with the vertical structure, discarding the diagonal structures.

The two structures, GSJ and Non GSJ (nGSJ) for diagonal and vertical orders, show completely different properties in computation and are thus examined separately. In the following section, we examine the two structures in more detail and eventually represent them using hardware algorithms, called *RE* and *FRE* machines, intermediate representations between software algorithm and Verilog design.

8.6 Relaxation Machine

Let us first examine the GSJ structure. For the Gauss–Seidel method, the order is $(t(y(x)))$ and the operation is

$$f(x,y,t) \leftarrow T(I(x,y),\ f(x,y,t-1),\ f(x-1,y,t),\ f(x,y-1,t),\ f(x+1,y,t-1), f(x,y+1,t-1)). \tag{8.50}$$

Among the five neighbors, two are new and three are old. Moving in the order, $(t(y(x)))$, the operation is obviously recursive. Meanwhile, the Jacobi method has computation order $O(t(x,y))$ and operations,

$$f(x,y,t) \leftarrow T(I(x,y),\ f(x,y,t-1),\ f(x-1,y,t-1),\ f(x,y-1,t-1),\ f(x+1,y,t-1), f(x,y+1,t-1)). \tag{8.51}$$

All the neighbor values are located below the current plane. The operation is also recursive if the computation order $(t(x,y))$ is maintained.

For a closer look at the Gauss–Seidel method, three side views of G are illustrated in Figure 8.6. The views are the *y-l*, *x-y*, and a part of the *x-y* planes. The *y-t* view shows the connection between neighbors,

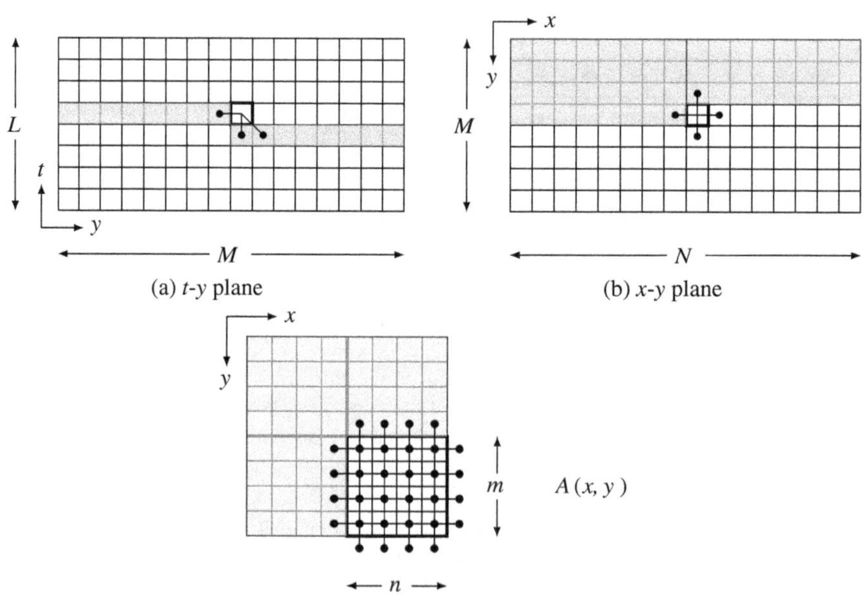

(a) *t-y* plane (b) *x-y* plane (c) A window

Figure 8.6 Configurations: storage and connections for a node and window located on the same layer and the lower layer. The shaded region is the minimal storage for recursive computation. The same computation is also observed in the x-y plane. The shaded region is the storage to be used later when the upper layer is updated. In the bottom is shown a window, $A(x, y)$, an expanded version of a pixel, for window processing. Inside the window, the nodes located around the upper and left boundaries can access the most recently updated values while the others access older values in the lower layer. In fact, a window possesses both Gauss–Seidel and Jacobi properties. The boundary nodes belong to the Gauss–Seidel connection and the inner nodes belong to the Jacobi connection. As $mn \rightarrow 1$, the system tends closer to the Gauss–Seidel method. Conversely, as $mn \rightarrow MN$, the system tends closer to the Jacobi method. Between $1 < mn < MN$, the system possesses properties of both the Gauss–Seidel and Jacobi methods.

In this manner, both the Gauss–Seidel and Jacobi methods are commonly represented by the window introduced. The RE becomes

$$f(A(x,y,t)) \leftarrow T(I(A(x,y)), f(N(A(x,y,t)))), \quad (t(y(x))|A), \tag{8.52}$$

which is a graphical representation of Equation (8.33). Here, $N(A(x, y, t)$ is connected to the most recently updated nodes as explained: boundary nodes to the same layer and inner nodes to the lower layer.

$$\begin{aligned} A(x,y,t) = {} & \{(x+i, y+j, t-1)|i \in [1, n+1], j \in [1, m+1]\} \\ & \cup \{(x+i, y-1, t)|i \in [0, n-1]\} \cup \{(x-1, y+j, t)|j \in [0, m-1]\}. \end{aligned} \tag{8.53}$$

If $mn = 1$, we have $A(x,y,t) = \{(x,y-1,t), (x-1,y,t), (x,y,t-1), (x+1,y,t-1), (x,y+1,t-1)\}$. If $mn = MN$, we have $A(x,y,t) = \{(x,y-1,t-1), (x-1,y,t-1), (x,y,t-1), (x+1,y,t-1), (x,y+1, t-1)\}$.

In addition to the updation equation, an algorithm needs more information about initial condition, boundary condition, control, and memory. It is summarized as follows:

Algorithm 8.2 (RE machine) *Given I, determine f.*

- *Input:* $\{I(x,y)|(x,y) \in \mathcal{P}\}$.
- *Memory:* $F = \{f(x,y)|(x,y) \in N(\mathcal{P})\}$.
- *Window:* $A(x,y) = \{(x+i, y+j)|i \in [0, n-1], j \in [0, m-1]\}$.
- *Boundary: global or local method.*
- *Output:* $\{f(x,y)|(x,y) \in \mathcal{P}\}$.

1. *Initialization:* $F \leftarrow I$.
2. *for* $t = 0, 1, \ldots, T-1$,
   (a) *for* $y = 0, m, 2m, \ldots, M-1$, *for* $x = 0, n, 2n, \ldots, N-1$,

$$\begin{aligned} & f(N(A(x,y))) \overset{read}{\leftarrow} F, \\ & f(A(x,y)) \leftarrow T(I(x,y), f(N(A(x,y)))), \\ & F \overset{write}{\leftarrow} f(A(x,y)). \end{aligned}$$

Let us call this the *RE machine* (relaxation equation machine). This machine needs two memories, a memory F and a window A, and a logic, global, or local boundary policy. In this algorithm, the detailed expression, represented by Equation (8.53), is not required, because the memory always contains the most recent values. Initially, the memory is simply overwritten with the image. The same operation is then repeated for all nodes in three nested loops. In each operation, a block of neighbors is read from the

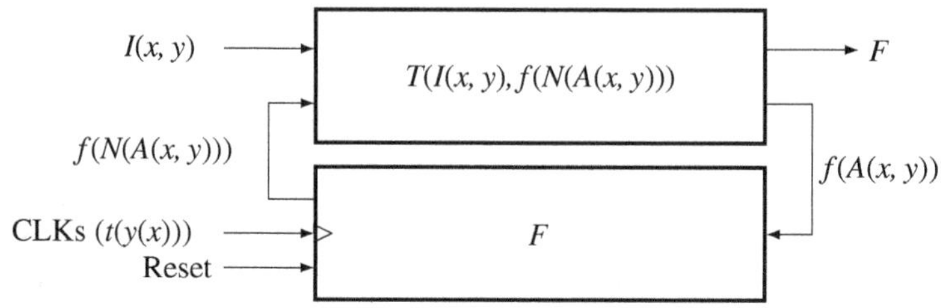

Figure 8.7 Architecture of the RE machine

memory and used in the updation equation. The updated window is then overwritten on the older values in the memory. When the operation reaches the top and is finally over, the final result is the contents in the memory.

Considered in the computational complexity, the variables are the neighborhood $N(\cdot)$ and the window size mn. This system requires $O(mn)$ processors, $O(MNT/mn)$ time, and $O(MN + mn)$ space. At one extreme, it approaches the Gauss–Seidel method as $mn \to 1$, which executes the algorithm with one processor, $O(MNL)$ time, and $O(MN)$ space. At the other end, as $mn \to MN$, it approaches the Jacobi method, which uses $O(MN)$ processors, $O(T)$ time, and $O(2MN)$ space. (Two memories are required in this case for input and output. The roles are alternatively changed in each iteration.) In general, the degree of serial and parallel computation is controlled by the parameter mn.

The corresponding architecture consists of a combinational circuit $T(\cdot)$, a memory plane F, a buffer memory $f(A)$, and three clocks $(t(y(x)))$ (Figure 8.7). The clocks are represented by the three nested loops, $(t(y(x)))$, with x for the innermost loop and t the outermost loop. There are no conditional jumps: the logic is completely deterministic. The image is stored in I and read in each clock period.

8.7 Affine Graph

In Figure 8.5, we observed that the computational order can be $(y - t(t(x)))$ or $(x - t(t(y)))$. However, the diagonal direction is somewhat complicated when counting node numbers and preserving memories and thus more convenient representation is needed. There are three possibilities for shift directions: x, y, and x-y directions. Of the three, the third option is the best because it can use more updated neighbors than the others.

This concept is shown in Figure 8.8. If we push the graph in both the x and y directions, proportionally to the layer height – an affine transformation, the shape becomes a parallelepiped – the top plane is still parallel to the image plane but the other walls are no longer orthogonal to the image plane. Between two adjacent layers, the amount of shift is just one unit in both directions. Therefore, the neighborhood connection must also be shifted properly. For better understanding, three views are provided. The proceeding direction is the raster scan in both the l-y and x-y planes. In this order and connection, the neighbor values are always the most recently updated ones. This is one of many possible variations of deformation (see the problems at the end of this chapter).

Because of the deformation, the original cube (rectangular parallelepiped) becomes a parallelepiped. To make the graph a rectangular parallelepiped, we fill the empty spaces with dummy nodes, which function the same way as the nodes. The resulting shape is a cube with $N' \times T'$ nodes, where $N' = (N + T - 1)$ and $M' = (M + T - 1)$. In this cube, the image input is still the $M \times N$ part of the bottom layer and the output is the same size as the top layer. Now, G' can be considered G, except that the cube is expanded and the nodes are connected differently.

Let us define the induced graph formally and call it an *affine graph*.

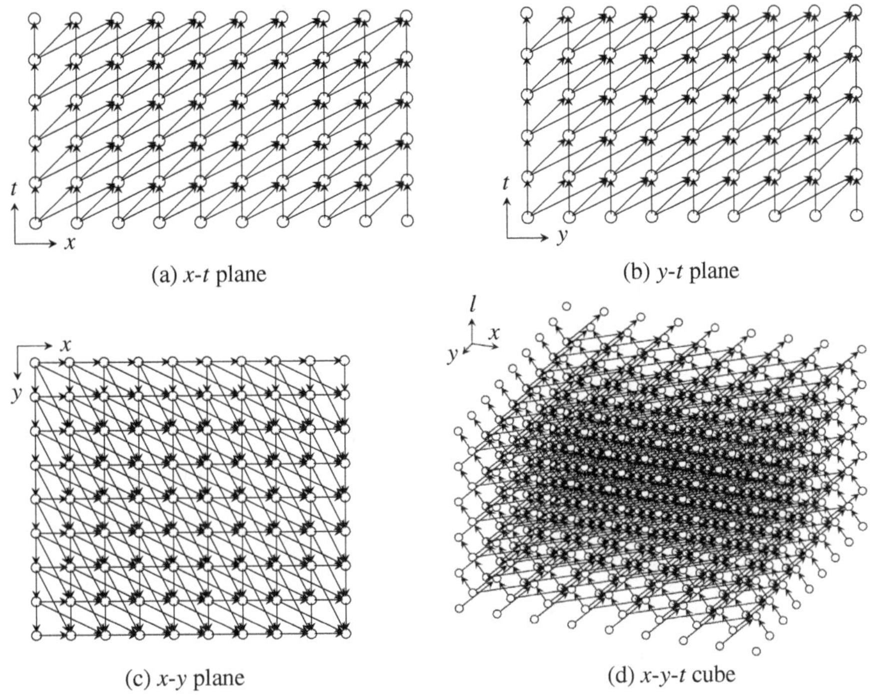

Figure 8.8 The induced graph, $G' = (V, E, F)$

Definition 8.2 (Affine graph) *An affine graph $G' = (V, E, F)$ is a graph that is induced from the relaxation graph G by applying the affine transformation, which transforms $(x, y, t) \in G$ to $(x', y', t') \in G'$, using*

$$\begin{bmatrix} x' \\ y' \\ t' \end{bmatrix} = \begin{bmatrix} 1 & 0 & 1 \\ 0 & 1 & 1 \\ 0 & 0 & 1 \end{bmatrix} \begin{bmatrix} x \\ y \\ t \end{bmatrix}, \quad (or\ \mathbf{x}' = A\mathbf{x}), \tag{8.54}$$

where A is an affine matrix, and padding nodes so that the graph becomes a rectangular parallelepiped with $V = \{(x, y, t)|x \in [0, N' - 1], y \in [0, M' - 1], t \in \mathcal{T}\}$, where $N' = N + T - 1$ and $M' = M + T - 1$.

The affine transformation can only be applied to one direction, in either x or y, but not both. In this case, we obtain different types of graphs in terms of neighborhood connections (see the problems at the end of this chapter). The two graphs differ in two aspects: first, the space is changed from $M \times N \times T$ to $M' \times N' \times T$. Second, the original neighborhood must also be transformed by $N' = AN$.

The neighborhood systems in Equation (8.32) become

$$\begin{aligned} N_4(x, y, t) = \{&(x-1, y-1, t-1), (x, y-1, t-1), (x-2, y-1, t-1), \\ &(x-1, y, t-1), (x-1, y-2, t-1)\}, \\ N_8(x, y, t) = \{&(x-1, y-1, t-1), (x, y-1, t-1), (x, y, t-1), (x-1, y, t-1), (x-2, y, t-1), \\ &(x-2, y-1, t-1), (x, y-2, t-1), (x-1, y-2, t-1), (x-2, y-2, t-1)\}. \end{aligned} \tag{8.55}$$

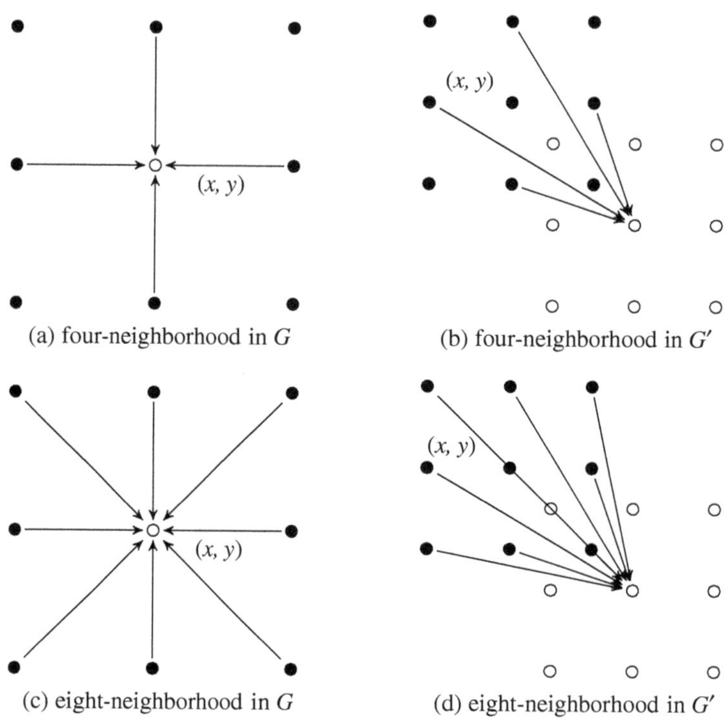

Figure 8.9 Neighborhood systems in G and G'. Empty circles are one level above the dark circles. The edge direction means data dependency

In this expression, all the neighbors are positioned below and withdraw one or two cell distances from the center node.

The connections are illustrated in Figure 8.9. The filled dots are on the lower layer and the empty dots are on the upper layer. In the new graph, the neighborhood connections look distorted and thus the original bearings – east, west, south, and north – are not correct; however, we will keep the same name for simplicity. The node distances are also changed. The east and south neighbors are in one pixel distance but the west and north neighbors are in two pixels distance (in one coordinate).

8.8 Fast Relaxation Machine

In G', one of the efficient schedules is $(y(x(t)))$, where the computation proceeds in the order, layer, column, and row. A node (x, y, t) can then be computed recursively using the previous values.

$$\begin{aligned} f(x,y,t) \leftarrow\ & T(I(x,y,t), f(x-1,y-1,t-1), f(x-2,y-1,t), f(x-1,y-2,t), \\ & f(x,y-1,t-1), f(x-1,y,t-1)). \end{aligned} \tag{8.56}$$

Here, $I(x,y)$ is the new input while all the other values are stored values that were computed in the previous stages.

Let us expand the recursive computation from a node, (x,y,t), to a small window, $A(x,y,t)$, whose position is represented by the first pixel position in it: $A(x,y) = \{(x+i, y+j) | i \in [0, n-1], j \in [0, m-1]\}$.

The value set is $f(A(x,y)) = \{f(x+i, y+j) | i \in [0, n-1], j \in [0, m-1]\}$. The relaxation equation thus becomes

$$f(A(x,y,t)) \leftarrow T(I(A(x,y)), f(N(A(x,y,t)))), \quad (y(x(t))|A), \tag{8.57}$$

where $y = 0, m, \ldots, M'-1$, $x = 0, n, \ldots, N'-1$, and $t = 0, 1, \ldots, L-1$. Notice that starting from Equation (8.33), we have derived Equation (8.52) and Equation (8.57). The three equations represent the same RE but in different spaces – time, G, and G'. This method divides the x-y plane into $m \times n$ blocks and scans the plane block by block.

Together with the scheduling and hardware resources, this method is described as follows:

Algorithm 8.3 (fast relaxation machine) *Given I, determine f.*

- *Input:* $\{I(x,y) | (x,y) \in \mathcal{P}\}$.
- *Queue:* $F = \{f(x,y) | (x,y) \in N(\mathcal{P})\}$.
- *Window:* $A(x,y) = \{(x+k, y+t) | k \in [0, n-1], l \in [0, m-1]\}$.
- *Boundary: global or local boundary policy.*
- *Output:* $f(A(x,y,T-1))$.

1. *Initialization:* $F \leftarrow I$.
2. *for* $y = 0, m, \ldots, M'-1$, *for* $x = 0, n, \ldots, N'-1$, *for* $t = 0, 1, \ldots, L-1$, *compute*
   (a) $f(N(A(x,y,t))) \overset{read}{\leftarrow} Q(x,y,t)$.
   (b) $f(A(x,y,t)) \leftarrow T(I(A(x,y,t)), f(N(A(x,y,t))))$.
   (c) $Q(x,y,t) \overset{push}{\leftarrow} f(A(x,y,t))$.
   (d) *if* $t = T-1$, *output* $f(A(x,y,T-1))$.

To differentiate this machine from the RE machine, let us call it the *FRE Machine* (fast relaxation equation machine). The major difference from the RE machine is the memory type: queue. The reading and writing positions, defined by $f(N(A(x,y,t)))$, are fixed but the memory must shift down as the node position changes. Alternatively, the opposite is possible: fixed memory and moving address. The memory position is determined by the neighborhood type and the window shape. At the bottom layer, the processors do not need neighborhood but input image. At the first column, only one neighbor is available and thus others must be empty. Otherwise, the image input is not available and thus the processors use neighbor values only. The state memory must also be avoided at the top layer, since it will never be used. Whenever the processors move upward, the neighbor values must be read from the state memory. The output is available when the processors complete the top layer. This algorithm uses $O(mn)$ processors and $((N'/n+1)(L-1))mn$ space. If $mn \to 1$ and $L \to 2$, it approaches the Jacobi machine but never approaches the Gauss–Seidel machine.

The architecture is shown in Figure 8.10. The system is driven by the three nested clocks, $(y(x(t)))$, where the variables respectively denote the block number, row, column, and layer, with t the fastest and y

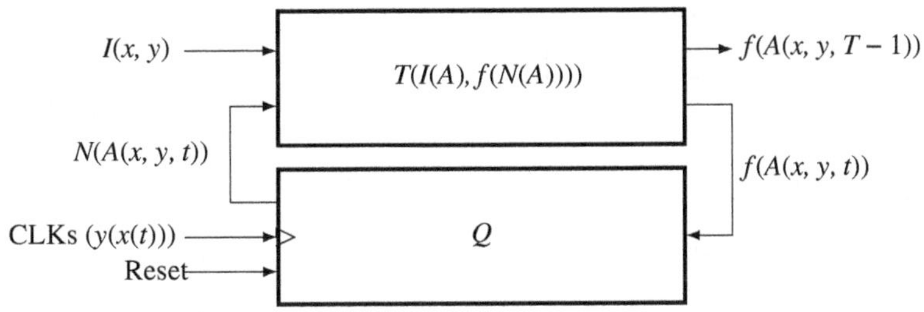

Figure 8.10 The block relaxation machine

the slowest. The addresses to the state memory blocks and pixels are all computed by the neighborhood relationship in a window. With image and neighbor values, the $m \times n$ processors compute the node values $f(A(x, y, t))$. After the updation, the state memory is written with this value when it is not on the top layer. This architecture is relatively easy to realize, because the memory structure is rather simple.

For a complete system, the machines are the major part in Algorithm 8.1, which includes hierarchical control. However, those controls are largely dependent upon the problems and applications.

8.9 State Memory of Fast Relaxation Machine

To completely describe FRE, we have to specify $f(N(A(x, y, t)))$, by computing the positions of the neighbors in the memory. There are two possibilities for the memory: RAM and queue. For RAM, the addresses $N(A(x, y, t))$ are changed to write and read the memory and thus no further explanation is needed. For queue, the addresses are fixed and the contents are shifted down in the queue whenever the window moves to the next position. Unless otherwise stated, we assume a queue.

Let us consider a 2×2 window, A, in a graph G' (Figure 8.11). The window moves according to the schedule, $(y(x(t)))$. The left figure indicates a y-t plane view, which consists of an $M' \times T$ grid, with bottom representing image plane and the top representing the result. In both views, the neighbor values are indicated by the connecting lines the state memory is denoted by the shaded region. In the y-t plane, the window moves in $(y(t))$ order. The state memory is a $4 \times T$ rectangular in this plane. As the window moves upwards, the top of the memory is filled and the tail is emptied, so that the queue moves upwards. On reaching the top layer, the window shifts from y to $y + 2$.

In the x-y plane, the window moves in $(y(x))$ order. The node inside the window accesses the neighbor nodes as the links indicate. The memory in this view occupies the $2 \times N'$ rectangular region. From both views, the state memory becomes a $2 \times T \times N'$ cube. The memory structure is primarily a queue, which can be conveniently realized with an array. To fully specify the neighborhood, we have to specify the addresses, relative to the present window. The addresses depend on the window position, (x, y, t) and the window size, (m, n).

Typical examples are depicted in Figure 8.12. The figure contains four windows and the neighbor connections. Nodes in a window access other nodes as indicated by the lines. The shaded area is a part

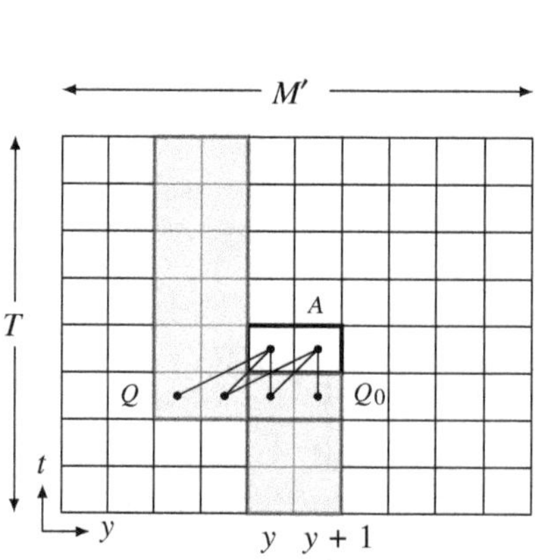

(a) y-t plane

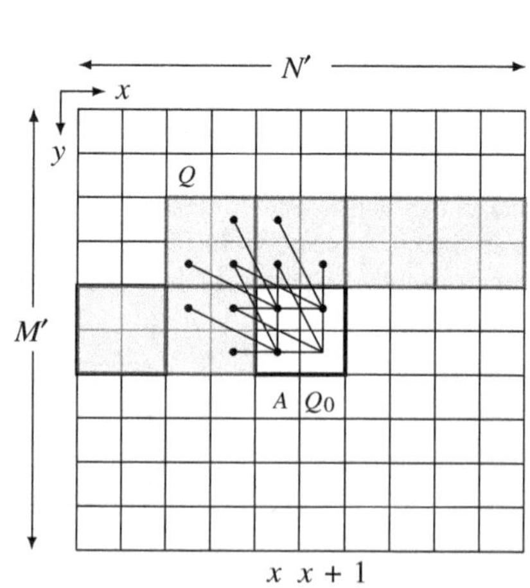

(b) x-y plane

Figure 8.11 System state in y-t and x-y planes. A block (2×4), a state memory, and a buffer

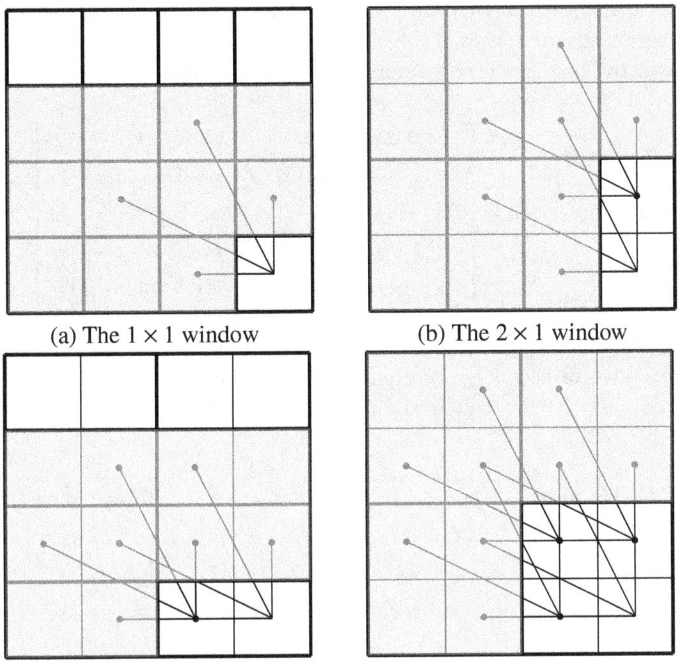

(a) The 1×1 window (b) The 2×1 window

(c) The 1×2 window (d) The 2×2 window

Figure 8.12 The windows and neighborhoods: 1×1, 2×1, 1×2, and 2×2

of the system memory that contains the neighbor values to be used presently and later. For simplicity, some unused memory cells are also included to make the memory structure more regular. The addresses indicated by the connecting lines clearly depend upon the window and image size.

Let us first consider the 1×1 window, which is located at (x, y, t). If a queue is used, the memory is a rectangular parallelepiped with $3N'T$ nodes. The neighborhood pixels are located in five different places in the memory. When ordered in east, west, south, and north, the neighbor values are as follows:

$$f(N(A(x,y,t))) = \{f(x,y,t-1), f(x,y-1,t-1), f(x-2,y-1,t-1), \\ f(x-1,y,t-1), f(x-1,y-2,t-1)\}. \tag{8.58}$$

The addresses represent the absolute positions in RAM. If a queue is to be used, the offset from (x, y, t) is the fixed address in memory. This concept is the same for other windows.

For a two-pixel window, we have two possibilities, specifically, 1×2 and 2×1 windows. There appears to be no preference about this but the 2×1 window seems to be somewhat simpler, because its height matches the state memory size. For the 2×1 window, two nodes independently access 10 cells in the memory, which has size $3N'T$. The absolute positions are defined by

$$f(N(A(x,y,t))) = \begin{bmatrix} f(x,y,t-1) & f(x,y+1,t-1) \\ f(x,y-1,t-1) & f(x,y,t-1)) \\ f(x-2,y-1,t-1) & f(x-2,y,t-1) \\ f(x-1,y,t-1) & f(x-1,y+1,t-1) \\ f(x-1,y-2,t-1) & f(x-1,y-1,t-1) \end{bmatrix}^T, \tag{8.59}$$

where the first row contains the neighbors of (x, y, t) and the second row the neighbors of $(x, y+1, t)$, all arranged in the order center, east, west, south, and north.

For the 1×2 window, the size of the memory is $2N'T$. The memory addresses are

$$f(N(A(x,y,t))) = \begin{bmatrix} f(x,y,t-1) & f(x+1,y,t-1) \\ f(x,y-1,t-1) & f(x+1,y-1,t-1) \\ f(x-2,y-1,t-1) & f(x-1,y-1,t-1) \\ f(x-1,y,t-1) & f(x,y+1,t-1) \\ f(x-1,y-2,t-1) & f(x,y-1,t-1) \end{bmatrix}^T . \tag{8.60}$$

Likewise, in the 2×1 window, this window also accesses 10 neighbors, but in different positions. The first and the second rows, respectively, correspond to the neighbors of (x, y, t) and $(x+1, y, t)$.

The 2×2 window has 20 elements in the memory, which has $4N'T$ nodes. The neighborhood is defined by

$$f(N(A(x,y))) = \begin{bmatrix} f(x,y) & f(x,y-1) & f(x-2,y-1) & f(x-1,y) & f(x-1,y-2) \\ f(x,y+1) & f(x,y) & f(x-2,y) & f(x-1,y+1) & f(x-1,y) \\ f(x+1,y) & f(x+1,y-1) & f(x-1,y-1) & f(x,y) & f(x,y-2) \\ f(x+1,y+1) & f(x+1,y) & f(x-1,y) & f(x,y+1) & f(x,y-1) \end{bmatrix}, \tag{8.61}$$

where time indices are dropped for simplicity. The neighbors are ordered in a row, for (x, y, t), $(x, y+1, t)$, $(x+1, y, t)$, and $(x+1, y+1, t)$, with the same four bearings.

In general, for an (m, n) window, the neighborhood values are determined by

$$f(N(A(x,y,t))) = f\left(\bigcup_{\substack{i\in[0,n-1] \\ j\in[0,m-1]}} N(x+i, y+j, t) \right). \tag{8.62}$$

The addresses denote absolute positions in RAM, which is organized in the shape of a 'V'. If the memory is organized in other multidimensional arrays, the addresses must be converted accordingly. Moreover, if a queue is used instead, the addresses must be converted to the fixed positions in that memory.

8.10 Comparison of Relaxation Machines

Thus far, we have derived various architectures that possess some major properties of relaxation operations. We have defined a relaxation equation and, based on a graphical representation, obtained RE and FRE machines (Park and Jeong 2008a,b). The machines are all summarized in Table 8.1 and compared with time, space, and space-time product.

The machines included in this table are classified into two classes: RE and FRE machines. The major difference between the two machines is the direction of computation, that is $(t(y(x)))$ and $(t(x, y))$ or $(y(x(t)))$. The RE machine is a unified concept of the Gauss–Seidel $(mn = 1)$ and the Jacobi methods $(mn = MN)$. The FRE machine is a rather different concept, whose extreme is also the Jacobi machine $(mn = MN)$. Thus, the Jacobi method is the common connection between the two machines. The memories are all RAM, but queue is more natural to FRE. In RAM, the address moves and the content remains in the same position. In queue, the address is fixed and the contents are shifted. All the methods are scalable

Table 8.1 Relaxation machines

Machine	PEs	Time	Space	Space-Time Product	Memory
Gauss–Seidel	1	MNT	MN	M^2N^2T	RAM
Jacobi	MN	T	$2MN$	$2MNT$	RAM
RE $(m \times n)$	mn	MNT/mn	$MN + mn$	$MNT(MN + mn)/mn$	RAM
FRE (1×1)	1	$M'N'T$	$3N'T$	$3M'N'^2T^2$	Queue
FRE (2×1)	2	$M'N'T/2$	$4N'T$	$2M'N'^2T^2$	Queue
FRE (1×2)	2	$M'N'T/2$	$3N'T$	$3M'N'^2T^2/2$	Queue
FRE (2×2)	4	$M'N'T/4$	$4N'T$	$M'N'^2T^2$	Queue
FRE $(m \times n)$	mn	$M'N'T/mn$	$(2 + m)N'T$	$(2 + m)M'N'^2T^2/mn$	Queue

cf. $M' = M + T - 1, N' = N + T - 1, m \in [1, M], n \in [1, N]$.

using the parameter mn, denoting the number of parallel processors. One of the advantages of the FRE over the RE machine is the far smaller memory.

Problems

8.1 [Euler–Lagrange Equation] Prove that the Gaussian distribution is the solution of the diffusion equation.

8.2 [Discretization] What stencils are possible, other than Equation (8.22), for $\nabla^2 f(x, y)$?

8.3 [Discretization] Derive Equation (8.23), which is a discretization of anisotropic diffusion operator.

8.4 [SOR] For the above anisotropic diffusion, derive the relaxation equation for Equation (8.6), similarly to Equation (8.28).

8.5 [Relaxation equation] The relaxation technique originated from the iterative solution of linear systems. Let $A\mathbf{x} = \mathbf{b}$, where $\mathbf{x} \in \mathcal{R}^n$ and $\mathbf{b} \in \mathcal{R}^m$. One of the approaches is to partition A into two matrices, $A = N - M$. Using this method, derive a relaxation equation and discuss the convergence conditions.

8.6 [Relaxation equation] In deriving relaxation for $A\mathbf{x} = \mathbf{b}$, we may partition A into three matrices. Using this method, derive the Jacobi method in matrix form.

8.7 [Relaxation equation] As a continuation of the previous problem, derive the Gauss–Seidel method in matrix form, using the three partitioned matrices.

8.8 [Relaxation equation] As a continuation of the previous problem, derive SOR in matrix form for the Gauss–Seidel method.

8.9 [Affine graph] In the affine graph, the transformation is applied in both directions, x and y. What happens to the neighborhood connection if the transformation is applied in only one direction?

8.10 [FRE machine] There is another type of algorithm that is different from the four-neighborhood processing, called *sum area table* (SAT). The SAT (also known as *integral table*) (Viola and Jones 2001) uses a three-neighborhood system and raster scan for computing area using just the previously stored values. It is a data structure and an algorithm for quickly and efficiently generating the sum of values in a rectangular subset of a grid. Write the updation equation for SAT and show that it is a one-pass algorithm.

8.11 [FRE machine] The original SAT algorithm means mainly fast summation, but inherently implies an efficient computational structure. In the SAT algorithm, show that the state memory can be realized with a queue, and rewrite the updation equation in terms of the queue.

8.12 [FRE machine] Derive the SAT in the above problem with corresponding algorithm and machine architecture, as we have done for the RE and FRE machines.

References

Alvarez L, Lions PL, and Morel JM 1992 Image selective smoothing and edge detection by nonlinear diffusion. ii. *SIAM Journal on Numerical Analysis* **29**(3), 845–866.

Boykov Y, Veksler O, and Zabih R 1998 Markov random fields with efficient approximations. *International Conference on Computer Vision and Pattern Recognition (CVPR)*.

Burt PJ 1984 *The Pyramid as a Structure for Efficient Computation*. Springer.

Chen G, Li Z, and Lin P 2008 A fast finite difference method for biharmonic equations on irregular domains and its application to an incompressible Stokes flow. *Advances in Computational Mathematics* **29**(2), 113–133.

Cohen FS and Cooper DB 1987 Simple parallel hierarchical and relaxation algorithms for segmenting noncausal Markovian random fields. *IEEE Trans. Pattern Anal. Mach. Intell.* **9**(2), 195–219.

Courant R and Hilbert D 1953 *Methods of Mathematical Physics*, vol. 1. Interscience Press.

Crow FC 1984 Summed-area tables for texture mapping. *Computer Graphics (SIGGRAPH '84 Proceedings)*, pp. 207–212. Published as Computer Graphics (SIGGRAPH '84 Proceedings), volume 18, number 3.

De Ma S and Li B 1998 Derivative computation by multiscale filters. *Image and Vision Computing* **16**(1), 43–53.

Ghosh K, Sarkar S, and Bhaumik K 2004 A bio-inspired model for multi-scale representation of even order Gaussian derivatives. *Intelligent Sensors, Sensor Networks and Information Processing Conference, 2004. Proceedings of the 2004*, pp. 497–502 IEEE.

Glazer F 1984 *Multilevel Relaxation in Low-level Computer Vision*. Springer.

Glowinski R and Pironneau O 1979 Numerical methods for the first biharmonic equation and for the two-dimensional Stokes problem. *SIAM Review* **21**(2), 167–212.

Golub GH and Van Loan CF 1996 *Matrix Computation* John Hopkins Studies in the Mathematical Sciences third edn. Johns Hopkins University Press, Baltimore, Maryland.

Gonzalez RC, Woods RE, and Eddins SL 2009 Digital image processing using MATLAB(R), 2nd edition *Gatesmark Publishing*.

Gu J and Wang W 1992 A novel discrete relaxation architecture. *IEEE Trans. Pattern Anal. Mach. Intell.* **14**(8), 857–865.

Hayes KC 1980 Reading handwritten words using hierarchical relaxation. *Computer Graphics and Image Processing* **14**(4), 344–364.

Heath M 2002 *Scientific Computing: an Introductory Survey*. McGraw-Hill Higher Education. McGraw-Hill.

Hinton GE 2007 Learning multiple layers of representation. *Trends in Cognitive Science* **11**(10), 428–434.

Horn BKP 1986 *Robot Vision*. MIT Press, Cambridge, Massachusetts.

Hummel RA and Zucker SW 1983 On the foundations of relaxation labeling processes. *IEEE Trans. Pattern Anal. Mach. Intell.* **5**(3), 267–287.

Jolion JM and Rosenfeld A 1994 *A Pyramid Framework for Early Vision: Multiresolutional Computer Vision*. Kluwer Academic Publishers.

Kamada M, Toraichi K, Mori R, Yamamoto K, and Yamada H 1988 A parallel architecture for relaxation operations. *Pattern Recognition* **21**(2), 175–181.

Kim J, Liu C, Sha F, and Grauman K 2013 Deformable spatial pyramid matching for fast dense correspondences. *Computer Vision and Pattern Recognition (CVPR), 2013 IEEE Conference on*, pp. 2307–2314 IEEE.

Kittler J and Illingworth J 1985 Relaxation labelling algorithms: Review. *Image and Vision Computing* **3**(4), 206–216.

Kittler J, Christmas WJ, and Petrou M 1993 Probabilistic relaxation for matching problems in computer vision. *Computer Vision, 1993. Proceedings, Fourth International Conference on*, pp. 666–673 IEEE.

Lindeberg T 1993 *Scale-Space Theory in Computer Vision*. Kluwer.

Marr D and Hildreth E 1980 Theory of edge detection. *Proceedings of the Royal Society of London. Series B. Biological Sciences* **207**(1167), 187–217.

Miranker WL 1979 Hierarchical relaxation. *Computing* **23**(3), 267–285.

Mori K, Horiuchi T, Wada K, and Toraichi K 1995 A parallel relaxation architecture for handwritten character recognition. *Communications, Computers, and Signal Processing, 1995. Proceedings, IEEE Pacific Rim Conference on*, pp. 74–77 IEEE.

Nagao and Matsuyama 2013 http://anorkey.com/nagao-matsuyama-filter/ (accessed May 3, 2013).

Park S and Jeong H 2008a High-speed parallel very large scale integration architecture for global stereo matching. *Journal of Electronic Imaging* **17**(1), 010501–3.

Park S and Jeong H 2008b Memory efficient iterative process on a two-dimensional first-order regular graph. *Optics Letters* **33**, 74–76.

Pearl J 1982 Reverend Bayes on inference engines: A distributed hierarchical approach. In *AAAI* (ed. Waltz D), pp. 133–136. AAAI Press.

Perona P and Malik J 1990 Scale-space and edge detection using anisotropic diffusion. *IEEE Trans. Pattern Anal. Mach. Intell.* **12**(7), 629–639.

Polyanin A and Zaitsev V 2012 *Handbook of Nonlinear Partial Differential Equations* second edn. CRC Press.

Press WH, Teukolsky SA, Vetterling WT, and Flannery BP 2007 *Numerical Recipes: The Art of Scientific Computing*. Cambridge Univ. Press.

Rudin LI, Osher S, and Fatemi E 1992 Nonlinear Total Variation based noise removal algorithms. *Physica D: Nonlinear Phenomena* **60**(1), 259–268.

Sochen N, Kimmel R, and Malladi R 1998 A general framework for low level vision. *IEEE Trans. Image Processing* **7**(3), 310–318.

ter Haar Romeny B 1994 *Geometry-driven Diffusion in Computer Vision*. Kluwer Academic Dordrecht.

Terzopoulos D 1986 Image analysis using multigrid relaxation methods. *IEEE Trans. Pattern Anal. Mach. Intell.* **8**(2), 129–139.

Ursell TS 2007 The diffusion equation a multi-dimensional tutorial http://dl.dropbox.com/u/46147408/tutorials/diffusion.pdf (accessed Nov. 1, 2013).

Viola P and Jones MJ 2001 Robust real time object detection. *Workshop on Statistical and Computational Theories of Vision*.

Wang W, Gu J, and Henderson T 1987 A pipelined architecture for parallel image relaxation operations. *IEEE Trans. Circuits and Systems for Video Technology* **34**(11), 1375–1384.

Weickert J 2008 Anisotropic diffusion in image processing http://www.lpi.tel.uva.es/muitic/pim/docus/anisotropic_diffusion.pdf (accessed April 15, 2014).

Wesseling P 1992 *An Introduction to Multigrid Methods*. Pure and applied mathematics. John Wiley & Sons Australia, Limited.

Wikipedia 2013a Discrete laplacian operator http://en.wikipedia.org/wiki/Discrete_Laplacian_operator (accessed Nov. 1, 2013).

Wikipedia 2013b Euler–Lagrange equation http://en.wikipedia.org/wiki/Euler%E2%80%93Lagrange_equation (accessed May 3, 2013).

Wikipedia 2013c Finite difference http://en.wikipedia.org/wiki/Finite_difference (accessed Nov. 1, 2013).

Wikipedia 2013d Hermite polynomials http://en.wikipedia.org/wiki/Hermite_polynomials (accessed Nov. 4, 2013).

Young DM 1950 *Iterative Methods for Solving Partial Difference Equations df Elliptical Type* Phd thesis Harvard University.

9

Dynamic Programming for Energy Minimization

As is the case with the relaxation algorithm and the BP algorithm, dynamic programming (DP) (Bellman 1954) is an important algorithm that can solve, under general settings, many problems in energy functions (Amini *et al.* 1990; Felzenszwalb and Zabih 2011). Dynamic programming is extremely fast and uses less memory space than other algorithms, but unfortunately, DP can only solve one-dimensional problems, such as line-by-line processing, until it finds local optimal solutions. Given that DP can only solve one-dimensional problems, this type of algorithm is especially useful for stereo matching, where the search space is limited to the epipolar line (Gong and Yang 2005; Jeong and Yuns 2000; Ohta and Kanade 1985). DP is also an important construct of the hidden Markov model (HMM), where hidden states must be recovered in decoding problems.

In this chapter, we study DP as a method for solving energy minimization problems. In addition to standard DP, we study various forms of DP: parallel DP, serial DP, and extended DP (EDP). Parallel and serial DPs are designed for extracting multiple best solutions in parallel and in series, respectively. The extended DP is tailored to solve multiple image lines by introducing the product space. We also study HMM and the inside-outside algorithm, which can be used in higher-level processing, such as image interpretation or image understanding.

In this chapter, we will examine the computation structures of DP in serial and vector forms, along with HMM and inside-outside algorithm, that will be designed in the next chapter on Verilog machines. More parallel forms of DP that use pipelined PEs are extended versions of these architectures, and they are also covered in the next chapter.

9.1 DP for Energy Minimization

We start with the energy function in Definition 5.1, in which

$$E(F) = \sum_{p\in\mathcal{P}} \phi(f(p)) + \sum_{p\in\mathcal{P}} \sum_{q\in N(p)\backslash p} \psi(f(p), f(q)), \tag{9.1}$$

where $F = \{f(p)|p \in \mathcal{P}, f \in \mathcal{L}\}$ is the target label map and $\mathcal{L} = [0, L-1]$ is the label space with maximum L labels. The two terms represent data and smoothness terms, respectively. To solve this energy

Architectures for Computer Vision: From Algorithm to Chip with Verilog, First Edition. Hong Jeong.

Companion Website: www.wiley.com/go/jeong

minimization in the DP paradigm, we have to convert this equation into a one-dimensional problem. Moreover, the neighborhood must be limited to the adjacent nodes on the same line only.

There is a class of problems where the relationship between lines is assumed to be statistically independent, and thus the lines can be processed independently. The total minimum energy is the summation of the local minimum energy defined over a line. A typical example is stereo matching, where the energy function is defined over an epipolar line, and thus the labels between the lines are independent. In these types of problems, the minimum energy can be obtained independently for each line, and then added up to comprise the total energy. Therefore, we have two forms,

$$E(F) = \sum_{y \in [0,M-1]} E(\mathbf{f}(y)) \quad \text{or} \quad E(F) = \sum_{x \in [0,N-1]} E(\mathbf{f}(x)), \tag{9.2}$$

where $\mathbf{f}(y)$ and $\mathbf{f}(x)$ are vectors such that $F = (\mathbf{f}(y)|y \in [0, M-1]) = (\mathbf{f}(x)|x \in [0, N-1])$. The local energy is defined as horizontal or vertical lines. (To adopt the MRF property, the line must be expanded to a set of consecutive lines as we will see shortly.) Without loss of generality, we assume a single horizontal image line. If the labels on each line are independent of each other, divide-and-conquer is a natural method:

$$F^* = \arg\min_F \sum_{y \in [0,M-1]} E(\mathbf{f}(y)) = \bigcup_{y=0}^{M-1} \arg\min_{\mathbf{f}(y)} E(\mathbf{f}(y)). \tag{9.3}$$

The problem reduces to energy minimization for each line.

In modeling the energy function for a line, we define the neighborhood as $N(x, y) = \{(x-1, y), (x, y), (x+1, y)\}$, and $f \in [0, L-1]$. Particularly on the boundaries, the neighborhood becomes, $N(0, y) = \{(0, y), (1, y)\}$ and $N(N-1, y) = \{(N-2, y), (N-1, y)\}$. Since the formula is the same for all the lines, we drop the y coordinates in the variables and energy. Considering all these together, we have the energy for a line:

$$E(\mathbf{f}) = \sum_{i \in [0,N-1]} \phi(f(i)) + \psi(f(i-1), f(i)), \quad \text{where } \psi(f(-1), f(0)) = 0. \tag{9.4}$$

The search space consisting of the nodes and edges can be represented by a graph and thereby the energy can be interpreted efficiently (Figure 9.1).

Definition 9.1 (DP graph) *The DP graph $G = (V, E, F, W)$ is a finite, rooted, vertex-weighted, edge-weighted, directed graph. The vertices are $V = \{(i, j)|i \in [0, N-1], j \in [0, L-1]\}$, where i and j denote the pixel and the label (or state), respectively. The edges are $E = \{e(i-1, k, i, j)|i \in [1, N-1], k, j \in [0, L-1]\}$, where $e(i-1, k, i, j)$ is a bidirectional edge between the nodes, $(i-1, k)$ and (i, j). The vertex has the weight $F = \{f(p)|f \in \mathcal{L}, p \in V\}$, where the label set is $\mathcal{L} = [0, L-1]$ for L labels. The node input is $\Psi = \{\phi(v)|\phi \in \mathcal{R}_+, v \in V\}$, where $\mathcal{R}_+$ is nonnegative real. The edge has the weight $\Psi = \{\psi(e)|\psi \in \mathcal{R}_+, e \in E\}$ for forward connection only.*

This definition describes a trellis, which consists of $N \times L$ vertices, nearest neighbor connections, weighted vertex, and weighted edge. As a result, the solution in Equation (9.4) is equivalent to the path in the graph and the energy minimization problem becomes the shortest path problem. In such graphs, the shortest path can be discovered efficiently with the Viterbi algorithm (Viterbi 1967). This algorithm uses two directional edges: forward connection and backward connection.

The system is also characterized by the edge weights. In the most general case, $\psi(i-1, k, i, j)$ is dependent on the nodes. In the space-invariant system, $\psi(i-1, k, i, j) = \psi(|k-j|)$. Furthermore, the connection range can be controlled by the truncated linear or Potts model. In such cases, the graph

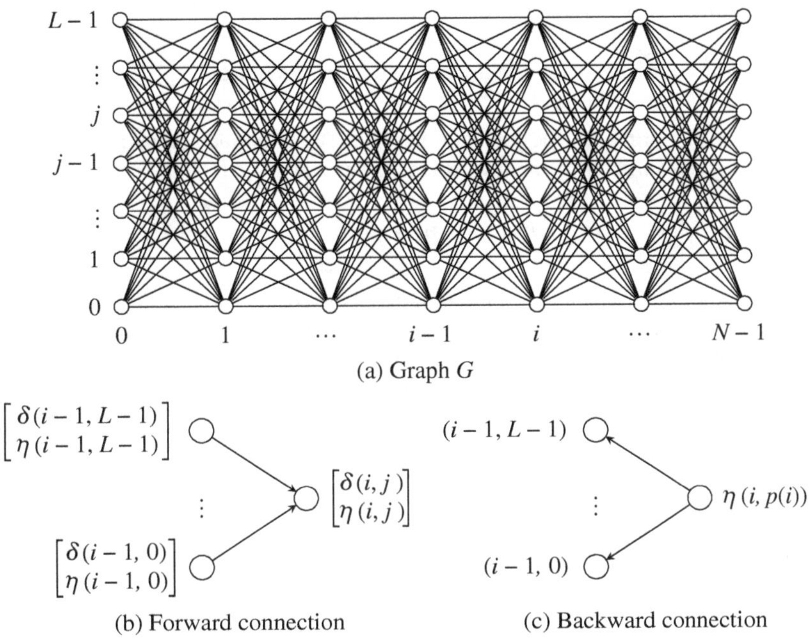

Figure 9.1 The graph $G = (V, E)$ and the two directional connections

connection will be very sparse. The matrix $\psi = \{\psi(|k - j|)\}$ becomes a symmetric Toeplitz matrix, which can be represented by L discrete numbers.

In this graph, the energy function can be defined on a path $p = \{(0, j_0)(1, j_1), \dots, (N - 1, j_{N-1})\}$, where $(0, j_0)$ is the starting node and $(N - 1, j_{N-1})$ is the ending node. If (k, j) are adjacent nodes on the path, Equation (9.4) becomes

$$E(p) = \sum_{i \in [0, N-1]} \phi(i, j) + \psi(k, j), \text{ where } \psi(\cdot, \cdot) = 0 \text{ at } i = 0. \tag{9.5}$$

If $\delta(i, j)$ is the 'partial cost' up to $(i, j) \in p$, then it can be represented by the recursion:

$$\delta(i, j) = \delta(i - 1, k) + \psi(k, j) + \phi(i, j), i = 0, \dots, N - 1. \tag{9.6}$$

The overall cost is $\delta(p) = \delta(N - 1, j_{N-1})$. Unfortunately, we have to try all possible paths to find the shortest path:

$$p^* = \min_p \delta(p). \tag{9.7}$$

The required computation is *exponential time*, $O(L^N)$, for N pixels and L labels.

To avoid the long computation time, we rely on Bellman's principle of optimality (Bellman 1954). We again define $\delta(p, q)$ as the 'minimum cost' (the cost of the shortest path) on the path between a pair of nodes, p and q. According to the triangular inequality,

$$\delta(p, q) = \min_{r \in V} \delta(p, r) + \delta(r, q), \quad \forall p, q \in V. \tag{9.8}$$

If there is a direct link between r and q with $\psi(r,q)$, this becomes

$$\delta(p,q) = \min_{r\in V} \delta(p,r) + \psi(r,q), \quad \forall p,q \in V. \tag{9.9}$$

To satisfy Bellman's principle, the problem must satisfy the *optimal substructure* and *overlapping subproblems* (Cormen *et al.* 2001). For any path in G, we have

$$\delta(i,j) = \min_{k\in[0,L-1]} \{\delta(i-1,k) + \psi(k,j)\} + \phi(i,j), i = 0, \dots, N-1, j \in [0, L-1].$$

This is a special case of the *Bellman equation*. Initially, the cost is assigned to the data term, $\delta(0,j) = \phi(0,j)$ ($j \in [0, L-1]$), because there is no parent (Figure 9.1(b)). In addition to the minimum cost, we are interested in the shortest path. The Viterbi algorithm (Viterbi 1967) is also the method that recovers the shortest path. Let us introduce an additional variable, $\eta(i,j)$, which is a pointer to the parent node. The pointer to the parent is

$$\eta(i,j) = \operatorname*{argmin}_{k\in[0,L-1]}\{(\delta(i-1,k) + \psi(k,j)\}. \tag{9.10}$$

The computation proceeds sequentially in $i = 0, \dots, N-1$ and concurrently in $j \in [0, L-1]$. Compared with the brute force method which requires an $O(L^N)$ search, this method uses only $O(L^2N)$ operations.

As a result of forward processing, the minimum cost is available at the last nodes:

$$\delta^* = \min_{j\in[0,L-1]} \delta(N-1,j). \tag{9.11}$$

In addition, the position of the minimum cost is given by

$$p(N-1) = \arg\min_{j\in[0,L-1]} \delta(N-1,j). \tag{9.12}$$

From this pointer, the next pointers can be extracted recursively by

$$p(i) \leftarrow \eta(i+1, p(i+1)), \quad i = N-2, \dots, 0. \tag{9.13}$$

(Figure 9.1(c)) The result is the shortest path, $(p(N-1), \dots, p(0))$, appearing in reverse order. The data structure of the pointer is a queue.

Let us consider an architectural model for this method. As a first step in this architectural design, we use a single processor and global memory, and accordingly, specify the control structure, memory, and operations. To begin with, look at Figure 9.2. Since we are using only one processor, it must scan all the nodes in the graph. The natural directions are forward and backward. In each direction, the processor moves vertically and then horizontally, alternately. The processor performs the required operations, reading and writing global memories.

The processor executes the operations differently according to four stages: initialization, forward processing, finalization, and backward processing. One of the major memory allocations is for cost, $\{\delta^1(j), \delta^2(j) | j \in [0, L-1]\}$, which stores two consecutive columns. At first, δ_1 is determined by δ_2, and then the two buffers are switched. The next memory allocation is for the pointer, $\{\eta(i,j) | i \in [0, N-1], j \in [0, L-1]\}$, defined over entire nodes. Arriving at each position, the processor receives the inputs, $\phi = \{\phi(i,j) | i \in [0, N-1], j \in [0, L-1]\}$. The processor contains the parameter $\{\psi(|k - j|) | k, j \in [0, L-1]\}$.

Considering all these together, we formally describe the algorithm.

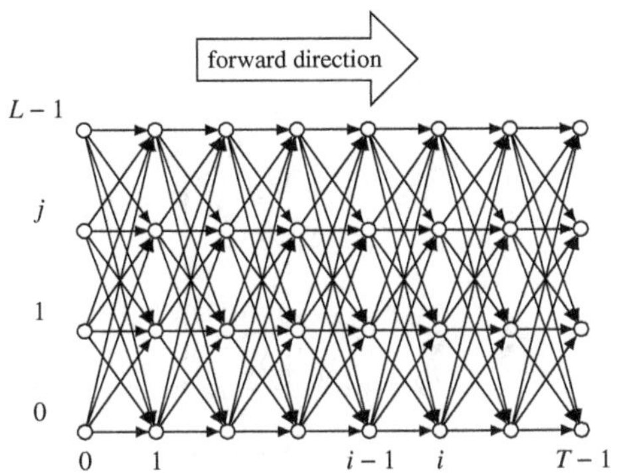

(a) Forward processing

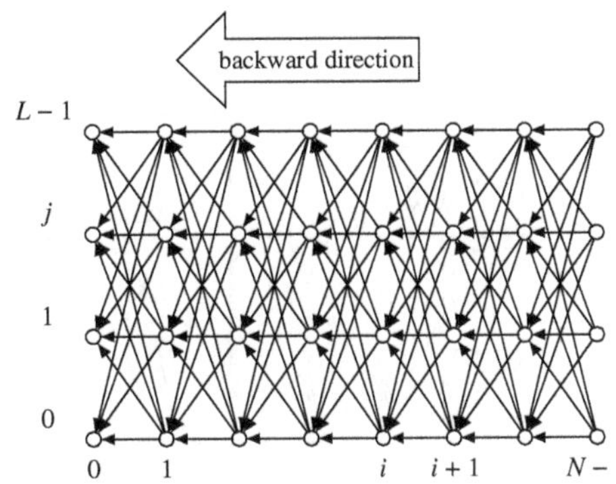

(b) Backward processing

Figure 9.2 Forward and backward processing

Algorithm 9.1 (DP for energy minimization) *For an image line, the energy minimization problem is solved serially in DP.*

Input: $\{\phi(i,j)|i \in [0, N-1], j \in [0, L-1]\}$.

Memory: $\{\delta^1(j), \delta^2(j)|j \in [0, L-1]\}$ *and* $\{\eta(i,j)|i \in [0, N-1], j \in [0, L-1]\}$.

Parameter: $\{\psi(|k-j|)|i \in [0, N-1], j \in [0, L-1]\}$.

Output: δ^* *and* $\{f(N-1), f(N-2), \dots, f(0)\}$.

1. *Initialization: for* $j \in [0, L-1]$, $\delta^1(j) \leftarrow \phi(0,j)$.
2. *Forward processing: for* $i = 0, \dots, N-1$.
   (a) for $j \in [0, L-1]$,

$$\delta^2(j) \leftarrow \min_{k \in [0, L-1]} \{\delta^1(k) + \psi(k,j)\} + \phi(i,j),$$

$$\eta(i,j) \leftarrow \arg\min_{k \in [0, L-1]} \{\delta^1(k) + \psi(k,j)\}.$$

   (b) for $j \in [0, L-1]$, $\delta^1(j) \leftarrow \delta^2(j)$.
3. *Termination:*

$$\delta^* \leftarrow \min_{j \in [0, L-1]} \delta^1(j),$$

$$f(N-1) \leftarrow \arg\min_{j \in [0, L-1]} \delta^1(j).$$

4. *Backtracking: for* $i = N-2, \dots, 0$, $f(i) \leftarrow \eta(i+1, f(i+1))$.

The pointer can be stored in either RAM or a queue, although RAM is easier to design. This algorithm takes $O(L^2N)$ operations and $O(LN)$ memory space. In this count, the forward processing and the pointers are the major factors in the algorithm's complexity.

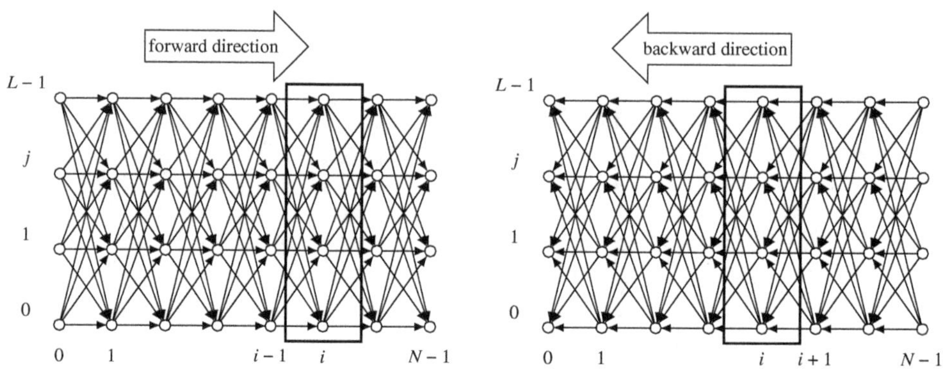

(a) Forward processing (b) Backward processing

Figure 9.3 Forward and backward processing

The next architectural model is a vector processor, which processes the column concurrently. The vector processor scans the network horizontally only. Inside the vector processor, all the nodes are independent and concurrent.

Let us consider the graph G in Figure 9.3. In the forward phase, and while maintaining the concurrent computation for each column, the computation proceeds in the right direction. All the nodes inside a block are concurrent. In this scheme, a node $(\cdot, j)$ experiences N nodes, and thus it computes $\delta(\cdot, j)$ and stores $\eta(\cdot, j)$. When the forward phase finishes, the processor searches the node that has the smallest cost by comparing all the L nodes. From this node, backward computation begins. During the backward phase, the processor finds parent nodes by repeatedly popping the stack until nothing remains. The popped indices are the pointers to the shortest path (or minimum energy).

The DP operations can be represented by a vector operation. For the input, transition, minimum cost, and pointer, let

$$
\begin{aligned}
\Phi &= (\phi(0), \dots, \phi(N-1)) = \{\phi(i,j) | i \in [0, N-1], j \in [0, L-1]\}, \\
\Psi &= \{\psi(k,j) | k, j \in [0, L-1]\}, \\
\boldsymbol{\delta}(i) &= (\delta(i,j) | j \in [0, L-1])^T, \\
\boldsymbol{\eta} &= (\boldsymbol{\eta}(0), \dots, \boldsymbol{\eta}(N-1)) = \{\eta(i,j) | i \in [0, N-1], j \in [0, L-1]\}.
\end{aligned} \tag{9.14}
$$

Define the operation:

$$\Psi \odot \boldsymbol{\delta}(i-1) \triangleq \{\max_{k \in [0, L-1]} \delta(i-1, k) + \psi(k, j) | j \in [0, L-1]\}. \tag{9.15}$$

Then, the cost evaluation becomes

$$\boldsymbol{\delta}(i) \leftarrow \Psi \odot \boldsymbol{\delta}(i-1) + \phi(i). \tag{9.16}$$

In addition, define another operation:

$$\Psi \oplus \boldsymbol{\delta}(i-1) \triangleq \{\arg\max_{k \in [0, L-1]} \delta(i-1, k) + \psi(k, j) | j \in [0, L-1]\}. \tag{9.17}$$

Then, the pointer operation becomes

$$\eta(i) \leftarrow \Psi \oplus \delta(i-1). \tag{9.18}$$

All the operations are summarized in the following algorithm.

Algorithm 9.2 (Vector DP) *For an image line, the energy minimization problem is solved concurrently in DP.*

Input: $\{\phi(i)|i \in [0, N-1]\}$.

Memory: $\boldsymbol{\delta}^1$, $\boldsymbol{\delta}^2$, *and* $\{\eta(i)|i \in [0, N-1]\}$.

Parameter: Ψ.

Output: δ^* *and* $\{f(N-1), \ldots, f(0)\}$.

1. *Initialization:* $\boldsymbol{\delta}^1 \leftarrow \boldsymbol{\phi}(0)$.
2. *Induction: for* $i = 0, 1, \ldots, N-1$,

$$\boldsymbol{\delta}^2 \leftarrow \Psi \odot \boldsymbol{\delta}^1 + \boldsymbol{\phi}(i),$$
$$\boldsymbol{\eta}(i) \longleftarrow \Psi \oplus \boldsymbol{\delta}^1,$$
$$\boldsymbol{\delta}^1 \leftarrow \boldsymbol{\delta}^2.$$

3. *Termination:*

$$\delta^* = \min \boldsymbol{\delta}^1,$$
$$f(N-1) = \arg\min \boldsymbol{\delta}^1.$$

4. *Backtracking: for* $i = N-2, \ldots, 0$, $f(i) \leftarrow \eta(i+1, f(i+1))$.

This is simply a vector representation of the original DP, but it reveals well the concurrent nature of forward processing. We have extended from single processor to vector processor. The next level of parallelism is obtained when the vector processor is further decomposed into an array of small processing elements, where all the processing elements are concurrent and memories are localized. However, in order to design such a system, we have to specify all the information about input, output, and communication between processors. This condition is possible only when the application is known. Chapter 13 extends the vector processor to the systolic array for stereo matching.

The shortest path in DP is related to the matrix structure of Ψ, which has the property of *transitive closure* (Aho *et al.* 1974). There are several issues with defining edges and limiting search space (Lawrence *et al.* 2007; Rabiner and Juang 1993). In the algorithm, we assume that the beginning point values are all determined (i.e. $\delta(0, \cdot)$). However, in speech recognition the beginning and ending points are usually undetermined. The *open-end problem* naturally needs more computation to deal with all the possible endings.

9.2 N-best Parallel DP

The standard DP algorithm only finds the best path. We can extend DP so as to find multiple best (or N-best) paths. There are two methods: parallel or serial (Rabiner and Juang 1993). The parallel algorithm finds all the best paths in parallel and the serial algorithm finds the best paths one by one from best to worst.

Let us first examine the parallel algorithm that finds T ($T \leq L$) best paths, differently from the name. For this purpose, we modify the variables, memories, and operators that were used in the original DP. Define $\delta_t(i, j)$ and $\eta_t(i, j)$ as the minimum cost and the pointer to the tth shortest path, where $1 \leq t \leq T \leq L$. We also provide a storage $\{(\delta_t(j), \eta_t(i, j))|i \in [0, N-1], j \in [0, L-1], 1 \leq t \leq T\}$. Replace 'min' by 'min$^{(t)}$', which chooses the tth minimum value from the arguments.

The key point is the operation for choosing the tth path from the previous nodes. Each node in the previous column already contains costs and pointers up to the Tth best. Among them, paths only up to the tth paths are the candidates in the tth path search. Since there are L such nodes, the number of candidate parents is tL. As such, the forward operation is

$$\delta_t(i, j) = \min^{(t)}_{\substack{0 \leq k \leq L-1 \\ 1 \leq \tau \leq t}} \{\delta_\tau(i-1, k) + \psi(k, j)\} + \phi(i, j). \tag{9.19}$$

The operation needs $O(tL)$ sorting operations for each node, and thereby $O(T^2L^2N)$ sorting operations as a whole.

With all other factors considered together, we write the complete operation and memories in the following definition.

Algorithm 9.3 (Parallel N-best) *For an image line, the energy minimization problem is solved by finding the T best solutions in parallel DP.*

Input: Φ.

Memory: $\{\delta_t^1(j), \delta_t^2(j)|j \in [0, L-1], 1 \leq t \leq T\}$ *and* $\{\eta_t(i, j)|i \in [0, N-1], j \in [0, L-1], 1 \leq t \leq T\}$.

Parameter: Ψ.

Output: δ_t^* *and* $(f_t(N-1), f_t(1), \ldots, f_t(1), f_t(0))$, $\quad 1 \leq t \leq T$.

1. *Initialization: for* $j \in [0, L-1]$, $\delta_t(0, j) \leftarrow \phi(0, j)$.
2. *Forward processing: for* $i = 0, \ldots, N-1$,
   (a) *for* $t \in [1, T]$ *and* $j \in [0, L-1]$,

$$\delta_t^2(j) \leftarrow \min^{(t)}_{\substack{0 \leq k \leq L-1 \\ 1 \leq \tau \leq t}} \{\delta_\tau^1(k) + \psi(k, j)\} + \phi(i, j),$$

$$\eta_t(i, j) \leftarrow \arg\min^{(t)}_{\substack{0 \leq k \leq L-1 \\ 1 \leq \tau \leq t}} \{\delta_\tau^1(k) + \psi(k, j)\}.$$

   (b) *for* $t \in [1, T]$ *and* $j \in [0, L-1]$, $\delta_t^1(j) \leftarrow \delta_t^2(j)$.

3. *Termination: for* $t = 1, \dots, T$,

$$\delta_t^* \leftarrow \min_{\substack{0 \le j \le L-1 \\ 0 \le \tau \le t}}^{(t)} \delta_t(N-1, j),$$

$$f_t(N-1) \leftarrow \arg\min_{\substack{0 \le j \le L-1 \\ 1 \le \tau \le t}}^{(t)} \delta_t(N-1, j).$$

4. *Backward processing: for* $i = N-2, \dots, 0$ *and* $t \in [1, T]$,

$$f_t(i) \leftarrow \eta_t(i+1, (f_t(i+1)).$$

This algorithm can also be represented by vector operations. The initialization is a vector operation. The forward processing is massively parallel, since all the nodes simultaneously compute T paths. Thus, a total of LT operations can be done concurrently. The following swap is a vector operation. Termination and backtracking are inherently serial operations.

This algorithm requires $O(T^2L^2N)$ operations and $O(TLN)$ spaces. Compared to the standard DP, this algorithm needs $T(T+1)/2$ and T times more operations and spaces, respectively. If $T = 1$, it returns to the standard DP. If maximum parallelism is utilized, $O(LT)$ processors can execute the algorithm in $O(N)$ steps. This scheme is an N-best version of the vector DP.

9.3 N-best Serial DP

The serial algorithm (Rabiner and Juang 1993) finds multiple best paths sequentially, starting from best to worst. The key idea is that the number of parent candidates is proportional to the number of visits. For this purpose, we modify the variables, memory, and operation in the parallel algorithm.

Let's provide a memory, $\{c(i,j), \delta_{\tau_1}(i,j), \dots, \delta_{\tau_{c(i,j)}}(i,j), p_{\tau_1}(i,j), \dots, p_{\tau_{c(i,j)}}(i,j) | i \in [0, N-1], j \in [0, L-1]\}$. The counter, $c(i,j)$, is the number of paths that passed through the node in the previous operations. The indices, $\tau_1 < \tau_2 \cdots < \tau_{c(i,j)}$, are the ranks of the previous paths, such that $\tau \in [1, T]$. Therefore, $(\delta_\tau(i,j), p_\tau(i,j))$ represents the sorted list of the cost and the pointer. After the tth path ends and during backtracking, the counter is increased by one and the costs and parents are added to the list of all the nodes along the path.

The central point is that each of the previous nodes contains up to 'c' costs. The parent exists among the '$1 + c$' costs.

$$\delta_t(i,j) \leftarrow \min_{\substack{0 \le k \le L-1 \\ 1 \le t_k \le 1 + c(i-1,k)}}^{(t)} \{\delta_{t_k}(i-1, k) + \psi(k, j)\} + \phi(i, j).$$

Another point is that, unlike other algorithms, all the costs must also be stored. Compared to the parallel DP, the required memory size is doubled. Other operations are similarly derived.

The following algorithm summarizes the complete operations and the required memory.

Algorithm 9.4 (Serial Multiple Best) *For an image line, the energy minimization problem is solved by finding T best solutions in serial DP.*

Input: Φ *and* Ψ.

Memory: $Q = \{c(i,j), \delta_{\tau_1}(i,j), \dots, \delta_{\tau_{c(i,j)}}(i,j), p_{\tau_1}(i,j), \dots, p_{\tau_{c(i,j)}}(i,j) | i \in [0, N-1], j \in [0, L-1]\}$.

Output: δ_t^* *and* $f_t(i)$, $t = 1, \ldots, T$, $i = N-1, \ldots, 0$.

1. *Initialization: for* $i \in [0, N-1]$ *and* $j \in [0, L-1]$, $c(i,j) \leftarrow 0$.
2. *for* $t = 1, 2, \ldots, T$,
   (a) *Initialization:* $\delta_t(0,j) \leftarrow \phi(0,j), \quad j \in [0, L-1]$.
   (b) *Forward processing: for* $i = 0, \ldots, N-1, j \in [0, L-1]$,

$$\delta_t(i,j) \leftarrow \min^{(t)}_{\substack{0\le k\le L-1\\ 1\le t_k\le 1+c(i-1,k)}} \{\delta_{t_k}(i-1,k) + \psi(k,j)\} + \phi(i,j),$$

$$\eta_t(i,j) \leftarrow \arg\min^{(t)}_{\substack{0\le k\le L-1\\ 1\le t_k\le 1+c(i-1,k)}} \{\delta_{t_k}(i-1,k) + \psi(k,j)\}.$$

   (c) *Termination:*

$$\delta_t^* \leftarrow \min^{(t)}_{\substack{0\le j\le L-1\\ 0\le t_k\le 1+c(i,j)}} \delta_{t_k}(N-1,j),$$

$$f_t(N-1) \leftarrow \arg\min^{(t)}_{\substack{0\le j\le L-1\\ 1\le t_k\le 1+c(i,j)}} \delta_t(N-1,j),$$

$$Q(N-1, f_t(N-1)) \leftarrow \{+c(N-1, f_t(N-1)),$$
$$\delta_t^*(N-1, f_t(N-1)), \eta_t(N-1, f_t(N-1))\}.$$

   (d) *Backward processing: for* $i = N-2, \ldots, 0$,

$$f_t(i) \leftarrow \eta_t(i+1, (f_t(i+1)),$$
$$Q(i, f_t(i)) \leftarrow \{+c(i, f_t(i)), \delta_t(i, f_t(i)), \eta_t(i, f_t(i))\}.$$

Here, '$+a$' means $a \leftarrow a + 1$. This algorithm needs T passes of DP using $O(T^2L^2N)$ operations and $O(LNT)$ space, just as the parallel DP. Essentially, the complexity ignores a two-time constant in the memory. This algorithm is T times slower than the parallel algorithm in terms of the overall number of iterations. Since $T = 1$, it becomes the standard DP.

The parallel and serial algorithms ignore all the previously calculated partial paths and compute all the required partial paths again in each path exploration. Remembering that the scores of all partial paths in a trellis, the tree-trellis algorithm efficiently uses them in a backward A* algorithm-based tree search (Rabiner and Juang 1993; Soong and Huang 1991).

9.4 Extended DP

Although DP is limited to one line – and thus useful for some applications, such as stereo matching – in typical vision problems where MRF properties are important, it should be extended to multiple lines, or better yet, to the entire image plane. However, the problem must be converted to a one-dimensional problem to satisfy the DP requirements.

A block of m $(1 \le m \le M)$ lines is defined by $F(y) = \{f(x, y+j) | x \in [0, N-1], j \in [0, m-1]\}$, which is arranged by

$$F(y) \triangleq (\mathbf{f}(0) \ldots \mathbf{f}(N-1)), \tag{9.20}$$

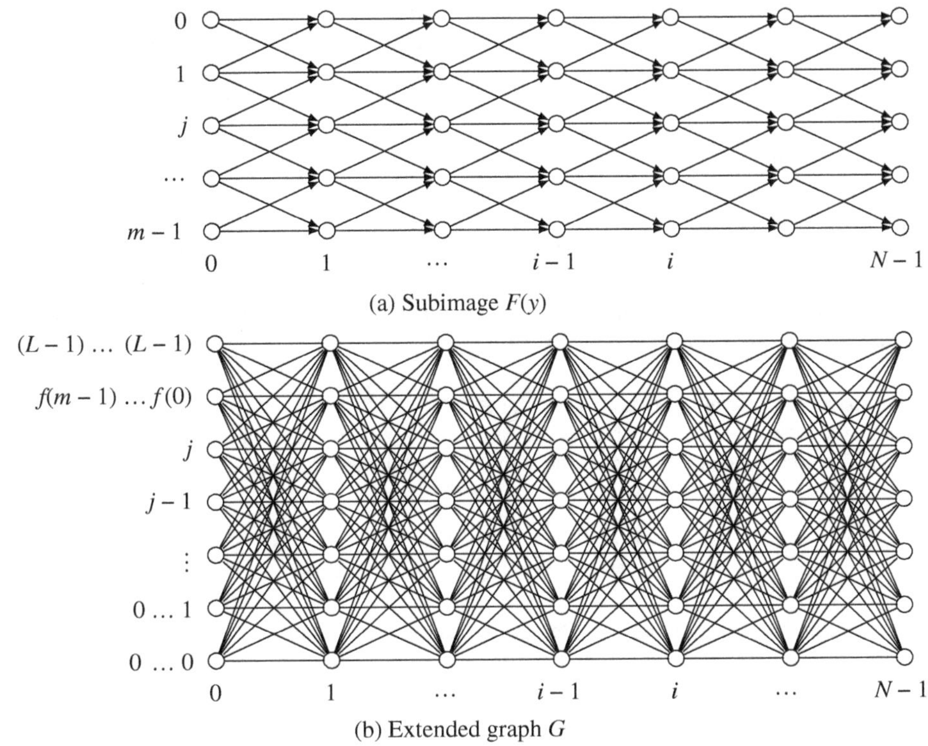

Figure 9.4 Neighbor connections: (a) subimage F with simple connections and (b) the DP graph

where $\mathbf{f}(i) = (f(i, y), f(i, y + 1), \ldots, f(i, y + m - 1))^T$, $\quad i \in [0, N - 1]$. (Figure 9.4(a).) The image plane consists of the blocks $F = \{F(y) | y = 0, m, \ldots, M - 1\}$ (potentially overlapped).

For such image blocks, assume that the minimum energy is a summation of the local minimum energy defined for the block:

$$E(F) = \sum_{y \in \{0, m, \ldots, M-1\}} E(F(y)). \tag{9.21}$$

Then, the problem reduces to minimizing block energy. This concept is a line minimization (Equation (9.3)) to a set of lines:

$$F^* = \arg\min_F \sum_{y \in [0, M-1]} E(F(y)) = \bigcup_{y=0}^{M-1} \arg\min_{F(y)} E(F(y)). \tag{9.22}$$

The single line problem occurs when $m = 1$. Since each block is processed individually, we drop the global coordinate and reorder the pixels: $F = \{\mathbf{f}(i) | i \in [0, N - 1]\} = \{f(i, j) | i \in [0, N - 1], j \in [0, m - 1]\}$.

For convenience, let us represent the label through concatenated labels for each $\mathbf{f}$ by

$$q \triangleq f(m - 1) f(m - 2) \cdots f(1) f(0). \tag{9.23}$$

Then, the label $q = q_{m-1} q_{m-2} \cdots q_0$ uniquely defines the labels of a vertical line by $q_k = f(k)$ $(k \in [0, m - 1])$. Then, the label space becomes a product space; $\mathcal{L}^m$ space consists of $L^m \times N$ nodes (Figure 9.4(b)). A point in this space means a unique labeling of the m points of a vertical line. A trajectory in this space means unique trajectories for the m lines. The problem of finding a shortest path in this space becomes the original DP problem. There are two important properties in this method. First, the shortest path is not necessarily the shortest paths for all lines, but is the shortest path in the collective sense. Second, the shortest path might be better than the collection of individual shortest paths, since the neighborhood constraints are utilized in the transition function.

Let us formally define the new graph.

Definition 9.2 (Extended DP graph) *For a label map, $F = \{\mathbf{f}(i)|i \in [0, N-1]\}$, defined over a subimage, we define a graph $G = (V, E, F, W)$, which is an extension of the DP graph. With all other aspects of the graph the same, the vertex is changed from $L \times N$ to $L^m \times N$, so that the new graph is a lattice, consisting of $L^m \times N$ nodes, where m is a nonnegative integer. For $\mathbf{f} \in F$, a label (or state) is assigned, $l = l_{m-1} \ldots l_0$, where $l_k = f(k)$ ($k \in [0, m-1]$).*

In this space, the cost $\delta(i, j)$ ($i \in [0, N-1], j \in [0, L^m - 1]$) is defined, as was the case when $m = 1$. Define also the local cost, $\phi(i, j)$, which is the case when the lines are labels represented respectively by $j_{m-1}, \ldots, j_0$. The overall cost is naturally the summation of the individual local cost:

$$\phi(i, j) = \sum_{k \in [0, m-1]} \phi(i, j_k), \quad j = j_{m-1} \cdots j_0. \tag{9.24}$$

The transition function is more comprehensive than a simple transition in the standard DP. Let us first consider the simple case, where the lines are all independent. The transition penalty is simply the summation of the individual transition functions:

$$\psi(k, j) = \sum_{n \in [0, m-1]} \psi(|k_n - j_n|). \tag{9.25}$$

Here, the missing indices mean 'doesn't care;' in other words, the rule holds regardless of what the other indices will be.

If the nearest neighbor is adopted, the transition function becomes

$$\psi(k, j) = \sum_{n \in [0, m-1]} \psi(k_{n+1} k_n k_{n-1}, j_n). \tag{9.26}$$

The function $\psi(k_{n+1} k_n k_{n-1}, j_n)$ describes the transition from $(f(i-1, l+1), f(i-1, l), f(i-1, l-1))$ to $f(i, l)$ for any i and l. If the function does not depend on n, it is space variant. Note that the neighborhood is different from the four-neighborhood system. For a point (i, j), the neighborhood consists of the three neighbors $\{(i, j), (i-1, j), (i-1, j+1), (i-1, j-1)\}$. Here and in the following, we assume that the transition function is treated especially around the boundary, since around the boundary the neighbors might not be available. (See the problems at the end of this chapter.)

The next level of neighborhood systems is the mapping from three points to three points:

$$\psi(k, j) = \sum_{n \in [0, m-1]} \psi(k_{n+1} k_n k_{n-1}, j_{n+1} j_n j_{n-1}). \tag{9.27}$$

In this case, the transition function is the possibility that the labels of the three points $(f(i-1, l+1), f(i-1, l), f(i-1, l-1))$ map to the labels of the three points $(f(i, l+1), f(i, l), f(i, l-1))$.

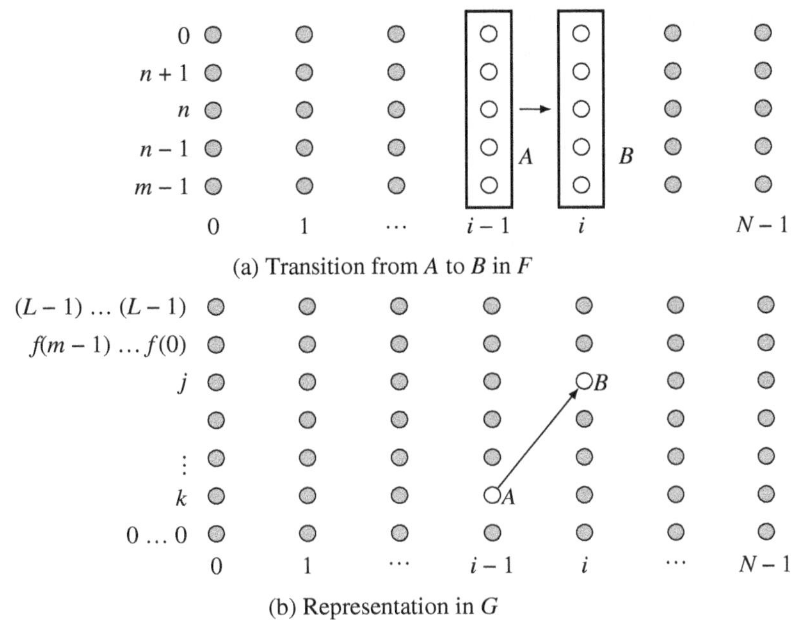

Figure 9.5 Representation of transition: (a) transition in the subimage and (b) transition in G (a label configuration appears as a point in the graph)

In this manner, the neighbor size can be extended up to m points (Figure 9.5). As a result, the general meaning of the transition function, $\psi(k, j)$, is the transition from a label $k_{m-1} \cdots k_0$ to $j_{m-1} \cdots j_0$. Each k and j is a specific label assignment for the vertical m points:

$$\psi(k, j) = \psi(k_{m-1} \dots k_0, j_{m-1} \dots j_0). \tag{9.28}$$

The transition is a collective meaning: transition from the labels of m pixels to the labels of the next m pixels: from $\{f(i-1, l+k)|k \in [0, m-1]\}$ to $\{(f(i, l+k)|k \in [0, m-1]\}$. That is, $\psi :\in \mathcal{L}^m \times \mathcal{L}^m \mapsto \mathcal{R}_+$. In Figure 9.5, the image and the corresponding space are shown. The configurations A and B in the image correspond respectively to the points A and B in the DP space. Through the transition function, we can provide a constraint that a certain transition is possible in an individual line, but it can be inhibited in the group sense. In this manner, we can now implement the rules needed between a configuration to another configuration through the transition function. Depending upon applications, we can define various types of transition functions. This concept implies MRF in a general formation and can be determined by rule or by learning method.

All things combined, we can compute the cost recursively in the $L^m \times N$ space by

$$\delta(i, j) = \min_{k=0}^{L^m-1} \left\{\delta(i-1, k) + \psi(k, j)\right\} + \phi(i, j), \quad i = 0, 1, \dots, N-1. \tag{9.29}$$

Pointers and other operations can be derived by following the standard DP.

Along with other details, we can summarize the algorithm as follows.

Algorithm 9.5 (Extended DP) *For a subimage, the energy minimization problem is solved in DP. Given a subimage, the optimal solution is obtained.*

Input: $\Phi = \{\phi(i,j) | i \in [0, N-1], j \in [0, L^m - 1]\}$.

Memory: $\{\delta^1(j), \delta^2(j) | j \in [0, L^m - 1]\}$ *and* $\{\eta(i,j) | i \in [0, N-1], j \in [0, L^m - 1]\}$.

Parameter: $\Psi = \{\psi(k,j) | k, l \in [0, L^m - 1]\}$.

Output: δ^* *and* $\mathbf{f}(N-1), \ldots, \mathbf{f}(0)$.

1. *Initialization:* $\delta^1(j) \leftarrow \phi(0,j) = \sum_{k \in [0,m-1]} \phi(0, j_k)$.
2. *Forward processing: for* $i = 0, \ldots, N-1$,
   (a) *for* $j \in [0, L^m - 1]$,

$$\delta^2(j) \leftarrow \min_{j \in [0, L^m - 1]} \delta^1(j) + \psi(k,j) + \phi(i),$$

$$\eta(i,j) \leftarrow \arg\min_{j \in [0, L^m - 1]} \delta^1(j) + \psi(k,j).$$

   (b) *for* $j \in [0, L^m - 1]$, $\delta^1(j) \leftarrow \delta^2(j)$.
3. *Termination:*

$$\delta^* \leftarrow \min_{j \in [0, L^m - 1]} \delta(N-1, j),$$

$$f(N-1)^* \leftarrow \arg\min_{j \in [0, L^m - 1]} \delta(N-1, j).$$

4. *Backward processing: for* $i = N-2, \ldots, 0, f(i) \leftarrow \eta(i+1, f(i+1))$.
   (a) *for* $k \in [0, m-1], f(i, y+k) \leftarrow f(i)_k$, *where* $f(i) = f(i)_{m-1} \cdots f(i)_0$.

This algorithm uses $O(L^{2m}N)$ operations and $O(L^m)$ space, an exponential complexity.

The concept is general in that the label space can be extended to the multidimensional space by way of product space. However, this is actually intractable, except that L and m are small. Nevertheless, the great advantage is when the lines are correlated, as is often the case in images. If applied, the result is generally much better than the single line solution. The neighborhood concept can be realized by a mapping from one configuration to another in a collective manner via the transition function. Depending on the transition function, the space might be highly sparse, and thus might be reduced greatly with appropriate encoding methods. As is the case with the standard DP, all the multiple best algorithms are also possible.

In general, the Bellman's DP suffers from the type of computational complexity that increases exponentially with dimensionality of the state, called *curse of dimensionality* (Bellman 2003), thus becoming impractical in large-scale applications. Therefore, we are compelled to seek for *dimensionality reduction* or *approximate dynamic programming* (Bertsekas 2007, 2012, 2013; Powell 2011).

9.5 Hidden Markov Model

A hidden Markov model (HMM) (Baum *et al.* 1970) is a simple, *dynamic Bayesian network* in which the observed process is produced by the unobserved (hidden) Markov process. In vision, HMM is appropriate in recognizing patterns in dynamically varying scenes. The DP principle is also used for finding the shortest path via the Viterbi algorithm.

The energy on a line is

$$E(\mathbf{f}) = \sum_{i\in[0,N-1]} \phi(f(i)) + \psi(f(i-1), f(i)), \text{where } \psi(f(-1), f(0)) = 0, \tag{9.30}$$

where $\phi(f(i)) = T(I(i), f(i))$ with some transformation $T(\cdot)$. The DP method is to find

$$\begin{cases} \delta(i,j) = \min_{i\in[0,N-1]}\delta(i-1,k) + \psi(k,j) + \phi(i,j), \\ \eta(i,j) = \arg\min_{i\in[0,N-1]}\delta(i-1,k) + \psi(k,j) + \phi(i,j). \end{cases} \tag{9.31}$$

HMM is ordinarily defined for Markov processes of time-varying signals. We also assume that the pixel label is a Markov process that has the following models.

We define the *parameter space* $\boldsymbol{\theta} = (A, B, \boldsymbol{\pi})$; the *observation space* $I = \{I(0), \dots, I(N-1)\}$, where $I(\cdot) \in \{I^k|k \in [0, n-1]\}$; and the *hidden state* $F = \{f(0), \dots, f(N-1)\}$, where $f \in \{f^k|k \in [0, L-1]\}$. The state starts with the *initial probability* $\boldsymbol{\pi} = (\pi_0, \pi_1, \dots, \pi_{L-1})$, where $\pi_i = p(f^i(0))$ and moves to the next state according to the *transition probability* $A = \{a(i,j)\}$, where $a(k,j) = p(f^j(i+1)|f^k(i))$. For each state, the output is generated by the *output probability* $B = \{b(i,k)|i \in [0, L-1], k \in [0, n-1]\}$, where $b(i,k) = p(I^k|f^i)$. The variables are nonnegative $(a(i,j), b(i,k), \pi_i \geq 0)$ and summed to one,

$$\sum_{j\in[0,L-1]} a(i,j) = 1, \quad \sum_{k\in[0,n-1]} b(i,k) = 1, \quad \sum_{i\in[0,L-1]} \pi_i = 1. \tag{9.32}$$

Assume that a label is the first-order Markov process, $p(f(i)|F_0^{i-1}) = p(f(i)|f(i-1))$, where F_0^{i-1} is the set of past states up to $i-1$. The other assumption is the *output independence* (or *context-free*) condition, $p(I(i)|I_0^{i-1}, F_0^i) = p(I(i)|f(i))$, where I_0^{i-1} denotes the sequence from $I(0)$ to $I(i-1)$. Assume a state vector $\mathbf{f} = (f_0, \dots, f_{L-1})$ such that $\sum_{k=0}^{L-1} f_k = 1$ (the probability distribution of the label). Then, the system can be represented by the state equation:

$$\begin{cases} \mathbf{f}(i) = \mathbf{f}(i-1)A, \quad \mathbf{f}_0 = \boldsymbol{\pi}, \\ \mathbf{I}(i) = \mathbf{f}(i)B, \end{cases} \tag{9.33}$$

where $\mathbf{I} = (I_0, \dots, I_{n-1})$ with $I_k = p(I^k)$. It is a Moore machine, where the output depends directly on the state. The system models between MRF and the Markov process are compared in Table 9.1.

In MRF, the label is regarded as MRF with a posterior distribution and energy function. In the Markov process, the state is regarded as a Markov process that changes dynamically. In the two system models, the following are a 1:1 correspondence: label vs. state, smoothness term vs. transition probability, data term vs. output. In finding the best solution, the two systems use the same Viterbi search method. MRF focuses on the relationship in space and the Markov process focuses on the relationship in time.

There are three basic problems in HMM (Rabiner and Juang 1993). The *evaluation problem* is a pattern-matching problem: given $\boldsymbol{\theta}$ and I, compute $p(I|\boldsymbol{\theta})$. The *decoding problem* is to find the hidden state: given $\boldsymbol{\theta}$ and I, find F such that $F^* = \arg\max_F p(F|I, \boldsymbol{\theta})$. The *learning problem* is to determine the parameters: given $\boldsymbol{\theta}$ and I, find $\boldsymbol{\theta} = \arg\max_{\boldsymbol{\theta}} p(\boldsymbol{\theta}|I)$.

The first problem can be solved by the *forward probability*,

$$\alpha(i,j) \triangleq p(I_0^i, f^j(i)|\boldsymbol{\theta}), \tag{9.34}$$

which can be determined recursively

$$\alpha(i,j) = \sum_{k\in[0,L-1]} \{\alpha(i-1,k)a(k,j)\}\, b(j, I(i)), \tag{9.35}$$

where $\alpha(0,j) = \pi_j(0)b(j, I(0))$ for $i = 0, 1, \dots, N-1$ and $j \in [0, L-1]$. The result is obtained by $p(I|\boldsymbol{\theta}) = \sum_{j\in[0,L-1]} \alpha(N-1, j)$.

The details are summarized in the following.

Table 9.1 The system models between MRF and Markov process

MRF	Markov process
Energy function $E(F) = \sum_{i\in[0,N-1]} \phi(f(i)) + \psi(f(i-1), f(i))$	State equation $\mathbf{f}(i) = \mathbf{f}(i-1)A$ $\mathbf{I}(i) = \mathbf{f}(i)B$
Data term: $\phi(i,j) = T(I(i), f(i,j))$	Output probability: $b(j, I(i)) = p(I(i)\vert q^j(i))$ $b(j, I(i)) = \exp\{-\phi(i,j)\}$
Smoothness term $\psi(k,j)$	Transition probability $a(k,j)$
Forward processing $\delta(i) = \min_{k\in[0,L-1]} \delta(i-1,k) + \psi(k,j) + \phi(i,j)$ $\eta(i) = \min_{k\in[0,L-1]} \delta(i-1,k) + \psi(k,j)$	Forward probability $\delta(i) = \max_{k\in[0,L-1]} \delta(i-1,k)a(k,j)b(j,I(i))$ $\eta(i) = \arg\max_{k\in[0,L-1]} \delta(i-1,k)a(k,j)$
Termination $f(N-1) \leftarrow \arg\min_{j\in[0,L-1]} \delta(N-1,j)$	Termination $f(N-1) \leftarrow \arg\max_{j\in[0,L-1]} \delta(N-1,j)$
Backtracking $f(i) \leftarrow \eta(i+1, f(i+1))$	Backtracking $f(i) \leftarrow \eta(i+1, f(i+1))$

cf. $i \in [0, N-1]$ and $k, j \in [0, L-1]$.

Algorithm 9.6 (Forward probability) *For an image line, the evaluation problem is solved with the forward probability.*

Input: θ and I.

Memory: $\{\alpha^1(j), \alpha^2(j) | j \in [0, L-1]\}$.

Output: $p(I|\theta)$.

1. *Initialization: for $j \in [0, L-1]$, $\alpha^1(j) = \pi_j b(j, I(0))$.*
2. *Induction: for $i = 1, \ldots, N-1$,*
   (a) for $j \in [0, L-1]$, $\alpha^2(j) \leftarrow \sum_{k\in[0,L-1]} \{\alpha^1(k)a(k,j)\} b(j, I(i))$.
   (b) for $j \in [0, L-1]$, $\alpha^1(j) \leftarrow \alpha^2(j)$.
3. *Termination: $p(I|\theta) \leftarrow \sum_{j\in[0,L-1]} \alpha^1(j)$.*

This algorithm is similar to the forward processing in the standard DP. The inputs are θ and I. The operations in the initialization stage are concurrent. The operations in the induction stage are recursive and concurrent. The termination stage is sequential. As is the case with the forward processing in DP, this algorithm needs $O(L^2N)$ operations and $O(L^2)$ space. Similar to the DP, the initialization and the induction stage can be represented by vector operations.

Equivalently, the evaluation problem can be solved by the *backward probability*:

$$\beta(i,k) \triangleq p(I_{i+1}^{N-1} | f^k(i), \theta). \tag{9.36}$$

This quantity can be obtained recursively

$$\beta(i,k) = \sum_{j\in[0,L-1]} \{a(k,j)b(j, I(i+1))\beta(i+1,j)\}, \tag{9.37}$$

where $\beta(N-1, \cdot) = 1/L$ and $i = N-1, \ldots, 0, k \in [0, L-1]$.

The detailed operations are summarized in the algorithm.

Algorithm 9.7 (Backward probability) *For an image line, the evaluation problem is solved by the backward probability.*

Input: θ *and* I.

Memory: $\{\beta^1(j), \beta^2(j) | j \in [0, L-1]\}$.

Output: $p(I|\theta)$.

1. *Initialization: for* $j \in [0, L-1]$, $\beta^1(j) = 1/L$.
2. *Induction: for* $i = N-2, \ldots, 0$,
   (a) *for* $j \in [0, L-1]$, $\beta^2(i) \leftarrow \sum_{k\in[0,L-1]} \{a(k,j)b(j, I(t+1))\beta^1(j)\}$.
   (b) *for* $j \in [0, L-1]$, $\beta^1(j) \leftarrow \beta^2(j)$.
3. *Termination:* $p(I|\theta) = \sum_{j\in[0,L-1]} \beta(0, j)$.

Given the inputs θ and I, this algorithm computes the backward probability in the induction stage and adds up the probabilities at the end. The complexities are identical to the forward probability.

The product of the forward and backward probabilities has the property:

$$\alpha(i, j)\beta(i, j) = p(I_0^i, f^j(i)|\theta)p(I_{i+1}^{N-1}|f^j(i), \theta) = p(I, f^j(i)|\theta). \tag{9.38}$$

Taking marginalization, we get

$$\begin{aligned} p(I, f(i)|\theta) &= \sum_{j\in[0,L-1]} \alpha(i, j)\beta(i, j), \\ p(I, f^j|\theta) &= \sum_{i\in[0,N-1]} \alpha(i, j)\beta(i, j), \\ p(I|\theta) &= \sum_{i,j} \alpha(i, j)\beta(i, j). \end{aligned} \tag{9.39}$$

Each of the above respectively means an expected state at i; the occurrence of a particular state along the input sequence; and the probability of the input sequence (i.e. evaluation problem), given the parameters. Thus, the evaluation can be achieved in three different ways:

$$\begin{aligned} p(I|\theta) &= \sum_{j\in[0,L-1]} \alpha(N-1, j) = \sum_{j\in[0,L-1]} \beta(0, j) \\ &= \sum_{i\in[0,N-1]} \sum_{j\in[0,L-1]} \alpha(i, j)\beta(i, j). \end{aligned} \tag{9.40}$$

Another property is

$$p(f^j(i)|I, \theta) = \frac{p(I, f(i)^j|\theta)}{p(I|\theta)} = \frac{\alpha(i, j)\beta(i, j)}{\sum_{j\in[0,L-1]} \alpha(N-1, j)}. \tag{9.41}$$

By this equation, we obtain the expected count of the rule, given the instance and parameters.

The decoding problem – where the shortest path is required as well as the minimum values (actually, the opposites) – is solved by the Viterbi algorithm. Let $\delta(t, j)$ be the 'maximum cost' up to the node (t, j).

Algorithm 9.8 (Decoding) *For an image line, the hidden states are found.*

Input: θ *and* I.

Memory: $\{\delta^1(j), \delta^2(j)|j \in [0, L-1]\}$ *and* $\{\eta(i, j)|i \in [0, N-1], j \in [0, L-1]\}$.

Output: A shortest path $\{f(N-1), \ldots, f(0)\}$.

1. *Initialization: for* $j \in [0, L-1]$, $\delta_0(j) = \pi_j b(j, I(0))$.
2. *Induction: for* $i = 1, \ldots, N-1$,
   (a) *for* $j \in [0, L-1]$,

$$\delta^2(j) \leftarrow \max_{k\in[0,L-1]} \{\delta^1(k)a(k, j)\}b(j, I(i)),$$

$$\eta(i, j) \leftarrow \arg\max_{k\in[0,L-1]} \{\delta^1(k)a(k, j)\}.$$

   (b) *for* $j \in [0, L-1]$, $\delta^1(j) \leftarrow \delta^2(j)$.
3. *Termination:*

$$\delta^* \leftarrow \max_{j\in[0,L-1]} \delta^1(j),$$

$$f(N-1) = \arg\max_{j\in[0,L-1]} \delta^1(j).$$

4. *Backtracking: for* $i = N-2, \ldots, 0, f(i) \leftarrow \eta(i+1, f(i+1))$.

The algorithm is similar to the forward algorithm. The big difference is the maximum instead of the summation operations at the induction stage. The required resources are $O(L^2N)$ operations and $O(LN)$ space.

The third problem is solved by the Baum–Welch algorithm (Baum *et al.* 1970), which is also derived from the expectation-maximization (EM) algorithm (Dempster *et al.* 1977). For this method, we need the *transition probability*,

$$\gamma(i, k, j) \triangleq p(f^i(t-1), f^j(t)|I, \theta), \tag{9.42}$$

which can be obtained by the forward and backward probabilities,

$$\gamma(i, k, j) = \frac{p(f^k(i-1), f^j(i), I|\theta)}{p(I|\theta)} = \frac{\alpha(i-1, k)a(k, j)b(j, I(i))\beta(i, j)}{\sum_{j\in[0,L-1]} \alpha(N-1, j)}. \tag{9.43}$$

Here, the denominator is a constant. This part is the major bottleneck in learning, that needs $3L^2T$ multiplications, in addition to the required multiplication for α and β.

The operations are summarized by the algorithm.

Algorithm 9.9 (Learning) *For an image line, the parameters are determined.*

Input: I.

Memory: $\theta = (A, B, \pi)$ *and* $\{\alpha(i, j), \beta(i, j), \gamma(i, k, j)|i \in [0, N-1], k, j \in [0, L-1]\}$.

Output: θ.

1. *Initialization:* $\boldsymbol{\theta}$.
2. *for convergence,*
   (a) *Algorithm 9.6 and Algorithm 9.7:* $\{\alpha(i,j), \beta(i,j) | i \in [0, N-1], j \in [0, L-1]\}$.
   (b) $\gamma(i,k,j) = \frac{\alpha(i-1,k)a(k,j)b(j,I(i))\beta(i,j)}{\sum_{k\in[0,L-1]}\alpha(N-1,k)}$, $k, j \in [0, L-1], i \in [0, N-1]$.
   (c) *for* $k, j \in [0, L-1]$,

$$\pi_j \leftarrow \gamma_0(j,j),$$

$$a(k,j) = \sum_{i\in[0,N-1]} \gamma(i,k,j) / \sum_{i\in[0,N-1]} \sum_{k\in[0,L-1]} \sum_{j\in[0,L-1]} \gamma(i,k,j),$$

$$b(j, I^k) = \sum_{i=0,I^k(t)}^{N-1} \gamma(i,k,j) / \sum_{i\in[0,N-1]} \sum_{k\in[0,L-1]} \sum_{j\in[0,L-1]} \gamma(i,k,j).$$

This computation needs $O(L^2N)$ operations for one iteration and $O(L^2N)$ space.

Computing forward, backward, and transition probabilities are all involved with multiplication, which can be converted into summation operations in the logarithmic space. The result is the integer forward, backward, Viterbi, and learning algorithms (Rabiner and Juang 1993).

In this section, we have considered only the standard HMM. There are advanced algorithms in HMM, such as continuous mixture HMM, semi-continuous HMM, hierarchical Dirichlet process HMM, maximum entropy Markov model, and factorial HMM (Jelinek *et al.* 1992; Rabiner 1989). See (Wikipedia 2013a) for further information about HMM. Among others, the forward-backward algorithm can be generalized into the inside-outside algorithm for probabilistic context-free grammar (Baker 1979).

9.6 Inside-Outside Algorithm

The inside-outside algorithm (Baker 1979) might be potentially important in the future for image understanding, since it provides a means by which to interpret the formation of hierarchical constructs in terms of grammatical rules. If the image contents comprise a hierarchy of progressively larger objects, and there exist rules among hierarchies, the image can be described by the parse tree, which is the basis of image interpretation.

A *probabilistic context-free grammar* (PCFG)) (aka *stochastic context-free grammar* (SCFG)) is a context-free grammar in which each production is augmented with a probability (Jelinek *et al.* 1992; Jurafsky *et al.* 2000; Manning 2001). PCFG extends context-free grammar in the same way that hidden Markov models extend regular grammar.

A PCFG system (W, N, P, G) consists of a set of terminal symbols $W = \{w^j | j \in [1, V]\}$, and grammar G, which is in CNF (Chomsky normal form):

$$\begin{cases} p(N^j \to N^k N^l), & N^j, N^k, N^l \in N, \\ p(N^j \to w^k), & w^k \in W, \end{cases} \tag{9.44}$$

which satisfies

$$\sum_{k,l} p(N^j \to N^k N^l) + \sum_k p(N^j \to w^k) = 1. \tag{9.45}$$

The start symbol N^1 is a node from which all others are derived as a binary tree. For n nonterminals and V terminals, the number of rules is theoretically $n^3 + nV$ but can be fewer. A string from p to q is represented by w_{pq}. A nonterminal symbol N^j that spans p through q is represented by N^j_{pq}.

Table 9.2 Problems in HMM and PCFG

Problems	HMM	PCFG
The evaluation problem	Given θ and I, compute $p(I\|\theta)$.	Given G and W, compute $p(W\|G)$.
The decoding problem	Given θ and I, $Q^* = \arg\max_Q p(Q\|I, \theta)$	Given G and W, $t^* = \arg\max_t p(t\|W, G)$.
The learning problem	Given θ and I $\theta^* = \arg\max_\theta p(\theta\|I)$	Given G and W, $G^* = \arg\max_G p(W\|G)$.

cf. HMM: $I = I_0^{N-1}$ and PCFG: $W = w_{1m}$.

Likewise in HMM, three basic problems are defined in PCFG (Table 9.2). The evaluation problem is to compute the probability of the observed sequence, conditioned by the grammar. The decoding problem is to determine the sequence of latent variables. The learning problem is to update the grammar from the old grammar by observing the given sentence.

The *parse tree* is t. In other words, HMM is a special case of PCFG, and PCFG is a special case of EM (Lafferty 2000; Sanchez *et al.* 1996).

There are three assumptions: place invariance, context-free, and ancestor-free. Similar to the time invariance in HMM, the place invariance indicates that the probability of a subtree does not depend on the location in the string where the words it dominates are found:

$$p(N^j_{k,k+a} \to \alpha), \quad \forall k \in [1, m], j \in N, \tag{9.46}$$

where α means terminal or nonterminal symbols. The context-free hypothesis states that the probability of a subtree does not depend on words not dominated by the subtree:

$$p(N^j_{kl} \to \alpha | w_{1,k-1}, w_{l+1,m}) = p(N^j_{kl} \to \alpha), \quad \forall k, l \in [1, m], j \in N. \tag{9.47}$$

The ancestor-free condition means that the probability of a subtree does not depend on nodes in the derivation outside the subtree:

$$p(N^j_{kl} \to \alpha | \text{ancestor nodes}) = p(N^j_{kl} \to \alpha), \quad \forall k, l \in [1, m], j \in N. \tag{9.48}$$

The outside and the inside probabilities are $\alpha_j(p, q)$ and $\beta_j(p, q)$. The forward-backward probabilities and the inside-outside probabilities are compared in Table 9.3.

The corresponding representations of the two systems are compared. Above all, the search space is $\{(i, j)|i \in [0, N-1], j \in [0, L-1]\}$ in HMM and $\{(i, j, k)|i \in [0, m], j, k \in [1, n]\}$ in PCFG. The pointer is one-dimensional in HMM (i.e. $\eta(i, j)$), but it is two-dimensional in PCFG (i.e. $\eta_j(p, q)$). The inside probability is the extension of the forward probability and the outside probability is the extension of the backward probability. For more information, see (Lari and Young 1990, 1991; Pereira and Schabes 1992; Xia 2006).

Let us first consider the evaluation problem. The inside probability $\beta_j(p, q)$ is the total probability of generating words $w_p \cdots w_q$, given the root nonterminal N^j and grammar G:

$$\beta_j(p, q) \triangleq p(w_{pq}|N^j, G). \tag{9.49}$$

Table 9.3 The forward-backward vs. inside-outside probabilities

HMM	PCFG
Forward probability: $\alpha(i,j) = p(I, f(i)^j)$ $\alpha(0,j) = \pi_j b(j, I(0))$ $p(I\|\theta) = \sum_{j\in[0,L-1]} \alpha(N-1,j)$	Inside probability: $\beta_j(p,q) = p(N^j_{pq} \to w_{pq})$ $\beta_j(p,p) = p(N^j \to w_p)$ $p(W\|G) = \beta_1(1,m)$
Backward probability: $\beta(i,j) = p(I\|f(i)^j)$ $\beta(N-1,j) = 1/L$ $p(I\|\theta) = \sum_{j\in[0,L-1]} \beta(0,j)$	Outside probability: $\alpha_j(p,q) = p(w_{1(p-1)}, N^j_{pq}, w_{(q+1)m})$ $\alpha_j(1,m) = \delta(j-1)$ $p(W\|G) = \sum_{j\in[1,n]} \alpha_j(p,p) p(N^j \to w_p)$
Cost and pointer: $\delta(0,j) = \pi_j b(j, I(0))$ $\delta(i,j) = \underset{k\in[0,L-1]}{\mathrm{argmax}} \delta(i-1,k) a(k,j) b(j, I(i))$ $\eta(i,j) = \underset{k\in[0,L-1]}{\mathrm{argmax}} \delta(i-1,k) a(k,j)$ $\eta(N-1) = \arg\max_j \delta(N-1,j)$	Cost and pointer: $\delta_j(p,p) = p(N^j \to w_p)$ $\delta_j(p,q) = \max_{\substack{1\le k,l\le n\\ p\le r<q}} p(N^j \to N^k N^l) \times \delta_k(p,r)\delta_l(r+1,q)$ $\eta_j(p,q) = \arg\max_{\substack{1\le k,l\le n\\ p\le r<q}} p(N^j \to N^k N^l) \times \delta_k(p,r)\delta_l(r+1,q)$ $\eta^* = \eta_1(1,m)$

*cf. HMM: $i \in [0, N-1], j \in [0, L-1]$ and PCFG: $p, q \in [1, m], j, k, l \in [1, n]$.

It can be computed recursively in bottom-up direction,

$$\beta_j(p,q) = \sum_{k,l\in[1,n]} \sum_{t\in[p,q-1]} p(N^j \to N^k N^l) \beta_k(p,t) \beta_l(t+1,q), \tag{9.50}$$

with the initial condition

$$\beta_j(k,k) = p(N^j \to w_k) \tag{9.51}$$

and termination

$$p(w_{1m}|G) = \beta_1(1,m). \tag{9.52}$$

The detailed operations are summarized in the algorithm.

Algorithm 9.10 (Evaluation by inside probability) *For a string of words, the evaluation problem is solved by the inside probability.*

Input: G and w_{1m}.

Memory: $\{\beta_j^1(p,q), \beta_j^2(p,q) | p, q \in [1,m], j \in [1,n]\}$.

Output: $p(w_{1m}|G) = \beta_1(1,m)$.

1. *Initialization: for* $k \in [1,m]$ *and* $j \in [1,n]$, $\beta_j^1(k,k) = p(N^j \to w_k)$.

2. *Induction: for $q-p=1,2,\dots,m-1$,*
   (a) *for $p\in[1,m-(q-p)]$ and $j\in[1,n]$,*

$$\beta_j^2(p,q)=\sum_{k,l\in[1,n]}\sum_{t\in[p,q-1]}p(N^j\to N^kN^l)\beta_k^1(p,t)\beta_l^1(t+1,q).$$

   (b) *for $p\in[1,m-(q-p)]$ and $j\in[1,n]$, $\beta_j^1(p,q)\leftarrow\beta_j^2(p,q)$.*

This algorithm begins with a word, proceeds with increasing width, and stops at the full sentence. There are vast parallelisms in initialization and induction. The algorithm needs $O(m^2n^2)$ operations and $O(m^2n)$ space, except for the grammar, which uses $O(n^3)$ space.

Similarly, the evaluation problem can be solved by the outside probability $\alpha_j(p,q)$, which is the total probability of grammar G beginning with N^1, generating N^j_{pq}, and having all the words outside $w_p\dots w_q$:

$$\alpha_j(p,q)\triangleq p(w_{1,p-1},N^j,w_{q+1,m}|G). \tag{9.53}$$

It has the recursion operations in top-down direction,

$$\alpha_j(p,q)=\sum_{f,k\neq j}\left\{\sum_{e=q+1}^{m}\alpha_f(p,e)p(N^f\to N^jN^k)\beta_k(q+1,e)\right.$$
$$\left.+\sum_{e\in[1,p-1]}\beta_k(e,p-1)p(N^f\to N^kN^j)\alpha_f(e,q)\right\}, \tag{9.54}$$

with the initial condition

$$\alpha_j(1,m)=\delta(j-1), \tag{9.55}$$

and termination

$$p(w_{1m}|G)=\sum_{j\in[1,n]}\alpha_j(k,k)p(N^j\to w_k),\quad k\in[1,m]. \tag{9.56}$$

However, the outside probability cannot be decided alone; it needs the inside probability. The operations are listed as follows:

Algorithm 9.11 (Evaluation by outside probability) *For a string of words, the evaluation problem is solved by the outside probability.*

Input: G, w_{1m}, and $\{\beta_j(p,q)|p,q\in[1,m],j\in[1,n]\}$.

Memory: $\{\alpha_j^1(p,q),\alpha_j^2(p,q)|p,q\in[1,m],j\in[1,n]\}$.

Output: $p(w_{1m}|G)=\sum_{j\in[1,n]}\alpha_j(k,k)p(N^j\to w_k)$, $k\in[1,m]$.

1. *Initialization: for $j\in[1,n]$, $\alpha_j^1(1,m)=\delta(j-1)$.*
2. *Induction: for $q-p=m-1,\dots,1$.*

(a) *for* $p \in [1, m-(q-p)]$ *and* $j \in [1, n]$,

$$\alpha_j^2(p,q) = \sum_{f,k\neq j} \left\{ \sum_{e\in[q+1,m]} \alpha_f^1(p,e)p(N^f \to N^j N^k)\beta_k(q+1,e) \right.$$
$$\left. + \sum_{e\in[1,p-1]} \beta_k(e,p-1)p(N^f \to N^k N^j)\alpha_f^1(e,q) \right\}.$$

(b) *for* $p \in [1, m-(q-p)]$ *and* $j \in [1, n]$, $\alpha_j^1(p,q) \leftarrow \alpha_j^2(p,q)$.

Here, $\delta(\cdot)$ means Kronecker delta. This algorithm begins with the full text, advances with decreasing width, and stops at a word. There are vast parallelisms in initialization and induction. This algorithm uses $O(m^2n^2)$ time and $O(m^2n)$ space. The inside and outside algorithms proceed in bottom-up and top-down directions, respectively, but their running time and space are identical.

Analogously to Equation (9.38), the product of the inside and outside probabilities becomes

$$\begin{aligned} \alpha_j(p,q)\beta_j(p,q) &= p(w_{1(p-1)}N_{pq}^j w_{(q+1)m})p(w_{pq}|N_{pq}^j G) \\ &= p(w_{1m}, N_{pq}^j|G). \end{aligned} \tag{9.57}$$

Taking marginalization, we get

$$\begin{aligned} p(w_{1m}, N_{pq}|G) &= \sum\nolimits_{j\in[1,n]} \alpha_j(p,q)\beta_j(p,q), \\ p(w_{1m}, N^j|G) &= \sum\nolimits_{p\in[1,m]} \sum\nolimits_{q\in[1,m]} \alpha_j(p,q)\beta_j(p,q), \\ p(w_{1m}|G) &= \sum\nolimits_{j\in[1,n]} \sum\nolimits_{p\in[1,m]} \sum\nolimits_{q\in[1,m]} \alpha_j(p,q)\beta_j(p,q). \end{aligned} \tag{9.58}$$

Each of the probabilities means, respectively, the average nonterminal for w_{pq}, the occurrence of the nonterminal N^j in the sentence, and the evaluation. The evaluation is especially possible in three ways:

$$\begin{aligned} p(w_{1m}|G) = \beta_1(1,m) &= \sum_{j\in[1,n]} \alpha_j(k,k)p(N^j \to w_k),\ k \in [1,m], \\ &= \sum\nolimits_{j\in[1,n]} \sum\nolimits_{p\in[1,m]} \sum\nolimits_{q\in[1,m]} \alpha_j(p,q)\beta_j(p,q). \end{aligned} \tag{9.59}$$

Another property is that

$$p(N_{pq}^j|w_{1m}, G) = \frac{p(w_{1m}, N_{pq}^j|G)}{p(w_{1m}|G)} = \frac{\alpha_j(p,q)\beta_j(p,q)}{\beta_1(1,m)}. \tag{9.60}$$

This means the expected count of the rule, given the instance and grammar.

The next problem is the decoding problem, which determines the syntax tree. This can be obtained by the cost $\delta_i(p,q)$, which is the highest inside probability parse of a subtree N_{pq}^i. The structure is similar to the inside probability.

Algorithm 9.12 (Decoding problem) *For a string of words, the decoding problem is solved.*

Input: G and w_{1m}.

Memory: $\{\delta_j^1(p,q), \delta_j^2(p,q) | p,q \in [1,m], j \in [1,n]\}$ *and* $\{\eta_j(p,q) | p,q \in [1,m], j \in [1,n]\} = \{(k,l,r,j,p,q) | p,r,q \in [1,m], j,k,l \in [1,n]\}$.

Output: Strings $\{(k,l,r)\}$.

1. *Initialization: for* $p \in [1,m]$ *and* $j \in [1,n]$, $\delta_j(p,p) = p(N^j \to w_p)$.
2. *Induction: for* $q - p = 1, \ldots, m-1$.
   (a) *for* $p \in [1, m-(q-p)]$ *and* $j \in [1,n]$,

$$\delta_j^2(p,q) = \max_{\substack{1 \le k,l \le n \\ p \le r < q}} p(N^j \to N^k N^l)\delta_k^1(p,r)\delta_l^1(r+1,q),$$

$$\eta_j(p,q) = \arg\max_{\substack{1 \le k,l \le n \\ p \le r < q}} p(N^j \to N^k N^l)\delta_k^1(p,r)\delta_l^1(r+1,q).$$

   (b) *for* $p \in [1, m-(q-p)]$ *and* $j \in [1,n]$, $\delta_j^1(p,q) \leftarrow \delta^2(p,q)$.
3. *Termination:* $\delta^* = \delta_1(1,m)$ *and* $(k,l,r) \leftarrow \eta_1(1,m)$.
4. *Backtracking: for* $q - p = m-2, \ldots, 1$ *and for* $p \in [1, m-(q-p)]$,

$$(k,l,r) \leftarrow \eta_j(p,q)(k,l,r).$$

The pointer stores (p,r,q,k,l), which means the tagging (N_{pr}^k, N_{rq}^l). During induction, the pointer (k,l,r) is stored at the position (j,p,q). During backtracking, the pointer (k,l,r) is read from the position (j,p,q), recursively. This algorithm needs immense complexity because of the sequence $p \le r < q$ and the labels (j,k,l). The computation time is the same as for the inside and outside probabilities. Therefore, we need $O(m^2n^2)$ operations and $O(m^3n^3)$ space. There are various alternatives to perform the iterations. Essentially, the parsing is realized with the Cocke–Younger–Kasami (CYK) algorithm (Hopcroft *et al.* 2006; Knuth 2011; Sudkamp 2005), which requires $O(m^3|G|)$ time for the worst-case scenario, where $|G|$ is the grammar size (or $O(n^3)$ worst-case) in the worst-case scenario.

The third problem is determining what differentiates the grammar from the instance. For this purpose, we need the transition probability:

$$\gamma_i(j,k,l,p,q) \triangleq p(w_{1,p-1}N^j w_{q+1,m}, N^j \to w_{pq}, N^j \to N^k N^l)/p(W_i) \tag{9.61}$$

with the property,

$$\gamma_i(j,k,k,p,p) = p(N^j \to w^k)/p(W_i), \tag{9.62}$$

where W_i is an instance. The transition probability can be obtained by the inside and outside probabilities:

$$\gamma(j,k,l,p,q) = \frac{1}{p(w_{1m})} \sum_{i \in [p,q-1]} p(N^j \to N^k N^l)\beta_k(p,i)\beta_l(i+1,q)\alpha_j(p,q). \tag{9.63}$$

For the sentences $\{W_i | i \in [1, \omega]\}$, with each having the size m_i, the grammar G can be updated by

$$p(N^j \rightarrow N^r N^s) = \frac{\sum_{i=1}^{\omega} \sum_{p=1}^{m_i - 1} \sum_{q=p+1}^{m_i} \gamma_i(j, r, s, p, q)}{\sum_{i=1}^{\omega} \sum_{r,s} \sum_{p=1}^{m_i - 1} \sum_{q=p+1}^{m_i} \gamma_i(j, r, s, p, q)},$$

$$p(N^j \rightarrow w^r) = \frac{\sum_{i=1}^{\omega} \sum_{h=1}^{m_i} \alpha_j(h, h) p(w_h = w^k) \beta_j(h, h)}{\sum_{i=1}^{\omega} \sum_{p=1}^{m_i} \sum_{q=p}^{m_i} \alpha_j(p, q) \beta_j(p, q)}. \tag{9.64}$$

The method is summarized in the following.

Algorithm 9.13 (Learning problem) *For a string of words, the grammar is determined.*

Input: w_{1m}.

Memory: Memories for α, β, *and* γ.

Output: G.

1. *Initialization:* G.
2. *Until convergence, do the following:*
   (a) *Algorithm 9.10 and 9.12:* $\{\alpha_j(p, q), \beta_j(p, q) | j \in [1, n],\ p < q \in [1, m]\}$.
   (b) *for* $p < q \in [1, m]$ *and* $j, k, l \in [1, n]$,

$$\gamma(j, k, l, p, q) = \frac{1}{p(w_{1m})} \sum_{i \in [p, q-1]} p(N^j \rightarrow N^k N^l) \beta_k(p, i) \beta_l(i + 1, q) \alpha_j(p, q).$$

   (c) *for* $j, r, s \in [1, n]$,

$$p(N^j \rightarrow N^r N^s) = \frac{\sum_{i \in [1, \omega]} \sum_{p=1}^{m_i - 1} \sum_{q=p+1}^{m_i} \gamma_i(j, r, s, p, q)}{\sum_{i=1}^{\omega} \sum_{r,s} \sum_{p=1}^{m_i - 1} \sum_{q=p+1}^{m_i} \gamma_i(j, r, s, p, q)},$$

$$p(N^j \rightarrow w^r) = \frac{\sum_{i=1}^{\omega} \sum_{h=1}^{m_i} \alpha_j(h, h) p(w_h = w^k) \beta_j(h, h)}{\sum_{i=1}^{\omega} \sum_{p=1}^{m_i} \sum_{q=p}^{m_i} \alpha_j(p, q) \beta_j(p, q)}.$$

   (d) *Update* G.

This algorithm needs all the inside, outside, and transition probabilities. The computation is iterated until convergence. The required operation is $O(m^2 n^3 \omega)$ for one iteration and the required space is $O(m^2 n + n^3)$.

As an example, let us consider an image that consists of horizontal pixels. An object or background consists of connected pixels. The goal is to identify the objects and backgrounds when the image is already segmented. A foreground might be further decomposed into one or more different objects. The ordering is specified by the production rule:

$S \rightarrow BS\,O(1)$	$O \rightarrow O\,O(.1)$	$O \rightarrow S(.1)$
$BS \rightarrow B\,BS(.5)$	$O \rightarrow B\,O(.2)$	$O \rightarrow D(.2)$
$BS \rightarrow B(.5)$	$O \rightarrow O\,B(.1)$	$O \rightarrow T(.3)$
$B \rightarrow E(1)$		

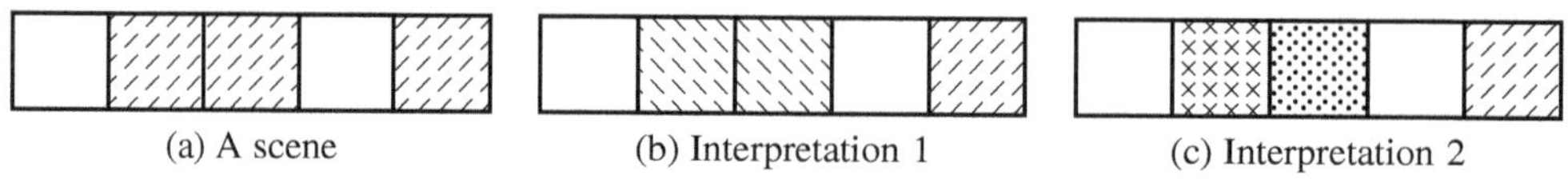

Figure 9.6 A toy scene and its interpretations: (a) original scene, (b) two objects, and (c) three objects

Here, 'BS', 'B', and 'E' mean backgrounds, background, and empty, respectively. The other symbols, 'O', 'S', 'D', and 'T' represent object, singleton, doubleton, and tripleton, respectively. The symbol 'O' is a set of one or more connected foreground pixels. The singleton, doubleton, and tripleton represent cliques consisting of one, two, and three pixels, respectively. The numbers beside the terminal and nonterminal symbols represent probabilities.

A simple example consists of five pixels, as shown in Figure 9.6(a). The shaded pixels are unknown objects and the empty pixels are backgrounds, represented by the sequence, $W = BOOBO$. The other two figures are two different interpretations. The shaded pixels might mean two objects or three objects. The interpretations are represented by parse trees (Figure 9.7).

The probability of the first parse tree is $1 \times .5 \times 1 \times .1 \times .2 \times .2 \times 1 \times .1 = 0.002$. The second parse tree has the probability $1 \times .5 \times 1 \times .1 \times .1 \times .1 \times .1 \times .2 \times 1 \times .1 = 0.000001$. Therefore, the first parse tree is more probable. In general, the probabilities of parse trees can be calculated with the inside-outside probabilities. Also, the most probable parse tree can be found through the decoding algorithm.

The one-dimensional scene can be interpreted by parsing the erroneous input strings by the inside-outside algorithm. However, the image problem seems to be beyond one-dimensional, unlike natural language processing. The 3D problem is decomposed into three or more one-dimensional problems, solved separately, and then combined together for the overall solution. Nevertheless, the sequential and symbolic descriptions might be the most general representation scheme for describing the three-dimensional scene, if the direct spatial reasoning is bypassed by more abstract representations. There are some clues about representation and *binding problem* in the area of *multisensory integration* (Bear *et al.* 2007; Calvert *et al.* 2004; Purves 2008; Stein and Meredith 1993; Wikipedia 2013c).

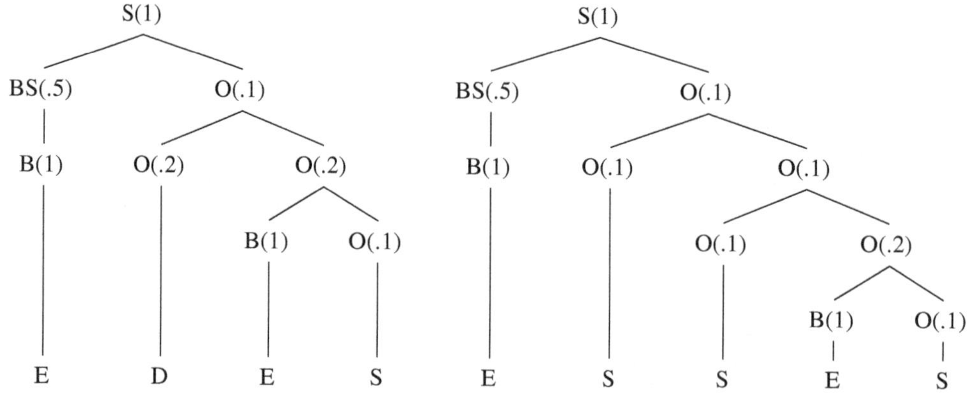

Figure 9.7 Parse trees for the two interpretations

Problems

9.1 [DP] How can you expand the DP algorithm, limited to one line of image, for better performance?

9.2 [DP] Consider multiplying three matrices in various orders.

$$ABC = \begin{bmatrix} 1 & 2 & 3 \\ 4 & 5 & 6 \end{bmatrix} \begin{bmatrix} 1 & 2 & 3 \\ 4 & 5 & 6 \\ 7 & 8 & 9 \end{bmatrix} \begin{bmatrix} 1 & 2 & 3 \\ 4 & 5 & 6 \\ 7 & 8 & 9 \end{bmatrix}.$$

Considered under the DP paradigm, what are the states? What is the optimal path and what are the minimum multiplications? This is a simple example of the *matrix chain multiplication* problem (Bradford *et al.* 1994; Cormen *et al.* 2001; Ramanan 1996; Wikipedia 2013b).

9.3 [Extended DP] Considering the boundary conditions, rewrite Equation (9.26).

9.4 [Extended DP] Similarly to the previous problem, rewrite Equation (9.27) with boundary considered.

9.5 [Extended DP] The extended DP is the only concept available, and it is impossible to apply because of the vast dimensionality in state. How can you manage such a limitation?

9.6 [Extended DP] In EDP, define $\psi(k, j)$ for a nearest neighbor connection and discuss the sparseness.

9.7 [Inside-outside] For a given consecutive N pixels, how many different objects are there for all cases of segmentation? Assume that continued pixels are identical objects or background.

9.8 [Inside-outside] Consider a *blocks world* (Slaney and Thiébaux 2001), where the objects are cubes as shown in Figure 9.8. The blocks world vision has been extensively explored by Winston and Waltz for an original concept (Cohen and Feigenbaum 1982; Winston 1992, 1984). (See also the references (Cohen and Feigenbaum 1982; Gupta *et al.* 2010; Jeong 1986; Jeong and Musicus 1989; Mörwald *et al.* 2010; Slaney and Thiébaux 2001)). David Waltz invented *constraint propagation* for solving the problem with a stack. Instead of the constraint propagation, can you interpret the scene by grammatical description and possibly in an inside-outside algorithm?

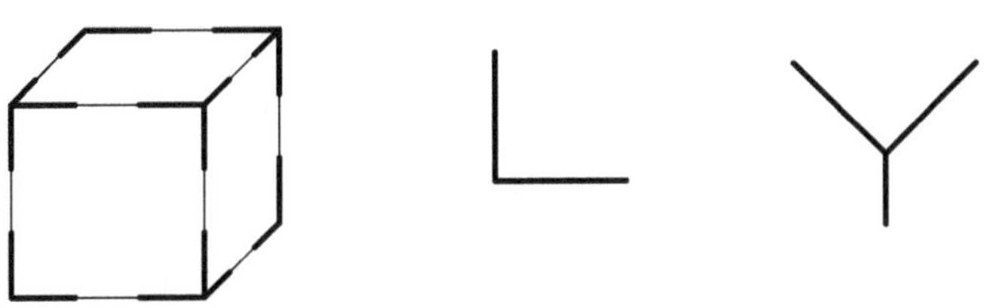

(a) A scene (b) Corners (L and Y)

Figure 9.8 Interpretation of a box scene in a blocks world

9.9 [Inside-outside] Given an algorithm that contains several loops, we need a systematic method to estimate computational complexity. One useful formula is $\sum_{i=1}^{N} i^s \to O(N^{s+1})$. For multiple loops, $\prod_{k=1}^{K} \sum_{i_k=1}^{N_k} 1 \to O(\prod_{k=1}^{K} N_k)$. Using this formula, obtain the complexity of nested loops $\prod_{k=1}^{K} \sum_{i_k=1}^{i_{k+1}} i_k$, where $i_{K+1} = N$.

9.10 [Inside-outside] Using the previous formula, analyze the running complexity of Algorithm 9.12.

9.11 [Inside-outside] The inside-outside algorithm can be converted to CYK by suitably arranging the loops and replacing the probability with binary decision for the production rules. How can you modify the loops for CYK?

References

Aho A, Hopcroft J, and Ullman J 1974 *The Design and Analysis of Computer Algorithms*. Addison-Wesley.

Amini AA, Weymouth TE, and Jain RC 1990 Using dynamic programming for solving variational problems in vision. *IEEE Trans. Pattern Anal. Mach. Intell.* **12**(9), 855–867.

Baker J 1979 Trainable grammars for speech recognition In *Speech communication papers presented at the 97th meeting of the Acoustical Society of America* (ed. Wolf JJ and Klatt DH), pp. 547–550 Acoustical Society of America.

Baum LE, Petrie T, Soules G, and Weiss N 1970 A maximization technique occurring in the statistical analysis of probabilistic functions of Markov chains. *Ann. Math. Stat.* **41**, 164–171.

Bear M, Conners B, and Paradiso M 2007 *Neuroscience: Exploring the Brain* third edn. Williams & Wilkins, Baltimore.

Bellman R 1954 The theory of dynamic programming. *Bulletin of the American Mathematical Society* **60**, 503–516.

Bellman R 2003 *Dynamic Programming* Dover Books on Computer Science Series. Dover Publications.

Bertsekas DP 2007 *Dynamic Programming and Optimal Control* vol. 1,2. Athena Scientific.

Bertsekas DP 2012 *Dynamic Programming and Optimal Control: Approximate Dynamic Programming* vol. 2 fourth edn. Athena Scientific.

Bertsekas DP 2013 *Abstract Dynamic Programming*. Athena Scientific.

Bradford PG, Rawlins GJ, and Shannon GE 1994 Efficient matrix chain ordering in polylog time *Parallel Processing Symposium, 1994. Proceedings, Eighth International*, pp. 234–241 IEEE.

Calvert GA, Spence C, and Stein BE 2004 *The Handbook of Multisensory Processes*. MIT press.

Cohen P and Feigenbaum EA 1982 *The Handbook of Artificial Intelligence* vol. 3. Morgan Kaufinann.

Cormen T, Rivest CLR, and Stein C 2001 *Introduction to Algorithms* second edn. The MIT Press.

Dempster A, Laird N, and Rubin D 1977 Maximum likelihood from incomplete data via the em algorithm. *Journal of the Royal Statistical Society, Series B* **39**, 1–38.

(ed. Purves D) 2008 *Neuroscience* fourth edn. Sinaur Associates.

Felzenszwalb PF and Zabih R 2011 Dynamic programming and graph algorithms in computer vision. *IEEE Trans. Pattern Anal. Mach. Intell.* **33**(4), 721–740.

Gong M and Yang YH 2005 Fast unambiguous stereo matching using reliability-based dynamic programming. *IEEE Trans. Pattern Anal. Mach. Intell.* **27**(6), 998–1003.

Gupta A, Efros AA, and Hebert M 2010 Blocks world revisited: Image understanding using qualitative geometry and mechanics *Computer Vision–ECCV 2010* Springer pp. 482–496.

Hopcroft JE, Motwani R, and Ullman JD 2006 *Introduction to Automata Theory, Languages, and Computation (3rd Edition)*. Prentice Hall.

Jelinek F, Lafferty JD, and Mercer RL 1992 *Basic Methods of Probabilistic Context Free Grammars*. Springer.

Jeong H 1986 *Mask Extraction of Optical Images of VLSI Circuits* PhD thesis MIT.

Jeong H and Musicus BR 1989 *Advances in Machine Vision* Springer Series in Perception Engineering Springer-Verlag chapter 6, pp. 214–254.

Jeong H and Yuns O 2000 Fast stereo matching using constraints in discrete space. *IEICE Transactions on Information and Systems* **83**(7), 1592–1600.

Jurafsky D, Martin JH, Kaehler A, Vander Linden K, and Ward N 2000 *Speech and Language Processing: An Introduction to Natural Language Processing, Computational Linguistics, and Speech Recognition* vol. 2. MIT Press.

Knuth DE 2011 *The Art of Computer Programming, Volumes 1-4A Boxed Set*. Addison-Wesley Professional.

Lafferty JD 2000 *A Derivation of the Inside-Outside Algorithm from the EM Algorithm*. IBM TJ Watson Research Center.

Lari K and Young SJ 1990 The estimation of stochastic context-free grammars using the inside-outside algorithm. *Computer speech & language* **4**(1), 35–56.

Lari K and Young SJ 1991 Applications of stochastic context-free grammars using the inside-outside algorithm. *Computer speech & language* **5**(3), 237–257.

Lawrence R, Rabiner R, and Schafer R 2007 *Introduction to Digital Speech Processing*. Now Publishers Inc., Hanover, MA USA.

Manning C 2001 Probabilistic linguistics and probabilistic models of natural language processing NIPS 2001 Tutorial.

Mörwald T, Prankl J, Richtsfeld A, Zillich M, and Vincze M 2010 Blort – the blocks world robotic vision toolbox *Proc. ICRA Workshop Best Practice in 3D Perception and Modeling for Mobile Manipulation*.

Ohta Y and Kanade T 1985 Stereo by intra- and inter-scanline search using dynamic programming. *IEEE Trans. Pattern Anal. Mach. Intell.* **7**(2), 139–154.

Pereira F and Schabes Y 1992 Inside-outside reestimation from partially bracketed corpora *Proceedings of the 30th annual meeting on Association for Computational Linguistics*, pp. 128–135 Association for Computational Linguistics.

Powell WB 2011 *Approximate Dynamic Programming: Solving the Curses of Dimensionality* Wiley series in probability and statistics second edn. Wiley.

Rabiner L and Juang B 1993 *Fundamentals of Speech Recognition* Prentice Hall signal processing series. Prentice Hall.

Rabiner LR 1989 A tutorial on hidden Markov models and selected applications in speech recognition. *Proceedings of IEEE* **77**(2), 257–286.

Ramanan P 1996 An efficient parallel algorithm for the matrix-chain-product problem. *SIAM Journal on Computing* **25**(4), 874–893.

Sanchez JA, Benedí JM, and Casacuberta F 1996 Comparison between the inside-outside algorithm and the Viterbi algorithm for stochastic context-free grammars *Advances in Structural and Syntactical Pattern Recognition* Springer pp. 50–59.

Slaney J and Thiébaux S 2001 Blocks world revisited. *Artificial Intelligence* **125**(1), 119–153.

Soong FK and Huang EF 1991 A tree-trellis based fast search for finding the N-best sentence hypotheses in continuous speech recognition *Acoustics, Speech, and Signal Processing, 1991. ICASSP-91, 1991 International Conference on*, pp. 705–708 IEEE.

Stein BE and Meredith MA 1993 *The Merging of the Senses*. The MIT Press.

Sudkamp TA 2005 *Languages and Machines: An Introduction to the Theory of Computer Science (3rd Edition)*. Addison-Wesley.

Viterbi A 1967 Error bounds for convolutional codes and an asymptotically optimum decoding algorithm. *IEEE Trans. Information Theory* **13**(2), 260–269.

Wikipedia 2013a Hidden Markov model http://en.wikipedia.org/wiki/Hidden_markov_model (accessed Nov. 13, 2013).

Wikipedia 2013b Matrix chain multiplication http://en.wikipedia.org/wiki/Matrix_chain_multiplication (accessed Nov. 14, 2013).

Wikipedia 2013c Multisensory integration http://en.wikipedia.org/wiki/Multisensory_integration (accessed Nov. 2, 2013).

Winston 1992 *Artificial Intelligence (3rd Edition)*. Addison-Wesley.

Winston PH 1984 *Artificial Intelligence*. Addison-Wesley.

Xia F 2006 Inside-outside algorithm LING 572, Lecture note.

10

Belief Propagation and Graph Cuts for Energy Minimization

In energy minimization, belief propagation (BP) (Pearl 1982; Yedidia *et al.* 2003) and graph cut (GC) (Boykov *et al.* 2001; Felzenszwalb and Zabih 2011) are two important algorithms that can be used to solve many intermediate vision problems. These two algorithms are general problem solvers, showing duality and, in many aspects, evolving competitively in performance, computational speed, and generality. BP is an excellent general solver, especially for MRF factor graphs because it guarantees reasonable solutions even for loopy graphs. This method models the system as a joint pmf given by the energy function, estimates marginals, and iteratively propagates messages between neighbors to enhance beliefs. Upon convergence, each node contains a belief that is the score of the marginal states. The computational structure is inherently parallel because all the operations are local and concurrent. However, because of the vector variables and matrix priors, this method involves significant computation and storage, which are usually beyond the capacities of serial computers, for real-time computation.

GC is an excellent general solver for graph problems and returns remarkably accurate solutions. It models the system as a flow graph, in which a graph cut is equivalent to the energy, and thus searches for the min-cut using the standard max-flow min-cut algorithms. It solves the problem of multiple labels by first converting the label pairs into the binary label problem. To arrive at the global solution, this method also iterates in the label space until the converged solution is obtained. The computational structure is inherently serial because of the core max-flow min-cut algorithms and preparation of the intermediate graphs. In addition, this method is NP-complete for multiple labels but is practical in polynomial time because of the *move-based algorithms* (specifically, swap move and expansion move) (Boykov *et al.* 2001).

In this chapter, we discuss BP and GC in terms of their principles, algorithms, and computational structures. In particular, we analyze the parallel operations of BP in vector space. The RE and FRE machines in Chapter 8 can be directly applied to the BP machine. The BP architecture will be designed in the next chapter. Although GC is primarily a serial algorithm, parallel approaches are also investigated. In the first part of this chapter, we discuss BP, after which we discuss GC. We focus solely on energy minimization for vision problems in a general setting, skipping the fundamentals of Bayesian estimation and graph theory.

Architectures for Computer Vision: From Algorithm to Chip with Verilog, First Edition. Hong Jeong.

Companion Website: www.wiley.com/go/jeong

10.1 Belief in MRF Factor System

Consider an MRF system, $G = (U, V, X, \Theta)$, as stated in Definition 5.3. Here, U and V denote, respectively, the factor and the variable sets. Further, the factors and variables are represented by $\{\theta_u(\mathbf{x}_u)|\mathbf{x}_u = \{x_v|v \in N(u)\}, u \in U\}$ and $\{x_v|v \in V\}$, respectively. In this system, the joint pmf is the product of the factor nodes,

$$p(\mathbf{x}) = \prod\nolimits_{u \in U} \theta_u(\mathbf{x}_u). \tag{10.1}$$

To estimate a node's variable, we need that node's pmf, which can be achieved by marginalizing other variables, retaining only one variable:

$$p(x_v) = \sum\nolimits_{X \backslash x_v} p(\mathbf{x}), \quad v \in V. \tag{10.2}$$

However, marginalization is an intractable task because the computational complexity involved is exponential. For an image with $M \times N$ pixels and L labels, the complexity is $O(L^{MN})$. This problem is one of the central issues in many problems based on Bayesian estimation and is solved by various methods. One approach is to estimate the states using DP, HMM, or Kalman filtering. The other approach is to simulate the integration by sampling, as in Monte Carlo sampling and simulated annealing. Yet another method is to find the stable state by local marginalization and iteration, that is mean field approximation and BP.

BP determines a node probability iteratively by using information from children nodes and parent nodes. If there is no loop as in *Bayesian trees*, BP provides an exact solution, just like dynamic programming/Viterbi. Otherwise, *loopy BP*, like our MRF model of an image, provides an approximate solution.

The purpose is to define the belief that approximates the marginal:

$$p(x_v) = \prod\nolimits_{u \in N(v)} \sum\nolimits_{\mathbf{x}_u \backslash x_v} \theta_u(\mathbf{x}_u), \quad v \in V. \tag{10.3}$$

The belief propagation concept links marginals with conditionals using a chain rule. A marginal at a site can be connected to other marginals by conditioning the factors. This is a recursive relationship, eventually connecting all the variables in the MRF relationship. The marginal is called a *belief* and the conditional is called a *message*.

Let us formally define belief and message in terms of the factor graph.

Definition 10.1 (Belief and messages) *For an MRF factor graph, $G = (U, V, X, \Theta)$, we define belief 'b' and message 'm' as*

$$b(x_v) \triangleq \prod\nolimits_{u \in N(v)} m_{uv}(x_v), \tag{10.4}$$

$$m_{vu}(x_v) \triangleq b(x_v), \tag{10.5}$$

$$m_{uv}(x_v) \triangleq \sum\nolimits_{\mathbf{x}_u \backslash x_v} \theta(\mathbf{x}_u) \prod\nolimits_{v^* \in N(u) \backslash v} m_{v^*u}(x_{v^*}), \tag{10.6}$$

where $p, q \in U \cup V$.

The belief is the product of the messages from the factor nodes. The variable and the factor nodes update alternately via messages. The message from the variable is the belief itself. The message from the factor node is the marginalization of the product of the factor and the messages. The underlying operation in the factor node is a convolution of the incoming messages with the factors.

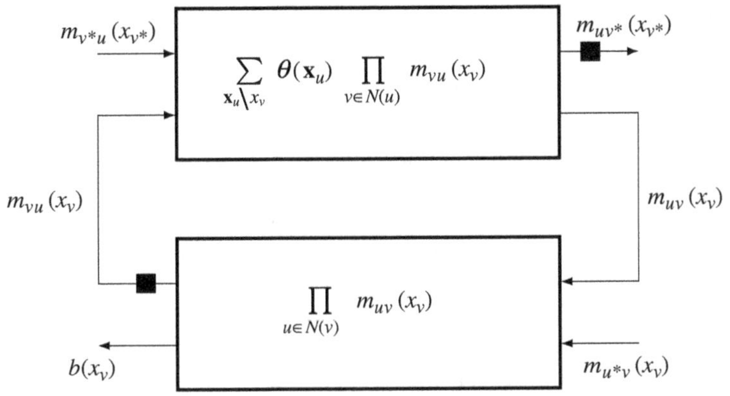

Figure 10.1 Belief and messages between variable and factor nodes (all outputs are blocked by registers, preventing infinity loops)

We apply the belief and message mechanism to the factor graph to obtain an iterative formulation. We start with a variable node, v, where the belief $b(x_v)$ is defined (Figure 10.1). In Figure 10.1, the top block is the factor node and the bottom block is the variable node. In accordance with Equation (10.6), the variable node sends a message to the factor node:

$$m_{vu}(x_v) = b(x_v), \quad u \in U, v \in V. \tag{10.7}$$

The factor node then assembles the incoming messages and convolves them to generate messages for the variable node:

$$m_{uv}(x_v) = \sum\nolimits_{\mathbf{x}_u \setminus x_v} \theta(\mathbf{x}_u) \prod\nolimits_{v^* \in N(u) \setminus v} m_{v^*u}(x_{v^*}), \tag{10.8}$$

where the destination node is excluded from the source node list to prevent oscillations. From the definition of belief, Equation (10.7) becomes

$$m_{vu}(x_v) = \prod\nolimits_{u^* \in N(v) \setminus u} m_{u^*v}(x_v), \tag{10.9}$$

where the destination node is also extracted from the source list. Consequently, we obtain a belief and two messages to describe the system.

Let us now formally define the belief propagation algorithm.

Algorithm 10.1 (Belief propagation for factor graph) *Given a Markov factor graph, $G = (U, V, X, \Theta)$, compute the following.*

1. *Initialization: m_{uv} and m_{vu} for $u \in U$ and $v \in V$.*
2. *for $t = 0, 1, \ldots, T-1$ and for $u, u^* \in U$ and $v, v^* \in V$,*

$$m_{vu}(x_v) \leftarrow \prod\nolimits_{u^* \in N(v) \setminus u} m_{u^*v}(x_v),$$

$$m_{uv}(x_v) \leftarrow \sum\nolimits_{\mathbf{x}_u \setminus x_v} \theta_u(\mathbf{x}_u) \prod\nolimits_{v^* \in N(u) \setminus v} m_{v^*u}(x_{v^*}).$$

3. for $u \in U$ and $v \in V$,

$$b(x_v) = \prod\nolimits_{u \in N(v)} m_{uv}(x_v).$$

The result is the belief $b(x_v)$ at a variable node, which is the estimated marginal, $p(x_v)$. In this manner, the marginal is obtained with iterative message passing.

It is known that BP converges to a fixed point that is also a stationary point of the Bethe approximation to the free energy (Yedidia *et al.* 2003). Thus, BP is naturally expandable to more general models (Ihler *et al.* 2005; Sudderth *et al.* 2010; Weiss 2014; Yedidia *et al.* 2005).

10.2 Belief in Pairwise MRF System

Let us now apply the concept of belief to the MRF model, stated in Chapter 5 (see also Figure 10.2(a)).

Each pixel, $p \in \mathcal{P}$, is assigned with a label $x_p \in \mathcal{L}$ and attached to a pixel, $I_p \in [0, n]$. The probabilistic properties of the system are described by the joint distribution, which is either in factored form or Gibb's

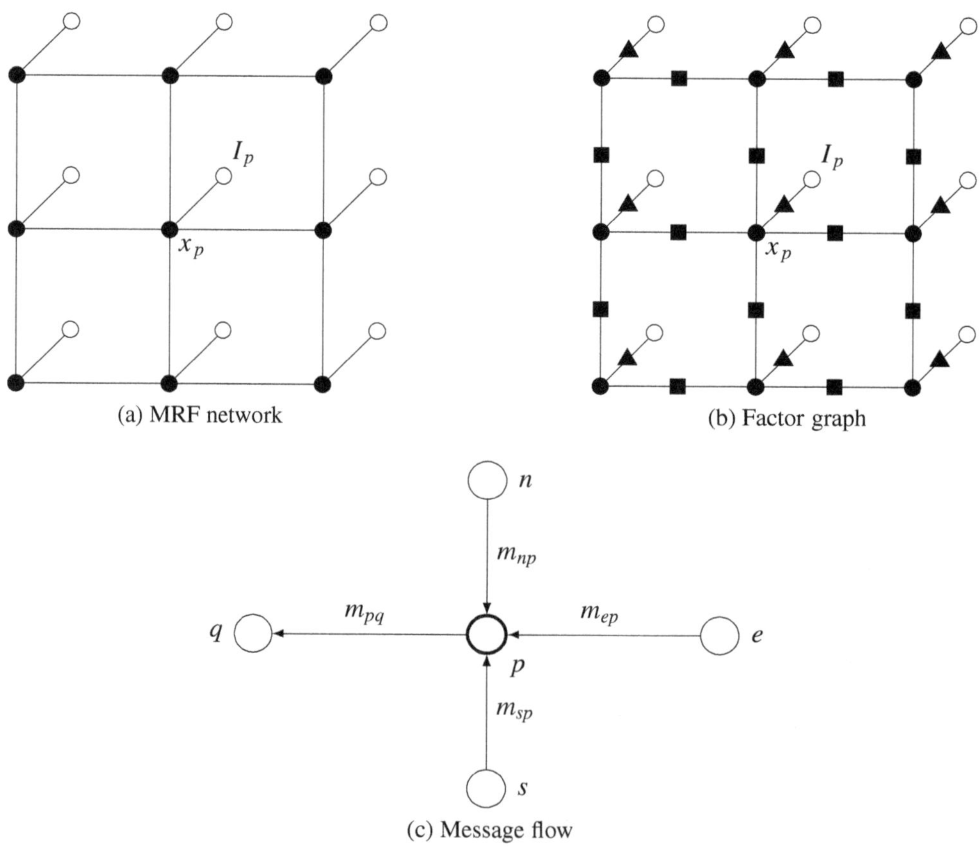

Figure 10.2 Representations of MRF network, factor graph, and message flow

distribution. For $I = \{I_p | p \in \mathcal{P}\}$, $\mathbf{x} = \{x_p | x \in \mathcal{L}, p \in \mathcal{P}\}$ is an MRF that has

$$p(\mathbf{x}|I) = \frac{1}{Z} \exp\left\{ - \left(\sum_{p \in \mathcal{P}} \phi(x_p|I_p) + \sum_{q \in N_p \backslash p} \psi(x_p, x_q) \right) \right\},$$

$$= \frac{1}{Z} \prod_{p \in \mathcal{P}} p(x_p|I_p) \prod_{q \in N_p \backslash p} p(x_p, x_q), \tag{10.10}$$

where ϕ and ψ denote, respectively, the data term and the smoothness term. Since the variable is discrete, all the distributions in the following are pmfs, unless otherwise stated.

The MRF graph model is depicted in Figure 10.2(b). Each pixel p is assigned with both unobserved node (x_p) and observed node (I_p). In the factor graph terms, the nodes are the variable nodes, and the connections between them are the factor nodes. Thus, the MRF model can be viewed as a simple bipartite graph. The general definition of message can be adapted to the MRF graph in the following way. Consider the path from a variable node p to a variable node q via a factor node $p(x_p, x_q)$. The variable node is attached to another factor node $p(x_p|I_p)$. Because there is only one factor node between two variable nodes, the same variable can be used for the variable node and the factor node.

Consequently, the factor graph is $G = (\mathcal{P}, \mathcal{P}, X, \Theta)$, the joint pmf is

$$p(\mathbf{x}) = \frac{1}{Z} \prod_{p \in \mathcal{P}} \left\{ p(x_p|I_p) \prod_{q \in N_p \backslash p} p(x_p, x_q) \right\} \tag{10.11}$$

and the factor at p is

$$\theta(p) = \frac{1}{Z} p(x_p|I_p) p(x_p, x_q), q \in N_p, \tag{10.12}$$

The factors consist of singletons and doubletons only. The message from a variable node p to a factor node p' (i.e. $\theta(p)$) is

$$m_{pp'}(x_p) = \prod_{s \in N_p} m_{sp}(x_p). \tag{10.13}$$

Since there is only one path from a factor node to a variable node, the message between variable nodes becomes

$$m_{pq}(x_q) = \sum_{x_p} p(x_p|I_p) p(x_p, x_q) \prod_{s \in N_p \backslash q} m_{sp}(x_p). \tag{10.14}$$

The message is now represented by transfers between variable nodes, bypassing the factor nodes (Figure 10.2(c)). When all the messages have propagated along the tree and are thus determined, the beliefs are available on the variable nodes:

$$p(x_q) = p(I_q|x_q) \prod_{p \in N(q)} m_{pq}(x_q), \quad p, q \in \mathcal{P}. \tag{10.15}$$

This representation means that the belief at a node is the marginal pmf, $p(x_p)$ $(p \in \mathcal{P})$. This is the original sum-product algorithm.

For a loopy MRF, the message must be iterated until convergence. In iterative form, the sum-product becomes

$$\text{sum-product:}\begin{cases} m_{pq}^{(t)}(x_q) = \sum_{x_p} p(x_p, x_q)p(I_p|x_p) \prod_{s\in N(p)\backslash q} p_{sp}^{(t-1)}(x_p), \\ p(x_q) \quad = p(I_q|x_q) \prod_{p\in N(q)} m_{pq}^{(T)}(x_q), \quad t = 0, 1, \ldots, T. \end{cases} \tag{10.16}$$

The message $m_{pq}^{(t)}$ at node p is calculated at iteration t and sent to neighbor node q. After T iterations, the $p(x_q)$ at each node is decided according to the read-out equation. This is known as the *sum-product* algorithm. To make the system stable, a normalization process is then needed:

$$\sum\nolimits_{x_q} m_{pq}(x_q) = 1, \tag{10.17}$$

which also means that the message is a marginal distribution. Although it is better than the original marginalization that does not use belief, the sum-product is still a prohibitively large problem. Because $f \in \mathcal{L}$, obtaining the message of a node requires $O(L^2)$ multiplications and $O(L^2)$ additions.

To simplify the operations, we replace the summation with the maximum, resulting in the *max-product* form:

$$\text{max-product:}\begin{cases} m_{pq}^{(t)}(x_q) = \max_{x_p} p(x_p, x_q)p(I_p|x_p) \prod_{s\in N(p)\backslash q} p_{sp}^{(t-1)}(x_p), \\ p(x_q) \quad = p(I_q|x_q) \prod_{p\in N(q)} m_{pq}^{T}(x_q), \quad t = 0, 1, \ldots, T. \end{cases} \tag{10.18}$$

In this algorithm, the summation is replaced with $O(L^2)$ 'max' operations. In this case, beliefs no longer estimate marginal but a sort of score of messages, and determine the maxima point to most likely states. As a consequence of computation, underflow and overflow might occur and must be prevented by applying some bias. Considering the variables as states, it can be seen that this method is very similar to the Viterbi algorithm in DP.

Taking the logarithm of the distributions $\phi(x) = -\ln p(I|x)$ and $\psi(x_p, x_q) = -\ln p(x_p, x_q)$, Equation (10.16) becomes

$$\text{sum-sum:}\begin{cases} m_{pq}^{(t)}(x_q) = \sum_{x_p} \left\{ \begin{array}{l} \psi(x_p, x_q) + \phi(x_p) \\ \quad + \sum_{s\in N(p)\backslash q} \left(m_{sp}^{(t-1)}(x_p) - \alpha \right) \end{array} \right\}, \\ \hat{x}_q = \arg\min_{x_q} \left\{ \phi(x_q) + \sum_{p\in N(q)} m_{pq}^{T}(x_v) \right\}, \end{cases} \tag{10.19}$$

where $\alpha = \sum_{x_p} m_{sp}^{(t-1)}(x_p)$. The term α is introduced to adjust the bias to prevent underflow. As a consequence of the logarithm, the multiplication is changed to addition. It requires $O(L^2)$ additions. Let us call this *sum-sum*, considering the two operations involved in the computation.

We can further simplify sum-sum to the min-sum algorithm.

$$\text{min-sum:}\begin{cases} m_{pq}^{(t)}(x_q) = \min_{x_p} \left\{ \begin{array}{l} \psi(x_p, x_q) + \phi(x_p) \\ \quad + \sum_{s\in N(p)\backslash q} \left(m_{sp}^{(t-1)}(x_p) - \alpha \right) \end{array} \right\}, \\ \hat{x}_q = \arg\min_{x_q} \left(\phi(x_q) + \sum_{p\in N(q)} m_{pq}^{T}(x_v) \right), \end{cases} \tag{10.20}$$

where $\alpha = \sum_{x_p} m_{sp}^{(t-1)}(x_p)$. We need $O(L^2)$ comparisons and $O(L)$ additions. This algorithm is similar to the Viterbi algorithm. However, we do not return to the previous state by storing the parent pointers. The computation proceeds only in the forward direction. We started from the marginal distribution but arrived again at the MAP estimate, which is free from multiplication.

From a computational point of view, we have the four dual equations: sum-product, max-product, sum-sum, and min-sum. Of these equations, min-sum is the one that is used in practical hardware systems, owing to its computational simplicity. In the following sections, we analyze the computational structure of these equations and derive efficient computational models that will be used later to design architectures.

10.3 BP in Discrete Space

Thus far, we have assumed that the variables are continuous, but from here onwards we consider BP in discrete space. The variable x is defined as $x \in [0, L-1]$, where L is the size of the discrete labels. The beliefs and messages are all discrete, that is $b, m \in [0, N_m - 1]$, where N_m represent the discrete levels. Without loss of generality, we use the four-neighborhood system, N_4, in which the neighbors are represented relative to the current node: center (0), east (1), south (2), west (3), and north (4). For $q \in \{1, 2, 3, 4\}$, the opposite node is $q' = ((q + 2))_4$, where $((x))_4$ signifies modulo-four division. We also assume that the prior is shift-invariant and symmetric: $\psi(x_p, x_q) = \psi(|x_p - x_q|)$. Therefore, for the prior, we have only L distinct values. In addition, ϕ and ψ are nonnegative and real. The only remaining unspecified value is the data term, $\phi(\cdot) \geq 0$, which depends on the application, and is therefore assumed to be given.

Although the min-sum formula is the one actually used in most applications, we use all four formulas in order to examine their computational aspects. If all assumptions are satisfied, the four equations can be represented in discrete space as follows. First, the sum-product has the form

$$\text{sum-product:} \begin{cases} m_{pq}^{(t)}(l) = \sum_k p(k, l) p(I_p|k) \prod_{s \in N(p) \backslash q} p_{sp}^{(t-1)}(k), \\ p(l) \quad = p(I_q|l) \prod_{p \in N(q)} m_{pq}^T(l), \quad t = 0, 1, \ldots, T-1. \end{cases} \tag{10.21}$$

Here, $\sum_{k=1}^{n} m_{pq}(k) = 1$ and $k, l \in [0, L-1]$. The discrete-form of the max-product is

$$\text{max-product:} \begin{cases} m_{pq}^{(t)}(l) = \max_k p(k, l) p(I_p|k) \prod_{s \in N(p) \backslash q} p_{sp}^{(t-1)}(k), \\ p(l) \quad = p(I_q|l) \prod_{p \in N(q)} m_{pq}^T(l), \quad t = 0, 1, \ldots, T-1. \end{cases} \tag{10.22}$$

Similarly, the discrete form of the sum-sum formula is

$$\text{sum-sum:} \begin{cases} m_{pq}^{(t)}(l) = \sum_k \left(\begin{array}{c} \psi(k, l) + \phi(k) \\ + \sum_{s \in N(p) \backslash q} \left(m_{sp}^{(t-1)}(k) - \alpha \right) \end{array} \right), \\ \hat{x}_q = \arg\min_l \left(\phi(l) + \sum_{p \in N(q)} m_{pq}^T(x_v) \right), \quad \alpha = \sum_k m_{sp}^{(t-1)}(k). \end{cases} \tag{10.23}$$

Finally, the min-sum form is

$$\text{min-sum:}\begin{cases} m_{pq}^{(t)}(l) = \min_{k\in[0,L-1]}\left(\begin{array}{c}\psi(|k-l|)+\phi_p(k)\\ +\sum_{q^*\in[1,4]\backslash q}\left(m_{q^*p}^{(t-1)}(k)-\alpha\right)\end{array}\right), \\ x_p = \arg\min_k\left(\phi_p(k)+\sum_{q^*\in[1,4]} m_{q^*p}^T(k)\right), \quad \alpha=\sum_k m_{q^*p}^{(t-1)}(k). \end{cases} \tag{10.24}$$

The four equations have the same computational structure, with the exception that the operations, product vs. sum and maximum vs. minimum, must be replaced appropriately in each equation.

We consider only the representative equation, the min-sum formula. The computation performed by Equation (10.24) is done in a number of steps. The first step builds an average vector for each port: a node receives four message vectors from four neighbors, chooses three of them, and builds four different average vectors.

$$\bar{m}_{pq}(k) = \sum_{q^*\in[1,4]\backslash q'} m_{q^*p}(k) = \sum_{q^*\in[1,4]\backslash q'} m_{q^*p}(k) - m_{qp}(k), \quad k\in[1,4], \tag{10.25}$$

where constant division for the averaging operation is omitted for simplicity.

The second step adds the prior vector to the averaged messages:

$$\phi(k)+\bar{m}_{pq}(k), k\in[1,4], \quad q\in[1,4]. \tag{10.26}$$

Note that the same prior vector is added to the four different message vectors. This is done because the prior does not depend on the neighbor but on the incoming data in the current node.

The third step adds the vector with the bias, depending on the difference of the element index between the k element in the p node and the l element of the q node:

$$\psi(|k-l|)+\phi(k)+\bar{m}_{pq}(k), k\in[1,4], l\in[1,4]. \tag{10.27}$$

This bias represents the smoothness factor between message indices. The final step chooses the minimum of the L elements, which is illustrated in Figure 10.3.

The data and the prior terms are added to the average input message, and all the components compared to determine the smallest value. This structure and operation are well-known in DP as the Viterbi algorithm. The input-output connection is just one part of the otherwise long sections in the DP graph

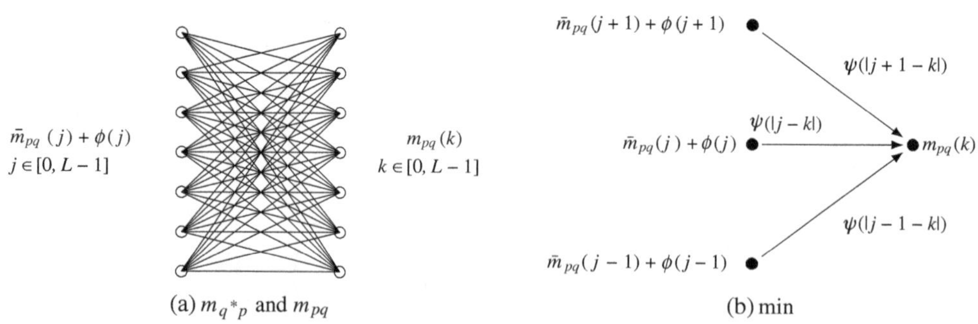

Figure 10.3 Message update in the min-sum algorithm

(refer to Chapter 9). However, the Viterbi algorithm cannot be applied here because the input is changed by external networks in each iteration. This operation can be represented by

$$m_{pq}(k) = \min_{j=1}^{n} \bar{m}_{pq}(j) + \phi(j) + \psi(|j-k|), k \in [1,4]. \tag{10.28}$$

The concept of choosing one of the L values and storing it in the node for the next iteration is the same as in the Viterbi algorithm. However, the same node cannot be visited until all other nodes are visited. This algorithm – which combines localized DP and global relaxation, and can therefore be considered a generalization of the DP algorithm – can be applied to multidimensional problems, unlike the DP algorithm, which can only be applied to one-dimensional problems. The parent index, as used in Viterbi, is not needed for backtracking: this system only has the forward phase. From a macroscopic viewpoint, the nodes on the graph may be the whole nodes MN, and the new value m^o is obtained from the old value m^i, replacing m^i with the previous m^o. The iteration proceeds until convergence occurs.

The full description is as follows:

Algorithm 10.2 (Min-sum in discrete space) *Given the data term, compute the MAP estimate* $\{x_p | p \in \mathcal{P}\}$.

Input: $\{\phi_p(k) | p \in \mathcal{P}, k \in [0, L-1]\}$.

Parameter: $\{\psi(|k-l|) | k, l \in [0, L-1]\}$.

Output: $\{x_p | p \in \mathcal{P}\}$.

1. *Initialization:* $\{m_{pq}(k) | p, q \in \mathcal{P}, k \in [0, L-1]\}$.
2. *Message: for* $t = 0, 1, \ldots, T-1$ *and* $p \in \mathcal{P}$, *and* $q \in N_p \setminus p$,

$$m_{pq}(k) = \min_{j=1}^{n} \left\{ \left(\sum\nolimits_{q^* \in N_p \setminus q} m_{q^*p}(j) \right) + \phi(j) + \psi(|j-k|) \right\}.$$

3. *Belief: for* $p \in \mathcal{P}$ *and* $k \in [0, L-1]$,

$$b_p(k) = \phi(k) + \sum\nolimits_{q \in N_p \setminus p} m_{qp}(k).$$

4. *Output: for* $p \in \mathcal{P}$, $x_p = \arg\min_{k \in [0, L-1]} b_p(k)$.

In this algorithm, each node needs $O(L^2)$ 'min' operations and $O(L)$ space to store ϕ and ψ. The entire system needs $O(MNTL^2)$ time and $O(MNL)$ space. This basic algorithm is used in the next chapter for circuit design.

10.4 BP in Vector Space

Since the state is discrete, the message is a vector-valued quantity, and thus the vector representation might be more useful for representation. In the min-sum algorithm, we replace all the scalar quantities, including variables, data terms, and prior terms, with vectors and matrices. The scalar operations are replaced by special operations on vectors or matrices.

To begin with, let us consider a pixel p and its surrounding neighbors (Figure 10.4). In Figure 10.4, the four neighbors are named $\{1, 2, 3, 4\}$, representing east, south, west, north, according to the current pixel under consideration. The coordinates of the center node are absolute but those of the neighbors are

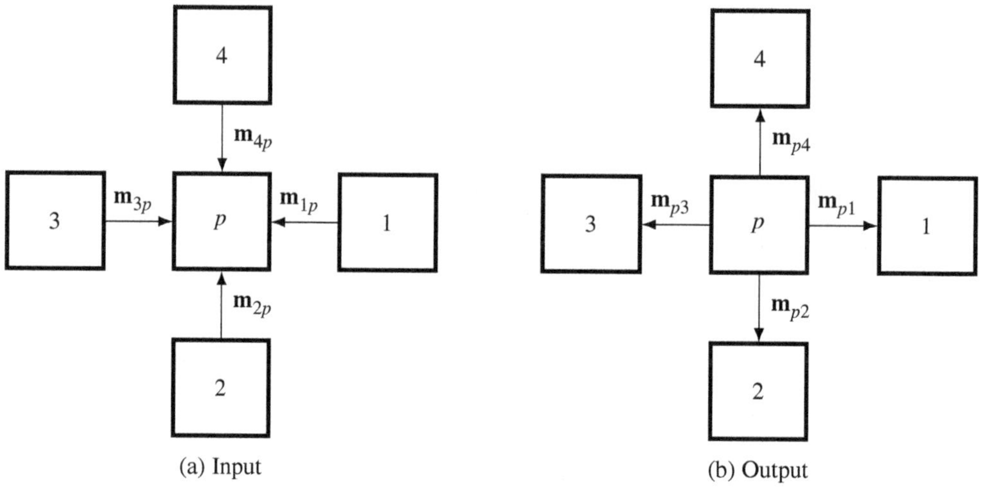

Figure 10.4 Passing message vectors between nodes (east, south, west, and north are represented by 1, 2, 3, and 4, respectively)

relative to the center node. Because the algorithm is defined for a single node, the mixed absolute and relative coordinates make the description very compact. In regard to the center node, the input data are the four incoming message vectors and the outputs are the four output message vectors.

The message vector from p to q is defined as a set of L scalar messages:

$$\mathbf{m}_{pq} \triangleq (m(1)_{pq}, \ldots, m(L-1)_{pq})^T, \quad m \in [0, \infty). \tag{10.29}$$

The message values must be nonnegative, as noted by $[0, \infty)$. The message is actually represented by an integer, and thus has a finite range in the circuit. This property, however, does not affect the underlying concept in any way. A node is surrounded by four neighbors, numbered from one to four, and receives and sends messages from and to them in a package of four messages. A package of four messages can be represented by a matrix, for each input or output.

$$M_p^o \triangleq \left(\mathbf{m}_{p1}^o, \mathbf{m}_{p2}^o, \mathbf{m}_{p3}^o, \mathbf{m}_{p4}^o\right), \quad M_p^i \triangleq \left(\mathbf{m}_{1p}^i, \mathbf{m}_{2p}^i, \mathbf{m}_{3p}^i, \mathbf{m}_{4p}^i\right), \tag{10.30}$$

where the superscript denotes the input and output. All the notations of the message direction and neighborhood directions are defined relative to a node, because all the other nodes have the same connection and operation. As a result, a node can be considered a transformation $T(\cdot)$ that receives M_p^i and outputs M_p^o with $M^o = T(M^i)$. This operation is iterative and concurrent for all nodes.

The data term is represented by both a vector ϕ_p and a diagonal matrix Φ:

$$\begin{aligned} L \times 1 &: \phi_p \triangleq (\phi_p(0), \ldots, \phi_p(L-1))^T, \\ L \times 4 &: \Phi_p = \mathbf{1}_4^T \otimes \phi_p, \end{aligned} \tag{10.31}$$

where $\mathbf{1}_4$ is a four-element vector with all ones, and $\otimes$ is the tensor product. The data term must be determined at the beginning and must always be available to nodes as the message updation always uses this value. Because it is a function of the input image, the data term may differ for all the nodes.

Unlike the data term, the prior term does not depend on the input image, and thus remains unchanged for all nodes. It is computed initially and stored inside nodes. Because it is a large two-dimensional matrix, the prior must be simplified, by using its properties, and coded compactly to save space. One important property is that, in most cases, the prior is shift-invariant and symmetric:

$$\psi(x_p, x_q) = \psi(|x_p - x_q|). \tag{10.32}$$

This means that the prior depends only on local neighbors, not on absolute position, and on the absolute difference of coordinates, which are the same for all neighbors and nodes. This property appears as an $n \times n$ matrix:

$$n \times n : \Psi = \{\psi(|i - j|) | i, j \in [0, L - 1]\}, \tag{10.33}$$

or as a symmetric *Toeplitz matrix*. Among the $n \times n$ elements, only $n/2$ values differ in the worst case, needing a small vector for the $n/2$ values.

A node receives four messages and builds four different averages by selectively choosing three input messages. For this selective average, we can define an operation, $(\mathbf{1}_4\mathbf{1}_4^T - I_{4\times4})$, where $\mathbf{1}_n$ is an $n \times 1$ vector with ones and $I_{4\times4}$ is a 4×4 identity matrix. Subsequently, using the vector-matrix notations and the new operations, we can represent sum-sum by

$$\begin{aligned} M_p^o &= \Psi(\Phi_p + M_p^i(\mathbf{1}_4\mathbf{1}_4^T - I_{4\times4})), \\ \mathbf{b}_p &= \Phi + M_p^i\mathbf{1}_4. \end{aligned} \tag{10.34}$$

During the iteration, the message matrices are updated iteratively, replacing M^i by M^o at the beginning of each iteration. Following convergence of the messages, the stabilized belief, $\mathbf{b}$, may be obtained as the aggregate of all the incoming messages. As a solution of the sum-product formula, the message vector represents the marginal distribution, $p(\mathbf{x}_p) = \mathbf{b}_p$.

To complete the min-sum algorithm in vector form, we need an additional operation. For an $n \times n$ matrix A and an $n \times 1$ vector $\mathbf{b}$, define the operation

$$A \odot \mathbf{b} = \left\{ \min_{j=1}^{n}(a_{ij} + b_j) | i = 1, 2, \ldots, n \right\}^T. \tag{10.35}$$

This operation is related to *transitive closure* and the *shortest path problem* (Aho *et al.* 1974; Cormen *et al.* 2001; Knuth 1997).

Combining all these, we obtain the following equations:

$$\begin{cases} M_p^o &= \Psi \odot (\Phi_p + M_p^i(\mathbf{1}_4\mathbf{1}_4^T - I_{4\times4})), \\ \mathbf{b}_p &= \phi_p + M_p^i\mathbf{1}_4, \\ x_p &= \arg\min \mathbf{b}_p, \quad p \in \mathcal{P}. \end{cases} \tag{10.36}$$

After initialization, to determine ϕ, the updation repeats, replacing M^i with M^o each time. After the messages have converged when the iteration is at a maximum, we can obtain the final message using the second and third equations. The elements of a message vector denote scores of the states inversely, and thus the best state must be chosen by comparing all the elements. The state with the minimum score is the solution for the node.

In vector space, the min-sum algorithm can be represented in a very compact form:

Algorithm 10.3 (Min-sum in vector space) *Given the data term, compute the MAP estimate* $\{x_p|p \in \mathcal{P}]\}$.

Input: $\{\phi_p|p \in \mathcal{P}\}$.

Parameter: $\Psi = \{\Psi(j,k)|j,k \in \mathcal{L}\}$.

Output: $\{x_p|p \in \mathcal{P}\}$.

1. *Initialization:* $\{M_p|p \in \mathcal{P}\}$.
2. *Message updation: for* $t = 0, 1, \ldots, T-1$ *and* $p \in \mathcal{P}$,

$$M_p^o \leftarrow \Psi \odot \left(\Phi_p + M_p^i \left(\mathbf{1}_4 \mathbf{1}_4^T - I_{4\times4}\right)\right).$$

3. *Belief: for* $p \in \mathcal{P}$, $\mathbf{b}_p \leftarrow \phi_p + M_p^i \mathbf{1}_4$
4. *Output: for* $p \in \mathcal{P}$, $x_p \leftarrow \arg\min \mathbf{b}_p(k)$.

The input is the image, from which the data term is computed. The data term must be computed for each node initially and must always be available for each node. The smoothness term is universal to the nodes and must always be available for each node. The first stage of updation is computation of the average matrix. The second stage is to choose the minimum value from the combined input average message, data term, and smoothness term. Computation in updation is fully parallel. Thus, the first stage of updation needs $12n$ addition operations with a single adder, but only one operation with $12n$ adders. For the second stage of updation, $4n^2$ min-operations are needed with a single processor, but $4n$ min-operations with L processors. The updation loop comprises $M \times N \times L$ iterations. Following the iterations, the message vectors are computed for all nodes. The elements of the message vector represent scores, and thus the best index with the largest element is chosen. The result is the MAP estimate.

Because of the iterative neighborhood operation, this algorithm is qualified for the RE and FRE machines (in Chapter 8). The computation space is the graph G, which consists of $M \times N \times L$ nodes and an N_4 neighborhood system. As a standard RE, a node p computes $M_p^o = T(M_p^i)$ with a transformation $T(\cdot)$.

BP can be separated into two main methods according to update style (Jordan 2004). The first method updates all the nodes synchronously and in parallel, while the second updates sequentially in the inward direction, from the leaf to the root, and the reverse direction on the tree. For each update, the sequential method does not need to calculate the messages of all the nodes during each iteration; thus, they can be fully propagated in a small number of operations. In the tree scenario, both algorithms produce exact solutions. For real-time computation, BP is realized as fast belief propagation (FBP), hierarchical BP (Felzenszwalb and Huttenlocher 2004), and hypertree BP (Bernier and Cheung-Mon-Chan 2006; Bernier *et al.* 2009; Grauer-Gray *et al.* 2008; Guo and Hsu 2002; Jeong and Park 2004; Park and Jeong 2008; Sun *et al.* 2003; Yang *et al.* 2006).

10.5 Flow Network for Energy Function

Thus far, the energy minimization problem has been studied in terms of the functional minimization in the relaxation paradigm, the shortest path problem in the dynamic programming paradigm, and the marginal estimation in the belief propagation paradigm. Another important paradigm is the graph cuts (GC) paradigm, in which the energy minimization problem becomes the min-cut problem.

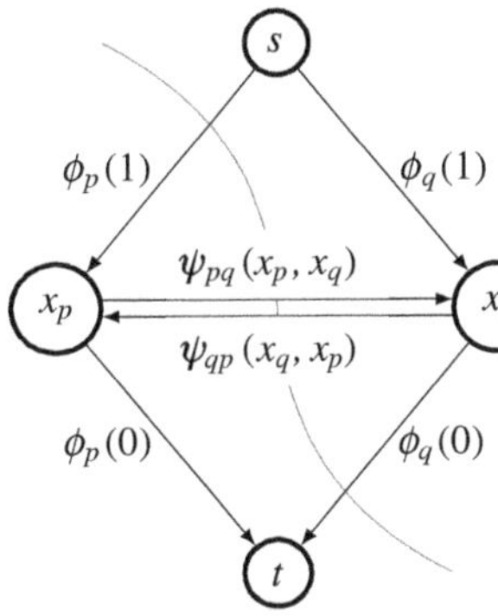

Figure 10.5 A flow graph for binary labeling (there are four possible cuts)

We focus on the flow network defined on the image plane, $\mathcal{P}$, and the energy function,

$$E(\mathbf{x}) = \sum_{p\in\mathcal{P}} \phi_p(x_p) + \sum_{p\in\mathcal{P},q\in N_p} \psi_{pq}(x_p, x_q), \tag{10.37}$$

where N_p is the neighborhood of p and the label is $x \in \mathcal{L}$. Using the Max-flow min-cut theorem, we can solve energy minimization by maximizing the flow over the network, which is determined by the min-cut algorithm. This computation can be achieved by the standard minimum cut algorithm.

For a label set $\mathcal{L} = \{0, 1\}$, the energy function $E(\mathbf{x})$ becomes

$$E(\mathbf{x}) = \sum_{p\in\mathcal{P}} \{\phi_p(0)(1 - x_p) + \phi_p(1)x_p\} + \sum_{p\in\mathcal{P},q\in N_p\backslash p} \psi_{pq}(x_p, x_q)(1 - x_p)x_q. \tag{10.38}$$

where $x_p \in \{0, 1\}$. This is a quadratic pseudo-Boolean function (QPBF), $E : \{0, 1\}^{\mathcal{P}} \mapsto \mathcal{R}$, which is a special case of the more general pseudo-Boolean function.

We can easily construct a flow graph, such as that shown in Figure 10.5, for the QPBF. The connection between a node and the terminal is called a t-link (terminal link) and a connection between nodes is called an n-link (neighbor link). The data term is assigned to the t-link capacity and the smoothness term is assigned to the n-link capacity. The label of the pixel is determined by the connected source (0) or sink (1). The construction of a flow graph means that the energy minimization can be solved by the min-cut algorithm. In this construction, any st-cut C corresponds to an assignment of label to the pixels $\mathbf{x}$ and the cost of the cut $|C|$ is equal to the energy of $E(\mathbf{x})$.

For the overall image plane, the graph is as shown in Figure 10.6. For simplicity, the image plane is illustrated as a linear array. Here, the nodes are $p \in \mathcal{P}$, and the t-link capacities are $t_p^s = \phi_p(1)$ and $t_p^t = \phi_p(0)$. The n-link capacity is $e_{pq} = \psi_{pq}(x_p, x_q)$.

Because all the discussions are based on this type of flow graph, we formally define the graph as follows below.

Definition 10.2 (Energy Network) *For the QPBF $E(\mathbf{x})$ in Equation (10.38), we define a flow graph $G = (V, E, X, \Phi, \Psi)$. V is the set of terminals, s and t, and the pixels $\mathcal{P}$. E is the set of t-links and n-links, $E = \{t_p^s, t_p^t, e_{pq} | p, q \in \mathcal{P}, p, q \in \mathcal{N}\}$. The source and sink are permanently labeled with zero and one, respectively. X denotes the labels of other vertices, $X = \{x_p | x_p \in \{0, 1\}, p \in \mathcal{P}\}$. D is the set of t-link capacities, $\Phi = \{\phi_p^s(1), \phi_p^t(0) | p \in \mathcal{P}\}$, and Ψ is the set of n-link capacities, $\Psi = \{\psi_{pq}(x_p, x_q) | p, q \in \mathcal{P}\}$.*

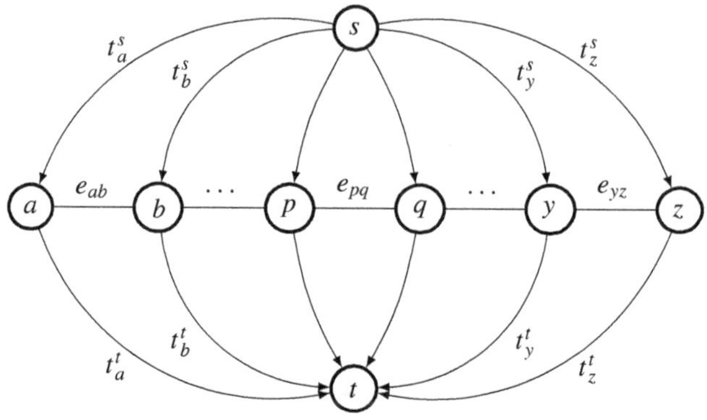

Figure 10.6 A flow graph for the labeling problem. The nodes are defined on the pixels and the source and sink are defined externally ($p, q \in \mathcal{P}$ and $p, q \in \mathcal{N}$. t: t-links and e: n-links)

The graph is different from an ordinary flow network because it is a grid in which the connectivity is very low, $O(MN)$. This definition connects the labeling problem and the graph problem. The purpose of the graph cut is to solve the energy minimization problem by finding a min-cut:

$$\mathbf{x}^* = \arg\min_{\mathbf{x}} E(\mathbf{x}) = \arg\min_{\mathbf{x}} |C|. \tag{10.39}$$

The characteristics of the graph are completely defined by the capacities $\{\phi, \psi\}$. In general, the data term and the smoothness function satisfy the properties:

$$\begin{aligned} &\phi(x_p) \geq 0, \quad \psi(x_p, x_q) \geq 0, \quad \psi(x_p, x_q) = \psi(x_q, x_p), \\ &\psi(x_{p+k}, x_{q+k}) = \psi(x_p, x_q), \qquad \forall p, q \in \mathcal{P}. \end{aligned} \tag{10.40}$$

Otherwise, the smoothness function may be semimetric or metric, which allows for different types of methods, such as the swap move and the expansion move algorithms.

For a given energy function, we may have more than one representation, which are all equivalent. Two functions $E_1(\mathbf{x})$ and $E_2(\mathbf{x})$ are *reparameterizations* if

$$E_1(\mathbf{x}) = E_2(\mathbf{x}), \quad \forall \mathbf{x}. \tag{10.41}$$

The smoothness function can be reparameterized as follows (Boykov and Kolmogorov 2004):

$$\begin{aligned} \psi_{pq}(x_p, x_q) &= \psi_{pq}(0,0) \\ &= (\psi_{pq}(1,0) - \psi_{pq}(0,0))x_p + (\psi_{pq}(1,0) - \psi_{pq}(0,0))x_q \\ &= (\psi_{pq}(1,0) + \psi_{pq}(0,1) - \psi_{pq}(0,0) - \psi_{pq}(1,1))(1 - x_p)x_q. \end{aligned} \tag{10.42}$$

The last term must satisfy

$$\psi_{pq}(1,0) + \psi_{pq}(0,1) - \psi_{pq}(0,0) - \psi_{pq}(1,1) \geq 0, \tag{10.43}$$

which is called *submodularity*. The energy function that satisfies the submodularity is called quadratic submodular pseudo-Boolean Function. All submodular QPBS are st-min-cut solvable.

There are some standard algorithms for *max-flow min-cut* problems (Cormen *et al.* 2001). The Ford–Furkerson algorithm is based on the DFS (depth first search)and runs in $O(E|f^*|)$, where E is the number of edges in the graph and $|f^*|$ is the maximum flow in the graph. The Edmond–Karp algorithm is based on the BFS (breadth first search) and runs in $O(VE^2)$ time. The Goldberg–Tarjan generic maximum-flow algorithm is based on *push-relabel* and has a simple implementation that runs in $O(V^2E)$ time. The relabel-to-front algorithm solves in $O(V^3)$ better for dense networks. After (Boykov *et al.* 2001), there appear numerous algorithms on graph cuts, such as tree recycling, flow recycling, cut recycling, and hierarchical methods (Wikipedia 2013). For this particular graph, there is an efficient algorithm, called *dual-search augmenting path algorithm* (Boykov and Kolmogorov 2004). It finds approximate shortest augmenting paths efficiently, shows high worst-case time complexity, and empirically outperforms other algorithms.

10.6 Swap Move Algorithm

The binary labels must be expanded to the multiple labels. The straightforward method is to try all the labels, using the binary labeling. However, searching L^{MN} space with the traditional algorithms is intractable. There are three methods: multiway cut, multilayer, and move algorithms. In the multiway cut, there are as many as terminals as labels. In the multilayer model, there are L layers of planes between the two terminals (Ishikawa 2003; Ishikawa and Geiger 1998; Roy and Cox 1998). In these algorithms, however, the multiple label problem is NP-complete (Dahlhaus *et al.* 1992; Greig *et al.* 1989). There are divide-and-conquer algorithms, called *move algorithm* (i.e. *swap move* and *move expansion*) (Boykov and Kolmogorov 2004; Boykov *et al.* 1998, 2001), that convert the labeling problems into binary labeling, having geometrical constraints. These algorithms solve the multiple label problem in polynomial time.

In this section, we consider the swap move algorithm. For a given pair of initial labels, $\{\alpha,\beta\}$ $(\alpha,\beta\in\mathcal{L})$, an image plane $\mathcal{P}$ is partitioned into P_α, P_β, and $P-P_{\alpha\beta}$ $(P_{\alpha\beta}=P_\alpha\cup P_\beta)$. Then, the energy function can be decomposed to

$$E(\mathbf{x}) = \underbrace{\sum_{\substack{p,q\notin P_{\alpha\beta}\\ q\in N_p}} E(x_p,x_q)}_{\text{constant}} + \underbrace{E_{\alpha\beta}(\mathbf{x}')}_{\text{variable}}, \tag{10.44}$$

where the first term belongs to $P-P_{\alpha\beta}$ and the second term belongs to $P_{\alpha\beta}$. The second term is again decomposed to

$$E_{\alpha\beta}(\mathbf{x}) = \underbrace{\sum_{\substack{p,q\in P_{\alpha\beta}\\ p,q\in N}} E(x_p,x_q)}_{\text{inside } P_{\alpha\beta}} + \underbrace{\sum_{\substack{p\in P_\alpha,q\in N_p\\ q\notin P_{\alpha\beta}}} E(x_p,x_q) + \sum_{\substack{p\in P_\beta,q\in N_p\\ q\notin P_{\alpha\beta}}} E(x_p,x_q)}_{\text{between } P_{\alpha\beta} \text{ and } P-P_{\alpha\beta}}.$$

This decomposition is possible because of the pairwise MRF. For higher-order MRF, the partition may be more complicated with additional pairs of neighbors. The complication of the energy computation occurs at the interface between two different partitions, where the edge weight depends on the labels of both ends. If we change α and β by switching labels in some nodes, $E_{\alpha\beta}$ changes but the first term in Equation (10.44) does not. Therefore, we can locally minimize $E_{\alpha\beta}$ only and thereby update the labels in $P_{\alpha\beta}$. As a result, G is updated and another pair of labels is chosen, and the same routine repeats.

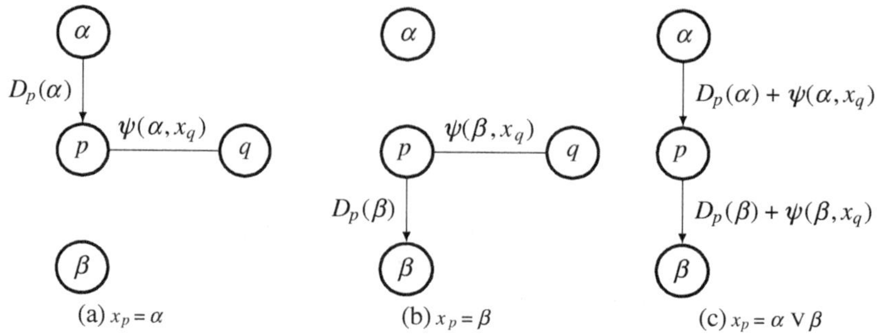

Figure 10.7 Node connections in a local flow graph: $p \in P_{\alpha\beta}$ and $q \notin P_{\alpha\beta}$

With respect to the data and smoothness terms, the energy function becomes

$$E_{\alpha\beta}(\mathbf{x}) = \underbrace{\sum_{\substack{p,q\in P_{\alpha\beta}\\ p,q\in N}} \psi_{pq}(x_p, x_q)}_{\text{inside } P_{\alpha\beta}} + \underbrace{\sum_{p\in P_{\alpha\beta}} \left\{ D(x_p) + \sum_{\substack{q\in N_p\\ q\notin P_{\alpha\beta}}} \psi_{pq}(x_p, x_q) \right\}}_{\text{between } P_{\alpha\beta} \text{ and } P - P_{\alpha\beta}}. \tag{10.45}$$

The second term in Equation (10.45) can be represented by the local connections in Figure 10.7(a) or (b). Choosing an edge connection is equivalent to a graph cut. If a graph cut contains both of the edges in Figure 10.7(a), it means the node is labeled with α. The same is true for Figure 10.7(b).

The two configurations can be combined to give Figure 10.7(c), ignoring the external node q. In the new graph, x_p can be readjusted locally, without concern for the external nodes. Our purpose is to build a graph $G_{\alpha\beta}$ for a pairwise MRF and readjust x_p using the min-cut algorithm to minimize Equation (10.45). In principle, this concept can be expanded to the higher-order MRF.

All the connection types are illustrated in Figure 10.8. In the graph shown, the set of vertices includes the terminals α and β, pixels $p \in P_\alpha$ with $x_p = \alpha$ and pixels $q \in P_\beta$ with $x_p = \beta$, where α and β are, respectively, source and sink. The set of pixels in $G_{\alpha\beta}$ is $P_{\alpha\beta} = P_\alpha \cup P_\beta$. Each pixel $p \in P_\alpha$ is connected

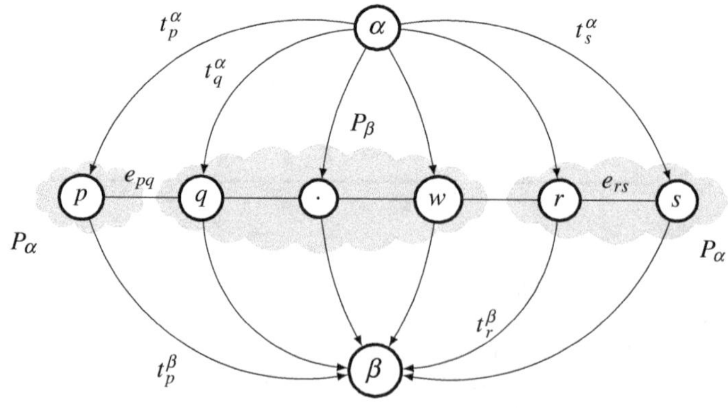

Figure 10.8 A subgraph $G_{\alpha\beta}$ in the swap move algorithm

Table 10.1 Edge weights in $G_{\alpha\beta}$

Edge	Weight	For
t_p^α	$\phi_p(\alpha) + \sum_{\substack{q\in\mathcal{N}_p \\ q\notin P_{\alpha\beta}}} \psi(\alpha, x_q)$	$p \in P_{\alpha\beta}$
t_p^β	$\phi_p(\beta) + \sum_{\substack{q\in\mathcal{N}_p \\ q\notin P_{\alpha\beta}}} \psi(\beta, x_q)$	$p \in P_{\alpha\beta}$
e_{pq}	$\psi(\alpha, \beta)$	$p, q \in \mathcal{N}, p, q \in P_{\alpha\beta}$

to the terminals by edges (t-link) t_p^α and t_p^β. Each pair of neighbor nodes is connected by edges (n-link) e_{pq}, where $\{p, q\} \subset P_{\alpha\beta}$ and $(p, q) \in \mathcal{N}$.

For $G_{\alpha\beta}$, Equation (10.45) becomes

$$E_{\alpha\beta}(\mathbf{x}) = \sum\nolimits_{p\in P_{\alpha\beta}} \left\{t_p^\alpha \delta(x_p - \alpha) + t_p^\beta \delta(x_p - \beta)\right\} + \sum\nolimits_{\substack{p,q\in P_{\alpha\beta} \\ q\in N_p}} \psi_{pq}(x_p, x_q)\delta(x_p - \alpha)\delta(x_q - \beta). \tag{10.46}$$

Here, $\delta(\cdot)$ is the Kronecker delta and the weights of the t-links are listed in Table 10.1. As already noted, the costs of t-links contain the edge weight between the nodes in $P_{\alpha\beta}$ and $P - P_{\alpha\beta}$. On those links, only the nodes on one side may change labels, while those on the other side have fixed labels.

Given $G_{\alpha\beta}$, the min-cut algorithm tries to minimize $E_{\alpha\beta}$ by cutting the edges in four different ways (Figure 10.9). To guarantee the graph cut, the smoothness function must be *semimetric*:

$$\psi(\alpha, \beta) \geq 0, \quad \psi(\alpha, \beta) = 0 \Longleftrightarrow \alpha = \beta. \tag{10.47}$$

One of the semimetric functions is the *truncated quadratic*, $\psi(\alpha, \beta) = \min(|\alpha - \beta|^2, K)$, where K is a constant. A stricter constraint is *metric*, which needs an additional requirement, specifically, *triangular inequality*:

$$\psi(\alpha, \beta) \leq \psi(\alpha, \gamma) + \psi(\gamma, \beta), \quad \forall \alpha, \beta, \gamma \in \mathcal{L}. \tag{10.48}$$

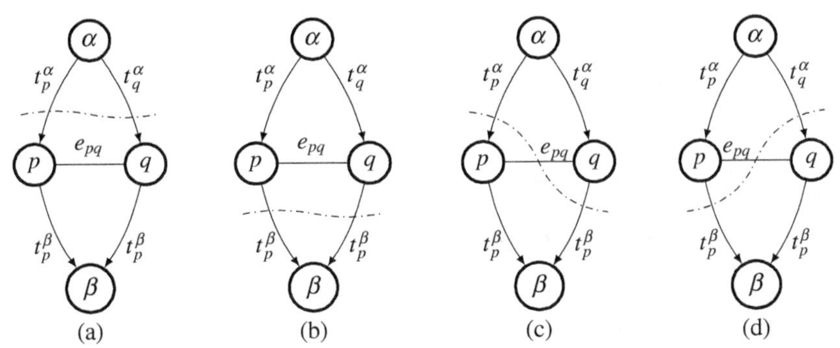

Figure 10.9 Legal edge cutting in $G_{\alpha\beta}$

The metric functions are the truncated absolute distance, $\psi(\alpha, \beta) = (|\alpha - \beta|, K)$, and the Potts model, $\psi(\alpha, \beta) = \delta(\alpha \neq \beta)$. Unlike the swap move, the expansion move requires these strict measures.

A cut, $C \subset E$, separates the terminals in the induced graph $G(C) = (V, E - C)$. No proper subset of C separates the terminals in $G(C)$. The cost of cut C, denoted $|C|$, is the sum of its edge weights. The min-cut problem is to find the minimum cost among all cuts separating the terminals. Any cut, C, on $G_{\alpha\beta}$, exactly severs one t-link for any $p \in P_{\alpha\beta}$ and thus labels the nodes:

$$x_p = \begin{cases} \alpha, & \forall t_p^\alpha \in C, p \in P_{\alpha\beta}, \\ \beta, & \forall t_p^\beta \in C, p \in P_{\alpha\beta}, \\ x_p, & \forall p \in P, p \notin P_{\alpha\beta}. \end{cases} \tag{10.49}$$

Under the semimetric condition, the min-cut algorithm guarantees that each node is connected to only one terminal. (In this graph notation, cutting the t-link actually means connecting, and cutting the n-link actually means separating.) As a result, cutting an n-link means that nodes on both sides have different labels. If the n-link is not cut, the connected nodes have the same labels.

If all the conditions are satisfied, it is shown that $|C| = E(x^C) - K$ for some constant K (Boykov *et al.* 2001):

$$\begin{aligned} E(x^C) &= \sum_{p \in P_{\alpha\beta}} \phi_p(x_p^C) + \sum_{\substack{p \in P_{\alpha\beta}, q \in N_p \\ q \notin P_{\alpha\beta}}} \psi(x_p^C, x_q) + \sum_{\substack{p,q \in P_{\alpha\beta} \\ p,q \in \mathcal{N}}} \psi(x_p^C, x_q^C) \\ &= \sum_{p \in P_{\alpha\beta}} \phi_p(x_p^C) + \sum_{\substack{p \wedge q \in P_{\alpha\beta} \\ p,q \in \mathcal{N}}} \psi(x_p^C, f_q^C), \end{aligned} \tag{10.50}$$

which is $E(x^C) - K$, where

$$K = \sum_{p \notin P_{\alpha\beta}} \phi_p(x_p) + \sum_{\substack{p,q \notin P_{\alpha\beta} \\ p,q \in \mathcal{N}}} \psi(x_p, x_q). \tag{10.51}$$

The swap move algorithm (Boykov *et al.* 2001) can be interpreted as follows.

Algorithm 10.4 (Swap move) *Compute in the following.*

Input: Φ.

Memory: G *and* $G_{\alpha\beta}$.

Parameter: Ψ.

Output: $\mathbf{x} = \{x_p | p \in \mathcal{P}\}$.

1. *Initialization:* $\mathbf{x}$.
2. *Cycle: until convergence for each pair of labels* $\{\alpha, \beta\} \subset \mathcal{L}$,
   (a) *Subgraph: build* $G_{\alpha\beta} \subset G$,
   (b) *Min-cut: solve* $\mathbf{x}_{\alpha\beta} = \arg\min_{\mathbf{x}} E_{\alpha\beta}(\mathbf{x})$ *by the min-cut algorithm,*
   (c) *Graph updation: update* G *with* $\mathbf{x}_{\alpha\beta}$.

Here, $G_{\alpha\beta}$ is given by Figure 10.8 and $E_{\alpha\beta}$ is given by Equation (10.50). This algorithm receives an input Φ and uses the memories to store G and $G_{\alpha\beta}$. The computation consists of a cycle for choosing the label pair and an iteration for computing min-cut. The swap move uses a new max-flow algorithm that has the best speed on these graphs over many modern algorithms; the running time is virtually linear in practice

(Boykov and Kolmogorov 2004). After each cycle, G is updated with the updated labels. For L labels, the label pairs are L^2. Therefore, the cycle is within the complexity range $O(L^2)$. The same label pairs may be tried more than once. The memory is proportional to the image size and labels, i.e. $O(MNL)$. Inside a cycle, we need more operations and memory for the binary min-cut.

The computational structure of this algorithm is sequential. In particular, building $G_{\alpha\beta}$ and using the min-cut algorithm require sequential and irregular operations.

10.7 Expansion Move Algorithm

The second of the move algorithms is the expansion move algorithm (Boykov *et al.* 2001). In a procedure analogous to that of the swap move, it converts the original problem into a series of binary labeling problems. The difference is that β is replaced with all the other labels. Therefore, the α region may expand to other regions.

An image plane $\mathcal{P}$ is partitioned into P_l, where $l \in \mathcal{L}$. The energy function can then be partitioned into

$$E(\mathbf{x}) = \underbrace{\sum_{\substack{p,q \in P_l \\ (p,q)\in N, l \in \mathcal{L}}} E(x_p, x_q)}_{\text{same label } E_s} + \underbrace{\sum_{\substack{p \in P_k, q \in P_l \\ (p,q)\in N, k\neq l \in \mathcal{L}}} E(x_p, x_q)}_{\text{different label } E_d}. \tag{10.52}$$

The first term is the energy for neighbor nodes that have the same labels, whereas the second term is the energy for neighbor nodes that have different labels. As in the swap move, this partition is possible because of the pairwise MRF. For higher-order MRF, two or more pairs of neighbors must be considered. Unlike the swap move, however, the expansion move deals with the entire plane.

For a label $\alpha \in \mathcal{L}$, the purpose is to change the labels of some nodes to α. Like the swap move, the complication occurs at the interface between two different partitions, where the edge weight depends on the labels of both ends. To make matters worse, one of the ends, but not both, may change to α. (In the swap move, a node in $\bar{P}_{\alpha\beta}$ is fixed in the label.) The effect of the label change is reflected on the edge weight, even though there is only one edge between a pair of neighbors. The expansion move algorithm solves this problem by introducing an auxiliary node between the nodes, creating two edges.

Between the partition, the energy can be either of those shown in Figures 10.10(a) and (b). The edge weight has two values depending on which node is changed to α. This can be remedied by introducing

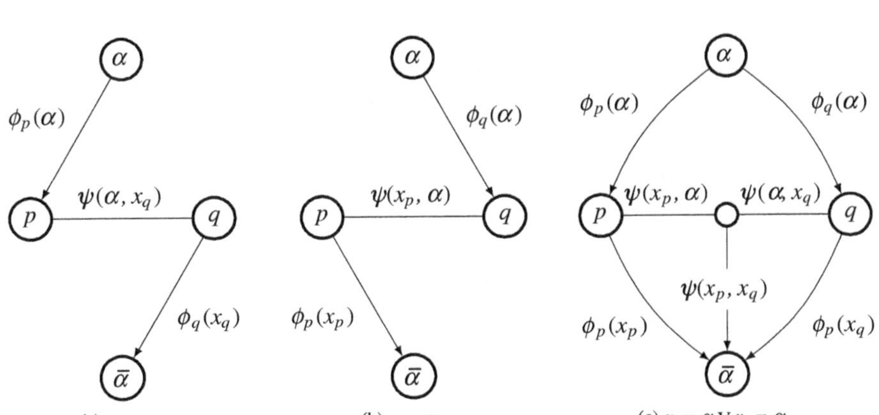

Figure 10.10 Node connections in a local flow graph: $p \in P_k$ and $q \in P_l$, where $k \neq l \in \mathcal{L}$

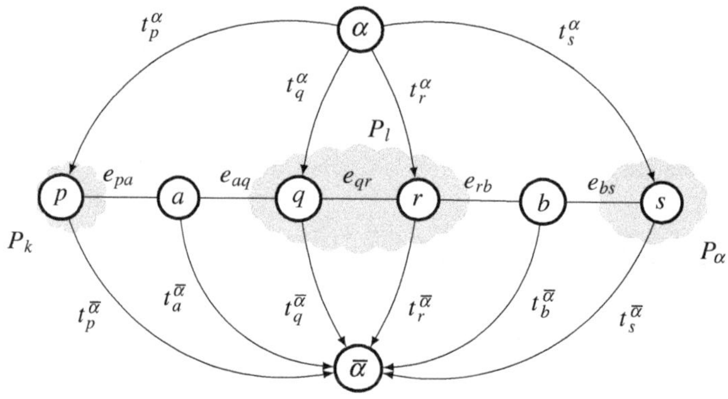

Figure 10.11 A graph G_α in the expansion move algorithm ($k \neq l \in \mathcal{L}$)

an auxiliary node a_{pq}, which is connected as shown in Figure 10.10(c). If the left edge is cut, $x_q = \alpha$, if the right edge is cut, $x_p = \alpha$, and if the t-link is cut, the labels remain unchanged. Other cuts must be prohibited by introducing the triangular inequality for the edge weights.

All the connection types are illustrated in the graph in Figure 10.11. In this graph, the set of vertices includes the terminals α and $\bar\alpha$, pixels $p \in P_k$ with $k \in \mathcal{P}$, where α and $\bar\alpha$ are, respectively, source and sink. Each pixel is connected to the terminals by edges (t-links) t_p^α and $t_p^{\bar\alpha}$. Each pair of neighbor nodes is connected by edges (n-links) e_{pq}, where $\{p,q\} \subset P_{\alpha\beta}$ and $(p,q) \in \mathcal{N}$. In addition, an auxiliary node a is created between every pair of neighbor nodes with different initial labels, that is $x_p \neq x_q$. The weights of the t-links and n-links are listed in Table 10.2. As already noted, the costs of t-links contain the edge weight between the nodes in $P_{\alpha\beta}$ and $P - P_{\alpha\beta}$. On those links, only the nodes on one side may change labels, while those on the other side have their labels fixed.

Given G_α, the min-cut algorithm tries to minimize E by cutting the edges in four different ways (Figure 10.12). To guarantee the graph cut, the smoothness function must be *metric*:

$$\begin{aligned}
&\psi(\alpha,\beta) \geq 0, \quad \psi(\alpha,\beta) = 0 \Longleftrightarrow \alpha = \beta, \\
&\psi(\alpha,\beta) \leq \psi(\alpha,\gamma) + \psi(\gamma,\beta), \quad \forall \alpha,\beta,\gamma \in \mathcal{L}.
\end{aligned} \tag{10.53}$$

Table 10.2 Edge weights in G_α

Edge	Weight	For
$t_p^{\bar\alpha}$	∞	$p \in P_\alpha$
$t_p^{\bar\alpha}$	$\phi_p(x_p)$	$p \notin P_\alpha$
t_p^α	$\phi_p(\alpha)$	$p \in P_\alpha$
e_{pa}	$\psi_{pq}(x_p,\alpha)$	
e_{aq}	$\psi_{pq}(\alpha,x_q)$	$p,q \in \mathcal{N}, x_p \neq x_q$
$t_a^{\bar\alpha}$	$\psi_{pq}(x_p,x_q)$	
e_{pq}	$\psi(x_p,\alpha)$	$p,q \in \mathcal{N}, x_p = x_q$

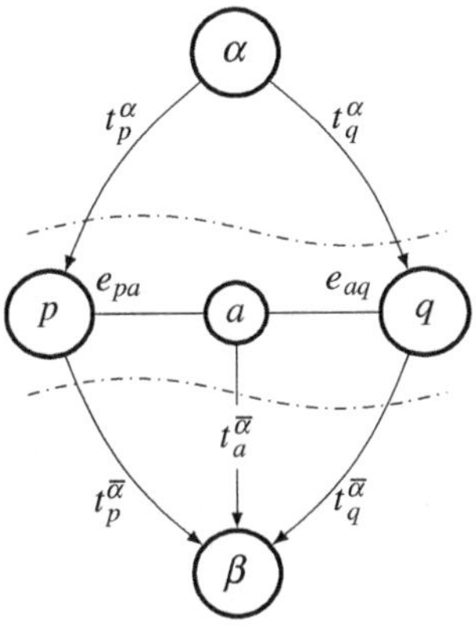

(a) two types

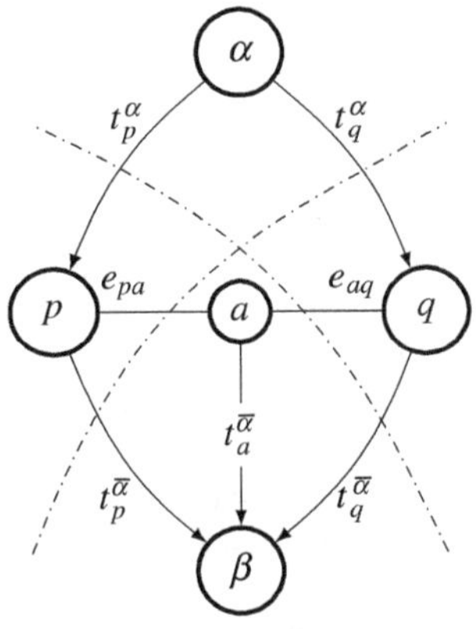

(b) two types

Figure 10.12 Legal edge cutting in G_α: four types

The metric functions are the truncated absolute distance, $\psi(\alpha, \beta) = (|\alpha - \beta|, K)$, and the Potts model, $\psi(\alpha, \beta) = \delta(\alpha \neq \beta)$. Unlike the swap move, the expansion move requires these strict measures.

A cut, $C \subset E$, separates the terminals in the induced graph $G(C) = (V, E - C)$. No proper subset of C separates the terminals in $G(C)$. The cost of cut C, denoted $|C|$, is the sum of its edge weights. The min-cut problem is to find the minimum cost among all cuts separating the terminals. Any cut, C, on $G_{\alpha\beta}$, severs exactly one t-link for any $p \in P_{\alpha\beta}$, and thus labels the nodes:

$$x_p = \begin{cases} \alpha, & \forall t_p^\alpha \in C, p \in P_{\alpha\beta}, \\ \beta, & \forall t_p^\beta \in C, p \in P_{\alpha\beta}, \\ x_p, & \forall p \in P, p \notin P_{\alpha\beta}. \end{cases} \tag{10.54}$$

Under the metric condition, the min-cut algorithm guarantees that each node is connected to only one terminal.

If all the conditions are satisfied, it is shown that $|C| = E(x^C)$ (Boykov *et al.* 2001):

$$\begin{aligned} |C| &= \sum_{p\in\mathcal{P}} \left|C \cap \{t_p^\alpha, t_p^{\bar\alpha}\}\right| + \sum_{\substack{p,q\in\mathcal{N}\\ x_p=x_q}} |C \cap e_{pq}| + \sum_{\substack{p,q\in\mathcal{N}\\ x_p\neq x_q}} |C \cap E_{pq}| \\ &= \sum_{p\in\mathcal{P}} \phi_p(x_p^C) + \sum_{p,q\in\mathcal{N}} \psi(x_p^C, f_q^C) = E(x^C), \end{aligned} \tag{10.55}$$

where $E_{pq} = \{e_{pa}, e_{aq}, t_a^{\bar\alpha}\}$.

In summary, the expansion move algorithm (Boykov *et al.* 2001) becomes as follows:

Algorithm 10.5 (Expansion move) *Compute in the following.*

Input: Φ.

Memory: G *and* G_α.

Parameter: Ψ.

Output: $\mathbf{x} = \{x_p | p \in \mathcal{P}\}$.

1. *Initialization:* $\mathbf{x}$.
2. *Cycle: until convergence for* $\alpha \in \mathcal{L}$,
   (a) *Subgraph: build* G_α,
   (b) *Min-cut: solve* $\mathbf{x} = \arg\min_{\mathbf{x}} E(\mathbf{x})$ *by the min-cut algorithm,*
   (c) *Graph updation: update G with* $\mathbf{x}$.

Here, G_α is given by Figure 10.11, and $E(\mathbf{x})$ is given by Equation (10.55). This algorithm receives an input Φ and uses the memories to store G and G_α. The computation consists of the cycle for choosing the label pair and the iteration for computing min-cut. Like the swap move, this algorithm uses a new max-flow algorithm that has the best speed on these graphs over many modern algorithms; the running time is virtually linear in practice (Boykov and Kolmogorov 2004). After each cycle, G is updated with the updated labels. For L labels, the cycle has a complexity of $O(L)$. The same label may be tried more than once. The memory is proportional to the image size and labels, that is $O(MNL)$. Inside a cycle, more operations and memory are needed for the binary min-cut. This algorithm is also highly sequential. In addition to the min-cut algorithm, the auxiliary node makes the algorithm highly irregular. (For more on graph cuts, refer to (Felzenszwalb and Zabih 2011; Middlebury 2013; Wikipedia 2013)).

The trouble with the expansion move algorithm is the irregular structure due to the auxiliary nodes, which may be placed unpredictably depending on the initial labeling. To make it regular, we may put auxiliary nodes in between pixels. The auxiliary nodes must function normally when they are in between different labels, otherwise they must function as dummy nodes. For this purpose, we have to define the links properly, so that the elementary cut can be used for this modified graph (Figure 10.13).

In Figure 12.13, $p \in P_k$, $s \in P_\alpha$, and $q, c, r \in P_l$. A normal auxiliary node a is inserted between two different partitions. In Pl, where all the nodes have the same labels, a new auxiliary node c is introduced.

Because of the additional auxiliary node, e_{pq} must be replaced with three edges, $e_q c$, $e_c r$, and $t_c^{\bar{\alpha}}$. We have to ensure that no two of the three edges are cut. This is the same metric constraint as a (Table 10.3). The circuit for these weights is highly regular. The status of the auxiliary nodes is determined by the initial labels, the three edges are determined by the neighbor labels.

The graph cut algorithms can be expanded to problems that are more general. The problems are expanded to the general non-submodular functions, which are NP-hard, but are commonly solved by a relaxation of the problem, such as roof dual relaxation (Rother *et al.* 2007, 2009). Further, because of the advantage inherent in QBFs, most difficult problems are converted to QBFs. For one thing, the higher-order pseudo-Boolean functions are converted to the quadratic pseudo-Boolean functions (Kohli

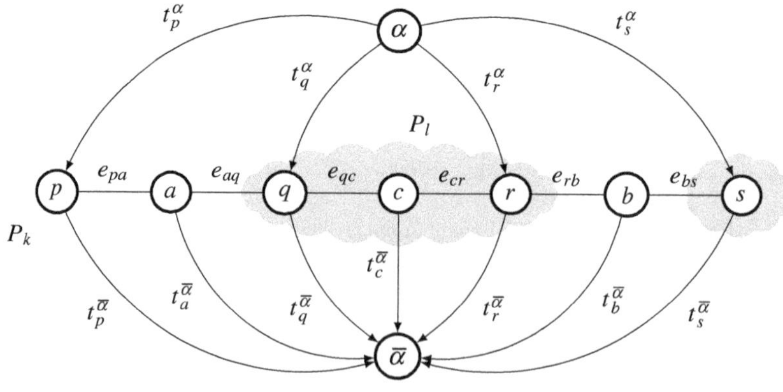

Figure 10.13 A graph G_α in the parallel expansion move algorithm ($k \neq l \in \mathcal{L}$)

Table 10.3 Edge weights in G_α

Edge	Weight	For
$t_p^{\bar{\alpha}}$	∞	$p \in P_\alpha$
$t_p^{\bar{\alpha}}$	$\phi_p(x_p)$	$p \notin P_\alpha$
t_p^{α}	$\phi_p(\alpha)$	$p \in P_\alpha$
e_{pa}	$\psi_{pq}(x_p, \alpha)$	
e_{aq}	$\psi_{pq}(\alpha, x_q)$	$p, q \in \mathcal{N}, x_p \neq x_q$
$t_a^{\bar{\alpha}}$	$\psi_{pq}(x_p, x_q)$	
e_{qc}	$\psi_{pq}(x_q, \alpha)$	
e_{cr}	$\psi_{pq}(\alpha, x_r)$	$p, q \in \mathcal{N}, x_p \neq x_q$
$t_c^{\bar{\alpha}}$	∞	

et al. 2007, 2008, 2009). In addition, the multi-label functions are converted to the pseudo-Boolean functions (Ishikawa 2003; Roy and Cox 1998; Schlesinger and Flach 2006; Veksler 2012).

The two general paradigms, BP and GC, are advancing toward better performance, complexity, and general problem-solving. Currently, BP is advancing towards faster computation and GC is moving towards a more general paradigm. Refer to (Tappen and Freeman 2003) for a comparison of the two methods, and (Middlebury 2013) for a listing in rated ranking of stereo matching and optical flow algorithms, which facilitates measurement of the status of BP and GC, as well as other algorithms.

Problems

10.1 [RE, DP, BP, and GC] For the $E(\mathbf{x}) = \sum_{p\in\mathcal{P}} \phi_p x_p + \sum_{p,q\in\mathcal{N}} \psi_{pq} x_p(1 - x_q)$, derive the formulation for relaxation. Here, assume that $x \in [0, 1]$.

10.2 [RE, DP, BP, and GC] For the $E(\mathbf{x}) = \sum_{p\in\mathcal{P}} \phi_p x_p + \sum_{p,q\in\mathcal{N}} \psi_{pq} x_p(1 - x_q)$, derive the formulation for DP. Assume that $x \in \{0, 1\}$.

10.3 [RE, DP, BP, and GC] For the $E(\mathbf{x}) = \sum_{p\in\mathcal{P}} \phi_p x_p + \sum_{p,q\in\mathcal{N}} \psi_{pq} x_p(1 - x_q)$, derive the formulation for sum-sum BP. Assume that $x \in \{0, 1\}$. Use the simple weight, $\psi_{pq} = 0$, between the same states and $\psi_{pq} = \psi$ between different states.

10.4 [RE, DP, BP, and GC] For the $E(\mathbf{x}) = \sum_{p\in\mathcal{P}} \phi_p x_p + \sum_{p,q\in\mathcal{N}} \psi_{pq} x_p(1 - x_q)$, derive the flow graph for GC. Assume that $x \in \{0, 1\}$. Use the simple weight, $\psi_{pq} = 0$, between the same states and $\psi_{pq} = \psi$ between different states.

10.5 [Flow graph] For the energy function, $E(x, y) = 2x + 5\bar{x} + 9y + 4\bar{y} + 2x\bar{y} + \bar{x}y$, find the reparameterizations (Kumar and Kohli 2008).

10.6 [Swap move] Explain why Equation (10.44) is an approximation.

10.7 [Swap move] Show that the truncated absolute distance is metric.

10.8 [Swap move] Show that the truncated quadratic is semimetric.

10.9 [Swap move] Prove that the truncated Potts model is metric.

10.10 [Swap move] Consider a rooted tree, T, whose edge lengths are non-negative and satisfy the following properties: (1) the edge lengths from any node to all of its children are the same; and

(2) the edge lengths along any path from the root to a leaf decrease by a factor of at least one. Given such a tree, an r-HST (Bartal 1998; Kumar and Koller 2009), $d(x, y)$ $(x, y \in T)$, is the sum of the edge lengths on the unique path between them. Show that it is a metric.

10.11 [RE, DP, BP, and GC] Compare the four algorithms, RE, DP, BP, and GC, for the same energy minimization, with the running time and space complexity.

References

Aho A, Hopcroft J, and Ullman J 1974 *The Design and Analysis of Computer Algorithms*. Addison-Wesley.

Bartal Y 1998 On approximating arbitrary metrics by tree metrics *Proceedings of the thirtieth annual ACM symposium on Theory of computing*, pp. 161–168 ACM.

Bernier O and Cheung-Mon-Chan P 2006 Real-time 3D articulated pose tracking using particle filtering and belief propagation on factor graphs. *BMVC*, pp. 27–36 Citeseer.

Bernier O, Cheung-Mon-Chan P, and Bouguet A 2009 Fast nonparametric belief propagation for real-time stereo articulated body tracking. *Computer Vision and Image Understanding* **113**(1), 29–47.

Boykov Y and Kolmogorov V 2004 An experimental comparison of min-cut/max-flow algorithms for energy minimization in vision. *IEEE Trans. Pattern Anal. Mach. Intell.* **26**(9), 1124–1137.

Boykov Y, Veksler O, and Zabih R 1998 Markov random fields with efficient approximations *International Conference on Computer Vision and Pattern Recognition (CVPR)*.

Boykov Y, Veksler O, and Zabih R 2001 Fast approximate energy minimization via graph cuts. *IEEE Trans. Pattern Anal. Mach. Intell.* **23**(11), 1222–1239.

Cormen T, Rivest CLR, and Stein C 2001 *Introduction to Algorithms* second edn. The MIT Press.

Dahlhaus E, Johnson DS, Papadimitriou CH, Seymour PD, and Yannakakis M 1992 The complexity of multiway cuts *Proceedings of the twenty-fourth annual ACM symposium on Theory of computing*, pp. 241–251 ACM.

Felzenszwalb P and Huttenlocher D 2004 Efficient belief propagation for early vision *Proceedings of the 2004 IEEE Computer Society Conference on Computer Vision and Pattern Recognition*, pp. I261–I268 number 1.

Felzenszwalb PF and Zabih R 2011 Dynamic programming and graph algorithms in computer vision. *IEEE Trans. Pattern Anal. Mach. Intell.* **33**(4), 721–740.

Grauer-Gray S, Kambhamettu C, and Palaniappan K 2008 GPU implementation of belief propagation using CUDA for cloud tracking and reconstruction *Pattern Recognition in Remote Sensing (PRRS 2008), 2008 IAPR Workshop on*, pp. 1–4 IEEE.

Greig D, Porteous B, and Seheult A 1989 Exact maximum a posteriori estimation for binary images. *Journal of the Royal Statistical Society Series B* **51**, 271–279.

Guo H and Hsu W 2002 A survey of algorithms for real-time Bayesian network inference *AAAI/KDD/UAI02 Joint Workshop on Real-Time Decision Support and Diagnosis Systems* Edmonton, Canada.

Ihler AT, Fisher III J, and Willsky AS 2005 Loopy belief propagation: Convergence and effects of message errors *Journal of Machine Learning Research*, pp. 905–936.

Ishikawa H 2003 Exact optimization for Markov random fields with convex priors. *IEEE Trans. Pattern Anal. Mach. Intell.* **25**(10), 1333–1336.

Ishikawa H and Geiger D 1998 Segmentation by grouping junctions *Computer Vision and Pattern Recognition, 1998. Proceedings. 1998 IEEE Computer Society Conference on*, pp. 125–131 IEEE.

Jeong H and Park S 2004 Generalized trellis stereo matching with systolic array *Lecture Notes in Computer Science*, vol. 3358, pp. 263–267.

Jordan MI 2004 Graphical models. *Statistical Science (Special Issue on Bayesian Statistics)* **19**(1), 140–155.

Knuth D 1997 *The Art of Computer Programming*. Addison-Wesley.

Kohli P, Kumar MP, and Torr PH 2007 P3 & beyond: Solving energies with higher order cliques *Computer Vision and Pattern Recognition, 2007. CVPR'07. IEEE Conference on*, pp. 1–8 IEEE.

Kohli P, Kumar MP, and Torr PH 2009 P3 & beyond: Move making algorithms for solving higher order functions. *IEEE Trans. Pattern Anal. Mach. Intell.* **31**(9), 1645–1656.

Kohli P, Ladicky L, and Torr P 2008 Graph cuts for minimizing robust higher order potentials *Proc. Int'l Conf. Computer Vision and Pattern Recognition*.

Kumar MP and Kohli P 2008 MAP estimation algorithms in computer vision – part ii (eccv8 tutorial) http://www.robots.ox.ac.uk/~pawan/eccv08.../Tutorial_Part2.ppt (accessed Dec. 3, 2013).

Kumar MP and Koller D 2009 Map estimation of semi-metric mrfs via hierarchical graph cuts *Proceedings of the Twenty-Fifth Conference on Uncertainty in Artificial Intelligence*, pp. 313–320 AUAI Press.

Middlebury U 2013 Middlebury computer vision pages http://vision.middlebury.edu/ (accessed May 3, 2013).

Park S and Jeong H 2008 Memory efficient iterative process on a two-dimensional first-order regular graph. *Optics Letters* **33**, 74–76.

Pearl J 1982 Reverend Bayes on inference engines: A distributed hierarchical approach In *AAAI* (ed. Waltz D), pp. 133–136. AAAI Press.

Rother C, Kohli P, Feng W, and Jia J 2009 Minimizing sparse higher order energy functions of discrete variables *Computer Vision and Pattern Recognition, 2009. CVPR 2009. IEEE Conference on*, pp. 1382–1389 IEEE.

Rother C, Kolmogorov V, Lempitsky V, and Szummer M 2007 Optimizing binary MRFs via extended roof duality *Computer Vision and Pattern Recognition, 2007. CVPR'07. IEEE Conference on*, pp. 1–8 IEEE.

Roy S and Cox IJ 1998 A maximum-flow formulation of the n-camera stereo correspondence problem *Computer Vision, 1998. Sixth International Conference on*, pp. 492–499 IEEE.

Schlesinger D and Flach B 2006 *Transforming an Arbitrary Minsum Problem into a Binary One*. TU, Fak. Informatik.

Sudderth EB, Ihler AT, Isard M, Freeman WT, and Willsky AS 2010 Nonparametric belief propagation. *Communications of the ACM* **53**(10), 95–103.

Sun J, Zheng NN, and Shum HY 2003 Stereo matching using belief propagation. *IEEE Trans. Pattern Anal. Mach. Intell.* **25**(7), 787–800.

Tappen M and Freeman W 2003 Comparison of graph cuts with belief propagation for stereo, using identical MRF parameters *Proceedings of Ninth IEEE International Computer Vision Conference*, pp. 900–906.

Veksler O 2012 Multi-label moves for MRFs with truncated convex priors. *International Journal of Computer Vision* **98**(1), 1–14.

Weiss Y 2014 *Belief Propagation (Synthesis Lectures on Computer Vision)*. Morgan & Claypool Publishers.

Wikipedia 2013 Graph cuts in computer vision http://en.wikipedia.org/wiki/Graph_cuts_in_computer_vision (accessed on Dec. 3, 2013).

Yang Q, Wang L, Yang R, Wang S, Liao M, and Nister D 2006 Real-time global stereo matching using hierarchical belief propagation. *BMVC*, vol. 6, pp. 989–998.

Yedidia J, Freeman W, and Weiss Y 2003 *Exploring Artificial Intelligence in the New Millennium* Morgan Kaufmann Publishers Inc. chapter Understanding Belief Propagation and Its Generalizations, pp. 239–269.

Yedidia JS, Freeman WT, and Weiss Y 2005 Constructing free-energy approximations and generalized Belief Propagation algorithms. *IEEE Trans. Information Theory* **51**(7), 2282–2312.

Part Four

Verilog Design

11

Relaxation for Stereo Matching

One of the classical approaches to the energy equation is the calculus of variations (Aubert and Kornprobst 2006; Courant and Hilbert 1953; Scherzer *et al.* 2008), especially functional minimization. In this paradigm, the solution is the function that minimizes the given energy function and, usually, the solution is in the form of an integro-differential equation. The resulting architecture, relaxation, belongs to the four major architectures: relaxation, DP, BP, and GC, which are used in general energy problems. Starting from an initial set of values, the concept underlying the relaxation architecture is the reuse of previous values to update new values recursively, so that the operation is a contraction mapping. The relaxation architecture is the poorest of the four but is often the starting point in designing a vision circuit because it is fast, simple, and general. It is particularly pertinent here because we are considering a machine for stereo matching that can be used in other vision problems after some modifications.

This chapter is a continuation of Chapter 8. In it, we learned how to interpret the energy equation in terms of the calculus of variation, how to derive the Euler–Lagrange equation, and how to derive relaxation equations from it. We will design the derived relaxation equation with the Verilog HDL (IEEE 2005), using the simulator FVSIM, introduced in Chapter 4: the relaxation equation is inherently frame-based computation. We will also design various components in the RE machine using efficient Verilog circuits.

11.1 Euler–Lagrange Equation

In this section, we will learn how to design the RE machine for stereo matching, step-by-step, from algorithm to architecture. The design method consists of three steps: energy function, relaxation equation, and the RE machine. First, we have to provide an energy function to model the functional disparity. We then have to derive a relaxation equation that gives a solution, after a certain number of iterations, from the energy function. In the final stage, we use the RE machine to realize the relaxation equation.

Numerous definitions for the stereo matching energy function exists, from a simple definition, consisting of data and smoothness terms only, to a complicated definition, consisting of highly nonlinear terms. We here begin with a basic form that consists of data and smoothness terms and which is differentiable. For a pair of stereo images, $\{(I^l(p), I^r(p))|p \in \mathcal{P}\}$ and the disparity, $d = \{d(p)|p \in \mathcal{P}\}$, we define the energy function:

$$E(d) = \sum_{(x,y)\in\mathcal{P}} (I^r(x,y) - I^l(x + d(x,y), y))^2 + \lambda|\nabla d(x,y)|^2, \tag{11.1}$$

Architectures for Computer Vision: From Algorithm to Chip with Verilog, First Edition. Hong Jeong.

Companion Website: www.wiley.com/go/jeong

where λ is a Lagrange multiplier. For the disparity function, the coordinates of the right image are adopted as reference. This equation holds for the epipolar constraint. A more advanced system may contain additional terms, which represent occlusion, geometry, and the local neighborhood relationship between two images, and further relax the epipolar constraint, modeling the problem as a general setting.

This energy function has the form

$$E(d) = \sum F(d, d_x, d_y), \tag{11.2}$$

where $F(\cdot)$ is a *functional* and d is the function we seek. The energy function can be differentiated to form the Euler–Lagrange equation (Courant and Hilbert 1953; Horn 1986; Wikipedia 2013a):

$$F_d - \partial_x F_{d_x} - \partial_y F_{d_y} = 0. \tag{11.3}$$

From Equation (11.1), the functional has the form

$$F(d, d_x, d_y) = (I^r(x,y) - I^l(x + d(x,y), y))^2 + \lambda\left(f_x^2 + f_y^2\right). \tag{11.4}$$

Substituting this into Equation (11.3) yields

$$\lambda \nabla^2 d = (I^l(x + d(x,y), y) - I^r(x,y))I_d^l(x + d(x,y), y). \tag{11.5}$$

Here, the smoothness term in the energy becomes the second derivative, which is in Laplacian form. As mentioned earlier, the Laplacian operator is related to diffusion, which has been intensively studied in computer vision as nonlinear scalar diffusion by Perona (Perona and Malik 1990) and nonlinear tensor diffusion by Weickert (Weickert 2008).

The same derivation can be applied to the optical flow, a generalization of the stereo matching that has the basic form of the energy function:

$$E(u,v) = \sum_{(x,y)\in\mathcal{P}} (I(x,y) - I(x+u, y+v))^2 + \lambda(|\nabla u|^2 + |\nabla v|^2). \tag{11.6}$$

The corresponding Euler–Lagrange equation is

$$\begin{aligned}\lambda(\nabla^2 u + \nabla^2 v) = &-(I(x,y,t) - I(x+u, y+v, t+1))(I_u(x+u, y+v, t+1) \\ &+ I_v(x+u, y+v, t+1)).\end{aligned} \tag{11.7}$$

Clearly, this equation must be decoupled so that the two variables can be obtained together. The consequent approximated equations are

$$\begin{cases} \lambda\nabla^2 u = -(I(x,y,t) - I(x+u, y+v, t+1))(I_u(x+u, y+v, t+1) \\ \qquad\quad + I_v(x+u, y+v, t+1)), \\ \lambda\nabla^2 v = -(I(x,y,t) - I(x+u, y+v, t+1))(I_u(x+u, y+v, t+1) \\ \qquad\quad + I_v(x+u, y+v, t+1)). \end{cases} \tag{11.8}$$

11.2 Discretization and Iteration

The next step is to convert the differential equation into a difference equation. For the first-order difference, ∂^f, there are three methods: forward, backward, and center difference (Fehrenbachy and Mirebeauz 2013; Weickert 2008):

$$\begin{cases} \partial_x^f f(x,y) = f(x+1,y) - f(x,y), & \partial_x^b f(x,y) = f(x,y) - f(x-1,y), \\ \partial_y^f f(x,y) = f(x,y+1) - f(x,y), & \partial_y^b f(x,y) = f(x,y) - f(x,y-1), \\ \partial_x^c f(x,y) = \frac{1}{2}(f(x+1,y) - f(x-1,y)), & \partial_y^c f(x,y) = \frac{1}{2}(f(x,y+1) - f(x,y-1)). \end{cases} \tag{11.9}$$

The templates for the difference operators are all 3×3 pixels. However, for the second derivative, the template size increases if the same types of differentials are used. We can instead alternate the derivatives with forward and backward and obtain a template size of the same size, that is 3×3 pixels (see the problems at the end of this chapter).

For the Laplacian, $\nabla^2 f(p) \approx \sum_{q \in N(p)} f(q) - |N| f(p)$, where $|N|$ denotes the neighborhood size. In addition, $I_d^r(x+d,y)$ must be discretized around $(x+d,y)$.

Once the equation is discretized, it must be transformed into iterative form. The iterative form can be obtained by partitioning the equation into two parts. For $ax = b$, we partition the coefficient a in such a way that $x = \alpha x + \beta b$, where α is a contraction mapping. This results in the successive-over-relaxation (SOR) equation $x^{(n+1)} = \alpha x^{(n)} + \beta b$. For further reading, refer to (Wikipedia 2013d; Young 1950).

Applying this method, we get the disparity equation,

$$\begin{aligned} d(x,y)^{(n+1)} &= \alpha d^{(n)} + \beta \bar{d}^{(n)}(x,y) + \gamma(I^r(x,y) - I^l(x + d^{(n)}(x,y),y)) \\ &\quad \times I_d^l(x + d^{(n)}(x,y),y), \end{aligned} \tag{11.10}$$

where $0 < \alpha, \beta, \gamma < 1$ (see the problems at the end of this chapter). The first term acts as a forcing term, which further represents the data term. The second term tends to make the disparity smooth. The third term determines the direction of the new solution. The mapping from RHS to LHS must be a contraction mapping, so that the solution converges to a fixed point, either local or global.

In hardware design, overflow and underflow must also be considered. To ensure that these conditions are met, each term must be within the number range. In addition, the intermediate result of the two terms must not deviate from the number range. This requirement needs some kind of saturation logic, in which the output is guaranteed within the number range. Incidentally, all the values in the disparity map must be well-defined, avoiding 'x' and 'z.' Otherwise, any part generating 'don't care' will propagate to all other parts of the map, spoiling the disparity map. For this reason, a strong guard must be provided for the computation and the boundary conditions.

For the optical flow, the discrete equation is

$$\begin{aligned} \lambda(\nabla^2 u + \nabla^2 v) &= (I(x+u,y+v,t+1) - I(x,y,t))(I_u(x+u,y+v,t+1) \\ &\quad + I_v(x+u,y+v,t+1)), \end{aligned} \tag{11.11}$$

and, after decoupling u and v, the relaxation equation becomes

$$\begin{cases} u^{(n+1)}(x,y) = \alpha u^{(n)} + \beta \bar{u}^{(n)}(x,y) + \gamma\{(I(x,y,t) - I(x+u,y+v,t+1)) \\ \qquad \times (I_u(x+u,y+v,t+1) + I_v(x+u,y+v,t+1))\}, \\ v^{(n+1)}(x,y) = \alpha v^{(n)} + \beta \bar{v}^{(n)}(x,y) + \gamma\{(I(x,y,t) - I(x+u,y+v,t+1)) \\ \qquad \times (I_u(x+u,y+v,t+1) + I_v(x+u,y+v,t+1))\}. \end{cases} \tag{11.12}$$

Direct differentiation is rarely used because of the noise. The image must be filtered with a smoothing filter such as Gaussian, $G(x, y; \sigma^2)$, with zero mean and σ^2 variance before differentiation. Otherwise, the filtering coefficients can be implemented in the relaxation:

$$J(x, y) = G(x, y; \sigma^2) * I(x, y). \tag{11.13}$$

The first-order differentiation then becomes

$$J_x(x, y) = G_x * I + G * I_x, \quad J_y(x, y) = G_y * I + G * I_y. \tag{11.14}$$

In Equations (11.10) and (11.12), I and its derivatives must be replaced with J and its derivatives. This results in a larger template weighted by the Gaussian coefficients. The design does not use any filtering, remaining faithful to the original relaxation.

11.3 Relaxation Algorithm for Stereo Matching

Let us now summarize the algorithm for Equation (11.10). We need two input images, and one memory plane to store the disparity. The computation proceeds in raster scan. As regards the neighborhoods, the most recently updated values are used, that is the Gauss–Seidel method. The disparity values are overwritten on the memory as soon as they are updated. For brevity, the algorithm is built only for the right reference mode.

Algorithm 11.1 (Relaxation algorithm for stereo matching) *Given the image pair, (I^l, I^r), determine the disparity map, D, with L iterations.*

Input: $\{I^l(x, y), I^r(x, y) | (x, y) \in \mathcal{P}\}$.
Memory: $D = \{d(x, y) | (x, y) \in \mathcal{P}, \}$.

1. *Initialization: Initialize the disparity map, D.*
2. *for* $l = 0, 1, \dots, L - 1$,
3. *for* $y = 0, 1, \dots, M - 1$,
4. *for* $x = 0, 1, \dots, N - 1$,

$$\begin{aligned} d(x, y) \leftarrow{} & \alpha d(x, y) + \beta \bar{d}(x, y) \\ & + \gamma(I^r(x, y) - I^l(x + d(x, y), y)) I^l_d(x + d(x, y), y). \end{aligned}$$

Output: D.

The disparity map can be initialized in many different ways. Because the final solution depends on the initial point, preparing a good initial value is crucial. The iteration is repeated after a fixed period of time instead of in accordance with a convergence test. Appropriate constants must also be provided so that the mapping converges eventually. In actual computation, all the computations must be kept within a specific number range. In addition, no disparity value is allowed to be uncertain with 'x' and 'z' during the computation.

This algorithm is based on the Gauss–Seidel method. For the Jacobi method, we can use two planes of the disparity maps and alternate the input and the output between them. For fast convergence, other

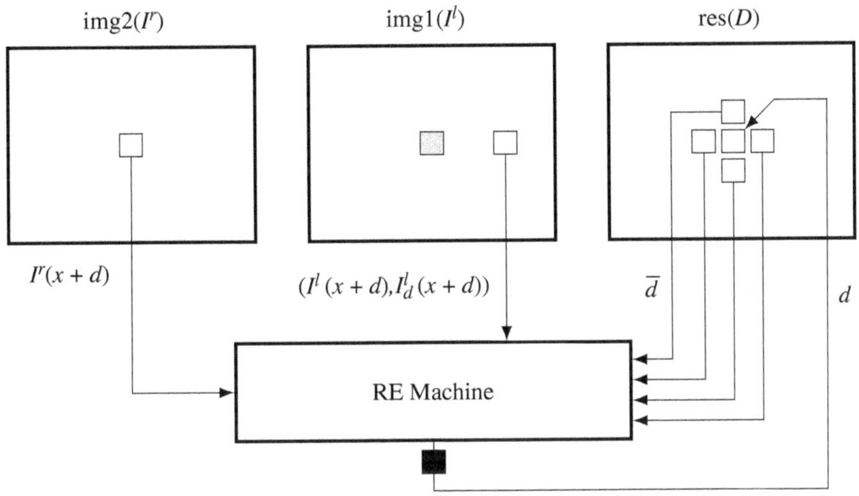

Figure 11.1 The flow of computation in the RE machine. Right reference mode. The shaded square is the current position. The RE machine is terminated by a pipelining register

techniques such as *multigrid* or adaptive *adaptive multigrid* (Ilyevsky 2010; Wikipedia 2013b) may be utilized.

11.4 Relaxation Machine

Now we will design the RE machine that conceptually executes Algorithm 11.1. Between the two simulators, LSIM and FSIM, we adopt FSIM because frame processing is required (Figure 11.1).

For legibility reasons, only the circuit for the right reference system is shown. For the left reference system, the role of the images must be switched. The top three elements are the memories (I^r, I^l) for the images, and D for the disparity map. They are the inputs and state memories of the RE machine. The other constructs are the sequential and combinational circuits, where the actual operations are executed. At a certain time, the memories are all fixed and the values in the combination circuits are actively being decided. Blocking the output port of the RE machine and connecting the combinational paths between the state memory and the blocking registers result in the system becoming a finite state machine (specifically, a Mealy machine), as a whole.

Within a given period, all the computation is done for $I^r(x, y)$ in the right image plane (in right reference mode). The conjugate point $I^l(x + d(x, y))$ is determined by reading the disparity at this pixel from the disparity map, D. The conjugate pairs and the neighborhoods around $d(x, y)$ are used to determine the new disparity $d(x, y)$, which is overwritten to the disparity map, D. In the next period, the same computation is executed for the next pixel. This computation is repeated for the frame until the disparity values converge. (Actually, in a simple design, the number of iterations is predetermined.)

11.5 Overall System

Keeping Figure 11.1 in mind, let us begin to design the Verilog HDL code. The header contains the parameters that characterize the images and the RE algorithm.

Listing 11.1 The header: head.v (1/9)

```
//file name
`define file_name "bear11394"                    //BMP file name

//image parameters
`define WIDTH      113                            //image width
`define HEIGHT     94                             //image height

//memory parameters
`define DATA_BITS  8                              //word size
`define ADDR_BITS  15                             //max image size

//reference modes
`define LEFT                                      //left and right mode

//RE parameters (log LAB\_DIM < LAB\_BITS)
`define LAB_BITS   8                              //disparity bits
`define LAB_DIM    32                             //disparity number
`define ITER       10                             //iteration number
```

The filename is used for the IO part of the simulator to open and read the image files in the RAM, imitating the camera output. The image size, defined by the height and the width, $M \times N$, is used in the specifying of the required resources throughout the circuit. The memory parameters specify the word length and the address range for the contents in the RAM. The image data is ordinarily stored in bytes – three bytes for RGB channels. These parameters are also used to define the arrays, `img1`, `img2`, and `res`, storing two images and a disparity map.

The next parameter is the key, `LEFT`, indicating the left or right reference mode. The window and the scan directions differ according to this parameter. The computation order is simply the raster scan direction in the right mode and the opposite of the raster scan direction in the left mode.

The RE parameters specify the word length of the disparity and also its maximum number. For a number of bits, B, the maximum disparity level, D, must be $D \leq 2^B$. Finally, the number of iterations is specified by `ITER`.

The template for the main part of the code is as follows.

Listing 11.2 The framework: `processor.v` (2/9)

```
`timescale 1ns / 1ps
`include "head.v"

module processor(                                        //RE processor
   input clock, reset,
   output reg [`ADDR_BITS - 1:0] i_raddr, r_raddr, r_waddr,//address bus
```

```
input ['DATA_BITS - 1:0] i_rdata1, i_rdata2, r_rdata, //data bus
output reg ['DATA_BITS - 1:0] r_wdata,          //data bus
output reg r_wen                                //write enable
);

//working arrays: image 1, image 2, and disparity map
reg ['DATA_BITS - 1:0] img1 [0: 'HEIGHT - 1][0: 3*'WIDTH - 1];//1st
reg ['DATA_BITS - 1:0] img2 [0: 'HEIGHT - 1][0: 3*'WIDTH - 1];//2nd
reg ['DATA_BITS - 1:0] res    [0: 'HEIGHT - 1][0: 3*'WIDTH - 1];//map

//variables
reg ['ADDR_BITS - 1:0]  idx, idx1,idx2;        //variables
reg [9:0] row, col, x, y, xx, yy, wx, wy;      //variables
reg [7:0] iter;
reg do_load, do_display, do_read, do_write;   //for control
reg [2:0] state, lstate;

//reading (IMAGE -> img)
always @ (posedge clock) begin: READING        //reading block
end

//writing (res -> RESULT)
always @(posedge clock) begin: WRITING         //writing block
end

//main
always @ (posedge clock) begin
   if (reset) begin
      state <= 0;
      x <= 0;
      y <= 0;
   end
   else begin
      case (state)
      0: begin: INITIALIZATION                 //initialization
      end
      1: begin: UPDATION                       //relaxation
         if (iter < 'ITER) begin               //iteration
            case (lstate)
            0: begin: DISPARITY                //updation
            1: begin: STORE                    //store the disparity map
            end
            default: lstate <= 0;
            endcase
         end
```

```
            else begin
               iter <= 0;
               state <= 0;
            end
         end
         default: state <= 0;
         endcase
      end
   end //always

   //neighbor disparity values

   //image and differential

   //the data term

   //functions

endmodule
```

The code has three parts: sequential circuits, combinational circuits, and functions. The sequential part consists of three concurrent parts: reading, writing, and updation. The reading and writing blocks are the IP interfaces to the external RAMs, RAM1, RAM2, and RES, and the internal buffers, `img1`, `img2`, and `res`. The updation block writes the updated disparity to the disparity map. In this code, the disparity map is encoded as an unpacked array, `res`. However, the data vectors, `data`, are all coded in packed format for computational simplicity. While the sequential part works for each clock tick, the combinational part works between the clock period, reading the data from the registers and stabilizing the result, so that in the next clock tick the result can be stored in the registers. The combinational circuits have three parts: a circuit that builds the conjugate pairs, one that builds the data term, and another that determines the final disparity. The combinational circuits are aided by various functions, which all operate in the same simulation time.

The complexity of the code is as a result of the boundary conditions and the two modes. The related variables are the neighbor disparities, `d0, d1, d2, d3`, and the image values, `Ir, Il, dI`. The boundaries used in this code are mirror images. Other definitions are also possible (see the problems at the end of this chapter).

The components filling this template are explained in the ensuing sections.

11.6 IO Circuit

Two of the sequential circuits are for reading and writing. The image data are located in the external RAMs, outside of the main processor, and must be accessed periodically. The circuit can be designed as follows:

Listing 11.3 The IO circuit (3/9)

```
//reading (IMAGE -> img)
always @ (posedge clock) begin: READING          //reading block
   if (reset) begin                              //initialize
      row <= 0;
      col <= 0;
      do_load <= 1;
   end
   else begin                                    //read RAM into buffers
      do_load <= 0;
      if (row < 'HEIGHT) begin                   //for a row
         if (col < 3 * 'WIDTH + 2) begin         //for a column
            i_raddr <= 3 * 'WIDTH * row + col;   //pixel address

            img1[row][idx1] <= i_rdata1;         //load 1st image
            img2[row][idx1] <= i_rdata2;         //load 2nd image
            //res [row][idx1] <= i_rdata1;

            idx1 <= idx;                         //delay 2
            idx <= col;                          //delay 1
            col <= col + 1;                      //next column
         end else begin
            col <= 0;
            row <= row + 1;                      //next row
         end
      end else begin
         row <= 0;
         do_load <= 1;
      end //else
   end
end

//writing (res -> RESULT)
always @(posedge clock) begin: WRITING           //writing block
   if (reset) begin
      xxx <= 0;
      yyy <= 0;
      do_display <= 0;
   end
   else begin
      if (yyy < 'HEIGHT) begin
         do_display <= 0;
         if (xxx < 3 * 'WIDTH) begin
            r_wdata <= res[yyy][xxx];            //data
```

```
            r_waddr <= 3*`WIDTH * yyy + xxx;     //address
            r_wen <= 1;                          //write enable
            xxx <= xxx + 1;                      //next
         end
         else begin
            xxx <= 0;
            yyy <= yyy + 1;
         end
      end
      else begin
         yyy <= 0;
         do_display <= 1;
      end
   end
end
```

The purpose of the reading part is to read `RAM1`, `RAM2`, and `RES` into the internal buffers, `img1`, `img2`, and `res`. The processor reads the images (I^l, I^r) and the disparity D from the buffers, processes them to determine the updated disparity, and writes the result into `res`. To match the address with the data, some small delays must be introduced into the address bus because a mismatch exists between the incoming data and the current address: the current data corresponds to the address two clocks ahead. These problems can be solved by the delay buffers `idx` and `idx1` and the two clock delays in the address loop.

Another concurrent always block is the writing block. The purpose of this block is to write the disparity map stored in the buffer, `res`, into the external RAM, `RESULT`, in RGB format so that the simulator can display the disparity map in BMP format. The flags `do_load` and `do_display` are used to control the simulator and thus are not part of the synthesis. Note that the counters representing pixel positions, (row, col), (x, y), (xx, yy), and (xxx, yyy) are all differently redefined in different always blocks, to avoid driving a net variable with multiple drivers.

For simplicity, the IO circuit can be bypassed for simulation purposes by the unsynthesizable codes in `io.v` (see the problems in Chapter 4).

The remaining circuit can be considered a system that receives `img1`, `img2`, and `res` as inputs and returns an updated `res` as output.

11.7 Updation Circuit

The computation is based on window processing. There must be a circuit that relocates the window around the image plane. The constraint is that as a consequence of window movement, the entire image plane must be completely scanned, without producing empty spaces. In actuality, the space to be scanned is (x, y, l), where $(x, y) \in \mathcal{P}$ and $l \in [0, L-1]$ for some maximum iteration L. There is an algorithm called FBP (Jeong and Park 2004; Park and Jeong 2008) that can scan in the iteration index. For hierarchical BP (Yang *et al.* 2006), sampling in this space must be made in the pyramid form. The order of visits may be deterministic or random. In this chapter, we follow the usual approach: scanning the image plane in raster scan manner.

Listing 11.4 The updation circuit (4/9)

```
always @ (posedge clock) begin
   if (reset) begin
      state <= 0;
      x <= 0;
      y <= 0;
   end
   else begin
      case (state)
      0: begin: INITIALIZATION //initialize the disparity
         if (y < `HEIGHT) begin: LAB_INT
            if (x < `WIDTH) begin
               x <= x + 1;                       //for the next column
               `ifdef LEFT                       //from right to left
               res[y][3*(`WIDTH-1-x)] <= argmin(data);
               `else                             //from left to right
               res[y][3*x] <= argmin(data);
               `endif
            end
            else begin
               x <= 0;
               y <= y + 1;                       //for the next row
            end
         end
         else begin
            state <= 1;                          //the next state
            lstate <= 0;                         //the next local state
            y <= 0;                              //reset the counter
            iter <= 0;                           //the iteration counter
         end
      end
      1: begin: UPDATION                         //relaxation
         if (iter < `ITER) begin                 //iteration
            case (lstate)
            0: begin: DISPARITY                  //updation
               if (y < `HEIGHT) begin            //for each row
                  if (x < `WIDTH) begin          //for each column
                     x <= x + 1;                 //next column
                     `ifdef LEFT                 //from right to left
                     res[y][3*(`WIDTH-1-x)] <=  sat(argmin(data)
                         + (av4(d0,d1,d2,d3)>>1) + sgn((Ir - Il)* dI ));
                     `else                       //from left to right
                     res[y][3*x] <=  sat(argmin(data)
                         + (av4(d0,d1,d2,d3)>>1) + sgn((Ir - Il) * dI));
```

```
                    `endif
                 end
                 else begin
                    x <= 0;                          //reset the column
                    y <= y + 1;                      //next row
                 end
              end
              else begin
                 lstate <= 1;                        //next local state
                 y <= 0;                             //reset the row
                 xx <= 0;                            //next state counter
                 yy <= 0;                            //next state counter
              end
           end
           1: begin: STORE                           //store disparity map
              if (yy < `HEIGHT) begin                //for each row
                 if (xx < `WIDTH) begin              //for each column
                    xx <= xx + 1;                    //next column
                    res[yy][3*xx+1] <= res[yy][3*xx]; //2nd channel
                    res[yy][3*xx+2] <= res[yy][3*xx]; //3rd channel

                 end
                 else begin
                    xx <= 0;                         //reset the column
                    yy <= yy + 1;                    //next row
                 end
              end
              else begin
                 lstate <= 0;                        //reset the local state
                 yy <= 0;                            //reset the row
                 iter <= iter + 1;                   //next iteration
              end
           end
           default: lstate <= 0;
           endcase
        end
        else begin
           iter <= 0;                                //reset the iteration
           state <= 0;                               //reset the state
        end
     end
     default: state <= 0;
     endcase
  end
end //always
```

In iteration notation, the circuit spans the $M \times N \times L \times m \times n$ space in (l, y, x) manner, where x is changed most rapidly and l is changed most slowly. Other iteration methods are also possible. For the right mode, the circuit scans from left to right, while for the left mode, it scans from right to left. The absolute positions of the pixels are $(I^r(y,x), I^l(y, x + d(x,y)))$ for the right mode and $(I^l(y, \texttt{WIDTH} - 1 - x), I^r(y, \texttt{WIDTH} - 1 - (x + d(x,y))))$ for the left mode.

In the updation block, the new disparity is determined by the combination of three terms: data, neighborhood, and differential. The data term functions as a forcing term, preventing the solution from deviating too much from this value. To balance the dynamic range, the neighborhood average is reduced by half. Next in line is the differential, which guides the solution in the direction it must move. This differential is determined by the difference of the conjugate pairs and the slope of the matching image. The dynamic range of the disparity is very small, and so a large differential may result in an overflow or an underflow. To prevent such cases, we may take only the unit direction of the differential vector. Addition of the three terms again must be protected by the saturation function, which limits the number within the maximum disparity.

11.8 Circuit for the Data Term

From here onwards, all the computations are realized with combinational circuits, unless otherwise stated. The data vector, $d^{(n)}$, in Equation (11.9), is the major source of the belief message, driven by the input images, and thus must be provided accurately.

The circuit that provides this vector is depicted in Figure 11.2. As shown in the figure, the sources of the data vector are the two image frames. The location of the current pixel is indicated by a position in a frame. A specific field, d, of the data vector is constructed by the data read from the two images. Therefore, a data vector can be constructed concurrently for all the pixels of the two images on the same epipolar line. All the elements of the vector are determined by the combinational circuits, as follows.

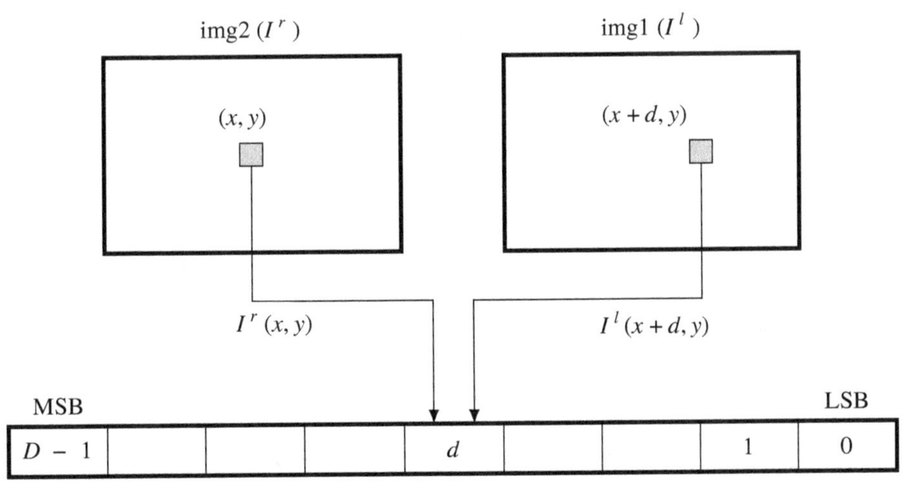

Figure 11.2 Building the data vector, $d(x, y)$. The vector is generated by the combinational circuits for all elements in parallel (right reference mode)

The data vector is encoded in a packed array of BD bits, because it must be often accessed as one complete set of data. In the right reference system, the data term is

$$d(x,y) = \{d_{D-1}, \dots, d_1, d_0\}, \tag{11.15}$$

where d_{D-1} is the MSB and d_0 is the LSB. Each element is a B bit number with

$$d_d = \min\left\{ \sum_{k\in\{R,G,B\}} \left|I_k^r(x,y) - I_k^l(x+d,y)\right|, 2^B - 1 \right\},$$
$$\forall d \in [0, D-1]. \tag{11.16}$$

Here, the data value is limited within B bit word length, preventing overflow.

For the left reference system, the data is defined as

$$d_d = \min\left\{ \sum_{k\in\{R,G,B\}} \left|I_k^l(N-1-x,y) - I_k^r(N-1-(x+d),y)\right|, 2^B - 1 \right\},$$
$$\forall d \in [0, D-1]. \tag{11.17}$$

Advanced algorithms may use different schemes to compute the data term, for example with better distance measure and perhaps an occlusion indicator. This code is the basic template and contains only the most basic features.

Keeping in mind the concept, we can code the algorithm as follows. Because there are numerous identical circuits, the Verilog generate construct is used. The code also contains the Verilog compiler directive to switch the design between the two reference modes.

Listing 11.5 The data term: `processor.v` (5/9)

```
//the data term
wire ['LAB_BITS * 'LAB_DIM - 1:0] data;
genvar vary;

for (vary = 0; vary < 'LAB_DIM; vary = vary + 1) begin: DATA_TERM
'ifdef LEFT                                    //left mode
   assign data['LAB_BITS * vary +: 'LAB_BITS] = (x+vary < 'WIDTH)?
      tadd(tadd(adistance(img1[y][3*('WIDTH-1-x)],
                img2[y][3*('WIDTH-1-(x+vary))]),
                adistance(img1[y][3*('WIDTH-1-x)+1],
                img2[y][3*('WIDTH-1-(x+vary))+1])),
                adistance(img1[y][3*('WIDTH-1-x)+2],
                img2[y][3*('WIDTH-1-(x+vary))+2])):
      tadd(tadd(adistance(img2[y][0],img1[y][3*vary]),
                adistance(img2[y][1],img1[y][3*vary + 1])),
```

```
                adistance(img2[y][2],img1[y][3*vary + 2]));
`else                                              //right mode
  assign data[`LAB_BITS * vary +: `LAB_BITS] = (x+vary < `WIDTH)?
     tadd(tadd(adistance(img2[y][3*x],   img1[y][3*(x+vary)]),
                adistance(img2[y][3*x+1],img1[y][3*(x+vary)+1])),
                adistance(img2[y][3*x+2],img1[y][3*(x+vary)+2])):
     tadd(tadd(adistance(img2[y][3*x],
                img1[y][3*(2*(`WIDTH-1)-(x+vary))]),
                adistance(img2[y][3*x+1],
                img1[y][3*(2*(`WIDTH-1)-(x+vary))+1])),
                adistance(img2[y][3*x+2],
                img1[y][3*(2*(`WIDTH-1)-(x+vary))+2]));
`endif
end
```

The circuits are compiled separately according to the two types of reference systems. Each reference system consists of D continuous assignments, with each assignment determining a B bit field in the data vector. The circuits are generated by the Verilog HDL generate construct. Consequently, this part of the circuit consists of D combinational circuits.

Two functions are used in the expression: `adistance` and `tadd`. The `adistance` function is an absolute function that returns the absolute distance between two arguments. The `tadd` function is an addition function that accounts for saturation math. The upper bound of the truncation is defined by $2^B - 1$. The functions, together with other functions, will be discussed together in a later section. The deciding minimum argument may be enhanced by introducing weights such as the truncated linear or Potts model.

The code is somewhat lengthy because of the boundary conditions. The mirror image is used around the boundary.

11.9 Circuit for the Differential

The next term related to the image inputs is the differential term. When the mirror image is adopted in the boundary values, the code becomes as follows.

Listing 11.6 The data term: `processor.v` (6/9)

```
//image and differential
`ifdef LEFT
assign Il = av3(img1[y][3*(`WIDTH-1-x)],img1[y][3*(`WIDTH-1-x)+1],
         img1[y][3*(`WIDTH-1-x)+2]);
assign Ir = (x + d < `WIDTH)? //Problem!
         av3(img2[y][3*(`WIDTH-1-(x+d))],
         img2[y][3*(`WIDTH-1-(x+d))+1],img2[y][3*(`WIDTH-1-(x+d))+2]):
```

```
        av3(img2[y][3*(('WIDTH - 1) - (x - d))],
        img2[y][3*(('WIDTH - 1) - (x - d))+1],
        img2[y][3*(('WIDTH - 1) - (x - d))]+2);
assign dI = (x + d < 'WIDTH - 1)?
        Ir - av3(img2[y][3*('WIDTH-1-(x+d+1))],
        img2[y][3*('WIDTH-1-(x+d+1))+1],
        img2[y][3*('WIDTH-1-(x+d+1))+2]):
        av3(img2[y][3*(('WIDTH-1)-(x-d))],
        img2[y][3*(('WIDTH-1)-(x-d))+1],
        img2[y][3*(('WIDTH-1)-(x-d))+2])-
        av3(img2[y][3*(('WIDTH-1)-(x-d-1))],
        img2[y][3*(('WIDTH-1)-(x-d-1))+1],
        img2[y][3*(('WIDTH-1)-(x-d-1))+2]);

'else
assign Ir = av3(img2[y][3*x],img2[y][3*x+1],img2[y][3*x+2]);
assign Il = (x + d < 'WIDTH)?
        av3(img1[y][3*(x+d)],img1[y][3*(x+d)+1],img1[y][3*(x+d)+2]):
        av3(img1[y][3*(2*('WIDTH - 1) - (x + d))],
        img1[y][3*(2*('WIDTH - 1) - (x + d))+1],
        img1[y][3*(2*('WIDTH - 1) - (x + d))]+2);
assign dI = (x + d < 'WIDTH - 1)?
        av3(img1[y][3*(x+d+1)],img1[y][3*(x+d+1)+1],
        img1[y][3*(x+d+1)+2])-Il:
        av3(img1[y][3*(2*('WIDTH-1)-(x+d))],
        img1[y][3*(2*('WIDTH-1)-(x+d))+1],
        img2[y][3*(2*('WIDTH-1)-(x+d))+2])-
        av3(img1[y][3*(2*('WIDTH-1)-(x+d+1))],
        img1[y][3*(2*('WIDTH-1)-(x+d+1))+1],
        img1[y][3*(2*('WIDTH-1)-(x+d+1))+2]);
'endif
```

For the right mode, the corresponding pixel on the left image is offset by d, and thus may be located outside of the image frame. The conditionals check this condition and add mirrored values for such pixels. For the differential, the description is much more complicated because both terms are offset by d and $d + 1$, which may deviate from the image boundary. A similar situation occurs for the left mode system, but in opposite coordinates.

11.10 Circuit for the Neighborhood

The input disparity vector must be constructed in parallel with the data vector because they will be combined immediately afterwards. The circuit consists of only five continuous assignments.

Listing 11.7 The neighborhood: `processor.v` (7/9)

```
//neighbor disparity values
wire signed [15:0] d,d0,d1,d2,d3,Ir,Il;
wire signed [15:0] dI;
`ifdef LEFT
assign d  = res[y][3*(`WIDTH-1-x)];
assign d0 = (x > 0)? res[y][3*(`WIDTH-1-(x-1))]:
          res[y][3*((`WIDTH-1)-(x+1))];
assign d1 = (y < `HEIGHT - 1)? res[y+1][3*(`WIDTH-1-x)]:
          res[2*(`HEIGHT - 1)-(y+1)][3*(`WIDTH-1-x)];
assign d2 = (x < `WIDTH - 1)? res[y][3*(`WIDTH - 1 - (x+1))]:
          res[y][3*(`WIDTH -  1 - (x-1))];
assign d3 = (y > 0)? res[y-1][3*(`WIDTH-1-x)]:
          res[y+1][3*(`WIDTH-1-x)];
`else
assign d  = res[y][3*x];
assign d0 = (x < `WIDTH - 1)? res[y][3*(x+1)]:
          res[y][3*(2*(`WIDTH-1)-(x+1))];
assign d1 = (y < `HEIGHT - 1)? res[y+1][3*x]:
          res[2*(`HEIGHT - 1)-(y+1)][3*x];
assign d2 = (x > 0)? res[y][3*(x-1)]: res[y][3*(x+1)];
assign d3 = (y > 0)? res[y-1][3*x]: res[y+1][3*x];
`endif
```

The circuit must also account for the boundary conditions. (Mirror image is used here.)

Note that the code is separated with the Verilog compiler directive for the right and left reference modes. The difference between the two modes is in their use of the counters to compute the coordinates. For the right mode, the conjugate point is on the right, while for the left mode, the conjugate point is on the left.

11.11 Functions for Saturation Arithmetic

The combinational circuits are aided by many functions. They provide a compact method to write the common codes in the function and task (although task is not used here). The restriction is that the codes must be executed within the same simulation time and the variables are all local. Because of the variable scopes, accessing the entire image or message matrix is very inefficient. Let us design the circuits for such functions.

The first function is `tadd`, which adds numbers and limits the size of the output to predefined bounds. Usually, the lower bound is zero and the upper bound is the full field, $2^B - 1$, where B is the word length of the message. This operation must be secured so that underflow and overflow are averted. All other functions doing any kind of addition may use this saturation math.

The second function is `av`, which takes two arguments and outputs their average value. To avoid any possible overflow, the arguments are halved before addition. All the arguments must be within the number range. The functions `av3` and `av4` are the expansions from two to three or four arguments. The function computes the average of the multiple arguments, calling `av` as required.

Listing 11.8 The functions (8/9)

```
//functions
//average of two arguments
function [15:0] av;
   input [15:0] a,b;
   begin
      av = (a>>1) + (b>>1);
   end
endfunction
//average of three arguments
function [15:0] av3;
   input [15:0] a,b,c;
   begin
      av3 = (a>>2) + (a>>4) + (b>>2) +(b>>4) + (c>>2) + (c>>4);
   end
endfunction
//average of the four arguments
function [15:0] av4;
   input [15:0] a,b,c,d;
   begin
      av4 = av(av(a,b),av(c,d));
   end
endfunction

//absolute distance
function [15:0] adistance;                          //absolute distance
   input [15:0] a, b;
   begin
      adistance = (a > b)? (a - b): (b - a);
   end
endfunction

//truncate math
function [15:0] tadd;                               //saturation logic
   input signed[15:0] a, b;
   reg signed [15:0] c;

   begin
      c = a + b;
      tadd = (c < 0)? 0: (c < 8'hFF)? c: 8'hFF;
   end
endfunction

//saturation lodic
```

```
function ['DATA_BITS - 1:0] sat;
   input [15:0] a;
   begin
      sat = (a <= 0)? 0:
         (a > 'LAB_DIM - 1)? ('LAB_DIM - 1): a;
   end
endfunction

//sign function
function signed [1:0] sgn;
   input signed [15:0] a;
   begin
      sgn = (a < 0)? -1:
         (a > 0)? 1: 0;
   end
endfunction
```

In computing averages, shift operations are used to avoid division. However, a problem arises when finding the average of the three arguments because getting the exact average of the three arguments is not possible with shift operations. In general, for n arguments, we have to determine the coefficients a_k, which is $a_k \in \{-1, 0, 1\}$:

$$\sum_{k=1}^{B-1} a_k 2^{-k} \leq \frac{1}{n}, \tag{11.18}$$

where B is the word length of the arguments. For the three arguments, one of the best approximations is $\frac{1}{4} + \frac{1}{16} < \frac{1}{3}$ (see the problems at the end of this chapter).

In addition to the additions, difference operations are needed to measure the likelihood of two numbers. The basic distance between two numbers is defined by the absolute distance, although other advanced distance measures can replace this. The function, `adistance`, serves this purpose in an integer word length.

11.12 Functions for Minimum Argument

At the end of the iteration, the messages are supposed to be in equilibrium. At this point, the final message is determined and therefore so is the disparity. This is the concept underlying the original theory. In actuality, the circuit executing this task is separated from the circuit utilized for the message updation and thus operates concurrently with the other circuits. Therefore, there is no reason to halt this circuit during the iteration.

In Equation (11.16), the required operation is

$$x = \arg \min_{k=0}^{D-1} d(k). \tag{11.19}$$

The function, `argmin`, returns the minimum argument, given the input vector.

This operation reads as follows in Verilog HDL.

Listing 11.9 The functions (9/9)

```
    //choose argument for the minimum
    //minimum argument
    function [15:0] argmin;                        //minimum argument
      input ['LAB_BITS * 'LAB_DIM - 1:0] a;
      reg [15:0] i, tmp, temp;
      begin
        tmp = 8'hFF;
        temp = 0;
        for (i=0; i < 'LAB_DIM; i=i+1) begin
          temp = (a['LAB_BITS * i +:'LAB_BITS] < tmp)? i: temp;
          tmp = (a['LAB_BITS * i +:'LAB_BITS] < tmp)?
                      a['LAB_BITS * i +:'LAB_BITS]: tmp;
        end
        argmin = temp;
      end
    endfunction
endmodule
```

It is important that a minimum near the center position be chosen when multiple minima exist throughout the elements in a vector. This is because the required value is not the message but its index, which must be as close to the current position as possible. The heavy weight must be designed so that this condition is guaranteed. Otherwise, the circuit will have to be redesigned in a more complicated manner.

11.13 Simulation

Thus far, we have derived the RE circuit. In order to successfully implement the design, it must first be optimized by removing as many of the warning signs as possible. If the design is correct, the synthesis parts, `processor.v`, `pe.v`, `RAM1`, `RAM2`, `RES`, excluding `io.v`, will all pass the synthesis stage. For the simulation, we used a pair of 225×188 images (CMU 2013; Middlebury 2013). The test images are depicted at the top of Figure 11.3. The lower images are the disparity maps, that is left and right reference modes.

The parameters for the RE were as follows. The entire image frame was processed in a raster scan manner and the total number of iterations was 10.

The right reference map has a poor region on the right end. Likewise, the left reference map has a poor region on the left side (see the problems at the end of this chapter). The result is poorer than the disparity map obtained by the DP and BP machines. However, more weight for the neighborhood and preprocessing with smooth filtering may help to improve the performance.

In complexity view, the RE machine needs $3MNB$ bits to store the images and $MNDB$ bits to store the disparity map, where B is the word length of the disparity and the image pixel, and D is the number of disparity levels. In later chapters, we will encounter the DP and BP machines. The RE machine is simple and fast. It is the starting point for all other vision processing circuits. Improvements can be made to it by modifying the relaxation equation with more sophisticated terms.

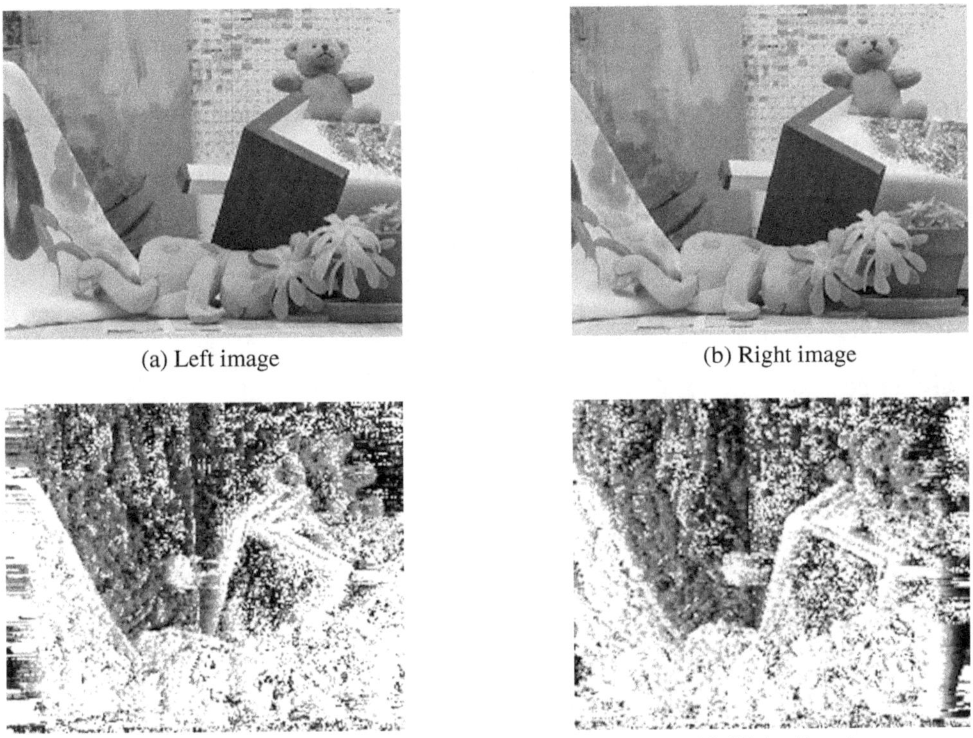

(a) Left image (b) Right image

(c) Left disparity (d) Right disparity

Figure 11.3 Disparity maps (image size: 225 × 188, disparity level: 32, iteration: 10, mirror-reflected boundary)

Problems

11.1 [Discretization] Derive the discretization of the second differential, $\partial_{xx}^{f} f$ and $\partial_{xx}^{fb} f$.

11.2 [Discretization] Derive the third difference, ∂_{xxx}^{fff} and ∂_{xxx}^{fbf}. Discuss its properties. The higher-order derivatives can be interpreted as the Sobel operator (Bradski and Kaehler 2008; OpenCV 2013; Wikipedia 2013c), which can be obtained by convolving templates of lower order.

11.3 [Discretization] Derive Equation (11.10).

11.4 [Overall system] In Listing 11.2, the computation is based on the Gauss–Seidel method. How can you convert the circuit into the Jacobi method?

11.5 [Overall system] In Listing 11.2, the pixel value beyond the boundary is set by the mirror image. Instead of the mirror image, fix the values to zero.

11.6 [Overall system] In Listing 11.2, the pixel value beyond the boundary is set by the mirror image. Instead of the mirror image, fix the values to the boundary values.

11.7 [Overall system] Listing 11.2 is for the stereo matching. How can you implement the circuit for motion estimation?

11.8 [Saturation arithmetic] In Listing 11.8, function `av3` is defined for the average of three arguments. The result should not exceed the maximum value and division must be avoided. Enhance the computation by introducing more terms.

11.9 [Simulation] In the right mode system, the disparity value becomes uncertain because the position is closer to the right boundary. The same is true for the left mode system on the left boundary. Derive the probability of the disparity located in the given region and discuss the uncertainty.

11.10 [Simulation] In the right mode system, the disparity value becomes uncertain because the position is closer to the right boundary. The same is true for the left mode system on the left boundary. Let the range of disparity be $N' \leq N$. Derive the probability and discuss the uncertainty.

References

Aubert G and Kornprobst P 2006 *Mathematical Problems in Image Processing: Partial Differential Equations and the Calculus of Variations (Applied Mathematical Sciences)*. Springer-Verlag.

Bradski GR and Kaehler A 2008 *Learning OpenCV*. O'Reilly Media, Inc.

CMU 2013 Cmu data set http://vasc.ri.cmu.edu/idb/html/stereo/ (accessed Sept. 4, 2013).

Courant R and Hilbert D 1953 *Methods of Mathematical Physics*, vol. 1. Interscience Press.

Fehrenbachy J and Mirebeauz J 2013 Small non-negative stencils for anisotropic diffusion http://arxiv.org/pdf/1301.3925v1.pdf (accessed May 3, 2013).

Horn BKP 1986 *Robot Vision*. MIT Press, Cambridge, Massachusetts.

IEEE 2005 *IEEE Standard for Verilog Hardware Description Language*. IEEE.

Ilyevsky A 2010 *Digital Image Restoration by Multigrid Methods: Numerical Solution of Partial Differential Equations by Multigrid Methods for Removing Noise from Digital Pictures*. Lambert Academic Publishing.

Jeong H and Park S 2004 Generalized trellis stereo matching with systolic array *Lecture Notes in Computer Science*, vol. 3358, pp. 263–267.

Middlebury U 2013 Middlebury stereo home page http://vision.middlebury.edu/stereo (accessed Sept. 4, 2013).

OpenCV 2013 Sobel operator http://docs.opencv.org/modules/imgproc/doc/filtering.html (accessed Sept. 24, 2013).

Park S and Jeong H 2008 Memory efficient iterative process on a two-dimensional first-order regular graph. *Optics Letters* **33**, 74–76.

Perona P and Malik J 1990 Scale-space and edge detection using anisotropic diffusion. *IEEE Trans. Pattern Anal. Mach. Intell.* **12**(7), 629–639.

Scherzer O, Grasmair M, Grossauer H, Haltmeier M, and Lenzen F 2008 *Variational Methods in Imaging* Applied Mathematical Sciences. Springer-Verlag.

Weickert J 2008 Anisotropic diffusion in image processing http://www.lpi.tel.uva.es/muitic/pim/docus/anisotropic_diffusion.pdf (accessed April 15, 2014).

Wikipedia 2013a Euler–Lagrange equation http://en.wikipedia.org/wiki/Euler%E2%80%93Lagrange_equation (accessed May 3, 2013).

Wikipedia 2013b Multigrid methods http://en.wikipedia.org/wiki/Multigrid_methods (accessed Sept. 23, 2013).

Wikipedia 2013c Sobel operator http://en.wikipedia.org/wiki/Sobel_operator (accessed Sept. 24, 2013).

Wikipedia 2013d Successive over-relaxation http://en.wikipedia.org/wiki/Successive_over-relaxation (accessed Sept. 24, 2013).

Yang QX, Wang L, and Yang RG 2006 Real-time global stereo matching using hierarchical belief propagation *BMVC*, p. III:989.

Young DM 1950 *Iterative Methods for Solving Partial Difference Equations df Elliptical Type* Phd thesis Harvard University.

12

Dynamic Programming for Stereo Matching

So far, we have discussed the following concepts: vision simulator (Chapter 4), stereo matching (Chapter 6), and DP machine (Chapter 9). As one of our final goals, in this chapter, we explain how to design a DP machine for stereo matching (Baker and Binford 1981; Ohta and Kanade 1985).

There are various types of stereo DP machines. One possible source of diversity is the reference system: left, right, or center. The various types of DP machines may have some parts of their code in common, but they may also have some dissimilar code that is reference-system-dependent. A good design contains as much code as possible in common, keeping the number of reference-system-dependent parts as small as possible. Another possible source of diversity is the number of processors: single processor or array processor. In a single processor system, all the computation is carried out within the same processor. The processor is actually a large FSM, driven only by a clock and a reset signal, together with RAMs storing the left and right images and the disparity map. On the other hand, in an array processor system, all computation is carried out via a network of identical processors. In this case, there must be a plan for supplying the images to the network, retrieving the disparity maps, and executing each processor in various states. Yet another possible source of diversity is the use of lines: one line or a set of lines. A minimal system may use only a pair of image lines for stereo matching. A more advanced system may use a set of image lines from both left and right images to compute neighborhood operations.

In this chapter, we explain how to design a DP machine for stereo matching, for the left and right reference systems, a single processor, and neighborhood computation. The reference systems can be selected by the Verilog compiler directives, making the three systems into the same Verilog HDL code. We review the stereo matching algorithm, hypothesize a DP machine, and design Verilog codes.

12.1 Search Space

We start again with the space in which the solution exists. The space consists of the points, $\{(x,d)|x \in [0,N-1], d \in [0,D-1]\}$ for the left right reference and $\{(x,d)|x \in [0,2N-1], d \in [0,D-1]\}$ for the center reference system (Figure 12.1). The first property of the disparity is that it depends on the reference system and thus must be explained in a general setting.

The second property is that the solution space must be further confined to the trapezoidal region within the rectangular space. This is because only points in this region can be observed by both images.

Architectures for Computer Vision: From Algorithm to Chip with Verilog, First Edition. Hong Jeong.

Companion Website: www.wiley.com/go/jeong

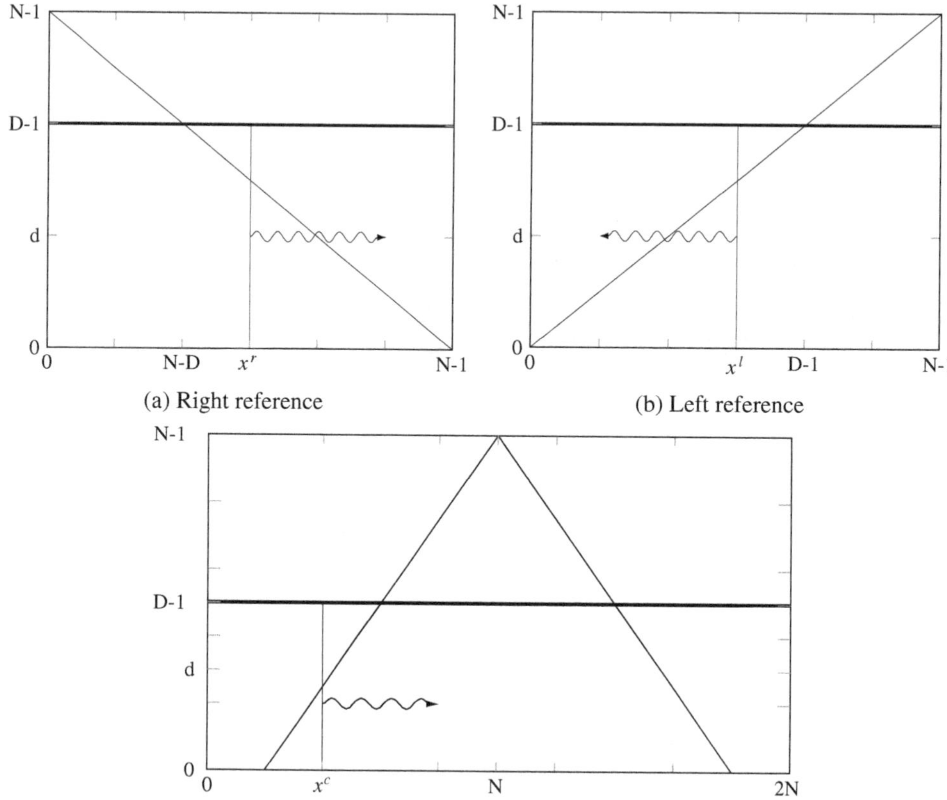

(a) Right reference (b) Left reference

(c) Center reference

Figure 12.1 The (x, d) space: left/right and center reference systems

Outside of this region, all the points are indeterminate, due to lack of observation. Consequently, when we consider the space as a graph, we call the observable nodes *matching nodes* and the unobservable nodes *occlusion nodes*. In the center reference system, occlusion nodes exist even inside the trapezoidal region. Both types of nodes are alternately distributed in this region. The identity of a node can be easily verified by observing whether $x + d$ is even or odd. (It depends on where the node origin is defined. For an $x \in [0, 2N]$ system, it is odd and for an $x \in [0, 2N - 2]$ system, it is even.) If the domain is defined as $x \in [0, 2N]$, $x + d$ is odd. The corresponding coordinates in the images are $x^r = (x - d - 1)/2$ and $x^l = (x + d - 1)/2$. If the domain is $x \in [0, 2N - 2]$, $x + d$ is odd. The corresponding image points are $x^r = (x - d)/2$ and $x^l = (x + d)/2$ (refer to Equation (6.80)). In designing the circuit, we need to know where the matching nodes are. If we represent such regions by R^r, R^l, and R^c, they are given by

$$\begin{aligned}
R^r &= \left\{ (x^r, d) | x^r \in [0, N - 1], d \leq D - 1 - \frac{D - 1}{N - 1} x^r \right\}, \\
R^l &= \left\{ (x^l, d) | x^l \in [0, N - 1], d \leq \frac{D - 1}{N - 1} x^l \right\}, \\
R^c &= \left\{ (x^c, d) | x^c \in [0, 2N - 2], d \leq \frac{D - 1}{N - 1}, d \leq \frac{D - 1}{N - 1}(2N - 2 - x^c), d \leq D - 1, x^c + d = even \right\}.
\end{aligned} \tag{12.1}$$

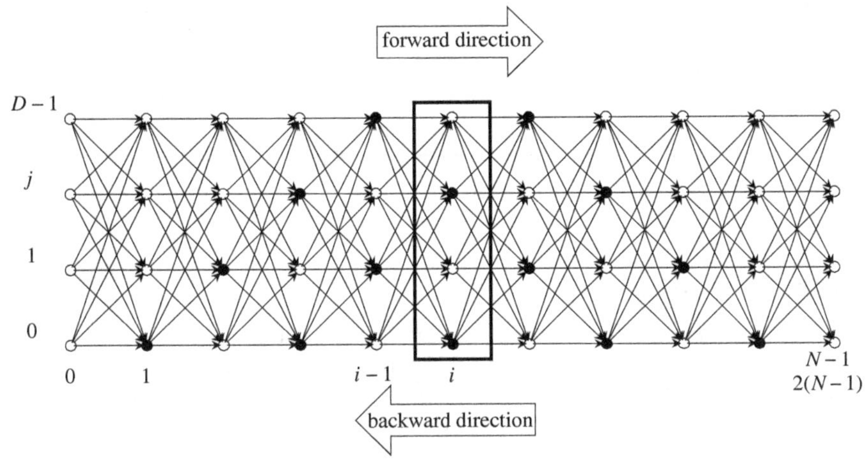

(a) Neighborhood size, $N_e = D$

Figure 12.2 A graph for the search spaces. The size is either $D \times N$ or $2D \times (N - 1)$

In order to find a feasible solution in the solution space, we can embed all the paths that we are looking for. In this manner, the search space can be defined over the solution space. To make the method clearer, we can represent the search method by a graph, $G = (V, E)$, which consists of nodes and edges (Figure 12.2). The nodes are the lattice points in Figure 12.1 and the edges are the feasible path of the desired object boundary. This graph is specific in that the edges are connected between adjacent nodes only, although there could be many other connections. This particular graph is very limited but also efficient in DP realization.

The graph consists of DN nodes for left right references and $2D(N - 1)$ nodes for center reference. Some nodes are in the trapezoid; these are called matching nodes, and some others, called occlusion nodes, are not. This graph shows the center reference as an example. The strategy is to compute column by column, as the nodes in a column are represented by a block in the figure.

From the previous two figures, we obtain the local connections, as shown in Figure 12.3. On the left a connection in the right or left reference system is shown. Any pair of nodes connected by the edge are assigned uniquely in different positions in the right or left image planes: $(x - 1)$ and x. The figure on the right side is the possible paths in the center reference system. If the coordinates are mapped to the image plane, the nodes $(x^c - 1, d - 1)$ and (x^c, d) are mapped to the same position in the right image plane (see

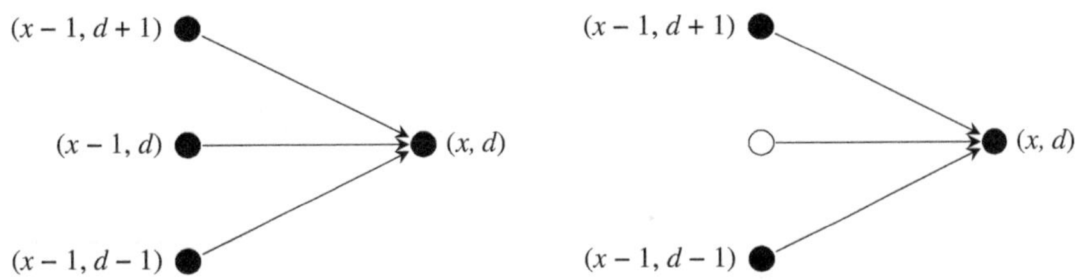

(a) Right or left reference (b) Center reference

Figure 12.3 Two cases of connections: (a) $x + d = odd$ (b) $x + d = even$

Equation (6.80)). They are actually $(x, d-1)$ and (x, d) in the left right reference, a path that is prohibited in the search path. Similarly, the nodes $(x^c-1, d+1)$ and (x^c, d) are actually the same point in the left image plane. They are the points, $(x, d-1)$ and (x, d), which must be avoided in building the search path. The search space of the center reference is the one skewed from the left right reference system. That is, $(x, d-1)$ and (x, d) are mapped to either $(x^c-1, d-1)$ and (x^c, d) or $(x^c-1, d+1)$ and (x^c, d) in the graph. We must expect the result of the center reference system to be very unreliable compared to that of the left right system.

12.2 Line Processing

From a computational point of view, a pair of conjugate images can be processed in one of three ways: line, strip, or plane (or frame). In the first method, the image is scanned in raster manner and processed for disparity computation between the line intervals. In the second method, the line is expanded to a block of lines, which shifts downwards in an overlapped or skipped manner. Finally, in the third method, the entire image plane is processed as a body. Before going any further, let us first define this concept.

For the image plane, $\mathcal{P} = \{(x, y)|x \in [0, N-1], y \in [0, M-1]\}$, the three schemes can be illustrated as depicted in Figure 12.4. Figure 12.4(a) depicts the three images, $I^l(\cdot, y)$, $I^r(\cdot, y)$, and disparity $d(\cdot, y)$. The computation uses the images on the epipolar lines, producing disparity on the same line:

$$d(\cdot, y) \leftarrow T(I^l(\cdot, y), I^r(\cdot, y)). \tag{12.2}$$

Here, $T(\cdot)$ represents the disparity computation operations. The computation progresses downwards line by line. In Figure 12.4(b), the line is expanded to a set of lines, $\{I^l(\cdot, y')|y' \in [y-(L-1)/2, y+(L-1)/2]\}$ and $\{I^r(\cdot, y')|y' \in [y-(L-1)/2, y+(L-1)/2]\}$, and disparity $d(\cdot, y)$. In this case, the disparity

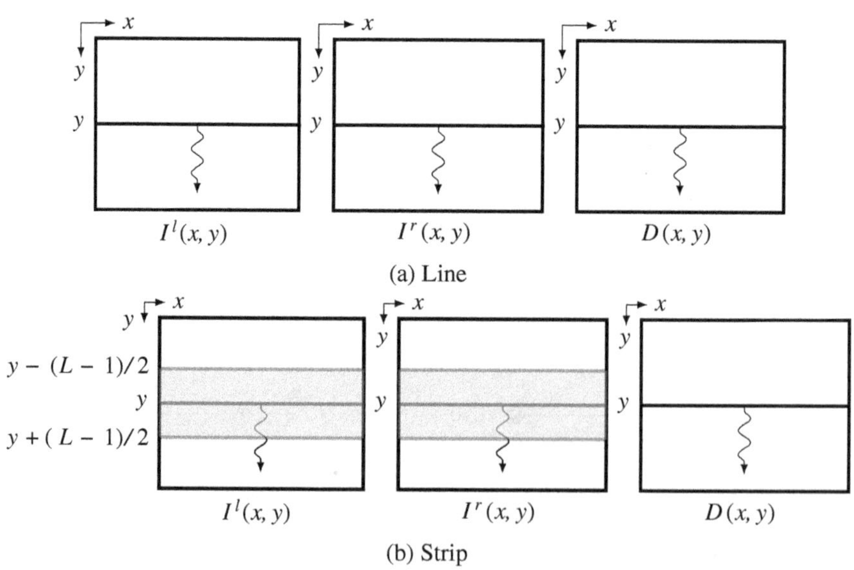

Figure 12.4 Computing line and strip: left image (I^l), right image (I^r), and disparity map D

computation becomes

$$d(\cdot, y) \leftarrow T(\{I^l(\cdot, y')|y' \in [y-(L-1)/2, y+(L-1)/2]\},$$
$$\{I^r(\cdot, y')|y' \in [y-(L-1)/2, y+(L-1)/2]\}). \tag{12.3}$$

Using more than one line potentially facilitates neighborhood computation. To make the strip symmetric on both sides of the centerline, the number of lines in a strip, L, must be an odd number. If $L = 1$, the strip becomes a line. If $L = M$, the image frame itself is signified.

Because the computation progresses downwards, the disparities of the previous lines are available to the current line and thus recursive computation is made possible:

$$d(\cdot, y) \leftarrow T(\{I^l(\cdot, y')|y' \in [y-(L-1)/2, y+(L-1)/2]\},$$
$$\{I^r(\cdot, y')|y' \in [y-(L-1)/2, y+(L-1)/2]\}, d(\cdot, y-1)). \tag{12.4}$$

Using the previous disparity may help in deciding the disparity of the present line.

In light of this, in designing the DP machine, we have to consider the computation structure (multiple lines, neighborhood computation, and recursive computation) and leave the details to the actual algorithm design.

12.3 Computational Space

As discussed in Chapter 6, the stereo images can be referenced in terms of the three coordinates system: left, right, and center reference. To design appropriate DP machines, we have to know the search space of these systems in detail.

Figure 12.5 shows the space observed by two cameras. The space containing the observed sites (black dots) is the epiplane, and the horizontal axis is the epipolar line. The apex of the inverted triangle is the nearest point with disparity $N-1$, while the base of the triangle and beyond are the farthest points with disparity zero. This space can be viewed from many directions, such as the right image axis, the left image axis, and the center between the two images, as illustrated. As a result, we can derive spaces (x^r, d), (x^l, d), and (x^c, d), respectively called *right reference*, *left reference*, and *center reference* system.

In the right reference system, the image on the right is used as the reference in computing the distance:

$$I^r(x^l, y) - I^l(x^l + d, y), \quad d \in [0, D-1], \tag{12.5}$$

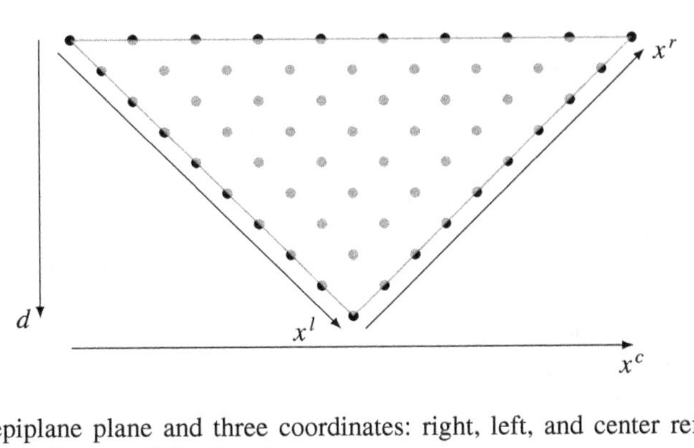

Figure 12.5 An epiplane plane and three coordinates: right, left, and center reference images (the disparity is shown as an inverse of the depth)

where d denotes disparity and x^l denote the coordinates in the left image. Similarly, in the left reference system, the image on the left is used as the reference in computing the disparity:

$$I^l(x^r, y) - I^r(x^r - d, y), \quad d \in [0, D-1], \tag{12.6}$$

where x^r are the coordinates in the right image plane. Note the difference in the sign placed before the disparity. Notice the difference in the sign attached before the disparity. In the center reference system (Jeong and Oh 2000; Jeong and Park 2004; Jeong and Yuns 2000; Jeong *et al.* 2002), the corresponding points are

$$I^l((x^c + d - 1)/2, y) - I^r((x^c - d - 1)/2, y), \forall x + d = odd, \tag{12.7}$$

where x^c are the coordinates in the center reference system. After the disparity is obtained, it can be mapped to the coordinates in the left or right image planes, according to Equation (6.80),

$$\begin{aligned} x^l &= \frac{1}{2}(x^c + d - 1), \\ x^r &= \frac{1}{2}(x^c - d - 1), \quad \forall x^c + d = odd. \end{aligned} \tag{12.8}$$

We will sometimes call the mapped coordinates, respectively, *center left reference* and *center right reference*, for convenience. The places where the occlusion nodes exist are the other positions that do not satisfy this condition. Those positions can be used for smoothing purposes, as we shall see.

Collectively, we can define a space (x, d), consisting of the coordinates and disparity, and examine possible computations there. We can derive the three spaces shown in Figure 12.6 from Figure 12.5. In the three spaces, the horizontal and vertical axes are labeled with pixel numbers and disparity values, respectively. At a glance, it can be seen that the space is separated into two parts, represented by black and white nodes. The difference between the two types of nodes is that the nodes below the diagonal are observed by both cameras, while the nodes above the diagonal are observed by only one camera. In the center reference system, the observable and unobservable nodes are alternately arranged even inside the triangle. We call the observable and unobservable nodes, matching nodes and occlusion nodes, for convenience. In the right reference system, the occlusion nodes exist only in the image on the right. Similarly, in the left reference system, the occlusion nodes exist only in the image on the left. In the center reference system, the occlusion nodes exist alternately in both images.

The space occupied by the left and right reference systems consists of $N \times N$ nodes, where the number of matching and occlusion nodes is $N(N + 1)/2$ and $N(N - 1)/2$, respectively. In the center reference system, the nodes, $(2N + 1)N$, consist of $N(N + 1)/2$ matching nodes and $N(3N + 1)/2$ occlusion nodes. If the disparity range is limited to $D < N$, the space becomes the set of $N \times D$ and $D(2N + 1)$ nodes, respectively. In designing the DP machine, the size of the space is a major factor because it correlates to the amount of space it consumes in the chip. Reducing D may therefore improve the space requirement significantly.

The given problem is to divide the space into two separate subspaces, above and below, so that the borderline becomes a disparity. The constraints are that the borderline must pass through the matching nodes – starting and ending nodes. The purpose of the DP algorithm (Aho *et al.* 1974; Bertsekas 2007; Cormen *et al.* 2001; Knuth 1997) is to find an optimal path along the x-axis. There are constraints associated with the optimal path. One constraint is that the path must travel through the matching nodes. The other constraint is the starting and ending nodes. In the right reference system, both ends must be $(0, \cdot)$ and $(N - 1, 0)$. In the left reference system, the two points must be $(N - 1, \cdot)$ and $(0, 0)$. In the center reference system, the extreme points must be $(0, 0)$ and $(2N, 0)$. Whether the path may go through the occlusion nodes is undetermined because there is no information on those nodes. The algorithm has

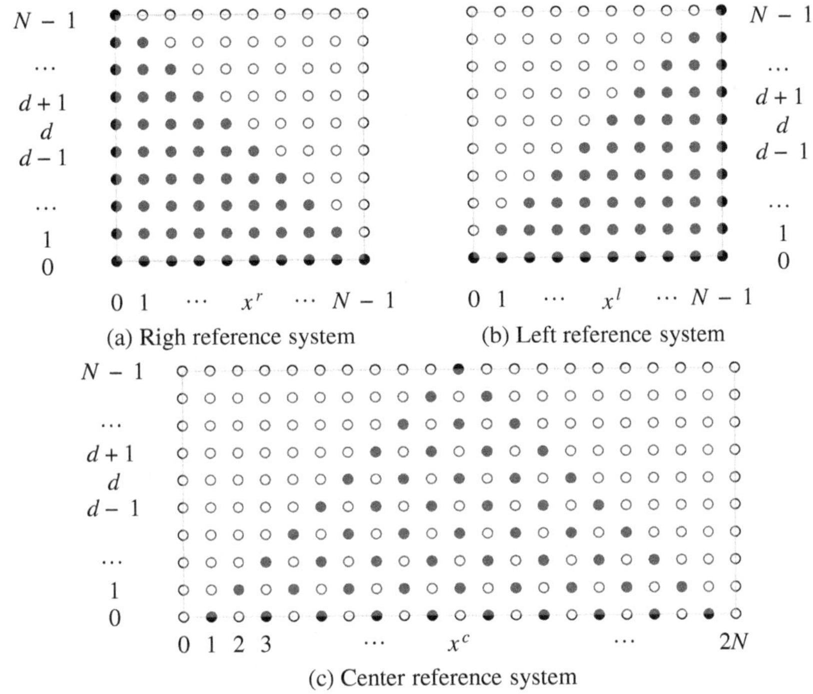

Figure 12.6 The search space: (x^r, d^r), (x^l, d^l), and (x^c, d^c): black and white dots represent, respectively, matching and occlusion nodes

the responsibility of deciding whether to include the occlusion nodes. The occlusion nodes may help to provide a smoother path but may also lead to wrong interpretation.

In both the left and right reference systems, it is expected that the matching result will become less reliable as the path progresses because the number of matching candidates will become smaller along the path. As a result, in the right reference system, the disparity is uncertain on the right side of the image. Likewise, in the left reference system, the disparity on the left end of the image is naturally uncertain. How the uncertainties are resolved depends on the algorithms, for example, by using the two types of disparity results. In the center reference system, there is no such bias depending on the direction of computation, except that the role of the starting and ending nodes can be changed, resulting in different disparity maps.

Finally, the left and right reference systems are not suitable for array design, although it is possible to use them. The data flow and the internal operations are very complicated. On the other hand, the center reference system is especially efficient when implemented in network arrays. In this chapter, we focus on single processor design, not array processor design, for the three reference systems.

12.4 Energy Equations

The next step is to define the energy function, defined on the search space, (x, d). In Chapter 6, we derived the energy equations for the three coordinate systems. To design the DP machines, we simplify the energy equations by including only the basic features and excluding higher order smoothness and occlusion constraints. However, more advanced energy functions can be applied to the DP machine by modifying the Verilog functions in later applications.

Consider a pair of epipolar lines, $I^l(\cdot, y)$ and $I^r(\cdot, y)$. The corresponding energy equation in the right reference system is

$$E(d) = \sum_{x=0}^{N-1} \rho(I^r(x), I^l(x + d)) + \lambda\mu(d(x), d(x - 1)), \tag{12.9}$$

where $\rho(\cdot)$ is the local distance measure and $\mu(\cdot)$ is the smoothness constraint. Similarly, in the left reference system, the corresponding energy equation is

$$E(d) = \sum_{x=0}^{N-1} \rho(I^l(x), I^r(x - d)) + \lambda\mu(d(x), d(x - 1)). \tag{12.10}$$

Here, the negative sign is used to retain the disparity nonnegative number. Finally, the center reference system has the energy equation

$$E(d) = \sum_{x=0}^{2N} \rho(I^l((x + d - 1)/2), I^r((x - d - 1)/2)) + \lambda\mu(d(x), d(x - 1)). \tag{12.11}$$

The major backbone of the DP machine is based on these underlying simplified energy equations. Higher-order terms and nonlinear time varying terms, which may appear in more specific algorithms, are all disregarded. Our purpose is to design a DP machine that is general in many ways – energy equation, DP algorithm, and architecture-so that more advanced terms can be easily imported later. Incorporating the advanced algorithms introduced in Chapter 6 is a challenging task. Even the distance measure for the local cost and smoothness will be defined in simplified forms.

12.5 DP Algorithm

Finding the optimal path that minimizes the energy equation can be conveniently explained with the connections between nodes in the search space, (x, d). For two nodes, $(x - 1, d')$ and (x, d), the connection has the configuration shown in Figure 12.7.

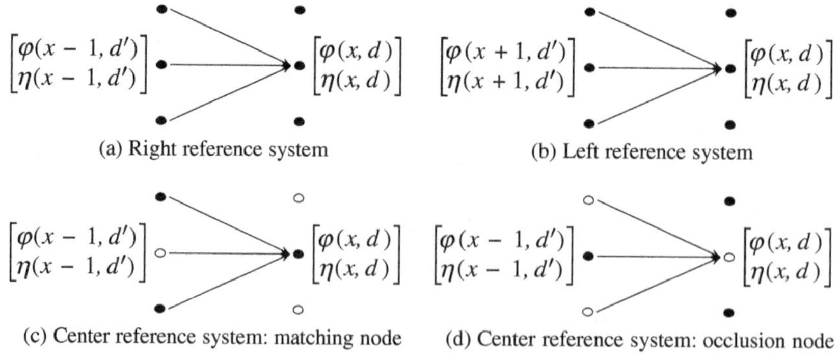

Figure 12.7 Paths from $(x - 1, d')$ to (x, d) in the three reference systems (only two neighbor nodes are shown)

As a part of the search space, (x, d), the horizontal axis denotes the computation direction and the vertical axis denotes the disparity levels. The direction in the left reference system is opposite to that of the right reference system. However, in the center reference system it does not matter because the search space is symmetric. In the center reference system, occlusion nodes are also included in the feasible paths for possible improvement of smoothness.

The concept is as follows. According to the previous computation, all the nodes, $(x-1, \cdot)$, already contain the cost, $\varphi(x-1, d')$, and the pointer, $\eta(x-1, d')$. In the current computation, (x, d) is resolved for the costs and pointers. For this purpose, (x, d) observes all the nodes in the previous column, $(x-1, \cdot)$, to choose the smallest cost and keep the node as a parent. In addition to the parent costs, some smoothness measure must be applied to the transition between the two nodes. The scope of parent search and the distance are often the major factors taken into consideration for smoothness. In the right and left reference systems, the transition is between two matching nodes, whereas in the center reference system it is between two types of nodes. There are four possible transitions: matching to matching, matching to occlusion, occlusion to matching, and occlusion to occlusion. In order to assign a suitable penalty to these transitions, we need to have some physical understanding of the geometry. Another observation is that the search range of the parent nodes can be limited to a small neighborhood. Smaller neighborhoods result in smoother disparities, even around object boundaries. Conversely, larger neighborhoods may result in noisy disparity distributions, although the disparities around object boundaries can be sharper.

From a computational point of view, choosing an optimal parent is a sequential operation, but the nodes, $(x, \cdot)$, are all concurrent because they do not refer to each other for any costs or pointers. In the DP machine, we can realize this computation in either of two ways: the loop operation may need less space but run slower. The parallel realization is the opposite of the serial realization. It depends upon the conditions of the given resources. We will design the DP machine using many loops, which can be parallelized easily if required.

The DP algorithms must be defined separately for the three reference systems. For the right reference system in the space $\{(x, d) | x \in [0, N-1], d \in [0, D-1]\}$, the DP algorithm is as follows:

Algorithm 12.1 (DP algorithm for the right reference system) *Given* $(I^l(\cdot, y), I^r(\cdot, y))$, *determine* $\{d(N-1), \ldots, d(0)\}$.

1. *Initialization:* $\varphi(0, d) = \rho(0, d)$, $\eta(0, d) = 0$, *for* $d \in [0, D-1]$.
2. *Forward pass: for* $x = 0, 1, \ldots, N-1$ *and* $d \in [0, D-1]$,

$$\varphi(x, d) = \min_{k \in [0, D-1]} (\varphi(x-1, k) + \mu(k, d)) + \lambda \rho(x, d),$$

$$\eta(x, d) = \arg\min_{k \in [0, D-1]} (\varphi(x-1, k) + \mu(k, d)).$$

3. *Finalization:* $d(N-1) = \arg\min_{d \in [0, D-1]} \varphi(N-1, d)$.
4. *Backward pass: for* $x = N-2, \ldots, 0$,

$$d(x) = \eta(x+1, d(x+1)).$$

The finalization is in fact trivial because the starting point is fixed, $d(N-1) = 0$. However, this condition may be somewhat relaxed in a more advanced algorithm where other nodes $(N-1, \cdot)$ may be allowed as candidates for the starting node. The direction of computation is from $x = 0$ to $x = N-1$ for the forward pass and from $x = N-1$ to $x = 0$ for the backward pass. However, designing this algorithm in Verilog is not straightforward. The effect of the finite D, assignment of occlusion nodes with costs and pointers, signed and unsigned numbers, and overflow and word length, must all be taken into consideration.

The left reference system has a similar algorithm, but the coordinates are reversed.

Algorithm 12.2 (DP algorithm for the left reference system) *Given* $(I^l(\cdot, y), I^r(\cdot, y))$, *determine* $\{d(0), \ldots, d(N-1)\}$.

1. *Initialization:* $\varphi(N-1, d) = \rho(N-1, d)$, $\eta(N-1, d) = 0$, *for* $d \in [0, D-1]$.
2. *Forward pass: for* $x = N-1, \ldots, 1, 0$ *and* $d \in [0, D-1]$,

$$\begin{aligned}\varphi(x, d) &= \min_{k \in [0, D-1]} (\varphi(x+1, k) + \mu(k, d)) + \lambda \rho(x, d),\\ \eta(x, d) &= \arg\min_{k \in [0, D-1]} (\varphi(x+1, k) + \mu(k, d)).\end{aligned}$$

3. *Finalization:* $d(0) = \arg\min_{d \in [0, D-1]} \varphi(0, d)$.
4. *Backward pass: for* $x = 1, \ldots, N-1$,

$$d(x) = \eta(x-1, d(x-1)).$$

The computation starts from $x = N-1$ and arrives at $x = 0$ in the forward pass. Next, in the backward pass, the computation starts from $x = 0$ and ends at $x = N-1$.

We have two options for combining the two algorithms. The first option is to keep the coordinates, x^l and x^r, in defining the costs and pointers. In this case, the computation proceeds in the direction of increasing x^r (or decreasing x^l), building the pointer array, ordered in the direction of increasing x^r (or decreasing x^l). The concept is intuitive but the shape of the search space and the pointer array are different in two coordinates system. The other choice is to define coordinates that increase in the direction of the forward pass. In this case, the structure of the pointer array is the same in both systems. We will use the latter option to design the DP machine.

Among the three coordinate systems, the algorithm structure of the center reference system is somewhat different from that of the others. Let us define the indicator functions: If x is even, $e_x = 1$, otherwise, $e_x = 0$. An odd indicator, o_x, is therefore, $o_x = 1 - e_x$.

Algorithm 12.3 (DP algorithm for the center reference system) *Given* $(I^l(\cdot, y), I^r(\cdot, y))$, *determine* $\{(x, d(x)) | i \in [0, 2N], d \in [0, D-1]\}$.

1. *Initialization:* $\rho(0, 0) = \rho(2N, 0) = 0$, $\rho(x, d) = \infty$ for $x - d \leq 0$ or $x + d \geq 2N$.
2. *Forward pass: for* $x = 0, \ldots, 2N$, $d \in [0, D-1]$,
   (a) *for matching node* ($x + d = odd$),

$$\begin{aligned}\varphi(x, d) &= \min_{d' \in [0, D-1]} \{\varphi(x-1, d') + e_{j-d'+1}\mu(d', d) + o_{j-k+1}\alpha\} + \rho(x, d),\\ \eta(x, d) &= \arg\min_{d' \in [0, D-1]} \{\varphi(x-1, d') + e_{j-d'+1}\mu(d', d)\}.\end{aligned}$$

   (b) *for occlusion node* ($x + d = even$),

$$\begin{aligned}\varphi(x, d) &= \varphi(x-1, d) + \beta,\\ \eta(x, d) &= d.\end{aligned}$$

3. *Finalization:* $d(2N) = 0$.
4. *Backward pass: for* $k \in [0, D-1]$,

$$d(x) = \begin{cases} 0, & x = 2N, \\ \eta(x+1, d(x+1)), & x = 2N-1, \ldots, 0. \end{cases}$$

5. *Map the disparity map:*

$$d(x^l) \leftarrow d(x), \quad \text{where } x^l = \frac{1}{2}(x + d - 1),$$

$$d(x^r) \leftarrow d(x), \quad \text{where } x^r = \frac{1}{2}(x - d - 1).$$

In the initialization, nodes outside of the triangular zone in the (x, d) space are assigned very large numbers, which may prevent the optimal path from being in that region. The exceptions are nodes $(0, 0)$ and $(2N, 0)$, the start and end nodes of the optimal path. In the forward pass, node updating is carried according to the matching and occlusion nodes. There are four cases: matching to matching, matching to occlusion, occlusion to matching, and occlusion to occlusion. Different penalties can be assigned to the various different types of transitions. Parameters α and β denote the penalties for the occlusion nodes. The algorithm considers only three types of transitions. The backtracking is the same as that used in the right and left reference systems. As the pointers are retrieved, they must be mapped to the coordinates in the left or right image planes.

In order to allow for expansion to more advanced algorithms if needed, only the basic form of the DP algorithm is considered here. For example, more advanced algorithms may use features such as occlusion, neighborhood operations, and previous results.

12.6 Architecture

The concept of DP in Algorithm 9.1 is applied to stereo matching, as summarized in Algorithm 12.1. Let us design a circuit that implements this algorithm. One approach is to use a large state machine that computes everything from reading, processing, and writing. Let us use the processor that was developed as a component of the LVSIM – although we will modify it a great deal to accommodate stereo matching (see Chapter 4). The other parts in the simulator are all the same and thus need not to be repeated. Conceptually, the processor computes an image, line by line from top to bottom, and then outputs the result before the next raster line enters. In this section, we expand this structure more to facilitate the management of neighborhood operations and recursive computation.

The major components of the DP machine are depicted in Figure 12.8. Three buffers function as the major data structure storing the intermediate data. Two buffers, called image buffers, store two rows of the images, left and right, that are read from the two external RAMs. The third buffer, called the disparity buffer, stores the previous disparity result read from the external RAM. The processor reads the images and the previous disparity results, computes the new disparities, and stores them in the disparity buffer. This computation progresses downwards in the image plane. For possible neighborhood operation, we expand the buffer to a set of rows, that is a strip. The buffers are actually FIFOs, in which the images enter the bottom and exit the top of the buffers. The three buffers are updated in synchrony. The objective is to update the contents of the center buffer with the corresponding images.

The machine computes the following mathematical equations:

$$D(\cdot, y, t) = F(I^l(\cdot, y), I^r(\cdot, y), D(\cdot, y, t - 1)), \tag{12.12}$$

where $I^l(\cdot, y)$ and $I^r(\cdot, y)$ are the image rows, $D(\cdot, y)$ is the desired disparity, and $F(\cdot)$ is the main engine that computes the stereo matching algorithm. In addition to $I^l(\cdot, y)$ and $I^r(\cdot, y)$, the computational structure allows us to use all the other components in the buffer, as a neighborhood. Further, the disparity buffer contains disparities, computed previously, in the current frame as well as the previous frame. The computational resources facilitate neighborhood and recursive operations, in addition to the primary algorithm, DP.

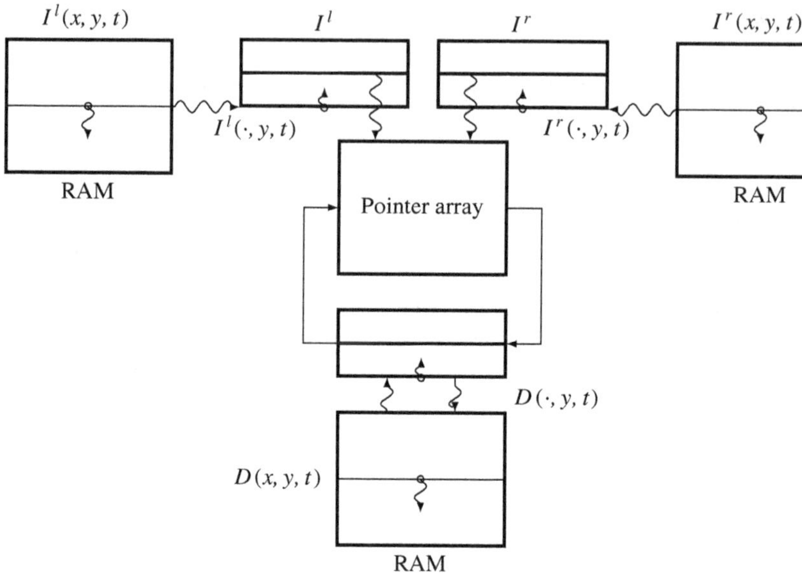

Figure 12.8 The concept of the Verilog DP machine

12.7 Overall Scheme

We design the system as a large state machine, with small sub-states within the big states. The required states are the buffer shift, reading, initialization, forward pass, finalization, backward pass, and writing states. Three states are associated with input and output, and four states with the DP algorithm. The states and their connections are illustrated by the state diagram depicted in Figure 12.9. The cycle starts

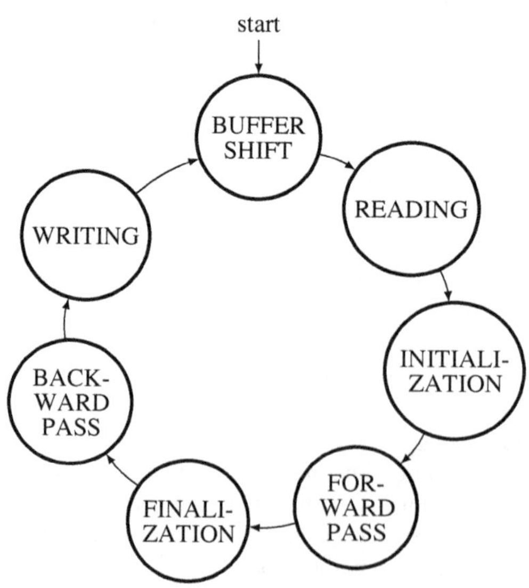

Figure 12.9 The state diagram of the DP machine

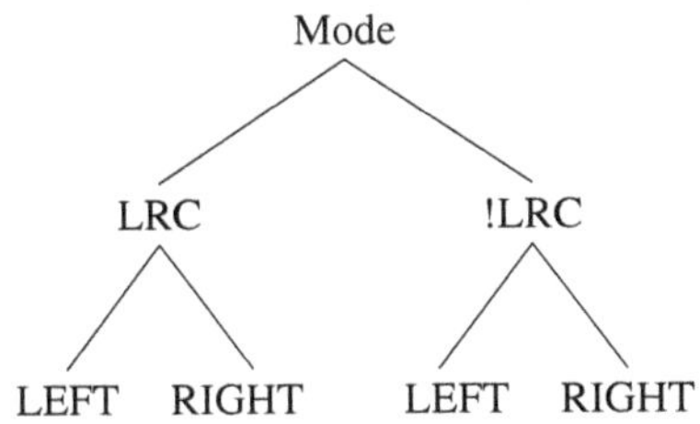

Figure 12.10 The three modes: left, right, and center (LRC) reference modes

from the buffer shift state. The three buffers, left image, right image, and disparity buffers, shift upwards, providing an empty line at the bottom. In the next state, the empty spaces are filled with the data from the external RAMs. Although the data at the bottom of the buffer are new, the data processed are those located along the center of the buffer. This arrangement is utilized in order to accommodate the possibility of neighborhood processing. The pixels along the buffer center can be grouped with their neighborhoods. The next state is DP computation, as specified in Algorithm 12.1. In the initialization state, the costs of the starting nodes are computed. The next state is the forward pass state, in which the costs and pointers are recursively computed and the pointers are written to the pointer matrix. When the forward pass ends at the final pixel position, the finalization process starts. Among the final nodes, the node with the minimum cost must be determined. In the three reference systems, this stage is trivial because the node with the minimum cost is already known. The backward pass process then starts, reading the pointers from the pointer matrix. When the process reaches the first pixel, it starts reading the next lines of images. For real-time processing, the computation in a loop must be completed within the raster scan interval.

The DP machine must be designed for the three reference systems we have studied: left, right, and center reference systems. Designing separate machines may be very inefficient because they may have a great many parts in common, which will need to be modified later for specific applications. In Algorithms 12.1–12.3, the basic structures are all the same and thus must be retained in the code in the same way. Including common and difference codes in one package can be done using the Verilog compiler directives, **`ifdef** (Figure 12.10). With the header keys, LRC and LEFT, we can specify one of four modes: left, right, center left, and center right. In the left and right modes, the left and right image planes are the reference coordinate planes. In the center reference mode, the disparity obtained must be mapped to an actual plane, either the left or the right image plane, as derived in Equation (12.8). This requirement produces two more modes. In fact, there could be two additional modes in each of the center left and center right modes. In one mode, the computation proceeds from $(0, 0)$ to $(2N, 0)$ in the forward pass and returns in the backward pass. The other mode is the opposite – it proceeds from $(2N, 0)$ to $(0, 0)$ then reverses itself. The pointers retrieved in the two different ways are also different.

Let us consider the overall framework of the DP machine. It has four main parts: header, variable declarations, procedural, and combinational.

Listing 12.1 The Verilog DP machine: framework (1/7)

```
`define WIDTH       113        //image width
`define HEIGHT      94         //image height
`define DATA_BITS   8          //word size
`define ADDR_BITS   15         //pixel counter
`define LINES       3          //strip size
`define LRC                    //LR or C reference
`define LEFT                   //LR reference
```

```
`define COST_BITS      10                                //max cost range
`define INFTY          `COST_BITS'hFFFF                  //upper bound
`define DISPARITY_BITS 8                                 //disparity counter
`define DMAX           4                                 //max disparity
`define ALPHA          10                                //penalty

module processor(                                        //DP stereo processor
    input clock, reset,
    output reg [`ADDR_BITS - 1:0] raddr, r_waddr,       //address bus
    input [`DATA_BITS - 1:0] i_rdata1, i_rdata2, r_rdata, //data bus
    output reg [`DATA_BITS - 1:0] r_wdata,              //data bus
    output reg r_wen                                     //write enable
    );

    //working array: window of images
    reg [`DATA_BITS - 1:0] img1 [0: 3*`WIDTH*`LINES -1]; //1st image
    reg [`DATA_BITS - 1:0] img2 [0: 3*`WIDTH*`LINES -1]; //2nd image
    reg [`DATA_BITS - 1:0] res  [0: 3*`WIDTH*`LINES -1]; //disparity map

    //variables
    reg [`ADDR_BITS - 1:0] k, idx, idx1;                 //pixel
    reg [9:0] i, j, J;                                   //column, row
    reg [`DISPARITY_BITS - 1:0] jj, pointer;             //pointer
    reg [`COST_BITS - 1:0] cost [0:`DMAX - 1], costp[0:`DMAX - 1];  //cost
`ifdef LRC //LR reference
    reg [`DISPARITY_BITS - 1:0] queue [0:`WIDTH - 1][0: `DMAX - 1]; //LR
`else //center reference
    reg [`DISPARITY_BITS - 1:0] queue [0:2*`WIDTH][0: `DMAX - 1];   //C
`endif
    reg [2:0] state, statef, stater;                     //state and substates
    reg [9:0] count;                                     //general counter

    wire [7:0] xl, xr;                                   //coordinates
    wire [`COST_BITS - 1:0] ldistance;                   //local distance

    //DP processing
    always @ (posedge clock) begin: PROCESSING           //processing block
        if (reset) begin                                 //initialize
            state <= 0;                                  //global state
            count <= 0;                                  //counter
            j <= 0;                                      //image line
            k <= 0;                                      //pixel in the strip
        end
        else begin: MAIN
            case (state)                                 //state machine
```

```
            0: begin: BUFFER
               end
            1: begin: READING                          //fill the bottom
               end
            2: begin: INITIALIZATION                   //DP initialization
               end
            3: begin: FORWARD                          //DP forward pass
               end
            4: begin: FINALIZATION                     //DP finalization
               end
            5: begin: BACKWARD                         //DP backward pass
               end
            6: begin: WRITING
               end
            default: state <= 0;                       //fault recovery
         endcase
           end //MAIN
      end //PROCESSING

      //combinational circuits
endmodule
```

The header part assumes an image pair $M \times N$ in size, three channels, with each channel represented by a byte, and the total number of pixels specified. The three buffers are sub-images that have one or more lines of images. The parameters also define the reference systems – left, right, center left, and center right modes – using the keys `LRC` and `LEFT`. In addition, some constant numbers are defined, which we discuss below.

Inside the module keyword, ports are provided for interfacing with the three RAMs, a clock, and a reset signal. Two of the RAMs are for left and right images from cameras; the other is for the disparity result. In the variable declarations, the three buffers are defined as two-dimensional arrays. Three-dimensional arrays may be more natural for representing images but are more complicated to design. A two-dimensional array needs only one counter to access the contents, while a three-dimensional array needs two counters. The pitfall is that we have to consider the pixel coordinates in terms of the array order, which is rather complicated but advantageous for hardware implementation.

The procedural block consists of six states, as explained in the state diagram. The most important data structure is the queue that contains the pointers along the shortest paths. This table is filled during the forward pass and read from during the backward pass. It is an array of $DMAX \times N$ cells, where $DMAX < N$ denotes the maximum disparity. The filled configuration follows that of the search space in the left, right, and center reference systems. If $DMAX < N$, the triangular region becomes trapezoid; the meaningful pointers are written inside this region. Outside the region, the pointers are meaningless and must be avoided by assigning high costs to them. The pointer array is huge, consisting of $N \times DMAX \log DMAX$ elements, and thus the major bottleneck to the implementation. The final part is a combinational circuit that continuously monitors variables in the procedural block and computes required quantities, such as smoothness weight and local distance. This part largely depends on the applications and algorithms.

In the template, the combinational circuits are the same for all the reference systems. They also have parts in common inside the procedural block: reading and writing. The remaining parts are mixtures of

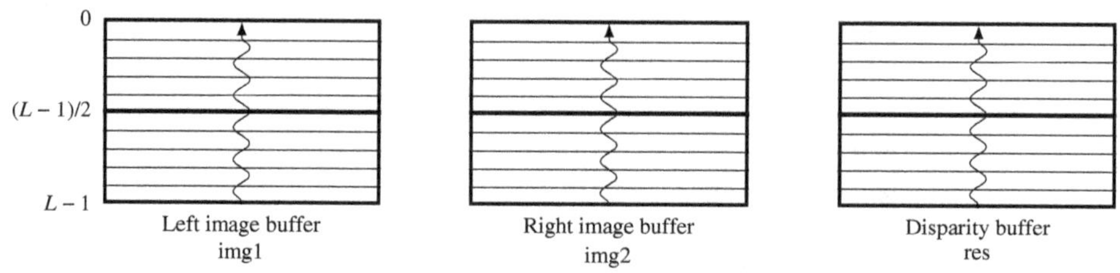

Figure 12.11 The operation of the three buffers: left image (I^l), right image (I^r), and disparity (D)

common and dissimilar parts. In the following sections, we discuss in detail each of the components comprising the DP template.

12.8 FIFO Buffer

The first state of the DP machine is the buffer shift state. In this state, all three buffers shift one line upwards and leave the last line empty. The purpose of the FIFO buffer is to store the raster line and keep it stable during the disparity computation. Without the buffer, the same data would have to be read from the external RAMs, possibly many times, because the disparity computation may use the same pixel many times. The buffer could be just one line of image, but it is expanded to a set of lines in order to accommodate the possibility of neighborhood computation. Wider neighborhoods require more lines, but we typically use a four-neighborhood system, which means three lines of images. The basic goal is to use the centerlines from each of the three buffers to compute the disparity and store the result in the disparity buffer. If the local distance measure uses neighborhoods, then the image lines above and below the centerlines are also used. Each pixel also signifies three RGB channels, even for the disparity buffer.

To design such a buffer, we may use a circular buffer or just an ordinary buffer. In a circular buffer, the insertion point changes every time a raster line is to be written. In a shift buffer, the insertion point is fixed. We will use the shift register method (Figure 12.11).

As depicted in Figure 12.11, let us represent the three buffers by `img1`, `img2`, and `res`. The size of each buffer is $L \times 3N$ bytes, where L is the number of image lines and N is the image width. To make the coordinates symmetric above and below the centerline, L must be odd. The disparity computation is applied to the centerline, $(L-1)/2$. The machine computes the following operations:

$$\texttt{res}(\cdot,(L-1)/2) = T(\texttt{img1}(\cdot,(L-1)/2), \texttt{img2}(\cdot,(L-1)/2), \texttt{res}(\cdot,(L-1)/2)). \quad (12.13)$$

Here, $T(\cdot)$ denotes disparity computation. In the array, the lines are numbered as $[0, L-1]$. In this manner, the centerline is always the $(L-1)/2$-th line, thus the neighborhood coordinates must be considered around it.

The pixel may appear in the image plane, buffer, and array and the exact coordinates must be calculated (Figure 12.12). The image plane is defined as $\{(x,y)|x \in [0,N-1], y \in [0,M-1]\}$. The buffer space is defined as $\{(a,b,c)|a \in [-(L-1)/2,(L-1)/2], b \in [0,N-1], c \in [0,2]\}$. The corresponding array is $\{i|i \in [0,3LN]\}$. If the origins are defined in each space as shown, a pixel appears at (x,y), representing column and row in the image plane – (a,b,c) in the buffer, representing row, column, and channel – and as (i) element in the array. A point (a,b,c) is mapped to i in the following way:

$$i = 3(Na + b) + c. \quad (12.14)$$

If the bottom of the buffer is written with the y' image line, a point (a,b,c) is mapped to (x,y) in the following manner:

$$x = 3b + c,$$
$$y = (y' - (L-1)/2 + a + M)\%M. \quad (12.15)$$

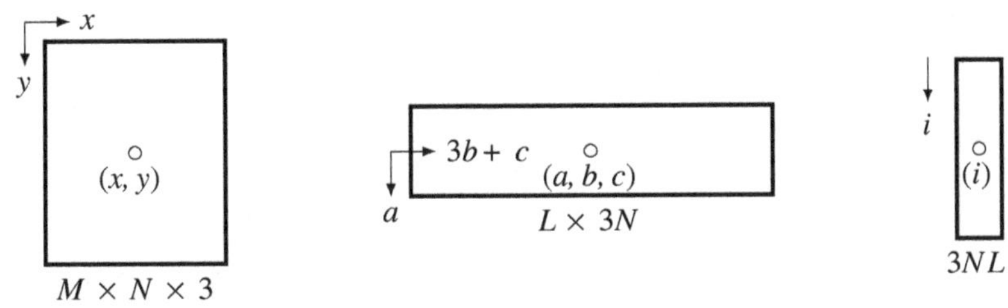

Figure 12.12 Three types of coordinates: image plane, buffer, and array

The transformation from buffer to array occurs often, so a dedicated function must be defined:

```
function ['ADDR_BITS - 1:0] id;
   input signed [9:0] row, column, channel;
begin
   id = 3*('WIDTH*((('LINES-1)>>1)+ row) +column) + channel;
end
endfunction
```

The shift operation of the buffer is as follows.

Listing 12.2 The Verilog DP machine: buffer (2/7)

```
//DP processing
0: begin: BUFFER                                 //shift buffer
     if (k < 3 * 'WIDTH * ('LINES -1)) begin     //3 * pixels
        img1[k] <= img1[k + 3*'WIDTH];
        img2[k] <= img2[k + 3*'WIDTH];
        res [k] <= res [k + 3*'WIDTH];
        k <= k + 1'b1;
     end
     else begin
        state <= 1;                              //go to the next state
        k <= 0;                                  //initialize variable
        idx1 <= 0;                               //for next state
        idx <= 0;                                //for next state
     end
  end
```

This is the first state in the main code. The three buffers are updated concurrently. Because the buffer is represented by a two-dimensional array, only one counter is used here, at the cost of more involved coordinates. Two contiguous lines are separated by the distance, $3N$, and thus shifting this amount is equivalent to shifting a row. Once the shift operation has been completed, the process moves to the next state, possibly by resetting variables. This stage uses $9NL$ space for three buffers and $3N(L-1)$ time for shift operations.

12.9 Reading and Writing

The next state is provided for filling the bottom of the buffer. We are now involved with three external RAMs and three internal buffers. The three pieces of data must be read from the RAMs and written to the buffers, concurrently:

$$\texttt{img1}(\cdot, L-1) \leftarrow I^l(\cdot, y), \texttt{img2}(\cdot, L-1) \leftarrow I^r(\cdot, y), \texttt{res}(\cdot, L-1) \leftarrow D(\cdot, y), \tag{12.16}$$

where I^l, I^r, and D are the quantities in the external RAMs, respectively representing left, right, and disparity map.

The action used when writing is opposite to that used when reading. However, in this case, only the disparity buffer is stored. Because the most recent result is the centerline, it must be copied to the external RAM:

$$D(\cdot, J) \leftarrow \texttt{res}(\cdot, L-1), \tag{12.17}$$

where J is the exact memory address defined by Equation (12.14).

The Verilog HDL code is as follows.

Listing 12.3 The Verilog DP machine: reading and writing (3/7)

```
1:  begin: READING                              //fill the bottom
      if (j < `HEIGHT) begin                    //line number
         if (k < 3* `WIDTH + 2) begin           //pixel
            state <= 1;                         //repeat state
            raddr <= 3 * `WIDTH * j + k;        //pixel address
            img1[3*`WIDTH*(`LINES-1) + idx1] <= i_rdata1;  //1st image
            img2[3*`WIDTH*(`LINES-1) + idx1] <= i_rdata2;  //2nd image
            res [3*`WIDTH*(`LINES-1) + idx1] <= r_rdata;
            idx1 <= idx;                        //delay
            idx <= k;                           //delay
            k <= k + 1'b1;                      //next block
         end else begin
            state <= 2;                         //go to the next state
            count <= 0;
            J <= (`LINES == 1)? j :             //row number
               ((j - ((`LINES - 1) >>1) + `HEIGHT) % `HEIGHT);
            j <= j + 1'b1;                      //next strip
         end
      end else begin
         j <= 0;                                //hit the bottom
      end //else
    end

6: begin: WRITING
     if (count < `WIDTH) begin
        if (k < 3) begin                        //make 3 channels
           r_wdata <= res[id(0,count,0)];       //data
```

```
            r_waddr <= 3*`WIDTH*J + 3*count + k;      //address
            r_wen <= 1;                               //write enable
            k <= k + 1;
         end
         else begin
            count <= count + 1'b1;                    //next
            k <= 0;
         end
      end
      else begin
         state <= 0;
         k <= 0;
         count <= 0;
      end
   end
```

Only one line must be read and the reading pauses until the large state loop is complete. Therefore, the line number and the center of the buffer must be kept in memory throughout the loop. This is explained in the buffer section. We have to be careful of delays that may be introduced between a piece of data and its corresponding address. This can be solved by using some auxiliary variables to store the previous addresses. The range of the loop must also be extended so that the address queue is emptied. Otherwise, the data in the last part of the loop may be lost.

In writing the state, the disparity buffer is written to the external RAM. Note that the disparity buffer is copied three times to make the three channels the same. The three RAM channels contain the same disparity map. This arrangement is necessary in order to provide grey level BMP files.

12.10 Initialization

The main part, Algorithm 12.1, starts at the initialization stage. The purpose of this stage is to provide two quantities: initial costs and pointers. For an $M \times N$ image, we consider the nodes defined in $\{(i,j)|i \in [0,N-1],\ j \in [0,D-1]\}$, where D is the maximum disparity, $D \leq N$. For the right reference system, the costs are defined between $I^r(0)$ and $\{I^l(j)|j \in [0,D-1]\}$. Therefore, the initial costs become

$$\varphi(0,j) = \left|I^r_R(0) - I^l_R(j)\right| + \left|I^r_G(0) - I^l_G(j)\right| + \left|I^r_B(0) - I^l_B(j)\right|, j \in [0,D-1]. \tag{12.18}$$

The three channels are treated separately. For the left reference system, the formula is somewhat different. The distance is defined between $I^l(0)$ and $\{I^r(j)|j \in [0,D-1]\}$:

$$\begin{aligned}\varphi(0,j) = &\left|I^l_R(N-1) - I^r_R(N-1-j)\right| + \left|I^l_R(N-1) - I^r_R(N-1-j)\right| \\ &+ \left|I^l_R(N-1) - I^r_R(N-1-j)\right|, \quad j \in [0,D-1].\end{aligned} \tag{12.19}$$

For the center reference system, the initial costs are

$$\varphi(0,j) = \begin{cases} 0, & j = 0, \\ \infty, & j \in [1,D-1]. \end{cases} \tag{12.20}$$

This condition holds whether the DP starts from $(0,0)$ or $(2N,0)$. A large number is necessary to mark all occlusion nodes apart from the starting node. The pointers can be anything, considering that the nodes have no parents at this point.

$$\eta(0,j) = 0, \forall j \in [0, D-1]. \tag{12.21}$$

At this stage, the first column of the pointer matrix is filled, that is, $\{\eta(0,j)|j \in [0, D-1]\}$. We use absolute distance measure for the three channels, but other measures can also be used.

The Verilog codes are as follows.

Listing 12.4 The Verilog DP machine: initialization (4/7)

```
2: begin: INITIALIZATION                                //DP initialization
     if (count < 'DMAX) begin                           //for each disparity
        queue[0][count] <= 0;                           //initialize the queue
        count <= count + 1'b1;                          //next in the queue
  'ifdef LRC //LR mode
     'ifdef LEFT                                        //left disparity
        costp[count] <=
           distance(img1[id(0,('WIDTH - 1),0)],
                 img2[id(0,('WIDTH - 1 - count),0)])
          + distance(img1[id(0,('WIDTH - 1),1)],
                 img2[id(0,('WIDTH - 1 - count),1)])
          + distance(img1[id(0,('WIDTH - 1),2)],
                 img2[id(0,('WIDTH - 1 - count),2)]);
     'else                                              //right disparity
        costp[count] <= distance(img1[id(0,count,0)],  img2[id(0,0,0)])
           + distance(img1[id(0,count,1)], img2[id(0,0,1)])
           + distance(img1[id(0,count,2)], img2[id(0,0,2)]);
     'endif
  'else //center reference mode
        costp[count] <= (count)? 'INFTY: 0;             //assign large number
  'endif
     end
     else begin
        state <= 3;                                     //next state
        statef <= 0;                                    //next sub-state
        i <= 1;                                         //1st pixel
        jj <= 0;                                        //zero disparity
     end
  end
```

Here, the distance measure is a function, which we will define later. In the distance measure, the coordinates of the buffer elements are rather complicated, due to the use of the Verilog array. The process is similar to that of delineating the two-dimensional image plane into a one-dimensional array. In calculating such coordinates, we have to take the image width and channels into account. Functions may simplify the coordinate transformation from the one-dimensional array to the two-dimensional array, and vice versa.

At the end of this process, there is a transition to the next state. The next state has both state and sub-states that must be clearly specified. In addition, variables, which will be used in the next state must be set to appropriate values. In this manner, we may reuse the same variables many times in different states, saving space but not the connections.

12.11 Forward Pass

The forward pass in Algorithm 12.1 comprises the core of DP. The key operation in this pass is the computation of cost and pointer for all the nodes. It provides a big table that stores the pointers. In the right reference system, the nodes are the elements in the space, $\{(x^r, d)|x^r \in [0, N-1], d \in [0, D-1]\}$. As a preliminary condition, the costs and pointers of the nodes, $\{(0, d)|d \in [0, D-1]\}$, must have been determined in the previous initialization stage. The remaining nodes are subsequently visited and computed, recursively (Figure 12.13). In the figure, the horizontal axis signifies the number of pixels, while the vertical axis signifies the disparity. The maximum disparity level is denoted with thick lines.

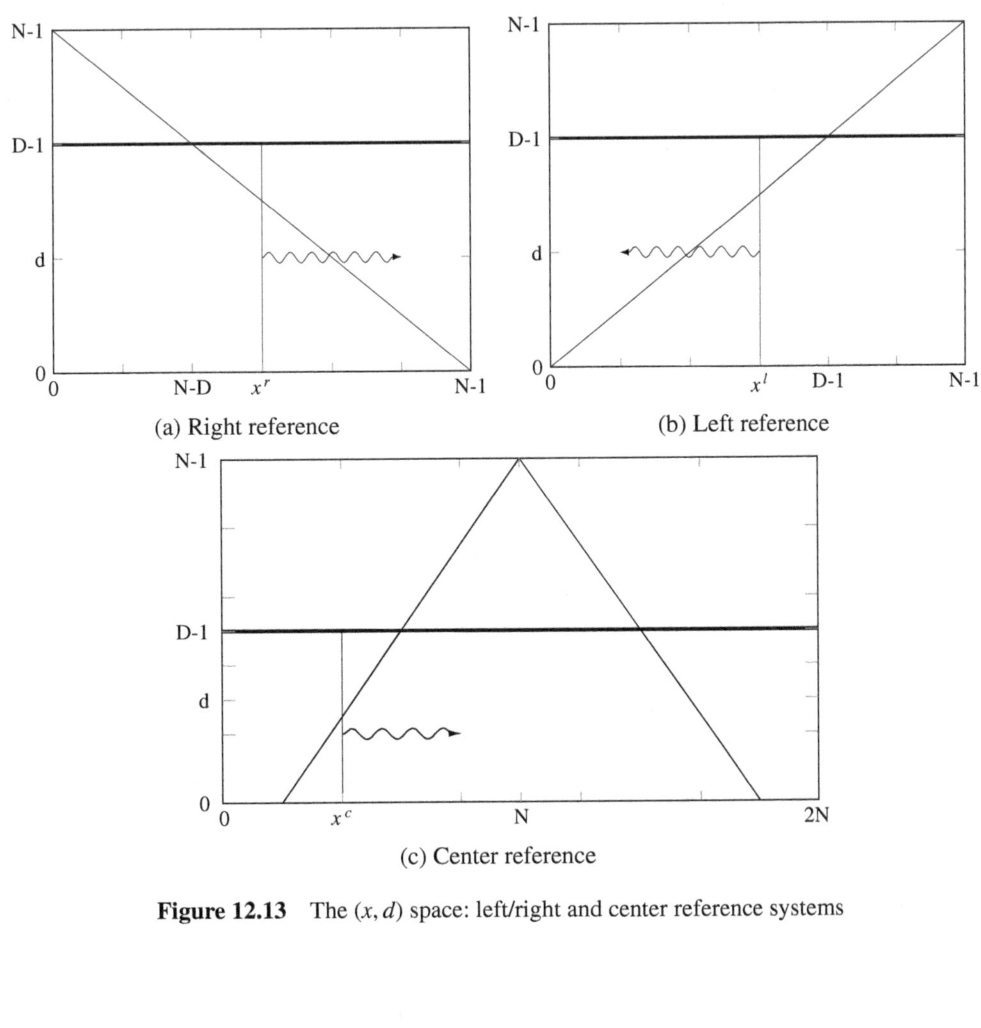

Figure 12.13 The (x, d) space: left/right and center reference systems

The arrows indicate the computing direction of the nodes in a column, and this is represented by a vertical line. In Figure 12.13(a), the search space is divided into two parts, inside and outside of the trapezoid. Inside the trapezoid, all the nodes are mapped to a pair of corresponding images. Outside the trapezoid, all the nodes are mapped only to the right image. In computing costs and pointers, the matching and occlusion nodes must be dealt with differently. The computation proceeds along the computing costs and pointers. The computation proceeds along the x^r axis. The costs and pointers of the nodes at a point on the computing costs and pointers. The computation proceeds along the x^r axis are computed using the costs and pointers of the nodes at the computing costs and pointers. The computation proceeds along the $x^r - 1$ axis. The nodes on the same axis are all independent, allowing for possible parallel computation. For the occlusion nodes, the costs must be very large to prevent the optimal path from infiltrating this forbidden region. The pointers, which will never be used, may be arbitrary in this region. The result is the pointer array $P = \{\eta(x,d)|x \in [0, N-1], d \in [0, D-1]\}$, where $x = x^r$.

The left reference system has a similar interpretation. In Figure 12.13(b), the search space is $S = \{(x^l, d)|x^l \in [0, N-1], d \in [0, D-1]\}$. The shape of the trapezoid and the search direction are all opposite to those of the right reference system. The pointer array is also indexed in accordance with the direction of the forward path: $P = \{\eta(x,d)|x \in [0, N-1], d \in [0, D-1]\}$, where $x = N - 1 - x^l$. This makes the pointer table the same type for both reference systems.

The forward pass operation for the center reference system is shown in Figure 12.13(c). The search space is $S = \{(x^c, d)|x^c \in [0, 2N], d \in [0, D-1]\}$ in this case. The shape of the search space is symmetric, and so the search direction can be either forward or backward, but the result obtained may be different. For the forward direction, the pointer table becomes $P = \{(x^c, d)|x_c \in [0, 2N], d \in [0, D-1]\}$. The difficulty of this system is that the region inside the trapezoid also contains both matching and occlusion nodes (Figure 12.6(c)), which must be treated differently.

In designing the forward pass, we first describe the algorithm with a state diagram (Figure 12.14). The diagram is common to both the right and left reference systems. The process starts at the initialization state,

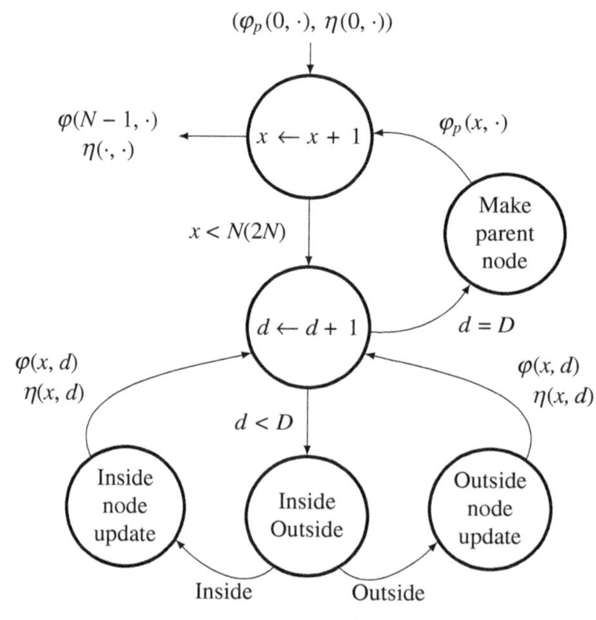

Figure 12.14 The computation of the forward pass: $\varphi(x,d)$ and $\eta(x,d)$ (the value in the parenthesis is for the center reference system)

with $\varphi(0,\cdot)$ and $\eta(0,\cdot)$. The first state represents the big loop that computes in the direction of the column, $x = 0, 1, \ldots, N-1$. The second state represents the sub-loop that computes the rows, $d = 0, 1, \ldots, N-1$. In each of the rows in a given column, the node-pointer update is different, depending on whether the node is a matching or an occlusion node. For a matching node, the costs and the pointers are updated according to the DP equation. For an occlusion node, the cost must be given as an arbitrarily large number, which prevents the backtracking from passing the region over the diagonal. However, this assignment is not sufficient to prevent the optimal path infiltrating this forbidden region. A small addition to the large number may cause an overflow, resulting in a wrong number. For this reason, the positions inside and outside of the trapezoid must be considered in the node update.

For the center reference system, there are two differences in the flow graph. First, the column is limited to $x \leq 2N$. Second, the nodes inside the trapezoid are not all matching nodes. The mixed matching and occlusion nodes inside the trapezoid must be dealt with differently.

Once all the nodes in a column are determined, the costs associated with the nodes present must be stored as the parent nodes, so that in the next column, the current column can be used as parent nodes. This series of computations completes one column and thus must proceed to the next column. When all the columns have been visited, the forward pass is complete, having $\varphi(N-1,\cdot)$ and $\eta(N-1,\cdot)$.

The concept in the diagram can be represented as the following Verilog code:

Listing 12.5 The Verilog DP machine: forward pass (5/7)

```
3: begin: FORWARD                                          //DP forward pass
   `ifdef LRC
   if (i < `WIDTH) begin: COLUMN                           //for each column
   `else
   if (i < 2*`WIDTH + 1'b1) begin: COLUMN                  //for each column
   `endif
   if (jj < `DMAX) begin: ROW                              //for each disparity
   case (statef)
   0:  begin: COST_INIT                                    //initialization
         statef <= 1;                                      //next sub-state
         count <= 0;                                       //parent index
         cost[jj] <=  `INFTY;                              //cost reset
         queue[i][jj] <= `DMAX - 1;                        //queue reset
      end
   1: `ifdef LRC
      if (jj <`WIDTH - i) begin: TRAPEZOID_IN              //matching
         if(count < `DMAX) begin: COMPARISON               //shortest path
           if (costp[count] < `INFTY) begin                //avoid overflow
             queue[i][jj]<= ((costp[count] + weight(count,jj))
                         < cost[jj])?(count): queue[i][jj];
             cost[jj] <= ((costp[count] + weight(count,jj))
                         < cost[jj])?(costp[count] + weight(count,jj))
                         : cost[jj];
           end
           count <= count + 1'b1;                          //for each parent
         end
```

```
        else begin: COST_UPDATE                     //add ldistance
           `ifdef LEFT                              //left disparity
           cost[jj] <= (ldistance + cost[jj])>>1;
           `else                                    //right disparity
           cost[jj] <= (ldistance + cost[jj])>>1;
           `endif
           statef <= 0;
           jj <= jj + 1'b1;                         //repeat disparity
        end
        stater <= 0; //if not upper TRAPEZOID
     end
  `else
     if ((jj <= i - 1) & (jj <= 2*`WIDTH - i - 1)) begin: TRAPEZOID_IN
        if ((i + jj) % 2 == 1) begin: MATCHING_NODE
           if (count < `DMAX) begin: COMPARISON
              if (costp[count] < `INFTY) begin //avoid overflow
                 queue[i][jj]<= ((costp[count] + weight(count,jj))
                 < cost[jj])?(count): queue[i][jj];
                 cost[jj] <= ((costp[count] + weight(count,jj))
                 < cost[jj])?(costp[count] + weight(count,jj))
                 : cost[jj];
              end
              count <= count + 1'b1;                //for each parent
           end
           else begin: COST_UPDATE                  //add ldistance
              cost[jj] <= (ldistance + cost[jj])>>1; //normalize
              jj <= jj + 1'b1;                      //repeat disparity
              statef <= 0;
           end
        end
        else begin: OCCLUSION_NODE                  //outside TRAPEZOID
           statef <= 0;
           jj <= jj + 1'b1;
           queue[i][jj] <= jj;
           cost[jj] <= costp[jj] + `ALPHA;          //assign penalty
        end                                         //smaller the smoother
        stater <= 0;//if not upper TRAPEZOID
     end
  `endif
     else begin: TRAPEZOID_OUT                      //unobservable region
        statef <= 0;
        stater <= 0;
        cost[jj] <= `INFTY;                         //assign big number
        jj <= jj + 1'b1;                            //next disparity
     end
```

```
      endcase
   end //ROW
   else begin
   case (stater)                                    //parent update
    0:  begin                                       //initialization
          stater <= 1;                              //next sub-state
          count <= 0;                               //reset variable
        end
    1:  begin: PARENT                               //main
          if (count < `DMAX) begin  //for each disparity
              stater <= 1;                          //repeat state
            costp[count] <= cost[count];            //copy
            count <= count + 1'b1;                  //next disparity
          end
          else begin
            stater <= 0;                            //reset sub-state
            jj <= 0;                                //reset disparity
            i <= i + 1'b1;                          //next pixel
          end
        end
     endcase
end
end //COLUMN
else begin
   state <= 4;                                      //go to the next state
end
end //FORWARD
```

The forward pass consists of two loops (`j` and `jj`) as explained in the diagram. The internal loop (`jj`) is further divided into two parts: `ROW_1` and `ROW_2`. The first part, `ROW_1`, is for updating node costs and pointers. The other part, `ROW_2`, is for collecting all the nodes and making them parent nodes. The two parts must be separated, otherwise the updated parents may be used too early in the current loop.

The node updating, `ROW_1`, also consists of two sub-parts: `TRAPEZOID_IN` and `TRAPEZOID_OUT`. One part is for updating the nodes inside the trapezoid; the other part is for updating the nodes outside the trapezoid. The state of the matching nodes inside the trapezoid also contains a loop, for comparing the costs of the possible parent nodes. In the center reference mode, the nodes inside the trapezoid are further divided into matching and occlusion nodes. All the conditions – matching to matching, occlusion to matching, matching to occlusion, and occlusion to occlusion – must be considered. In this code, the transition from occlusion to occlusion is excluded.

Note that, in computing local costs, there are transformations from buffer to image plane. Some parts of the code can be parallelized, whereas some other parts cannot be parallelized. The blocks, `COST_INIT`, `COST_UPDATE`, `TRAPEZOID_OUT`, and `PARENT` are possible candidates for parallelization. The block, `TRAPEZOID_IN`, however, is inherently serial. Note also that in `COST_UPDATE`, the cost update is significantly different among the reference systems and thus must be chosen appropriately by the compiler directives, **`` `ifdef ``**, **`` `else ``**, and **`` `endif ``**.

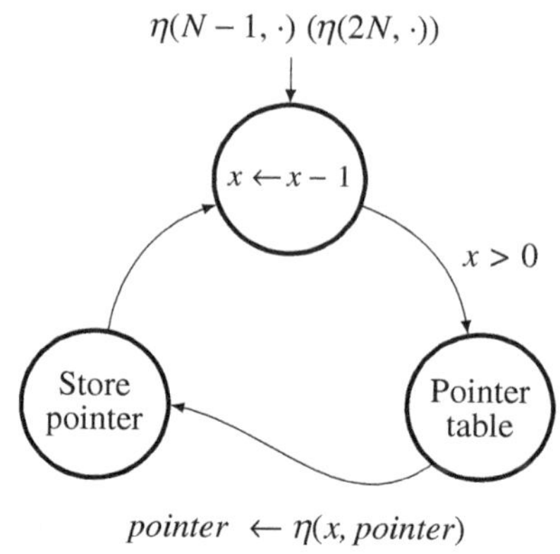

Figure 12.15 The backward pass (The expression in the parenthesis is for the center reference system. Others are for the left and right reference systems.)

12.12 Backward Pass

In Algorithm 12.1, the finalization is the computation stage that follows the forward pass and appears before the backward pass. The purpose of this stage is to choose a starting point for the backward pass. The starting point must be a node whose cost is minimal among the nodes in the final column. In the three reference systems, this starting point is fixed to the last point of the triangle, making this stage almost trivial. For the left and right reference systems, the starting point is $\eta(N-1, 0)$, because the configuration of their pointer matrix is the same. However, the center reference system may start from either $\eta(2N, 0)$ or $\eta(0, 0)$.

The backward pass (illustrated in Figure 12.15) starts when the finalization state is complete. Starting from the end of the image pixel for the right reference system (reverse for the left reference system), the pointers in the pointer array are read in succession. For each reading, the pointer is written as a result on the disparity map. This concept is represented in the Verilog HDL as follows:

Listing 12.6 The Verilog DP machine: backward pass (6/7)

```
4:  begin: FINALIZATION                        //DP finalization
        state <= 5;                            //go to the next state
        pointer <= 0;                          //starting pointer
        count <= 0;                            //reset counter
    end
5:  begin: BACKWARD                            //DP backward pass
    `ifdef LRC //LR reference
    if (count <`WIDTH)  begin
       pointer <= queue[`WIDTH - 1 - count][pointer];    //recursion
       `ifdef LEFT
       res[id(0,count,0)] <= queue[`WIDTH - 1 - count][pointer];
       `else
       res[id(0,(`WIDTH-count),-3)] <= queue[`WIDTH-1-count][pointer];
       `endif
```

```
`else  //center reference
if (count < 2*`WIDTH + 1'b1)  begin
   pointer <= queue[`WIDTH*2 - count][pointer];
`ifdef LEFT //center left reference
   res[id(0,(`WIDTH - ((count+pointer-1)>>1)),- 3)]
      <= queue[2*`WIDTH - count][pointer];
`else //center right reference
   pointer <= queue[`WIDTH*2 - count][pointer];
   res[id(0,(`WIDTH - ((count-pointer-1)>>1)),- 3)]
      <= queue[2*`WIDTH - count][pointer];
`endif
`endif
   count <= count + 1'b1;
end else begin
   state <= 6;                                    //next state
   count <= 0;
end
end
```

The disparity result is written to the first channel only. The two other channels are not used, but are instead reserved for other possible algorithms. Note that there are coordinate transformations from the buffer space to the image space. A combinational circuit is provided for monitoring the variables and providing the appropriate coordinate values.

In this code, the disparity map is exactly the same size as the image, including the three channels. The coordinates of the center reference system are also transformed to either the left or the right image plane. The disparity buffer and RAM can more than store the disparity. Usually $D \ll N$, and so the three channels can more than represent the disparity range D, $\log_2 D \ll 24$. This makes it possible to use the disparity buffer and RAM otherwise, that is to store information other than the disparity, such as features and other temporary results. We leave this possibility up to the actual applications that use the DP machine.

12.13 Combinational Circuits

The remaining parts are the combinational circuits and functions, which finish in the current simulation time. There are three parts: coordinates transform, weight computation, and local cost computation. The coordinates transform is for computing an array index from the given buffer coordinates, according to Equation (12.14). This can be easily realized by the Verilog function.

The cost computation needs two distance measures: smoothness measure and local distance measure. The smoothness measure is defined as an absolute of the two arguments:

$$\mu(k,j) \triangleq |k-j|. \tag{12.22}$$

The local distance measure uses the same absolute measure:

$$\rho(i,j) \triangleq |I^l_R(i) - I^r_R(j)| + |I^l_G(i) - I^r_G(j)| + |I^l_B(i) - I^r_B(j)|. \tag{12.23}$$

However, in the actual code, it becomes somewhat complicated because of the boundary effect, neighborhood computation, and the size of the strip. The use of neighborhoods can also be adopted in many different ways. Instead of the sum of individual differences, average features or edges may be used.

All three effects are considered in the following listing:

Listing 12.7 The Verilog DP machine: functions (7/7)

```
//coordinates transformation: (row,column,channel) -> id
function ['ADDR_BITS - 1:0] id;
   input signed [9:0] row, column, channel;
begin
   id = 3*('WIDTH*((('LINES-1)>>1)+ row) +column) + channel;
end
endfunction

//absolute distance measure with threshold
function ['DATA_BITS - 1:0] weight;           //smoothness constraint
   input ['DATA_BITS - 1:0] a, b;
   begin
      weight = (((a > b)? (a-b) : (b - a)) < 5)?
         ((a > b)? (a-b) : (b - a)):  'DMAX;  //threshold
   end
endfunction

//image intensity distance measure
function ['DATA_BITS - 1:0] distance;         //intensity distance
   input ['DATA_BITS - 1:0] a, b;
   begin
      distance = (a > b)? (a-b): (b - a);     //distance measure
   end
endfunction

//corresponding points for the given disparity
'ifdef LRC
   'ifdef LEFT                                //left coordinate
      assign xl = 'WIDTH-1-i;
      assign xr = 'WIDTH-1-i-jj;              //right coordinate
   'else                                      //right coordinate
      assign xl = i + jj;                     //left coordinate
      assign xr = i;                          //right coordinate
   'endif
'else
   assign xl = (i + jj - 1)>>1;               //left coordinate
   assign xr = (i - jj - 1)>> 1;              //right coordinate
'endif

//local distance: four-neighborhood
assign ldistance =
   distance(img1[id(0,xl,0)],img2[id(0,xr,0)]) //center pixel
```

```
+ distance(img1[id(0,xl,1)],img2[id(0,xr,1)])
+ distance(img1[id(0,xl,2)],img2[id(0,xr,2)])
//south neighborhood
+ ((`LINES < 2)? 0:
(((distance(img1[id(1,xl,0)],img2[id(1,xr,0)])   //south neighbor
+ distance(img1[id(1,xl,1)],img2[id(1,xr,1)])
+ distance(img1[id(1,xl,2)],img2[id(1,xr,2)])
//north neighborhood
+ distance(img1[id(-1,xl,0)],img2[id(-1,xr,0)]) //north neighbor
+ distance(img1[id(-1,xl,1)],img2[id(-1,xr,1)])
+ distance(img1[id(-1,xl,2)],img2[id(-1,xr,2)])
//east neighborhood
+ (((xl < `WIDTH - 1) && (xr < `WIDTH - 1))?    //east neighbor
  distance(img1[id(0,(xl+1),0)],img2[id(0,(xr+1),0)]) //boundary
+ distance(img1[id(0,(xl+1),1)],img2[id(0,(xr+1),1)])
+ distance(img1[id(0,(xl+1),2)],img2[id(0,(xr+1),2)]): 0)
//west neighborhood
+ (((xl > 0) && (xr > 0))?                 //west neighbor
  distance(img1[id(0,(xl-1),0)],img2[id(0,(xr-1),0)]) //boundary
+ distance(img1[id(0,(xl-1),1)],img2[id(0,(xr-1),1)])
+ distance(img1[id(0,(xl-1),2)],img2[id(0,(xr-1),2)]): 0))>>2)));
```

This template contains a local distance measure that uses four pixels from four-neighborhoods, together with the center pixel. To turn on the neighborhood computation, the buffer must contain at least three lines. Pixels beyond the boundary are assigned boundary values. However, mirror images or other types of boundary definitions may be adopted in this function. Moreover, even though the neighborhood is defined as a four-neighborhood system, it can be expanded to become a larger neighborhood system. All the neighborhood definitions are possible because the buffer has a general design for storing a strip instead of a single raster line. For better performance, the distance measure can be expanded to other measures such as Pott's model, edges, and features, instead of simple intensity values.

12.14 Simulation

We tested the code for both simulation and synthesis. There were numerous warning signals because we emphasized readability over optimization. However, before actual implementation, the code must be cleaned and optimized by rectifying as many of the warnings as possible.

The test images used were a pair of 225×188 images. The test images allowed us to test various versions of the DP machine. The first possibility was the reference modes: left reference, right reference, center reference right, and center reference left. The center reference has two modes, depending on where the disparity map is projected: left image or right image plane. In terms of the distance measures, there are numerous variations. The point operation and the neighborhood operations, in particular, must be compared for performance.

The first sets of tests were point operations in the DP machine (Figure 12.16). Figures 12.16(a) and 12.16(b) are a pair of stereo images that have 225×188 pixels in three channels. The other images are the disparity maps obtained by the DP machine. The performance depends on the parameters and distance measures. As a first attempt, the disparity level, D, was restricted to 32, in order to observe

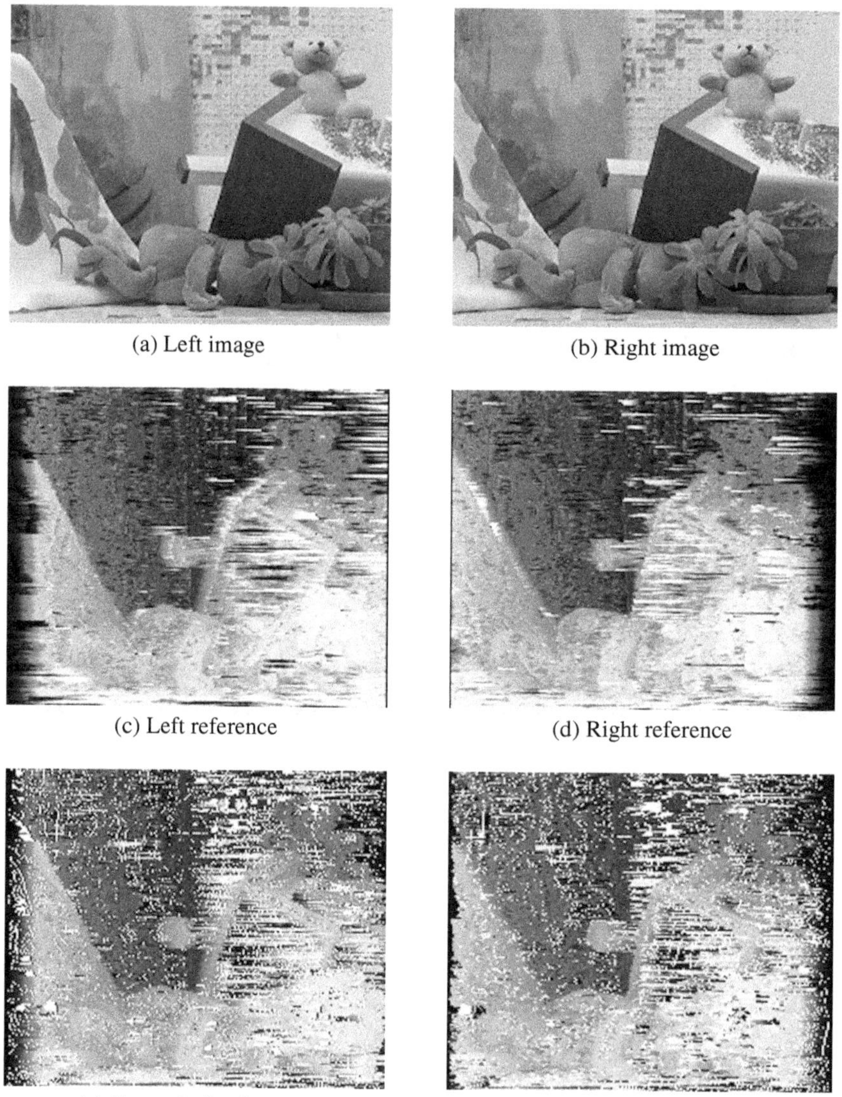

(a) Left image (b) Right image

(c) Left reference (d) Right reference

(e) Center Left reference (f) Center Right reference

Figure 12.16 Disparity maps: point operations

the range of the disparity. The smoothness parameter was also limited to 5. The penalty from matching node to occlusion node was set to 10. In addition, the buffers contained only one line of images, which automatically turned off the local neighborhood operations, retaining only point operations. The original disparity map was a single channel gray map. For better rendering, the disparity map was made to three channels, histogram equalized, and color-coded. The result was a color map, with each level represented by a different color.

Figure 12.17 depicts the simulation results. Three lines are used to compute local distance in a four-neighborhood system. The images in the second row (Figures 12.17(c) and 12.17(d)) are the

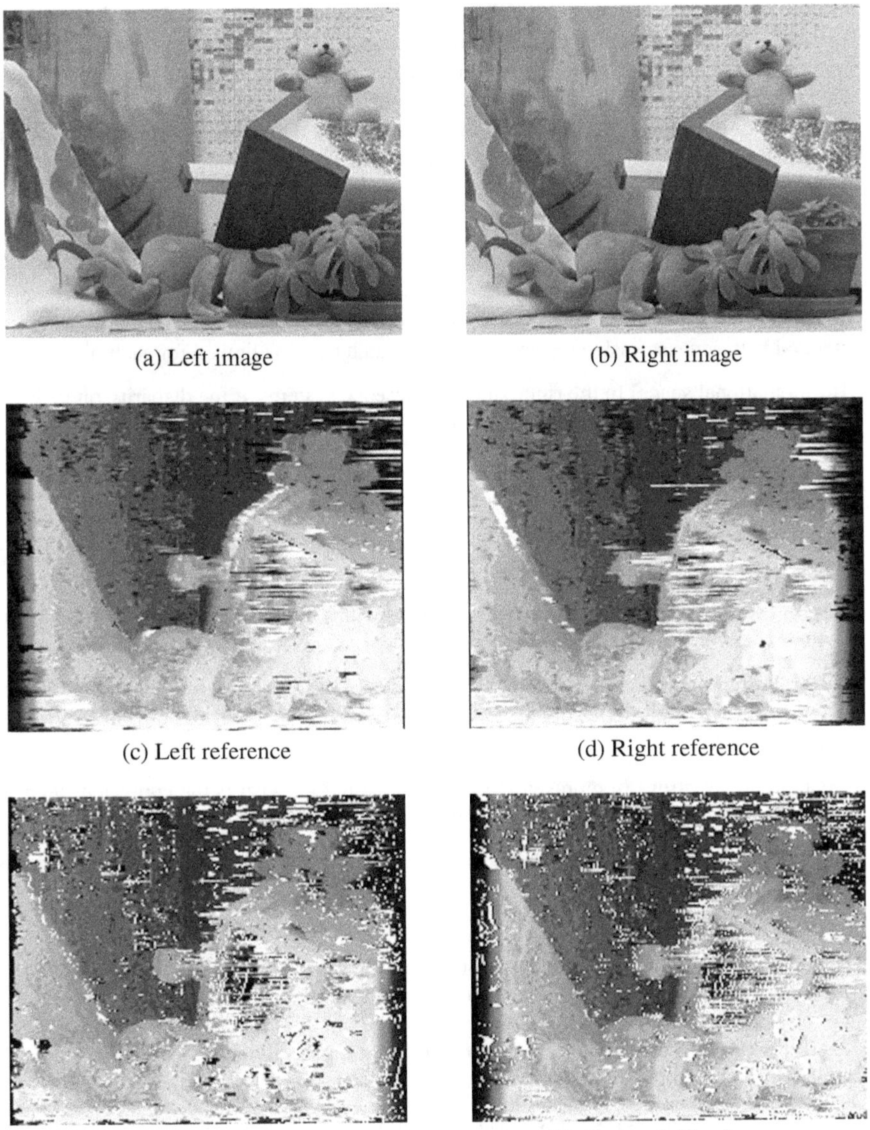

(a) Left image (b) Right image

(c) Left reference (d) Right reference

(e) Center left reference (f) Center right reference

Figure 12.17 Disparity maps: four-neighborhood operations

disparity maps for the left and right reference systems, respectively. Of note is the fact that the left side is poor in the left reference and vice versa in the right reference. The disparity maps for the center reference are in the third row (Figures 12.17(e) and 12.17(f)). The disparity map is mapped to the left and right image planes.

A comparison of the two sets of simulations, that is point operation and neighborhood operation, easily shows the difference between them. The neighborhood operation provides a better disparity map but uses more combinational circuits and functions.

Because the purpose of designing the DP machine is to provide a standard template, it is generally configured with three buffers, which contain multiple lines, allowing possible neighborhood operations. Equally important, the reference systems are all counted in the design, which can be turned on and off by the header parameters. A simple condition on the transition between nodes is used in the center reference system. The size of the images and the level of disparities are defined by the parameters. As a result, advanced algorithms can be imported into this DP machine.

Problems

12.1 [Line processing] In a real-time system, the disparity for a line must be computed between the intervals of two successive lines. For an $M \times N$ pixel with a 30 fps video stream, what is the time interval between successive raster lines? How much time is allowed for each pixel?

12.2 [Computational space] In the right and left reference systems, if the disparity range is limited to $D \leq N$, how many matching nodes and occlusion nodes are there?

12.3 [Computational space] In the center reference system, if the disparity range is limited to $D \leq N$, how many matching nodes and occlusion nodes are there?

12.4 [Architecture] The three buffers are updated by shifting upwards and filling the bottom. What else could be done instead of shifting?

12.5 [Overall scheme] The DP machine was designed with a large state machine. How can you design it otherwise?

12.6 [FIFO buffer] The buffer is designed with the Verilog array. How can it be implemented using a Verilog multidimensional array? What are the advantages and disadvantages of the two methods?

12.7 [Reading and writing] In representing a line in the buffer, what is the equivalent representation for `res[0,0,k]`, where $k \in [0, 3 * \mathit{WIDTH} - 1]$?

12.8 [Forward pass] In the forward pass, the previous column is searched for all nodes, with the expectation that the occlusion nodes have a high cost. How can `if (costp[count] < 'INFTY)` be replaced otherwise?

12.9 [Forward pass] In choosing the smallest parent, the occlusion nodes are already assigned very high costs in the previous loop, and thus, adding a smoothness penalty does not allow them to be the parents. According to this observation, the conditions in the previous problem are not necessary. What is the problem in this method for treating all the nodes in the column the same way?

12.10 [Combinational circuits] What is the critical path that determines the fastest clock period?

References

Aho A, Hopcroft J and Ullman J 1974 *The Design and Analysis of Computer Algorithms*. Addison-Wesley.

Baker H and Binford T 1981 Depth from intensity and edge based stereo *Proc. Seventh Int'l Joint Conf. Artificial Intelligence*, pp. 631–636.

Bertsekas DP 2007 *Dynamic Programming and Optimal Control* vol. 1,2. Athena Scientific.

Cormen T, Rivest CLR and Stein C 2001 *Introduction to Algorithms* second edn. The MIT Press.

Jeong H and Oh Y 2000 Trellis-based parallel stereo matching *Proceedings of the IEEE International Conference on Acoustics, Speech, and Signal Processing*, Istanbul, Turkey.

Jeong H and Park S 2004 Generalized trellis stereo matching with systolic array *Lecture Notes in Computer Science*, vol. 3358, pp. 263–267.

Jeong H and Yuns O 2000 Fast stereo matching using constraints in discrete space. *IEICE Transactions on Information and Systems* **83**(7), 1592–1600.

Jeong H, Oh Y, Park J, Koo B and Lee SW 2002 Vision-based adaptive and recursive tracking of unpaved roads. *Pattern Recognition Letters* **23**(1), 73–82.

Knuth D 1997 *The Art of Computer Programming*. Addison-Wesley.

Ohta Y and Kanade T 1985 Stereo by intra- and inter-scanline search using dynamic programming. *IEEE Trans. Pattern Anal. Mach. Intell.* **7**(2), 139–154.

13

Systolic Array for Stereo Matching

In this chapter, following the single processor designed in Chapter 12, we design a systolic machine for stereo matching. Although the two machines are structurally different, they are both based on the line processing method (i.e. LVSIM) introduced in Chapter 4, which processes a frame line by line (or strip by strip), using small internal buffers. The systolic array introduced in Chapter 4 is a linear array consisting of many identical processors connected in a neighborhood fashion. This type of architecture is especially effective for VLSI implementation because it has many advantages, such as a regular structure, identical processors, neighborhood connections, and simple control.

This chapter first deals with the search space, because the problem is to find the path that incurs the least cost. We derive a systolic array, which is an efficient machine for such problems, in a systematic manner, following (Jeong 1984; Kung and Leiserson 1980; Leiserson and Saxe 1991). Using huge broadcasting, we spatially and temporally transform a simple circuit that matches the left and right image streams for disparity computation into the form of systolic arrays. The result is eight fundamental circuits that can be classified into two types: forward backward (FB), in which the two signal streams flow in opposite directions, and backward backward (BB), in which the two signals flow in the same direction. The multitude of circuits arises from the dualism or degree of freedom originating from the data direction, the head and tail, and the left right reference, resulting in the eight fundamental circuits.

We start designing FB and BB circuits, separately, as representative circuits, in Verilog HDL. The major components of the circuits are the systolic array, where actual computation is executed, and a control unit that drives the array. Although they look like datapath methods, both systems work in perfect synchrony with a common system clock, without any intervening handshake messages except for a starting signal, resulting in a very fast machine.

13.1 Search Space

For a pair of epipolar lines $(I^l(\cdot, y), I^r(\cdot, y))$, the purpose of stereo matching is to find the disparity that exists in the space $\{(x, d)|x \in [0, N-1], d \in [0, D-1]\}$, for the left right reference systems, and $\{(x, d)|x \in [0, 2N-2], d \in [0, D-1]\}$, for the center reference system. The three types of spaces are shown in Figure 13.1. The measurable region is the trapezoids, a subset inside the rectangular region, formed by cutting the triangles. Areas out of this region are not observed by both cameras and are thus are indeterminate in nature. An object surface must appear as a line connecting $(0, d)$ and $(N-1, 0)$

Architectures for Computer Vision: From Algorithm to Chip with Verilog, First Edition. Hong Jeong.

Companion Website: www.wiley.com/go/jeong

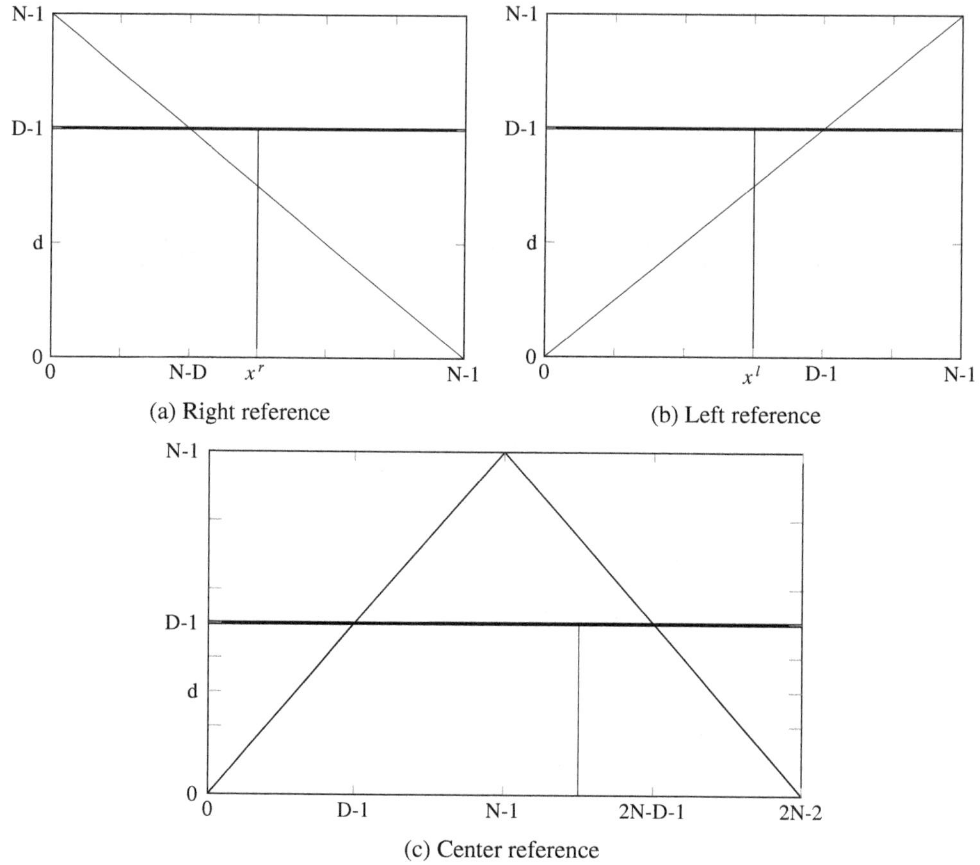

Figure 13.1 The (x, d) space: left, right, and center reference systems

in the right reference, $(0, 0)$ and $(N - 1, d)$ in the left reference, and $(1, 0)$ and $(2N - 2, 0)$ in the center reference. For the three reference systems, the regions inside the trapezoid are defined by

$$\begin{aligned} R^r &= \{(x^r, d)|x^r \in [0, N-1], d \leq \min\{D-1, N-1-x^r\}\}, \\ R^l &= \{(x^l, d)|x^l \in [0, N-1], d \leq \min\{D-1, x^l\}\}, \\ R^c &= \{(x^c, d)|x^c \in [0, 2N-2], d \leq \min\{D-1, x^c, N-1-x^c\}, x^c + d = even\}. \end{aligned} \tag{13.1}$$

Note that in the center reference, only the nodes that satisfy $x^c + d = even$ can be projected onto both images. In computing disparity, we use this equation as constraints on the search region.

In Chapter 12, we designed a DP machine that searches the solution space, column by column, as indicated by the vertical line. However, in this chapter, we present other methods for scanning the space, leading to the systolic array. We start the derivation of the array from a purely computational point of view below.

13.2 Systolic Transformation

We consider an array, $\{PE(d)|d \in [0, D-1]\}$, where the processing elements are connected only between neighbors. In Chapter 3, we encountered a linear systolic array that computes convolution. In that system, the signal and the weights were the inputs, and the output was a weighted summation. The timing relationship between filter weights, the input signal, and the output was the key to the design of that array. Although seemingly different, the linear convolution and the disparity computation are, in fact, the same concept. The disparity is the result of the spatial relationship between two images. If the images are supplied by streams, the spatial relationship becomes the timing relationship. This transformation is possible by tilting the vertical scan line, as shall soon be seen.

Let us derive such an array in a more systematic way. The general idea is to begin with a simple circuit that we can easily understand; then we will modify the simple circuit to a more desirable form, following some intermediate stages. The techniques used in this approach consist of topological and timing transformation (Jeong 1984).

Before beginning, let us establish some data representation conventions. First, the image streams consist of the right and left images, $I^r(t)$ and $I^l(t)$, where $t \in [0, N-1]$. In the array circuit, the timing relationship between the two streams is the most important factor and we therefore consider only the sequence order. The order of the stream might be head first, $I = 0, 1, \dots, N_1$, or tail first, $I = N_1, N_2, \dots, 0$, where N_x is an abbreviation for $N - x$. Second, the disparity is a nonnegative integer, satisfying

$$d(x^r) = x^l - x^r \geq 0, \quad d(x^l) = x^r - x^l \geq 0. \tag{13.2}$$

That is, in the right reference, the corresponding point in the left image is on the right of that in the right image. Conversely, in the left reference, the corresponding point in the right image is on the left of that in the left image. This property is essential in deriving the pipelined array with the two image streams, where the processing elements are numbered with disparities.

Let us first start with the right reference system. One of the simplest forms is a circuit in which the right image is broadcast to all the nodes and the left image is shifted into the nodes in a pipelined manner (Figure 13.2(a)). The numbered nodes denote the processing elements $PE(d)$ with $d \in [0, D-1]$, where $D = 3$. The other two nodes are the hosts supplying the right and left images, as specified by the node labels. In this case, the image stream advances in head-first order. There are two things to note about the circuit. First, while the left image enters the array in its original order, the right image enters late, in the amount of $D - 1$ clocks. This delay is indicated by introducing 'don't care' in front of the right image stream. Note that this delay keeps the two streams synchronized correctly, in such a way that at PE(d), the right signal x^r always encounters the left signal $x^l = x^r + d$.

Second, every edge between two nodes is blocked by a clocked register, although the edges from the two sources are free from this constraint. This small circuit with $D = 3$ operates as follows. After two clock periods, the two signals meet at the three nodes in pairs, $PE(0) : (I^r(0), I^l(0))$, $PE(1) : (I^r(0), I^l(1))$, and $PE(2) : (I^r(0), I^l(2))$. The relationship subsequently holds at all times, $PE(0) : (I^r(t), I^l(t))$, $PE(1) : (I^r(t), I^l(t+1))$, and $PE(2) : (I^r(t), I^l(t+2))$. Each node has only to compute the two incoming data streams for its disparity computation. In this dynamical system, the spatial relationship $(x^r, x^r + d)$, is changed to the time relationship $(t, t + d)$.

To describe the node behavior quantitatively, we use the notations $I_i(d)$ and $I_o(d)$, respectively, for the input and output to a node $PE(d)$. Consequently, node $PE(d)$ performs the following.

$$\begin{aligned} I_o^l(d) &\leftarrow I_i^l(d), \\ y(d) &\leftarrow T(I_i^r(d), I_i^l(d)), \quad \forall d \in [0, D-1], \end{aligned} \tag{13.3}$$

where $T(\cdot)$ denotes the operations for forward pass and $y(d)$, the intermediate result.

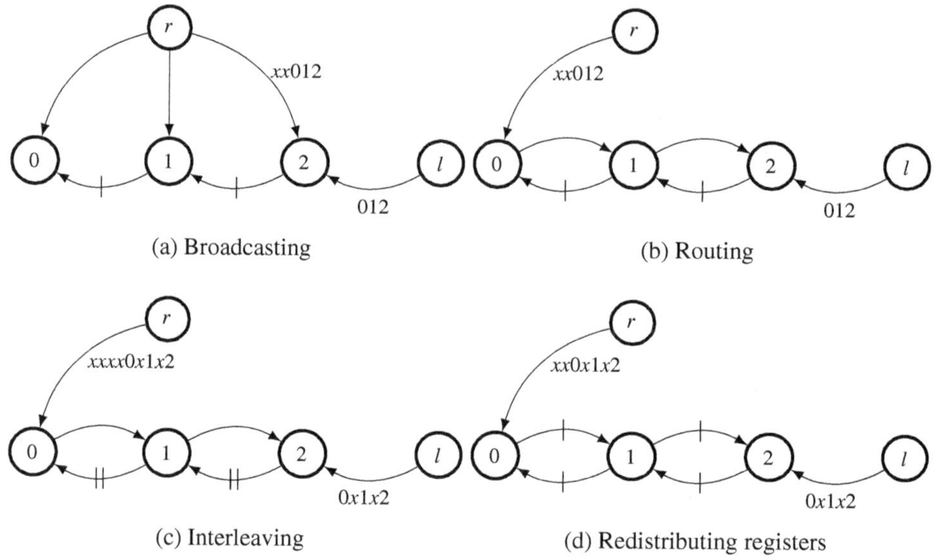

Figure 13.2 Deriving a systolic array, in which two image streams, I^r : $xx012$ and I^l : 012, flow in the opposite direction (the edges are pipelined, and the leading 'x' denotes 'don't care')

This structure is very inefficient due to the broadcasting, which may be a major barrier to chip implementation. To remedy this situation, we have to modify the circuit topology so that the connection becomes regular and locally connected. Figure 13.2(b) depicts one way, among many, of delineating the topology (Jeong 1984). (There are numerous different ways. See the problems at the end of this chapter.) The three broadcasting edges from the right image source are reduced to one, while passing through all the nodes. To be an equivalent circuit, the node functions must be changed in such a way that an additional dummy input and output port that is internally connected to pass the input data to the output, is added to the node:

$$\begin{aligned} I_o^r(d) &\leftarrow I_i^r(d), \\ I_o^l(d) &\leftarrow I_i^l(d), \\ y(d) &\leftarrow T(I_i^r(d), I_i^l(d)), \end{aligned} \tag{13.4}$$

where the port I_o^r is added. This kind of node modification is trivial, and perfectly feasible.

The circuit topology is now regular, but the long combinational path still exists. We have to block all such paths with registers. However, we cannot arbitrarily insert registers or change the number of registers in the circuit because the timing relationship between data may be harmed. We have to consider using a pipelining technique, after examining the circuit topology. The point to note is that the circuit consists of three loops, each pipelined with a register. We need one more register to block the combinational path in the loop. One way to increase the number of registers without violating the circuit function is *interleaving* (or *k-slow*, in systolic terms). The penalty is that the circuit works at every other clock, slowed down twice, although the interleaved data can be used otherwise. (See the problems at the end of this chapter.) In Figure 13.2(c), the number of registers is doubled at all edges. Furthermore, the data streams, including the leading delays, are also interleaved. Check that the interleaved 'don't care' data, apart from preserving correct synchronization of the data streams, do not affect the computation on the normal data.

The next step is to redistribute the registers so that all the edges are pipelined. This task can be done by employing the retiming technique (Kung and Leiserson 1980). In Figure 13.2(d), the registers are redistributed correctly. In fact, the two leading 'don't cares,' which are equivalent to two register delays, are carried along the paths. The result is that the leading 'don't cares' are reduced by two and the registers along the broadcasting path are increased by two. Consequently, the critical path is reduced to the node delay, making the system very fast.

Incidentally, obtaining systolic arrays by topological and timing transformation has been studied in detail (Jeong 1984; Leiserson and Saxe 1991). Starting from a basic circuit, we can derive many functionally equivalent alternative arrays. The concept involves a combination of timing, spatial regularity, and duality. The circuit can be represented by an incidence matrix, whose elements represent vertex and edge registers. The topological and timing transformation can be represented by similarity transformations. In this chapter, we simply encapsulate the concept in an algorithm.

Algorithm 13.1 (Systolic transformation) *Consider an array, $\{PE(k)|k \in [0, K-1]\}$, having K nodes, all connected between neighbors only. The input streams are $x(t)$ and $y(t)$ for $t \in [0, T-1]$.*

1. *Start from a basic circuit that has a large fan-out and a large fan-in. The node performs*

$$x_o(k) \leftarrow x_i(k),$$
$$z(k) \leftarrow T(x_i(k), y_i(k)),$$

   where $T(\cdot)$ is the internal operation and y is the intermediate result. The input streams are augmented by leading 'don't cares,' if necessary, to meet synchronization needs.
2. *Remove the fan-in and fan-out edges by routing them in one of many directions through the nodes. The node becomes*

$$x_o(k) \leftarrow x_i(k),$$
$$y_o(k) \leftarrow y_i(k),$$
$$z(k) \leftarrow T(x_i(k), y_i(k)).$$

3. *If a loop consists of E edges and R registers, multiply all the edges by a constant 'c' so that $c = \arg\min_c\{cR \geq E\}$ and interleave the signals, including the leading delays, by $c - 1$ 'don't cares'.*
4. *Redistribute the registers so that all the edges are blocked by at least one register.*
5. *For dual circuits, repeat the process from the beginning.*

In this formula, the broadcasting is generalized to the fan-in and fan-out, which are convenient for representing computation but inconvenient for circuit implementation. For the dual circuit, the following factors must be considered: the direction of routing, the signal directions, and the possibility of moving the three signals – input data and the result. It is potentially possible to make all the data move around the circuit, as evidenced by the circuits in Figure 3.10 in Chapter 3. With this concept as our basis, we will further derive the dual circuits.

13.3 Fundamental Systolic Arrays

Thus far, we have derived one type of systolic array, in which the image streams move in opposite directions. Intuitively, there must be another type of systolic array, one in which the two data streams move in the same direction. Let us derive this type of array using Algorithm 13.1. (Figure 13.3.) The starting graph is the same as before. In the second stage, however, the right image is routed in another

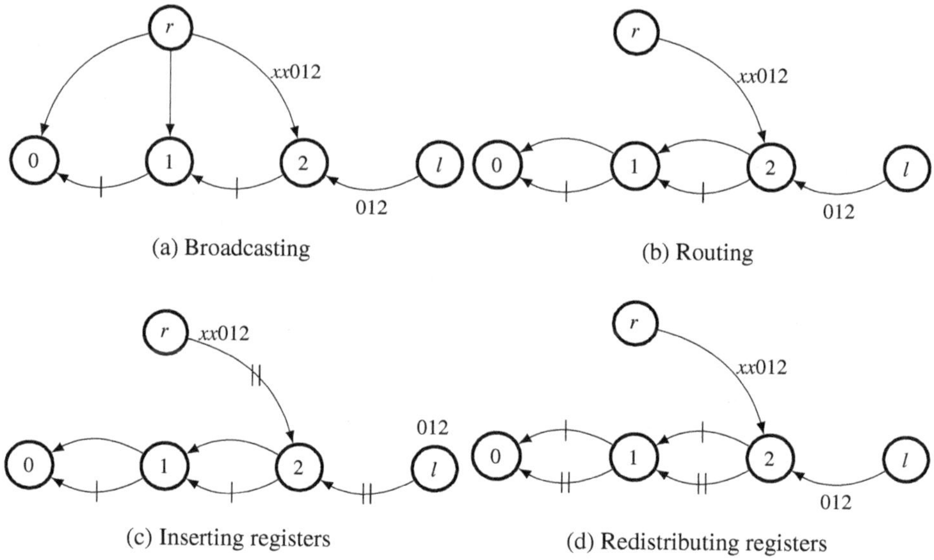

Figure 13.3 Deriving a systolic array, in which two image streams flow in the same direction

direction and, as a result, the two streams flow in the same direction. In this circuit, there is no loop involved, so no interleaving is necessary. Consequently, pipelining can be easily achieved by supplying registers from the source side. Of course, the number of additional registers must be just enough to pipeline all the edges. Because there are two combinational edges, we need two additional registers. As such, two registers can be inserted in front of the sources, without violating data synchronization. (You may have to put in the lowest number of registers possible to save the registers and speed. In this case, the number is $D - 1$.) The inserted registers are moved along the paths and allotted to each edge in equal numbers (just one in this circuit). In addition, note that the transformation does not alter the overall function. Each node receives the input data in the correct order. The only change is the lead or lag between the host nodes and the arrays, which are not a problem from the viewpoint of the host. The result is that the edges on the upper path are pipelined with one register, while the edges on the lower path are pipelined with two registers. Like the original circuit, between the two paths, the time difference is preserved. In this manner, the upper stream moves twice as fast as the lower stream but must initially wait $D - 1$ clocks for correct synchronization. That is, the right image starts late but runs faster; the left image starts fast but runs slower. Because of this difference, four cases of time difference, which we call disparity, are possible. (We may call this circuit 'tortoise and hare.')

If duality is considered, many more circuits can be derived. In Figure 13.2, we assumed that the data are entering head first. The duality to this data order is that the data enter in tail-first order. Although there seems to be no benefit to this circuit, such a dual circuit actually exists. The basic circuit can be redrawn as depicted in Figure 13.4. As a perfect dual condition, no leading 'don't care' is needed at this time. As before, the broadcasting paths can be detoured in two directions. When the detour path is chosen as shown, the upper and lower paths are in the same direction. This circuit has no initial latency as in Figure 13.2, but has final latency. We must wait $D - 1$ clocks more for output depletion after the last set of data enters the circuit.

The last dual circuit is obtained by detouring the broadcasting path in another direction. This is the dual circuit to Figure 13.3 Let us examine this circuit (Figure 13.5). When the right image is connected to the last node, the resulting path consists of loops. The newly introduced path contains no registers

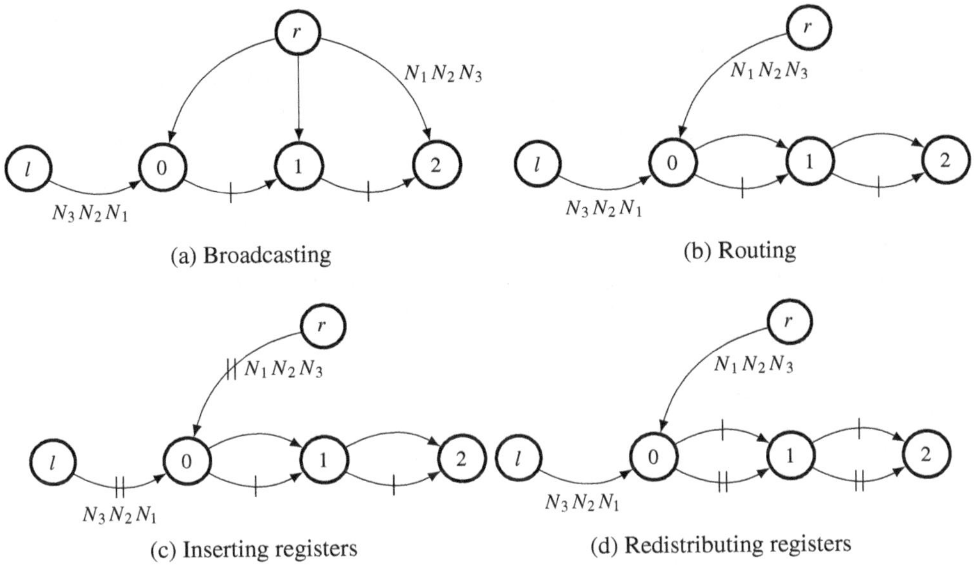

Figure 13.4 Dual to Figure 13.2. The data with bigger address (tail) comes first

and must be blocked. To secure more registers in the loops, we rely on an interleaving technique. As in the previous examples, the number of registers is doubled and the input data streams are interleaved. The resulting circuit is equivalent to the original only at even periods. The registers are redistributed so that the combinational path is blocked. During this transformation, the input to the zero disparity must be delayed with $D - 1$ clocks, the number of edges along the upper path. The result is a pipelined circuit.

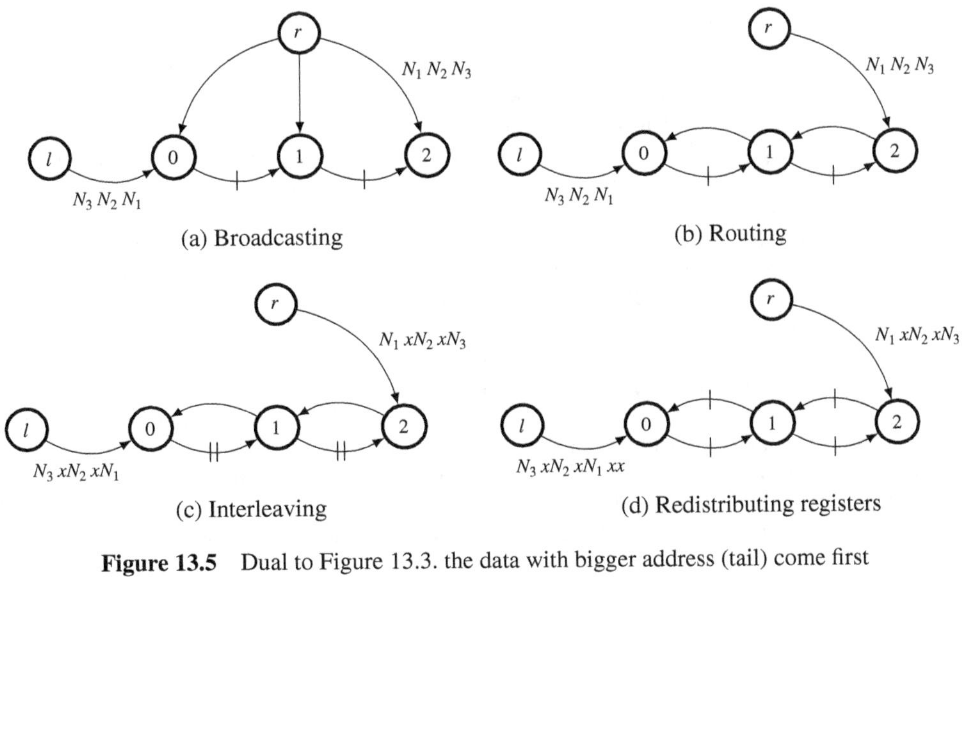

Figure 13.5 Dual to Figure 13.3. the data with bigger address (tail) come first

So far, we have derived four circuits for the right reference. If duality is considered, there must be four more equivalent circuits for the left reference, in which only the two streams are switched as inputs compared with the right reference system. Because there are so many circuits, we need a naming convention that differentiates them. One important factor is the direction of the streams, forward or backward, according to the array number. The other factor is the stream order, head or tail first. Yet another factor is the reference system, right or left reference. Combining these factors, we arrive at the eight circuits: FBR, FBL, BBR, BBL, FFR, FFL, BFR, and BFL, where F, B, R, and L represent, respectively, forward, backward, right, and left. They are in some way or another all dual to each other. Because many more circuits can be derived from these basic forms, we may call them *fundamental circuits*. All the circuits are listed in Figure 13.6. The first four circuits are interleaved and the others are not. The last four circuits need more registers, at the cost of original data ordering. All these circuits have different properties. The circuits are, in fact, all computing with the center reference system. Actually, the center reference is mapped to the right and left image coordinates, which we call center right and center left systems. Among the center left and right reference systems, FBR, FBL, BFR, and BFL are interleaved circuits. Circuits BBR and BBL have head-first streams but need initial delays, while circuits FFR and FFL do not need initial delays but need tail-first streams.

According to Algorithm 13.1, there can be more equivalent circuits (see the problems at the end of this chapter). However, the eight fundamental circuits are the most efficient in terms of complexity and resource usage. Among the fundamental circuits, FBR is an identical circuit for center reference and has been extensively studied (Jeong and Oh 2000; Jeong and Yuns 2000; Jeong *et al.* 2002). In the following sections, we examine the properties of the fundamental circuits in more detail and choose the best candidates for circuit design.

13.4 Search Spaces of the Fundamental Systolic Arrays

We can compare the eight circuits by observing how they behave in the search space. Conceptually, the linear array is possible due to the slanted form of the scanning line, as opposed to the vertical line in Figure 13.1. This interpretation gives us an idea of the properties of the circuits as well as other possibilities (Figure 13.7). The solution space is defined by $\{(x, d)|x \in [0, N-1]\}$. Depending on the reference system, the region of observation is determined, as indicated by the shaded area. A linear array corresponds to a line that scans the space. All the nodes in a line operate concurrently, finding their parent pointers and updating their costs. A node, $PE(d)$, must access previous nodes, $PE(d)$, $PE(d+1)$, and $PE(d-1)$, as shown, to determine a parent. The interleaved system, (a)–(d), corresponds to the circuits where the line slope is greater than one (empty circles are introduced between filled ones). In a scan line, two types of nodes operate alternately to match images. The remaining nodes must hold previous costs and pointers, in order to operate again when their turns come. The circuits with slope one, (e)–(h), do not need interleaving.

Although all the eight circuits are valid, they are not all the same in terms of performance. The first factor affecting the performance is the starting points. Finding reliable parents heavily depends upon the costs of the parent nodes. In BF and FF, the computation proceeds in the space from fewer nodes to more nodes. On the other hand, in FB and BB, the computation proceeds in the opposite direction. Thus, the latter circuits will provide us with results that are more reliable. As a result, we will design circuits FBR (FBL) and BBR (BBL). The next factor is the form of the neighborhoods. In FBR, the parent candidates are $(x, d-1), (x-1, d), (x-1, d+1)$. Among the nodes, $(x-1, d)$ must be stored in the previous scan line, where the corresponding node does not match anything but preserves the previous cost and pointer. The node $(x, d-1)$ means that paths through this node are all mapped to the same image point, which may give poor results. These properties hold for all the FB and BF type circuits. In BBR, no occlusion node is involved, so all the nodes are busy during the forward computation. There is one

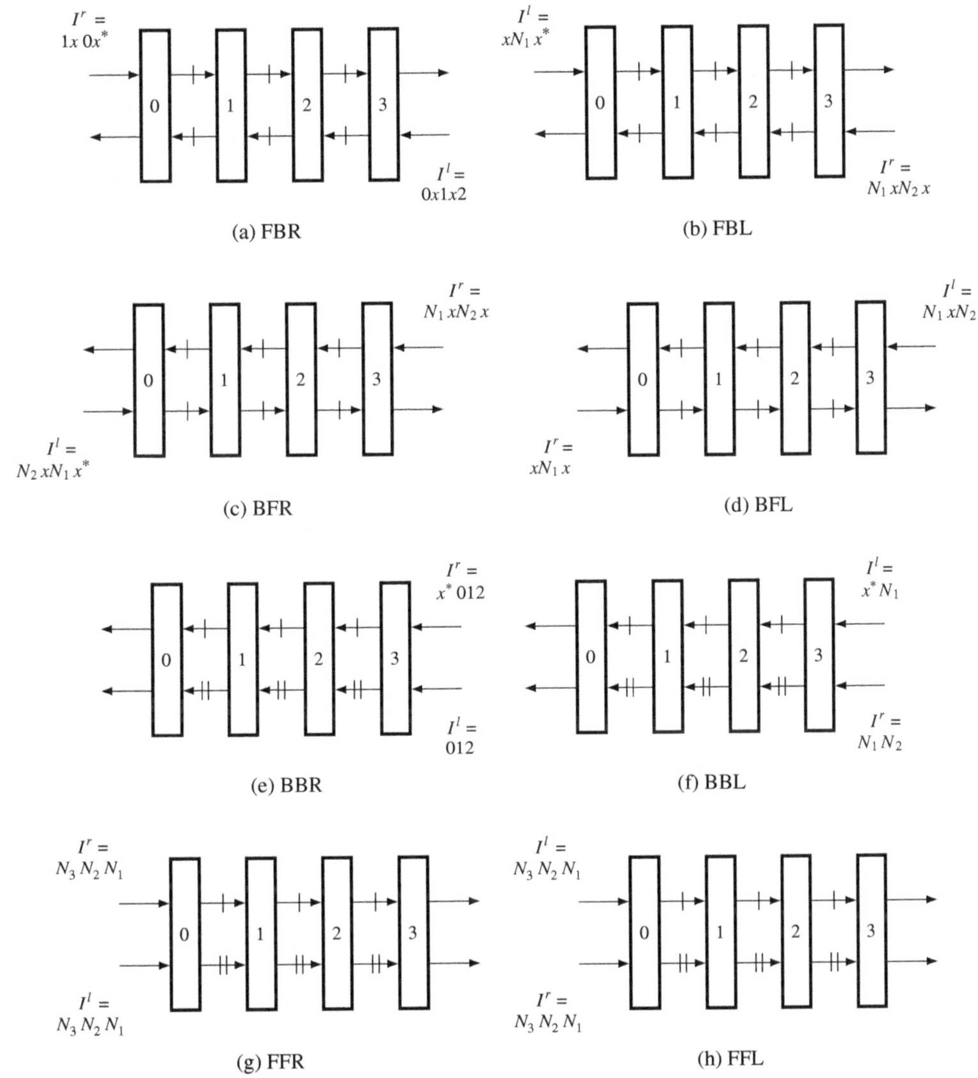

Figure 13.6 Eight fundamental systolic arrays for disparity computation (N_a denotes $N - a$. x^* denote $D - 1$ number of 'don't cares'. In this case, $D = 4$)

constraint that limits the performance, the parent $(x, d + 1)$, along which all the points map to the same image point.

It is obvious that the scan line has two degrees of freedom – slope and direction – and thus results in various dual circuits. If the slope is infinite, the scan line is a vertical line. In such cases, the computation deviates from array, because one of the images must broadcast to the other every time the scan line moves. The serial algorithm in Chapter 12 was designed for such cases. If the slope is less than unity, the range of the neighborhood becomes large, deviating from the nearest neighborhoods.

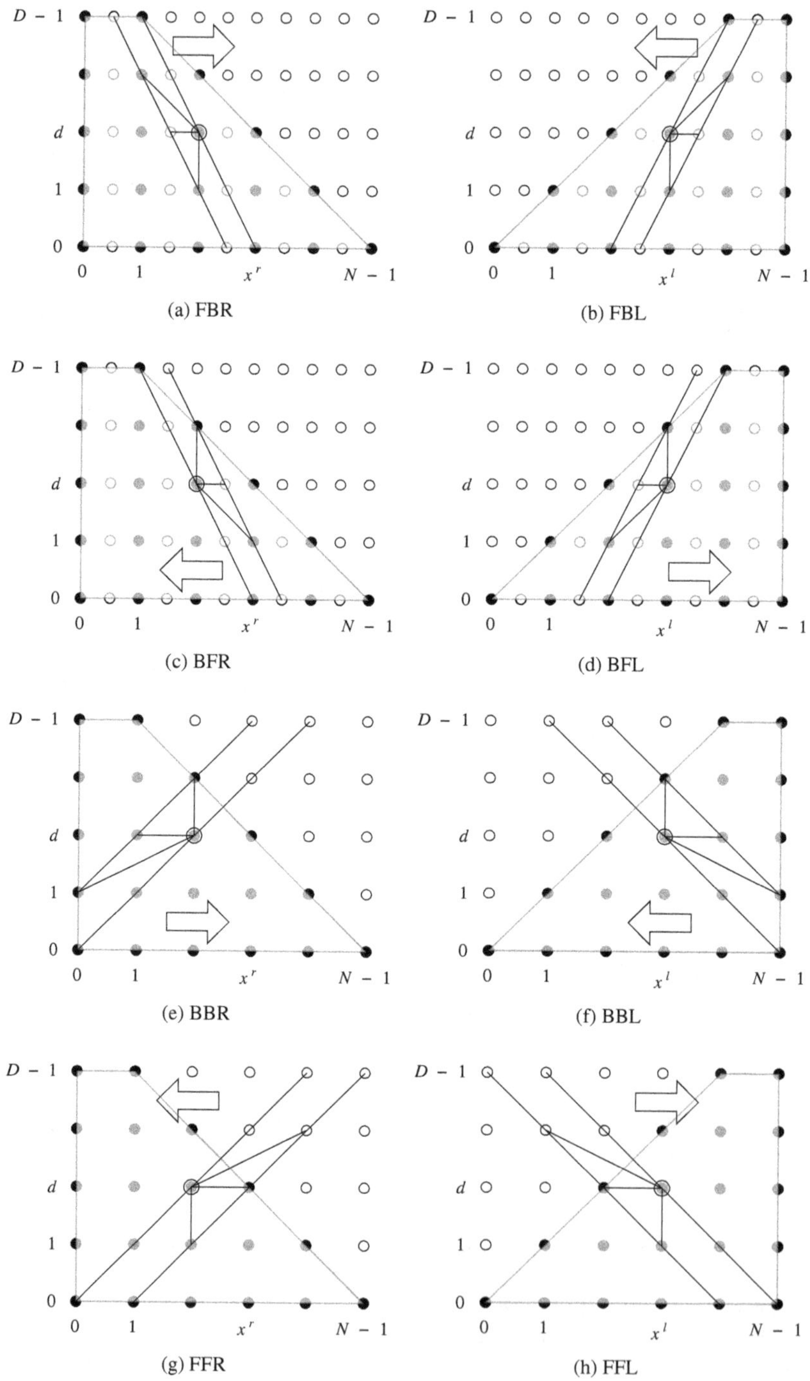

Figure 13.7 The relationship between computation and linear array in the left right reference systems. In this case, $D = 5$ and $N = 6$

13.5 Systolic Algorithm

Let us now build a systolic system and algorithm on the basis of the eight fundamental systolic arrays. In addition to forward processing, each processor must execute backward processing and other forms of processing. This means that additional ports need to be added to the fundamental circuits. Fortunately, these additional ports are the same for all of the fundamental circuits. In addition to passing image streams, the internal operations are all associated with maintenance of the pointer table. The required values are the costs from neighbor nodes and a bit, called the *activation* bit, denoting whether the neighbor node is on the shortest path. Because the communication is bidirectional, the number of input and output ports must be the same.

Considering all these facts, we can build two types of arrays, one type to perform forward processing and the other to perform backward processing (Figure 13.8). The array consists of the processors $PE(k)$, where $k \in [0, D-1]$, and neighborhood connections among them. Although the registers are explicitly shown, they must be absorbed into the output ports of the processors. A PE has a pair of input and output ports for image, cost, and activity bits. Only the two end elements are connected outside as inputs. An output port may be directly connected to the input port or driven by the internal register. The pointer output is a two-bit line. All the outputs are connected by tri-state, driving a bus.

The two types of arrays can be further decomposed into two types of processors (Figure 13.9). In one type of processor, the directions of the image ports are opposed, while in the other, they are the same. When we build the algorithm, the controller must be described in terms of the arrays in Figure 13.8. The algorithm for the processor must be based on the two types of processors depicted in Figure 13.9. The following systolic algorithm must describe the internal operations of this basic element.

In order to be a systolic system, the systolic array must be aided by a control unit. Therefore, unlike single processor algorithms, the array algorithm generally consists of two parts, one for the control unit and the other for a single processing element. While the control unit drives the array as a whole, feeding data and receiving the result, the processor only carries out its job on the entering data and outputs the

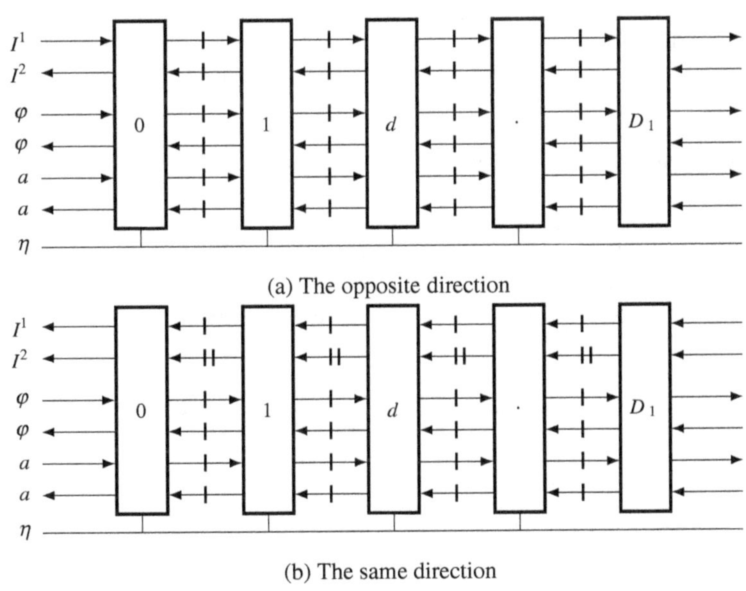

Figure 13.8 Complete form of fundamental systolic arrays for disparity computation (D_1 means $D-1$ for simplicity)

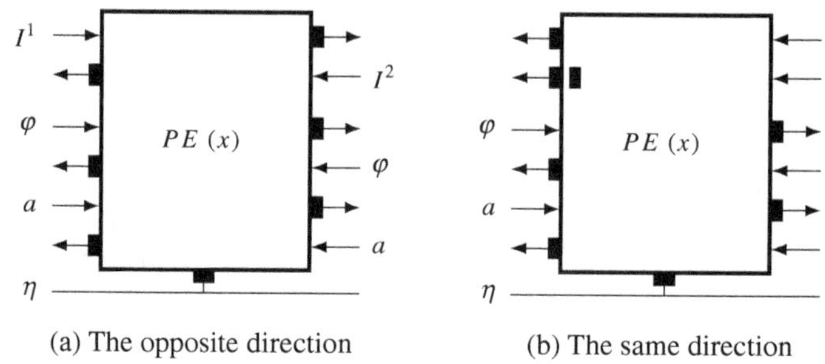

Figure 13.9 Two type of fundamental processing elements (the outputs ports are buffered by one or two registers)

results. The job of a processor can be recognized by its identification and clock counts, as a node is specified by (x, d) in the graph.

The control unit and systolic array are connected as depicted in Figure 13.10. The systolic array is one of the two types shown in Figure 13.8. The control unit provides the image stream differently for each of the eight types of systolic arrays in Figure 13.6 and receives the output from all the array elements via a wired-OR bus. To avoid conflict, only one of the elements is allowed to emit the pointer, while the others are in tri-state or all zero. In this manner, the pointer can be obtained by bit reduction. The control mechanism is very simple because there is no handshake mechanism included between the control unit and the systolic array. After the controller initiates the systolic array, the two systems work independently but in synchrony with the common clock. Initially, the array element is in an idle state, waiting for the initiation signal from the controller. However, the controller needs more time than the array because it must do other jobs, such as updating the buffers, reading images from the RAMs into the buffers, and writing results back to the RAM.

Because there are eight types of systolic arrays, we have to write a general algorithm. Algorithms that are more detailed will follow in the later sections for particular circuits. As already explained, the algorithm consists of two parts: control unit and systolic element. The control unit performs the operations outlined in Algorithm 13.2.

Algorithm 13.2 (Control unit) *Given (I^r, I^l), do the following.*

1. *Initialization: align the two image streams in the array.*
2. *Forward pass: for $t = 0, 1, \ldots, N-1$, continue to feed the image stream.*
3. *Finalization: wait for the finalization, setting $d(N) \leftarrow 0$ (or $d(0) \leftarrow 0$).*
4. *Backward pass: for $t = N-1, N-2, \ldots, 0$, $d(t) \leftarrow d(t+1) + \eta(t)$.*

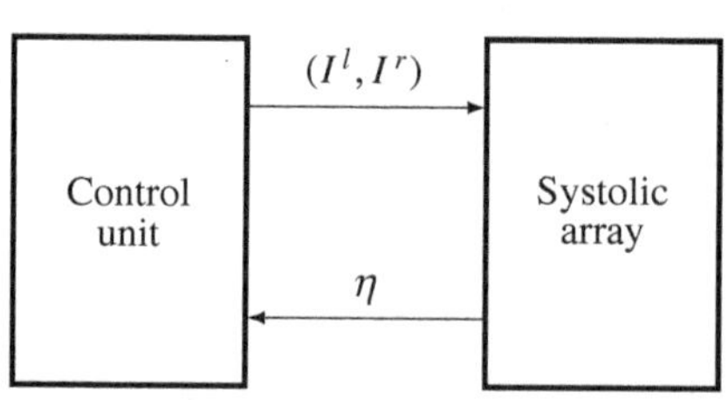

Figure 13.10 The systolic array system

The controller drives the systolic array, treating it like a black box. The purpose of the initialization is to make the array satisfy a state just one clock before the forward pass. This condition can be met by shifting the streams into the systolic array until the two streams fill all the registers but the last one. This condition is necessary because in the beginning of the forward pass, the first data of the two streams must meet at the last processor. The purpose of the forward pass is to feed the systolic array with the two streams in synchrony. After waiting a period for the systolic to finalize its operation, the controller starts to receive the disparity results from the systolic array. This value is differential, $\eta \in \{1, 0, -1\}$, instead of an absolute value and must therefore be accumulated. The initialization and forward pass depend on the eight types of circuits but the finalization and the backward pass are all the same. This is because all eight types of arrays use the same data structure for the pointers. It can be realized by an array or a queue. (See the problems at the end of this chapter.)

As a companion to the control unit, an element of the systolic array is executing a predetermined operation, as others, in synchronization with the system clock. The inputs are image, cost, and activity bit, while the outputs are image data, cost, and activity bit.

Algorithm 13.3 (Processing element) *For a processor PE(d), do the following.*

1. *Initialization: pass the image data.*
2. *Forward pass: for* $t = 0, 1, \ldots, N-1$, *read* $\varphi(d+1)$ *and* $\varphi(d-1)$, *determine* η, *and update* $\varphi(d)$.
3. *Finalization: set* $a(0) \leftarrow 1$.
4. *Backward pass: for* $t = N-1, N-2, \ldots, 0$, *retrieve the pointer. If the active bit is true, set the activity bit of one of the two neighbor PEs, as indicated by the pointer and output the pointer. Otherwise, output high impedance.*

The algorithm is designed for an individual element. All the elements carry out the same operation, in perfect synchrony. Each element knows its state by the two values, node ID, which is the disparity number, and the clock count, which is common to all. Once started by the controller, it operates itself up to the end of the backward pass, and then returns to the wait state. In the initialization state, an element simply passes the input image data in a predetermined number of times. In the end, its registers will all be filled with the image data. It subsequently enters forward pass, executing the predefined operations on the input images, passing the cost, and storing the pointer in its internal array. Finally, in the finalization stage, a particular element is set with its activity bit, which is predetermined as the node for disparity zero. The state then enters the backward pass, in which the pointer array is read, one of the two neighbors are set or reset with the activity bits, and the pointer is issued. The pointer output may be disabled by tri-state if it is not an active node.

The difficulty of the systolic array design lies in the preparation of the initial condition and the correct synchronism in the data streams. Once synchronized perfectly, the system becomes a very fast circuit, with no more intervening control messages. To cover the eight fundamental circuits in a compact code, we have to make as many common constructs as possible. To design the circuit, let us first consider the hardware platform that is commonly used for all types of circuits.

13.6 Common Platform of the Circuits

The basic structure of the systolic machine is analogous to the LVSIM but varies somewhat, as shown in Figure 13.11. (Compare this with Figure 12.8.) Three buffers are the major data structures storing the intermediate data. Two buffers, called the image buffers, store two rows of the images, left and right, that are read from the two external RAMs. The difference is that these buffers are expanded with more channels so that feature vectors can be stored too. The third buffer, called the disparity buffer, stores the new disparity, updated in this period or the previous disparity result, read from the external RAM.

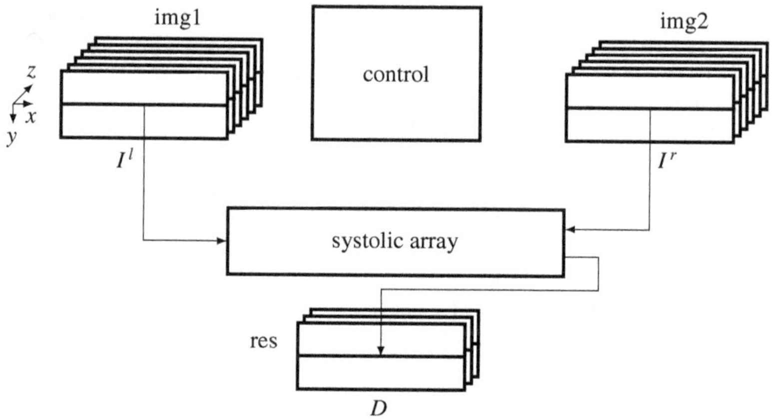

Figure 13.11 The concept of the systolic systolic machine. The three buffers, img1, img2, and res, respectively, store I^l, I^r, and D, and the control unit controls the buffers and the systolic array

The three buffers are arrays with a three-dimensional structure in column (x), row (y), and channel (z), following the image, $I(x, y, z)$, where z signifies the channel. We usually store RGB in the first three channels and the feature maps in the remaining channels. However, the number of channels may vary from one to multiple channels, depending on the application. In addition to the expanded channels of the image buffers, one more component is added – the systolic array.

With the four major resources, the processor executes the following operations, supervised by the control unit. First, the processor reads the images and the previous disparity results, into the three buffers. It then processes the images in the buffers (i.e. RGB channels in img1 and img2) and stores the features in the remaining channels of the two buffers (i.e. channels 3, 4, 5, or 6 in img1 and img2). The control unit constructs two streams of feature vectors out of the two image buffers and feeds them to the systolic array as inputs. In the end, as the array emits a stream of disparity values, the control unit stores them in the disparity buffer. The control unit returns to the beginning and repeats the same series of operations. In this manner, the computation proceeds downwards for a pair of epipolar lines in the image frames.

For possible neighborhood operation, we expand the buffer to a set of rows, that is strip instead of a line of an image. The buffers are actually FIFOs, in which the images enter the bottom and leave the top of the buffers. The three buffers are updated in synchrony. In this manner, the three buffers indicate the same window of the image frame at all times. For the added preprocessing, the image buffers contain more than three channels to store the feature maps. The intention is to update the contents of the buffer center with the corresponding images.

Mathematically, the machine computes the following equations:

$$D(\cdot, y, t) = T(I^l(\cdot, y), I^r(\cdot, y), D(\cdot, y, t-1)), \tag{13.5}$$

where $I^l(\cdot, y)$ and $I^r(\cdot, y)$ are the image rows, including feature vectors, $D(\cdot, y)$ is the desired disparity, and $T(\cdot)$ signifies the main operations of the stereo matching algorithm. In addition to $I^l(\cdot, y)$ and $I^r(\cdot, y)$, the computational structure may enable us to use all the other components in the buffer, as a neighborhood. Moreover, the disparity buffer contains disparities, computed previously, in the current frame as well as the previous frame. The computational resources enable us to conduct preprocessing, neighborhood, and recursive operations, in addition to the primary algorithm, DP.

In the following sections, this system is used as a platform for the design of FB and BB circuits.

13.7 Forward Backward and Right Left Algorithm

The first choice of the eight fundamental circuits is the FB system, which is characterized by the right reference and the image streams moving in opposite directions. As dual circuits, FBR and FBL are the same except for the fact that the roles of their two inputs are reversed. As a result, we can explain the algorithm primarily in terms of FBR. The architecture of the FBR system is shown in Figure 13.12. Initially, the left image shifts down the array to fill all the buffers but the last one. Subsequently, the right image also enters the array, first meeting the left image at $PE(0)$. During the forward pass, the cost ports, φ, are active. The state then enters the backward pass, in which state the activity ports, a, are active. The results drive the bus so that the output reaches the controller. As boundary conditions, the input ports at the end processors must be terminated with suitable values. In this case, the terminal conditions are $\varphi = \infty$ and $a = 0$. The processors use the same values as the others, executing the same operations as the others, and avoiding complicated logic for testing boundary conditions.

The search space and circuits are not enough to define a detailed algorithm. We need the most detailed description, the timing diagram. This diagram may provide the precise operations of the controller and the array element on the basis of clock ticks. Let us return to FBR in Figure 13.7(a). The figure describes the search space, (x, d), and the computational order. By following the activities of the elements, we can build a new space, (t, d), which we may call a timing diagram (Figure 13.13). The horizontal axis is the time and the vertical axis is the disparity. In actuality, the graph, (t, d), is an affine transformation of (x, d), in which the originally slanted scan line is erected into the vertical direction. Further, this space is equivalent to that of the center reference. In the forward pass, the computation proceeds as indicated, and the direction is reversed in the backward pass. The nodes on the computation line try to match images for the costs and pointers or retain the previous costs and pointers, depending on the costs being compared. The result is the pointer table, (η, t). A possible solution may be the lines from 'A' to 'B', which can be

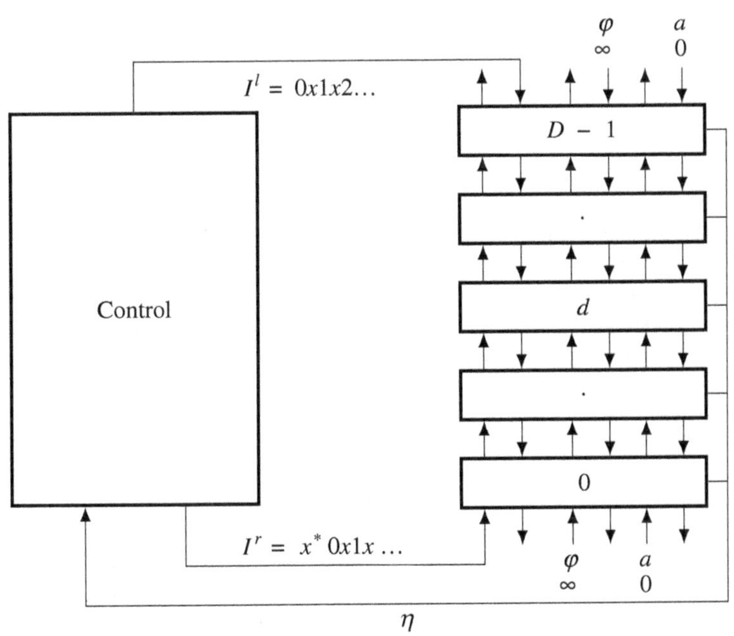

Figure 13.12 The FBR system (x^* denotes $D - 1$ 'don't cares'. Each out port is buffered by one register. The input terminals are fixed with $\varphi = \infty$ and $a = 0$.)

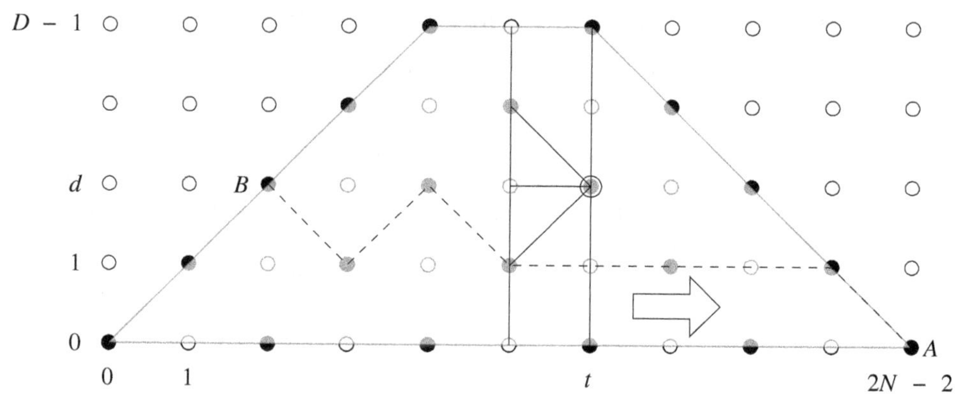

Figure 13.13 The computational space, (t, d), of FBR. In this case, $D = 5$ and $N = 6$. The dashed line is a possible solution

traced during the backtracking. Note that the start point is fixed but the end point may be any point on the left side of the trapezoid.

The algorithm must respect the trapezoid region and its boundary. The region is an affine transform of that in the (x, d) space (refer to Figure 13.2(a)). For both FBR and FBL, the trapezoid is defined by

$$R = \left\{(t, d)|d \leq t, \quad d \leq N - 1 - \frac{1}{2}t, \quad t \in [0, 2N - 2]\right\}. \tag{13.6}$$

The spaces (x, d) and (t, d) have the following relationship:

$$\begin{aligned} FBR : x^r &= (t - d)/2, \quad \forall t + d = even, \\ FBL : x^l &= (t + d)/2, \quad \forall t + d = even, \end{aligned} \tag{13.7}$$

where t is again equivalent to the center reference coordinates.

Each processor must know where it is located in the space, especially in terms of the trapezoid. In the forward pass, a processor is in one of the four states: out of the right side, on the left side, out of the left side, matching node inside the trapezoid, and occlusion node in the trapezoid. The region located out of the right side is the forbidden region and thus all the nodes there are assigned tri-state for the pointer and a very large number for the cost. The tri-state logic allows us to bundle the outputs from D processors into a line. (See the problems at the end of this chapter. The tri-state output can be used for a wired-OR gate. The other alternative is logic zero; in which case, we can use bit reduction.) The high cost simplifies the comparison in the event of parent decision. Even the boundary processors – $PE(D - 1)$ and $PE(0)$ – are arranged to receive very high costs from their pseudo-neighbors. The nodes along the left side are all the same points on the right image. They must be treated specially because they must be the end of the shortest path. Beyond this side, the nodes are visited in the backtracking but should not change the disparity value, which has already been determined on the left side. This policy needs to be implemented using some technique during coding. Inside the trapezoid, the matching node is the major place where the pointer and cost must be determined on the bases of neighbor costs and input images. The comparison can be done without worrying about the boundary conditions because illegal nodes have already been assigned very large numbers in the previous stages. The occlusion nodes do no matching but play the role of keeping cost and point to the previous matching node. The role of the node alternates between matching and occlusion as we move along the timeline.

In the backtracking, node $(2N - 2, 0)$, is the only starting node. There is only one starting node but there are D possible end nodes, all located on the left side. The pointers must be compact, indicating relative positions to the parents with three possible values, $(-1, 0, 1)$. The true disparity is the accumulated value of the pointers. After recovering the shortest path, the positions must be mapped to the right image, in accordance with Equation (13.7).

Let us now formally describe the algorithm. To denote the connecting ports, we use the subscripts 'i' and 'o' for input and output ports, respectively, and 'u' and 'd' for upper and lower PE, respectively, keeping in mind the structure, Figure 13.8.

Algorithm 13.4 (FBR: control) *Given* $I^r = \{I^r(0), x, I^r(1), \cdots, I^r(N-1)\}$ *and* $I^l = \{I^l(0), x, I^l(1), x, \ldots, I^l(N-1)\}$, *do the following.*

1. *Initialization: for* $t = 0, 1, \ldots, D-2$, $I^l_i(D-1) \leftarrow I^l(t)$.
2. *Forward pass: for* $t = 0, 1, \ldots, 2N-2$, $I^r_i \leftarrow I^r(t)$ *and* $I^l_i \leftarrow I^l(t + D - 2)$.
3. *Finalization:* $d(2N-2) \leftarrow 0$.
4. *Backward pass: for* $t = 2N-2, 2N-3, \ldots, 0$,

$$d(t) \leftarrow d((t+1)) + \eta(t),$$
$$disparity((t-d)/2) \leftarrow d(t), \quad \text{if } (t+d) = \text{even}.$$

The system is interleaved and thus twice the image width is needed for the clock period. As a result, the length of the pointer array is $2N - 1$. In the initialization state, the left image flows into the array, filling the $D - 1$ registers. In the forward pass, there is an offset, $D - 2$, between the left and right image streams. After the end of the left image stream, the flow continues with $D - 2$ more values, which may be arbitrary. During the backward pass, the pointers are accumulated but sampled at even periods only.

All $PE(d)$, $d \in [0, D-1]$, do the same operations. For convenience, let us use an indicator function, $I(x) = 1$ if $x \neq 0$ and $I(x) = 0$ if $x = 0$.

Algorithm 13.5 (FBR: processing element) *For a processor* $PE(d)$, *do the following.*

1. *Initialization: for* $t = 0, 1, \ldots, D-2$, $I^r_o \leftarrow I^r_i$ *and* $I^l_o \leftarrow I^l_i$.
2. *Forward pass: for* $t = 0, 1, \ldots, 2N-2$, *do the following.*
   (a) $I^r_o \leftarrow I^r_i$, $I^l_o \leftarrow I^l_i$, $\varphi^u_o \leftarrow \varphi$, *and* $\varphi^d_o \leftarrow \varphi$.
   (b) *If* $d > t$ *or* $d > 2N - 2 - t$, *then* $\eta \leftarrow 0$ *and* $\varphi \leftarrow \infty$. *else if* $d = t$, $\eta(0) \leftarrow 0$, *then* $\varphi \leftarrow |I^r_i - I^l_i|$, *else if* $t + d =$ *even*,

$$\eta(t) \leftarrow \arg\min \left\{\varphi^u_i, \varphi, \varphi^d_i\right\},$$
$$\varphi \leftarrow \min \left\{\varphi^u_i + \alpha, \varphi^d_i + \alpha, \varphi\right\} + |I^r_i - I^l_i|.$$

   else, $\eta(t) \leftarrow 0$ *and* $\varphi \leftarrow \varphi$.
3. *Finalization:* $a \leftarrow I(d = 0)$.
4. *Backward pass: for* $t = 2N-2, 2N-4, \ldots, 0$,

$$a^u_o \leftarrow a \cdot I(\eta(t) = 1),$$
$$a^d_o \leftarrow a \cdot I(\eta(t) = -1),$$
$$a \leftarrow a \cdot I(\eta(t) = 0) + a^u_i + a^d_i.$$

In the initialization phase, $PE(d)$ with $d \neq 0$ is also assigned $\eta = 0$. This simplifies the logic during the backward pass operation. During that period, all PEs issue η to the bus. Among them, only one PE issues the desired pointer, the others do not. However, all the outputs are connected together, making a bus. Therefore, the output of the unactivated PE must be zero (wired-OR) or tri-state (bus). We prefer the former method, due to its simplicity. In the forward pass, $\eta \in \{1, 0, -1\}$ represents one of the three parents, $PE(d+1)$, $PE(d)$, and $PE(d-1)$. The search region is within the trapezoid, R in Equation (13.6). A unmatched node within the trapezoid simply retains its previous cost and zero pointer.

For the FBL, I^r and I^l are reversed in their roles and switched for their ports in the controller. However, the systolic array is exactly the same. The algorithm describes the overall scheme but still misses some details that are possible only in the actual coding. The following section explains the overall framework of the Verilog HDL code.

13.8 FBR and FBL Overall Scheme

The specifications of the circuits can be defined by a header file, `head.v`.

Listing 13.1 The framework: `head.v`

```
//image property
`define WIDTH       225     //image width (225)
`define HEIGHT      188     //image height (188)

//memory property
`define DATA_BITS   8       //word size
`define ADDR_BITS   20      //max image size (17)
`define LINES       3       //strip size -(L-1)/2, 0, (L-1)/2
`define CHANNELS    6       //buffer channel, CHANNEL =1,2,3,...
`define DMAX        32      //max disparity

//mode
//`define LEFT              //right or left reference mode
```

With the header keys, `LEFT`, we can specify one of the two modes: FBR and FBL. All the image and disparity specs are defined by an $M \times N$ image, three buffers with L lines, and the disparity level D. There can be one or more channels. One channel may signify mono, while additional channels may signify RGB colors or feature maps. The maximum disparity level is $D < N$.

Next, for the main part, we design the system with two subsystems, one for the control, Algorithm 13.4, and the other for the systolic element, Algorithm 13.4. However, the control contains additional tasks, in addition to the systolic control, such as buffer management, reading, and writing. The states and their connections are illustrated by the state diagram in Figure 13.14. The system starts from buffer shift for the control and from the waiting state for the array. The three buffers, left image, right image, and disparity buffers, shift upwards, providing an empty line at the bottom of each buffer. In the next state, the empty lines are filled with the data from the external RAMs. Although the data on the bottom of the buffer are new, the data to be processed are located along the center of the buffer. The philosophy underlying this arrangement is facilitation of the possibility of neighborhood processing. In this scheme, the pixels along the buffer center can be grouped with their neighborhoods. The two systems are completely synchronized

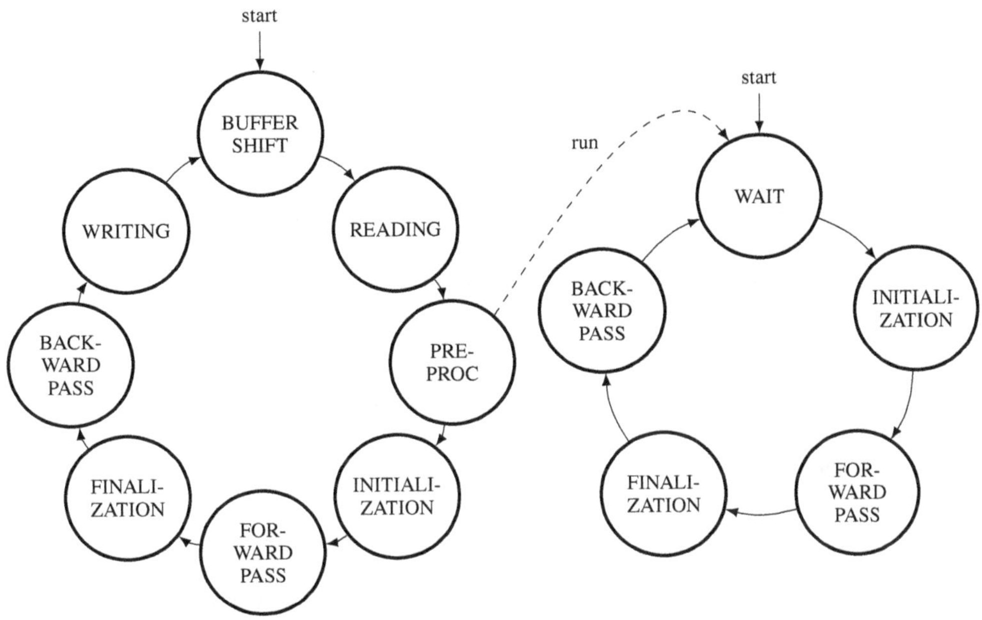

Figure 13.14 The state diagrams of the controller and the systolic array. The controller activates the systolic array and synchronizes itself up until the end of backward pass

only in the DP computation – initialization, forward pass, finalization, and backward pass and decoupled during the other periods. This synchronization is activated by a semaphore, which invokes the idling processors. In the initialization state, the costs of the starting nodes are computed. The following state is the forward pass, which recursively computes the costs and pointers, and writes the pointers into the pointer matrix. When the forward pass ends at the final pixel position, the finalization process starts. Among the final nodes, a node with the minimum cost must be determined. In BF circuits, this stage is the most trivial because the node with the minimum cost is already known. From there on, the backward pass starts, reading the pointers from the pointer matrix. When the computations hit the endpoint, they restart and read the next lines of images. For real-time processing, the computation in a loop must be completed within the raster scan interval.

The code, `processor.v`, is used to realize the control unit, Algorithm 13.4. Let us look at the overall control framework, in which the states are removed and labeled instead.

Listing 13.2 The framework: `processor.v`

```
'include 'head.v'

module processor(                                        //DP stereo processor
   input clock, reset,
   output reg ['ADDR_BITS - 1:0] i_raddr, r_raddr, r_waddr, //address bus
   input ['DATA_BITS - 1:0] i_rdata1, i_rdata2, r_rdata,     //data bus
   output reg ['DATA_BITS - 1:0] r_wdata,                    //data bus
```

```
output reg r_wen                                   //write enable
);

//working array: window of images
reg ['DATA_BITS - 1:0] img1 [-(('LINES-1)>>1):('LINES-1)>>1]
    [0: 'CHANNELS* 'WIDTH - 1];                    //1st image
reg ['DATA_BITS - 1:0] img2 [-(('LINES-1)>>1):('LINES-1)>>1]
    [0: 'CHANNELS* 'WIDTH - 1];                    //2nd image
reg ['DATA_BITS - 1:0] res  [-(('LINES-1)>>1):('LINES-1)>>1]
    [0: 3* 'WIDTH - 1];                            //disparity map

//variables
reg ['ADDR_BITS - 1:0] k,  K,  idx, idx1,idx2; //variables
reg [9:0] row;                                 //pointer
reg signed [9:0] J;                            //row in an image
reg [2:0] state;                               //state variables
reg [15:0] count;                              //count variable

reg run;                                       //activate array
reg signed [7:0] disparity;

 //inputs to the systolic array
reg [0:'CHANNELS*'DATA_BITS - 1] left_image, right_image;

//main part for the systolic system
always @ (posedge clock) begin: PROCESSING
   if (reset) begin                            //initialize
      state <= 3'b000;                         //global state
      row <= 0;
      k <= 0;                                  //pixel address
      count <= 10'h0;
      run <= 1'b0;
   end
   else begin: MAIN
      case (state)                             //state machine
         3'b000:   begin: BUFFER               //buffer management
               end
         3'b001:   begin: READING              //RAM reading
               end
         3'b010:   begin: PREPROCESSING
               end
         3'b011:   begin: INITIALIZATION       //fill the array
               end
         3'b100:   begin: FORWARD              //forward processing
               end
```

```
        3'b101:    begin: FINALIZATION             //finalization
                end
        3'b110: begin: BACKWARD                    //backward processing
                end
        3'b111:    begin: WRITE                    //RAM writing
                end
        default: state <= 3'b000;
      endcase
   end //MAIN
end //PROCESSING

//connection nets for the array
wire ['CHANNELS*'DATA_BITS-1:0]up[0:'DMAX],down[0:'DMAX];//image net
wire [7:0] upcost[0:'DMAX],downcost[0:'DMAX];  //cost net
wire upactive[0:'DMAX], downactive[0:'DMAX];   //active flag net
wire signed [1:0] disp[0:'DMAX - 1];           //pointer net
wor  signed [1:0] dispbus;                     //pointer bus

//feed the systolic array with the two image streams
'ifdef LEFT                                    //left reference
assign up[0] =  left_image;                    //upward image
assign down['DMAX]  = right_image;             //downward image
'else                                          //right reference
assign up[0] =  right_image;                   //upward image
assign down['DMAX]  = left_image;              //downward image
'endif

//boundary conditions for the top and bottom PEs
assign upcost[0] = 8'hFF;               //top boundary cost
assign downcost['DMAX] = 8'hFF;         //bottom boundary cost
assign upactive[0] = 0;                 //bottom boundary active bit
assign downactive['DMAX] = 0;           //top boundary active bit

//build a linear network of PE arrays by instantiation
genvar varx;                                   //systolic array
generate
for (varx = 0; varx < 'DMAX; varx = varx + 1) begin: SYSTOLIC_ARRAY
   systolic  #(varx) SYSTOLIC (                //array ID
      .clock(clock),
      .reset(reset),
      .upin(up[varx]),                   //image upstream link
      .upout(up[varx + 1]),
      .downin(down[varx+1]),             //image downstream link
      .downout(down[varx]),
      .upcostin(upcost[varx]),           //cost upstream link
      .upcostout(upcost[varx+1]),
```

```
        .downcostin(downcost[varx+1]),          //cost downstream link
        .downcostout(downcost[varx]),
        .upactivein(upactive[varx]),            //active bit upstream link
        .upactiveout(upactive[varx+1]),
        .downactivein(downactive[varx+1]),      //active bit downstream link
        .downactiveout(downactive[varx]),
        .disp(disp[varx]),                      //pointer output (tri-state)
        .run(run)                               //control signal
    );
  end
  endgenerate

  //combine the outputs of the systolic array to obtain a pointer
  genvar p;                                          //00, 01, 10, or ZZ
  for (p =0; p < `DMAX; p = p + 1) begin: BUS
     assign dispbus = disp[p];                       //wired-OR D pointers
  end                                                //0 or 1 bit.
endmodule
```

Conceptually, the code realizes Algorithm 13.4. It consists of four parts: a procedural block, instantiation, input, and output. The code instantiates the systolic array, SYSTOLIC, linking individual processing elements to net arrays. Through the links, the streams of images (I^l and I^r), cost (φ), and activation bits (a) flow upwards and downwards, so that an element can receive the necessary data from both neighbors and send the processed data to both neighbors. Note also that the processors located at the top and bottom of the array are missing in one of the two neighbors. The streams from the missing neighbors must be provided appropriately: $\varphi = \infty$ and $a = 0$. The terminal processor can then execute the same neighborhood operations as the others. The control also plays the role of driver, supplying the array with two image streams, in both directions. In FBR, the upstream is the right image and the downstream is the left image. In FBL, the roles of the two images are reversed. Finally, the output is the pointers from the array. Among the D elements, only one emits a valid pointer, a two-bit binary, while the others emit tri-states or zero. To detect the valid pointer, we can combine the output lines via wired-OR. (See the problems at the end of this chapter.)

The code for the processing element, `systolic.v`, realizes Algorithm 13.5. This code is instantiated by the control to form an array, consisting of D elements. Each element executes the same operations, depending only on the time and processor ID. The ID is assigned by the instantiation and the time is known by the synchronized clock. No more handshaking is needed, sparing unnecessary communication overhead. The system behaves like an engine, where all the operations are already predetermined by the clock and processor identification.

Listing 13.3 The framework: `systolic.v`

```
`include head.v

module systolic #(parameter ID = 0) (             //processing element ID
   input clock, reset,
```

```
input ['CHANNELS*'DATA_BITS - 1:0] upin,      //image upstream input
output reg ['CHANNELS*'DATA_BITS - 1:0] upout,//image upstream output
input ['CHANNELS*'DATA_BITS - 1:0] downin,    //image downstream input
output reg ['CHANNELS*'DATA_BITS - 1:0] downout, //image down output
input [7:0] upcostin,                         //cost upstream input
output [7:0] upcostout,                       //cost upstream output
output [7:0] downcostout,                     //cost downstream output
input [7:0] downcostin,                       //cost downstream input
input upactivein,                             //active upstream output
output  upactiveout,                          //active upstream output
input downactivein,                           //active down input
output  downactiveout,                        //active down output
output signed [1:0] disp,                     //pointer output
input run                                     //control input
);

reg [2:0] state;                              //state variable
reg [9:0] count;                              //count variable
reg signed [1:0] queue [0:2*('WIDTH - 1)];    //pointer array
reg [7:0] cost, costp;                        //child parent costs
wire [7:0] ldistance;                         //local distance
reg active;                                   //activity bit

//state machine
always @(posedge clock) begin
   if (reset) begin
      state <= 3'b000;
      count <= 10'h0;
   end
   else case (state)
      3'b000: begin: IDLE                     //wait for activation
            if (run) begin state <= 3'b001;   //start processing
            else state <= 3'b000;             //idling
         end
      3'b001: begin: INITIALIZATION           //pass the image streams
         end
      3'b010: begin: FORWARD_PASS             //forward processing
         end
      3'b011: begin: FINALIZATION             //define the start point
         end
      3'b100: begin: BACKWARD_PASS            //backward processing
         end
      default: state <= 3'b000;
   endcase
end
```

```
//drivers
//cost port drive
assign upcostout = costp;                         //output cost
assign downcostout = costp;
//active port drive                               //drive active bit
assign upactiveout    = ((active) &
     (queue[2*('WIDTH - 1) - count] == 1))? 1:0;
assign downactiveout  = ((active) &
     (queue[2*('WIDTH - 1) - count] == -1))? 1:0;
//disparity port drive                            //drive  pointer
assign disp = (active == 1)? queue[2*('WIDTH - 1) - count]: 2'bZZ;

//functions                                       //distance measure
function ['DATA_BITS - 1:0] distance;             //intensity distance
   input ['DATA_BITS - 1:0] a, b;
   begin
      distance = (a > b)? (a-b): (b - a);         //absolute distance
   end
endfunction

//local distance measure                          //local distance
assign ldistance =
     (distance(upin[0  +: 8], downin[0  +: 8])>>2)     //channel 0
   + (distance(upin[8  +: 8], downin[8  +: 8])>>2)     //channel 1
   + (distance(upin[16 +: 8], downin[16 +: 8])>>2)     //channel 2
   + (distance(upin[24 +: 8], downin[24 +: 8])>>1)     //channel 3
   + (distance(upin[32 +: 8], downin[32 +: 8])>>1)     //channel 4
   + (distance(upin[40 +: 8], downin[40 +: 8])>>1);    //channel 5
endmodule
```

The code consists of four parts: a procedural block, driver, and cost computation parts. The procedural block is a companion to that of the control unit and thus will be explained shortly together as a pair. The purpose of the processor is to send the correct output to the output ports after undergoing internal operations. The values to be sent to the output ports are the costs and the activation bits. Next, for internal operation, local cost is needed in updating parent costs. This computation is realized with the combinational circuit, which takes the two image data, computes the distance between them and supplies it to the forward pass operation. The template shows a basic example, in which all the six channels are used to compute the distance measure. In terms of the distance measure and the combination of channels, schemes that are more elaborate must be adopted for better performance.

Now let us examine the parts of this system one by one in more detail.

13.9 FBR and FBL FIFO Buffer

The first state of the systolic machine is the buffer management. In this state, all the three buffers shift upwards just one line and leave the last line empty. The purpose of the FIFO buffer is to store the raster

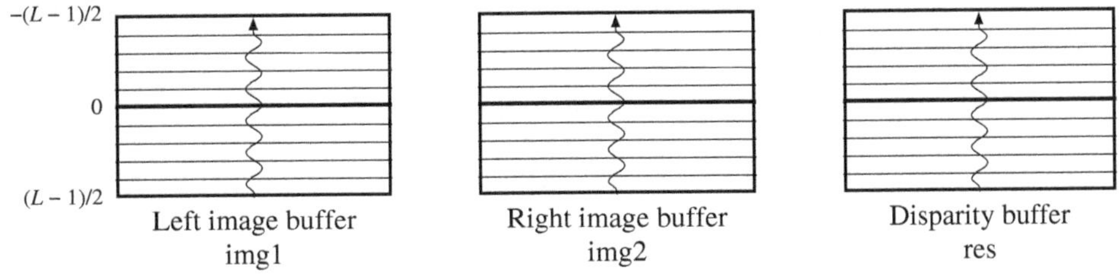

Figure 13.15 The three buffers: left image, right image, and disparity buffers

line and keep it stable during the disparity computation. Without the buffer, the same data must be read from the external RAMs, possibly many times, because the disparity computation may use the same pixel many times. The buffer could be just one line of an image or a set of lines. In the latter case, neighborhood computation is possible. The neighborhood operation needs more than one line, typically three lines for the four-neighborhood scenario. The three buffers are the windows, mapping the same positions of the image plane. The basic goal is to update the centerline of the disparity buffer, using all the other buffers. Because the position of the image that corresponds to the buffer center is changing, it is required that that position be remembered in order to write the result back to the memory later. If the local distance measure uses neighborhoods, then the image lines above and below the centerlines are also used (Figure 13.15).

We may use a circular buffer or just an ordinary buffer in the design of such a buffer. For the circular buffer, the insertion position changes every time a raster line is to be written. In the shift buffer, the insertion position is fixed. We will follow the shift register method. The system contains three buffers, one for the left image, one for the right image, and one for the disparity. The left right image buffers have dimension, $L \times N \times C$, characterized by the number of lines, L, and channels, C. The image buffers have more channels than required for the input images. The extra channels are used to store the features' vectors obtained after preprocessing. Conversely, the disparity buffer has a smaller number of channels, just enough to store the disparity map.

To code the buffers, we need to define the coordinates for the pixels in the buffers. The underlying concept is that the array is numbered $[-(L-1)/2, (L-1)/2]$, instead of $[0, L]$. This is done so as to always make the centerline the origin and thereby the neighborhood pixels can be easily located. Consequently, a pixel appears with different coordinates in image, buffer, and array. We have to know the exact relationship among the coordinates (Figure 13.16). The image plane is defined as $\{(x,y)|x \in [0, N-1], y \in [0, M-1]\}$. The buffer space is defined as $\{(a,b,c)|a \in [-(L-1)/2, (L-1)/2], b \in [0, N-1], c \in [0, C-1]\}$. The corresponding Verilog array is $\{i|i \in [0, CLN-1]\}$. If the origins are defined in each space as shown, a pixel appears as (x,y), meaning column and row in the image plane,

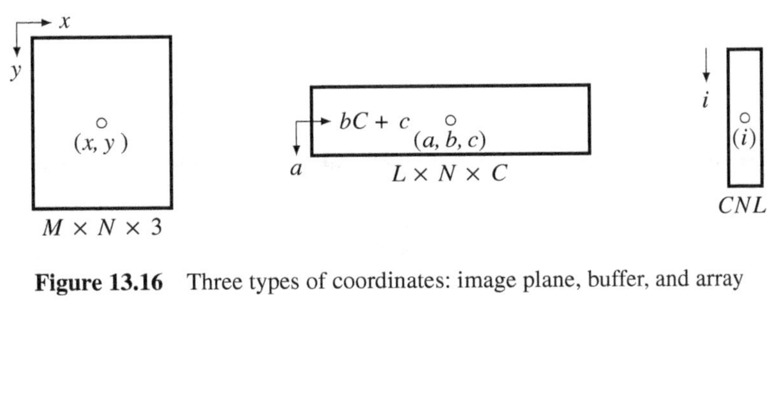

Figure 13.16 Three types of coordinates: image plane, buffer, and array

(a, b, c) in the buffer, meaning row, column, and channel, and as (i) element in the array. A point (a, b, c) is mapped to i in the following way:

$$i = C(Na + b) + c. \tag{13.8}$$

If the bottom of the buffer is written just with y' image lines, a point (a, b, c) is mapped to (x, y) in the following manner:

$$\begin{aligned} x &= Cb + c, \\ y &= (y' - (L-1)/2 + a + M)\%M. \end{aligned} \tag{13.9}$$

The modulo arithmetic is necessary to manipulate the case when the raster line is located at the bottom of the image. The transform from buffer to RAM is needed whenever the disparity map is to be written to the external RAM.

The shift operation of the buffer is as follows:

Listing 13.4 Buffer: `processor.v`

```
3'b000:  begin: BUFFER
      if (count < 'LINES - 1) begin: BUFFER_SHIFT            //shift
        if (k < 'CHANNELS * 'WIDTH) begin                    //pixels
          img1[count-(('LINES-1)>>1)][k]                     //buffer img1
              <= img1[count-(('LINES-1)>>1)+1][k];
          img2[count-(('LINES-1)>>1)][k]                     //buffer img2
              <= img2[count-(('LINES-1)>>1)+1][k];
          res  [count-(('LINES-1)>>1)][k]                    //buffer res
              <= res  [count-(('LINES-1)>>1)+1][k];
          k <= k + 1;                                        //next pixel
        end
        else begin
          k <= 0;                                            //reset pixel
          count <= count + 1;                                //next line
        end
      end
      else begin
          state <= 3'b001;                                   //next state
          k <= 0;                                            //for next state
          count <= 0;                                        //for next state
          idx1 <= 0;                                         //for next state
          idx <= 0;                                          //for next state
      end
    end
```

This is the first state in the main code. Three buffers are updated concurrently. Because the buffer is represented by a three-dimensional array, in the sense of the Verilog array, two counters are used here, rewarded by the easy coordinates. (See the problems at the end of this chapter.) Two contiguous lines are separated by the distance, CN, and thus shifting this amount is equivalent to shifting a row. Once the shift operation has been completed, the operation moves to the next state, possibly by resetting variables. This stage uses $(2C + 3)NL$ space for three buffers and $CN(L - 1)$ time. If the buffer contains a line, no time is consumed here. For larger buffers, this part may take the longest time of all and thus must be optimized by using dedicated buffers, or altered by directly reading from RAM, although some of the functionality of the system may inevitably be lost.

13.10 FBR and FBL Reading and Writing

The next state is provided for filling the bottom of the buffer. We are now involved with three external RAMs and three internal buffers. The three sets of data must be read from the RAMs and written to the buffers, concurrently. The writing action is opposite to that of reading. However, in this case, only the disparity buffer is stored. Because the most recent result is the centerline, it must be copied to the external RAM.

The code reads as follows:

Listing 13.5 Reading and writing: `processor.v`

```
3'b001:  begin: READING
      if (row < 'HEIGHT) begin:                        //fill the bottom
         if (k < 'CHANNELS * 'WIDTH + 2) begin  //for a row
            i_raddr <= 3 * 'WIDTH * row + k;          //pixel address
            if ((idx1%3) == 2) begin                  //RGB or feature maps
               count <= count + 1;                    //count
            end
            //RGB channels
            img1[('LINES-1)>>1][idx1+('CHANNELS - 3)*count]
              <= i_rdata1;//load 1st image
            img2[('LINES-1)>>1][idx1+('CHANNELS - 3)*count]
              <= i_rdata2;//load 2nd image
            res [('LINES-1)>>1][idx1] <= r_rdata; //load result buffer

            idx1 <= idx;                              //2nd delay
            idx <= k;                                 //1st delay
            k <= k + 1;                               //next block
          end else begin
            state <= 2;                               //go to the next state
            k <= 0;                                   //reset variable
            J <= ('LINES == 1)? row :                 //keep row number
              ((row - (('LINES - 1) >>1) + 'HEIGHT) % 'HEIGHT);
            row <= row + 1;                           //next strip
         end
      end else begin
            row <= 0;                                 //hit the bottom
   end
```

```
3'b111:  begin: WRITING                           //write the result
   if (k < 3 * 'WIDTH) begin
      r_wdata <= res[0][k];                       //data
      r_waddr <= 3*'WIDTH * J + k;                //compute actual addr
      r_wen <= 1;                                 //write enable
      k <= k + 1;                                 //next
   end
   else begin
      state <= 0;                                 //return to the top
      k <= 0;                                     //reset the variable
      count <= 0;                                 //reset the variable
   end
   end
```

The reading is somewhat involved because the RAM and the buffer has a different number of channels. While a pixel is assigned three channels in RAM, the same pixel is represented by more than three channels in the buffer. The read data must be written to the first three channels in each pixel.

This state reads a line and then stops until the whole loop is completed. Therefore, the line number and the center of the buffer must be kept, throughout the loop. Two unit delays are introduced between an item of data and the corresponding address. In the loop end, the range is extended so that the address queue may be emptied and thus the data in the last part of the loop may not be lost.

The last state is reserved for writing, in which the disparity buffer is written to the external RAM. The same contents of the disparity buffer is written into three channels, to make a gray level bitmap.

13.11 FBR and FBL Preprocessing

After the buffers are loaded, we can conduct preprocessing to extract features or filtering. In the image buffers, the first three channels contain the source images in RGB format. The other channels, if available, are provided for storing features. The preprocessing stage is a template provided for processing the image channels and filling the feature channels. A basic example is to average vertically to obtain feature vectors.

Listing 13.6 Preprocessing: `processor.v`

```
3'b010:  begin: PREPROCESSING                     //compute the features
   if (k < 'WIDTH -1) begin                       //for each pixel
     img1[0]['CHANNELS*k+3] <= (img1[0]['CHANNELS*k]>>1)
        + (img1[-1]['CHANNELS*k]>>2) + (img1[1]['CHANNELS*k]>>2);
     img1[0]['CHANNELS*k+4] <= (img1[0]['CHANNELS*k+1]>>1)
        + (img1[-1]['CHANNELS*k+1]>>2) + (img1[1]['CHANNELS*k+1]>>2);
     img1[0]['CHANNELS*k+5] <= (img1[0]['CHANNELS*k+2]>>1)
        + (img1[-1]['CHANNELS*k+2]>>2) + (img1[1]['CHANNELS*k+2]>>2);
     img2[0]['CHANNELS*k+3] <= (img2[0]['CHANNELS*k]>>1)
        + (img2[-1]['CHANNELS*k]>>2) + (img2[1]['CHANNELS*k]>>2);
     img2[0]['CHANNELS*k+4] <= (img2[0]['CHANNELS*k+1]>>1)
        + (img2[-1]['CHANNELS*k+1]>>2) + (img2[1]['CHANNELS*k+1]>>2);
```

```
    img2[0]['CHANNELS*k+5] <= (img2[0]['CHANNELS*k+2]>>1)
       + (img2[-1]['CHANNELS*k+2]>>2) + (img2[1]['CHANNELS*k+2]>>2);
    k <= k + 1;
  end
  else begin
     state <= 3;                        //go to the next state
     run <= 1;                          //start the array
     k <= 0;                            //reset the variable
  end
end
```

If the neighborhood operation is to be extended to the four neighbors, boundary conditions must be considered, as in Listing 4.17. Note that, due to the new definition of the coordinates, the neighborhood pixels can be easily located.

If the incoming image is black and white, the number of channels is just one or greater. If preprocessing is needed, an additional channel may be added to store the feature map. In an actual system, this part must be elaborated in such a way that the feature maps may affect the distance measure and the good disparity result.

Up to this state, the controller does not yet invoke the systolic array. As soon as the preprocessing is finished, a control signal, that is, 'run,' must be sent to the array, preemptively one clock before, so that from the next initialization state, both control and systolic array can be synchronized.

13.12 FBR and FBL Initialization

From this state to the end of the backtracking, the control and the systolic array execute concurrently in perfect synchrony. Therefore, the two systems must be explained together. According to Algorithms 13.4 and 13.5, the control supplies one stream of images and the array fills itself with the stream. Through $D-1$ clocks, $D-2$ registers must be filled because, in the next state, the two streams must meet head to head in FBR (tail to tail in FBL) at $PE(0)$.

The control unit must build two streams of feature vectors, out of the image buffers, and possibly with the disparity buffer and supply them on both terminals of the array.

Listing 13.7 Initialization: `processor.v`

```
3'b011:   begin: INITIALIZATION                           //fill the array
      if (k < 'DMAX - 1) begin                            //D-2 deep
         'ifdef LEFT
         right_image <= (!((2*'WIDTH - 1 - k)%2))? 1'hx:{
            img2[0]['CHANNELS*((2*'WIDTH-1 - k)>>1)],   //R channel
            img2[0]['CHANNELS*((2*'WIDTH-1 - k)>>1)+1],//G channel
            img2[0]['CHANNELS*((2*'WIDTH-1 - k)>>1)+2],//B channel
            img2[0]['CHANNELS*((2*'WIDTH-1 - k)>>1)+3],//feature map
            img2[0]['CHANNELS*((2*'WIDTH-1 - k)>>1)+4],//feature map
            img2[0]['CHANNELS*((2*'WIDTH-1 - k)>>1)+5] //feature map
            };
         'else
```

```
        left_image <= (k%2)? 1'hx: {
            img1[0]['CHANNELS*(k>>1)],              //R channel
            img1[0]['CHANNELS*(k>>1)+1],            //G channel
            img1[0]['CHANNELS*(k>>1)+2],            //B channel
            img1[0]['CHANNELS*(k>>1)+3],            //feature map
            img1[0]['CHANNELS*(k>>1)+4],            //feature map
            img1[0]['CHANNELS*(k>>1)+5]             //feature map
            };
        'endif
        k <= k+1;
    end
    else begin
        state <= 3'b100;
        run <= 0;                                   //reset control
        K <= k;
        k <= 0;
    end
end
```

In FBR, the left image flows down the array just before the bottom array, before the right image enters. In FBL, the right image flows down while the left image is waiting. The difficulty is that the two streams must be interleaved.

On the array side, the state is idle and waiting for the semaphore from the control unit. As soon as this bit enters, the state changes to the initialization process:

Listing 13.8 Initialization: `systolic.v`

```
3'b000:   begin: IDLE                           //wait for activation
      if (run) begin state <= 3'b001;           //start processing
      else state <= 3'b000;                     //idling
   end
3'b001:   begin: INITIALIZATION                 //pass the image streams
      if (count < 'DMAX - 1) begin              //for DMAX-2 times
         downout <= downin;                     //downwards only
         count <= count + 1'b1;                 //next clock
      end
      else begin
         state <= 3'b010;
         count <= 10'h0;
      end
   end
```

In this instance, the control and array are in perfect synchrony. Each processor passes the downstream for the predetermined number of times: $D-2$.

13.13 FBR and FBL Forward Pass

The forward pass in Algorithms 13.4 and 13.5 is the core of DP. In this state, the control continues to supply the image streams and the array while passing the streams, and computes the required operations, through $2N - 1$ clocks. The key operation is the computation of the cost and pointer for each processor, providing a $2N - 1$ long pointer array.

The control is relatively simple because the operation is simply to supply the data stream.

Listing 13.9 Forward pass: `processor.v`

```
3'b100:    begin: FORWARD                              //forward processing
   if (k < 2*'WIDTH - 1) begin
      k <= k + 1;
      'ifdef LEFT                                      //left reference
      if ('DMAX % 2) begin: DMAX_ODD                   //DMAX odd
         right_image  <= ((k%2))? 1'hx: {
            img2[0]['CHANNELS*('WIDTH-1-((K+k)>>1))],
            img2[0]['CHANNELS*('WIDTH-1-((K+k)>>1))+1],
            img2[0]['CHANNELS*('WIDTH-1-((K+k)>>1))+2],
            img2[0]['CHANNELS*('WIDTH-1-((K+k)>>1))+3],
            img2[0]['CHANNELS*('WIDTH-1-((K+k)>>1))+4],
            img2[0]['CHANNELS*('WIDTH-1-((K+k)>>1))+5]
            };
      end else begin: DMAX_EVEN                        //DMAX even
         right_image  <= (!(k%2))? 1'hx: {
            img2[0]['CHANNELS*('WIDTH-1-((K+k)>>1))],
            img2[0]['CHANNELS*('WIDTH-1-((K+k)>>1))+1],
            img2[0]['CHANNELS*('WIDTH-1-((K+k)>>1))+2],
            img2[0]['CHANNELS*('WIDTH-1-((K+k)>>1))+3],
            img2[0]['CHANNELS*('WIDTH-1-((K+k)>>1))+4],
            img2[0]['CHANNELS*('WIDTH-1-((K+k)>>1))+5]
            };
      end
         left_image <= (k%2)? 1'hx: {
            img1[0]['CHANNELS*('WIDTH-1-(k>>1))],
            img1[0]['CHANNELS*('WIDTH-1-(k>>1))+1],
            img1[0]['CHANNELS*('WIDTH-1-(k>>1))+2],
            img1[0]['CHANNELS*('WIDTH-1-(k>>1))+3],
            img1[0]['CHANNELS*('WIDTH-1-(k>>1))+4],
            img1[0]['CHANNELS*('WIDTH-1-(k>>1))+5]
            };
      'else                                            //right reference
      if ('DMAX % 2) begin: DMAX_ODD                   //DMAX odd
         left_image  <= (k%2)? 1'hx: {
            img1[0]['CHANNELS*((K+k)>>1)],
            img1[0]['CHANNELS*((K+k)>>1)+1],
```

```
            img1[0][`CHANNELS*((K+k)>>1)+2],
            img1[0][`CHANNELS*((K+k)>>1)+3],
            img1[0][`CHANNELS*((K+k)>>1)+4],
            img1[0][`CHANNELS*((K+k)>>1)+5]
            };
      end else begin: DMAX_EVEN                              //DMAX even
         left_image  <= (!(k%2))? 1'hx: {
            img1[0][`CHANNELS*((K+k)>>1)],
            img1[0][`CHANNELS*((K+k)>>1)+1],
            img1[0][`CHANNELS*((K+k)>>1)+2],
            img1[0][`CHANNELS*((K+k)>>1)+3],
            img1[0][`CHANNELS*((K+k)>>1)+4],
            img1[0][`CHANNELS*((K+k)>>1)+5]
            };
      end
         right_image <= (k%2)? 1'hx: {
            img2[0][`CHANNELS*(k>>1)],
            img2[0][`CHANNELS*(k>>1)+1],
            img2[0][`CHANNELS*(k>>1)+2],
            img2[0][`CHANNELS*(k>>1)+3],
            img2[0][`CHANNELS*(k>>1)+4],
            img2[0][`CHANNELS*(k>>1)+5]
            };
      `endif
   end
   else begin
      state <= 3'b101;
      k <= 0;
      count <= 0;
   end
end
```

The stream must be a smooth continuation from that of initialization. Complications arise, however, from the combined effect of the left right mode, the interleaving, and the even and odd D. As a result, the four cases shown arise. The control unit packs two image streams with the buffer contents and supplies them in the predefined order to the systolic array.

The purpose of the array element in the forward pass is twofold: buffering two image streams and determining a pointer and a cost value.

Listing 13.10 Forward pass: `systolic.v`

```
3'b010:   begin: FORWARD_PASS                       //forward processing
   if (count < 2*`WIDTH - 1) begin                  //for 2N-1 clocks
      downout <= downin;                            //pass downward stream
```

```
    upout <= upin;                                  //pass upward stream
    count <= count + 1;                             //next clock
    if ((ID > count) | (ID > (2*`WIDTH - 2 - count)))
      begin: TRAPEZOID_OUT                          //out of the trapezoid
      queue[count] <= 2'bZZ; costp <= 8'hFF;        //tri-state pointer
    end
    else if (ID == count) begin: TRAPEZOID_LEFT_SIDE//left boundary
      queue[count] <= 0; costp <= ldistance;        //end points
    end
    else if ((count+ID)%2) begin: OCCLUSION_NODE//occlusion nodes
      costp <= costp;                               //pass cost
      queue[count] <= 0;                            //pass pointer
    end
    else begin: MATCHING_NODE                       //matching node
      if ((costp <= downcostin) & (costp <= upcostin)) begin
          costp <= (costp + ldistance)>>1;
          queue[count] <= 0;
      end
      else if ((upcostin <= costp) & (upcostin <= downcostin))
        begin
          costp <= (upcostin + ldistance)>>1;
          queue[count] <= -1;
      end
      else begin
          costp <= (downcostin + ldistance)>>1;
          queue[count] <= 1;
      end
    end
  end
  else begin
    state <= 3'b011;
    count <= 0;
  end
end
```

The details of the task depend on where the element is located in (t, d) space. There are four possibilities. The first possibility is that the position is located out of the right side of the trapezoid. In that case, the cost is assigned a large number and the pointer is arbitrarily assigned, because it will never be accessed. The second possibility is that the position is on the left side of the trapezoid, which is the end position in the backtracking. Therefore, the cost and pointer are assigned a local cost and zero pointer, respectively. Beyond the left side, the cost that was determined already in the previous endpoint must be maintained until the loop ends. Inside the trapezoid, the position might be an occlusion, in which case the cost and pointer must be retained until it becomes a matching node in the next clock. (A node alternates between matching and occlusion.) Otherwise, it is the matching node and must be computed using the normal Viterbi method. The basic operation is to compare the neighbor costs and decide on a parent.

The pointer is an incremental disparity, relative to the current node. This operation is the same for the terminal elements in the bottom or top of the array because those processors are terminated with very high costs, which prevent the possible shortest path intervening in those positions.

As shown in Listing 13.3, the local cost is computed with the image inputs by the combinational circuit. There are many variations on the cost computation and weights on the neighborhood.

13.14 FBR and FBL Backward Pass

In Algorithms 13.4 and 13.5, the finalization is the computation stage that follows the forward pass; it appears before the backward pass. The purpose of this stage is to choose a starting point for the backward pass. The starting point must be a node whose cost is minimal among the nodes in the final column. In FBR and FBL, this point is fixed to the last point of the triangle, making this stage almost trivial. However, there are D candidate points in BFR and BFL, necessitating a full finalization process. As such, the starting point is $PE(0)$, which means the first pointer, $\eta = 0$.

In the control side, this concept is represented in Verilog HDL as follows:

Listing 13.11 Backward pass: `processor.v`

```
3'b101:    begin: FINALIZATION                              //synchronize
   if (count <1) count <= count + 1;
   else begin
      state <= 3'b110;
      k <= 0;
      disparity <= 0;                                      //initial disparity
   end
end

3'b110:    begin: BACKWARD                                 //backward processing
   if (k < 2*'WIDTH - 1) begin
      k <= k + 1;
      disparity <= disparity + dispbus;                    //accumulate pointer
      if ((disparity < 2*('WIDTH - 1) - k + 2)|
            (!((2*('WIDTH - 1) - k - disparity)%2)))
         begin: TRAPEZOID_LEFT    //end boundary
         'ifdef LEFT                                        //left reference
         res[0][(3*(k+disparity)>>1)]   <= disparity;
         res[0][(3*(k+disparity)>>1)+1] <= disparity;
         res[0][(3*(k+disparity)>>1)+2] <= disparity;
         'else                                              //right reference
         res[0][(3*(2*('WIDTH-1)- k - disparity)>>1)]   <= disparity;
         res[0][(3*(2*('WIDTH-1)- k - disparity)>>1)+1] <= disparity;
         res[0][(3*(2*('WIDTH-1)- k - disparity)>>1)+2] <= disparity;
         'endif
      end
   end
   else begin
```

```
        state <= 3'b111;
        k <= 0;
    end
end
```

In the backward block, the control receives the pointer via a wired-OR network. Among the D pointers, only one is valid and the others are tri-states. The values are signed and thus accumulation gives the disparity. This computation is done by the combinational circuit in Listing 13.2. One of the complicated parts is the ending points along the left side of the trapezoid. The other part is the assignment of the disparity to the correct pixel.

In the systolic array side, the role is to provide the control circuit with the pointer, driving a port with a combinational circuit, as shown in Listing 13.3. The code for the systolic array is as follows.

Listing 13.12 Backward pass: `systolic.v`

```
3'b011: begin: FINALIZATION                          //define the start point
        state <= 3'b100;
        active <= (ID)? 0:1;                         //node (2N-2,0)
        count <= 0;
    end
3'b100:    begin: BACKWARD_PASS                      //backward processing
        if (count < 2*'WIDTH - 1 ) begin
            active <= (((active)&(queue[2*('WIDTH - 1) - count] == 0))
                |(upactivein)|(downactivein))? 1:0;  //update activity bit
            count <= count + 1'b1;
        end
        else begin
            state <= 3'b000;
            count <= 10'h0;
        end
    end
```

Setting and resetting a one-bit flag, called *the activation bit*, is the key point in the operation. In the finalization, the processor sets or resets its activation bit depending on whether its ID is $d = 0$. The combination of the activation bit and the output of the pointer array create various cases. As such, the activation bit is set or reset depending on the combined states. The pointer is output to the bus when its activation bit is set. Otherwise, the output is a tri-state, which has no effect on the wired nets.

13.15 FBR and FBL Simulation

For simplicity, we did not correct the codes for numerous warnings. Most of the warning signals were for the number casting from long to short word length. After checking whether the codes were synthesizable, we observed the outputs.

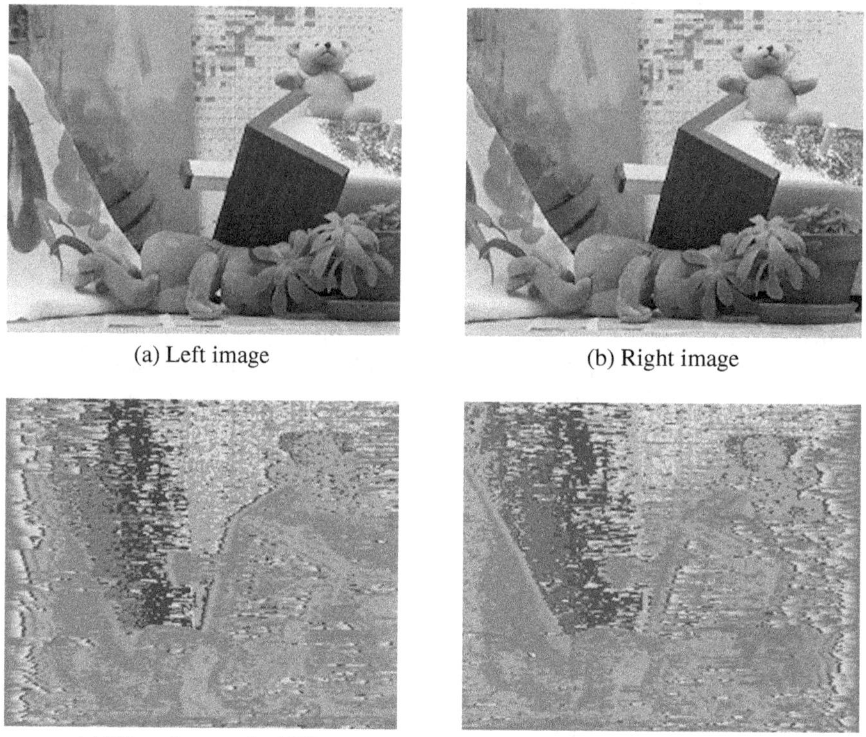

(a) Left image (b) Right image

(c) Disparity map by FBL (d) Disparity map by FBR

Figure 13.17 Disparity maps: point operations ($D = 32$)

As before, the test images were a pair of 225 × 188 images. With these test images, we could test FBR and FBL. The purpose of the simulation was to check the correctness of the code, not to optimize the performance by applying advanced techniques, which are unclear and dependent on applications.

The starting point was the circuit with point operations (Figure 13.17). The top figures are a pair of stereo images, having 225 × 188 pixels in three channels. The remaining images are the disparity maps obtained by the systolic machines. The performance varied depending on the parameters and distance measures. As one of the parameters, the disparity level, D was restricted to a value of 32, observing the range of the disparity. No other parameters, such as smoothness, were adopted in the coding. For point operation, the buffers were allowed to contain only one line of images, which automatically turned off the local neighborhood operations. The original disparity map was a single channel gray map; however, for better rendering, it was expanded to three channels, histogram equalized, and color-coded. The result was a color map, with different levels represented by difference color.

Figure 13.18 depicts another set of simulation results. Three lines were used in computing local distance in the four-neighborhood scenario. The images in the second row are the disparity maps for left reference and right reference, respectively. Note that the left side is poor in the left reference, and vice versa.

A comparison of the two sets of simulations – point operation and neighborhood operation – easily shows the difference. The neighborhood operation provides a better disparity map but uses more combinational circuits and functions.

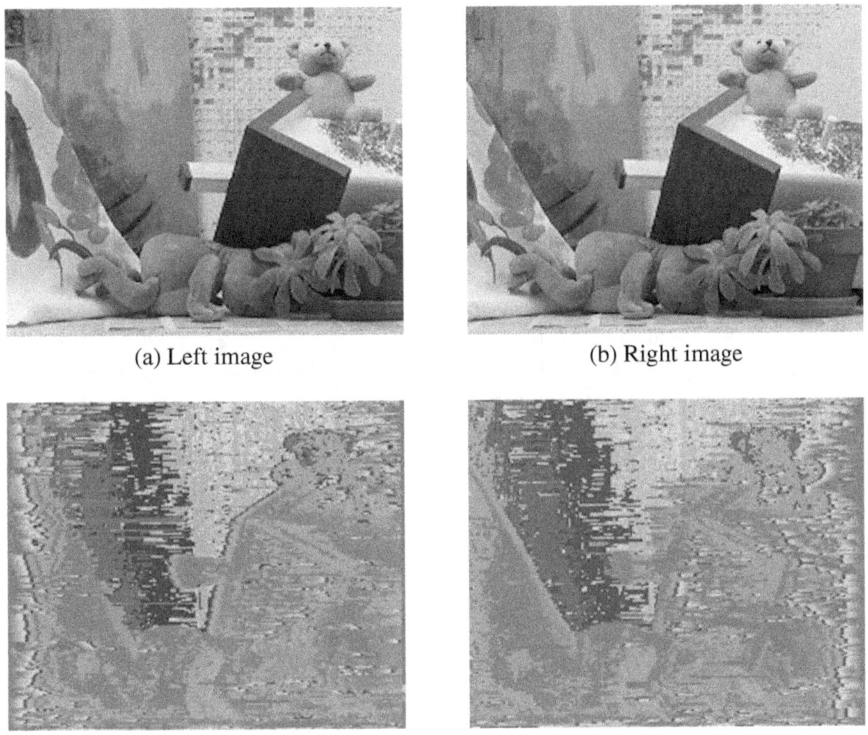

(a) Left image (b) Right image

(c) Disparity map by FBL (d) Disparity map by FBR

Figure 13.18 Disparity maps: four-neighborhood operations ($D = 32$)

Because the systolic machine is being designed in order to provide a standard template, it is generally configured with three buffers, containing multiple lines, which allow for possible neighborhood operations. Of equal importance is the fact that the reference systems are all counted in the design, which can be turned on and off by the header parameters. A simple condition on the transition between nodes is used in the center reference system. The size of the images and the level of disparities are defined by the parameters. As a result, advanced algorithms can be imported into this systolic machine.

13.16 Backward Backward and Right Left Algorithm

Of the eight fundamental systolic arrays, the second type is the arrays, BBR, BBL, FFR, and FFL, in which the two image streams flow in the same direction (Figure 13.6). With the exception of their flow directions and data ordering (head or data first), they are all equivalent. The BBR (and thus BBL) is the most natural choice for a design because it features right reference and head-first data direction. Let us proceed to the design of BBR and BBL.

The architecture of the BBR system is illustrated in Figure 13.19. Initially, while the left image shifts down the array to fill all the buffers, the right image waits at $PE(0)$. Subsequently, the two flows meet and enter the forward pass. During this state, the cost ports, φ, are actively used to transfer costs between neighbor processors. After the input streams are exhausted, the state enters the backward pass, in which

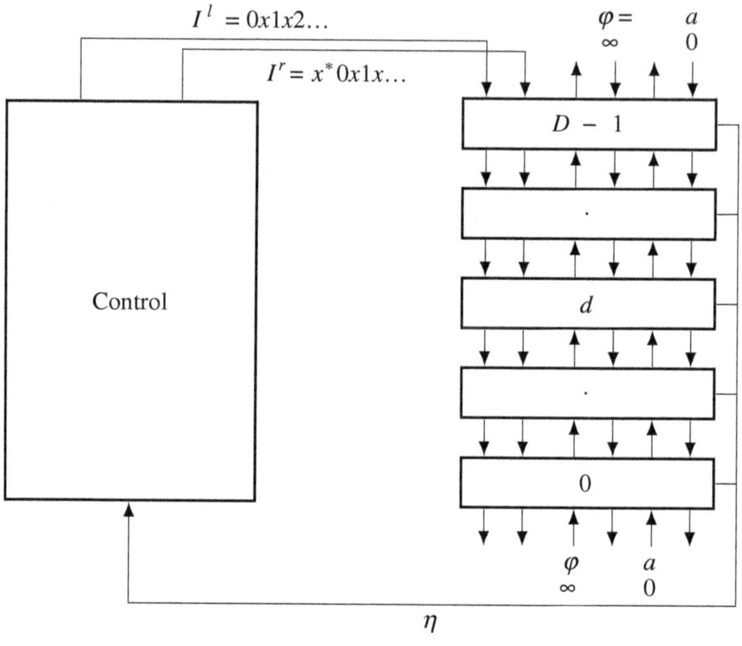

Figure 13.19 The BBR system (x^* denotes $D-1$ 'don't cares'. Each out port is buffered by one or two registers. The input terminals are fixed with $\varphi = \infty$ and $a = 0$.)

the activity ports, a, are activated to trace the processor along the shortest path. The results of all the processors drive the same bus so that the output reaches the controller. The input ports located on both ends of the array must be terminated with suitable values, $\varphi = \infty$ and $a = 0$, which are analogous to boundary conditions. The end processors use these values and the values from others to execute the same operations as others, free from testing boundary conditions, which make the computation very complicated.

In order to design the system, it is essential that the algorithm be understood at the level of events. That is, the exact tasks carried out by the controller and the array element in each clock tick have to be known. Let us observe BBR in Figure 13.7(a). The figure describes the search space, (x, d), and the computational order. Following the activities of the elements, we can build the space, (t, d), as shown in Figure 13.20. The diagram shows the disparities computed and their respective times. In the forward pass, the computation proceeds to the right, building pointers. The nodes on the computation line match images for the costs and pointers or retain the previous cost and pointers. The result is the pointer table, (d, t). In the backward pass, the direction is reversed, retrieving the pointers. A possible solution might be the lines from 'A' to 'B', which must be traced in the backtracking. Notice that the ending point is on the left side of the trapezoid. The actual matching occurs at $t = N - D$; thus, this position must be redefined as the starting point of the computation. The repositioning may significantly reduce the amount of computation because the time saved, $N - D$, is great if $D \ll N$.

The side of the trapezoid is defined by the lines,

$$d = N - 1 - t, \quad d = N - 1 - \frac{1}{2}t, \quad \forall t \in [0, 2N - 2]. \tag{13.10}$$

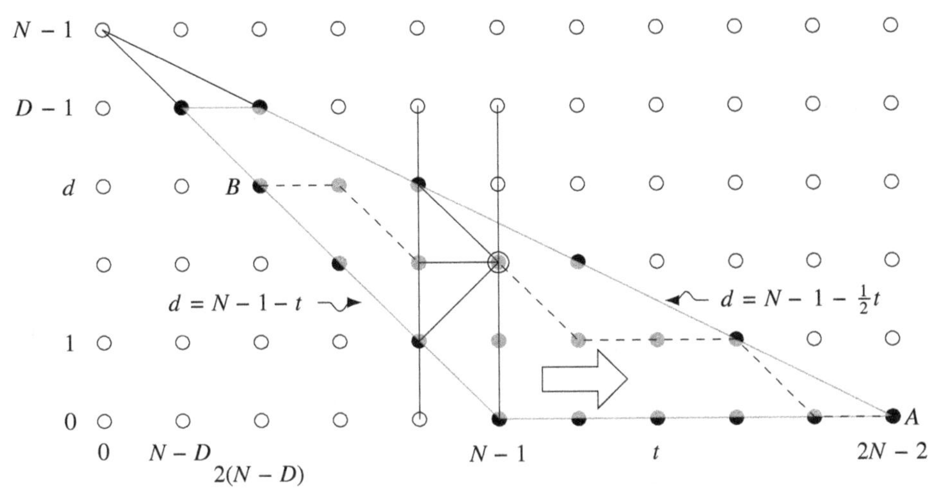

Figure 13.20 The computational space, (t, d), of BBR. Here, $D = 5$ and $N = 6$

In the graph, a node (t, d) corresponds to the point in both BBR and BBL:

$$x = t + d - N + 1, \quad \forall t \in [N - D, 2N - 2]. \tag{13.11}$$

(Compare this with Equation (13.7.)

Instead of designing the circuit from scratch, we can simply modify circuits that have already been designed – in this case, FBR and FBL. One difference between the FB and BB types lies in the direction of the data streams and the number of registers. Another important difference lies in their search spaces. Before designing the circuit, let us first clarify the algorithm. Our objective is to build the circuit, depicted in Figure 13.19, in accordance with the illustration in Figure 13.20.

Algorithm 13.6 (BBR: control) *Given* $I^r = \{I^r(0), x, I^r(1), \dots, I^r(N-1)\}$ *and* $I^l = \{I^l(0), I^l(1), \dots, I^l(N-1)\}$, *do the following.*

1. *Initialization: for* $t = 0, 1, \dots, D-2$, $I^l_i(D-1) \leftarrow I^l(t)$.
2. *Forward pass: for* $t = 0, 1, \dots, N+D-2$, $I^r_i(D-1) \leftarrow I^r(t)$ *and* $I^l_i(D-1) \leftarrow I^l(t+D-2)$.
3. *Finalization:* $d(N+D-2) \leftarrow 0$.
4. *Backward pass: for* $t = N+D-2, \dots, 1, 0$,

$$d(t) \leftarrow d(t+1) + \eta(t),$$
$$disparity(d + t - N + 1) \leftarrow d(t).$$

Notice that the time is reduced to $N + D - 1$ and so is the length of the pointer array. In the initialization state, the left image flows into the array, filling the first $D - 1$ registers among the $2(D - 1)$ registers. (Note that each processor has two output registers in the I^l ports. Other ports are terminated with a register, for example, in the FB series.) In the forward pass, there is an offset, $D - 2$, between the left and right image streams. At the end of the left image, the flow continues with $D - 2$ more values, which may be arbitrary. During the backward pass, the pointers are accumulated and mapped to the pixel in every period.

Because they form a concurrent array, all $PE(d)$, $d \in [0, D-1]$, do identical operations. The major difference with respect to the FB series is the time period and boundary conditions.

Algorithm 13.7 (BBR: processing element) *For a processor PE(d), do the following.*

1. *Initialization: for* $t = 0, 1, \ldots, D-2$, $I^r_o \leftarrow I^r_i$, $B \leftarrow I^l_i$, *and* $I^l_o \leftarrow B$.
2. *Forward pass: for* $t = 0, 1, \ldots, N+D-2$, *do the following.*
   (a) $I^r_o \leftarrow I^r_i$, $B \leftarrow I^l_i$, $I^l_o \leftarrow B$, $\varphi^u_o, \varphi^d_o \leftarrow \varphi$.
   (b) *If* $d < D-t-1$ *or* $d > (N+D-2-t)/2$, $\eta \leftarrow 0$ *and* $\varphi \leftarrow \infty$. *else if* $d = D-t-1$, $\eta(0) \leftarrow 0$, $\varphi \leftarrow |I^r_i - I^l_i|$, *else*

$$\eta(t) \leftarrow \arg\min \left\{ \varphi^u_i + \alpha, \varphi^d_i + \alpha, \varphi \right\},$$

$$\varphi \leftarrow \min \left\{ \varphi^u_i + \alpha, \varphi^d_i + \alpha, \varphi \right\} + |I^r_i - I^l_i|.$$

3. *Finalization:* $a \leftarrow I(d = 0)$.
4. *Backward pass: for* $t = N+D-1, \ldots, 1, 0$,

$$a^u_o \leftarrow a \cdot I(\eta(t) = 1),$$

$$a^d_o \leftarrow a \cdot I(\eta(t) = -1),$$

$$a \leftarrow a \cdot I(\eta(t) = 0) + a^u_i + a^d_i.$$

Note how one buffer, B, is introduced for delay in the left image stream. The algorithms are basic frameworks and so have many details missing; these details are explained in the code section.

For BBL, I^r and I^l, are reversed and switched for their ports in the controller. However, the systolic array is exactly the same.

13.17 BBR and BBL Overall Scheme

Some parts of the code are exactly the same as that of the FB system – specifically, header (Listing 13.1), buffer (Listing 13.4), reading and writing (Listing 13.5), and preprocessing (Listing 13.6) – and so only the remaining parts (i.e. the parts that are different), namely, initialization, forward pass, finalization, and backtracking, are explained in the following.

Algorithm 13.6 is realized by the code, `processor.v`. The overall framework of the code is:

Listing 13.13 The framework: `processor.v`

```
'include 'head.v'

module processor(                                          //DP stereo processor
   input clock, reset,
   output reg ['ADDR_BITS - 1:0] i_raddr, r_raddr, r_waddr, //address bus
   input ['DATA_BITS - 1:0] i_rdata1, i_rdata2, r_rdata,    //data bus
   output reg ['DATA_BITS - 1:0] r_wdata,                   //data bus
   output reg r_wen                                         //write enable
   );
```

```
//working array: window of images
reg ['DATA_BITS - 1:0] img1 [-(('LINES-1)>>1):('LINES-1)>>1]
    [0: 'CHANNELS* 'WIDTH - 1];                   //1st image
reg ['DATA_BITS - 1:0] img2 [-(('LINES-1)>>1):('LINES-1)>>1]
    [0: 'CHANNELS* 'WIDTH - 1];                   //2nd image
reg ['DATA_BITS - 1:0] res    [-(('LINES-1)>>1):('LINES-1)>>1]
    [0: 3* 'WIDTH - 1];                           //disparity map

//variables
reg ['ADDR_BITS - 1:0] k,  K,  idx, idx1,idx2; //variables
reg [9:0] row;                                  //pointer
reg signed [9:0] J;                             //row in an image
reg [2:0] state;                                //state variables
reg [15:0] count;                               //count variable

reg run;                                        //activate array
reg signed [7:0] disparity;                     //disparity value

 //input streams to the systolic array
reg [0:'CHANNELS*'DATA_BITS - 1] left_image, right_image;

//DP processing
always @ (posedge clock) begin: PROCESSING
   if (reset) begin                             //initialize
      state <= 3'b000;                          //initial state
      row <= 0;
      k <= 0;                                   //pixel address
      count <= 10'h0;
      run <= 1'b0;                              //stop systolic array
   end
   else begin: MAIN                             //main part
      case (state)                              //state machine
         3'b000:   begin: BUFFER                //buffer management
               end
         3'b001:   begin: READING               //RAM reading
               end
         3'b010:   begin: PREPROCESSING
               end
         3'b011:   begin: INITIALIZATION        //fill the array
               end
         3'b100:   begin: FORWARD               //forward processing
               end
         3'b101:   begin: FINALIZATION          //finalization
               end
         3'b110: begin: BACKWARD                //backward processing
```

```
              end
         3'b111:    begin: WRITE                     //RAM writing
              end
         default: state <= 3'b000;                   //fault recovery
      endcase
   end //MAIN
end //PROCESSING

//connections between array elements
wire ['CHANNELS*'DATA_BITS - 1:0] down1[0:'DMAX], down2[0:'DMAX];
wire [7:0] upcost[0:'DMAX],downcost[0:'DMAX];  //cost net
wire upactive[0:'DMAX], downactive[0:'DMAX];   //active flag net
wire signed [1:0] disp[0:'DMAX - 1];           //pointer net
wor  signed [1:0] dispbus;                     //pointer bus

//feed the systolic array with the image streams
'ifdef LEFT                                    //left reference
assign down1['DMAX]      =  left_image;        //downward image 1
assign down2['DMAX]      = right_image;        //downward image 2
'else                                          //right reference
assign down1['DMAX]      =  right_image;       //downward image 1
assign down2['DMAX]      = left_image;         //downward image 2
'endif

//boundary conditions for the top and bottom array element
assign upcost[0]          = 8'hFF;             //bottom boundary cost
assign downcost['DMAX]    = 8'hFF;             //top boundary cost
assign upactive[0]        = 0;                 //bottom active bit
assign downactive['DMAX]  = 0;                 //top active bit

//build the systolic array by instantiation
genvar varx;                                   //systolic array
generate
for (varx = 0; varx < 'DMAX; varx = varx + 1) begin: SYSTOLIC_ARRAY
   systolic  #(varx) SYSTOLIC (                //assign ID
      .clock(clock),                           //to each element
      .reset(reset),
      .downin1(down1[varx+1]),                 //image input stream 1
      .downout1(down1[varx]),
      .downin2(down2[varx+1]),                 //image input stream 2
      .downout2(down2[varx]),
      .upcostin(upcost[varx]),                 //cost link
      .upcostout(upcost[varx+1]),
      .downcostin(downcost[varx+1]),
      .downcostout(downcost[varx]),
```

```
        .upactivein(upactive[varx]),              //active bit link
        .upactiveout(upactive[varx+1]),
        .downactivein(downactive[varx+1]),
        .downactiveout(downactive[varx]),
        .disp(disp[varx]),                        //pointer output
        .run(run)                                 //control signal
    );
  end
  endgenerate

  //combine the $D$ systolic outputs
  //one PE issues a pointer and others 00 or ZZ
  genvar p;
  for (p = 0; p < `DMAX; p = p + 1) begin: BUS
     assign dispbus = disp[p];                    //wired-OR
  end

  //compute the image pixel coordinates for the systolic array output
  wire [15:0] pixel;
  `ifdef LEFT                                     //left reference
  assign pixel =  k - disparity;                  //right image plane
  `else                                           //right reference
  assign pixel =  disparity - k + `WIDTH  - 1;    //left image plane
  `endif
endmodule
```

Conceptually, the code realizes the circuit in Figure 13.19. The code consists of four parts: procedural block, instantiation, data input, and data output. The procedural block realizes the state diagram in Figure 13.14(a). Instantiation is done to build the systolic array, SYSTOLIC, linking individual processing elements with net arrays. Through the links, the streams of image (I^l and I^r), cost (φ), and activation bits (a) flow upwards and downwards, so that an element can receive the necessary data from both neighbors and send the processed data to both neighbors. Note also that the processors located on the top and bottom of the array miss one of the two neighbors and thus must be terminated properly. The terminal values are $\varphi = \infty$ and $a = 0$. In this manner, all the elements execute the same neighborhood operations without worrying about their positions. This control unit also plays the role of driver, supplying the array with two image streams, in the same direction. In BBR, the first port, with one buffer register, is for the right image and the second port, with two buffer registers, is for the left image. In BBL, the roles of the two images are changed. Finally, the output is the pointers from the array. Of the D elements, only one emits a valid pointer, a two-bit binary, while the others are either tri-states or zero. To detect the valid pointer, we can combine all the output lines via wired-OR logic (see the problems at the end of this chapter).

The code for the processing element, `systolic.v`, is used to realize Algorithm 13.7. This code is instantiated by the control unit to form an array of D elements. Each element executes the same operations, depending only on the time and processor ID. The ID is assigned at the time of instantiation and is kept by the synchronized clock. Thus, no handshake is needed, sparing unnecessary communication overhead.

The system behaves like an engine, in which all the operations are predetermined by the clock and processor identification.

Listing 13.14 The framework: `systolic.v`

```
'include 'head.v'

module systolic #(parameter ID = 0) (             //processing element ID
   input clock, reset,
   input ['CHANNELS*'DATA_BITS - 1:0] downin1,    //stream input  1
   output reg ['CHANNELS*'DATA_BITS - 1:0] downout1,  //stream output 1
   input ['CHANNELS*'DATA_BITS - 1:0] downin2,    //stream input  2
   output reg ['CHANNELS*'DATA_BITS - 1:0] downout2,  //stream output 2
   input [7:0] upcostin,                          //cost upstream input
   output [7:0] upcostout,                        //cost upstream output
   output [7:0] downcostout,                      //cost downstream output
   input [7:0] downcostin,                        //cost downstream input
   input upactivein,                              //active up input
   output  upactiveout,                           //active up output
   input downactivein,                            //active down input
   output  downactiveout,                         //active down output
   output signed [1:0] disp,                      //pointer output
   input run                                      //control input
   );

   reg [2:0] state;                               //state variable
   reg [9:0] count;                               //count variable
   reg signed [1:0] queue [0:'WIDTH+'DMAX-2];     //pointer array
   reg [7:0] costp;                               //child parent costs
   wire [7:0] ldistance;                          //local distance
   reg active;                                    //activity bit
   reg ['CHANNELS*'DATA_BITS - 1:0] downbuffer;   //delay buffer

   //state machine
   always @(posedge clock) begin
      if (reset) begin
         state <= 3'b000;
         count <= 10'h0;
      end
      else case (state)
         3'b000:   begin: IDLE                    //wait for activation
               if (run) begin                     //check run
                  state <= 3'b001;                //start processing
                  count <= 10'h0;
               end
```

```
            else state <= 3'b000;              //idling
         end
      3'b001:   begin: INITIALIZATION          //pass the streams
         end
      3'b010:   begin: FORWARD_PASS            //forward processing
         end
      3'b011:   begin: FINALIZATION            //find the start point
         end
      3'b100:   begin: BACKWARD_PASS           //backward processing
         end
      default: state <= 0; //fault recovery
   endcase
end

//cost port drive
assign upcostout = costp;                      //cost output
assign downcostout = costp;

//active port drive                            //activity outputs
assign upactiveout    = ((active)
   & (queue['WIDTH+'DMAX-2 - count] == 1))? 1:0;
assign downactiveout  = ((active)
   & (queue['WIDTH+'DMAX-2 - count] == -1))? 1:0;

//disparity port drive                         //pointer output
assign disp = (count > 'WIDTH + ID - 1)? 2'b00:
   (active == 1)? queue['WIDTH+'DMAX-2 - count]: 2'bZZ;//three regions

//distance measures
function ['DATA_BITS - 1:0] distance;          //intensity distance
   input ['DATA_BITS - 1:0] a, b;
   begin
      distance = (a > b)? (a-b): (b - a);      //distance measure
   end
endfunction

//local distance measure                       //local distance
assign ldistance =
    (distance(downin1[0  +: 8],downin2[0  +: 8])>>2)       //channel 5
    +(distance(downin1[8  +: 8],downin2[8  +: 8])>>2)      //channel 4
    +(distance(downin1[16 +: 8],downin2[16 +: 8])>>2);     //channel 3
    //+(distance(downin1[24 +: 8],downin2[24 +: 8])>>2)    //channel 2
    //+(distance(downin1[32 +: 8],downin2[32 +: 8])>>2)    //channel 1
    //+(distance(downin1[40 +: 8],downin2[40 +: 8])>>2);   //channel 0
endmodule
```

The code comprises four parts: procedural block, data output, and cost computation. The procedural block is the companion to that of the control unit. The data output drives the ports to send the costs, activation bits, and the pointer. In the internal operation, local cost is needed in order to update parent costs. Therefore, the inputs are compared with appropriate distance measures. The template shows a basic example, in which all the six channels are compared for absolute distance measure. The basic scheme is to assign the first three channels to the RGB images and the remaining channels to the feature maps. However, the number of channels is variable and any assignment to deal with various types of images is possible.

13.18 BBR and BBL Initialization

This part of the code realizes the initiation in Algorithms 13.6 and 13.7. In these algorithms, the two image streams flow into the array in a head-first manner. The purpose is to align the two image streams before the main operation begins. The left image always leads the right image by $D-1$ clocks; thus, in this stage the first $D-2$ registers are filled with the left image first. Then, at $D-1$ clock tick, the two streams first meet at $PE(D-1)$. In BBL, the streams flow in a tail-first manner and the right image stream fills the array before the left image stream.

The control unit must build two streams of feature vectors from the image buffers, and possibly with the disparity buffer, and supply them on the top of the array.

Listing 13.15 Initialization: `processor.v`

```
3'b011:   begin: INITIALIZATION                          //fill the array
      if (k < 'DMAX - 1) begin                           //D-2 deep
          'ifdef LEFT                                    //left reference
          right_image <= {
             img2[0]['CHANNELS*('WIDTH-1 - k)],          //R channel
             img2[0]['CHANNELS*('WIDTH-1 - k)+1],        //G channel
             img2[0]['CHANNELS*('WIDTH-1 - k)+2],        //B channel
             img2[0]['CHANNELS*('WIDTH-1 - k)+3],        //feature map
             img2[0]['CHANNELS*('WIDTH-1 - k)+4],        //feature map
             img2[0]['CHANNELS*('WIDTH-1 - k)+5]         //feature map
             };
          'else                                          //right reference
          left_image <= {
             img1[0]['CHANNELS*k],                       //R channel
             img1[0]['CHANNELS*k+1],                     //G channel
             img1[0]['CHANNELS*k+2],                     //B channel
             img1[0]['CHANNELS*k+3],                     //feature map
             img1[0]['CHANNELS*k+4],                     //feature map
             img1[0]['CHANNELS*k+5]                      //feature map
             };
          'endif
          k <= k+1;
      end
      else begin
```

```
            state <= 4;
            run <= 0;                                   //reset control
            k <= 0;
         end
      end
```

Unlike FBR and FBL, the streams are not interleaved and the coding is straightforward. The code is switched from BBR and BBL by the Verilog compiler directive.

On the array side, the system is originally in an idle state, waiting for the semaphore from the control unit. As soon as this bit enters, the state changes to the initialization process. There exists one clock tick, and thus the signal is sent just before entering this initiation state in the control side.

Listing 13.16 Initialization: `systolic.v`

```
3'b000:    begin: IDLE                         //wait for activation
        if (run) begin state <= 3'b001;        //start processing
        else state <= 3'b000;                  //idling
   end
3'b001:    begin: INITIALIZATION               //pass the image streams
        if (count < 'DMAX - 1) begin           //for DMAX-2 times
           downbuffer <= downin2;              //downwards only
           downout2 <= downbuffer;             //introduce register
           count <= count + 1'b1;              //next clock
        end
        else begin
           state <= 2;
           count <= 10'h0;
        end
   end
```

At this instance, the control and array are in perfect synchrony. Each processor passes the downstream for the determined times, i.e. $D - 2$. There is a difference in FB and BB circuits in the amount of delays. That is, there is a new buffer in the side of the left image stream and thus the input stream must pass two registers before coming out of an element.

13.19 BBR and BBL Forward Pass

Compared to the FB algorithm, the forward pass in Algorithms 13.6 and 13.7 has a lot of differences, especially in the systolic array.

On the control unit side, the code is relatively simple because the image streams flow in their original ordering, without any interpolation involved. The period of this state is $N + D - 2$, greatly depending on the disparity level. Compared with the period, $2N - 2$, in the FB algorithm, we expect that this algorithm is potentially very fast.

Listing 13.17 Forward pass: `processor.v`

```
3'b100:   begin: FORWARD                        //forward processing
      if (k < 'WIDTH + 'DMAX - 1) begin
         k <= k + 1;
         'ifdef LEFT                            //left reference
            right_image  <= {                   //build rightstream
               img2[0]['CHANNELS*('WIDTH-1-('DMAX-1+k))],  //offset
               img2[0]['CHANNELS*('WIDTH-1-('DMAX-1+k))+1],
               img2[0]['CHANNELS*('WIDTH-1-('DMAX-1+k))+2],
               img2[0]['CHANNELS*('WIDTH-1-('DMAX-1+k))+3],
               img2[0]['CHANNELS*('WIDTH-1-('DMAX-1+k))+4],
               img2[0]['CHANNELS*('WIDTH-1-('DMAX-1+k))+5]
               };
            left_image <=  {                    //build left stream
               img1[0]['CHANNELS*('WIDTH-1-k)],
               img1[0]['CHANNELS*('WIDTH-1-k)+1],
               img1[0]['CHANNELS*('WIDTH-1-k)+2],
               img1[0]['CHANNELS*('WIDTH-1-k)+3],
               img1[0]['CHANNELS*('WIDTH-1-k)+4],
               img1[0]['CHANNELS*('WIDTH-1-k)+5]
               };
         'else                                  //right reference

            left_image  <= {                    //build left stream
               img1[0]['CHANNELS*('DMAX-1+k)],  //offset
               img1[0]['CHANNELS*('DMAX-1+k)+1],
               img1[0]['CHANNELS*('DMAX-1+k)+2],
               img1[0]['CHANNELS*('DMAX-1+k)+3],
               img1[0]['CHANNELS*('DMAX-1+k)+4],
               img1[0]['CHANNELS*('DMAX-1+k)+5]
               };

            right_image <= {                    //build right stream
               img2[0]['CHANNELS*k],
               img2[0]['CHANNELS*k+1],
               img2[0]['CHANNELS*k+2],
               img2[0]['CHANNELS*k+3],
               img2[0]['CHANNELS*k+4],
               img2[0]['CHANNELS*k+5]
               };
         'endif
      end
      else begin
         state <= 5;
```

```
            k <= 0;
            count <= 0;
        end
    end
```

The control unit constructs two image streams by concatenating one or more channels from the image buffers. The two streams flow in either a head-first (right reference) or a tail-first (left reference) manner. Between the two streams, there is a $D - 1$ delay. The stream must be a smooth continuation from that of initialization.

On the systolic array side, the goal is to determine the pointers and update the costs. This is the most delicate part of the BBR circuit.

Listing 13.18 Forward pass: `systolic.v`

```
3'b010:   begin: FORWARD_PASS                          //forward processing
      if (count < `WIDTH + `DMAX - 1) begin
         downbuffer <= downin2;                        //pass downward stream 2
         downout2 <= downbuffer;                       //introduce register
         dout <= din;                                  //pass downward stream 1
         count <= count + 1;                           //next clock

         if (((ID < `DMAX - count - 1)&(count < `DMAX)) //left outside
            |(ID > ((`WIDTH + `DMAX - 2 - count)>>1)))  //right outside
         begin: TRAPEZOID_OUT
            queue[count] <= 2'bZZ;                     //tri-state pointer
            costp <= 8'hFF;                            //big cost
         end
         else if (ID == `DMAX - count - 1)
         begin: TRAPEZOID_LEFT_SIDE                    //left boundary
            queue[count] <= 0;                         //end of path
            costp <= ldistance;                        //end points
         end
         else begin: TRAPEZOID_IN                      //inside region
            if ((costp <= downcostin) & (costp <= upcostin))
            begin                                      //φ(d)≤φ(d+1), φ(d-1)
                  costp <= (costp + ldistance)>>1;
                  queue[count] <= 0;
            end
            else if ((upcostin <= costp) & (upcostin <= downcostin))
            begin                                      //φ(d-1)≤φ(d), φ(d+1)
                  costp <= (upcostin + ldistance)>>1;
                  queue[count] <= -1;
            end
            else begin
```

```
                    costp <= (downcostin + ldistance);
                    queue[count] <= 1;
                end
            end
        end
        else begin
            state <= 3;
            count <= 0;
        end
    end
```

As in the FB circuit, the operation depends on where the element is located in (t, d) space, which is characterized by the trapezoid. In the BB circuit, the shape of the trapezoid is somewhat complicated. Because the left side is slanted, one more region appears on the left side of the search space. The first case is when the position is located completely outside of the trapezoid. In this case, the cost is assigned a large number and the pointer is assigned tri-state, because it may not affect the bus when connected with other elements. The second case is when the position is on the left side of the trapezoid, which is the end position in the backtracking. Therefore, the cost and pointer are assigned with local cost and zero pointer, respectively. Inside the trapezoid, the normal forward operations must be performed. The basic operation is to compare the neighbor costs in deciding on the parent. The pointer is an incremental disparity relative to the current node. This operation is the same for the terminal elements in the bottom or top of the array because those processors are terminated with very large costs, which prevent the possible shortest path from advancing in those positions.

As shown in Listing 13.14, the local cost is computed with the image inputs by the combinational circuit. This part, in particular, must be changed in more advanced schemes.

13.20 BBR and BBL Backward Pass

In Algorithms 13.6 and 13.7, the finalization is the computation stage that follows the forward pass and appears before the backward pass. The purpose of this stage is to choose a starting point for the backward pass. The starting point must be a node whose cost is minimal among the nodes in the final column. In BBR and BBL, this point is fixed to the point of the trapezoid, that is $PE(0)$, making this stage almost trivial.

Unlike FB circuits, this part is somewhat complicated because of the introduction of a new region in the search space. The region, outside of the left side, must be passed, with no effect on the accumulation and pixel mapping. The more important operation is to compensate the missing pixels when $\eta = -1$. The circuits are characterized with the three parent candidates, $(t-1, d)$, $(t-1, d+1)$, and $(t-1, d-1)$. Of the three candidate parents, $(t-1, d+1)$ and $(t-1, d)$ map to the same pixel, x^r, meaning step changes in disparity. The point $(t-1, d-1)$, however, maps to $x^r - 2$, meaning that $x^r - 1$ is undetermined. Therefore, we have to fill this position, with the disparity at either of the two ends.

Listing 13.19 Backward pass: `processor.v`

```
3'b101:    begin: FINALIZATION                              //synchronize
       if (count <1) count <= count + 1;
       else begin
          state <= 3'b110;
```

```
        k <= 0;
        disparity <= 0;                            //initial disparity
      end
    end
3'b110:    begin: BACKWARD                         //backward processing
      if (k < 'WIDTH + 'DMAX - 1) begin
        k <= k + 1;
        disparity <= disparity + dispbus;          //accumulate pointer

        'ifdef LEFT                                //left reference
        if (pixel < 'WIDTH - 1) begin: BOUND       //out of bound
        if (dispbus ==  -1) begin: INTERPOLATION   //interpolation
          res[0][3*(pixel+1)]   <= disparity;
          res[0][3*(pixel+1)+1] <= disparity;
          res[0][3*(pixel+1)+2] <= disparity;
        end
          res[0][3*pixel]   <= disparity;
          res[0][3*pixel+1] <= disparity;
          res[0][3*pixel+2] <= disparity;
        end
        'else                                      //right reference
        if (pixel <='WIDTH + 'DMAX - 1) begin: BOUND  //out of bound
        if (dispbus == - 1) begin: INTERPOLATION   //interpolation
          res[0][3*(pixel-1)]   <= disparity;
          res[0][3*(pixel-1)+1] <= disparity;
          res[0][3*(pixel-1)+2] <= disparity;
        end
          res[0][3*pixel]   <= disparity;
          res[0][3*pixel+1] <= disparity;
          res[0][3*pixel+2] <= disparity;
        end
        'endif
      end
      else begin
        state <= 7;
        k <= 0;
      end
    end
```

The disparity value is computed by the combinational circuit in Listing 13.13. The concept is as follows. Each element issues a disparity output to the common bus. Of the D elements, only one element outputs the disparity; all others output tri-state. Therefore, the feasible output can be detected by wired-OR logic. In addition, the computation region must be restricted, because the path ends early at the left side of the trapezoid; thus, the disparity sequence may be shorter than $N + D - 2$.

In the systolic element, the backward pass reads as follows:

Listing 13.20 Backward pass: `systolic.v`

```
3'b011: begin: FINALIZATION                                  //start point
        state <= 3'b100;
        active <= (ID)? 0:1;                                 //node (N+D-2,0)
        count <= 0;
    end
3'b100:    begin: BACKWARD_PASS                              //backward processing
        if (count < 'WIDTH + 'DMAX - 1 ) begin
            active <= (((active)&(queue['WIDTH+'DMAX-2 - count] == 0))
            |(upactivein)|(downactivein))? 1:0;              //update activity bit
            count <= count + 1'b1;
        end
        else begin
            state <= 0;
            count <= 10'h0;
        end
    end
```

The active bits are the major mechanism to trace back the shortest path. The disparity output is computed by the combinational circuit in Listing 13.14. A somewhat complicated situation occurs when the computation crosses the region left of the trapezoid: in order not to affect the accumulation operation, the pointer is set to zero.

A review of the codes shows that this circuit is simpler than FB in data streaming but complicated in its management of boundary conditions. Interleaving is not involved in the filling of the empty pixels, but interpolation is. We can expect the disparity result to be jumpy on the right side and smooth on the left side in the BBR circuit. The reverse holds for the BBL circuit.

13.21 BBR and BBL Simulation

We used sample images – a pair of 225 × 188 images-to test BBR and BBL. Figure 13.21 depicts the simulation results. Three lines are used in computing local distance in four-neighborhood. The images in the second row are the respective disparity maps for left reference and right reference. Notably, the left side is poor in the left reference and vice versa for the right reference. The disparity maps for the center reference are placed in the third row. The disparity map is mapped to the left image plane and the right image plane.

By comparing the two sets of simulations – FB and BB, a difference can easily be seen. The FB circuits provide better performance. One of the reasons for this is that in BB circuits one of the three parent nodes is abnormal. Unlike FB circuits, in which all three candidate nodes denote three different pixels, in a BB circuit one of the parent nodes maps to the same pixel. In addition, the other parent candidate maps to the pixel that is two units away from the current pixel. Therefore, the pixel that is skipped must be interpolated one way or another. The template simply copies the previous node to fill in for the node that has been skipped, which may raise problems around boundaries.

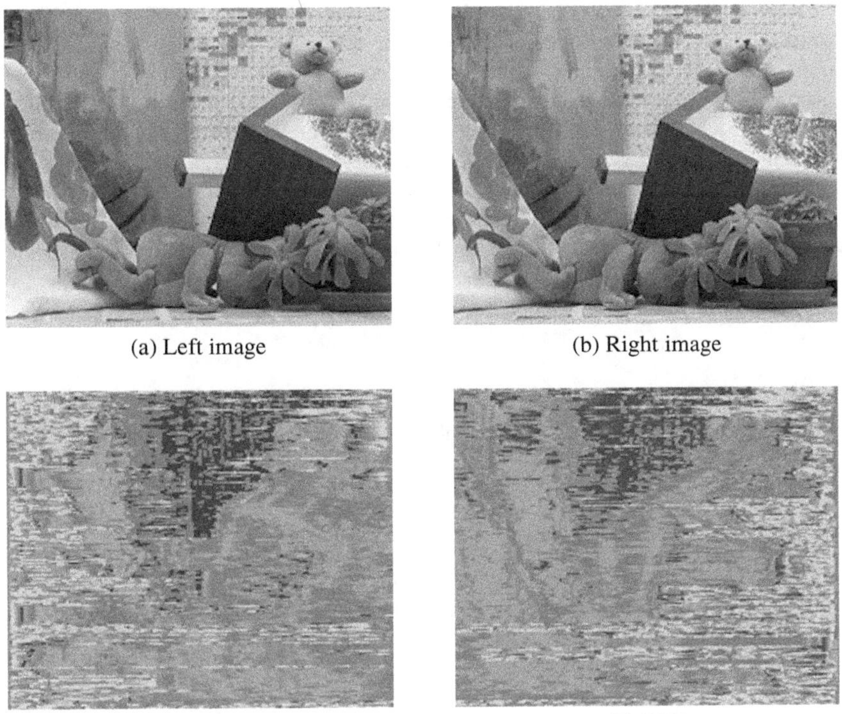

(a) Left image (b) Right image

(c) BBL (d) BBR

Figure 13.21 Disparity maps: four-neighborhood operations ($D = 32$)

From a performance standpoint, the FB series appears to be better than the BB series circuits. Conversely, from a computational standpoint, the opposite holds. The FB series is somewhat complicated because of the need for leading delays in the image streams and the use of interleaving. The BB series does not need such complications; the left boundary of the trapezoid is instead somewhat complicated, resulting in the array element needing more logic. In the BB series, the computation range is significantly shorter, specifically, $N + D$, than $2N - 1$ in the FB series.

The eight fundamental circuits are defined in Figure 13.6. Of these eight circuits, we have so far designed only four: FBR, FBL, BBR, and BBL. The remaining circuits, BFR, BFL, FFR, and FFL, can however be derived from FBR, FBL, BBR, and BBL, respectively, by inverting either their data directions or their data streams. The duality occurs due to their coordinates systems, stream directions, and data directions.

The DP algorithm for stereo matching has been realized in two directions: a single processor (specifically, a DP machine) and an array (specifically, a systolic machine), in Chapter 12 and in this chapter, respectively. As all the circuits are now available, we can compare the two systems. From a computational standpoint, the array implementation is very fast: $O(N^2D)$ vs. $O(N)$. One of the reasons is the fact that the D nodes are executed serially in single processors while they are processed concurrently in array processors. It is natural that the need for space is opposite to the need for speed. The other reason is that there is a full range of parent candidates in the single processor while it is limited to neighborhoods in the array processor. The smaller neighborhood contributes a speed factor of N to the array processor. Thus, from a performance standpoint, the single processor is much better than the array processor. The main reason is of course the wider neighborhood range.

In any case, the DP algorithm is based on line processing, which is naturally faster than the others, but is destined to be poorer than frame processing. The results are always horizontal noise (or vertical instability), because the lines are processed independently. To compensate for this weakness, we can use various methods. One such method is to combine the results from the right and left references. This requires some kind of occlusion detection and a filling of the gaps with suitable disparity. Another method is preprocessing for vertical smoothing, because the line-based method is poor in the vertical variation. To remedy the vertical independence, we may rely on segmentation such as soft matting. When the segmented result is used as the input features, the resulting disparity map is more likely to be stable in vertical variation. The final attempt might be the fusion of other vision modules or the expanded DP, which may help the stereo matching.

Problems

13.1 [Systolic transform] In the text, the possibility of many more equivalent circuits was mentioned. Explain this possibility.

13.2 [Systolic transform] In Figure 13.2, the array size is $D = 3$. For a general D, how many ways are there to route the broadcast paths?

13.3 [Systolic transform] In Figure 13.2, the routing is chosen in such a way that the right image enters $PE(2)$. Derive a new circuit in which the right image enters $PE(1)$. Discuss the property of the new circuit in terms of FB and BB type circuits.

13.4 [Systolic transform] Repeat the previous problem for the circuit in Figure 13.4.

13.5 [Systolic transform] In Figure 13.2, the edges are multiplied by two for the number of registers, and the resulting system becomes an interleaved circuit, called 2-slow. This operation must affect both the number of registers and the input streams. Derive an equivalent circuit that is 3-slow. Check the correctness of the circuit by counting the number of delays from each node.

13.6 [Systolic transform] It is possible to create another circuit from the above circuit by distributing the registers differently. Derive the equivalent circuit that has the registers distributed differently.

13.7 [Systolic transform] By analyzing the previous two examples, draw a general principle for *k-slow* circuits.

13.8 [Systolic algorithm] In FBR, what are the coordinates of the parent nodes? What kind of performance can be expected from such a parent formation?

13.9 [Systolic algorithm] Repeat the same discussion as above for BBR (Figure 13.6(e)).

13.10 [Overall scheme] In Listings 13.2 and 13.13, the output of the D elements are gathered by wired-OR.

```
wor signed[1:0] dispbus;
genvar p;
for (p =0; p < `DMAX; p = p + 1) begin: BUS
   assign dispbus = disp[p];
end
```

If the elements emit `2'b00` instead of `2'bZZ`, how must this combinational circuit be changed?

13.11 [Overall scheme] Discuss the new ideas for improving the systolic arrays.

References

Jeong H 1984 *Modeling and transformation of systolic network* Master's thesis Massachusetts Institute of Technology.

Jeong H and Oh Y 2000 Trellis-based parallel stereo matching *Proceedings of the IEEE International Conference on Acoustics, Speech, and Signal Processing*, Istanbul, Turkey.

Jeong H and Yuns O 2000 Fast stereo matching using constraints in discrete space. *IEICE Transactions on Information and Systems* **83**(7), 1592–1600.

Jeong H, Oh Y, Park J, Koo B, and Lee SW 2002 Vision-based adaptive and recursive tracking of unpaved roads. *Pattern Recognition Letters* **23**(1), 73–82.

Kung H and Leiserson C 1980 Algorithms for VLSI processor arrays In *Introduction to VLSI Systems* (ed. Mead C and Conway L) Addison-Wesley Reading, MA pp. 271–291.

Leiserson C and Saxe J 1991 Retiming synchronous circuitry. *Algorithmica* **6**(1), 5–35.

14

Belief Propagation for Stereo Matching

In Chapter 1, we surveyed vision systems in terms of algorithms and implementations. Especially good surveys have been done on real-time systems with BP (Tippetts *et al.* 2011) and with others (Tippetts *et al.* 2013). Unfortunately, most of the published works do not provide us with any source codes for actual designs, without which we cannot reconstruct an actual system. The purpose of this chapter is to develop an actual BP machine in Verilog HDL code (IEEE 2005) in order to equip readers to develop more advanced systems.

Belief propagation is a general method for solving optimization problems (Yedidia *et al.* 2003). In this chapter, we will design a BP circuit especially for stereo matching (Jian *et al.* 2003). However, although it is targeted at stereo matching, the design is general because by changing the data term together with other parameters, it can be used in many other vision problems, such as segmentation and motion estimation (Szeliski *et al.* 2008).

BP searches for the global optimal solution by iterative message passing. Since these messages are computed simultaneously for overall pixels per single iteration step, massive amount of computation and memory are required. Nevertheless, there are several high-speed implementations of stereo BP algorithm (Felzenszwalb and Huttenlocher 2004; Grauer-Gray and Kambhamettu 2009; Yang *et al.* 2006, 2009).

Due to high complexity of the algorithm, various works have tried to reduce computations and memory requirement in message computation by hierarchical BP (Felzenszwalb and Huttenlocher 2004; Yang *et al.* 2006), message compression (Montserrat *et al.* 2009; Yu *et al.* 2007), plane fitting to over-segmented regions (Klaus *et al.* 2006; Stankiewicz and Wegner 2008; Taguchi *et al.* 2008), or tile-based subgraph (Liang *et al.* 2011).

Due to the nature of BP, between the two simulators, the line-based vision simulator (LVSIM) and the frame-based vision simulator (FVSIM) in Chapter 4, we select FVSIM because we have to deal with window processing. In this chapter, we will design the BP circuit based on FVSIM.

In the design of pipelined circuits, synchronization is very important for the coordination of different circuit components. Therefore, those systems are designed with sequential circuits that are driven by one or more finite state machines. In contrast, in the BP machine, combinational circuits play the major

Architectures for Computer Vision: From Algorithm to Chip with Verilog, First Edition. Hong Jeong.

Companion Website: www.wiley.com/go/jeong

roles in computing various quantities, such as input belief matrix, output belief matrix, and data term. Therefore, the design is a collection of many different combinational and sequential circuits, together with functions. Unlike in DP and GC, the most significant bottleneck in a BP circuit is the fact that it uses a large amount of memory. Among the many data structures, the message matrix is the main data structure, which needs $4mnDB$ bits, where mn is the window size, D is the disparity level, and B is the number of bits used for the message. We will focus on the window processing, together with boundary conditions.

Starting from the BP equations developed in the previous chapter, we first examine the computational scheme. We note here that the operations must be designed with the overflow and underflow in mind because every piece of data must be represented using a finite word length, and every operation must be secured within the number range. We will then examine how to use FVSIM to compute the BP operations and derive the overall structure of the BP machine.

We develop the code for the right and left reference modes, with some customizable parameters. Even though the template is designed for stereo matching, it can be generalized to other applications, such as optical flow computation, by changing the message matrix and the data terms.

14.1 Message Representation

In Chapter 10, we discussed the BP algorithm in general and derived expressions, in component and vector form, of some essential equations for various formulations: sum-product, max-product, sum-sum, and min-sum. As the formulation evolves, the meaning of messages becomes more abstract, from marginal probability to some scores. Of the four formulations, the one most suitable for the circuit design is the min-sum formulation.

In Equation (10.36), we derived the min-sum equation in vector form, which we represent here as

$$\begin{cases} M_p^o &= \Psi \odot \left(\Phi_p + M_p^i\left(\mathbf{1}_4\mathbf{1}_4^T - I_{4\times 4}\right)\right), \\ \mathbf{m}_p &= \phi_p + M_p^i \mathbf{1}_4, \\ x_p &= \arg\min_{k=0}^{D-1} m_p(k), \quad p \in [1, MN]. \end{cases}$$

These three equations completely describe the BP algorithm. However, to transform the equations into circuits, we need to add numerous constraints and sometimes modify the original intentions slightly. The first equation signifies iterations for message updation, although the iteration index is not shown. The second equation signifies the message vector at equilibrium, after suitable iterations. The third equation shows the process in which the optimal disparity is extracted from the message vector.

In this equation, the belief message m is originated from the pdf p:

$$m \triangleq -\log p \geq 0. \tag{14.1}$$

In the design, the message must be represented by a finite word length. For stereo matching with D disparity levels, the belief vector is defined by

$$\mathbf{m} = \left(m_0, m_1, \ldots, m_{D-1}\right)^T. \tag{14.2}$$

Thus, the messages can be interpreted as scoring functions for the desirable disparity at a pixel. In the circuit design, we further process the messages numerically to prevent overflow and underflow and to secure normalization. After undergoing more numerical transformations, the scoring values further become a sort of preference order. The operations between such vectors may transform from linear operations to nonlinear operations. In the design, the vector must be represented by an array either in packed or unpacked format.

According to the formula, a node p receives four belief vectors from its neighbors,

$$M^i = \left(\mathbf{m}^i_{0p}, \mathbf{m}^i_{1p}, \mathbf{m}^i_{2p}, \mathbf{m}^i_{3p}\right) \tag{14.3}$$

and outputs another four belief vectors to its neighbors

$$M^o = \left(\mathbf{m}^o_{p0}, \mathbf{m}^o_{p1}, \mathbf{m}^o_{p2}, \mathbf{m}^o_{p3}\right). \tag{14.4}$$

The subscript denotes the pixel positions, which may be absolute or relative. The four neighbors are represented by the relative positions, 0, 1, 2, and 3, referring to east, south, west, and north, encoded in clockwise direction. Conversely, the current pixel is represented by the absolute coordinate, $p \in \mathcal{P}$. The message matrix must also be represented by an array, which is multidimensional.

Let us now design this algorithm with Verilog HDL, by adding more operations and also modifying the original algorithm appropriately to suit the nature of the numerical computation. The first step is to represent the belief message, m, in B bits: $m \in [0, 2^B - 1]$. The word length must be enough to uniquely identify D disparity levels and thus, $B \geq \log D$. However, in actual applications, the entropy of the message is much smaller than $\log D$ and needs a much smaller word length. The determination as to the word length actually depends on the statistics of the application. Generally, the upper bound of B is $\log D$. A fair decision on the word length may rely on the *perplexity* (Wikipedia 2013),

$$B = 2^{-\sum_k p(m_k)\log_2 p(m_k)}, \tag{14.5}$$

for a sufficiently large number of messages.

The next step is to define the normalization on this data. Because the belief value was derived from the probability, it must satisfy

$$\sum_{k=0}^{D-1} \exp\{-m_k\} = 1. \tag{14.6}$$

Because of the finite word length and the smallness of D, this condition is not met exactly. Nevertheless, the message has already lost the meaning of probability and instead stands for relative magnitude between vector elements. Therefore, there are numerous ways of defining normalization for the belief message. One practical operation is to subtract the minimum from all the elements to make the elements unbiased. This operation is necessary because the message values may diverge due to continuous positive bias during the iteration.

The other operation is to amplify the messages so that the magnitude variation is maximal, consuming as many of the bits in B as possible. Otherwise, the distinction between vector elements may become vague due to small variances. To achieve this, let

$$\mathbf{m} \leftarrow \alpha(\mathbf{m} - \mathbf{1}\min_k m_k), \tag{14.7}$$

where

$$\alpha = \min_\alpha(2^B - 1 - \alpha \max_k(m_k - \min_k m_k))^2. \tag{14.8}$$

If α is small, it means that the message variation is small and therefore we can use a lower number of bits, B, to code the message value. If α is large, we have to use a large B. The message variation depends on the problems, which require adaptive values for the word length B. Because we are concerned with hardware design, the word length is assumed to have been determined appropriately and fixed.

The output message matrix, M^o, is the state memory with which the subsequent states are determined, along with the input images. The circuit needs to store the message matrix in an array. There are several key points to bear in mind in representing the message matrix. The message matrix is not for a single pixel but for the entire image plane and is also defined for the four output message vectors. The storing of the messages is the main bottleneck in designing the BP. Usually, the spatial complexity in BP is $O(MND)$. (In graph cuts, the spatial complexity is $O(MN)$.) To represent the message matrix we may use small windows, $m \times n$, which is much smaller than $M \times N$, and use either a packed array or an unpacked array. The packed array is convenient for communicating data between modules but needs a field that is too long in the packed part: BD bits. Conversely, the unpacked array needs only B bits in the packed field but must be aided by counters for data communications. Considering all things together, let us represent the message matrix in an unpacked array but represent the incoming message in a packed array, so that the various operations in the combinational circuit can be more easily designed. This requires conversions from unpacked to packed and vice versa, which can be done with combinational circuits.

14.2 Window Processing

The basic platform for the BP algorithm is the FVSIM, in which full frame operations are available, as shown in Figure 14.1. The system consists of three buffers, storing two images (I^l, I^r) and a disparity map D, and a circuit for computing the BP algorithm. The sizes of the three buffers are all $M \times N$ RGB pixels. The BP circuit is the main engine that reads the two images, computes the disparity, and stores the result in the disparity map. Unlike the buffers in the line-based algorithms, the buffers here are all full-sized frames.

In the BP circuit, the major data structure is the belief message matrix, $M = \{M^o(x, y) | x \in [0, n-1], y \in [0, m-1]\}$, for an $m \times n$ window. The total size is $m \times n \times 4 \times D$, which is the bottleneck of the computation. To design the circuit, we have to restrict the window size, $m \times n$, to meet the available resources.

Therefore, the BP circuit is based on window processing. The working window is illustrated in Figure 14.2. The image plane can be scanned in two opposite directions, as shown. The first type is the raster scan and is used in the right reference system, where the reference image is the right image plane. The second type is the opposite of the raster scan and is useful for the left reference

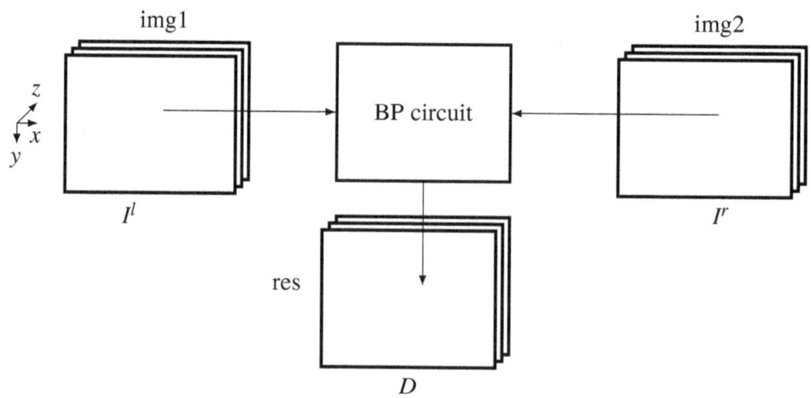

Figure 14.1 The components of the BP system. The three buffers, img1, img2, and res, respectively, store I^l, I^r, and D. The BP circuit reads the two image buffers, computes the disparity, and then stores the result in the disparity buffer

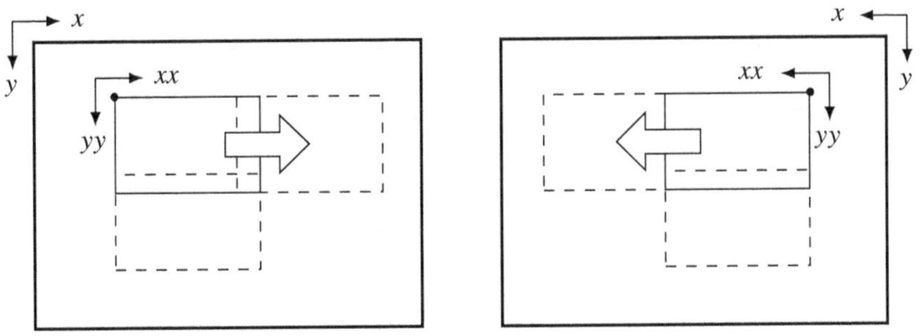

(a) Right scan (b) Left scan

Figure 14.2 The frame, window, and scan directions

system, where the reference coordinates are for the left image plane. A window is a rectangular area comprising $m \times n$ pixels. It is characterized by the origin, (x, y), defined by the top left corner (right mode) or the top right corner (left mode), and by the coordinates inside the regions. In addition, it is characterized by the shift intervals x_s and y_s between consecutive rectangles. If $x_s < n$ or $y_s < m$, the windows are overlapped; otherwise, they are not overlapped. The coordinates inside the region are defined by (xx, yy), as shown. (Note that xx is a single variable.) Therefore, a window $W(x, y)$ is a set of points, $\{(xx, yy)|xx \in [0, n-1], yy \in [0, m-1]\}$. This definition is adopted because it is convenient to locate the conjugate points in the other image. For the type 1 scan, the conjugate pair is $(I^r(x + xx, y + yy), I^l(x + xx + d, y + yy))$, where the disparity $d \geq 0$. Similarly, for the type 2 scan, the conjugate pair is $(I^l(N - 1 - (x + xx), y + yy), I^r(N - 1 - (x + xx + d), y + yy))$ also $d \geq 0$.

Associated with each window is the belief matrix, $M(x, y) = \{M^o(xx, yy)|xx \in [0, n-1], yy \in [0, m-1]\}$, where $M^o(xx, yy) = (\mathbf{m}(0), \mathbf{m}(1), \mathbf{m}(2), \mathbf{m}(3))$, indicating east, south, west, and north output belief vectors. A belief vector is a set of D belief messages, $\mathbf{m} = (m(0), m(1), \ldots, m(D-1))^T$, where D is the disparity level. The message m is encoded in a B bit binary number, as explained in the previous section.

The window scheme is quite general in that it can represent a pixel, $m \times n = 1$, a line $1 \times N$ in a row, a line in a column, $M \times 1$, or the entire image plane, $M \times N$. There is also freedom in the amount of overlap between contiguous windows. Reusing previous values is equivalent to the use of boundary conditions on the local windows.

14.3 BP Machine

Using the data representation and window processing in the FVIM framework, we can build a BP machine that computes the BP operations, as shown in Figure 14.3. The illustration shows the major constructs and operations of the machine. For the sake of clarity, the circuits are drawn only for the right reference system. For the left reference system, the role of the images must be switched. The top four elements are the memories, $M(x, y)$ for the belief matrix at the window $W(x, y)$, (I^r, I^l) for the images, and D for the disparity map. They are the inputs and state memories. The other constructs are the sequential and combinational circuits, in which actual operations are executed. At a given time period, the memories are all fixed and the values in the combinational circuits are actively decided. Blocked at two sites, M^o and $\mathbf{m}$, and connected by the combinational paths between the state memory and the blocking registers, the system as a whole becomes a finite state machine (specifically, a Mealy machine).

In one period, all the computation is done for a pixel (xx, yy) in a window. The first step is to construct the input message matrix M^i by reading the state memory M. The vectors in the input matrix are the components of the four neighbors in the state memory. In parallel with the input matrix, the data vector

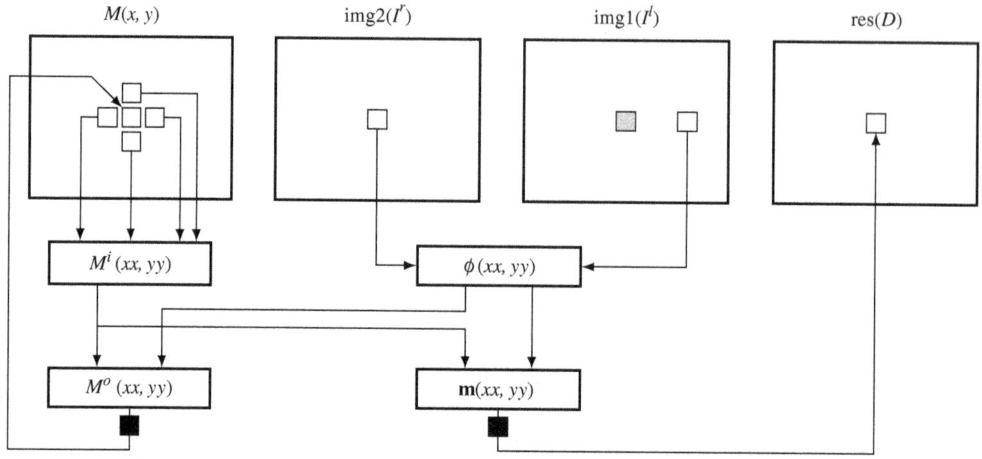

Figure 14.3 The flow of computation in the BP machine. Right reference mode. Two places are terminated by pipelining registers

is also composed from the image pairs. Combining the input message matrix and the data vector, we can build the output message matrix, following some extensive computations, as we will see. The determined matrix is held until the next clock. Eventually these data are overwritten to the state memory at the position (xx, yy), replacing the old one with the new one. Unlike the other parts, this section is realized with a sequential circuit. This cyclic process is repeated for a predetermined number of times and then the stabilized values in M and the data vector are used to build the message vector, $\mathbf{m}$. The argument of the minimum element is the quantity that we are seeking and thus is to be stored in the buffer. The contents of the buffer are the disparity map.

14.4 Overall System

On the basis of Figure 14.3, let us now begin to design the Verilog HDL code. The header contains the parameters that characterize the images and the BP algorithm.

Listing 14.1 The header (1/12)

```
//file name
`define file_name "bear11394"                    //BMP file name

//image parameters
`define WIDTH    113                             //image width
`define HEIGHT    94                             //image height

//memory parameters
`define DATA_BITS  8                             //word size
`define ADDR_BITS  15                            //max image size
```

```
//reference modes
`define LEFT                         //left and right mode

//window parameters
`define WIDTH1    20                 //window width
`define HEIGHT1   20                 //window height
`define XSHIFT    20                 //window x-axis shift
`define YSHIFT    20                 //window y-axis shift

//BP parameters
`define MESS_BITS  5                 //message word
`define MESS_DIM   30                //message dimension
`define ITER       10                //iterations
`define LOCAL      10                //local range
`define SLOPE      25                //smoothness slope
```

The filename is used for the IO part of the simulator to open and read the image files in the RAM, imitating the camera output. The image size, defined by the height and the width, $M \times N$, is used to specify the required resources throughout the circuit. The memory parameters specify the word length and the address range for the contents in the RAM. The image data is ordinarily stored in bytes – three bytes for RGB channels. These parameters are also used to define the arrays, `img1`, `img2`, and `res`.

The next parameter is the key indicating the left or right reference modes. The window and the scan directions vary, depending on this parameter (Figure 14.2). The window parameters comprise the window width, height, horizontal shift, and vertical shift. The shift amount must be less than or equal to the window size. Otherwise, there will be empty regions in the disparity map.

The BP parameters specify the word length of the message, the number of states, the slope of the smoothness function, and the iteration number. The message length and dimension are important parameters as they determine the performance, the computational speed, and the space. The larger values may be better for better performance but they also require more space and computation. The message dimension must be the maximum disparity range, which can be observed only after experimentation. The message word length must be enough to encode the smallest and the largest messages. This decision is also possible only after observing the computation. The bits must be enough to uniquely differentiate the disparity levels, $2^B \leq D$. This gives us, $B \leq \log D$. Usually, most of the disparities are labeled with the same index, making $B \ll \log D$. The most important factor determining the window is the belief matrix, which has a complexity of $4mnBD$ bits. The disparity size D is usually over 30, and thus the space complexity is overwhelmingly large to be applied to an entire frame. For larger disparity and message word, the window size must be small to be implemented in a chip. Next comes the smoothness function, which is characterized by the slope and local range and is the truncated linear function. The product of the slope and the local range must not exceed the maximum number range. More advanced algorithms may be implemented for the smoothness function, replacing the slope with appropriate parameters, such as the Potts model. Finally, the iteration number must be chosen so that the computation process reaches a stable state, at which time the disparity is determined as the index of the belief vector.

The main part of the code is as follows:

Listing 14.2 The framework: `processor.v` (2/12)

```
`include 'head.v'

module processor(                                     //BP segment processor
   input clock, reset,
   output reg [`ADDR_BITS - 1:0] i_raddr, r_raddr, r_waddr,//address bus
   input [`DATA_BITS - 1:0] i_rdata1, i_rdata2, r_rdata,   //data bus
   output reg [`DATA_BITS - 1:0] r_wdata,             //data bus
   output reg r_wen                                   //write enable
   );

   //parameters
   parameter MESS_MAX = {`MESS_BITS1{'b1}};           //message maximum

   //working array: window of images
   reg [`DATA_BITS - 1:0] img1 [0: `HEIGHT - 1][0: 3*`WIDTH - 1];//image
   reg [`DATA_BITS - 1:0] img2 [0: `HEIGHT - 1][0: 3*`WIDTH - 1];//2image
   reg [`DATA_BITS - 1:0] res  [0: `HEIGHT - 1][0: 3*`WIDTH - 1];//result
   reg [`MESS_BITS - 1:0] mmat [0: `HEIGHT1 - 1][0: `WIDTH1 - 1]
                         [0:3][0:`MESS_DIM - 1];      //message matrix

   //variables
   reg [`ADDR_BITS - 1:0]  idx, idx1,idx2;            //variables
   reg [9:0] row, col, x, y, xx, yy, xxx, yyy, dim;   //variables
   reg [4:0] iter;
   reg [2:0] dir;
   reg do_load, do_display, do_read, do_write;        //for control

   //net variables
   wire [`MESS_BITS * `MESS_DIM - 1:0] mess_in [0:3]; //input message
   wire [`MESS_BITS * `MESS_DIM - 1:0] mess_out [0:3];//output message
   wire [`MESS_BITS * `MESS_DIM - 1:0] data;          //data vector

   //sequential circuits
   //reading (IMAGE -> img)
   always @ (posedge clock) begin: READING            //reading block
   end

   //writing (res -> RESULT)
   always @(posedge clock) begin: WRITING             //writing block
   end
```

```
    //sampling
    always @ (posedge clock) begin: SAMPLING          //sampling block
    end //always

    //updating the message matrix (mmat)
    always @ (posedge clock) begin: MMAT              //belief matrix block
    end

    //combinational circuits
    //determining the disparity

    //computing the data term


    //building the input message matrix

    //building the output messages matrix

    //functions

endmodule
```

The code consists of three parts: sequential circuits, combinational circuits, and functions. The sequential part consists of four concurrent parts: reading, writing, sampling, and updation. The reading and writing blocks are the IP interfaces to the external RAMs, RAM1, RAM2, and RES, and the internal buffers, `img1`, `img2`, and `res`. The sampling block controls the window by moving around the image plane. This is common to both the left and right reference modes. Finally, the updation block writes the updated output message vector to the belief matrix, M. In this code, the message matrix is encoded as an unpacked array, `mmat` (refer to the problems at the end of this chapter). However, the message vectors, `mess_in` and `mess_out`, and the data vector, `data`, are all coded in packed format for computational simplicity (refer to the problems at the end of this chapter).

While the sequential part works for each clock tick, the combinational part works between the clock period, reading the data from the registers and stabilizing the result, so that in the next clock tick the result can be stored in the registers. The combinational part consists of four sections: a circuit building the input belief matrix, another building the data term, another building the output message matrix, and a circuit for determining the final disparity. The combinational circuits are aided by various functions, which all work in the same simulation time.

The components filling this template are explained in the following sections.

14.5 IO Circuit

Two of the sequential circuits are for reading and writing. The image data are located in the external RAMs, outside of the main processor, and must be accessed periodically. The circuit can be designed as follows.

Listing 14.3 The IO circuit (3/12)

```
//reading (IMAGE -> img)
always @ (posedge clock) begin: READING          //reading block
   if (reset) begin                              //initialize
      row <= 0;
      col <= 0;
      do_load <= 1;
   end
   else begin                                    //read RAM into buffers
      do_load <= 0;
      if (row < 'HEIGHT) begin                   //for a row
         if (col < 3 * 'WIDTH + 2) begin         //for a column
            i_raddr <= 3 * 'WIDTH * row + col;//pixel address

            img1[row][idx1] <= i_rdata1;         //load 1st image
            img2[row][idx1] <= i_rdata2;         //load 2nd image
            //res [row][idx1] <= i_rdata1;

            idx1 <= idx;                         //delay 2
            idx <= col;                          //delay 1
            col <= col + 1;                      //next block
         end else begin
            col <= 0;
            row <= row + 1;
         end
      end else begin
         row <= 0;
         do_load <= 1;
      end //else
   end
end

//writing (res -> RESULT)
always @(posedge clock) begin: WRITING           //writing block
   if (reset) begin
      xxx <= 0;
      yyy <= 0;
      do_display <= 0;
   end
   else begin
      if (yyy < 'HEIGHT) begin
         do_display <= 0;
         if (xxx < 3 * 'WIDTH) begin
```

```
                r_wdata <= res[yyy][xxx];            //data
                r_waddr <= 3*`WIDTH * yyy + xxx;     //address
                r_wen <= 1;                          //write enable
                xxx <= xxx + 1;                      //next
            end
            else begin
                xxx <= 0;
                yyy <= yyy + 1;
            end
        end
        else begin
            yyy <= 0;
            do_display <= 1;
        end
    end
end
```

The purpose of the reading part is to read RAM1 and RAM2, and possibly RES into the internal buffers, `img1`, `img2`, and `res`. The processor reads the images I^l and I^r from `img1` and `img2`, processes them to determine the disparity, and writes the result into `res`, which finally stores the disparity map, D. To pair the address and data, some small delays must be introduced in the address bus. A mismatch exists between the incoming data and the current address, as the current data corresponds to the address two clocks ahead. These problems can be solved by the delay buffers `idx` and `idx1` and the two-clocks delay in the address loop.

Another concurrent always block is the writing block. The purpose of this block is to write the disparity map, stored in the buffer, `res`, into the external RAM, RESULT, in RGB format so that the simulator can display the disparity map in BMP format. The flags, `do_load` and `do_display`, are used to control the simulator and therefore are not part of the synthesis. Note: the counters representing pixel positions (`row`, `col`), (x, y), (xx, yy), and (xxx, yyy) are all differently redefined in different always blocks in order to avoid multiple drivers for a net variable.

The remaining circuit can be considered a system that receives `img1` and `img2` as inputs and produces `res` as output.

14.6 Sampling Circuit

The computation is based on the window processing. A circuit that relocates the window around the image plane must be present. The constraint is that as a consequence of window movement, the entire image plane must be completely scanned, without producing empty spaces. In actuality, the space to be scanned is (x, y, l), where $(x, y) \in \mathcal{P}$ and $l \in [0, L-1]$ for some maximum iteration L. There is an algorithm that scans in the iteration index, called FBP (Jeong and Park 2004; Park and Jeong 2008). For hierarchical BP (Yang *et al.* 2006), sampling in this space must be made in the pyramid form. The order of the visit may be deterministic or random. In this chapter, we follow the usual approach, scanning of the image plane in a raster scan manner.

Listing 14.4 The sampling circuit (4/12)

```
//sampling
always @ (posedge clock) begin: SAMPLING   //sampling block
   if (reset) begin                        //initialize
      x <= 0;
      y <= 0;
      xx <= 0;
      yy <= 0;
      iter <= 0;
   end
else begin
   if (y < 'HEIGHT) begin
      if (x < 'WIDTH) begin
         if (iter < 'ITER) begin           //iteration
            if (yy < 'HEIGHT1) begin       //for a row
               if (xx < 'WIDTH1) begin     //for a column
                  xx <= xx + 1;
               end
               else begin
                  xx <= 0;
                  yy <= yy + 1;
               end
            end
            else begin
               yy <= 0;
               iter <= iter + 1;
            end
         end
         else begin
            iter <= 0;
            x <= x + 'XSHIFT;
         end
      end
      else begin
         x <= 0;
         y <= y + 'YSHIFT;
      end
   end
   else begin
      y <= 0;
   end
  end //else
end //always
```

In iteration notation, the circuit spans the $M \times N \times L \times m \times n$ space in a $(y(x(l(xx)))$ manner, where xx is changed most rapidly and y is changed most slowly. Other iteration methods are also possible. The sampling circuit guides the window so that the image plane may be scanned in a certain way with counters. The amount of skipping in the horizontal and vertical directions is specified by the parameters, x_s (`XSHIFT`) and x_y (`YSHIFT`). The circuit has to generate three types of counters for the purpose: the window position on the image plane, the pixel position in a window, and the iteration number. With the auto-incrementing counter, $x \le N - 1$ and $y \le M - 1$, the window is positioned by the top left corner, (x, y), for the right reference mode and the top right corner, $(N - 1 - x, y)$, for the left reference mode. Inside the window, the pixel is positioned by the counter, $xx = 0, 1, \ldots, n - 1$ and $yy = 0, 1, \ldots, m - 1$. Therefore, the absolute positions of the pixel are $(x + xx, y + yy)$ and $(N - 1 - (x + xx), y + yy)$, respectively, for both reference systems.

The amount of overlap between two contiguous windows is determined by the window size and the shift parameter. In both directions, the overlapped regions are $N - x_s$ and $M - y_s$. To be seen through the contiguous windows, suitable schemes for the boundary conditions must be considered. One way is to store the previous results around the boundary so that the next window can use them. The results may be the disparity values or the belief values. The other option is to use the data so that each window is independent of the other window processing. The former method needs a complicated scheme for storing the previous values, to use them in later windows, but leads to better performance. The latter scheme is the simplest of all but may result in poor performance around the window boundary.

The sampling scheme naturally involves a high degree of freedom, which is governed by the three counters, shift amount, and boundary policy. Here in the template, we consider only the basic one, two types of scanning, no overlap, and an independent window free from boundary preservation (see the problems at the end of this chapter).

In any case, the most important thing is that all the computation is described in terms of the current position and the time period. The current position is (xx, yy) in the message matrix and the current iteration is `iter` $<$ `ITER`. The current position is $I^r(x + xx, y + yy)$ for the right reference system and $I^l(N - 1 - (x + xx), y + yy)$ for the left reference system.

14.7 Circuit for the Data Term

From here onwards, all the computations are realized with combinational circuits, unless otherwise stated. The data vector, ϕ, is the major source of the belief message, driven by the input images, and thus must be provided accurately (Figure 14.3).

The concept for the provision of this vector is drawn in Figure 14.4. As shown in the figure, the sources of the data vector are the two image frames. The location of the current pixel is indicated as a position in a window, which is not shown here. A specific field, d, of the data vector is constructed by the data read from the two images. Therefore, a data vector can be constructed concurrently for all the pixels of the two images on the same epipolar line. All the elements of the vector are determined by the combinational circuits as follows.

The data vector is encoded in a packed array of BD bits, because it must often be accessed as one complete set of data (see the problems at the end of this chapter). In the right reference system, the data term is

$$\phi(x + xx, y + yy) = \{\phi_{D-1}, \ldots, \phi_1, \phi_0\}, \tag{14.9}$$

where ϕ_{D-1} is the MSB and ϕ_0 is the LSB. Each element is a B bit number with

$$\phi_d = \min\left\{ \sum_{k \in \{R,G,B\}} |I_k^r(x + xx, y + yy) - I_k^l(x + xx + d, y + yy)|, 2^B - 1 \right\},$$
$$\forall d \in [0, D - 1]. \tag{14.10}$$

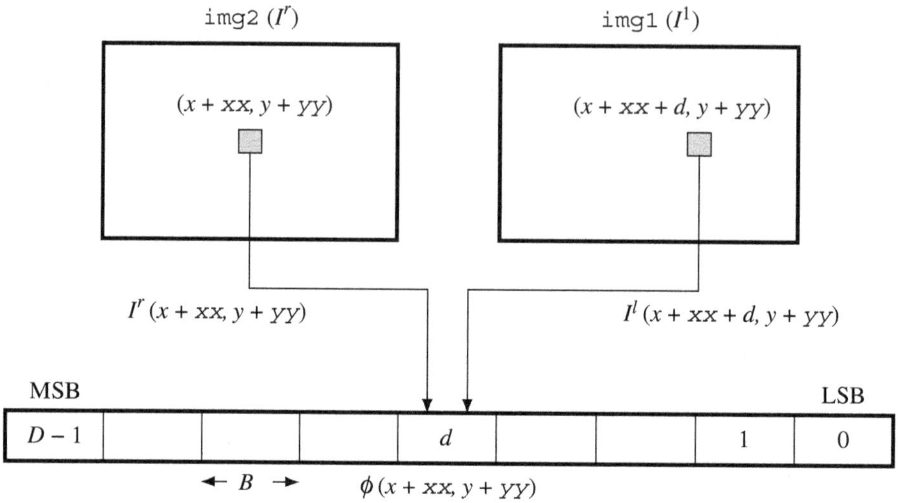

Figure 14.4 Building the data vector, $\phi(x + xx, y + yy)$, where (x, y) is the window position and (xx, yy) is the pixel position within the window. The vector is generated by the combinational circuits for all elements in parallel

Here, the data value is limited within a B bit word length, preventing overflow.

For the left reference system, the data are defined as

$$\phi_d = \min\left\{ \sum_{k\in\{R,G,B\}} |I_k^l(N-1-(x+xx), y+yy) - I_k^r(N-1 - (x+xx+d), y+yy)|, 2^B - 1 \right\}, \qquad \forall d \in [0, D-1]. \tag{14.11}$$

Advanced algorithms may use different schemes for computing the data term, for example, with better distance measure and maybe an occlusion indicator. This code is a basic template that contains only the most basic features.

Keeping in mind the concept, one can code the algorithm as follows. (Because there are a lot of identical circuits, the Verilog generate construct is used. The code also contains the Verilog compiler directive to switch the design between the two reference modes.)

Listing 14.5 The data term (5/12)

```
//computing the data term
genvar vary;
for (vary = 0; vary < 'MESS_DIM; vary = vary + 1) begin: DATA_TERM
'ifdef LEFT                                          //left mode
  assign data['MESS_BITS * vary +: 'MESS_BITS] =
     (x+xx+vary < 'WIDTH)?
     tadd(tadd(adistance(img1[y+yy][3*('WIDTH-1-(x+xx))],
                img2[y+yy][3*('WIDTH-1-(x+xx+vary))]),
```

```
            adistance(img1[y+yy][3*('WIDTH-1-(x+xx))+1],
              img2[y+yy][3*('WIDTH-1-(x+xx+vary))+1])),
            adistance(img1[y+yy][3*('WIDTH-1-(x+xx))+2],
              img2[y+yy][3*('WIDTH-1-(x+xx+vary))+2]))
      : MESS_MAX;
'else                                                   //right mode
   assign data['MESS_BITS * vary +: 'MESS_BITS] =
      (x+xx+vary < 'WIDTH)?
      tadd(tadd(adistance(img2[y+yy][3*(x+xx)],
            img1[y+yy][3*(x+xx+vary)]),
        adistance(img2[y+yy][3*(x+xx)+1],
            img1[y+yy][3*(x+xx+vary)+1])),
        adistance(img2[y+yy][3*(x+xx)+2],
            img1[y+yy][3*(x+xx+vary)+2]))
    : MESS_MAX;
'endif
end
```

The circuits are compiled separately according to the two types of reference systems. Each reference system consists of D continuous assignments, with each assignment determining a B bit field in the data vector. The circuits are generated by the Verilog HDL generate construct. Consequently, this part of the circuit consists of D combinational circuits.

Two functions are used in the expression: `adistance` and `tadd`. Function `adistance` is an absolute function that returns the absolute distance between two arguments. Function `tadd` is an addition that accounts for saturation math. The upper bound of the truncation is defined as $2^B - 1$. The functions, together with other functions, will be discussed in later sections.

Knowing the distribution of elements in a vector is very important, because the data vector is to be combined with message vectors. If either of the two vectors dominates the other, the combined result may be less efficient. This is part of the reason for normalizing the messages, as will be seen. Considering the sum of three differences in the RGB channels, the range of ϕ is between 0 and 255×3. To limit the number in B bits, which are used for message encoding, the data vector must also be normalized appropriately. This issue is also postponed to a later section.

14.8 Circuit for the Input Belief Message Matrix

The input message vector must be constructed in parallel with the data vector because they are combined soon afterwards (Figure 14.3). For this purpose, the required circuit is to build M^i in Equation (14.3) out of M^o.

The concept is depicted in Figure 14.5. Consider that the current position is $p = (x + xx, y + yy)$, with (x, y) for the window and (xx, yy) for the pixel within the window. At this window, the input belief matrix, $M^i(x, y)$, is decided. First, take the output belief matrix from the four neighbors, as shown in the figure. Each matrix contains four vectors, indicating four directions. Next, extract a vector from each matrix, west for east, north for south, east for west, and south for north vector, as shown, and build a matrix, M^i_p. The matrix is in the ordinary set of four vectors and thus must be converted to the packed array form.

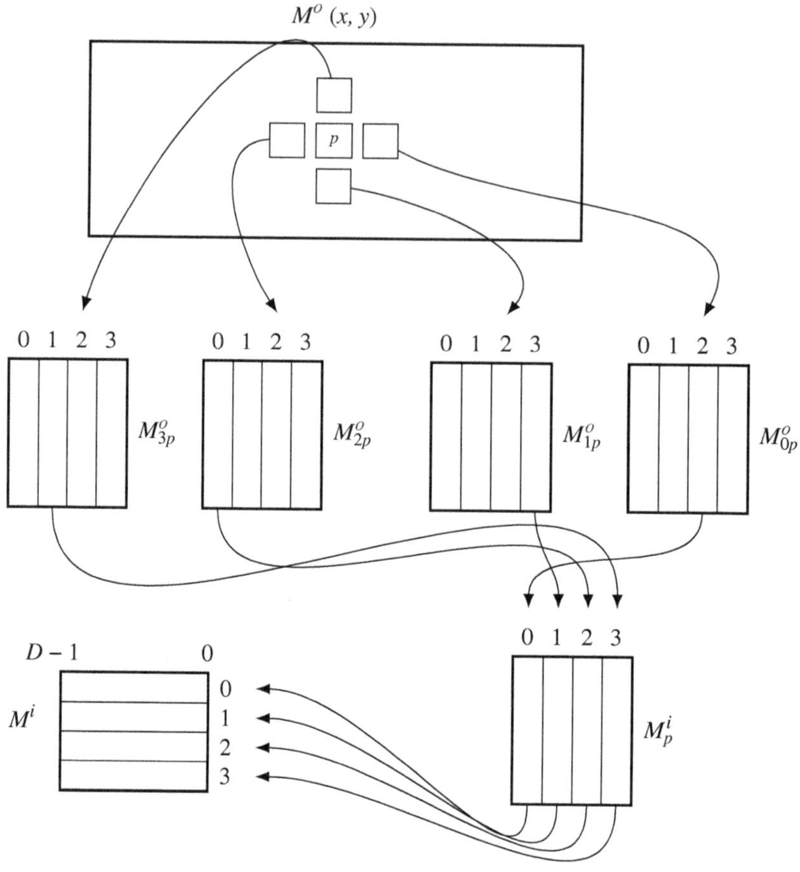

Figure 14.5 Building the input belief message matrix at $p = (xx, yy)$

This can be explained precisely with equations. In Equation (14.1), this stage corresponds to the computation: M^i_p. Consider a position $p = (x + xx, y + yy)$. At this position, we are going to build the input matrix:

$$M^i_p = \left(\mathbf{m}^i_{0p}, \mathbf{m}^i_{1p}, \mathbf{m}^i_{2p}, \mathbf{m}^i_{3p}\right). \tag{14.12}$$

The neighbors at p have the output matrices:

$$\begin{aligned}
M^o_0 &= \left(\mathbf{m}^o_{00}, \mathbf{m}^o_{01}, \mathbf{m}^o_{02}, \mathbf{m}^0_{03}\right),\\
M^o_1 &= \left(\mathbf{m}^o_{10}, \mathbf{m}^o_{11}, \mathbf{m}^o_{12}, \mathbf{m}^0_{13}\right),\\
M^o_2 &= \left(\mathbf{m}^o_{20}, \mathbf{m}^o_{21}, \mathbf{m}^o_{22}, \mathbf{m}^0_{23}\right),\\
M^o_3 &= \left(\mathbf{m}^o_{30}, \mathbf{m}^o_{31}, \mathbf{m}^o_{32}, \mathbf{m}^0_{33}\right),
\end{aligned} \tag{14.13}$$

where all the subscripts are the relative directions, east, south, west, and north. Extracting a vector from each matrix, we can construct the input matrix:

$$M_p^i = \left(\mathbf{m}_{02}^o, \mathbf{m}_{13}^o, \mathbf{m}_{20}^o, \mathbf{m}_{31}^o\right). \quad (14.14)$$

The criterion for choosing an element is based on the neighborhood. For example, the east input must be the west output of the east neighbor and the north input must be the south output of the north neighbor.

Although this seems complicated, the core operation is just reading and building the matrix in packed array format. The circuits consist of only four continuous assignments. Considering the D fields, we need to generate $4D$ combinational circuits.

Listing 14.6 The input message matrix: `processor.v` (6/12)

```
//building the input message matrix
genvar varx;
for (varx = 0; varx < `MESS_DIM; varx = varx + 1) begin: MESS_IN
`ifdef LEFT                                    //left mode
   assign mess_in[0]['MESS_BITS * varx +:'MESS_BITS] = //east vector
      (xx > 0)?
      mmat[yy]   [xx - 1][2][varx]:data['MESS_BITS * varx +:'MESS_BITS];
   assign mess_in[1]['MESS_BITS * varx +:'MESS_BITS] = //south vector
      (yy < 'HEIGHT1 - 1 & y+yy < 'HEIGHT - 1)?
      mmat[yy+1][xx][3][varx]:data['MESS_BITS * varx +:'MESS_BITS];
   assign mess_in[2]['MESS_BITS * varx +:'MESS_BITS] = //west vector
      (xx > 0 & yy > 0 & xx < 'WIDTH1 - 1 & x+xx < 'WIDTH - 1)?
      mmat[yy]   [xx+1][0][varx]:data['MESS_BITS * varx +:'MESS_BITS];
   assign mess_in[3]['MESS_BITS * varx +:'MESS_BITS] = //north vector
      (yy > 0)?
      mmat[yy-1][xx][1][varx]:data['MESS_BITS * varx +:'MESS_BITS];
`else                                          //right mode
   assign mess_in[0]['MESS_BITS * varx +:'MESS_BITS] = //east vector
      (xx > 0 & yy > 0 & xx < 'WIDTH1 - 1 & x+xx < 'WIDTH - 1)?
      mmat[yy]   [xx + 1][2][varx]:data['MESS_BITS * varx +:'MESS_BITS];
   assign mess_in[1]['MESS_BITS * varx +:'MESS_BITS] = //south vector
      (yy < 'HEIGHT1 - 1 & y+yy < 'HEIGHT - 1)?
      mmat[yy+1][xx][3][varx]:data['MESS_BITS * varx +:'MESS_BITS];
   assign mess_in[2]['MESS_BITS * varx +:'MESS_BITS] = //west vector
      (xx > 0)?
      mmat[yy]   [xx-1][0][varx]:data['MESS_BITS * varx +:'MESS_BITS];
   assign mess_in[3]['MESS_BITS * varx +:'MESS_BITS] = //north vector
      (yy > 0)?
      mmat[yy-1][xx][1][varx]:data['MESS_BITS * varx +:'MESS_BITS];
`endif
end
```

In addition to choosing the vectors and rotating them into packed field format, the circuit must also account for the boundary conditions. Around the image boundary, one or two neighbors may be missing. There are two kinds of boundaries: the window boundary and the image boundary. The neighbor may be out of the window but within the image frame. In another case, the neighbor may be completely outside the image frame.

One method is to replace the belief with the data terms. That is, for the first kind of neighbor, the belief is replaced with the data term in that pixel. For the second kind of neighbor, the belief is replaced with the data term of the current pixel. In effect, the image is expanded with the boundary values. Using this method, the windows are independent of each other and glued by the data terms. We will follow this approach to make the circuit simple. In the code, this concept is reflected as the conditional statements. A more sophisticated method that stores the actual messages, instead of using the data terms, and reuses them later in other windows is possible. This kind of strategy is needed for better performance and iteration over the entire image plane, following the iteration inside the window.

Note that the code is separated with the Verilog compiler directive for the right and left reference modes. The difference between the two modes is the use of the counters for computing the coordinates. For the right mode, the conjugate point is on the right and for the left mode, the conjugate point is on the left.

14.9 Circuit for the Output Belief Message Matrix

Given the data vector and message matrix, we can design the main circuits for generating the output message. This part is the most complicated circuit, where the variance between the data term and the message term, as well as the variance between messages in a message vector, must be properly regulated. Moreover, the smoothness function must be applied and the operation of minimum selection must be introduced. This operation requires four stages: selective averaging, adding of data terms, adding of smoothness function, and choosing the minimum. These complicated operations must be aided by the specialized functions.

In Equation (14.1), the output message matrix has the form

$$M_p^o = \Psi \odot \left(\Phi + M_p^i\left(\mathbf{1}_4\mathbf{1}_4^T - I_{4\times 4}\right)\right), \tag{14.15}$$

where

$$A \odot \mathbf{b} = \{\min_{j=1}^{n}(a_{ij} + b_j) | i = 1, 2, \ldots, n\}^T, \tag{14.16}$$

for a matrix A and vector $\boldsymbol{b}$. Let $M_p^o = (\mathbf{m}_0^o, \mathbf{m}_1^o, \mathbf{m}_2^o, \mathbf{m}_3^o)$ and $\mathbf{x} = \Phi + M_p^i(\mathbf{1}_4\mathbf{1}_4^T - I_{4\times 4})$. Then, the expressions mean

$$\mathbf{m}_i^o = \psi \odot \mathbf{x}_i, \quad \forall i \in [0, 3], \tag{14.17}$$

where $\odot$ means that the vector elements satisfy

$$m_{ik} = \min_{j=1}^{n} \left\{x_{ij} + \psi(|k - j|)\right\}, \quad \forall k \in [0, 3]. \tag{14.18}$$

Because Ψ is already known and stored as parameters, this operation can be designed into a function, `mess_min`, which receives a vector and produces the desired output. This function is one of the most complicated in the BP circuit, as we will see.

To design the circuit, we divide the equation into several stages, as illustrated in Figure 14.6. In the first stage, three of the input vectors are selected and then added to the data vector. This is realized with

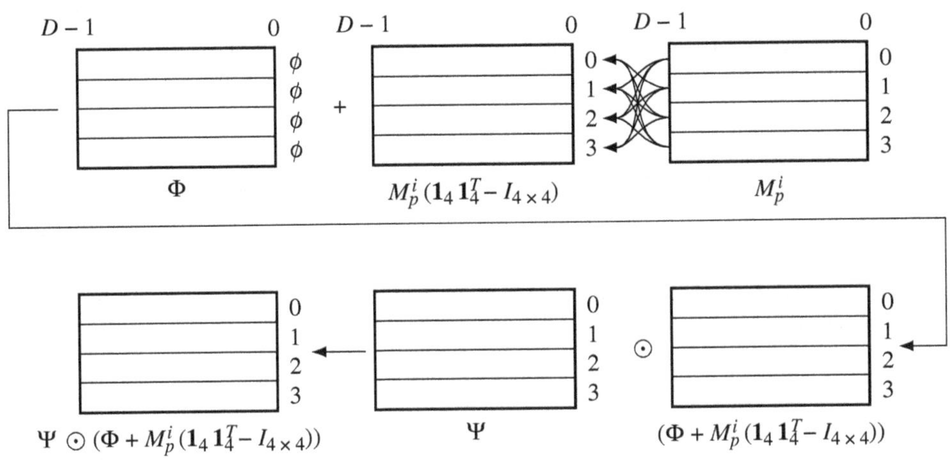

Figure 14.6 Building the output message matrix

the function mess_4av in the Verilog HDL code. This function operates field by field to take the average of the four elements.

In the second stage, the vectors are weighted with a smoothness function and the minimum elements are chosen. This is realized by the function mess_min. The functions will be discussed in more detail in a later section.

The actual code is as follows.

Listing 14.7 The output belief matrix (7/12)

```
//building the output messages matrix
assign mess_out[0]  = (iter)? mess_min(mess_4av
   (data,mess_in[1],mess_in[2],mess_in[3])): 0; //east vector
assign mess_out[1]  = (iter)? mess_min(mess_4av
   (data,mess_in[0],mess_in[2],mess_in[3])): 0; //south vector
assign mess_out[2]  = (iter)? mess_min(mess_4av
   (data,mess_in[0],mess_in[1],mess_in[3])): 0; //west vector
assign mess_out[3]  = (iter)? mess_min(mess_4av
   (data,mess_in[0],mess_in[1],mess_in[2])): 0; //north vector
```

The four output vectors are independently generated by calling the function mess_min. In the code, the initialization is also encoded. At the start, which can be recognized by the first iteration, the message matrix must be initialized. In this case, the initial values are all the same, zero. However, other values may be used instead of zero.

14.10 Circuit for the Updation of Message Matrix

The output matrix is overwritten to the current position of the output message matrix. This operation must be sequential, storing the result until the next clock, because the path from $M^o(x, y)$ to the output message matrix is a combinational path. The formats of M and M^o are different: M is encoded and unpacked while M^o is encoded in packed array format. Therefore, the message format must be transformed from packed to unpacked array before updation.

This operation is realized by the following circuit.

Listing 14.8 The framework: `processor.v` (8/12)

```
//updating the message matrix (mmat)
always @ (posedge clock) begin: MMAT             //belief matrix block
   if (reset) begin
   end
   else begin
      for (dir = 0; dir < 4; dir = dir + 1) begin: MESSAGE_MATRIX
         for (dim = 0; dim < 'MESS_DIM; dim = dim + 1) begin: UNPACK
            mmat[yy][xx][dir][dim] = mess_out[dir]
                  ['MESS_BITS * dim +:'MESS_BITS];
         end
      end
   end
end
```

In the code, each field is read and written to the vector element. The iteration is converted to $4D$ different circuits.

14.11 Circuit for the Disparity

The operations between the input message matrix and the output message matrix form a cycle. The iteration is aimed at a convergent system. Eventually, when the iteration ends, the message matrix M must be used for the final operation, which is to determine the disparity from the message vector and to write it to the result buffer. In Equation (14.1), the corresponding operation is

$$\mathbf{m}_p = \phi_p + M_p^i \mathbf{1}_4,$$

$$x_p = \arg \min_{k=0}^{D-1} m_p(k), \quad p \in [1, MN]. \tag{14.19}$$

This can be realized by two functions: `mess_4av` and `argmin`. Function `mess_4av` takes the average of the four vectors, while function `argmin` chooses the argument of the minimum element. The concept is depicted in Figure 14.7. In the figure, M^i is the input belief message matrix at a point. The matrix is reduced to a vector by `mess_4av`. This vector is then added to the data vector at this pixel by another average function, `mess_av`. From the vector, the minimum and corresponding index, which is the optimal disparity at this pixel, is computed.

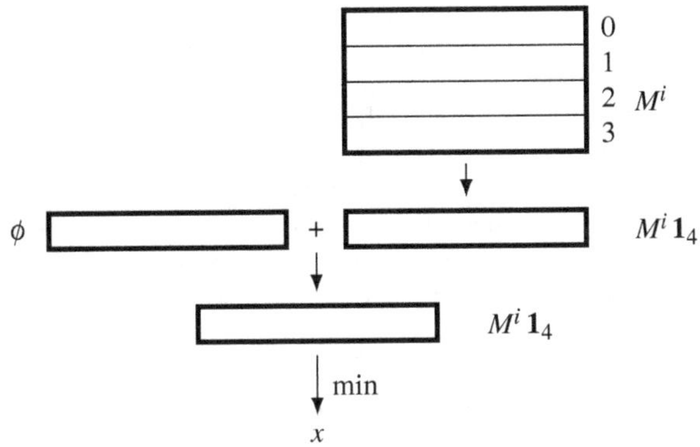

Figure 14.7 Building the result vector

The operations are designed by the following code.

Listing 14.9 The framework: `processor.v` (9/12)

```
//determining the disparity
wire ['DATA_BITS - 1:0] result;
assign result =  argmin(mess_av(data, mess_4av
   (mess_in[0],mess_in[1],mess_in[2],mess_in[3]))); //final message
always @(posedge clock) begin
'ifdef LEFT                                          //left mode
   res[y+yy][3*('WIDTH - 1 - (x+xx))]   <= result;
   res[y+yy][3*('WIDTH - 1 - (x+xx))+1] <= result;
   res[y+yy][3*('WIDTH - 1 - (x+xx))+2] <= result;
'else                                                //right mode
   res[y+yy][3*(x+xx)]   <= result;
   res[y+yy][3*(x+xx)+1] <= result;
   res[y+yy][3*(x+xx)+2] <= result;
'endif
end
```

The major operation is realized with the combinational circuit. However, an additional sequential operation is needed for terminating the flow of the combinational circuit and writing the vector to the internal buffer, `res`, at each clock tick. The buffer finally stores the disparity map. For the BMP display, the disparity map is copied into three channels.

14.12 Saturation Arithmetic

Thus far, the combinational circuits are aided by many functions, and are a compact method of writing the common codes in the function. The restriction is that the codes must be executed within the same simulation time and the variables should all be local. Due to the variable scopes, accessing the entire image or message matrix is very inefficient. Let us design the circuits for such functions.

The first function is `tadd`, which adds numbers limiting the size within the predefined bounds. Usually, the lower bound is zero and the upper bound is the full field: $2^B - 1$, where B is the word length of the message. This operation must be secured so that underflow and overflow are avoided. All the other functions using any kind of addition may use this saturation math.

The second function is `mess_av`, which takes two vectors in packed array form and takes averages field by field. This function uses the truncated addition mentioned above. Function `mess_4av` is an expansion of `mess_av` from two to four variables. The function computes the average of the four vectors, using `mess_av` twice.

Listing 14.10 The functions (10/12)

```
//functions ////////////////////////////////////////////
//truncate math
function [15:0] tadd;                              //saturation logic
   input signed[15:0] a, b;
   reg signed [15:0] c;

   begin
      c = a + b;
      tadd = (c < 0)? 0: (c < MESS_MAX)? c: MESS_MAX;
   end
endfunction


//average 2-vector
function ['MESS_BITS * 'MESS_DIM - 1:0] mess_av;   //vector average
   input ['MESS_BITS * 'MESS_DIM - 1:0] a, b;
   reg [7: 0] i;

   for (i = 0; i < 'MESS_DIM; i = i + 1) begin
      mess_av['MESS_BITS*i +:'MESS_BITS] =
         tadd(a['MESS_BITS*i +:'MESS_BITS]>>1,
            b['MESS_BITS*i +:'MESS_BITS]>>1);
   end
endfunction

//average 4-vector
function ['MESS_BITS * 'MESS_DIM - 1:0] mess_4av;  //vector average
   input ['MESS_BITS * 'MESS_DIM - 1:0] a, b, c, d;
   begin
      mess_4av = mess_av(mess_av(a,b),mess_av(c,d));
      //$display("4av=%d", mess_4av);
   end
endfunction
```

```
//absolute distance
function [15:0] adistance;                              //absolute distance
   input [15:0] a, b;
   begin
      adistance = (a > b)? (a - b): (b - a);
   end
endfunction
```

As well as the additions, difference operations are needed to measure the likelihood of two numbers. The basic distance between two numbers is defined by the absolute distance, although other advanced distance measures can replace this. The function, `adistance`, works for this purpose, in an integer word length.

14.13 Smoothness

The output message uses the function `mess_min`, as described in Equation (14.18). For a given vector **x** and the function, ψ, the function evaluates

$$m_k = \min_{j=1}^{n} \left\{ x_j + \psi(|k-j|) \right\}.$$

In the Verilog design, the vectors are all represented by packed arrays. The smooth function is predefined and thus may not be supplied as an additional argument to the function.

The underlying concept of the circuit is illustrated in Figure 14.8. The input vector is a message vector among the four, represented in packed array. The D weighted message vectors, **y**, are obtained by

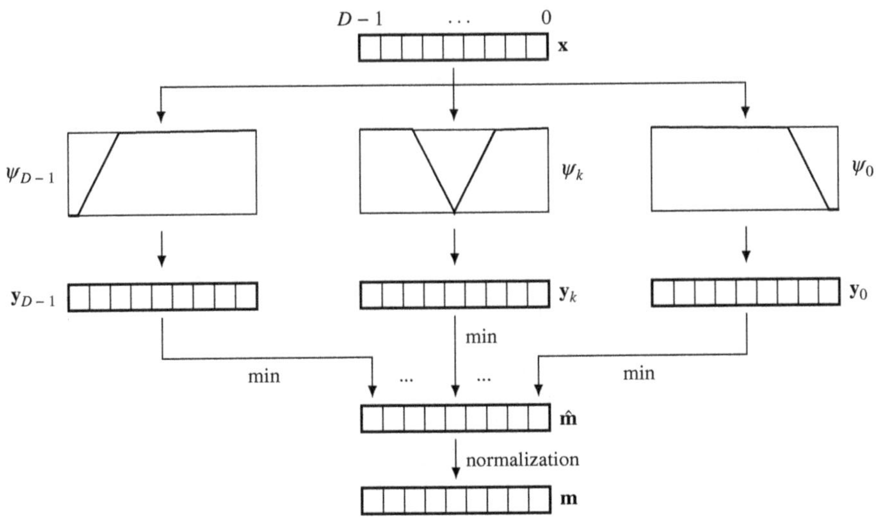

Figure 14.8 Building an output belief message vector with the operations: weighting (truncated linear), minimum selection, and normalization

weighting with D different smooth functions. The smoothness function here is the truncated linear model but can be any model, such as the quadratic model or the Potts model. Each field of the intermediate vector, $\hat{\mathbf{m}}$, is obtained by selecting the minimum of the corresponding weighted vector. This vector undergoes some more processes, collectively called normalization.

In the following, the concept is coded in Verilog HDL.

Listing 14.11 The functions (11/12)

```
//smoothness distance measure
function [15: 0] smoothed;                              //truncated linear
   input[15:0] center, position, value;
   begin
      smoothed = (adistance(center,position) < 'LOCAL)?
         tadd(value, adistance(center,position) * 'SLOPE): {15{1'b1}};
   end
endfunction

//minimum with smoothness weight
function ['MESS_BITS * 'MESS_DIM - 1:0] mess_min;  //weighted minimum
   input['MESS_BITS * 'MESS_DIM - 1:0] a;
   reg [7:0] i, j;
   reg [15:0] tmp, temp, sum;
   reg signed [15:0] delta;

   begin
      //choose the minimum with smoothness constraint
      for (i=0; i <'MESS_DIM; i = i + 1) begin: SMOOTHNESS
         tmp = a['MESS_BITS * i +:'MESS_BITS];
         for (j = 0; j <'MESS_DIM; j = j + 1) begin
            temp = smoothed(i,j,a['MESS_BITS*j +:'MESS_BITS]);
            tmp = (tmp <  temp)? tmp: temp;
         end
         mess_min['MESS_BITS * i +:'MESS_BITS] = tmp;
      end

      //shift
      tmp = {'MESS_BITS{1'b1}};
      for (i=0; i<'MESS_DIM; i=i+1) begin
         tmp = (tmp < mess_min['MESS_BITS * i +:'MESS_BITS])?
            tmp :mess_min['MESS_BITS * i +:'MESS_BITS];
      end
      for (i=0; i<'MESS_DIM; i=i+1) begin
         mess_min['MESS_BITS * i +:'MESS_BITS] =
            mess_min['MESS_BITS * i +:'MESS_BITS] - tmp;
      end
```

```
        //normalization: choose max
        tmp = 0;
        for (i=0; i<'MESS_DIM; i=i+1) begin: DISTRIBUTION
              tmp = (tmp > mess_min['MESS_BITS * i +:'MESS_BITS])?
                 tmp: mess_min['MESS_BITS * i +:'MESS_BITS];
        end

        //normalization: division                   //normalization
        delta = {'MESS_BITS{1'b1/tmp}};
        for (j=0; j<'MESS_DIM; j=j+1) begin
           mess_min['MESS_BITS * j +:'MESS_BITS] =
              mess_min['MESS_BITS * j +:'MESS_BITS] * delta;
        end
     end
endfunction
```

For the weighting, $\psi + \mathbf{x}$, a function, called `smoothed`, is defined. The given vectors $\mathbf{x}$ and the smoothness vector ψ in this function evaluate

$$\psi + \mathbf{x}. \tag{14.20}$$

Function `mess_min` computes Equation (14.20) in two steps: minimum selection of the weighted vector and normalization. For the first operation, the circuit uses `smoothed`. The normalization stage involves a number of sequential stages. The first stage shifts the element down to base zero:

$$m_k \leftarrow m_k - \min_{j=0}^{D-1} m_j, \quad \forall k \in [0, D-1]. \tag{14.21}$$

This operation is necessary because the message may be increased during the BP operations to the upper bound, $2^B - 1$, threatening overflow. The normalization starts with the selection of a maximum number. Subsequently, all the elements are divided by the common divisor so that the message is in the range $[0, 2^B - 1]$.

Observing the statistical distribution of the message values, we may notice that the dynamic range is very small and thus the full B bits may not be necessary. In fact, the nature of the images and the applications, and the chosen smoothness function, all contribute to the message distribution (see the problems at the end of this chapter). In some cases, normalization may not be necessary. From the given template, we can further develop circuits that are more efficient in both complexity and performance.

14.14 Minimum Argument

After the iteration is complete, the messages are supposed to be in equilibrium. At this instant, the final message is determined and, thus, the disparity. This is the concept of the original theory. In actuality, the circuit executing this task is separate from the circuit for the message updation and is thus concurrent, as are the other circuits. Therefore, there is no reason to halt this circuit during the iteration.

In Equation (14.1), the corresponding operation is

$$x = \arg \min_{k=0}^{D-1} m(k). \tag{14.22}$$

Function `argmin` returns the argument of the minimum given the input vector.

In the Verilog HDL, this operation reads:

Listing 14.12 The functions (12/12)

```
//choose argument for the minimum
function [15:0] argmin;                          //minimum argument
   input ['MESS_BITS * 'MESS_DIM - 1:0] a;
   reg [15:0] i, tmp, temp;
   begin
      tmp = MESS_MAX;
      temp = 0;
      for (i=0; i < 'MESS_DIM; i=i+1) begin
         temp = (a['MESS_BITS * i +:'MESS_BITS] < tmp)? i: temp;
         tmp = (a['MESS_BITS * i +:'MESS_BITS] < tmp)?
            a['MESS_BITS * i +:'MESS_BITS]: tmp;
      end
      argmin = temp;
   end
 endfunction
endmodule
```

It is important to choose the minimum near the center position when multiple minima exist throughout the elements in a vector. This is because the required value is not the message but its index, which must be as near to the current position as possible. An appropriate weight must be designed so that this condition is guaranteed. Otherwise, the circuit must be redesigned in a more complicated manner.

14.15 Simulation

Let us observe the testing of the BP circuit. The test images used were a pair of 225×188 images (CMU 2013; Middlebury 2013). They can be seen at the top of Figure 14.9, with the lower images being the disparity maps. The parameters for the BP were as follows. The window size was 40×40 and was moved un-overlapped in raster scan manner. Each window was iterated 10 times, somewhat earlier than complete convergence. The smoothness function was the truncated linear function with slope 25 in a 10 pixel range. Beyond the range, the smoothed value was saturated to the upper bound.

The right reference map had a poor region at the right side. In like manner, the left reference map had a poor region at the left side. Compared to the disparity map obtained by the DP machines, the result was less noisy, even if the result was not yet fully saturated. There were some remnants, some of the marks of the windows, due to the window processing. To avoid such window traces, the windows must be overlapped slightly around boundaries. The major differences between the two disparity maps are the important clues for computing occluding regions.

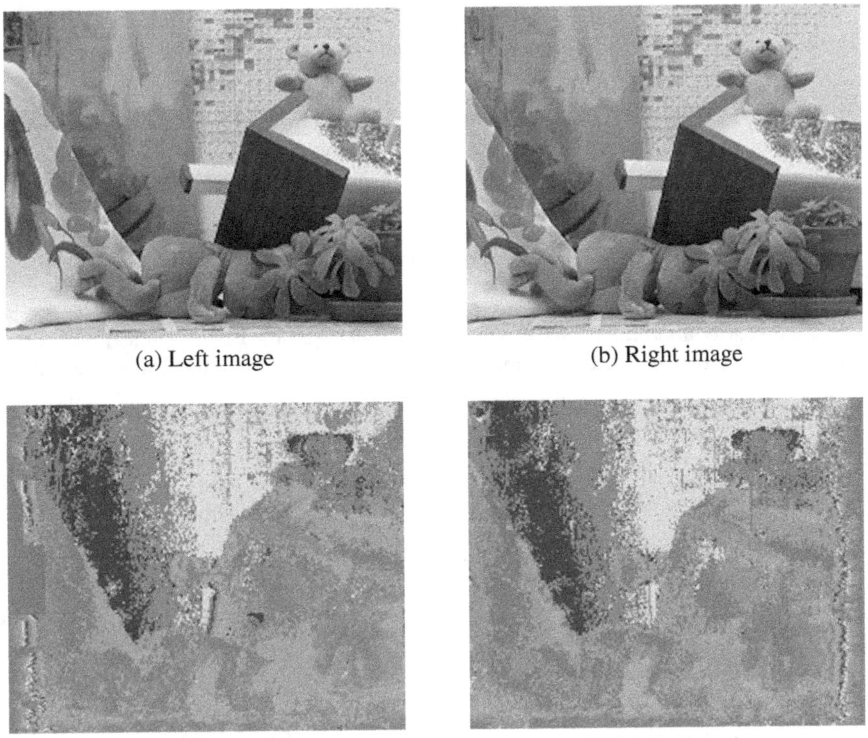

(a) Left image (b) Right image

(c) Left disparity (d) Right disparity

Figure 14.9 Disparity maps (image size: 225 × 188, disparity level: 32, window size: 40 × 40, iteration: 10, truncated linear function: 25)

In complexity view, the BP machine needed $4mnDB$ bits to store the message matrix and MNT time for computation, where T signifies iteration. Compared with the DP $O(N^2D)$ for a single processor and $O(N)$ for the D processor array, the BP consumed more space and time than DP but generally gives better results. The competitive algorithm, graph cuts, gives similar results, but takes less space, $O(MN)$, though the control structure is more complicated. It is known that the two algorithms have evolved in this direction: BP gets faster and GC gets more general.

Problems

14.1 [Data representation] A message is represented by the scoring function. If the abstraction process continues further, the message loses its meaning as a probability and score function. Instead, the quantities in the message vector will relate to preference order. Thus, $\mathbf{m} = (m_0, m_1, \ldots, m_{D-1}$, where $m \in [0, D-1]$. In such a case, what are the proper operations that correspond to the addition and average?

14.2 [Overall system] How is the message matrix, `mmat`, represented in packed form?

14.3 [Overall system] How can a message be sent in the packed and unpacked forms for the message matrix `mmat`?

14.4 [Overall system] In the code, the message and data vectors are coded in a packed array in contrast to the message matrix, which is in an unpacked array. Represent the message and data vectors in unpacked forms. Discuss their advantages and disadvantages.

14.5 [Overall system] In Listing 14.2, the message matrix was defined for disparity computation. What is the equivalent matrix representation for optical flow? Discuss using the spatial complexity. For instance, let the velocity vector (u, v) and their limits be U_DIM and V_DIM. For disparity, the message matrix is

```
reg ['MESS_BITS - 1:0] mmat [0: 'HEIGHT1 - 1][0: 'WIDTH1 - 1]
        [0:3][0:'MESS_DIM - 1];
```

In the disparity matrix, the spatial complexity is $4mnDB$ bits. For the optical flow, the message matrix has spatial complexity comprising UV, where U and V are the limits of u and v.

14.6 [Overall system] In Listing 14.2, the IO and sampling circuits are separately designed. Build a circuit that combines the three into one using an FSM.

14.7 [Sampling circuit] In Listing 14.4, the space is scanned in a $(y(x(l(xx)))$ manner, where xx changes most rapidly and y changes most slowly. What other scanning methods could be used?

14.8 [Data term] In Listing 14.5, the neighbors outside the window are assigned data along the boundary. However, we instead want to expand the outside in mirror image. Change the data term for such a mirror image case. Actually, there can be many more cases, which may need more computation. This modification is provided for the right mode only. However, similar changes can be made for the left mode also.

14.9 [Input message matrix] In Listing 14.6, the outside neighbors are bounded by the data on the boundary. Change the code so that the mirror image is used instead for the neighbors around the boundary.

14.10 [Functions] In Listing 14.10, the average of vectors is defined for the packed array. Modify the operation for an addition.

14.11 [Functions] In Listing 14.11, the distance measure is absolute. The Potts model is often more robust in many noisy environments. Design a function for the Potts model.

References

CMU 2013 Cmu data set `http://vasc.ri.cmu.edu/idb/html/stereo/` (accessed Sept. 4, 2013).

Felzenszwalb P and Huttenlocher D 2004 Efficient belief propagation for early vision *Proceedings of the 2004 IEEE Computer Society Conference on Computer Vision and Pattern Recognition*, pp. I261–I268 number 1.

Grauer-Gray S and Kambhamettu C 2009 Hierarchical belief propagation to reduce search space using CUDA for stereo and motion estimation *In Proceedings of 2009 Workshop on Applications of Computer Vision*, pp. 1–8.

IEEE 2005 *IEEE Standard for Verilog Hardware Description Language*. IEEE.

Jeong H and Park S 2004 Generalized trellis stereo matching with systolic array *Lecture Notes in Computer Science*, vol. 3358, pp. 263–267.

Jian S, Zheng N, and Shum H 2003 Stereo matching using belief propagation. *IEEE Trans. Pattern Anal. Mach. Intell.* **25**(7), 787–800.

Klaus A, Sormann M, and Karner K 2006 Segment-based stereo matching using belief propagation and a self-adapting dissimilarity measure *ICPR (3)*, pp. 15–18. IEEE Computer Society.

Liang C, Cheng C, Lai Y, Chen L, and Chen H 2011 Hardware-efficient belief propagation. *IEEE Trans. Circuits and Systems for Video Technology* **21**(5), 525–537.

Middlebury U 2013 Middlebury stereo home page `http://vision.middlebury.edu/stereo` (accessed Sept. 4, 2013).

Montserrat T, Civit J, Escoda O, and Landabaso J 2009 Depth estimation based on multiview matching with depth/color segmentation and memory efficient belief propagation *16th IEEE International Conference on Image Processing*, pp. 2353–2356.

Park S and Jeong H 2008 Memory efficient iterative process on a two-dimensional first-order regular graph. *Optics Letters* **33**, 74–76.

Stankiewicz O and Wegner K 2008 Depth map estimation software version 2 ISO/IEC MPEG meeting M15338.

Szeliski RS, Zabih R, Scharstein D, Veksler OA, Kolmogorov V, Agarwala A, Tappen M, and Rother C 2008 A comparative study of energy minimization methods for Markov random fields with smoothness-based priors. *IEEE Trans. Pattern Anal. Mach. Intell.* **30**(6), 1068–1080.

Taguchi Y, Wilburn B, and Zitnick C, 2008 Stereo reconstruction with mixed pixels using adaptive over-segmentation *CVPR*, pp. 1–8.

Tippetts BJ, Lee DJ, Archibald JK, and Lillywhite KD 2011 Dense disparity real-time stereo vision algorithm for resource-limited systems. *IEEE Trans. Circuits Syst. Video Techn* **21**(10), 1547–1555.

Tippetts BJ, Lee DJ, Lillywhite K, and Archibald J 2013 Review of stereo vision algorithms and their suitability for resource-limited systems `http://link.springer.com/article/10.1007%2Fs11554-012-0313-2` (accessed Sept. 4, 2013).

Wikipedia 2013 Perplexity `http://en.wikipedia.org/wiki/Perplexity` (accessed Sept. 2, 2013).

Yang Q, Wang L, Yang R, Stewenius H, and Nister D, 2009 Stereo matching with color-weighted correlation, hierarchical belief propagation, and occlusion handling. *IEEE Trans. Pattern Anal. Mach. Intell.* **31**(3), 492–504.

Yang QX, Wang L, and Yang RG 2006 Real-time global stereo matching using hierarchical belief propagation *BMVC*, p. III:989.

Yedidia J, Freeman W, and Weiss Y 2003 *Exploring Artificial Intelligence in the New Millennium* Morgan Kaufmann Publishers Inc. chapter Understanding Belief Propagation and Its Generalizations, pp. 239–269.

Yu T, Lin R, Super B, and Tang B 2007 Efficient message representations for belief propagation *ICCV*, pp. 1–8.

Index

Architectures for Computer Vision: From Algorithm to Chip with Verilog, First Edition. Hong Jeong.

Companion Website: www.wiley.com/go/jeong

www.ingramcontent.com/pod-product-compliance
Lightning Source LLC
LaVergne TN
LVHW062108200926
848484LV00007B/1619